# BIRDING IN THE AMERICAN WEST

# BIRDING
# IN THE
# AMERICAN
# WEST A HANDBOOK

## Kevin J. Zimmer

**Comstock Publishing Associates** a division of

**Cornell University Press** | ITHACA AND LONDON

First published 2000 by
Cornell University Press
First printing, Cornell Paperbacks, 2000

Printed in the United States of America

Cornell University Press strives to use environmen-
tally responsible suppliers and materials to the
fullest extent possible in the publishing of its books.
Such materials include vegetable-based, low-VOC
inks and acid-free papers that are recycled, totally
chlorine-free, or partly composed of nonwood
fibers. Books that bear the logo of the FSC (Forest
Stewardship Council) use paper taken from forests
that have been inspected and certified as meeting
the highest standards for environmental and social
responsibility. For further information, visit our
website at www.cornellpress.cornell.edu.

Library of Congress Cataloging-in-Publication Data

Zimmer, Kevin J.
Birding in the American West : a handbook / by
Kevin J. Zimmer
p.   cm.
Includes bibliographical references (p.    ).
ISBN 0-8014-3257-X (cloth) —
ISBN 0-8014-8328-X (paper)
1. Bird watching—West (U.S.)   2. Birds—West
(U.S.)—Identification.   I. Title.
QL683.W4 Z55 2000
598'.07'23478—dc21          99-053727

Cloth printing
10   9   8   7   6   5   4   3   2   1
Paperback printing
10   9   8   7   6   5   4   3   2   1

# Contents

Preface   vii

Acknowledgments   ix

**1 Techniques of Finding Birds  1**

Habitat Recognition  1
Elevation  2
Key Plant Species  3
Nest Site Availability  4
Time of Day  6
Time of Year  7
Tapping the Hotline  13
Finding Pelagic Birds  17
Calling Birds In  20
Ethics  22

**2 Techniques of Identifying Birds  27**

Form and Structure  28
Trophic Structures  29
Wing and Tail Shape and Flight
   Characteristics  29
Body Proportions  35
Color and Plumage Patterns  35
Vocalizations  42
Behavior  43
Gestalt, or Jizz  45
Accessory Information  47
Importance of Preparation  47
Ready Reference to Key
   Characters  48
Psychological Influences  57

**3 Keeping Field Notes  58**

Why Keep a Journal?  58
How to Keep a Journal  59
Species Accounts  65
Some Useful Tips  66

**4 Difficult Identifications: Beyond the Field Guides  67**

Nonbreeding-Plumaged Loons  69
Arctic versus Pacific Loon  73
Clark's versus Western Grebe  77
Horned versus Eared Grebe  79
Sooty versus Short-tailed
   Shearwater  80
Double-crested versus Neotropic
   Cormorant  82
Pacific Coast Cormorants  85
Immature Night-Herons  87
Tundra versus Trumpeter Swan  89
Ross's versus Snow Goose  92
Female Teals  94
Greater versus Lesser Scaup  96
Female Goldeneyes  98
Female Common versus Female
   Red-breasted Merganser  100
Immature Eagles  102
Accipiters  104
Buteos and Other Soaring
   Hawks  106
Shorebirds  117
Jaegers  140
Identifying Gulls  150

Slaty-backed Gulls   163
Thayer's Gulls   168
Kittiwakes   174
Common versus Arctic versus
    Forster's Tern   179
Elegant versus Royal versus Caspian
    Tern   189
Common versus Thick-billed
    Murre   192
Kittlitz's Murrelets   195
Craveri's versus Xantus's
    Murrelet   197
Common versus Lesser
    Nighthawk   199
Hummingbirds   200
Sapsuckers   206
*Myiarchus* Flycatchers   210
*Empidonax* Flycatchers   213
Swallows with a Brown Back   228
*Aphelocoma* Jays   231
Female Bluebirds   234
Bendire's versus Curve-billed
    Thrasher   236
American versus Sprague's
    Pipit   239

Wing-Barred Vireos   242
Baird's versus Savannah
    Sparrow   248
Clay-colored versus Chipping versus
    Brewer's Sparrow   251
Basic-Plumaged Longspurs   254
Eastern versus Western
    Meadowlark   257
*Carpodacus* Finches   258
Hoary versus Common Redpoll   262

**5  Finding the Western
    Specialties   267**
What Is a Specialty Bird?   267
Format   268
Species Accounts   269

**Appendix: Bird Species Mentioned
    in the Text   374**

**Bibliography   383**

**Index   391**

# PREFACE

This book is intended as a companion handbook to aid in finding and identifying birds in the American West. It is not a field guide, nor is it a bird-finding guide in the strictest sense. Instead, it is meant to fill the gaps left by those resources, first, by providing birders with the general concepts and framework needed to develop good bird-finding and identification skills, and second, by probing the intricacies of microhabitat and difficult-to-identify species complexes at a depth that is beyond the scope of most bird-finding guides or field guides. As such, the book should prove useful to all birders, from beginners to advanced, in their explorations of the West. The geographic coverage of this book includes all of the western United States from the eastern boundaries of the Dakotas, Nebraska, Kansas, Oklahoma, and Texas westward, including Alaska (Fig 1).

Chapter 1 deals with concepts of bird finding; it covers everything from habitat recognition to pelagic trips, rare bird alerts (RBAs), and using tape-recorders to attract birds. Finding the birds is only half the battle. You must also be able to identify the birds encountered. Accordingly, Chapter 2 treats the basics of bird identification, dwelling in particular on concepts that have been largely ignored until recent years: detailed knowledge of feather topography, gestalt birding, the study of molt patterns, geographic variation, and so on. Chapter 3 serves as a guide to keeping field notes, a desirable practice that will enhance both the pleasure and the importance of your birding activities.

Chapter 4 builds on the foundation laid in Chapter 2 by applying many of the generalized techniques to detailed treatments of some of our hardest to identify birds. These treatments go beyond the information found in most field guides by synthesizing a growing but scattered body of literature on advances in the field recognition of birds. As such, it is this chapter (and Chapter 5) that will be of most interest to more advanced birders. My decisions on which identification problems to treat are explained in detail at the beginning of Chapter 4.

Chapter 5 provides specific information on when and where to go to find the special birds of the American West. *Specialty bird* (as I have defined the term for this chapter) has a broad, and somewhat arbitrary, meaning. My main criterion was that the birds covered must be essentially western birds. Species whose ranges include large areas east of the Mississippi were left out, regardless of how common or rare they are in the West, but exceptions to that general rule were made. My rea-

Figure 1. The shading indicates the area covered in the text.

sons for including species and a list of excluded species are given in Chapter 5. Besides providing state-by-state breakdowns of specific spots, this chapter emphasizes specifics of microhabitat and behavior so that readers may become more proficient in discovering their own sites for various desired species and in some cases it provides identification tips and other ancillary information such as how to behave when observing lekking grouse.

Finally, although the focus is on the West, I hope that eastern birders will find this book of value. The general concepts of finding and identifying birds and of note taking (as laid out in Chapters 1–3) apply across the continent, and many of the specific identification problems discussed in detail in Chapter 4 are also of primary concern in the East. Also, it is inevitable that active eastern birders will eventually want to head west to experience the fascination of the country and its birds.

# ACKNOWLEDGMENTS

To paraphrase the late Roger Tory Peterson, this book has been written *by* the birders of North America as much as *for* them. The advances in knowledge of bird identification and distribution that have come about in the past two decades are the product of the efforts of hundreds of individuals. Jon Dunn, Kimball Garrett, and Kenn Kaufman have been particular inspirations, not only because of their numerous contributions to our knowledge of identification but also because of their willingness to share them with birders by means of the written word. Jon and Kimball's pioneering series of identification articles published in *The Western Tanager* and similar in-depth articles by Kenn in the short-lived but excellent publication *Continental Birdlife* played significant roles in furthering my own interest in the intricacies of bird identification. In the past decade Paul Lehman has made a major contribution through his editorship of *Birding*, the flagship publication of the American Birding Association. Under Paul's guiding hand, *Birding* evolved into a timely publication that has consistently produced state-of-the-art papers on bird identification (among other topics).

All birders owe a staggering debt to a handful of birding greats whose deaths in the past few years have left a tremendous void. Among them are Roger Tory Peterson, Peter Grant, Claudia Wilds, and Ted Parker. Peterson's contributions are too numerous to reiterate, but it must be stated that he provided the foundation upon which all modern discourses on bird identification are based. Grant, too, made numerous contributions to our knowledge of bird identification, but he is perhaps best known for his monumental work on gulls, which set the standard for study of that difficult group. Wilds authored pioneering papers on the identification of dowitchers and yellowlegs, was a noted authority on tern identification, and contributed in many other areas as well. Parker was best known for his unmatched knowledge of South American birds, but his influence was also felt in North America. His accomplishments and friendship serve as continuing sources of inspiration to me.

Conversations with colleagues have proved invaluable in sharpening my own field skills by introducing me to (or refining my grasp of) subtle field marks long before they appeared in print. Chief among these contributors have been Jon Dunn, Paul Lehman, Kenn Kaufman, and my brother and favorite field companion over the years, Barry Zimmer. Others who have shared their expertise include

Jonathan Alderfer, John Arvin, Victor Emanuel, Shawneen Finnegan, Kimball Garrett, Dan Gibson, Jim Lane, Curtis Marantz, Van Remsen, Don Roberson, Gary Rosenberg, Brad Schram, Bob Sundstrom, Richard Webster, David Wolf, and Dale and Marian Zimmerman.

The artwork by Shawneen Finnegan, Mimi Hoppe Wolf, and Dale Zimmerman has greatly enhanced this book, as have the many photographs provided by Barry Zimmer, Bob Sundstrom, and Shawneen Finnegan. Special thanks to Doug Weschler and VIREO (Visual Resources for Ornithology) for coordinating the use of several photos from their fine collection. Jon Dunn, Steve Howell, Jeff Kingery, Paul Lehman, Michael O'Brien, Gary Rosenberg, and Will Russell all made helpful comments for improving several of the illustrations.

Brad Schram and Bob Sundstrom reviewed Chapter 5 and made numerous suggestions regarding birding spots in California and Washington, respectively. Similarly, Gary Rosenberg made several useful suggestions regarding finding certain difficult birds in Arizona, as did Victor Emanuel for Texas, and Barry Zimmer for Texas, New Mexico, Arizona, and southern California. Mark Wimer and Dave Janiger kindly lent their map-making skills in the production of Figure 1.

Robb Reavill (formerly of Cornell University Press) got this project off the ground, and Peter J. Prescott and Nancy J. Winemiller have provided editorial guidance through the middle and final portions of the process. My thanks to all of them.

I owe a major debt to Victor Emanuel and Victor Emanuel Nature Tours, Inc. They have provided me with a stimulating work environment and rare travel opportunities that have, in large part, made this book possible.

I would be remiss if I did not mention some of the many field companions (in addition to those colleagues mentioned earlier) who have shared countless birding experiences over the years. My thanks to Beth Anderson, Carol Anderson, Rick Bowers, John Coons, Joe DiPasquale, Jeff Donaldson, Richard Gilliland, Jeff Gordon, Randy Hill, Charlie Jensen, Dan Jones, Barry Lyon, Sherry Nelson, Jorge Nocedal, Bill Principe, Robert Ridgely, Lorraine Schulte, Ken Seyffert, Dave Sonneborne, Barbara and Bernie Steinau, Drew Thate, Steve West, Deanne White, Geth and Ed White, Nat Whitney, Scott Wilson, Eleanor Wootten, and Jim Zimmer.

Special thanks go to my major professor, Ralph J. Raitt, who has inspired my keen interest in avian ecology. The numerous members of the Zimmer and Rucci families have provided much encouragement over the years. I owe a special debt to my parents, Bernie and Mary Zimmer, who provided the original stimulus that got me into birding, and whose encouragement and support throughout my life have truly made this book possible.

Final thanks go to my wife, Susan, and daughter, Marina, whose love and understanding are constant sources of inspiration in everything I do.

# BIRDING IN THE AMERICAN WEST

# CHAPTER 1

# TECHNIQUES OF FINDING BIRDS

This chapter deals with the techniques necessary for finding birds. Included are discussions of useful literature, how to plan pelagic trips, luring birds with tape recorders, using rare bird alerts, and other practicalities for finding birds. Good bird-finding ability, however, involves more than these straightforward methods. It involves developing a conceptual framework that enables one to understand why a bird might be found in one place and not in another. Most people have developed such a framework on a broad scale but lack knowledge of the subtleties of bird distribution and habitat selection. For that reason, several factors that influence the distribution and movements of birds at various times of the day and year are discussed. Several examples have been included to help illustrate each concept, but the list is by no means comprehensive. Specific information on where and when to find Western birds is given in Chapter 5.

## Habitat Recognition

Any discussion of the techniques of finding birds should begin with a discussion of habitat recognition. Being adept at finding birds goes beyond knowing the specific locations of desired species. By understanding the habitat preferences of bird species, expert birders can predict the likelihood of finding a certain species in areas with which they are not personally familiar. Such an ability is not contingent on being a master of plant identification, although being able to identify plants certainly would not hurt. Rather, it calls for a feeling for the overall physiognomy of a given habitat, along with recognition of a small number of important plant species.

Some habitats are broadly defined and easily recognized: open ocean, freshwater lakes, coniferous forest, deciduous forest, desert, grassland. Each of these habitats has its own characteristic suite of birds, and knowledge of these associations is the first step in developing good bird-finding technique. Most neophytes learn very rapidly not to expect albatrosses in the desert or woodpeckers on the beach. It may be less apparent that there are subtleties of habitat selection that go far beyond the broad categorizations of freshwater versus saltwater and conifer forest versus deciduous forest.

Some species, such as the Great Horned Owl, are supreme generalists that survive and prosper across a broad range of conditions. Still others may be more specialized but may still occupy two or three habitats. For instance, many desert species that are typical of arid desert scrub, are also found along well-forested river floodplains in the Southwest. Still other species may be specialists typical of ecotones, areas in which one habitat blends with another.

Many factors of the physical and biological environment define the niche that a particular species occupies. However, the degree to which the birder must be able to recognize specific environmental requirements in order to find the desired bird can vary substantially between species. Some birds are capable of occupying an incredible diversity of habitats, and finding them is only a matter of recognizing habitats on a broad scale. Others may be keyed into one specific factor or combination of factors. To find these birds, you must be aware of and able to recognize minute differences in habitat. Some important considerations that may determine or influence microhabitat selection include elevation, presence of key plant species, and nest site availability, all of which may be related.

## Elevation

Clinton H. Merriam (1855–1942) was among the first naturalists to devote considerable attention to the influence of elevation on the distribution of plants and animals. On his explorations of the West, Merriam noted elevational similarities of plant and animal life from one mountain range to the next. This observation led to the formulation of his life zone concept, based on the belief that temperature was the most important environmental factor in the distribution of plant species. Merriam believed that discrete plant communities yielded to one another along an elevational gradient based on temperature. Thus, the Sonoran Zone gives way to the Transition Zone, which in turn is followed by the Canadian Zone, Hudsonian Zone, and Alpine Zone. Along with these elevational changes in plant life are associated changes in the species composition of animals, including birds. Many authors have in fact described various bird species and groups of species as being characteristic of one life zone or another.

As have many classification schemes, the life zone concept has proved to be too simplistic in its approach and has been generally discarded by scientists. Neither the plants nor the birds vary so rigidly and predictably across the continent with elevation, and numerous underlying environmental factors can lead to great local and interregional variation in the distribution of species. Two examples are the Band-tailed Pigeon and Steller's Jay. Both species range widely across the pine-fir forests of Northern America's western mountain ranges, usually at elevations above 6000 ft. (1829 m). As such, they could be considered Transition Zone or more probably Canadian Zone species. Both species, however, are also common residents of the oak-covered hills and lowlands of the California coast, an entirely different habitat, at elevations that are thousands of feet lower. Still other species may inhabit two life zones within the same geographic area. For example, in the mountains of southeastern Arizona, the Northern Pygmy-Owl may range from oak-wooded canyons at 5000 ft (1524 m) to pine-fir forests above 8500 ft (2590 m). Despite the numerous exceptions, the life zone concept still has some use to the birder as a way of grouping species that is convenient, makes sense, and often works.

Often, several species within a family replace one another (with some overlap) altitudinally. In the mountains of Arizona, White-breasted Nuthatches are common in the oaks and sycamores of the canyon bottoms. They are replaced higher up in the ponderosa pine belt by Pygmy Nuthatches, which in turn give way to Red-breasted Nuthatches at still higher elevations. In California, finches of the genus *Carpodacus* show a similar pattern. House Finches inhabit the lowlands; Purple Finches inhabit the wooded foothills up into the mountains; and Cassin's Finches inhabit the highest-elevation conifer forests at the edge of timberline.

Elevation is often intimately linked to the distribution of particular species or groups of species. Its influence may be largely an indirect one, with birds selecting areas on the basis of plant species, which are more directly influenced by parameters of the physical environment. There are also undoubtedly many instances in which elevation indirectly determines the distributional boundaries of birds through differing temperature, moisture, and radiation regimes. The influence of elevation is probably at least partly responsible for the fact that many boreal forest birds have ranges extending much farther south in western North America than they do in the eastern half of the continent. The high elevations of the Rockies, Sierras, Cascades, and other western mountain ranges duplicate the climatic conditions of more northern latitudes and serve to pull such northern species as the Great Gray Owl, Boreal Owl, Black-backed Woodpecker, Three-toed Woodpecker, Gray Jay, and Evening and Pine grosbeaks far south into the central United States. In the East, where such high-elevation ranges are lacking, the same species typically reach their southern boundaries in Canada or the extreme northern edge of this country.

## Key Plant Species

Many bird species seem intimately bound to one plant species, genus, or family. In other cases it is the life form (that is, sapling, mature tree, senescent tree) and not the taxon that is important. In any event, finding these specialized birds becomes much easier once you are aware of the association and can recognize the plants involved.

Examples of specific bird–plant associations are numerous. The Golden-cheeked Warbler is found only where cedar (*Juniperus*) stands exist on the Edwards Plateau region of Texas. Two southwestern warblers of conifer forests, the Grace's and Olive, are also associated with specific types of trees. The Grace's is a bird of the ponderosa pine forest, whereas the Olive seems to require the presence of firs. The two species can be found together where either Douglas-fir, or white fir, or both are mixed with the pines. Red-faced Warblers are found in the same pine–fir forests, but they are most common in draws or on slopes with thickets of Gambel oak beneath the conifers. More specific still is the Kirtland's Warbler of Michigan. It not only requires one type of tree (the jack pine); it will inhabit forests only where that type of tree is of a certain height (6–20 ft, 1.8–6 m).

Slightly more generalized are several species of woodpeckers that key into whole genera (rather than one species) of trees. Even here, however, one sees specialization directed at the age or health of the tree. Acorn Woodpeckers require large numbers of oaks (no one species) to provide the mast that is the staple of their diet. Areas with a multitude of oak species may even be preferred because it is unlikely that the acorn crop of several species will fail simultaneously. Red-cockaded Woodpeckers are totally dependent on old-growth pine trees that are infected with red heart disease to use as nesting sites. Where there are several pines infected with this disease the birds form small colonies. This constraint leads to a very patchy distribution; localized regions that have high densities of woodpeckers are surrounded by large tracts of similar forest that have none. Similarly, Black-backed and Three-toed woodpeckers often invade and loosely colonize burn areas or disease-infested tree-kills in conifer forests while leaving adjacent unburned or disease-free areas unoccupied.

Hummingbirds of all species depend on the presence of flowers for nectar. Many species of hummers have distinct preferences for a few select species of flowering plants (For example, Lucifer Hummingbirds are especially attracted to penstemons, *Anisacanthus,* and flowering *Agave*). Areas that have large numbers of suitable flowers are usually swarming with hummers, whereas identical macrohabitat that lacks these plants may have few or none.

Many prairie birds are not tied to one species of plant but to recognizable physiognomic types of grasslands. Bobolinks and Dickcissels prefer the weedy, tall-grass meadows or old fields; Sprague's Pipits, Baird's Sparrows, and Chestnut-collared Longspurs do best in medium-height, mixed-grass prairies; and Mountain Plovers, Brewer's Sparrows, and McCown's Longspurs stick to more xeric shortgrass prairie. In all instances, species composition seems less important than the general structure of the grassland.

## Nest Site Availability

An additional consideration in locating some species during the breeding season is the availability of suitable nest sites. For most songbirds in most habitats nest sites are not limiting factors of distribution. For some larger birds and for colonial species, the availability of nest sites may be of overriding importance.

For example, some swifts and falcons depend on cliffs or rock faces for the placement of their nests. Areas that lack these features are usually unoccupied even though they are within the geographic ranges of the birds and provide otherwise suitable habitat. Black Swifts are even more specific, seemingly requiring cliff faces with waterfalls or overlooking the ocean for their nesting areas. American Dippers range widely along fast-moving streams but are dependent on rock ledges or bridges for the placement of their nests. By concentrating your search near appropriate nest sites, you may save a lot of time in locating this bird. Where trees are lacking (as in some deserts and grasslands) such species as Red-tailed, Ferruginous, and Zone-tailed hawks and Great Horned and Barn owls may be dependent on canyon walls, cliff faces, or steep sandbanks for the location of their nests. Likewise, Bank Swallows and kingfishers require sandbanks; Cliff Swallows and phoebes use bridges or building eves; and Cave Swallows need caves. The latter species has steadily expanded its range in recent years by finding substitutes for cave walls, such as concrete road culverts, highway bridges, and overpasses.

More generally, many species require some sort of cavity in which to place their nest, and the absence of such cavities may result in local gaps in the geographic ranges of these birds. Birds such as Elf Owls and Screech-Owls, *Myiarchus* flycatchers, Tree and Violet-green swallows, Purple Martins, Bridled and Juniper titmice, chickadees, House and Bewick's wrens, and bluebirds use old woodpecker holes to a large extent. Where permanent or semipermanent streams and rivers support gallery forest with trees of sufficient size, these birds abound. Intervening expanses of desert without true trees may lack the same species entirely. In parts of the Sonoran Desert of Arizona, Gila Woodpecker holes in the giant saguaro cacti provide homes for Elf Owls and Ferruginous Pygmy-Owls, Ash-throated and Brown-crested flycatchers, Purple Martins, and Lucy's Warblers. Although most of these cavity dwellers are found in areas where the woodpeckers and the cacti are common, available nest sites may be limited by the presence of large numbers of Starlings, which aggressively displace other species from cavities. Burrowing Owls depend largely on the burrows of prairie dogs, badgers, and the like for their nest holes. In parts of the West, the distribution of these little owls is largely coincident with the distribution of prairie dog towns.

Ground-nesting colonial species, such as some procellarids, gulls, and alcids, require remote rocky islands for nesting. Such islands must be far enough from shore so as not to be exposed to invasion at low tides by land predators.

In parts of the Chihuahuan and other deserts many species may be limited to arroyos (desert washes) because of the lack of large shrubs suitable for nest placement elsewhere. Such is the case in much of western Texas and southern New Mexico, where the divides between arroyos are often vegetated by nothing but creosotebush, tarbush, snakeweed, and other shrubs of spindly or small stature. Only the Black-throated Sparrow uses these shrubs to any great extent for nesting. Consequently, large expanses of desert may host little more than Black-throateds and the ground-nesting Scaled Quail and Lesser Nighthawk. Visiting birders should concentrate their search along the arroyos where sumac, desert willow, and mesquite provide nest sites for such species as the Greater Roadrunner, Black-chinned Hummingbird, Ladder-backed Woodpecker, Western Kingbird, Ash-throated Flycatcher, Verdin, Black-tailed Gnatcatcher, Cactus Wren, Crissal Thrasher, and Canyon Towhee.

## Time of Day

Knowing when to look for particular birds is almost as important as knowing where to look. Birds exhibit cyclic patterns of daily activity that make them easy to find during some hours and difficult to find during others. This is yet another case where doing some preparatory homework on the life histories of sought-after species can save much time and frustration.

Passerines (perching birds) are typically most active during the early morning. Cooler morning temperatures allow for maximum foraging activity with minimum heat stress. Song activity usually peaks at this time as well. Many forest-dwelling species can be almost impossible to locate unless they are calling, so an early start is all the more crucial in finding them. Most desert birds shut down all activity during the heat of the day. Desert thrashers are particularly difficult to find after the first few hours of daylight. They usually sing from a conspicuous perch early and then spend the rest of the day running quietly through arroyos or sitting in the inner shade of some densely vegetated shrub. A predawn start is also usually essential for seeing prairie grouse on their leks. The birds begin their booming or dancing in the dark, and activity usually peaks shortly after dawn. Within an hour or two most birds will have left the lek for the day, scattering to their feeding areas, where they can be very difficult to find.

Waterbirds such as herons, ducks, shorebirds, gulls, and terns are rarely affected by rising daytime temperatures and can be found in appropriate locations throughout the day. When a day's birding activities call for both landbirding and waterbirding, it is usually best to save the aquatic habitats for later in the day when songbird activity has slowed down.

There are several exceptions to this line of reasoning. Although any hour may be good for shorebirds in freshwater areas, in coastal locations tidal fluctuations must be taken into account. At high tide, certain stretches of coastline may be completely inundated, leaving little or no suitable foraging habitat for shorebirds. In these areas, high tide can make it particularly difficult to find the rock-inhabiting species such as Black Oystercatcher, Wandering Tattler, Surfbird, and Black Turnstones. Conversely, in some areas, high tides may make finding these species easier, because only the rocks closest to shore remain exposed, and the birds are concentrated in a few locations within easy viewing range. Low tides may expose too much good habitat, leaving the observer with the problem of having to view distant flocks of shorebirds across impassable mudflats or treacherous surf. Shorebirds often concentrate in particular locations immediately after high tide, when receding waters expose a new supply of invertebrate prey.

Shorebirds are not the only birds whose activity patterns are dictated by tidal changes. At many localities, the best time to see rails (particularly the secretive Black Rail) is when high tides force them from the concealment of marsh vegetation into the open. It often takes an exceptionally high tide to force them from cover, so searching for rails on a day with average tides might be a waste of time.

A current tide table should be consulted before planning a day of coastal birding. Each coastal location has its own nuances depending on micro- and macro-geography, prevailing winds, and tidal regime. Becoming acquainted with these nuances and regularly consulting tide tables can make a huge difference in the success of your coastal birding.

Black Swifts typically forage far from their nest cliffs during the day and return just before dusk. Watching at the nesting area at any time other than late afternoon is often an exercise in futility. A knowledge of such variations in daily activity patterns can save much time and energy when searching for such species.

Nocturnal species also exhibit marked changes in activity within the course of an evening, and these patterns may affect your chances of finding the birds. Some owls, such as the Burrowing, Northern Pygmy, Ferruginous Pygmy, Snowy, and Great Gray, are at least partially diurnal, and your chances of finding them may be better during the day. Many of the nocturnal species call continuously for some time after dusk but stop for long periods in the middle of the night to hunt. They may resume calling at different points, particularly just before dawn. Some caprimulgids, such as the Common Poorwill and the Whip-poor-will have similar patterns. It is generally easiest to track nocturnal birds down or lure them in when they are calling, although vocal responses can still be elicited at other times.

## Time of Year

As would be expected, time of year has a great influence on which birds can be seen in an area. Every locale has its unique combination of resident, summering, wintering, and migrant species. Areas situated at high northern latitudes typically have an abundance of summering species with few winter residents. The number of permanent residents in an area usually increases with decreasing latitude, as does the number of wintering species. There is also much temporal variation in species composition within seasons, because birds often fail to define summer, fall, winter, and spring on the same calendar as we do. Precise timing on the part of the birder can make the difference in seeing or not seeing many of the more transient species.

### Summer

Most breeding birds are easiest to find early in the nesting season, when territorial and nesting activity is at its peak. Passerines typically sing almost continuously at the onset of the breeding season. Males of most passerine species actively assist in caring for the young. Because they invest a lot of time and energy in each brood, they tend to be strongly territorial at the onset of the nesting season, lest another male enter their territory and "steal" a copulation from the female. Such a theft could result in the resident male's investing energy in raising young that are not his own. Frequent song bouts are a way of warning other males that a territory is occupied and being defended. Once the female is on the eggs the male tends to sing less. Males sing even less when feeding young, and they greatly restrict or even cease singing once the young have fledged. Many species are particularly conspicuous when feeding nestlings because of great increases in foraging activity and the number of trips to and from the nest. The Colima and Golden-cheeked warblers are good examples of birds that should be looked for early in the breeding season. Colima Warblers are found only in the Chisos Mountains of southwestern Texas. They arrive on the breeding grounds in April and are fairly easy to find until June, when many of the birds stop singing. They are drably colored and can become difficult to find when they are not singing. Golden-cheeked Warblers are restricted to the Edwards Plateau region of Texas and, like the Colima, are relatively easy to find when territorial singing is at its peak (March through May). Song activity tapers off rapidly in June, and the birds become progressively harder to locate through the summer. Flammulated Owls and Elf Owls are two more examples of birds that are infinitely easier to find early in the breeding season than later.

Postbreeding dispersal is another fairly common occurrence that birders must take into account. Although we tend to think of breeding birds as ones that stay through the summer, many species will breed once or twice early in the season and then leave the nesting area in midsummer. This pattern is common among hummingbirds. Desert populations of Costa's Hummingbirds breed especially early, arriving in Arizona and southern California in February. Breeding continues through March, and many of the birds disperse by the end of April. The Allen's Hummingbird of coastal California exhibits a similar dispersal pattern. Males may arrive on territory as early as the first week of January. As are other hummingbirds, Allen's Hummingbirds are polygamous breeders (one male may mate with multiple females) and the males provide no parental care. Once copulations have been made and the eggs have been laid, the males disperse, leaving the females to raise the young. After midsummer, visiting birders are therefore likely to see only female and immature Allen's Hummingbirds, which are impossible to distinguish from female and immature Rufous Hummingbirds.

Similarly, birders who time their trip to Alaska too far into summer are bound for disappointment. The breeding season at northern latitudes is remarkably compressed. Birds rush in at the earliest opportunity and begin breeding. Because food resources are often superabundant and daylight is continuous or nearly so, the parent birds can feed their offspring around the clock, accelerating the normal pace of nestling development. Larger birds with more protracted incubation periods will get only one shot at nesting before the short summer begins winding down. If their nests are lost to predators or foul weather, they will abandon all thoughts of nesting for the year and will leave the nesting grounds. Even the birds that are successful in their nesting attempts will leave the nesting grounds much earlier than more-southern birds do. The adults of precocial species (such as shorebirds) may migrate within a few weeks of the hatching of the young. By late July, many of the "summer" species of northern Alaska may be far to the south.

An opposite course is followed by Cassin's and Botteri's sparrows in southeastern Arizona. These two species are apparently stimulated by rain in their breeding cycles, responding to the midsummer rains common to the Southwest. They are either mostly absent or silent before the rainy season in July. Once the rains have started, they become very conspicuous, either skylarking (singing in flight; Cassin's) or singing from prominent perches (both species). When the birds are not singing, they are extremely difficult to find. This pattern of delaying singing or breeding until midsummer is rare in this country, but it is common to several species in the deserts of western Mexico.

Postbreeding dispersal is far from being a totally negative phenomenon for the birder. On the contrary, many Mexican or tropical species are seen in the United States only in late summer or early fall after a northward postbreeding dispersal from their nesting areas farther south. Postbreeding dispersal accounts for the regular midsummer appearances in Arizona of White-eared, Berylline, and Violet-crowned hummingbirds. Except for the latter species (which breeds in Guadalupe Canyon and in the Patagonia area in Arizona), these rare visitors are almost impossible to find before to July. More spectacular is the annual or semiannual northward movement of many waterbirds from their nesting areas along the Gulf of California to the California coast and the Salton Sea (southern California). Included in this procession are Red-billed Tropicbirds and Least and Black storm-petrels offshore and Brown Pelicans, Magnificent Frigatebirds (also coastal), Blue-footed and Brown boobies, Wood Storks, various southern herons, and Laughing and Yellow-footed gulls to the Salton Sea. Most of these birds cannot be found in California before July and will have vacated the state or expired by October. Although some of the species are commonly found in other parts of the country (for example, the Wood Stork and the Laughing Gull), others, such as the Red-billed Tropicbird, Blue-footed Booby, Least Storm-Petrel, and Yellow-footed Gull, are almost impossible to find elsewhere or at other times of the year.

## Winter

Winter often offers a greater diversity of birds than does summer (except in inland areas in the northern part of the country), and the chances of finding rarities are almost always better. Winter is the time for the best variety of hawks and sparrows in the Southwest; of loons, grebes, waterfowl, gulls, and alcids on the West Coast; and northern owls and finches in the upper Midwest and in the Rocky Mountain states. Montane species such as Band-tailed Pigeons, woodpeckers, jays, chickadees, nuthatches, creepers, kinglets, and bluebirds also periodically descend into adjacent lowlands, where they may spend all or part of the winter. Winter is an especially good time for finding vagrant Mexican species (for example, Hook-billed Kite, Clay-colored Robin, Blue Bunting, White-collared Seedeater) in southern Texas, whereas mid- to late summer is the better time for similar rarities in southeastern Arizona.

As is the case in summer, not all wintering species should be looked for at the same time. In most locales, more species can be found in early winter than in late winter, because of the presence of late migrants and semihardy species that can persist until very cold weather sets in. In inland areas in the north, most large lakes are still open in December, providing habitat for lingering waterfowl and gulls. This is a good time to look for northern ducks (Oldsquaw, scoters, goldeneyes) and gulls (Glaucous and Thayer's gulls, Black-legged Kittiwake), which are likely to move through later than other members of their families.

Winter is also the time when many boreal species stage major invasions into the northern tier of states. The onset and duration of these invasions vary from species to species and from year to year. Northern owls (Snowy, Hawk, Great Gray, and Boreal) are most likely to be found in late winter (after extreme cold spells in Canada and subsequent declines in rodent populations), but irruptions of Bohemian Waxwings and various finches (Evening and Pine grosbeaks, Pine Siskins, Common and Hoary redpolls, and Red and White-winged crossbills) may occur as early as November. The arrival of longspurs in the southern states may also depend on the weather farther north. Lapland Longspurs, for example, reach the Texas panhandle during very cold winters or after late winter blizzards to the north. They are rarely present before January.

## Migration

Few things are as exciting to birders as the onset of spring or fall migration. Along with the return of birds not seen all winter or summer comes the greatly increased opportunity for finding rare birds. Birds may appear in out-of-range localities because of errors in following the migratory route or because of weather events that blow the birds off course. These occurrences are most likely to take place when large numbers of birds are making transoceanic or transcontinental trips. The discovery of a rare bird is not the random event that one might imagine it to be. Just as there are particular places and times that are more productive for finding breeding and wintering species, so there are places and times that provide maximum opportunity for finding vagrants.

Spring is often the more predictable of the two migratory periods. Although spring migration in much of the West is less concentrated than it is in the East, there is still a somewhat finite quality to the flow and duration of bird movement. In the interior, waterfowl and cranes usually move first. These are followed by raptors, blackbirds, sparrows, and shorebirds and later by a rush of insectivorous passerines such as flycatchers, thrushes, vireos, warblers, orioles, and tanagers.

The large buildups or waves of migrant passerines common to eastern North America are not often encountered west of the Great Plains. However, it is still possible to find good concentrations of migrant songbirds in many areas along the central flyway from Canada through the Great Plains and on to the Gulf Coast of Texas. These concentrations usually coincide with weather events that bring a temporary halt to further northward flights, thereby causing birds to "stack up" at the edge of a frontal system. Nowhere is this type of phenomenon better observed than along the upper Texas coast during April. When a cold front blows in from the north, trans-Gulf migrants drop out of the sky upon reaching land, often totally exhausted from hours of battling the wind. If the front brings rain, truly spectacular "fallouts" of birds may occur, especially at High Island and Galveston. Every clump of trees may be swarming with birds, all in immaculate spring plumage. It is not uncommon on such occasions to find 20 to 25 species of warbler in a single hour. A single fruiting mulberry may host dozens of Gray Catbirds, Baltimore Orioles, Scarlet Tanagers, and Rose-breasted Grosbeaks, and the ground may be covered with Indigo Buntings and thrushes of three or four species.

Even calm-weather days can produce exciting birding at High Island. Wooded areas that are devoid of birds in the morning may come alive in late afternoon as migrants hit the coast in waves. If the winds are light and the sky is clear, the birds will be less exhausted and will not stack up. Instead they will be leapfrogging through the trees, feeding voraciously, and then leaving as fast as they came. Turnover may be rapid, with new groups of birds appearing as rapidly as the first ones leave. On such occasions each walk around even the smallest wooded area will produce new birds, providing the observer a rare chance to actually watch migration take place.

Although a day of spring birding often produces more species and individuals than does a day of fall birding, it is generally less likely to produce rarities. Seeing a rare bird in spring migration is especially unlikely for such groups as waterfowl, shorebirds, gulls, pelagics, and almost any Asiatic species along the coast south of Alaska. The primary spring vagrant excitement is generated by the appearance of numbers of eastern passerines in the West. Although such vagrants may occur anywhere west of the Great Plains, they are most likely to be found in the Southwest, particularly at small desert oases. These oases serve to concentrate birds in small areas, making them fairly easy to find. Heavily forested areas to the north undoubtedly get their share of rarities too, but the extensive nature of the habitat may allow such birds to go unnoticed. The first two weeks in May seem to be the most productive for eastern vagrants in western Texas and southern New Mexico, whereas the latter half of May and throughout early June are usually best in Arizona and southern California. California birders visit Death Valley and other desert sites each Memorial Day weekend expressly for the purpose of finding eastern vagrants (particularly warblers).

Spring is a time of special excitement on the Aleutians and the Bering Sea islands and along Alaska's western shores. Birds that nest in the high latitudes of Siberia winter farther south in Asia, Africa, and the south Pacific. They migrate northward to the breeding grounds in spring in the same manner as most of our

North American migrants. Because the outer Aleutians, St. Lawrence Island, and the Seward Peninsula are not far from Siberia, only a small shift in winds or a slight miscalculation on the part of the birds can bring northbound palearctic migrants to North American shores. Increasing numbers of birders position themselves each May and June at strategic points in the Bering Sea and Gulf of Alaska, hoping for westerly winds to dump exotic Eurasian species on our shores.

Away from Alaska, fall is the most exciting time of year for many birders. There are typically many more vagrants to be found in this season than in spring, probably owing to the large number of juveniles that are migrating for the first time. Lack of experience with the migratory route is undoubtedly the cause of many errors in migration, and, indeed, a large percentage of fall vagrants are juveniles.

The fall migratory period also lasts longer than than the spring migration; when all taxa are considered, it may stretch from late June to December. Hummingbirds and shorebirds are often the first to begin heading south. Rufous, Calliope, and Broad-tailed hummingbirds begin appearing at lowland feeders in the Southwest in early July. Adult males often predominate early, with adult females and juveniles following in subsequent months. Shorebirds also begin moving by midsummer. Some individual shorebirds forgo breeding to spend the entire summer well south of the nesting grounds. These are typically birds that are sexually immature or in some way physiologically incapable of breeding. Most species breed in the Arctic, and the adults begin heading south shortly after the young have fledged. Consequently, most adult shorebirds pass through in July and August, and the juveniles arrive later from August through October. Wilson's Phalaropes, which have a more southerly breeding range, return to many areas as early as mid-June. The earliest to migrate are the females because of the Wilson's sex role reversal; the females do nothing but lay the eggs, leaving the males to incubate the clutch and care for the young. Thus, females are free to travel much earlier than are the males.

Many passerine species are also on the move by August, and in the northern states, numbers of some migrants may peak before September 1. For many groups, fall migration is a mirror image of spring in that the early arrivals on the way north are the last to arrive on the way south. Waterfowl; raptors; montane species of many taxa; and northern finches, juncos, and sparrows usually form the bulk of migrants from late October through December.

As noted earlier, patterns of vagrancy of many species in many areas are decidedly nonrandom. Most rarities are found by birders who have studied the pattern of past occurrences and who plan their searches accordingly to be in the best places at the best times. The examples are too numerous to mention here, but a few deserve inclusion as points of illustration.

The postbreeding dispersal of boobies, frigatebirds, Wood Storks, and the like to the Salton Sea involves a predictable pattern of vagrancy that has already been discussed. Some of those species as well as more-pelagic ones (for example, Red Phalarope, all jaegers, Sabine's Gull) regularly appear far inland after late-summer tropical storms in the Gulf of California. The storms are not a requisite for the wanderings of the phalarope, jaegers, and gulls, because they all routinely travel the length of the coast from Alaska to Mexico. Periodic searches of large bodies of water from late August through November may reveal regular incursions of jaegers and Sabine's Gulls into many parts of the western and central United States. Likewise, Red Phalaropes frequently appear at sewage lagoons or wherever other phalarope species gather everywhere from Minnesota to Texas.

There is ample evidence that some vagrant individuals return to the exact same areas year after year: for example, Sky Lark: six consecutive winters (1979–85) at Point Reyes, California; Smew: a male at the same pond in Foster City, California, for two consecutive years (1981 and 1983); and individual Black-headed and Little gulls at the Stockton sewage ponds, Stockton, California, for seven consecutive years (1978–85).

## Tapping the Hotline

Some species will be hard to find even when one knows their general distribution, habitat requirements, and daily and seasonal activity patterns. Species whose continental or regional populations are very small and that, therefore, do not begin to saturate the available preferred habitat are particularly hard to find.

Several examples of such birds come to mind. The Great Gray Owl is a rare resident of high-elevation conifer forests that border grassy meadows in Yosemite National Park. At first, one might think that this is a fairly restricted niche and that the owls would be easy to find. But one need travel to the Yosemite high country only once to see that there are scores of seemingly appropriate meadows. The abundance of meadows, combined with the fact that relatively few pairs of owls inhabit the park in a given year, makes for a bird that is very difficult to find without prior knowledge of a specific location. Similarly, Buff-collared Nightjars and Five-striped Sparrows are found in only a few of the countless desert canyons of southeastern Arizona, and Buff-breasted Flycatchers are known to inhabit only a handful of pine-forested canyons in the same state. All three species reach the northern limits of their ranges in southern Arizona, and these fringe populations are apparently not large enough or fecund enough to expand into all of the available habitat. The result is the same for the birder: without prior knowledge of specific locations for these birds, a search may be futile.

Given all these difficulties, how can one learn the precise locations for the tougher species? The first course of action should be a check of the proper literature.

Two periodicals that are almost essential to avid field birders are *North American Birds* (formerly *Field Notes*) and *Birding*. The former is published quarterly by the American Birding Association (ABA) in alliance with the National Audubon Society (North American Birds, P.O. Box 6599, Colorado Springs, CO 80934–6599) and serves as *the* journal of North American bird distribution. Four issues each year are devoted to region-by-region seasonal reports of bird occurrences, reflecting the fieldwork of thousands of observers. Records of rare birds and vagrants and reports on population trends of all species are emphasized. Although specific directions to birding locales are seldom given, this journal provides the reader with a wealth of information on what to expect, where, and when.

*Birding* is the bimonthly journal of the ABA (American Birding Association, Inc., P.O. Box 6599, Colorado Springs, CO; 800-850-2473), an organization dedicated to the promotion of field birding as a hobby and sport. As such, it features a wide variety of articles aimed primarily at finding and identifying birds. The association's newsletter, *Winging It,* typically contains one or more short bird-finding "inserts," which provide explicit directions to various "hot spots" across the continent. Feature-length articles on major areas, on foreign countries, and on finding particular species are also included in both the magazine and the newsletter.

In addition to these useful but widescope journals, there are a number of bird-finding books for particular geographic areas. The first real bird-finding guides were conceived and written by Olin Sewall Pettingill, who published *A Guide to Birdfinding East of the Mississippi* in 1951 and *A Guide to Birdfinding West of the Mississippi* in 1953. Both books included separate chapters on each state in their area of coverage. The basic format centered on providing precise directions and mileages to the better birding areas in each state, as well as a list of what birds to expect in each season. These guides were subsequently revised (*East* in 1977, *West* in 1981), and much of the material remains useful today.

Although Pettingill's guides were of wide utility, they were of necessity less than comprehensive, given the large areas covered. Since the 1980s, there has been a proliferation of bird-finding guides that cover only one state or part of one state. Notable among these were the numerous guides authored by the late James A. Lane (and now expanded and regularly revised by the American Birding Association), which highlighted such diverse locales as Churchill, Manitoba and southeastern Arizona. These single-area guides have many advantages. First, they devote extensive coverage to a restricted area, thereby offering the birder more than just a skimming off the top. Second, an author who focuses on one region is more likely to be intimately familiar with all aspects of finding birds in that area than is one who covers half a continent. Last, guides to smaller areas are more readily revised, a matter of great importance considering how quickly bird-finding information can become outdated. Most of the state guides are similar in general format to the earlier Pettingill volumes. One notable difference for many is the inclusion of detailed maps and bar-graph checklists denoting details of seasonal occurrence and abundance; those helpful features were lacking in the Pettingill guides.

The ABA offers a comprehensive selection of pertinent books (including all of the finding guides) at discount prices to members. For more information, contact ABA Sales (P.O. Box 6599, Colorado Springs, CO 80934; 800-634-7736).

Although published material is invaluable in locating most birds, it lacks immediacy and can never present the true up-to-the-minute picture for any given area. Therefore, when traveling you will want to tap the local grapevines for current news of birding possibilities. You can obtain advance information by writing or telephoning experts who live in the area of your intended visit. One source of names, addresses, and phone numbers, is the ABA's membership directory, which indicates the degree of each member's willingness to provide information. When contacting these people, use common courtesy. Write well in advance of your trip, leaving ample time for them to respond. Always include a self-addressed, stamped envelope for their reply. If you are going to phone them, remember time-zone differences, and avoid early morning, late evening, and mealtime calls. Keep in mind that many of these experts are swamped with such requests for information every year and that the more effort you put into getting information on your own, the less they will have to put forth in giving it.

An excellent way to stay on top of birding conditions in many areas is to use the rare bird alert (RBA) hotlines. Rare bird alerts typically have a phone number that can be called day or night that will give you a prerecorded message of bird news from the area. Some tapes are updated weekly, others more frequently or as the need arises. Most give the name and number of someone to call for more information or to report details of rare birds seen (but think before reporting a rare or nesting bird; see Ethics, below). Because many of these RBAs are maintained by local Audubon Societies, news of society meetings, field trips, and so forth, is often included on the tape.

The main emphasis of most RBAs is the reporting of birds rare to the area. When such birds first appear, there are usually explicit directions given for finding them. If your shorthand skills are rusty you may want to tape record the call because route directions are often given quite rapidly. If the rare bird hangs around for some time, later tapes are likely to skip directions and just give the locale (for example, "The Sky Lark is still being seen at Point Reyes." ). Occasionally the tapes report on sightings of birds regular to the area but of particular interest to visitors. Less frequently, the tapes may report on outstanding rarities currently being seen in another part of the country

The RBA phone numbers for most Western states and several smaller subregions are provided below. Such lists have a tendency to become dated within a short time. The ABA updates these numbers periodically in its publications. Many electronic mail and bulletin board "chat services" that cater to birders are springing up. The best way to locate one is to use a search engine such as Excite or Alta-Vista to search for "birding."

Alaska
    Fairbanks 907-451-9213
    Kachemak Bay 907-235-7337
    Seward 907-224-2325
    Statewide 907-338-2473

Arizona
    Phoenix 602-832-8745
    Tucson 520-798-1005

California
    Arcata 707-822-5666
    Los Angeles 213-874-1318

Monterey 408-375-9122
Morro Bay 805-528-7182
northern 415-681-7422
Orange 949-487-6869
Sacramento 916-481-0118
San Diego 619-479-3400
Santa Barbara 805-964-8240
San Joaquin / southern Sierra 209-271-9420
Colorado 303-424-2144
Idaho
northern 208-882-6195
southeastern 208-236-3337
southwestern 208-368-6096
Kansas
Kansas City 913-342-2473
statewide 316-229-2777
Wichita 316-681-2266
Montana
Big Fork 406-756-5595
statewide 406-721-9799
Nebraska 402-292-5325
Nevada
northwestern 702-324-2473
southern 702-390-8463
New Mexico 505-323-9323
North Dakota 701-250-4481
Oklahoma
Oklahoma City 405-373-4531
statewide 918-669-6646
Oregon
Klamath Basin 541-850-3805
northeastern 208-882-6195
statewide 503-292-0661
South Dakota 605-773-6460
Texas
Abilene 915-691-8981
Austin 512-926-8751
Corpus Christi 512-265-0377
Lubbock 806-797-6690
Rio Grande Valley 956-969-2731
San Antonio 210-308-6788
statewide 713-964-5867
north-central 817-329-1270
northeast 903-234-2473

Utah 801-538-4730
Washington
    lower Columbia Basin 509-943-6957
    southeastern 208-882-6195
    statewide 425-454-2662
    western 206-933-1831
Wyoming 307-265-2473

# Finding Pelagic Birds

Pelagic (open-ocean) birding is very different from land-based birding, but it can be the most exciting, challenging, frustrating, taxing, and rewarding kind of birding. The excitement comes partly from the mystery of the high seas and partly from the unpredictable nature of the birds themselves. We have only recently begun to unravel some of the complexities of pelagic bird distribution and biology. The challenge stems from the need to identify these fast-flying, subtly different birds under what are usually less than ideal conditions. Frustration comes from the often poor or fleeting views, unidentifiable birds, and occasional birdless stretches of ocean. Pelagic birding can be taxing depending on one's inherent equilibrium and ability to tolerate a prolonged period with no firm ground underfoot. In the end, it is extremely rewarding, because by its very nature it requires a marshaling of most of one's skills of spotting and identifying birds, as well as a certain amount of physical stamina.

The first consideration is finding a boat. The best option is to obtain passage on one of the regularly scheduled boat trips run by various bird clubs or individuals. The Los Angeles Audubon Society (213-876-0202 or 213-874-1318) schedules several trips each year that depart from San Pedro, Ventura, and occasionally other ports in southern California. The Western Field Ornithologists (information often available from the Los Angeles Audubon Society number listed above, or try the San Diego RBA) usually sponsor a spring trip and a fall trip from San Diego to San Clemente Island. The most comprehensive program of birding and marine mammal trips to a variety of areas off the central coast of California is offered by Debra Love Shearwater (Shearwater Journeys, P.O. Box 190, Hollister, CA 95024–0190; 831-637-8527). The emphasis is on Monterey Bay, but Shearwater Journeys also offer trips to the Cordell Banks, Davidson Seamount, and other "deep-water" areas. Similarly, Terry Wahl (Westport Seabirds, c/o Terry Wahl, 3041 Elridge, Bellingham, WA 98225; 360-733-8255) runs many quality trips each year out of Westport, Washington. The Portland Audubon Society (Portland Audubon Society, Audubon House, 5151 NW Cornell Road, Portland, OR 97210; 503-292-6855) also runs several trips to Oregon and Washington waters. Finally, the Alaska Marine Highway System (P.O. Box 25535, Juneau, AK 99802; 800-642-0066, or 907-465-3946) offers ferry trips that can provide excellent seabirding, among them the Homer to Dutch Harbor ferry. Several commercial charters offer day trips from

Seward to nearby Kenai Fjords National Park, a trip that takes in stretches of open water as well as impressive seabird colonies in the Chiswell Islands (try Kenai Fjords Tours, Inc., Box 1889, Seward, AK 99664; (707) 224-8068). Other organizations and individuals offer one to several trips each year. The American Birding Association typically publishes a fairly comprehensive list of offerings each year in its newsletter.

Ticket prices for these trips vary, depending largely on the length of the trip. Most boats leave early (5:30–7:30 A.M.) and return later the same afternoon (3:00–5:00 P.M.). There are a few overnight trips to areas far offshore, and hours for these may vary considerably. All of these trips are quite popular, and reservations should be made well in advance.

The alternative to the organized birding boat is to latch onto one of the numerous commercial fishing boats that leave most large ports daily. Tickets for these one-day trips are usually sold right on the harbor on a first come, first-served basis. The length of these outings is usually comparable to that of most of the birding trips, but the price may be somewhat less (if you don't rent tackle and purchase a fishing license). Be sure to inquire how far offshore the skipper plans to go. Trips of less than 5 miles out usually produce little that cannot be seen from shore.

There are advantages and disadvantages to both types of boat trips. Most of the advantages lie with the organized birding trips which emphasize finding and observing birds. The skipper will not linger in birdless areas but will actively chase flocks of birds. When birds are spotted resting on the water the boat will stop for optimal viewing. Chumming is a common practice on organized birding trips; bits of squid, fish entrails, suet, popcorn, bread, and so forth are thrown into the wake of the boat to attract birds. Another advantage is in having 25 to 50 people (many of whom are avid seabirders) helping to spot and identify birds. The disadvantages of the organized trips stem mainly from the fact that there are relatively few of them and scheduling may be a problem. Most trips are concentrated in the fall, when the quality of pelagic birding is generally at its best. If your vacation time falls in summer or over the Christmas season you may be out of luck.

The main advantage of taking a fishing boat is that you can almost always find a boat, and advance scheduling is usually not required. Another nice point for those who enjoy the thrill of discovery is the opportunity to spot and identify all of the birds yourself. This chance is rarely afforded when there are 50 other eager birders on board. The disadvantages are many. The objectives of everyone on the boat but you are fish and fishing. So the boat does not stop for birds and does not chase birds. And do not get in the way of all the rods, reels, tangled lines, and fishers. Most true pelagic birds will be seen only when the boat is going out, coming back, or otherwise moving across the ocean from one fishing spot to another. This travel time may account for 3 hours of an 8-hour day. The rest of the time will be spent sitting in a couple of choice fishing spots for up to 2 or 3 hours at a time. During these periods you are likely to see little except the same gulls and cormorants that could have been seen from shore.

No matter what type of boat you find yourself on, you may have to cope with the problem of seasickness. There are few, if any, absolutes on how to avoid this unpleasant malady. Almost every veteran pelagic birder has suffered from it at least once, and some fall victim on nearly every trip. Weather conditions and underwater geographic features make every trip different in terms of motion. The size of the boat is another consideration (bigger is usually better). Even where you stand on the boat makes a difference; the bow is the liveliest spot.

Traditional over-the-counter remedies such as Dramamine and Marazine are helpful to some people and useless to others. One possible unpleasant side effect of these nonprescription drugs (as well as of many prescription drugs) is extreme drowsiness. If you do use these pills, it is best to start taking them the night before the trip so that the drug has a chance to work its way through your system. A light, nongreasy breakfast should be eaten at least 1 to 2 hours before departing. Snacks for the trip are also good, both to soak up the gastric juices and to renew energy levels. An empty stomach usually aggravates nausea, and, regardless of how you feel at the time, eating something may be the needed cure. A few strategically eaten crackers each hour can make all the difference in the world. Finally, if all else fails, head to the rail and get it over with. Do not use the restroom for this purpose unless you wish to be lynched by your fellow passengers.

Be sure to bring plenty of warm clothes that can be shed in layers. It is difficult to overdress for the first few hours of a pelagic trip regardless of time of year. You may also wish to bring popcorn, bread, and the like to add to the chum. Do not bother to bring a spotting scope, because boat motion will render it useless.

Above all, this is the time to really do your homework on the finer points of identification. Most pelagic birds appear suddenly, flash by the boat, and are gone before you know it. Many have a tendency to fly low between the swells, so keeping them in your binocular field is very difficult. Add to these problems light conditions that are often less than ideal, fog, boat motion that is sometimes severe, and several species that are extremely similar in appearance and you have the makings of a very frustrating day if you are not prepared to identify the bird instantly. There is seldom time to peruse your field guide while the bird is in sight. That is something that can be done later when activity slows.

There is no one time or place to take a pelagic trip. Although many of the West Coast pelagics can be found anywhere from San Diego to Seattle (and beyond), some are much better seen in one place than another. Likewise, different times of the year are good for different species.

Monterey Bay is usually the most consistent area for maximum diversity and lots of birds. Areas farther north tend to have fewer storm-petrels, whereas areas farther south are poor for alcids, skuas, and albatrosses. San Diego used to be a must for Red-billed Tropicbird, but that species is no longer consistently seen anywhere off the west coast and is probably best seen over deep water 100 miles or more offshore (Davidson Seamount and Cordell Banks trips are probably as good as any). Fall San Diego trips are probably still the best for seeing Least Storm-

Petrels, and Washington trips are probably the best for the South Polar Skua and Black-footed Albatross (although the albatross can be abundant on summer California trips). Trips off the Gulf Coast of Texas can produce species such as Cory's and Audubon's shearwaters, Band-rumped Storm-Petrel, and Masked Booby, none of which can be expected off the West Coast. For pure numbers, summer trips in the Gulf of Alaska can be hard to match, although the alcids that make up the bulk of the species present can usually be seen better from shore. Alaska is the place to go for numbers of Short-tailed Shearwaters and Fork-tailed Storm-Petrels, and it is the only place to see several of the alcids.

South of Alaska, winter is the best time for alcids, Northern Fulmar, Short-tailed Shearwater, Fork-tailed Storm-Petrel, Laysan Albatross, and Black-legged Kittiwake. Fall produces the greatest variety of birds no matter what the location. August through mid-September is generally best for Red-billed Tropicbird, Sabine's Gull, Long-tailed Jaeger, Arctic Tern, and Craveri's Murrelet. Late September through mid-October may produce more variety, and it is the time when thousands of storm-petrels raft on Monterey Bay. Spring usually offers slightly less variety, but some birds (such as Sabine's Gull and the alcids) are in their best plumages. June through July is generally the dullest time, but this is the easiest time to find Black-footed Albatross out of Monterey.

Keep in mind that it takes many boat trips out of several places and at different times of the year to build a good pelagic list. You cannot expect to find all or even most of the possible species on any one trip. It is also the nature of pelagic birding that almost any seabird is theoretically possible (witness a recent California record of Light-mantled Sooty Albatross), so even veterans of scores of trips can hold out hope for something new.

## Calling Birds In

Birders use a variety of sounds to lure birds out of cover. Two of the most universal are "squeaking" and "pishing." To squeak, purse your lips and draw air through in either rapid or prolonged bouts. The same effect can be generated by kissing the back of your hand very loudly. More widely effective is "pishing," a hissing sort of sound that sounds like "pissssh pissssh pissssh." This is similar to the alarm calls of many passerine birds (e.g., wrens, gnatcatchers, some vireos), and by varying the cadence and volume you may produce a fair imitation of a large group of birds mobbing some would-be predator. Both squeaking and pishing are directed primarily at calling in passerines, although some hawks, owls, hummingbirds, and woodpeckers may also respond. Some species respond well to these sounds; others respond little; and some show no interest at all. Chickadees, titmice, nuthatches, wrens, and gnatcatchers will almost always respond. The trick is to get these rather vocal birds agitated and let their alarm calls attract still more species. Many mimids, vireos, warblers, and sparrows will also react strongly to your efforts. Many birds respond best early in the breeding season when, territoriality is at its peak, when young are in the nest. When squeaking or pishing, you should not stand in the open, because a bird that sees that that is coming from a human will not reveal itself.

A more specific (and often more reliable) method of calling birds is to imitate the call of the bird you are trying to attract. However, only a few bird voices are easily duplicated by people. With the advent of the compact, battery-operated cassette recorder this problem has been alleviated. One way to use the tape recorder is to record the vocalizations of a singing bird and then play them back to lure the singer in. The drawback to this method is that, unless the bird is close and is a particularly explosive singer, the average recorder will not pick up the song or the song will be lost in background noise.

Making good field recordings of birds used to be an arduous process involving the use of some expensive and bulky equipment. In the past 10–20 years, innovations in the development of lightweight, highly directional, shotgun microphones, along with cassette tape recorders geared for louder playback, have made tape recording birds a much easier and more enjoyable (if still somewhat expensive) proposition. *Birding* (the journal of the American Birding Association) occasionally carries articles on the latest tape-recording equipment. Cornell University's Library of Natural Sounds (which has the single largest collection of bird recordings in the world) regularly conducts workshops on tape-recording techniques and equipment for persons interested in field recording birds.

Rather than investing in parabolic reflectors, shotgun microphones, and other expensive recording equipment, most birders simply use prerecorded cassette tapes. There are numerous commercially available tapes of bird songs. Many of these are also available as compact discs. The American Birding Association's ABA Sales carries a full line of tapes and CDs of bird vocalizations, including many for other parts of the world. The advent of portable CD players is a welcome development for field birders, because the random access offered by these digital systems saves valuable time formerly spent rewinding or fast-forwarding tape to get to the desired song.

Probably the most complete tape/CD set is *A Field Guide to Western Bird Songs* (revised in 1992), which corresponds by page number to Roger Tory Peterson's *Field Guide to Western Birds* (a companion set is available for eastern North America). This tape/CD set is available from ABA Sales. Although songs or calls of some (mostly rare or local) species are missing, these tapes and CDs include the primary vocalizations for most birds likely to be encountered in western North America. Also recommended is the *Birding by Ear* series by Richard K. Walton and Robert W. Lawson. To date, this series includes three separate sets of tapes and CDs that focus on techniques of learning bird vocalizations using a comparative approach. This series is available from ABA Sales. The third tape and CD set by these authors, *Birding by Ear: Western*, applies the learning approach of the first two volumes to western species. There are also an increasing number of tapes that focus on a single family of birds or on a more restricted geographic area.

Once you have the tape and the recorder in your hands, there are definite dos and don'ts for using it. A frequent mistake is to play the tape too loudly. Most birds have pretty acute hearing, so if it sounds loud to you, it may sound even louder to them. The typical reason for birds' responding to tapes of specific calls is that they are attempting to chase a possible rival from their territory. If your tape is extremely loud, the bird may be too intimidated to approach. Another mistake is to play the tape continuously without letup. Birds that are calling territorially to one another often pause between songs to listen for a response. Once you start to play a tape, the resident bird will often fall silent and begin homing in on your tape recorder. As long as the tape is playing, the bird will have a clear signal of your whereabouts and can approach quietly to check you out. Once it sees that the sound is coming from a human, it may slip quietly away without your even knowing it was there. Conversely, if you play the tape a few times and then stop, the defending bird will no longer have a homing signal to use. Typically, the bird will then deliver a few cautious songs of its own, in an attempt to coax its "rival" into the open. In so doing, the bird reveals its location to you. You should also avoid standing in the open when attempting to call birds in. The bird may respond well until it sees you standing where the song is originating. Once you have lured a bird into view, stop playing the tape. The bird will likely become curious and pause to sing, making it easy to study. Continuous playing of the tape will only agitate most birds and is actually counterproductive, because, in their excitement, they seldom sit still long enough for you to focus your binoculars.

Another technique that is useful in attracting many passerine birds is to play tapes of owl calls. Many of the smaller owls include birds in their diet, and the birds recognize these owls as enemies. Whenever they locate a small owl, most passerines engage in mobbing behavior; they dive at the owl and make scolding calls until the owl is driven from the area. Consequently, a tape recording of the appropriate small owl will often drive birds wild, and you may be absolutely surrounded by scolding birds. Northern Pygmy-Owl calls are almost certain to elicit mobbing behavior in any of the western mountains where they occur, probably because their diurnal nature brings them into relatively frequent contact with small birds. Western Screech-Owl calls will also work well throughout much of the West; tapes of Eastern Screech-Owl calls should be used in the Midwest, eastern Great Plains, and eastern Texas. Ferruginous Pygmy-Owl calls may be equally as effective as Eastern Screech-Owl calls when working in the lower Rio Grande Valley of Texas. In fact, Ferruginous Pygmy-Owl calls can be effective in many parts of the United States, simply because many of "our" birds spend their winters in Mexico or Central America, where these little owls are common. Great Horned Owl calls in the lower Rio Grande Valley may bring in a flock of Green or Brown jays.

## Ethics

A discussion of ethics should probably accompany every discourse on finding birds. With ever-increasing numbers of birders taking to the field, more and more instances of rude and careless behavior are causing reproductive failure for birds and the closure of privately owned lands to birders. Both problems stem from a lack of consideration by birders who will do anything to see their bird.

Birding ethics is an increasingly common topic within the birding community. Unfortunately, too much of the discussion has centered on the use of tape recorders to attract birds. Well-intentioned but misinformed people have created an atmosphere of near hysteria regarding tape playback and its alleged impact on birds. Well-intentioned as it might be, the argument that an individual bird is unduly stressed by a single encounter with tape playback has no basis in biological fact.

Territorial birds defend their territories repeatedly through the breeding season. At the onset of breeding, males will skirmish with other males time and again throughout the day; many of these encounters are sustained, and some are violent. Territorial defense is a natural and essential part of a bird's daily time-and-energy budget. Early in the season a territorial bird may allocate more time and energy to advertisement and defense than to any other activity. As the season progresses and boundaries become well established, the need to defend the territory gradually yields to other needs, such as procuring food for dependent young. Although these are to an extent competing activities, much slack is built into the system. A bird that takes a few minutes out of a day to respond to a tape has not been dealt a severe blow in its struggle to find food. If birds were indeed so tightly time constrained in their search for food or care of young, it is doubtful that they would bother with territorial defense at all. Certainly, if time or energy budgets of birds were so inflexible, we would see massive avian mortality every time the weather shifted in a way that negatively affected foraging efficiency.

Is a territorial bird upset or agitated when it hears a tape? Certainly. In fact, it may have an extremely strong response, flying rapidly from perch to perch with wings flicking and crown feathers erected. The important thing to remember is that this is a *normal* response to an intruder. When the territorial bird is responding to a real bird rather than a tape, the encounter frequently involves not only the aforementioned responses but also a prolonged, high-speed pursuit around trees, through bushes, and sometimes right onto the ground until the intruder is driven off. Such scenarios will be repeated many times throughout each day of the breeding season with no harm to the birds involved.

Can tapes be overdone? Again, the answer is definitely yes. A resident bird that is lured in repeatedly may become frustrated in its search for the phantom voice. Overusing tapes early in the territory-establishment part of the breeding season might drive a given individual away from its territory. Typically, however, another individual of the same species will move into the vacated space. The more likely scenario (especially later in the breeding season) is that, after a given period of time with no success in locating the intruder, the territorial bird will simply "burn out" in its responsiveness to tapes. It will not abandon ship; it will simply cease to respond to what it has learned is an artificial stimulus, a voice whose source cannot be seen. Birds with dependent young tend to become unresponsive particularly fast.

A tape played to an Arctic Warbler along a back road in Alaska, to a Wrentit in California, or to a Crissal Thrasher in western Texas will in all likelihood be the only tape heard by that individual bird in a season, if not in its lifetime. It may become temporarily agitated and will be taken out of its routine for a few minutes. That is the sum total of the tape's impact.

The birding alternative to using tapes, especially when groups of birders are involved, is not attractive. Abstention from using a tape could result in a prolonged pursuit of a single bird of a shy, skulking species. Inevitably, some people will still not obtain "countable" looks, even after near-constant harassment of the first bird. So the group will similarly pester the next individual of this species that it encounters. In an ecologically sensitive area the decision to leave the trail, particularly with numbers of people, may well lead to harmful trampling of vegetation, increased erosion, and other environmental disturbance. This is a scenario destined to be repeated until each person has seen the bird. On the other hand, judicious use of tapes under such circumstances can reduce the period of time that the bird is disrupted to a minimum, allowing every birder in the group a good view without unnecessary disturbance to the surrounding area.

Although an individual encounter with tape playback has negligible impact on a bird, the risks of stressing a bird or its environment may be unacceptable in the case of locally rare or endangered species in areas with high birder visitation. For that very reason, responsible birders do not play Elegant Trogon tapes on the South Fork Trail in Cave Creek Canyon, Arizona. On the other hand, Buff-collared Nightjars in McCleary Wash, Arizona persisted for years despite having been bombarded with tapes. Similarly, Ferruginous Pygmy-Owls have maintained territories below Falcon Dam in Texas, even though tape-playing birders have been going there for nearly 20 years. Rather than leaving the area, both the nightjars and owls have virtually stopped responding to tapes.

Some would argue that even a negligible impact from tapes is unacceptable. But pishing, squeaking, and whistled owl imitations also disturb birds. Although none of those activities directly involves a territorial response, they do temporarily agitate a bird and take it away from some other activity. And who among us has never pulled up alongside a raptor on a telephone pole or walked close to those shorebirds on the flats? Doing so often results in the birds' flying away, temporarily or even permanently driven from a particular spot. Our very pursuit of birds constitutes a disturbance, of which there is a continuum of degrees. Whereas the repeated use of tapes directed at rare species in areas of heavy birder visitation might be considered unreasonable disturbance, the prudent use of tapes with more common birds and in areas where there is not as much birding activity falls at the low end of the disturbance spectrum.

With the number of birders in the field today, the larger villain is not the tape recorder but the overreliance on "stake-outs" and the dissemination through efficient grapevines of pinpoint directions to specific territories. Each spring on the Texas coast, some birder locates a territorial Bachman's Sparrow and then passes on to other birders the directions and precise mileage to the spot. Before long, the information has been shared by scores of people. When you drive by the spot, it usually looks as if a herd of cattle had recently been driven through it. On a weekend, there may be 10 or more cars parked in the same spot. Over the course of a few weeks, more than a hundred people may stomp their way through the grassy woodland to chase down that one pair of birds. Whether or not any of these people use tapes, the birds at this site will be harassed. Meanwhile, a few miles down that road or along any one of several nearby side roads there may be other Bachman's Sparrows, but birders who have tapped the grapevine are unlikely to look for them. If more birders took the initiative to learn microhabitats and to explore a little rather than relying exclusively on the hotline, the negative impact on both birds and habitats would be reduced and the use of tapes would remain an issue only in the most heavily visited areas. Because of the potential for abuse, birders should use caution in reporting to hotlines the location of nesting territories or active nests. Although it may be perfectly acceptable for hundreds of birders to chase after a vagrant, nonbreeding shorebird or warbler (with little or no impact on the bird), the same frenzied pursuit of a nesting pair of birds attempting to incubate eggs or to feed young could be disastrous.

Particular caution should always be exercised in the vicinity of nest sites. Some species can tolerate a fair amount of disturbance near their nests, but others cannot. Caution is especially critical in the case of rare species and many raptors. Birds are most likely to abandon nests early in the breeding process, particularly when the nests are under construction. At this point, the birds have very little time and energy invested in the nest, and even slight disturbance may cause them to move elsewhere. Once the eggs have been laid, and particularly once the young have hatched, the parents will usually tolerate more disturbance. You should let the behavior of the birds act as your guide. If the parents are making trips to feed young in your presence, then you are probably not a major disturbance to them. If, however, the parents scold in agitation or refuse to deliver food to nestlings in your presence, you should leave. Remember that even when human disturbance does not precipitate actual nest desertion, the mere act of flushing the parent from the nest exposes the eggs or young to heat, cold, and possible predation. Flushing the parent is most harmful when dealing with colonial birds such as herons and terns; one disturbance at the wrong time of day could lead to massive nest failure for the colony.

Appropriate behavior regarding the use of private property is also of concern. Many of the better birding spots across the country are located on private property. Most landowners do not object to birders' entering their land as long as they are courteous and responsible in their use of the area. In a few instances, however, all birders have been barred from wonderful places because of the actions of a few inconsiderate people. The following are a few commonsense rules that should be observed.

1.  Do not enter posted land without permission from the owner. It is best to acquire permission before entering unposted land, too, unless the area is known to be open to birders.

2. Close all gates behind you.
3. Avoid contact with livestock whenever possible.
4. Keep vehicles on roads at all times.
5. Do not litter.
6. Do not smoke, or at least use all due caution.
7. Do not harass the wildlife or trample the vegetation.
8. Always act in a way that will assure other birders of being welcome.

# CHAPTER 2

# TECHNIQUES OF IDENTIFYING BIRDS

Field identification of North American birds is reasonably simple compared with the problems encountered in many other parts of the world. Several factors contribute to this simplicity. Among them are:

1. a relatively sparse avifauna when compared with much of the tropics;
2. our development of a relatively stable taxonomic classification with reasonably adequate knowledge of sexual, age, and geographic variation; and
3. availability of good field guides to help speed the identification process.

The innovation of the field guide has changed bird identification in this country into a skill that can be acquired with some proficiency by anyone in a relatively short period of time. Unfortunately, field guides by their very nature have several shortcomings when used as a sole reference and have even created new problems in the identification of birds.

Because of publishing considerations of cost and space, and because of the need to simplify the identification process from the incredibly lengthy plumage descriptions of earlier works, field guides have traditionally focused on one or two key field marks for each species. Indeed, this approach has great use and is probably adequate for the identification of most species. The goal of efficiency, however, has exacted a price, and that price is one of oversimplification. Many species have been written off as unidentifiable in the field or unidentifiable except by voice because current knowledge or publishing considerations, or both, did not allow the publication of workable techniques. Worse yet, the separation of many species complexes has been made to appear much easier than it is, thus causing and perpetuating a multitude of identification errors (many of which have found their way into print). In the process, much information that is useful and often necessary for identification (such as geographic and polymorphic variation, molt sequences, and subtle structural and behavioral differences) has been ignored.

This chapter and Chapter 4 attempt to fill in the gaps left by most field guides and supplement what is already there. This chapter is largely conceptual in nature and is intended to point out vital considerations in the identification of birds. It is intended to provide a conceptual framework upon which to build identification skills. Numerous specific examples of the various points are included.

# Form and Structure

Taxonomists have arranged birds and other organisms into a hierarchy of categories based on degree of relatedness. For categories above the species level, such relatedness is inferred from the sharing of certain evolutionarily derived characters, implying a common ancestry. There are seven major levels in this hierarchy:

- Kingdom
- Phylum
- Class
- Order
- Family
- Genus
- Species

Moving down the scale from kingdom to species, each category is less inclusive, so the higher levels contain many organisms that are often distantly related and the lower levels have fewer but more closely related members. By way of example, an American Crow is:

1. an animal (kingdom Animalia)
2. a chordate (phylum Chordata)
3. a vertebrate (subphylum Vertebrata)
4. a bird (class Aves)
5. a perching bird (order Passeriformes)
6. a corvid (family Corvidae)
7. a crow/raven–type bird (genus *Corvus*)
8. an American Crow (species *Corvus brachyrhynchos*)

Usually, the more closely related two species are, the more they will resemble one another in overall appearance.

For identification purposes it is often easiest to place an unknown bird in a higher category first, before attempting to identify it to species. Characters within an order are often so broad that one order includes many highly dissimilar birds, so ordinal characters are of little use in the recognition process. Family characters, however, are usually consistent for most members of the group and are often distinctive enough to make visual separation of families relatively easy. A correct family identification will serve to narrow your choices of species considerably and will save you from having to page laboriously through a field guide (for example, identify a bird first as a hummingbird, then narrow it down to Broad-tailed).

Color and other plumage characters are often used by untrained observers as the primary or only clues to bird identification. On many occasions, however, it is impossible to accurately determine a bird's color or plumage patterns because of distance, light conditions, and so forth, *or* color may not be diagnostic for the particular species under observation. Color is, in fact, a poor separator of families, because color differences within families are usually as great as differences between families; for example, such unrelated birds as storm-petrels, cormorants, some ducks, some hawks, crows, blackbirds, and some finches may be mostly or entirely black. Much more reliable in placing a bird in the correct family are overall form and structure. Characters to note include size, bill shape, leg and foot structure, size of head and bill relative to body size, wingspread and wing shape, and length of tail relative to body length.

## Trophic Structures

Trophic structures—those used in gathering food—are often the best indicators of family status, and they may vary dramatically between groups. Avian bill morphology is adapted to a variety of feeding modes and diets. Bills may be stout and conical for crushing seeds, hooked for tearing meat, chisel-like for drilling through bark, long and needle-like for obtaining nectar, and so forth. Leg and foot structure may also be related (at least indirectly) to food procurement and indicative of family status. Examples include long stiltlike legs for wading, strong and heavily clawed feet for snaring vertebrate prey, and zygodactylous toe arrangement (two toes forward and two back) for clinging to tree trunks.

Such structural variation can also be important in separating species within a family. For example, the trophic structures (particularly bills) of loons, cormorants, ducks, shorebirds (Fig. 2.1), gulls, terns, alcids, corvids, and mimids are often as important as plumage in separating otherwise similar species.

## Wing and Tail Shape and Flight Characteristics

Equally or more important to the identification of some families and of species within families is the overall shape of the bird, particularly of the wings and tail. Wing shape and associated flight characteristics are among the best ways to immediately recognize such groups as shearwaters, albatrosses, storm-petrels, raptors, terns, hummingbirds, swifts, and swallows. They are also extremely important clues to separating species within groups.

An appreciation for differences in flight characteristics is especially invaluable in the identification of species within such groups as hawks, shearwaters, storm-petrels, jaegers, gulls, and terns. For example, the combination of wing and tail structure and flight habits is of primary importance in narrowing the identification of an unknown raptor to one or a few species. Consequently, the following discussion will focus on the use of wing and tail structure and of flight characteristics in the identification of raptors and pelagic birds. These groups provide the best examples of the importance of learning wing and tail structures and flight characteristics.

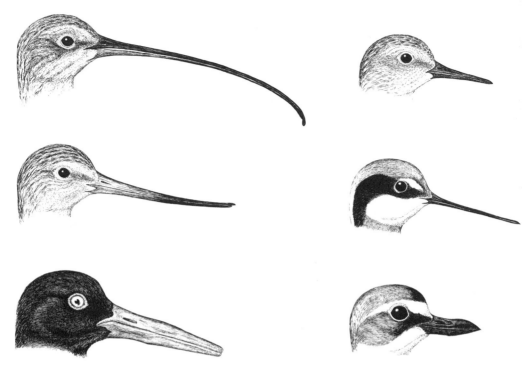

Figure 2.1. Shorebird bill diversity. Long-billed Curlew (top left), Marbled Godwit (center left), Black Oystercatcher (bottom left), Least Sandpiper (top right), Wilson's Phalarope (center right), Wilson's Plover (bottom right). (Artwork by Mimi Hoppe Wolf.)

## Raptors

When dealing with raptors, you should first place an unknown bird into one of five major structural groups. Excluding owls and vultures, these groups are:
1. eagles
2. soaring hawks
3. accipiters
4. falcons
5. kites

The kites and eagles are, to a certain extent, artificial groups containing multiple genera (that are not necessarily closely related), but the other groups are for the most part monogeneric. Descriptions of wing and tail shapes and flight habits for each group follow (see also Fig. 2.2).

**Eagles.** Eagles are huge soaring raptors with broad wings that are also very long. The primaries form distinct "fingers" at the ends of the wings. Their tails are broad and of short to medium length. Both of the two species in the continental United States can be found in the West.

Figure 2.2. *Buteo* outline (left), *Accipiter* outline (center), falcon outline (right). (Artwork by Mimi Hoppe Wolf.)

**Soaring hawks.** Soaring hawks are mostly members of the genus *Buteo*. These are large hawks that soar or glide lazily, high in the air. They have broad, rounded wings (not as proportionately long as eagles' wings) and a short, broad tail. Of the 12 species that occur in the United States, 11 can be found in the West.

**Accipiters.** Accipiters are bird-eating, small to medium-sized hawks of the forest. Members of the genus *Accipiter* have relatively short, rounded wings, with a proportionately long tail. They are typically sit-and-wait predators, remaining perched and chasing passing prey in short, rapid bursts. They also occasionally soar. The typical flight pattern consists of two to four flaps followed by a glide, usually at low to medium heights above ground. (The flight pattern is different when a bird is in direct chase or riding a thermal.) The wing shape and manner of flight are most helpful in separating these hawks from falcons. All three species that occur in the United States can be found in the West.

**Falcons.** Members of the genus *Falco,* are mostly small to medium-sized hawks with long, pointed wings, and a long, squared tail (which may appear rounded when fanned). Their straight-away flight is rapid and powerful, with continuous choppy strokes. When hunting, they typically soar high until prey (usually birds) is spotted and then fold their wings and dive (stoop) on their quarry from above, striking it on the wing. When doing so they achieve tremendous speeds. Kestrels hunt by hovering and then dropping to the ground. There are six species of falcon in the United States; all can be found in the West.

**Kites.** Kites are a polygeneric group of medium-sized raptors that show extreme variation in wing and tail structure and flight characteristics. Some species are falconlike in appearance. They have a long tail and long, pointed wings. These species typically have white and black or gray and black plumage, and they are more buoyant and graceful fliers than falcons; they bank and sail frequently while ruddering with their tails. Other kites are more *Buteo*-like in appearance, with broad, rounded wings. Their proportionately long tail will help separate them from the buteos. Only three of the five species that occur in the United States are likely to be seen in the West.

Three species of diurnal raptors do not fall easily into any of the above categories, and each is the sole representative of its genus in the United States. **Northern Harriers** have a long tail and long, slender wings that are somewhat intermediate between those of buteos and falcons. They typically fly low over the terrain, with wings held in a strong dihedral, and frequently tilt back and forth. A dihedral is simply the angle between two planes. In this case it refers to the angle that the wings of a soaring bird are held inclined above the body. A bird that soars on perfectly flat wings exhibits no dihedral, because the wings and body are on the same plane. **Ospreys** are very large and somewhat eagle-like, but their wings are flexed backward at the carpals (see Figure 2.7 for location of carpal), giving a distinctive crook to the wings and a gull-like appearance in flight. The **Crested Caracara** has a wingspan equivalent to that of the larger buteos, but its wings are narrower and the tail is longer. All three of the above species are so distinctively plumaged as to make misidentification unlikely.

Once you have properly placed an unknown raptor into the correct group, identification as to species can often be made on the basis of plumage characters. However, wing and tail structure and flight habits should not be ignored when making species-level identifications, because they can still provide important clues, particularly when dealing with immature or aberrantly plumaged birds or when viewing conditions do not allow ready color differentiation.

Some structural points to note are the width of the wings relative to their length and the length and width of the tail relative to wing shape. For example, adult Common Black-Hawks and White-tailed Hawks have wings that are very broad and a tail that is somewhat short, giving both species a diagnostic wide-winged look in flight. This feature is more pronounced in the Common Black-Hawk, because its wings are shorter and more rounded at the tips. On the other hand, Swainson's Hawks have long, very slender wings with pointed tips, giving them a look that is quite unlike that of other buteos. Likewise, Rough-legged Hawks have long, somewhat slender wings, whereas their close relatives, the Ferruginous Hawks, have long broad wings that may still appear narrow because of their longer tail. The relation of wing shape to tail length is age-related in several species of raptors. The differences in shape between adults and juveniles of some raptors of the same species may be greater than the differences between that species and another.

Once again, such terms as *slender* or *broad* are relative and require some comparative experience to assess. Carefully and repeatedly studying the structure of a common species (such as the Red-tailed Hawk) is the best way to develop a feel for structural differences in the group as a whole. Keep in mind that the relative proportions of wing breadth to tail length of many species of hawk differ markedly between young birds and mature adults. The tail of many species of soaring hawk, particularly, is often proportionately longer in juveniles. Additional flight characteristics to note include the following.

1. Does the bird frequently hover while hunting? (Ferruginous and Rough-legged hawks, American Kestrel, White-tailed Kite)
2. Does it tip or teeter back and forth while soaring or cruising? (Turkey Vulture, Zone-tailed Hawk, Northern Harrier)
3. What is its flight attitude when soaring (that is, are the wings held flat or raised in a dihedral)?

Be aware that flight habits can vary tremendously depending on wind conditions, so a bird that normally soars with a flat-winged attitude may have a pronounced dihedral at any given time. Also, many raptors will hover on occasion, although only Ferruginous and Rough-legged hawks, the American Kestrel, and White-tailed Kite do it habitually.

## Pelagic Birds

Identifying many pelagic birds involves problems not encountered on land. The viewing conditions are often poor, and observations must be made in a short time at a distance. Consequently, flight characteristics take on added importance because it is difficult to discriminate plumage characters in those circumstances.

Different characters of flight are important for the different groups of pelagic birds. Accordingly, the important points to note for each group are listed separately. The following flight characteristics are in some cases obvious and in other cases subtle. They require much practice and experience to master, but once you have done so your success on pelagic trips will increase manyfold. Take every opportunity to study the flight of even the most common pelagic species, and use their flight patterns as a yardstick with which to measure less familiar species. As do those of raptors, the flight habits of pelagic birds can vary tremendously with wind conditions and should not be used as the sole basis for an identification.

**Albatrosses.** The master fliers of the ocean, albatrosses glide on long bowed wings above the water, seemingly without effort. They flap their wings only once in a great while. Flight characteristics are fairly inconsequential in the separation of the few albatross species seen in our waters.

**Shearwaters.** Shearwaters are amazing fliers. They all have a characteristic alternation of relatively rapid wingbeats with stiff-winged glides over the water. Their glides are similar to those of albatrosses, but they flap more frequently. There are numerous subtle differences within this diagnostic style of flight that can aid in nailing down the specific identification of a distant bird. Ask yourself the following questions.

- Are the glides long or short? How are the wings held during the glides (e.g., bowed, straight out, flexed?)

- How frequent are the beats between glides?
- Does the bird rise and fall in height above the surface?
- Does the bird arc or wheel above the water. If it does, how high and how frequently?
- Does the bird bank frequently, alternately showing upper and lower surfaces?

***Pterodroma* Petrels.** *Pterodroma* Petrels are another group of master fliers. All of the points important in judging the flight of shearwaters apply to them also.

**The Storm-Petrels.** Storm-petrels include many extremely similar species, and plumage is of little help. Consequently, flight habits are of vital importance in separating members of the group. Storm-Petrels are highly variable in their manner of flying, but nearly all are fast, low fliers that occasionally glide. Their flight is often bounding or somewhat erratic. When feeding, they usually skip or patter across the surface. Points to note include
- depth of wingbeat (Are the wings brought above the horizontal plane of the body? If they are, how far?
- timing and constancy of beats
- flight path (Is it direct or zigzag? Level or up-and-down?)

**Jaegers.** Jaegers are frequent kleptoparasites (they steal food from other birds by chasing them until they disgorge), and much can be told from the birds they chase and how well they keep up. The large and heavy Pomarine Jaeger is a strong flier that chases larger, not overly maneuverable gulls. At the other end of the spectrum is the Long-tailed Jaeger, which is small enough and maneuverable enough to chase such aerobatic fliers as terns. The Parasitic Jaeger is intermediate in size and bulk and usually confines its chases to terns or small to medium-sized gulls. If other birds are not present for comparison, note the degree of power or buoyancy of the flight.

## General Comments about Tail Shape

Tail structure is probably more important in helping to separate species within groups than it is in differentiating one family from another. However, it is still an important aid in the recognition of such groups as frigatebirds, adult jaegers and tropicbirds, terns, some wrens and mimids, and gnatcatchers.

Within groups, tail structure can be extremely important in the separation of species, especially among the gulls, jaegers (length of tail points as well as their shape), kites, hummingbirds, swallows, some corvids, some sparrows, and some icterids. Certain species in other families have a tail that is so long or unusually shaped as to make them instantly recognizable on the basis of tail structure alone (for example, Scissor-tailed Flycatcher).

# Body Proportions

General body proportions should also be taken into account when identifying birds. Especially important are the head, bill, and tail relative to the body. The large head and short tail of many species give them a top-heavy, sawed-off look. A large bill will accentuate such an impression. Alternatively, a bird's head, including the bill, may be about the same length as its tail, lending a symmetrical look to the bird as a whole. These contrasting impressions of relative proportions are especially important clues to the identification of *Sterna* terns and *Empidonax* flycatchers.

The combination of a relatively small head with a somewhat plump body gives many groups, such as grouse, quail, doves, and thrushes, a rotund look that is instantly recognizable.

Head shape is just as critical as head size to the identification of many species. It is particularly helpful in the separation of grebes (Horned versus Eared), scaup, goldeneyes, eiders, scoters, swans, and diving ducks in general. Many of these species and others (for example, Canvasback, Ring-necked Duck, Tufted Duck) can be distinguished in poor light on the basis of the head and bill profile alone. Special structures such as crests or prominent head plumes should always be noted.

Neck structure (particularly relative thickness), too, should be used as an aid to identification, particularly when dealing with loons, grebes, cormorants, and waders.

# Color and Plumage Patterns

Despite the importance of the various structural features, plumage patterns and color remain the primary characters of identification for most species. Although structure is more important in the recognition of families or orders, plumage is most useful in separating species.

Plumage goes beyond color, to the presence or absence of such features as eye rings, eye stripes, eye lines, malar stripes, spectacles, median stripes, wing bars, rump patches, and tail spots. Also important to note are the presence, boldness, and extent of patterns of barring, streaking, spotting, or scalloping on the breast, belly, flanks, back, and upper and under surfaces of the wings.

Bright patches of color on the crown, back, shoulders, crissum (collective term used for the undertail coverts when they are of one color that contrasts with the surrounding feathers of the belly and lower flanks), and axillaries (also called axillars, these are the innermost wing lining feathers that cover the "armpit" region between the spread wing and the underbody) are important in the identification of many species, as is the presence of contrastingly colored caps, hoods, breast and belly bands, bibs, collars, outer tail feather, and others. Because of the diversity and complexity of bird plumages, it is important to become familiar with bird

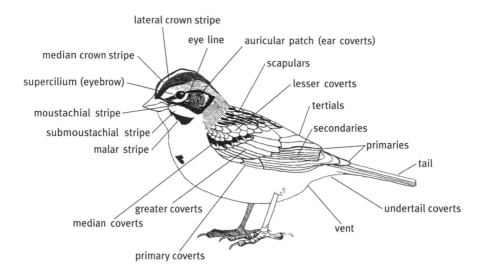

Figure 2.3. Bird topography. Lark Sparrow. (Artwork by Shawneen Finnegan.)

feather anatomy. A thorough review of the bird topography illustrated in Figures 2.3 through 2.7 should provide you with the necessary background information.

Different feather groups are more prominent on some groups of birds than on others. For example, the tertials and scapulars are most prominent on a dowitcher, whereas the secondaries and primaries are most prominent on the flycatcher.

### Plumage Variation

Recognizing birds by their plumage is complicated by the facts that the plumage of a given individual of any species changes throughout its life, and the plumage of males of most species differs from that of females. There may also be sources of variation other than age and sex.

One of the most common types of variation is geographic or racial variation. A subspecies (sometimes called a race) is an aggregate of local populations of a species that occupies some subdivision of the range of that species and that is morphologically or vocally different from other populations of that species. Such variation is maintained by low gene flow between populations and by at least slightly different selection pressures between different geographic areas. The list of species that vary geographically is long, and the nature and extent of that variation is different from one species to the next. Some species show more or less continuous variation from one extreme to another (e.g., light to dark). Such continuous (not exhibiting breaks) character variation usually coincides with some environmental gradient, such as latitude, and is termed *clinal variation*. Others species have discretely different races that may differ greatly or slightly but with no intermediate types.

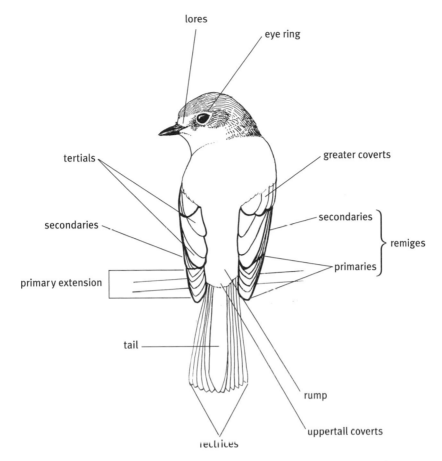

lores

eye ring

tertials

greater coverts

secondaries

secondaries

remiges

primary extension

primaries

tail

rump

rectrices

uppertail coverts

Figure 2.4. Bird topography. *Empidonax* flycatcher. (Artwork by Shawneen Finnegan.)

Some of the species that exhibit marked geographic variation are Leach's Storm-Petrel; Red-tailed Hawk; Merlin; Peregrine Falcon; Gyrfalcon; Bar-tailed Godwit; Short-billed Dowitcher; Clapper Rail; Western Gull; Northern Flicker; Gray Jay; Cliff Swallow; Tufted Titmouse; thrushes of the genus *Catharus;* Yellow-rumped Warbler; Savannah, Song, Grasshopper, and Fox sparrows; and Dark-eyed Junco. This list is not comprehensive, but it does demonstrate the existence of geographic variation in most families of birds. Your knowledge of geographic variations in plumage could be the vital factor in correctly identifying some birds. In addition, taxonomic thinking about how to define species is undergoing major changes, coincident with advances in techniques of studying genetic variation at the molecular level. Molecular studies are now revealing that many populations previously considered to be subspecies of one wide-ranging species, are, in fact, genetically different enough to be considered a separate species. The implications are enormous, and, no doubt, many forms currently considered subspecies will be elevated to full-species rank in the near future.

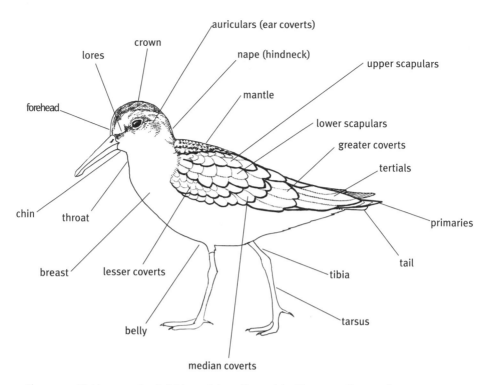

Figure 2.5. Bird topography. *Calidris* sandpiper. (Artwork by Shawneen Finnegan.)

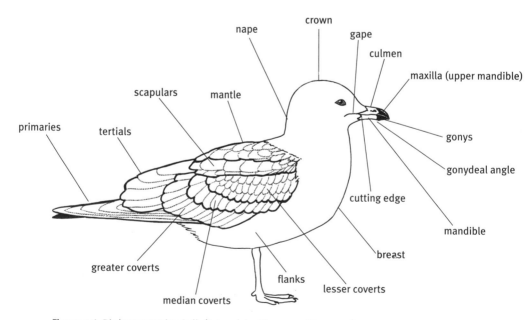

Figure 2.6. Bird topography. Gull. (Artwork by Shawneen Finnegan.)

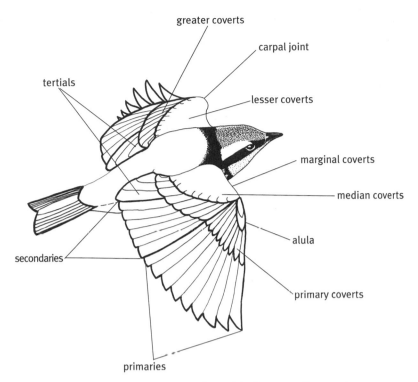

greater coverts

carpal joint

tertials

lesser coverts

marginal coverts

median coverts

alula

secondaries

primary coverts

primaries

Figure 2.7. Bird topography. Flying passerine. (Artwork by Shawneen Finnegan.)

Plumage variation also can occur within a single population. A species that has two distinct plumage types (morphs) within a population is said to be dimorphic. If more than two morphs occur in a population, the species is polymorphic. The most common types of dimorphism result from plumage differences between males and females and between young and adults. Sexual dimorphism is extremely common (particularly among passerines) but is most pronounced in groups such as ducks, gallinaceous fowl, hummingbirds, warblers, finches, icterids, and tanagers. In many cases the differences between male and female plumages in a species are greater than they are between species. Age dimorphism is also common, and in such groups as sulids, waders, hawks, jaegers, and gulls, the plumage of immature birds may be radically different from that of adults.

Still another type of dimorphism involves inherited traits that are not correlated with age or sex. Such morphs (frequently called phases, which inaccurately suggests a temporary condition) are often markedly different from one another, as demonstrated by the white and blue morphs of Snow and Ross's geese, the white and dark morphs of the Reddish Egret, the light and dark morphs of many buteos, and the red and gray morphs of the Eastern Screech-Owl.

The term *polymorphism* is usually reserved for cases in which more than two variants that are not the result of age and or sexual differences exist within a population. This situation is most closely approached among North American species by the Ruff, a rare but regular vagrant from Europe and Asia that probably occasionally breeds in Alaska. Male Ruffs in breeding plumage have a ruff of feathers around the head and neck that is erected during courtship. The ruff may be orange, black, or white. Females (called Reeves) are not polymorphic.

More frequent are cases in which a species shows a continuum of color variation between individuals in a population. This is not true polymorphism, because there is a gradation of plumage types, without discretely different morphs. Populations of Northern Fulmars, jaegers, and some buteos contain all manner of intermediate forms between dark-morph and light-morph birds.

## Molt and Plumage Sequence

The plumage of an individual of a given species undergoes seasonal or age variation resulting from molt and feather wear. Molt is a periodic replacement of old feathers with new ones. Feathers are subject to extreme abrasion, and because of their vital role in flight, insulation, and protection, it is important that they be constantly renewed and maintained. Molt is very expensive from an energy standpoint and must be timed so as not to compete with other energy-expensive activities such as nesting or migration. Consequently, most species have a yearly complete molt. All or most of the feathers are replaced immediately after the breeding season, just before or after their southbound migration. Most species molt on the breeding grounds before migration or on the wintering grounds after migration. However, some species will molt at least some feathers even while migrating. Others may molt some groups of feathers before migration then suspend their molt and complete it after arriving on the wintering grounds.

Feather loss during molt usually follows an orderly and bilaterally symmetrical pattern. Particularly important is the molt of the flight feathers: the primary and secondary feathers of the wings (called remiges). There are numerous patterns of wing and tail molt, but only a couple need to be mentioned here. Most common is a sequential feather replacement from the first primary (innermost) outward, and the first secondary (outermost) inward; the tail feathers are molted from the central pair outward in both directions. Many waterbirds (notably waterfowl, loons, grebes, and alcids) undergo a synchronous molt in which all primaries are lost simultaneously. Because most of these birds would be rendered nearly flightless by the loss of even one or two primaries, it is best that they compress the molt into a short period and get it over with all at once. During this time they are incapable of flying and must swim or dive to escape predation. Alternatively, some large birds, such as eagles, may require more than a year to completely recycle their plumage.

In addition to the yearly complete molt, many species also undergo a partial molt of head and body feathers just before the breeding season. This prebreeding molt accounts for the bright breeding dress of the males of many species. Most species have acquired essentially adult plumage by their first or second winter, but many larger species such as sulids, albatrosses, raptors, and gulls may take 3 to 8 years to attain full adult plumage. Identification of these groups is greatly complicated by their lengthy and often complex plumage sequences.

Birders must gain some understanding of patterns of molt and plumage sequence if they are to attain full competence in the field identification of birds. Although there can be extreme variation in molt sequence from one family or species to the next, there are some common threads that run through all taxonomic lines. A thorough understanding of these makes it much easier to pick up the nuances of specific groups. For that reason, a "typical" plumage sequence is outlined below. There are two popular systems of molt terminology. I have chosen to use the Humphrey and Parkes (1959) system, which uses the terms *basic* and *alternate* rather than *winter* and *nuptial* (or summer and breeding). This system avoids the confusion that comes from some birds' being in "winter" plumage during our summer months or vice versa. (Note the spelling: juvenal feathers are found on juvenile birds.)

1. The young bird starts out wearing natal down.
2. Natal down is replaced by a complete molt into juvenal plumage by time of fledging.
3. The juvenal plumage undergoes a partial or complete prebasic molt in fall into first-basic plumage.
4. The first-alternate plumage is acquired in spring either through feather wear or by a partial prealternate molt.
5. The first-alternate plumage is lost by a complete prebasic molt after the breeding season, at which time the second-basic plumage is acquired. In many species, this is equivalent to adult basic plumage.
6. Steps 4 and 5 of this cycle are repeated throughout the life of the bird, with either feather wear or partial molts in spring producing the alternate plumage and complete molts after breeding producing the basic plumage.

As can be seen above, birds acquire their alternate plumage through feather wear or by way of a prealternate molt. Feather wear involves the gradual wearing away of the usually dull-colored tips of winter feathers to reveal what are usually much brighter colors below. This phenomenon is found in hawks and most passerines, including parids, mimids, thrushes, vireos, some warblers, many finches, orioles, blackbirds, grackles, and Summer and Hepatic tanagers.

Birds that molt into alternate plumage usually do so by a partial molt of head and body feathers. Included in this group are such birds as gulls, shorebirds, most flycatchers, some warblers, and most sparrows. A few birds (e.g., Marsh Wrens) undergo a complete prealternate molt, and others undergo a nearly complete prealternate molt.

There are numerous variations on the so-called typical molt sequence, and, often, closely related species may show different patterns of molt. One striking variation on the common theme is found in ducks, which undergo a partial molt each fall. This molt produces a very dull *eclipse plumage* in the normally striking males. It is no coincidence that males acquire this dull plumage at a time when they are rendered vulnerable to predation by the simultaneous loss of their flight feathers. This plumage is retained for about 2 months, after which the ducks undergo a complete molt into basic plumage.

An ability to correctly determine a bird's age is a prerequisite for identification in many difficult groups such as sulids, shorebirds, and gulls. To determine the age of a bird in one of these groups, you must know their molt timing and plumage sequence. For other birds, it is important to realize that prebasic molts often produce plumages that are much brighter than the worn breeding dress, thereby dramatically changing the color of familiar species in fall. This realization, combined with a knowledge of the timing of molt in a particular species, is especially important when attempting to identify flycatchers of the genera *Empidonax* and *Myiarchus* during late summer and fall. The groups whose patterns of molt and plumage sequence are critical points in identification are treated in detail in Chapter 4.

There is often confusion regarding the terms *juvenile, immature*, and *subadult*. Juvenile has a precise meaning and refers to birds in juvenal plumage, the first set of true feathers worn by a bird. Once a bird has undergone a molt into its first basic plumage it is no longer a juvenile. Immature has a less precise meaning and is typically used for any grown bird that is not sexually mature or that has something less than adult or definitive plumage. All juveniles are therefore immature birds, but not all immatures are juveniles. Subadult is typically a collective term that refers to all stages between those of juvenile and adult. Some larger birds do not attain their first adult or definitive plumage until 2 to 5 years after their postjuvenal molt. During this time they would be considered subadults.

## Vocalizations

Understandably, most beginning birders rely heavily or entirely on visual clues to a bird's identity. The lesson that auditory discrimination is often as easy or easier comes with experience. Experienced birders may identify 75% or more of the birds encountered in a day's work by voice alone. Voice identification is particularly important in forests, where the vegetation can make it difficult to obtain more than a fleeting glance of a bird.

Vocalizations are generally most important in the identification of passerines, but they are also important when identifying rails, shorebirds, doves, cuckoos, owls, caprimulgids, hummingbirds, and woodpeckers and are of supplementary use in almost every group of birds.

Some species complexes cannot be identified safely in the field solely on the basis of visual characters. Others can be identified, but only by experienced birders and under good viewing conditions. Often these same species can be instantly separated by their songs or calls. Examples include basic-plumaged dowitchers, Western Screech-Owl versus Whiskered Screech-Owl, Common Nighthawk versus Lesser Nighthawk, female hummingbirds of several species (especially Black-chinned versus Costa's), Couch's Kingbird versus Tropical Kingbird, Eastern

Wood-Pewee versus Western Wood-Pewee, Willow Flycatcher versus Alder Flycatcher (as well as almost any other pair of *Empidonax* species), Northwestern Crow versus American Crow, Cassin's Sparrow versus Botteri's Sparrow, and Eastern Meadowlark versus Western Meadowlark.

As are visual identification skills, auditory skills are best acquired and perfected by spending many hours in the field. An excellent way to speed your progress in this area is to purchase some of the many cassette tapes and compact discs of bird songs and calls. These can be played repeatedly until the vocalizations are firmly entrenched in your mind. Be aware, however, that widespread species may have regional populations that sing dialects quite different from those recorded on the records or tapes. The vocal repertoire of many species is extensive, and some species are so prone to individual variation that no two individuals will sound precisely alike. Because of these differences, there is no substitute for extensive field experience over a wide geographic range when it comes to learning bird vocalizations.

Another technique that is especially helpful for remembering songs heard in the field is putting a song or call into words or distinct phonetic syllables. The vocalizations of many species will defy your best efforts in this regard, but others will lend themselves well to such a memory device. Examples include the "FITZ-bew" of the Willow Flycatcher, the "ho-SAY ma-REE-ah" of the Greater Pewee; the "WITchety WITchety WITchety" of the Common Yellowthroat, the "what-CHEER" of the Northern Cardinal, the "drink your TEA" of the Eastern Towhee, and the calls of the Plain Chachalaca, Whip-poor-will, Common Poorwill, Chuck-will's-widow, Eastern Wood-Pewee, Great Kiskadee, and chickadees, all of which say their names.

When learning songs and calls in this way, be sure to note which syllable is accented and whether the cadence is varied or constant for the duration of the vocalization. Are the notes delivered explosively or in a lazy, slow manner? Are they combined in a trill or warble, or is each note distinct? Is the sound sharp, metallic, nasal, harsh, lispy, or gutteral? How is the song paced (does the song speed up or slow down from start to finish, or is it evenly delivered)? These are just a few of the questions that you should ask yourself when committing a vocalization to memory.

By all means do not confine your work to songs or to distinctly different call notes. Even such seemingly similar calls as the "chip" notes common to warblers and sparrows can be separated with much practice. Such an ability can be of great value in keying into one rare bird from among a rapidly moving flock of more common species.

## Behavior

A bird's behavior is often among the most useful of clues in identifying it to the family level and perhaps even further. As noted earlier, trophic structures are useful clues to a bird's identity. As might be expected, unique structural adaptations usually coincide with characteristic behavioral adaptations, allowing birds to maximize their foraging efficiency. Because most birds spend a great deal of their time foraging, foraging behavior is an easily seen character that may greatly facilitate identification. When watching birds forage, try asking yourself some of the following questions:

- Does it feed in large flocks, small groups, or by itself?
- Does it swim? If it swims, does it periodically dive under water, disappearing from view for periods of time (e.g., loons, grebes, diving ducks), or does it tip forward leaving its tail up (dabbling ducks)? Does it spin in circles (phalaropes)? Does it swim with only its head and neck above water (cormorants and Anhinga)?
- If it dives into the water from the air, does it hover over the surface first and come up immediately (e.g., terns and kingfishers), or does it dive from a great height without hovering and stay under longer (e.g., pelicans, tropicbirds, sulids)?
- If it is a large wader (heron, crane, ibis, or stork-type bird), does it wade in deep water or close to the shore? Does it remain motionless or wade very slowly most of the time, only to dart its bill out after passing prey (many herons and egrets), or does it dash back and forth, stirring up prey as it goes (e.g., Tricolored Heron)? If the latter strategy is adopted, does the bird also hold its wings out to the side to shade the water below (canopy feeding) as does the Reddish Egret? Instead of stabbing at prey, does the bird swish its bill back and forth in the water (e.g., Roseate Spoonbill)?
- If you are dealing with a shorebird (sandpiper-, plover-, curlew-, or godwit-type bird), does it feed in the water and, if it does, how far out does it go? Does the bird pick (most sandpipers), probe deeply into the substrate (godwits, dowitchers), skim the water (avocets and stilts), or turn rocks over (turnstones)?
- If you are dealing with a terrestrial species, does it do most or all of its foraging on the wing (aerial), feed above ground in the trees and shrubs (arboreal), or run about on the ground (cursorial)?
- If it is an aerial forager, is it constantly flying in the manner of a nighthawk, swift, or swallow, or does it spend most of its time perched, flying out only to nab passing prey (e.g., most flycatchers)?
- If arboreal, does the bird travel up and down tree trunks and limbs while probing the bark? If so, does it remain upright (creepers and woodpeckers), or does it often move upside down (nuthatches)? Does it pick insects from leaf and twig surfaces (foliage gleaning), often hanging from under leaves to do so? Does it use the central, middle, or outer part of the canopy? Does it feed at high, medium, or low height?
- If the bird is cursorial, does it run, walk, or hop? Does it feed in the open or under heavy cover? Does it scratch back and forth vigorously in the litter (towhees, some sparrows) or pick quietly with its bill?
- Regardless of the foraging substrate used, what is the general foraging strategy (sit-and-wait or active searcher)? If it is an active forager (as most birds are), does it forage at a slow, deliberate pace (vireos) or more rapidly (warblers, kinglets, titmice, and chickadees)? Does it flick its wings or tail while moving

(e.g., kinglets, some warblers)? Does it keep its tail cocked (some wrens and gnatcatchers)?

Although foraging behaviors are usually the ones most likely to be observed, other behaviors may be just as visible and diagnostic. Because they are used to form and cement pair bonds and to ensure the integrity of the gene pool, mating displays tend to be highly specific and therefore make for valuable identification clues when observed. Most passerines have little in the way of special ritualized displays because song serves the same purpose. However, many larger birds such as grebes, ducks, some raptors, cranes, some shorebirds, and grouse have elaborate and colorful mating displays that are both visual and vocal.

Even some passerines have rather outstanding mating display behaviors that are diagnostic. Most of these involve aerial singing by the males. This may involve only a short vertical flutter accompanied by a fluffing of throat and breast feathers and a burst of song (Cassin's Sparrow), a more sustained horizontal flight (Vermilion Flycatcher, Bobolink), or a very prolonged higher-flight song given while circling or while increasing altitude in steplike fashion (larks and pipits). Male grackles and cowbirds often engage in bizarre posturing and feather erecting when courting females.

Also useful to the identification process are the alarm or escape behaviors of many birds. Most puddle ducks will fly when scared, leaping directly out of the water into full flight. Diving ducks have structural modifications that negate such a fast takeoff, so they must get a running start on the surface before getting airborne. Grebes and loons are more awkward still; they usually dive rather than fly to escape. Bitterns freeze with bill pointed to the sky when alarmed, but other herons will fly. When flushed, most grassland sparrows will fly low for a short distance and drop swiftly back into cover. Pipits, larks, and longspurs under the same conditions will often bounce high into the air and circle before returning to the ground.

Not to be overlooked are nest-building behaviors and the form of the nest. The nests of orioles, swallows, woodpeckers, hummingbirds, and others are good indicators of family or group status, and some individual species, such as the Rose-throated Becard and Altamira Oriole, have nests that are impossible to mistake (within the United States) for the nests of any other species.

If you are searching for Cave Swallows in southern Texas, a knowledge of nest structure can help you quickly distinguish the Cave Swallow from the very similar Cliff Swallow. Both species will place their mud nests in concrete culverts under highways, but the nests of the Cave Swallows are open cups whereas those of the Cliff Swallows are closed with only a small entrance hole. A quick inspection of the nests clustered on the culvert walls will reveal whether Cave Swallows are present and will save you from vainly sifting through scores of Cliff Swallows.

## Gestalt, or Jizz

An important component of identification that has been generally ignored until recent years is the concept of gestalt birding. This concept holds that each species has its own unique elemental character that is more than just the sum of its component parts. This character, in turn, yields a general impression to the birder that may be ill-defined yet instantly recognizable.

Gestalt, then, combines all of the previously discussed features of structure, flight characteristics, plumage, and behavior into an overall impression that can often be discerned even when specific characters cannot. The British have popularized the term *jizz*, which connotes a meaning similar to gestalt.

The approach is essentially the same as that used subconsciously when glancing at a bird and immediately placing it into a family on the basis of a general impression rather than any specific characters. For example, when specific plumage characters are considered, a Ruby-crowned Kinglet is reasonably similar in appearance to several *Empidonax* flycatchers and some vireos; all are olive above, light below, and have two wing bars and an eye ring. However, the Ruby-crowned Kinglet's plump appearance, small bill, and nervous behavior (constant motion and wing twitching) combine for a gestalt that allows instant separation from the other species.

It is this type of impression that allows us to describe a bird as being fierce, powerful, bold, elegant, graceful, delicate, dainty, and so forth. Although such an approach and terminology are somewhat subjective, gestalt birding is, in fact, an extremely useful approach whose value in identification (particularly in identification of certain groups) cannot be denied. Gestalt may play a major, or at least an initial, role in securing the identification of such difficult-to-identify families as storm-petrels, hawks, shorebirds, jaegers, gulls, terns, and flycatchers.

A ready example is provided by the Mew Gull. There is little in the way of plumage characters to separate adults of this species from several other gulls. Overall, it is smaller than similar gulls, and its bill is smaller. But size and subtleties of bill shape are relative, and there may be no other gulls nearby with which to compare the bird. This is where the gestalt, or jizz, of the bird can make identification easy. Mew Gulls have a small head and a small bill with a gently curved culmen and little gonydeal angle (see Fig. 2.6). These features, along with the large, dark eye, combine to give the bird a very delicate, almost dovelike look. No direct comparison with other gulls is needed to gain this impression, although it is certainly accentuated when such comparison is possible.

As are other subtleties of bird identification, gestalt is something that can be safely used only with experience. However, the beginning birder can speed his or her progress toward field excellence by remaining cognizant of such advanced techniques. This should not remain a passive back-of-the-mind awareness but should become an active, diligent search for new ways to recognize birds. When viewing a common familiar species, take an extra few seconds to really study the bird: its structure, its plumage, and how it moves. When seeing a species (or a morphological variant) for the first time, make a special effort to register impressions that can aid in its identification the next time. For the true student of bird identification, every sighting should be a challenge to the senses. When this philosophy is assumed, no field trip is a waste no matter how short the day's list.

Although the concept of gestalt or jizz is an important one, many birders misuse it. General impressions should never replace a solid notation of real field marks, and every attempt should be made to articulate as accurately as possible the various structural features or plumage patterns that impart the jizz of a particular bird. Certainly, identifications of rarities or out-of-range birds should not be based on something as vague as "it had a different jizz."

## Accessory Information

Knowledge of a species' life history, distribution, and habitat preferences can serve as valuable accessory information for making identifications. For example, adult shorebirds migrate earlier in fall than do their offspring. Because adult and juvenal plumages are markedly different for many species, knowing each species' migration timetable may provide a clue to the age, and hence to the identity, of an unknown shorebird. Dowitchers provide a real problem in identification. There are some reliable methods of separating Long-billeds from Short-billeds (see Chapter 4), but before you can separate them you must have some idea of which of the three geographic subspecies of Short-billeds is involved. If you know the respective distributions of these three subspecies, you can concentrate on the proper set of distinguishing field marks. On the West Coast, Short-billeds are usually found in saltwater or brackish habitats, leaving the freshwater, inland locales to the Long-billeds. (There are, however, many places where the two species are found together.) Habitat is also a valuable clue when dealing with *Empidonax* flycatchers during the breeding season (see Chapter 4).

## Importance of Preparation

An underlying thread of this entire chapter has been the need for preparation. The successful birder is cognizant of structures; plumage patterns; molt sequences; age, sex, and flight characteristics; behaviors; life histories; distributions; and habitats. But awareness of such vital factors should not come after the fact. The birders who develop real competence in bird identification are those who have done their homework.

Too often one sees birders who pick up their field guides only to identify an unknown bird. They flip aimlessly through the pages until they see something that looks like their bird. By this time, the barrage of pictures and information in the field guide has confused the memory of any observed details that might have been important to the identification. Many field-trip participants have come to me with the news that "I don't know what I just saw, but I'll recognize it when I see it in the book." They then confidently describe it as being "olive above and light below, with two white wing bars and an eye ring." Imagine their dismay when they come to the page with the *Empidonax* flycatchers (most of which fit the above description), and then follow that with the kinglets, vireos, and nonbreeding warblers (many of which also fit the description). The common reaction at this point is to either give up in disgust or to make a guess based upon some point in the field guide that was never actually observed in the field.

Such trial-and-error birding may eventually produce good results, but the process is long and arduous. Identification of birds becomes much easier if you have spent hours at home studying pictures and descriptions first. Then, when a bird flashes across the trail, you will already have a mental reference collection with which to compare it.

The sighting of a bird often takes place in a matter of a second or two, with visibility obscured by foliage or poor light conditions. In that short time you need to gather enough information to make identification possible. Identifying some species is easy because they are sufficiently distinct from everything else. But accurate identification of many more species depends on catching one specific detail that, often, is obscure. It is not enough to observe the facial pattern, wing bars, and upper and under coloration of a bird if the critical mark for separation is the presence or absence of tail spots. The birder who goes to the field without sufficient preparation cannot possibly hope to observe all pertinent details on every bird he or she sees. The prepared birder, on the other hand, will know to look immediately for certain characters, depending upon the family or genus of the bird.

## Ready Reference to Key Characters

To help birders prepare, I have included the following list of key characters in the identification of most each groups (usually by order or family, but often to smaller groups). The list is by no means comprehensive, and learning the key characters should not preclude the acquisition of other information. However, the list should provide a helpful starting point for the identification of birds within each group. The relative difficulty of identifying members of the groups is characterized as being *straightforward, subtle,* or *difficult to identify.* Simple attention to details mentioned in field guides should ensure identification of the straightforward complexes. *Subtle* implies the presence of distinctive characters that require attention to minute detail (and possibly some comparative experience). *Difficult* implies that knowledge of complex plumage patterns; geographic variability; and details of structure, flight characteristics, and so forth may be necessary. Even then, identification may not always be possible.

Groups that have only one member living in a particular area may be excluded from this list because identification can be made on the basis of geography alone. More-detailed information on specific identification problems within these groups is provided in Chapter 4.

**Loons.** Breeding plumages and bill color are diagnostic. In winter, look at the bill shape and color; face and crown coloration; back pattern; size of head, neck, and body; and posture on water. Identification of basic-plumaged individuals is subtle or difficult, often depending on viewing conditions.

**Grebes.** Breeding plumages are diagnostic, and identification is straightforward, except for separation of Western Grebe and Clark's Grebe, which is subtle. Separation in winter is sometimes subtle (mainly for Horned Grebe versus Eared Grebe). Look at head and neck shape and color, bill shape and color, size, and eye color.

**Albatrosses.** For adults, bill size and color combined with mantle, wing, and body color are diagnostic, and identification is straightforward. For immatures, the critical points are bill size and color and an understanding of plumage sequences. Identification in U.S. waters is fairly straightforward.

**Shearwaters.** Identifications range from straightforward to difficult. Look primarily at head and rump patterns and colors, underwing patterns, flight characteristics, and leg and bill color.

***Pterodroma* Petrels.** Identification of U.S. species is subtle to difficult. Focus on head markings and upper and under wing patterns.

**Storm-Petrels.** This is a subtle to difficult group. Concentrate on flight and feeding characteristics, rump markings, tail shape, and gestalt.

**Tropicbirds.** Concentrate on bill color, pattern of upper and lower wing surfaces, presence or absence of barring on the back (adults), color of tail streamers (adults), and size. Identification of adults is straightforward; identification of juveniles is subtle to difficult.

**Pelicans.** Bill color and overall plumage are diagnostic. Identification of all age classes is straightforward.

**Sulids.** This is a subtle to difficult group. For adults, look at the color of bare parts (bill, facial skin, feet) and overall plumage (particularly on the head, tail, wings, and breast and belly). For subadults, look at the underwing pattern; head, neck, breast and belly coloration; presence or absence of a white rump, collar, or patch at the base of the neck; size; and bare part coloration.

**Cormorants.** Focus on the throat pouch shape and color, facial skin color, bill size, body size, and neck thickness. Identification is subtle.

**Egrets.** Bill and leg combinations are, for the most part, diagnostic. Look secondarily at plumage, size, facial skin color, habitat, and behavior. Identification is straightforward.

**Herons, Storks, Ibises, Cranes, Spoonbills.** Look first at bill shape, body size and build, overall plumage, and soft-part coloration. Look second at feeding behavior and habitat. Identification is usually straightforward.

**Swans.** This is a difficult group. Focus on the head and bill profile, the skin color and shape of the face, posture when swimming, and call.

**Geese.** Look at overall plumage, leg and bill coloration, and size. Identification is straightforward.

**Puddle (Dabbling) Ducks.** Focus on the color of the head, speculum (a small patch of usually iridescent feathers, especially in ducks, showing in the secondary feathers of each wing and contrasting with the differently colored feathers surrounding it), rump, and tail coverts. Identification (except for birds in eclipse plumage) is usually straightforward.

**Diving Ducks.** Most males have either a distinctive plumage or a distinctive bill color and shape or both. Also note the head and bill profile. For females, check the head and bill profile and the overall color pattern. Identification is straightforward except for scaup, female and subadult goldeneyes, subadult scoters, and female eiders.

**Rails.** Focus on bill structure and color, overall size and color pattern, calls, habitat, and leg color. Identification is straightforward except for King Rail versus Clapper Rail.

**Gallinules and Coots.** Look at the color of the frontal shield and the body and legs. Identification is straightforward.

**Shorebirds.** This diverse group contains many species whose identification is straightforward, but it also has many subtle to difficult ones. Focus on bill structure and length; leg length; overall size; bare-part colors; wing, rump, and tail patterns; breast and belly plumage; feeding behaviors; and habitat. Knowledge of aging and plumage sequences is vital for the separation of some complexes.

**Jaegers.** The identification of alternate-plumaged adults is usually straightforward, but identification of immatures is difficult. For adults, concentrate on tail points (length and shape), flight characteristics, gestalt, coloration of the upper parts, nature of the breast band, presence or absence of mottling below (light-morph birds), presence or absence of contrast on upper wing surfaces, and size. For immatures, focus on size, flight characteristics, structure, the nature of barring on under and upper tail coverts, the degree of white flash in the wings, and the color tone of the body.

**Gulls.** The identification of adults is generally subtle, whereas that of immatures can be exceedingly difficult. When dealing with adults, focus on bill and leg colors, bill size and shape, upper and lower surfaces of the wings, mantle color, size and structure, presence or absence of a hood, tail shape and color pattern, and (to a lesser extent) iris color. Knowledge of molt sequence is critical when identifying immatures. Focus on bare-part colors, bill size and shape, wing pattern (particularly the contrast of the primaries with the rest of wing), size, tail bands, gestalt, and flight habits. Because there is frequent hybridization in this group, there will always be individuals that cannot be identified.

**Terns.** Identifications range from subtle to difficult. Concentrate on bill and leg colors, bill size and shape, body size, contrast of upper and under surfaces of primaries with the rest of the wing, the presence or absence of translucent areas (windows) in the wings, the presence or absence of a carpal bar (on juveniles), head and face color patterns, the relative protrusion of the head and bill versus the tail, and gestalt.

**Alcids.** Given good views, most identifications are relatively straightforward. Unfortunately, views are often poor, and then identifications can be difficult. Look at bill size, shape, and color (the combination is often diagnostic); size; presence or absence of a crest; head and neck color patterns (particularly eye rings, special plumes in breeding season, and the like); white on wings or scapulars; and overall color pattern.

**Raptors (Excluding Owls).** Identification of birds in this diverse group range from straightforward to difficult. Focus on wing and tail shapes and associated flight habits, color pattern of underparts (belly, wings, and tail), size, and plumage (or bare parts) of the head. To a lesser extent, look at the upper surface of the wings and tail, the scapulars, the rump, and gestalt. Most identification problems are caused by extreme plumage variation within species.

**Gallinaceous Fowl.** Identification is straightforward. Look at overall plumage; presence of special plumes, crests, combs, and so forth; tail shape, bare-part colors, habitat; and displays. Listen to calls.

**Pigeons and Doves.** Identification is straightforward. Focus on size, tail shape and color, color pattern of the wings, special marks (bands, spots, scaling) or colors on the neck, bill color, and overall color or pattern (scaled versus plain).

**Trogons.** Identification is straightforward and is made easier in this country by the regular presence of only one species. Note the bill and tail color and the presence or absence of a white breast band.

**Cuckoos.** Focus on bill color, pattern on the underside of the tail, color of the primaries, and call. Identification is generally straightforward.

**Owls.** Identification is relatively straightforward. Note size; the presence or absence of "ears" ; eye color; the shape, color, and pattern of the facial disc; breast and belly pattern (i.e., streaked, barred, or spotted); relative length of the tail; habitat; and activity patterns (diurnal versus nocturnal).

**Caprimulgids.** Vocal identification is straightforward, but visual identification ranges from subtle to difficult. Focus on wing and tail shape, tail length and color pattern, size, presence or absence of white in wings, warmth or coldness to overall color tone (i.e., rusty or gray), and behavior and habitat.

**Swifts.** Look at size and color patterns, particularly on the throat and rump. Identification in our area is generally straightforward because the breeding ranges of Vaux's Swift and Chimney Swift do not overlap.

**Hummingbirds.** Identification of adult males is usually straightforward. Look at face pattern (mask, eye stripe, and so on) and color of gorget (the iridescent feathers that make up the throat patch in hummingbirds), crown, and bill. Look secondarily at size, tail shape, and back and underpart colors. Field identification of females and immatures ranges from subtle to inseparable. Note bill color, face pattern, tail shape, size, habitat, and call.

**Kingfishers.** Identification is straightforward. Note the size, back and belly colors, and calls.

**Woodpeckers.** Identification of most species is straightforward. Note the presence or absence of horizontal barring on the back, head and face pattern, back and rump color, wing pattern in flight, and calls.

**Kingbirds.** Focus first on the coloration of the underparts. If they are largely white, focus on bill size and the presence or absence and nature of white on the tail. If the underparts are largely yellow, note the presence or absence and nature of white on the tail, the contrast of the breast with the throat and belly, calls, and the size of the bill. Separation is usually straightforward, but separating Tropical from Couch's and these two from Western may be difficult.

***Myiarchus* Flycatchers.** Identification is subtle. Focus on voice, head and bill proportions, size, contrast of breast with throat and belly, extent of reddish color on tail, lower mandible color, and range and habitat. A knowledge of plumage sequences is helpful.

***Empidonax* Flycatchers.** Identification is subtle to very difficult. The combination of calls, range, and habitat can make the identification of breeding birds fairly easy. At other times, check bill and tail proportions; conspicuousness and shape of the eye ring; size and overall proportions; color of the throat, breast, back, and outer rectrices; primary length; and calls.

**Pewees.** Identification is subtle, but vocalizations are generally diagnostic. For visual separation, note the presence or absence of conspicuous wing bars; contrast on the ventral surface of the body (particularly the contrast between the flanks and the breast); size and relative proportions of bill, body, and tail; and the presence or absence of white on the side of the rump. Separation of Eastern Wood-Pewee and Western Wood-Pewee except by voice may be impossible.

**Phoebes and other Flycatchers.** The Plumages of these remaining flycatchers are generally diagnostic, and identification is straightforward. Beware of confusing Eastern Phoebe with pewees, and tyrannulet with empids, kinglets, or vireos.

**Swallows.** Identification is straightforward. Note back, rump, and underpart colors; tail shape; and presence or absence of a breast band.

**Jays.** Identification is straightforward except for *Aphelocoma*. If the general body color is blue, note the presence or absence of a crest, the color of the head and breast, the presence or absence of white in the wings, face and throat pattern, tail length, and calls. If the bird is not blue, then the overall plumage plus bill and tail proportions (nutcracker versus Gray Jay) are diagnostic.

**Magpies.** Identification is straightforward, and the two species are nearly allopatric. Note the bill color and the presence or absence of yellow skin around the eye.

**Crows and Ravens.** Identification is subtle to difficult. Note the size, call, tail shape, habitat, bill proportions, and distribution.

**Titmice.** Identification is straightforward, especially given the allopatry of Tufted Titmouse, Juniper Titmouse, and Oak Titmouse. Note the color of the crest and flank, presence or absence of a black-and-white face pattern, and distribution.

**Other Parids.** Identification is straightforward except for Carolina Chickadee versus Black-capped Chickadee and young Verdin versus Bushtit. If the bird has a black bib, note the extent of the bib; crown, back, and flank colors; presence or absence of an eye stripe; presence or absence of white edgings to secondaries; and calls and distribution. If the bird does not have a black bib, note head and shoulder color, calls, relative tail length and habitat.

**Nuthatches.** Identification is straightforward given the allopatry of the Pygmy Nuthatch and the Brown-headed Nuthatch. Note the crown and face color and pattern, color of the underparts, calls, and distribution.

**Wrens.** Identification is generally straightforward. If an eye stripe is present, focus on size, the presence or absence of streaking on the back, underpart color and pattern, relative tail length, presence of white in the tail, calls, and distribution. If no eye stripe (or a very inconspicuous one) is present, note the throat and belly color, presence or absence and boldness of barring on undertail coverts, voice, and habitat.

**Kinglets.** Identification is straightforward. Crown color and calls are diagnostic, but the presence of an eye ring versus an eye stripe may be the easiest mark to observe on birds that are seen from below.

**Gnatcatchers.** Identification is subtle. Breeding-plumaged males are easily separated (except for Black-tailed Gnatcatcher versus possible Black-capped Gnatcatcher in Arizona). Note the color of the crown and the underside of the tail, habitat, voice, and distribution. Females and winter males can present problems. Note undertail color pattern, voice, habitat, and distribution.

**Bluebirds (and Solitaires).** Identification of males is straightforward. Note the overall color, particularly of the throat, chin, and central back but also of the belly and the shade of blue of the upper parts. Identification of females is subtle. Focus on the color of the throat and flanks, the wing color and feather edging, and the relative length of the wings. Solitaires are similar to female bluebirds but have wing bars, a longer tail with white outer feathers, and no hint of blue.

**Spot-Breasted Thrushes.** Identification is subtle. A knowledge of the geographic variation present in this group is necessary for accurate identification. Note the boldness and extent of spotting below; upperpart coloration (warm rusty brown, cold gray brown, or intermediate); color of face and flanks; presence or absence and pattern of an eye ring or spectacles; presence or absence of a buffy wash on breast; tail or back contrast; and voice.

**Shrikes.** Identification is straightforward to subtle. Note size, presence or absence of barring on underparts (adults), back color (juveniles), and range.

**Mimids.** Identification is straightforward except for Long-billed Thrasher versus Brown Thrasher and Curve-billed Thrasher versus Bendire's Thrasher. If the bird is streaked or spotted below, check the back and face color, length and decurvature of the bill, streaks versus spots (and how bold) on breast, voice, and distribution. If the bird is plain-breasted, note the length and decurvature of the bill, color of the undertail coverts, presence or absence of white in the wings, overall coloration, voice, habitat, and distribution.

**Pipits.** Identification of North American breeders is straightforward to subtle. Focus on back pattern (scaly, lightly streaked, or strongly streaked), boldness and extent of streaking on breast, face color and pattern, leg color, habitat, range, and voice.

**Wagtails.** Identification is straightforward except for immature-plumaged Black-backed Wagtails and White Wagtails, which are difficult. If the plumage is essentially black and white or gray and white, focus on the color of the flight feathers, back, and chin. If the bird is yellow and gray, check the color of the rump.

**Waxwings.** Identification is straightforward. Note the color of the undertail coverts and wings, body size, whether the body coloration is warm or cold, voice, and range.

**Vireos.** Identification is straightforward to subtle. Vireos can be readily divided into two groups: those with wing bars and spectacles or eye rings and those with plain wings and an eye stripe. If your bird belongs to the first group, note the boldness of the eye markings (and whether it is an eye ring or true spectacles) and wing bars, color of the lores and iris, general coloration, contrast between crown and back, flank color, voice, habitat, and range. If your bird belongs to the second group, check the color of the underparts (particularly the throat), contrast between crown and back, presence or absence of a black line through the eye or bordering eyebrow, eye color, and voice.

**Warblers.** Identification is straightforward for breeding males, most females, and most fall-plumaged birds. Waterthrushes, *Oporornis*, and some fall birds may be difficult. For breeding males, note the overall color patterns (particularly of the head and breast), voice, and the presence or absence of wing bars, tail spots, eye stripes, eye rings, and rump patches. For females, immatures, and fall-plumaged males, note the color of the flanks and undertail coverts, chip notes, and the presence or absence of wing bars, tail spots, eye stripes, eye rings, rump patches, and streaking on the back.

**Buntings.** Identification of males is straightforward; identification of females is subtle. The general plumage patterns of males are diagnostic. For females, note the overall coloration, presence or absence of buffy wing bars, contrast between the rump and back, and the presence or absence of indistinct streaking on the breast.

**Towhees.** Identification is straightforward, with overall plumage patterns diagnostic.

**Goldfinches.** Identification of males is straightforward, of other plumages somewhat subtle. For males, the overall plumage pattern is diagnostic. For females, immatures, and winter males, note the color of vent, back, and rump; amount of contrast between the throat and lower breast and between the wings and the rest of the body; wing color; and boldness of wing bars.

**Redpolls.** Identification is subtle to difficult. Focus on the presence or absence of streaking on the rump, bill size, extent of streaking on the flanks and undertail coverts, and degree of frostiness to overall color.

**Carpodacus Finches.** Identification is straightforward to subtle. For males, note the color and extent of red on the head, nape, and breast; the nature of streaking on the vent and flanks; voice; habitat; and distribution. For females and immatures, note the boldness of the face pattern, boldness and extent of ventral streaking (especially on the vent), ground color of the underparts (clean white or dingy), bill and tail proportions, habitat, and distribution.

**Grosbeaks and Other Finches.** Identification is straightforward except for female Rose-breasted Grosbeak versus female Black-headed Grosbeak and immatures of the same species. For these, focus on degree of streaking below, underpart coloration, underwing coloration, calls, and distribution. For other members of this group, overall coloration is diagnostic.

**Sparrows.** Identification is straightforward to subtle. Note the presence or absence, boldness, and extent of streaking on the underparts; face, throat, and crown color pattern (presence of median stripes, eye stripes, eye rings, malar stripes, and so on); presence or absence of a distinctive central breast spot; back pattern; wing coloration and presence or absence of wing bars; color of lores; size; tail length; voice; and habitat.

**Juncos.** Identification is straightforward. Eye color is diagnostic for adults of the two species. To separate subspecies, note the back, flank, and belly colors; presence or absence of wing bars; presence or absence of a dark hood; and distribution.

**Longspurs.** Identification of breeding males is straightforward, and separation can be made on the basis of the general plumage pattern. For females, juveniles, and winter males, identification is subtle. Focus on the distribution of white in the tail, the face pattern, the presence or absence of a shoulder patch, the bill color and shape, the primary projection, calls, and distribution.

**Meadowlarks.** Auditory identification is straightforward. Visual identification is difficult. Note the song, cheek color, amount of white in the tail, breeding habitat, and distribution.

**Orioles.** Identification of adult males is straightforward. Note the overall plumage (color and pattern), bill shape, size, and voice. Identification of females and immatures is subtle. Focus on size, overall coloration (particularly the contrast of breast with belly and of upper parts with underparts), bill shape and size, presence or absence of streaking on the back, presence or absence and nature of black on the face or throat, calls, and habitat during the breeding season.

**Other Icterids.** Identification is straightforward to subtle. For adult males, check tail shape and length, eye color, color of head and neck, color of gloss (if present) to the body, presence or absence of bright colors in the wings, bill shape, voice, and distribution. For females and juveniles, check the presence or absence of streaking above and below, tail length and shape, eye color, color or pattern of face and breast, size, bill shape, habitat, and distribution.

**Tanagers.** Identification is straightforward. Overall color is diagnostic for all breeding males except Hepatic Tanager versus Summer Tanager. For these two, note bill color, cheek color, shade of red in plumage, voice, and habitat. For females and juveniles, check overall color, bill color, presence or absence of wing bars, cheek color, calls, and breeding habitat.

## Psychological Influences

One of the driving influences behind the sport of birding is the thrill of finding and identifying new or rare birds. The discovery of an unusual bird carries with it not only intrinsic rewards but also extrinsic ones in the form of admiration from peers. These psychological influences create a situation that can lead to problems in identification.

Birders often go afield with the hope of finding something unusual. It is easy to let this desire cloud our judgment when making identifications, particularly when the circumstances of an observation are less than ideal because of distance, light, brevity of observation, and so forth. All too often a bird will rush past your path, giving a tantalizing glimpse of one or two field marks that might indicate a rarity. If the bird is not relocated, frustration takes over, and subconsciously your mind may begin to fill in details that were not seen, thereby pushing the identification in the desired direction.

This kind of situation must be strenuously avoided if we are to maintain high standards of accuracy in the reporting of bird movements and distributions. Although birds are more mobile than most other organisms and are therefore subject to more frequent vagrancy, the odds of finding a rare bird are slim. Statistically, you are always playing against a stacked deck. (If you weren't, the birds wouldn't be considered rare.) Keep this idea in mind when struggling with an identification. Prove to yourself that the bird in question cannot possibly be an expected species; only after you have eliminated expected species should you try to prove that it is something unusual. Avoid single-character identifications. If there remains any sliver of doubt as to the identification, make your uncertainty known when reporting the bird. As for the bird that reveals just enough to whet your appetite before vanishing, remember that birding is a lot like fishing—the big ones often get away!

Such a philosophy will inevitably produce moments of frustration, but the benefits will far outweigh the costs. You will have contributed nothing but "sanitary" records to the literature; your integrity among fellow birders will remain spotless; and you will feel much better about your bird list and about any rarities whose identity you are able to confirm.

# CHAPTER 3

# KEEPING FIELD NOTES

One of the most productive exercises that a field birder can engage in is keeping a field journal to chronicle his or her activities. Besides providing a record of what birds were seen where, a journal is an ideal repository for notes on identification, behavior, and other aspects of natural history.

## Why Keep a Journal?

There are numerous reasons for keeping a field journal. The most logical is the simple desire to have a record of all field trips taken. This is worthwhile if for no other reason than the pleasure derived from pouring over the accounts of fun days in the field.

If you are list-oriented a journal is essential. Who knows when a geographically variable species may get split by taxonomists? Without a written record, you may not be able to recall whether you saw yellow-legged "Western Gulls" (now Yellow-footed Gull, a separate species) several years ago at the Salton Sea, after having seen thousands of pink-legged ones up and down the California coast on the same trip. A well-kept journal will also save much time and memory searching when you are attempting to compile lists of any kind.

As an active birder you never know when you may be called upon to contribute information to an area checklist, an article, or even a book. Under such conditions memory is an unreliable tool, and there are few things more frustrating than trying vainly to recall the events of a day or an hour of birding that took place months or even years earlier.

Equally or more important, a journal provides a permanent record for others to use. Researchers routinely search the field notes of birders to gain insight into population trends of birds. By maintaining a journal and ensuring that photocopies are deposited with a local museum, library, or university, you may be making a significant contribution to our future understanding of bird distribution. Do not make the mistake of thinking that your records show nothing of value. Ornithology is more advanced as a science than are most fields of organismal biology, thanks in no small part to the contributions of an unparalleled number of active amateurs.

# How to Keep a Journal

Keeping a field journal is like choosing a pair of binoculars; it is a highly personal activity that must reflect the nature of the individual. Just as there is no one best binocular, there is also no absolute right or wrong way of keeping a journal. However, some methods are more desirable than others simply for their capacity for efficient information storage and retrieval.

The method that I suggest is essentially the same as that developed decades ago by Joseph Grinnell, founder of the Museum of Vertebrate Zoology, University of California at Berkeley. Almost everyone uses this basic method, with minor modifications, and you will no doubt wish to incorporate your own changes to reflect a style with which you are comfortable.

At the core of every field journal is a chronological log of every field trip taken, with a list of species seen and locations visited (Fig. 3.1). The date should be listed somewhere at the top of the page (be sure to include the year) and should be repeated for as many pages as are necessary to write up the trip. Putting the date on each page becomes vital if pages get torn or separated from their proper sequence. To indicate that there is another page I put "continued" at the bottom of a page and after the date on the subsequent page. Record the date in a manner that will be clear to everyone (for example, June 9, 1999, or 9 June 1999). Spelling out the month is important because dates written "6/9/99 may be read as either June 9, 1999, or September 6, 1999. It is also desirable to place your name at the top of each page, allowing lost or separated pages some chance of finding their way back to you.

Next, list the localities and habitats visited, in chronological order. Again, keep in mind that others may have use for your notes. Make locality headings as specific as possible. A locale such as Hueco Tanks State Park may need no further explanation, but names such as The Old Refuge or Randel's Pool do. The primary concern is that others should at least be able to pinpoint all spots on a detailed county map. Accordingly, the county and state of all areas visited should be recorded in the locality section. If locations listed are not readily apparent on most maps, then detailed directions (for example, 5 miles north on County Rd. 450 from its jct. with U.S. Hwy. 70) are in order. Too much detail is almost always better than not enough. It is common practice to place wavy lines under all of the localities listed in order to highlight them for quick reference. After the locality section you should list other accessory details of your outings. Minimally, this list should include

1. starting and finishing times,
2. some summary of weather conditions, and
3. a list of field companions, if any.

The starting time and duration of a field trip are important to consider when reviewing the results of a trip. For example, the fact that a formerly common species is missed during a 15-minute stop at noon means little. On the other hand, if that species is missed after a full day of birding that began at dawn, then you may

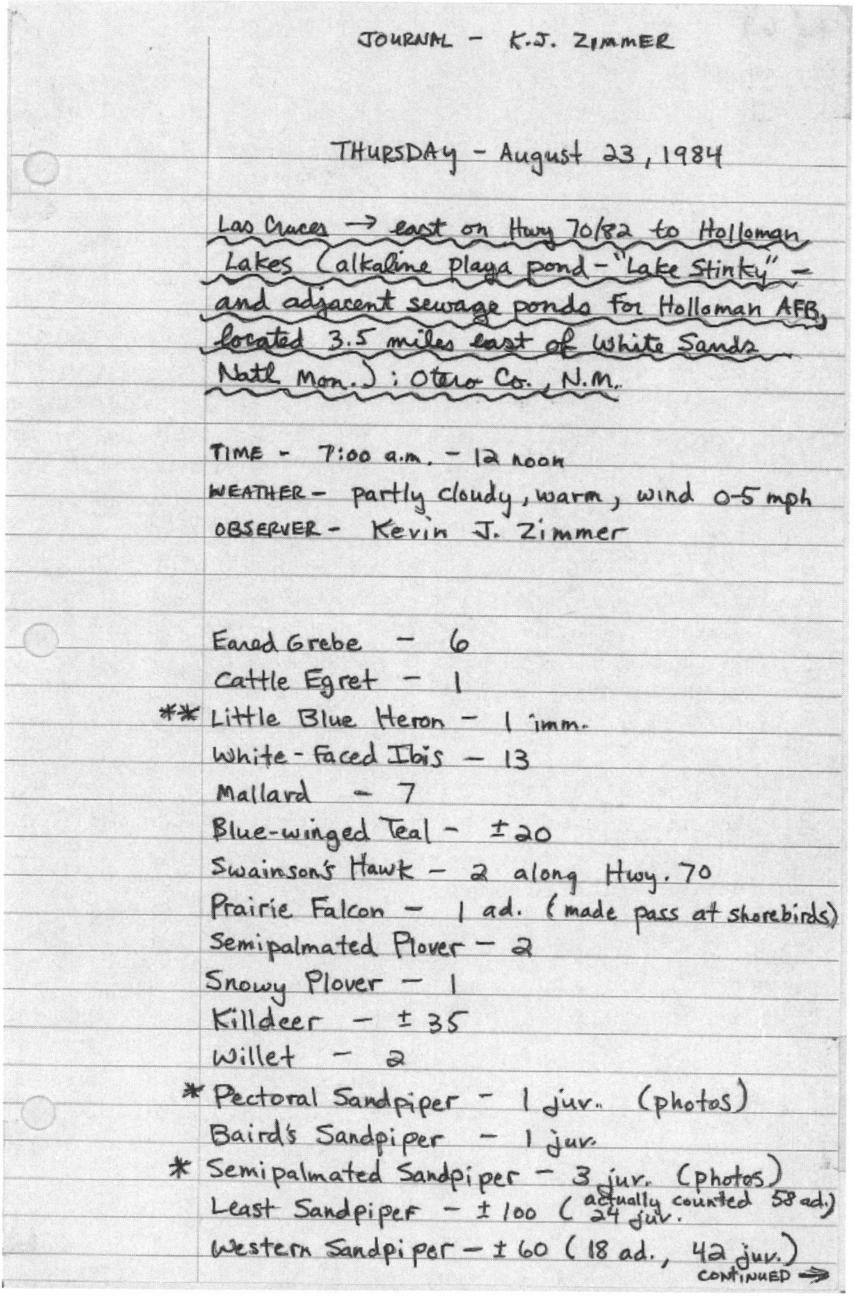

JOURNAL — K.J. ZIMMER

THURSDAY — August 23, 1984

Las Cruces → east on Hwy 70/82 to Holloman
Lakes (alkaline playa pond — "Lake Stinky" —
and adjacent sewage ponds for Holloman AFB,
located 3.5 miles east of White Sands
Natl. Mon.); Otero Co., N.M.

TIME — 7:00 a.m. — 12 noon
WEATHER — partly cloudy, warm, wind 0-5 mph
OBSERVER — Kevin J. Zimmer

Eared Grebe — 6
Cattle Egret — 1
** Little Blue Heron — 1 imm.
White-faced Ibis — 13
Mallard — 7
Blue-winged Teal — ±20
Swainson's Hawk — 2 along Hwy. 70
Prairie Falcon — 1 ad. (made pass at shorebirds)
Semipalmated Plover — 2
Snowy Plover — 1
Killdeer — ±35
Willet — 2
* Pectoral Sandpiper — 1 juv. (photos)
Baird's Sandpiper — 1 juv.
* Semipalmated Sandpiper — 3 juv. (photos)
Least Sandpiper — ±100 (actually counted 58 ad., 24 juv.)
Western Sandpiper — ±60 (18 ad., 42 juv.)
CONTINUED →

Figure 3.1. Sample page from a field journal.

put more stock in your discovery. Again, such information is of great concern to others who may be using your records.

Likewise, a statement of existing weather conditions for the day of a field trip is also critical for placing the results of the trip in proper perspective. Low numbers of birds seen may result mainly from high winds or some other weather condition rather than from a true paucity of bird life. The reverse situation may also hold. Large numbers of migrants on a given day could easily result from some prevailing weather pattern such as north winds and cold fronts. These bits of information may seem trivial at the time, but when records are kept over a number of years, the cumulative total may reveal some consistent trends.

The list of other observers is of primary importance when submitting your rarities records for publication or when others are doing research based on your notes. The more witnesses to an unusual sighting the better, and there is always the chance that one of your companions may have included important details in his or her field notes that you neglected to mention in yours. The list of your companions gives the outside researcher a lead on where to find further information. An observer list may also be helpful to you in recalling the events of a particular outing. Some people combine all of this accessory information in one paragraph. I prefer to give each category a separate line and heading (for example, Time, Weather, Observers) to make the information easier to read at a glance. You may wish to include other types of introductory information such as miles traveled (by car and foot), elevation, habitat descriptions, or, if multiple sites are visited, a breakdown of how much time was spent at each spot. This type of information may also be included in a Notes section at the end of the write-up. The introductory material is followed by the meat of the write-up: a list of all species of birds and the number of individuals of each species seen. Species are typically listed in taxonomic order, although some people prefer to subdivide by locality and then order the birds taxonomically within that framework. Avoid using any ambiguous abbreviations in your listing; for example, "B.t. Hummingbird" could refer either to Broad-tailed or Blue-throated. Using unambiguous abbreviations for common names is especially important because they tend to change over the years. The safest course is to avoid abbreviations altogether.

Birds not identified to species but narrowed to family or genus should be inserted in the sequence with the designation "sp.?" (read "species unknown" ) following the broader classification (e.g., "*Buteo* sp.?" for an unidentified soaring hawk). I typically use brackets to set these partially identified species apart from others on the list. Birds seen by companions but missed by you should still be cited with some symbol in front of the species name to indicate that you did not personally see the bird. The initials of the persons who did see the bird should be included somewhere after the name of the species.

A species list is the minimal amount of information that should be recorded regarding the birds seen on the day. If more than one locality is visited, the specific locale of the sighting should follow each bird name. This locale should be spelled out the first time it is used and can be abbreviated thereafter, providing that the abbreviation is cited parenthetically after the full name: for example, "Killdeer—1 at Hueco Tanks State Park (hereafter HT)." An alternative is to provide a key at the head of the list and then abbreviate throughout. If your notes for a given day require more than one page, the full name of each locale should be used the first time it is cited on each page.

Preferably, the numbers of individuals seen of each species would take the form of exact counts or at least accurate estimates. When large numbers of a species are encountered throughout the day and no attempt has been made at keeping a running tally, it is probably more honest to record a descriptive term (e.g., common or abundant) rather than a number. Even the most imprecise designations, such as "many" or "several" are better than no information at all.

Estimates of numbers may be indicated by a plus (+) sign in front of the figure. Estimates should be rounded to the nearest 10 for numbers under 100 and to the nearest 25 to 50 for numbers from 100 to 1000. Numbers over 1000 should not be estimated to a level finer than the nearest 100. If you have estimated 500 individuals in one flock and then see 3 individuals of the same species at another location, it would be misleading to record 503 as the total count. You may wish to indicate the occurrence of flocks parenthetically: for example, "Surf Scoter—250 (95 in one flock)."

It is often desirable to record the age and sex of a bird in your notes. This is essential information when detailing rarities, but it is also useful under other circumstances. It is well known that the different age classes of many migratory birds move south at different times in fall. Adult shorebirds, for example, migrate before juveniles. By recording the ages of the shorebirds seen on each trip, you can determine the typical timing and pattern of fall shorebird migration in your area. Likewise, the timing of migration of many species is separated by sex; for example, many adult male hummingbirds move south well ahead of the females. By carefully recording the age and sex of the birds seen, you may reveal patterns of differential movement that are still not known for a given species. Because raptors are always of special concern, it is useful to record ages for all the birds seen. This information may lend clues as to how well the populations are maintaining themselves. Large percentages of adults with few young birds may indicate low rates of reproduction.

The age and sex breakdowns do not have to be exact counts. Trying to count large numbers of birds and separating the numbers by age and sex would be extremely tedious, and few birders have enough time in the field or the motivation to make the effort. But it takes little time to note percentages or ratios: "Western Sandpiper—150 (75% adult, 25% juvs.)."

When various breeding behaviors are noticed, make a note of them beside the bird's name; you may want to expand on this description in the Notes section at the end of the write-up. Behaviors that should be noted include food carrying by adults, territorial singing and calling, nest building, mating displays, copulations, and so forth. Such information is vital in determining the true breeding status of birds at a given locale. It is always surprising to discover how many species that are assumed to breed in an area have never actually been documented to do so.

Rare birds listed in your account should be highlighted in some way so as to make them stand out. I usually denote unusual species with an asterisk in the left margin. Rare species merit two asterisks, and extremely rare ones receive three. Other people underline the names of rare birds and use a similar system of one, two, or three lines to denote differing degrees of rarity. I make note of unusually high numbers of individuals by underlining the number. I put unusually low numbers in parentheses. You may wish to include a "heard only" comment for birds that were heard but not seen.

The Notes section at the end of the write-up is the repository for more detailed information that does not conveniently fit into the preceding list (Fig. 3.2). You may have nothing special to write about short outings to familiar spots, but your Notes section for birding trips in unfamiliar places may be longer than the rest of the entry.

One important item to include under Notes is a detailed description of any rare bird that is seen. You may be the best field birder in your area, but a future researcher or someone from another region may have no knowledge of your abilities. Therefore, the simple fact that you recorded a rare species in your journal is not enough. You need to document it.

Documenting rare birds is an art in itself, and there are definite right and wrong ways to go about it. First, descriptions should be written in the field, either while viewing the bird or as soon after as possible. I prefer not to take my journal into the field for fear of losing it, but I do take some sort of notebook from which notes can be transcribed later. Microcassette recorders are handy for dictating in the field notes that can be transcribed later. It is preferable to record (either on tape or in writing) details before looking at a field guide, because our minds often subconsciously alter remembered details to fit those pictured in the book. No records are more tainted than those that say "looked exactly like the picture in the book" instead of containing an original description.

Details should include time of day, light conditions, distance of the observer from the bird, optical equipment used, duration of the sighting, and number of observers and their previous experience (if any) with the species or with similar species. This information should be followed by a detailed description of the bird, including remarks on plumage, size, shape, bill structure, habitat, and any behaviors or vocalizations that were noted. Next should come a discussion of how and why other similar or more likely (or both) species were eliminated from consideration.

Rarities should be reported to the appropriate regional editor of *North American Birds* (formerly *Field Notes*), the journal of North American bird distribution (see Chapter 1 for information on contacting the journal). If you keep a field journal, complete with detailed notes on rarities, it will be easy to report unusual sightings and your observations will become part of the published record.

The Notes section of your journal should not be limited to details of rare birds. This is the place for detailed notes on behaviors or vocalizations of more common birds; remarks on previously unnoted field marks; discussions on apparent population trends, migration patterns, habitat changes, or ecological theories; maps

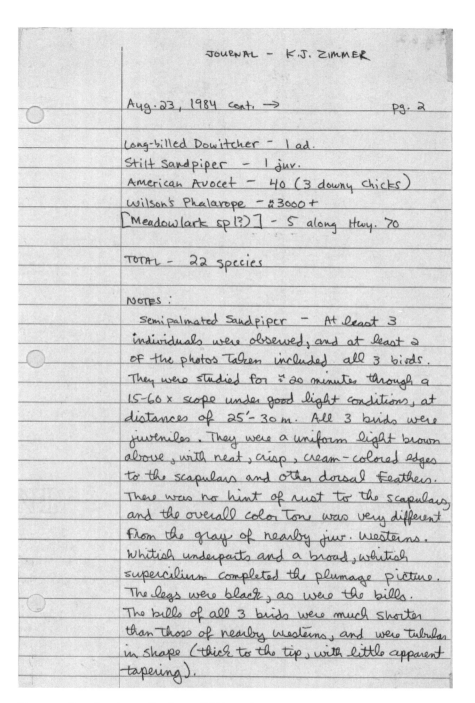

Figure 3.2. Sample notes section from a field journal.

and detailed directions to new birding spots; names, addresses, and phone numbers of birders met in the field; and so on. As such, the Notes section often makes for both interesting and informative reading and can be great fun to read again at some future date.

## Species Accounts

Many birders maintain separate species accounts as a supplement to their field journals. Unlike the journal, which is arranged chronologically by field trip, species accounts are ordered taxonomically, with whole pages devoted to individual species (Fig. 3.3). Within a species account, sightings of that species are entered chronologically, with all pertinent locality and numbers data included. This system makes it easy to retrieve data on any species; you need only turn to the proper species account to retrieve all sightings of that species for the year rather than having to laboriously page through several years of journals to extract the needed information. For this reason, many people prefer to place detailed notes on a given species under the species account rather than in the Notes section of the journal.

Because species accounts are maintained as running, cumulative lists for each species, it is best to keep them in a loose-leaf binder. You can add pages when necessary, and you can always have separate years or groups of years bound at a book bindery at low cost.

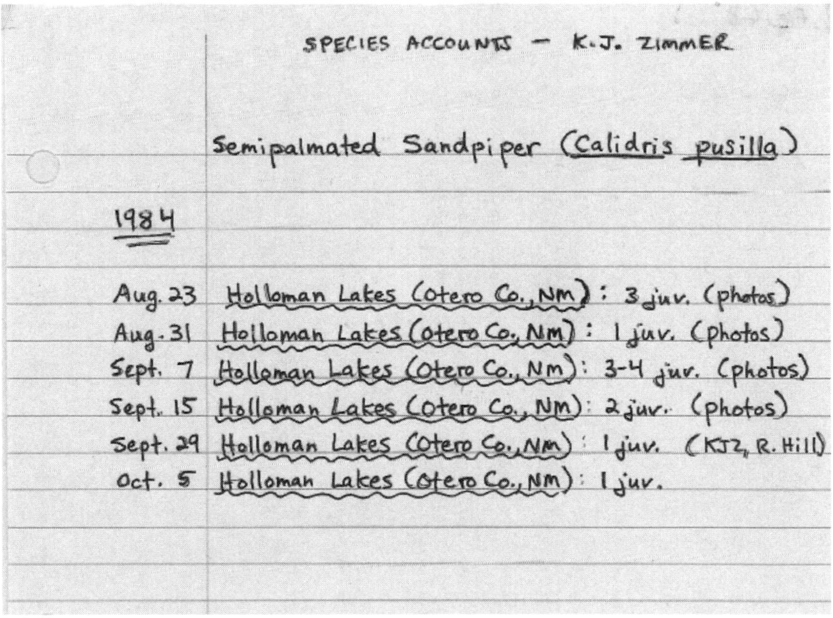
SPECIES ACCOUNTS — K.J. ZIMMER

Semipalmated Sandpiper (Calidris pusilla)

1984

Aug. 23 Holloman Lakes (Otero Co., NM): 3 juv. (photos)
Aug. 31 Holloman Lakes (Otero Co., NM): 1 juv. (photos)
Sept. 7 Holloman Lakes (Otero Co., NM): 3-4 juv. (photos)
Sept. 15 Holloman Lakes (Otero Co., NM): 2 juv. (photos)
Sept. 29 Holloman Lakes (Otero Co., NM): 1 juv. (KJZ, R. Hill)
Oct. 5 Holloman Lakes (Otero Co., NM): 1 juv.

Figure 3.3. Sample species account.

## Some Useful Tips

A final word concerning the maintenance of a field journal is appropriate here. All of the foregoing may seem like too much work, but if it is done regularly it can be easily incorporated into your daily routine. The most important rule is to write your notes while the experiences are still fresh in your mind. There is nothing like procrastination to turn note taking into a chore. Trying to catch up on multiple field trips is not only time-consuming but also leads to errors. Errors are particularly likely to occur in accounts of long birding trips, in which large numbers of birds are seen every day Under these conditions, the days tend to run together in one's mind, and if you allow your note writing to slide for even a couple of days you may find yourself hopelessly behind.

Good note takers learn to take advantage of "dead time" to write up their notes. The time spent driving from one location to another is an excellent time to at least jot numbers down on a field checklist from which they can later be transcribed. If you are the driver, have a companion do the actual recording. This is a good chance for all observers to provide input concerning the numbers of individuals seen of each species. Field notes can be readily written while watching television, listening to the stereo, or relaxing in the heat of the day with a cool drink. Keeping an accurate, useful journal takes discipline, but you'll soon find that with practice, note taking takes little time and provides many real rewards.

# CHAPTER 4

# DIFFICULT IDENTIFICATIONS:
# BEYOND THE FIELD GUIDES

Although the North American avifauna presents relatively few identification problems when compared with some regions, there still remain many species complexes that present real challenges to birders of all ranks. Birders who are confronted by one of these difficult identification problems often take one of two courses: they either overextend their abilities and make some sort of guess or they give in to confusion and write the bird off as unidentifiable. A guess is likely to be shaped by psychological influences and often ends in misidentification. Writing the bird off as unidentifiable is preferable but still unsatisfactory. Either situation results in a clouding of knowledge concerning the true status of the given species in that area.

Fortunately, North American birders are blessed with an abundance of available field guides, which are more than adequate in covering the vast majority of potential identification problems. As noted in Chapter 2, however, the field guides have spawned some problems of their own. Some groups or species have been written off as unidentifiable in the field, when in fact they can be identified. Still other groups have received an overly simplified treatment that makes identification seem easier than it is. Because the guides are often taken as gospel by birders, the printed errors are perpetuated time after time in the field.

The past two decades have seen the gradual adoption of a new approach to field identification by North American birders. This approach reflects a desire to go beyond the field guides, to push our identification capabilities to the limits. Such an attitude has long been in vogue in England, where birders have been subjecting hard-to-identify birds to minute inspection for many years. Questions of molt sequence; geographic variation; and subtle behavioral, vocal, and morphological criteria are all being addressed.

The result has been a rapid expansion of our knowledge of identification. Recent years have seen a proliferation of in-depth papers detailing the secrets to identifying some species or group formerly considered next-to-impossible to separate. Unfortunately, these papers are scattered throughout the literature, and many of the advances have yet to be disseminated to the majority of birders.

This chapter attempts to synthesize much of the current knowledge concerning the tougher species of Western birds. I have arbitrarily decided which species or groups to include. My decisions are based on more than 20 years of leading field trips and birding tours, editing observations columns, serving on records committees, and teaching classes in bird identification. These experiences have given me a feel for which birds are presenting the greatest identification problems. The choices no doubt reflect some personal and regional bias, and other authors would probably produce at least slightly different lists. Some of the more challenging groups (for example, gulls) are given only minimal treatment because the scope of this book precludes the necessary feather-by-feather treatment. For the same reasons a few groups are neglected altogether (e.g., *Pterodroma* petrels). I have also declined to treat most identification problems involving the numerous Siberian vagrants that regularly find their way to the Aleutians and Bering Sea islands of Alaska. Most birders will never encounter those species in North America, and dealing with all of the potential identifications problems involving vagrants is a subject worthy of its own book. I have made a few exceptions for some of the visitors that reach the Alaskan mainland and that are routinely misidentified by birders (e.g., Common Ringed Plover and Slaty-backed Gull).

This chapter, more than any other, is as much written by the birders of North America as for them. The many field marks presented have been discovered by a multitude of top birders. Some have been published; others have been passed by word of mouth. In every case, I have extensive field experience with the species involved and have emphasized the field marks that I find most useful. Where I cannot vouch for a particular character, I have cited the reference from which it came. At the end of many identification problems I have listed additional references on the topic that I consider of special interest. These lists are not implied or intended to be comprehensive.

Species complexes are presented in taxonomic order. Illustrations have been included where useful. Finally, you should not consider any of the following to be the last word in identification. Our knowledge of these groups is still incomplete, and you should constantly look for new field marks to secure difficult identifications.

It should also be emphasized that this material is supplemental to (not a replacement for) that found in standard guides. There are many commercially popular field guides available, and nearly all are adequate for beginning-level birders. The one that I recommend most strongly (particularly for intermediate and advanced birders) is the *National Geographic Society Field Guide to the Birds of North America* (3rd edition, 1999). This guide incorporates far more of the recent advances in field identification than do the others, and it is the most comprehensive in illustrating geographic variation, immature plumages, and so forth.

There now exist some fine books dealing with the identification of specific groups of birds. The ones that I would consider essential references for North American birders interested in in-depth identification of some of the most difficult groups of birds are those by Grant (1986) on gulls; Hayman, Marchant, and Prater (1986) on shorebirds; Harrison (1985, 1987) on seabirds; Paulson (1993) on shorebirds; Clark and Wheeler (1987) on hawks; Olsen and Larsson (1995) on terns; and Dunn and Garrett (1997) on warblers. Also highly recommended is the first installment in The Advanced Birding Video Series (Peregrine Video Productions), *The Large Gulls of North America*, narrated by Jon Dunn. This video offers a wealth of information and technically excellent footage, including stop-action looks at spread wing patterns and other details. The book *A Field Guide to Advanced Birding* (Kaufman 1990) offers in-depth discussions of many of the same problems tackled in this book, as does *The Western Birdwatcher* (Zimmer 1985). Also valuable are the excellent seminal articles by Jon Dunn and Kimball Garrett, which were published in the *Western Tanager* (the newsletter of the Los Angeles Audubon Society) over a period from 1976 to 1983. Each of these is recommended reading, even for the same field problems, because no two authors approach an identification challenge in precisely the same way. By comparing different approaches and opinions, you create your own synthesis, which can influence and be influenced by your own field experiences.

## Nonbreeding-Plumaged Loons

The world's five species of loons (Common, Yellow-billed, Arctic, Pacific, and Red-throated) are readily identified in breeding plumage (with the exception of Pacific versus Arctic Loon: see the next section). Basic-plumaged birds and juveniles, however, present a solvable but subtle challenge. This problem is of greatest concern to birders on the West Coast, where four species occur regularly, but it should not be ignored by inland birders. Both Red-throated and Pacific loons are regular vagrants to inland bodies of water, and in recent years there has been an increase in records of vagrant Yellow-billeds from the Southwest to the Great Lakes.

Throughout the interior of North America the Common Loon is indeed the most common loon species. Because it is also common in coastal locales, it serves as a good yardstick against which to compare the other species.

The Common Loon is a large-bodied, big-headed, big-billed loon. It could be confused with the even larger Yellow-billed or with the smaller Pacific. It is not likely to be confused with the much smaller, slender-billed Red-throated, and the Red-throated is not likely to be mistaken for the massive Yellow-billed. The critical problems then are: (1) Common versus Yellow-billed, (2) Common versus Pacific, and (3) Pacific versus Red-throated. The widespread Pacific Loon and the Arctic Loon, which is only a remote possibility outside of Alaska, differ from Common, Yellow-billed, and Red-throated loons in much the same ways. Therefore, and because Arctic and Pacific loons are difficult to separate, they are treated in detail in the next main section.

### Common versus Yellow-billed Loon

Most guides tend to stress bill shape and color as being critical field marks in the differentiation of these two species. Indeed, the combination of bill color and structure can be diagnostic for many individuals, but accessory marks should also be examined.

Yellow-billed Loons typically have a larger bill than most Commons. In both species the lower mandible angles sharply upward from the gonydeal angle to the tip. However, the culmen of the Common angles or curves down to the tip and that of the Yellow-billed is straight, accentuating the sharp gonydeal angle (Fig. 4.1). The sharp angle of the Yellow-billed is pronounced in some individuals (adults more than juveniles), and such birds have a distinctive upturned look to the bill. Such a look is further shown off by the tendency of Yellow-billeds to tilt their head with the bill pointed upward, much like the posture of the much smaller Red-throated Loon. Common Loons hold their bills in a horizontal position, and because the angle of the culmen and that of the gonys are more nearly equal, they appear to have a straighter, daggerlike bill (Fig. 4.1). Despite these distinctions, bill shape is not an infallible character for separating the two species because it is subject to some amount of variation.

Figure 4.1. Basic-plumaged loons. From top to bottom: Red-throated, Pacific, Common, and Yellow-billed. Compare bill shapes and sizes, postures, head shapes, and distribution and pattern of light and dark feathering on the face and sides of the neck. (Artwork by Shawneen Finnegan.)

Likewise, bill color is an important factor but should be viewed with caution. Some Yellow-billeds will show an entirely straw-yellow bill. Such individuals are readily identified. Most others (particularly first-year birds) have a paler bill with some duskiness to the base. These birds are not overly dissimilar to many Commons, whose bills may lighten to a very pale gray. The more common error is to mistake pale-billed Commons for Yellow-billeds, but the reverse error is conceivable. In any event, you should focus on the color of the culmen. Even the paler-billed Commons will have a dark culmen, whereas the culmens of Yellow-billeds (at least the distal half) are always pale (Fig. 4.1). Many Yellow-billeds have dusky coloring on the proximal one-third to one-half of the culmen.

Some excellent plumage characters have been largely ignored by most guides. Common Loons (Fig. 4.1) are darker brown on the crown and nape (hindneck) than on the back. The border between the dark nape and the white throat and foreneck is irregular and often vaguely defined. Virtually all individuals show one or two indentations of white from the foreneck into the dark feathering of the hindneck, making for a jagged border between dark and white on the sides of the neck. The dark feathering of the crown extends well into the auriculars on the rear of the face, but the foreface is more extensively pale. A diffuse white eye ring surrounds the eye. On some individuals this may take the form of a large whitish crescent separating the eye from the dark feathering of the crown. In these birds the dark feathering of the crown extends down only to about the midline of the eye. In other individuals (particularly juveniles, which can be identified by their more strongly barred backs), the dark feathering extends below the eye, and such birds will show a more complete, but somewhat diffuse, white eye ring. In all cases, the division between white and dark on the sides of the face and neck is both irregular in outline and fuzzy in delineation.

The Yellow-billed Loon has a similar overall pattern to the head and neck (Fig. 4.1), but its head is distinctly paler. This species is noticeably lighter on the crown and hindneck than it is on the rest of the upper parts. The crown and hindneck tend to be pale sandy brown; on the face, this color typically extends no farther than eye level and often does not reach that far. The face of most individuals is mostly pale, except for a conspicuous brown smudge on the auriculars. This smudge can be highly visible on some individuals but hard to distinguish on others.

Most Yellow-billeds show a distinctive pattern of transverse barring on the back, created by pale fringes to the back and scapular feathers. This pattern, which is typical of juveniles of all loons except Red-throated, is particularly pronounced in juvenile Yellow-billeds and is even typical of basic-plumaged adults. Beware, however, that juvenile Commons, although not as strongly patterned, still show conspicuous cross-barring on the upper parts. In any event, Yellow-billeds average browner on the upper parts, and most Commons appear darker.

Other differences are structural. Yellow-billeds have a larger body, a thicker neck, and a flatter crown. These subtle distinctions, however, may not be obvious except when the two species are in view at the same time.

See also Binford and Remsen 1974.

## Common versus Pacific Loon

Most standard guides do little to point out the many differences between these two species. Size and structural distinctions are usually noted, but plumage differences are largely ignored.

Commons are larger and bulkier than Pacifics. They have a thicker neck and a flatter crown, and most have a block-headed look that is created by the steep rise of the forehead from the bill (Fig. 4.1). In flight, they appear more hunched with a proportionately larger head and larger feet. Their wingbeats are noticeably slower. Both species have a bill that appears straight and daggerlike, but that of the Common is notably heavier (Fig. 4.1). All of these characters are useful and often instantly recognizable to those with much comparative experience. Birders lacking such experience, however, may be misled by individual variation or postural differences. Plumage differences lend themselves to more objective discrimination by those with little or no experience with one or the other species.

As pointed out in the preceding account, Commons are darker brown on the crown and hindneck than on the back. They also have conspicuous white eye rings or crescents that separate the eye from the dark crown. Although they lack the extremely patchy look of the Yellow-billed (presented by the white face and dark auricular smudge), Commons still have a somewhat patchy look to the face that results from an uneven, often fuzzy border between the dark crown and white lower face (Fig. 4.1). The lores may be dark or white, but if dark, they are the same color as the rest of the crown. The division between dark and light on the side of the neck is also uneven and somewhat erratic and may show a patchiness that differs from bird to bird. The back appears dark at any distance.

In contrast, Pacifics are paler on the rear of the crown and on the hindneck than on the back or forehead. In this species, the crown and hindneck are an evenly colored silver-gray (adults) or gray-brown (juveniles), lending a smooth look. This look is accentuated by a sharp division between white and dark on the side of the neck and on the face (Fig. 4.1). At close range you may see a thin blackish border separating the white foreneck from the gray nape and hindneck. This border often looks as if it were outlined by a fine-point pen. Many Pacifics show a row of dark spots across the white throat which form a sort of chinstrap. This chinstrap is individually variable and may be bold in some individuals, broken or indistinct in others, and absent in still others. A chinstrap is present on most adults, but it may be absent or indistinct on the majority of juveniles. The dark color of the crown extends downward to encompass the eye and then breaks off sharply, giving the species a dark-capped look. The area around the eye is typically dark (with only a thin white eye ring that is typically visible only at close range) and the lores and forehead are noticeably blacker than the rest of the face or crown. The back of this species is distinctly darker than either the crown or the hindneck and appears black at a distance or in poor light.

Some attention has been paid to diving differences between these two as an aid to identification. Commons tend to slide under the water, whereas Pacifics jump up and then go under. As do other such behavioral points, this one requires further testing because it could depend heavily on wind and water movements, water depth, and so forth. Another behavioral characteristic that could be considered supplemental concerns flocking behavior. Pacifics are often encountered in huge feeding flocks (often numbering hundreds of birds), whereas Commons and Red-throateds are rarely found in groups of any real size.

### Pacific versus Red-throated Loon

Red-throated Loons in basic plumage (Fig. 4.1) are noticeably paler in overall color than are the other loons and are particularly paler than Pacifics. Like the latter species, Red-throated is paler on the crown and hindneck than on the back. However, the entire upper parts are a light gray-brown that is very different from the blackish brown back and lighter (but still dark) gray hindneck and crown of the Pacific. The pale appearance of the Red-throated is heightened by the diagnostic white speckling to the back feathers, scapulars, and wing coverts (formed by paired white spots at the tip of each feather), a feature that is absent in Pacifics. In juvenile Red-throateds, the division between the gray-brown of the crown and hindneck and the white of the face and foreneck is usually somewhat uneven, and the line of demarcation is not nearly as sharply defined as in the Pacific. Instead, the lower face and sides of the neck are usually streaked and washed with gray. (This distinction does not hold for basic-plumaged adult Red-throateds, which have a sharper delineation between gray and white, although still not as sharp as in Pacific Loons.) This color pattern, combined with the highly speckled back, gives the Red-throated a variegated look that is very different from the smooth, evenly colored look of the Pacific. Adult Red-throated Loons in basic plumage are also particularly pale-faced. The dark feathering of the crown ends above the eye, leaving the lores and feathering above the eyes white, and therefore making the eyes appear more prominent.

Structural differences are also important. Red-throateds are smaller, a difference that is not always obvious in the field. A character that is obvious is the shape of the bill. As already noted, Pacifics have a straight bill. Red-throateds have a straight culmen, but there is a distinctive upturn to the distal end of the lower mandible (Fig. 4.1). The bill of the Red-throated is also distinctly thin, almost like that of a large grebe rather than a loon. The upturned bill of the Red-throated is accentuated by its habit of swimming with its bill angled up toward the sky, giving it a "snobby" look.

# Arctic versus Pacific Loon

Formerly considered conspecific, these two forms were formally elevated to full specific status in 1985. The Pacific Loon is a common breeder across much of Alaska and northern Canada and is an abundant nearshore migrant and winter resident along the length of our Pacific Coast south of Alaska. It is also an irregular winter vagrant to the interior West. The Arctic Loon breeds across much of northern Europe and Asia and is represented in North America by the subspecies *Gavia arctica viridigularis,* which breeds in northeastern Siberia (and at least occasionally in western Alaska) and winters south to the Baltic Sea and Japan. The true status of *G. a. viridigularis* in Alaska has remained clouded by its similarity to the widespread Pacific Loon and by the general remoteness of the areas in western Alaska where it is most likely to occur. Nesting has been confirmed in the Cape Prince of Wales and Kotzebue areas, and Arctic Loons are regular (albeit rare) spring migrants past Gambell (St. Lawrence Island) and Nome. It should be noted that some authorities have argued that *G. a. viridigularis* should be considered specifically distinct from nominate *arctica* of Europe and western Asia. Records of vagrant "Arctic Loons" in the eastern United States may refer to nominate *arctica.* All subsequent discussion of "Arctic Loons" in this account will refer to *G. a. viridigularis.*

Arctic Loons are bigger and stockier than Pacific Loons. On the basis of wing chord and tarsus measurements, Walsh (1988) found Arctic Loons to be 10% to 12% larger than Pacifics. Although others have pointed to overlap in measurements between the two species, my own examination of specimens and field observations of a number of Arctic Loons in Alaska would suggest that a 10% to 12% size difference may be conservative. Of course, judging the size of birds under field conditions is always fraught with peril, and accurate assessment is heavily dependent on a thorough knowledge of at least one of the species involved. Nonetheless, observers who are intimately familiar with Pacific Loons may notice the size difference on flying birds; Arctics appear closer in size to the Common Loon, or at least intermediate between Common and Pacific loons in size and bulk. It is more difficult to judge the size of swimming loons because the apparent size is highly dependent on how high or low the loon is riding on the water. If you are fortunate enough to find a Pacific Loon and an Arctic Loon close to each other on the water, the size differences may be obvious.

Shape is easier to judge than size, and the two species differ here as well. The Arctic Loon has a head shape that is more reminiscent of the Common Loon or the Yellow-billed Loon, with a steep, angular rise to the forehead and a flattish crown (Fig. 4.2). This similarity is heightened by the size and shape of the bill, which is longer and heavier than that of Pacific, and which (at least in the few individuals that I have studied on the water) seems to have a straighter culmen and a more pronounced gonydeal angle. This slight difference in bill shape is accentuated by the tendency of Arctic Loons to swim with their bill pointed up (Pacifics usually hold the bill straight out), more like a Yellow-billed Loon. Pacific Loons have a more gently rounded head, usually lacking any angular look to the forehead or obvious flatness to the crown (Fig. 4.2), and their bill is straighter in appearance. Although these shape differences have held for all of the Arctic Loons that I have seen on the water, it must be noted that we are still talking about a very small sample size. To my knowledge, no North American observers have truly extensive field experience with *viridigularis* given its rarity and localized, remote range in this country, and most of us who have seen a number of individuals would have to list flyby migrants at Gambell as the bulk of our sightings. Also, it is likely that the size, head shape,

Figure 4.2. Pacific Loon (top) versus Arctic Loon (bottom) (both in alternate plumage). On swimming birds, note particularly the head shape, bill size, posture, and boldness of neck striping, as well as the color of the flanks at the waterline. On flying birds, note the extension of white onto the sides of the rump and the bolder neck striping of Arctic Loons and the ventstrap and black sides of the rump of Pacific Loons. (Artwork by Shawneen Finnegan.)

and bill shape of both species are subject to sexual and individual variation. Therefore, size and shape should be used as supporting evidence in the identification an Arctic Loon, but they should never be the sole basis for such an identification.

Alternate (breeding)-plumaged birds can be separated by a few plumage characters. The best mark, but one that is often misunderstood, is the presence or absence of a white flank patch (Fig. 4.2). Both species are white on the underbody to about the level of the midline (when viewed in profile), but in Arctic Loons this white extends all of the way to the folded wing on sitting or swimming birds, whereas Pacific Loons have a band of dark (blackish in summer, dark brown in winter) feathering between the wing and the white belly that runs the length of the body. Consequently, a swimming Arctic Loon is more likely to show extensive white on the sides above the waterline than is a swimming Pacific Loon. Furthermore, on Arctics, this white extends higher behind the wing than in front, intruding onto the corners of the rump in much the same way as the white of a Violetgreen Swallow (although not as pronounced). On Pacific Loons the division between dark upper parts and white underparts is a straight line on the same level behind the wing as in front of it. A swimming Arctic Loon will usually show a white patch on the flanks at the rear of the folded wing. On an Arctic Loon that is riding low in the water (as when alarmed or actively diving), this patch may be isolated as an oval of white breaking the waterline. On a bird that is relaxed and riding high in the water, the patch may look like nothing more than a slight bulge at the terminus of an extensive band of white running the length of the waterline. Pacific Loons will usually look blackish to the waterline, although there are conditions under which some white shows: individuals riding high in the water may show some white, and preening birds that are rolling slightly to one side may expose the white belly. In no case should a Pacific Loon show white extending onto the sides of the rump in the form of an oval patch, although, again, careful observation is needed: the position of the legs when a bird is just taking off from the water may temporarily push white feathers up higher onto the sides. The white flank patch is readily seen on Arctics flying past in profile (Fig. 4.2). Again, the thing to look for is the dividing line between dark upper parts and white underparts along the midline of the body. If this dividing line is at the same level anterior and posterior to the wing, the bird is a Pacific Loon. If the white rides up significantly higher behind the wing than in front of it, the bird is probably an Arctic. (Another cautionary note: Red-throated Loons, can show a similar white flank patch in flight, but they lack the conspicuous black-and-white patches running down the scapulars that are so prominent on flying Pacific and Arctic loons.)

Another excellent mark for separating alternate-plumaged birds involves the black-and-white longitudinal striping on the sides of the neck. This striping is found in both Arctic and Pacific loons, but it is coarser and much more prominent on Arctic Loons (Fig. 4.2), being visible on swimming and flying birds at impressive distances. On Pacific Loons, the striping is finer and is not conspicuous except at close range. The difference in the boldness of the striping is due in part to the fact that the white stripes of Arctics are wider relative to the black stripes than are those of Pacifics. Similarly, the black-and-white striped chinstrap that borders the top of the iridescent throat is conspicuous on Arctic Loons at a great distance, whereas the same feature on Pacific Loons can be seen only at relatively close range.

Nape color is another good accessory mark. The hindcrown and nape of Arctic Loons are a medium to dark gray, whereas these same areas on Pacific Loons are a pale, silvery gray. One mark of limited use is the presence or absence of a dark "ventstrap" or "garter" crossing the white vent. This strap is visible on high-flying Pacific Loons at some distance. Most Arctic Loons lack such a strap. Least useful is the much-touted color of the iridescent throat patch. At long distances or in poor light this appears black in both species, but proper light reveals it to be glossed purple in the Pacific Loon and green in the Arctic Loon. Our field perceptions of these iridescent colors can rarely be trusted because of the tricky influence of ambient light.

Basic-plumaged birds give us less to go on in separating the two species. The white flank patch of the Arctic Loon remains the best field mark, and this should be supported by size and structural characters before attempting to identify this rare bird in North America. The presence of either a dark chinstrap (see the previous section on nonbreeding loons) or a dark ventstrap should be considered evidence supporting the identification of Pacific Loons.

For further discussions, see Walsh 1988, Roberson 1989, Schulenberg 1989, McCaskie et al. 1990, Dunn and Rose 1992, and Reinking and Howell 1993.

# Clark's versus Western Grebe

Clark's Grebe was elevated to full-specific status in only 1985. Before that it was considered merely a light-morph of the Western Grebe. The taxonomic split left birders groping for solid identification criteria for separating the two species. It also raised the question of distributional limits. Precise distributional limits of the two species are still being worked out, but it is clear that Clark's and Western grebes overlap broadly throughout much of the West. (Clark's is rarer to the north and east and Western is generally more common, with local exceptions, almost throughout the shared range.) In addition, there is still confusion about the identity of many birds that have seemingly intermediate appearances.

Part of the confusion stems from seasonal differences in plumage and bill color of both species. Alternate-plumaged adults are usually readily separable, and few intermediate types are reported from April through August. However, grown immatures and nonbreeding adults often have a slightly different facial pattern and bill color that approach those of the other species. This complication is compounded by a certain amount of individual variation, at least some of which may be due to limited hybridization between the two forms. Some individuals will defy certain identification; however, with good views, most birds can be confidently identified.

The most reliable field mark, and the one that is most easily discerned at great distances, is bill color. The Western Grebe has a dull, greenish yellow bill, with an extensively dusky culmen and a variable amount of dusky wash on the lower mandible. The Clark's Grebe typically has a bright, orangey-yellow bill, with a sharply defined dusky ridge to the culmen. At great distances, the bright bill color of a Clark's Grebe amongst several Westerns will stand out when facial patterns and other field marks are impossible to judge. Immatures and nonbreeding adults of both species have a duller-colored bill than do breeding adults. An immature or nonbreeding Clark's Grebe may have a bill that is more of a bright straw-yellow, with a more extensively dusky culmen. On direct comparison these birds will still appear brighter-billed than Westerns, which are particularly dull in the nonbreeding season, but the differences are much less obvious.

After bill color, facial pattern is the most important character, but it can also be difficult to assess. On a typical alternate-plumaged Western Grebe (Fig. 4.3), the black cap extends down through the eye so that the eye is completely surrounded by dark feathering. A small patch of bare skin extends from the eye to the gape of the bill. This skin may be blackish or may be paler gray, but the eye should nonetheless be surrounded by dark feathering or skin. On a typical alternate-plumaged Clark's Grebe (Fig. 4.3), the black cap stops above the eye, leaving the eye surrounded by white feathering. On many individuals, the gap between the black cap and the top of the eye is narrow, but the lores and the feathering behind and below the eye should be conspicuously white. As in Western Grebes, there is a small patch of bare skin leading from the eye to the gape of the bill. This will appear as a narrow dark line, which isolates the white lores from the white feathering

Figure 4.3. Clark's Grebe (left) versus Western Grebe (right). Compare the bill color, distribution of white on the face, and flank color. (Photo by Barry R. Zimmer.)

below the eye. The net effect is that the red eye is much more prominent in Clark's Grebe than it is in Western because it is set against a white (rather than a black) background.

Unfortunately, the facial patterns of nonbreeding birds are often more difficult to assess. Outside of the breeding season, many Westerns have gray feathering on the lores and below and behind the eyes that is distinctly paler than the black feathering of the cap. The key point is that this feathering is gray, not white. Similarly, many nonbreeding Clark's Grebes have more extensive black caps that extend down lower on the face, bisecting the eyes. The key on such birds is the color of the lores and of the feathering on the bottom side of the eye, both of which should be white (as opposed to gray or black as in Western). Some intermediate birds may be encountered; for such individuals you should look to bill color and lesser accessory characters. If a bird appears intermediate or indeterminate in both bill color and facial pattern, it should probably be left unidentified.

A few other characters should be considered accessory or supporting evidence, but they should never be the sole basis for an identification. Clark's Grebes tend to have flanks that are much more extensively mottled with white, giving them a paler-sided appearance. Western Grebes are more uniformly dark on the flanks. This distinction is subject to much individual variation, and birders may be misled by Western Grebes that are rolling slightly to one side to preen, thus exposing the white feathers of the belly and giving the appearance of having whitish flanks. Nonetheless, this is often a good way to pick a Clark's out of a group of sleeping grebes, when neither the bill color nor the face pattern can be determined. Another mark that can be helpful is the width of the dark stripe on the back of the neck. On Clark's Grebes this stripe is very thin; on Westerns it is much wider, occupying most of the back of the neck. This feature is best seen on birds swimming directly away from you. Clark's Grebes also tend to be slightly paler-backed in general than do Westerns. The downy young of Clark's Grebes are entirely white, whereas those of Westerns are bicolored (gray above and white below); this distinction is useful only until the chicks are about 45 days old. The advertising calls of the two species are similar in quality, but Western typically gives a reedy, two-note "kree-KREEK," whereas Clark's gives a single upslurred "krrrick."

For more information see Ratti 1981, Storer and Neuchterlein 1985, Kaufman 1990, and Eckert 1993.

## Horned versus Eared Grebe

The Horned and Eared Grebes present an identification problem that is caused mostly by an overemphasis of some field guides on one particular field mark. Most birders have no problem in separating the two species during the breeding season. The problem comes later when the birds are in basic plumage.

Most guides emphasize the white face and neck of the Horned Grebe as being the best mark for separation in winter. Although it is true that Horned Grebes are distinctly whiter in these regions than most Eared Grebes, it is also true that Eared Grebes show considerable variation in the extent of white versus dusky on the face and side of the neck. Consequently, birders often report Horned Grebes on lakes in the southwest (where the species is rare) solely on the basis of the presence of white facial areas.

It is much easier and safer to identify the two species by the overall structure of the head, neck, and bill and by the general color pattern of those areas rather than by the presence or absence of white in one specific area.

The Eared Grebe (Fig. 4.4) has a thin neck and a head that peaks at the midpoint of the crown. Grebes can erect or slick-down their crown feathers depending on their mood and what they are doing; (for example, the crown is more depressed when the bird is actively feeding and is more erect when it is alarmed. When seen in profile, however, the midcrown peak of the Eared Grebe is still apparent under most circumstances. Eared Grebes also have a relatively longer, thinner bill with an essentially straight culmen and a lower mandible that angles up toward the tip. By contrast, the Horned Grebe (Fig. 4.4) has a shorter, thicker neck with a flatter-crowned, triangular (when viewed from above) head that peaks at the rear crown. The stockier look of the head or neck region is accentuated by a shorter bill that is thicker and straighter in profile.

The distribution pattern of light and dark feathering on the face and neck of the two species is also quite different (Fig. 4.4). Although Eared Grebes often show varying amounts of clean white on the face, this white is usually located well below the eye, which is surrounded by dark gray feathers. The dark color of the

Figure 4.4. Horned Grebe (left) versus Eared Grebe (right) (both in basic plumage). Note particularly the differing head shapes and pattern of light and dark feathering on the sides of the face, as well as the pale loral spot of the Horned Grebe. (Artwork by Shawneen Finnegan.)

crown dips down into the auricular region behind the eye, lending a somewhat helmeted look, which, at the same time, partially isolates a whitish, rear auricular patch at the rear of the face. Thus, the blackish color dips lower onto the face behind the eye than in front of it. The line separating the dark color of the crown from the white of the lower face may be sharply demarcated in a minority of Eared Grebes, but it is more often uneven and somewhat blurred (gray around the edges) in nature.

Conversely, Horned Grebes typically have a sharp line of demarcation between the dark crown feathering and the white feathering of the face. This line of demarcation is a nearly horizontal line at the level of the eye (both in front of and behind the eye) and lends a capped (rather than a helmeted) appearance (somewhat like a small version of a Western Grebe). The auriculars are clean white in most birds, lightly washed with gray in a few, but always sharply delineated from the black cap. Some Horned Grebes have a distinct white loral spot between the eye and the bill; this spot is diagnostic when present. The amount of white or gray on the sides of the neck is somewhat variable in both species, but Horneds are typically much cleaner looking, and the black of the nape usually forms a narrow line up an otherwise white neck.

For further discussion see Dunn and Garrett 1982a, and Kaufman 1992.

## Sooty versus Short-tailed Shearwater

Separating the Sooty from the Short-tailed shearwater is one of the most intractable field problems in all of North America. Field guides and other identification literature have oversimplified the identification of these two species and have failed to take into account the difficulty of accurately perceiving subtle differences in shape and plumage at sea. In-hand differences between the two species are recognizable in most individuals, but such differences rarely are useful for field identification given the difficulty of observing birds from a rocking boat in what is often poor or harsh light. Experienced birders can identify "classic" examples of both species with some confidence, but cautious individuals will rightly treat most birds (in areas and times of likely overlap) as "dark shearwater sp.?."

The Sooty Shearwater breeds on islands in the southern Hemisphere during our winter then disperses northward to winter (our summer) off both coasts of North America. It is by far the most abundant shearwater off our Pacific Coast south of Alaska, and flocks numbering in the hundreds of thousands are frequently seen in August and September. As such, it should be learned well as a basis of comparison with less common dark tubenoses.

The Short-tailed Shearwater is an abundant postbreeding visitor to the the cold, plankton-rich waters of the Bering Sea and the northern Pacific from its nesting areas on islands off Australia and Tasmania. It breeds during our winter, spending the austral winter months (our summer) primarily in Alaskan waters. Nonbreeders move down the length of our Pacific Coast later in fall. On the basis of specimen records, Short-tailed Shearwaters are most likely to be found south of Alaska from November through March. The true status of the Short-tailed Shearwater throughout its North American range is clouded by its extreme similarity to the Sooty Shearwater.

Both species are medium-sized, and the body of both is entirely dark sooty-brown but slightly paler on the underparts. Short-taileds in fresh plumage (late fall and early winter) appear more uniformly dark, almost velvety-brown. Many individuals have a distinctly whitish chin and contrasting darker crown. In worn plumage, Short-taileds appear warmer brown, and the pale-chinned, dark-crowned appearance is frequently lost. Sooty Shearwaters are often paler on the throat too, but this paler color tends more toward buff or light gray-brown (rather than whitish) and is less defined in extent, typically spreading from the chin through the upper breast.

The color of the underwing linings (Fig. 4.5) is helpful in identifying "classic" individuals. The average Sooty shows a bright silvery white flash to the outer wing linings, whereas the typical Short-tailed is dull smoky gray in the same area. Birders must be aware, however, that many individuals of both species have underwing patterns that closely approximate those of the other species. Part of this variation is caused by differences in feather wear. By late spring and early summer, most Short-taileds are very worn and in heavy molt. This condition exposes pale bases to the underwing feathers, making for an overall whitish underwing that is impossible to distinguish from that of the Sooty.

The best identification characters may be structural. Short-taileds have shorter, more slender bills than Sooties. Their forehead rises steeply (more perpendicularly) from the bill, and the crown is more rounded, lending a gentler, dove-headed aspect (Fig. 4.5). Sooty Shearwaters have a larger, heavier bill and a sloping forehead with flatter crown (Fig. 4.5). The differences in head and bill shape are similar to those between Thayer's or Iceland gulls (short-billed, round-headed)

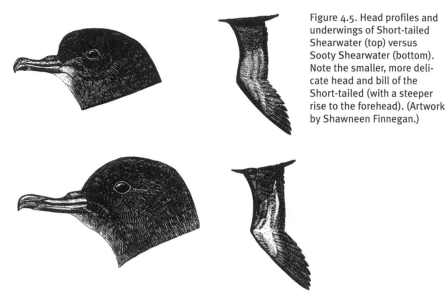

Figure 4.5. Head profiles and underwings of Short-tailed Shearwater (top) versus Sooty Shearwater (bottom). Note the smaller, more delicate head and bill of the Short-tailed (with a steeper rise to the forehead). (Artwork by Shawneen Finnegan.)

and Herring Gulls (long-billed, flat-crowned). Unfortunately, these characters are difficult to assess on flying birds that are streaking past a bouncing boat. They can also be influenced by molt. A Short-tailed that is molting forehead and crown feathers may appear flatter-crowned. If feathers from the forehead are missing, our perception of bill length may be thrown off as well, because the bill of such a bird would be more exposed and would appear longer.

In summary, a specific identification of one of these birds, from a place and season where either species is possible, is likely to boil down to your best guess. As long as you recognize the inherent uncertainty (given our present level of knowledge), best guesses may be acceptable. Just don't bet the farm on your identification!

## Double-crested versus Neotropic Cormorant

These are the only two cormorants found in our area away from the West Coast. The Neotropic is locally common in Texas, Louisiana, and New Mexico, but reports from Arizona and southern California are increasing. Certainly, it should be watched for in freshwater areas throughout the Southwest.

The Neotropic is a much smaller bird than the Double-crested, even more in bulk than in length. This size difference is immediately obvious when the two species are side by side and is even quite apparent to experienced observers on lone birds at reasonable distances. However, swimming cormorants of any species often look deceptively small, and observers should not rely on this criterion alone.

In addition to absolute size differences, Neotropic Cormorants are differently proportioned from Double-cresteds. They are much more slender birds and have a thinner neck and bill and proportionately longer tail.

Besides structure, the best way to separate adults of the two species is by the shape and color of the gular pouch (a skin pouch of the throat that is most developed in pelicans but is bare of feathers and contrastingly colored in cormorants and sulids as well) on the throat (Figs. 4.6 and 4.7). In the Double-crested, this area of bare skin extends from behind the eye downward and encircles the throat. In profile it presents a large semicircular outline. Because it covers a large area and is either bright orange or yellow, the gular pouch of the Double-crested is usually obvious at even great distances. The Neotropic, on the other hand, has a much smaller gular pouch that angles posteriorly from the eye and then cuts back sharply toward the chin. It ranges in color from a dull pink-orange to a dull yellow. The combination of dull color with small size makes the gular pouch of the Neotropic somewhat inconspicuous, especially at longer distances. The gular pouch of adult Neotropics is bordered by a narrow line of white feathers, a character that will immediately separate them from adult Double-cresteds.

One distinguishing mark that has received attention in recent years is the color of the supraloral region: the area above the lores, between the eye and the bill. Double-cresteds of all ages appear to have a patch of bare, orange or orange-yellow skin in the supraloral region. Neotropic Cormorants have dark feathers (black in adults, brown in immatures) covering the supraloral region. This difference seems to be diagnostic, at least in North America. However, occasional Neotropic Cormorants that I have examined in South America seem to have a patch of bare (albeit dull gray or olive, not bright orange or orange-yellow) skin in

Figure 4.6. Double-crested Cormorant. Note particularly the shape of the gular pouch. (Photo by Allen Cruickshank/VIREO.)

Figure 4.7. Neotropic Cormorant. Note the size and shape of the gular pouch and the surrounding white border. (Photo by Barry R. Zimmer.)

the supraloral region. Whether this is a geographic difference between different populations of Neotropic Cormorants or merely a rare expression of an individually variable character is not clear.

Adults (and some immatures) of the two species can also be separated by the shape of their scapular feathers, which are very pointed on Neotropics and more rounded on Double-cresteds. But if you are close enough to accurately determine this feature, you will likely already have identified the bird by something more obvious.

Immatures of the two species can also be separated by the same characteristics of size and proportions, but they can show some convergence of gular pouch characteristics. Many immature Neotropic Cormorants have a larger, brighter gular pouch than adults. Similarly, the gular pouch of many immature Double-cresteds appears slightly pointed (rather than rounded) at the rear margin. Some of these same birds may have a vaguely defined band of whitish feathering bordering the gular pouch (which is typically a duller yellow than in adults), thus pushing the resemblance to Neotropic Cormorant even closer. When confronted with an immature bird with indeterminate gular and throat characteristics, check the supraloral region to see if it is feathered or if there is a patch of yellow or orange skin.

Other plumage characters offer accessory information in separating immatures. Young Double-cresteds tend to be very pale (almost cream-colored) on the underside of the neck and breast. This coloring contrasts strongly with the dark brown belly, giving these birds a bicolored appearance. Young Neotropics may be uniformly dark brown (slightly lighter with buffy tones below) or quite pale below, but they lack the bicolored look. Beware, however, that some immature Double-cresteds may be entirely pale below (without the bicolored look), and a smaller percentage may appear as dark as a typical young Neotropic. Young Double-cresteds also have a yellowish bill, whereas the bill of young Neotropics tends to be indistinctly colored.

## Pacific Coast Cormorants

Three species of cormorant (Double-crested, Brandt's, and Pelagic) are found along the West Coast from Canada to Mexico. The Brandt's and Pelagic are extremely unlikely to be seen away from the immediate coast or open sea, so any cormorant seen inland is likely to be a Double-crested by default. However, Double-cresteds are routinely seen in numbers at coastal locales, so cormorants in marine environments must be studied before being labeled as to species. Double-crested and Pelagic cormorants also overlap with the Red-faced Cormorant in south-coastal Alaska, and in some places all three species can be found side by side. Double-cresteds of all ages should be immediately separable from the other three species by their conspicuous yellow-orange gular pouch and supraorbital marks. Hence, the real difficulties arise from trying to separate Brandt's Cormorants from Pelagics, and (in Alaska) Pelagics from Red-faced. In all cases, separation of breeding-condition adults is straightforward, given reasonable views of the diagnostic facial skin and gular pouch colors. Non-breeding adults (whose soft parts have a color much duller) and immature birds can cause identification problems, however, as can distant or flying birds.

One immediate way to separate the Pelagic Cormorant from the Brandt's and Double-crested is on the basis of size and shape (Figs. 4.6, 4.8, and 4.9). Double-crested and Brandt's are large, bulky cormorants with a thick neck, large head, and thick bill. The Pelagic, on the other hand, is a small, slender cormorant, built more along the lines of a Neotropic Cormorant. Pelagics have a thin neck and bill, and a small head. When perched on a rock alongside either of the other two species, Pelagics appear noticeably smaller. Perched or swimming birds can also be picked out by their different head shape. Both the forehead and the throat of the Pelagic Cormorant appear to angle steeply from the base of the bill, whereas on Brandt's Cormorant the base of the bill seems to blend more smoothly into the contours of the head and throat (Figs. 4.8 and 4.9). Conversely, Pelagic Cormorants in flight appear almost headless, as the small head blends with the straight-necked profile in tapering to a fine, pencil-like point.

Pelagic Cormorants have dark red facial skin that can be seen at close range (very difficult in winter) and a dull red gular pouch that is relatively inconspicuous. Perched birds in good light show a more uniform "oily" (purple-green) iridescent sheen than do Brandt's Cormorants. Breeding-plumaged Pelagics show two white oval patches on the flanks that are very conspicuous in flight. Immature birds can be distinguished by their combination of small, slender build and uniformly dark-brown plumage.

Adult Red-faced Cormorants in breeding condition are instantly identifiable by their yellow bill, powder-blue gular pouch, and bright-red facial skin, which ex-

Figure 4.8. Pelagic Cormorant. Note the slender build, small head, and thin bill. (Photographed late November at Pacific Grove, California, by Kevin J. Zimmer.)

tends broadly across the forehead. Like Pelagic Cormorants, they have white flank patches during the breeding season. Unlike Pelagics, adult Red-faced Cormorants show contrast between the oily, iridescent body plumage and the flatter, duller, brownish black of the wings, a feature that can be helpful in identifying flying birds. Red-faced Cormorants of all ages are larger, stockier birds than Pelagic Cormorants, and they have a proportionately bigger head and bill.

Immature Red-faced Cormorants present the primary identification challenge. They are uniformly dark brown, as are the immature Pelagics. Immature Pelagic Cormorants have extremely reduced bare skin on the face, and these areas are dull

Figure 4.9. Brandt's Cormorant. Note the heavy build, stout bill, and pale gular area. (Photographed late November at Pacific Grove, California, by Kevin J. Zimmer.)

and lack any contrasting color. Most immature Red-faced Cormorants show at least some bare skin between the eye and the bill and at the base of the throat. The exact color of these bare areas seems to be individually variable (from pale orange-brown to pinkish and even light blue around the throat), but they are all light-colored and contrast with the brown feathering of the face. At close range, a dull vermilion eye ring can be seen on many individuals. Bill shape and color are probably more helpful. An immature Red-faced has an echo of the adult condition, with a dusky culmen (or, frequently, the entire upper mandible or maxilla is dusky) and tip contrasting with a mostly (basal three-quarters) pale yellow mandible. The bill of young Pelagics is uniformly dull gray or horn colored. Bill shape also differs; Red-faced Cormorants have a longer bill with a noticeable concave scoop to the base of the culmen, whereas Pelagics have a shorter bill that is more nearly parallel-sided.

As stated previously, Brandt's Cormorants are large, bulky cormorants built along the lines of Double-cresteds. Breeding adults have beautiful blue-centered gular pouches surrounded by yellow. In other age classes and nonbreeding adults the blue is replaced by dull slate-gray and is inconspicuous, but these birds may be recognized by the dull, buffy border to the throat that is smaller and much paler than the bright yellow-orange throat of a Double-crested. This light buff contrasts as a paler band across the rest of the darker plumage. Immature Brandt's show more contrast between upper parts (darker) and underparts (lighter) than do immature Pelagics and Red-faced, but they are darker and more uniformly colored than the bicolored immature Double-cresteds.

When flying in a straight line, the Brandt's tends to leave its neck straight out (but not always), whereas the Double-crested routinely flies with its head up and neck crooked. Brandt's Cormorants are often seen feeding in the nearshore ocean in sizable flocks (up to several hundred birds). Double-cresteds tend to feed in small groups in sheltered bays and onshore lakes and are rarely seen in the nearshore ocean. Pelagics are normally encountered as individuals or in small groups. Despite its name, the Pelagic Cormorant is not pelagic, at least not south of Alaska. The Pelagic Cormorant tends to be a strictly nearshore species, whereas the Brandt's Cormorant is routinely seen many miles out to sea.

## Immature Night-Herons

Identifying immature night-herons is a problem of increasing concern to western birders, as more and more Yellow-crowned Night-Herons are turning up west and north of their normal ranges. Adult birds of both species are instantly recognizable, but the identification of immatures is somewhat subtle.

Yellow-crowned Night-Herons of all ages have a positively huge bill (Fig. 4.10) that is noticeably thicker than the bill of Black-crowneds (although some experience with the latter species may be necessary to get a feel for this difference). This look is accentuated by the more slender-necked appearance of the Yellow-

Figure 4.10. Immature Yellow-crowned Night-Heron. Note the huge, entirely black bill and the fine speckling on the wing coverts and neck. (Photo by Kevin J. Zimmer.)

crowned. Young Black-crowneds (Fig. 4.11) typically have a bill that is at least partially greenish yellow, whereas young Yellow-crowneds usually have an all-black bill. The latter species also has longer legs that trail well beyond the tail in flight, as compared with Black-crowneds, whose feet only partially protrude beyond the tail.

Figure 4.11. Immature Black-crowned Night-Heron. Note the smaller bill (in comparison with the Yellow-crowned) and the contrasting pale base to the mandible, as well as the more prominent pale streaking. (Photo by Allen Cruickshank/VIREO.)

A good mark for identifying young Yellow-crowneds is the contrast in the upper surface of the wings, seen when the bird is flying. The dark gray flight feathers of young Yellow-crowneds contrast strongly with the browner forewing, giving the wings a distinctive bicolored look that is very conspicuous and that is somewhat similar to the upperwing pattern of Great Blue Herons. Young Black-crowneds have an essentially uniformly brown wing that looks very different.

Yellow-crowneds are a cooler gray-brown, whereas Black-crowneds are a warmer brown. The upper parts of Yellow-crowneds also look smoother in color because they have fewer and smaller white spots on the dark ground color. These smaller white spots (against a grayer background) are almost reminiscent of the spotting on the upper parts of a Yellowlegs. By contrast, young Black-crowneds have large, elongate white spots (many of which are closer to stripes) on the wing coverts, scapulars and mantle.

See also Zimmer 1985 and Kaufman 1988a.

## Tundra versus Trumpeter Swan

One of the most difficult field problems in North America is separating the Tundra Swan from the Trumpeter Swan. The two species have largely allopatric breeding ranges, but they do overlap somewhat in Alaska (where they are nonetheless mostly separated by habitat). Overlap also occurs in the Pacific Northwest, where both species winter, and, to a lesser extent, throughout much of the Great Plains and surrounding areas, where migrant Tundra Swans could occur near introduced populations of Trumpeters. Small numbers of both species occur as migrants or winter visitors virtually throughout the West.

It is crucial to determine the age of a swan before attempting to identify it to species. Many of the characters most useful in the field separation of the two species are age-related and can be seriously misinterpreted if the bird is not correctly aged. Dusky or brown feathering anywhere, but especially on the head, neck, and wing coverts is a sign of immaturity (but beware of rusty-brown staining of adult feathers, which occurs when birds forage in oxide-rich water). So is pink coloring to the bill (aside from the reddish tomial stripe, discussed below). Juvenile Tundra Swans begin and complete their first prebasic molt earlier in the year than do juvenile Trumpeters. Most Tundra Swans begin this molt in December, and it is largely completed by March. By March, first-year birds are nearly as white as adults, although close inspection will usually reveal at least some gray feathering throughout the first year or more. Juvenile Trumpeters typically begin their first prebasic molt in January, and the molt continues late into the spring. Thus, many young Trumpeter Swans retain significant amounts of dusky or brownish feathering well into April and May (or later), long after most young Tundra Swans appear essentially all white.

Trumpeter Swans are, on average, noticeably larger than Tundra Swans. However, this size difference is not obvious except in direct comparison. The size question is further complicated by sexual dimorphism, because males of both species are substantially larger than the females. Size overlap between small female Trumpeters and large male Tundras has been demonstrated.

The most useful distinctions between the two species all involve the head and bill. Trumpeter Swans have a proportionately larger head and bill than Tundra Swans. Proportionate bill size can be roughly judged by comparing the length of the bill (tip to gape) with the distance from the eye to the nape. In Tundra Swans the ratio between the two measurments varies from roughly 1:1 to 1.5:1, whereas in Trumpeters the ratio of the bill length to the eye-nape distance varies from more than 1.5:1 to 2:1 (Patten and Heindel 1994). Nostril placement also differs between the two species. The nostrils of Trumpeters are located about midway between the eye and the tip of the bill, whereas the nostrils of Tundras are noticeably closer to the tip of the bill than they are to the eyes.

Head and bill shape (Fig. 4.12) can also be useful clues, but they are very much age-dependent. Adult Tundra Swans, when viewed in profile, typically have a rounded crown (highest in the center) and a concave culmen. Adult Trumpeters, by contrast, have a heavier, more angular head that peaks at the rear of the crown and a straight culmen. The large, angular head, combined with the proportionately large bill and straight culmen, create a profile that is suggestive of Canvasback or Common Eider. Although this mark generally works well for adults (occasional adult Tundras may have a straight culmen), it is useless in identifying immature birds. Young birds of both species have a straighter or even slightly convex culmen (Bailey 1991), with the adult bill shape developing slowly over the first year and a half.

Some of the better clues involve the way in which the feathering of the head and face meet the bill and bare facial skin (Figs. 4.12 and 4.13) Particularly important is the interface between the base of the culmen and the feathering of the forehead. On adult Trumpeters, the forehead feathering extends deeply onto the culmen to form a pronounced V. On adult Tundras, the feathering does not extend as deeply onto the culmen, and the resulting interface is more of a shallow U. The difference

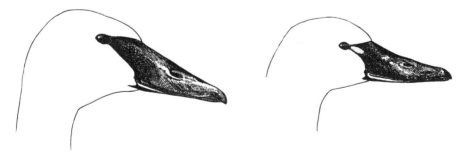

Figure 4.12. Head profiles of Trumpeter Swan (left) versus Tundra Swan (right). Compare bill shapes and breadth of contact point between facial skin and eye. Note also the yellow loral spot present in many (but not all) Tundra Swans. (Artwork by Shawneen Finnegan.)

Figure 4.13. Head-on views of adult Trumpeter Swan (left) versus adult Tundra Swan (right). Note that the forehead feathering extends forward on the Trumpeter, forming a distinct V. On the adult Tundra Swan, the feathering forms a shallow U across the forehead. (Artwork by Shawneen Finnegan.)

is usually quite prominent when birds are viewed head-on. Again, this character is useful only on adult birds; immatures of both species have the forehead feathering extending well onto the culmen in a pronounced V.

Most adult Tundra Swans have a bright yellow loral spot (variably sized) between the eye and the bill. Trumpeters lack such a spot. Because a significant minority of adult Tundras also lack a yellow loral spot, the absence of a spot tells us nothing about the identity of a bird. The way in which the black skin at the base of the bill meets the eye can be helpful. The black facial skin of Tundras is constricted where it meets the eye (which is also black), and thus the eye is nearly isolated against the white face, and therefore, stands in greater contrast. The black facial skin of Trumpeters meets the eye more broadly so that the eye tends to blend with the facial skin rather than being isolated against the white face. This mark is subtle and can be difficult to judge at greater distances.

The shape of the cheek feathering where it meets the gape of the bill can also be instructive. On Trumpeters, the edge of the feathering often extends in a fairly straight, angled line from the eye to the gape. On Tundras, it more often extends down from the eye at an angle before dropping perpendicularly to the base of the bill, thus presenting a shelflike, or squared-off edge to the base of the bill. Although this edge is distinct on many individuals, other birds will be encountered that appear intermediate.

Some references have suggested that the pinkish or reddish tomial stripe (or "lipstick line") is diagnostic for Trumpeters, but it is also found on many Tundra Swans, some of which will also lack the diagnostic yellow loral spot. Bill color differences in immature birds can be difficult to interpret. Early in fall, young Tundras are likely to have a mostly pink bill, with the pink actually meeting the feathering at the base of the bill. Young Trumpeters at the same stage should have an extensive black base to the bill, with the pink confined to the center of the bill. Because young Tundra Swans steadily acquire their adult bill color through their first winter (being mostly black-billed by spring), immature swans with a black-based bill after late fall could be of either species. However, a swan that has a pink bill base should be a Tundra.

Vocalizations are diagnostic for both species, but the differences do not lend themselves well to written description. To birders not familiar with the more resonant, hornlike honking of the Trumpeter Swan, the calls of Tundra Swans could easily be interpreted as trumpeting. My best advice is to obtain commercially available tapes of bird recordings that contain calls of the two species.

Most references refer to the behavioral tendency of Trumpeters to swim or stand with their neck kinked back at the base, whereas Tundras more commonly hold their neck straight up. Alarmed swans (which can be any swan that sees you) of either species will hold their neck straight up, and I've seen enough Tundras with a kinked neck to put little value on this feature as being helpful.

For more information see Jordan 1988, Bailey 1991, and, especially, Patten and Heindel 1994.

## Ross's versus Snow Goose

Ross's Goose and Snow Goose have similar plumage, but they can usually be identified by a combination of structural characters. Ross's Geese are turning up as regular migrants throughout the West, so it is particularly important that birders be aware of reliable methods for identifying them.

Because the blue-morph of Ross's Goose is extremely rare, it is white-morph birds of both species that are likely to be confused. There is nothing in the plumage of adult birds that can be safely used to distinguish between species. Plumage is a helpful cue in identifying immature birds. Young Snow Geese are very dingy looking, with extensive amounts of gray on the wing coverts, back, head, and neck. They also have a blackish bill and grayish legs and feet before January of their first year. Young Ross's Geese, on the other hand, closely resemble adults; they are almost entirely clean white with only small amounts of gray (mostly confined to the crown and nape) and have a pinkish bill and pinkish legs and feet.

The defining characteristics for these geese at any age come from an examination of the bill, head, and neck structure and of overall body size. Ross's Geese are decidedly smaller than are Snow Geese. This difference is usually evident when the two species are side by side, but it may be very hard to judge on lone birds. Even in mixed flocks, size differences can be difficult to judge because of uneven terrain (such as plowed fields) or postural differences.

The best mark by far is the size and shape of the bill. Snow Geese have a large bill that shows a distinct black "lip" or "grinning patch" at the juncture of the upper and lower mandibles (Fig. 4.14) This mark is extremely prominent and easy to see. In addition, the culmen of a Snow Goose is slightly humped at the base and then dips distally, appearing somewhat concave. Still another important point to check is the interface between the base of the bill and the feathering of the foreface. In Snow Geese, the upper portion of the base of the upper mandible pro-

Figure 4.14. Snow Goose. Note the head and bill shape and the distinctive black "lip" or "grinning patch." (Photo by Kevin J. Zimmer.)

trudes into the feathering between the eye and the bill, forming an extension of the bill base. Concomitantly, the feathering of the foreface angles forward below this extension toward the gape. Viewed in profile, the division between bill base and feathers is then an angled line from the gape up toward the lores.

In comparison, Ross's Geese have a very short, stubby bill (Figs. 4.15 and 4.16) that appears sawed off. This sawed-off look is due in part to the interface between the base of the bill and the feathering of the foreface. In Ross's Geese this division takes the form of a straight, vertical line, from the top of the bill to the bottom. There is no extension to the top of the bill, and, viewed in profile, the division between bill and feathers is a straight (not angled) line perpendicular to the gape. The culmen is essentially straight, giving the bill a triangular appearance that is in-

Figure 4.15. Ross's Goose. Note the compact build and stubby, triangular bill. The slight amount of dusky feathering on the nape marks this bird as an immature. (Photo by Kevin J. Zimmer.)

Figure 4.16. Adult Ross's Goose. Note especially the bill shape and the band of blue-gray, "warty" skin surrounding the base of the bill. (Photo by Kevin J. Zimmer.)

stantly recognizable as being different from that of a Snow Goose. Also, Ross's lacks the conspicuous lips or grinning patch of the Snow Goose.

One mark that is somewhat overplayed is the presence of warty protruberances at the base of adult Ross's bills. These are not conspicuous on most individuals, particularly at longer distances. What is noticeable is that Ross's Geese usually have a distinctive blue-gray or purplish band around the base of the bill. This band contrasts strongly with the pink color of the rest of the bill. This blue-gray band is not found in Snow Geese.

The head and neck shapes of the two species are also somewhat different. Snow Geese have a long neck (beware of postural influences), and the head is somewhat flat-crowned, or angular. Ross's Geese have a short, stubby neck and a very rounded, or domed, head. The head and neck shapes, combined with the stubby bill, give Ross' Goose a gentle, cute look that is very different from that of the Snow Goose.

There have been many documented cases of presumed hybrid Ross's × Snow Goose that have intermediate character expression or a variable combination of parental characters (Roberson 1993). Such birds may defy certain field identification.

For more information see Simon 1978 and Roberson 1993.


## Female Teals

The identification of female teal is a source of frustration for many birders. The biggest problem comes from attempting to separate females of Blue-winged and Cinnamon teal, which are so similar as to be a real identification problem in areas of overlap. Unfortunately, most existing field guides do little to point out the few differences that can be reliably used to sort out these two species.

Female Cinnamons are evenly colored with warm brown tones that tend toward the rusty end of the spectrum. Female Blue-wingeds, on the other hand, typically have a cold look and are more gray-brown with no hint of rust (eclipse-plumaged males are warmer brown). In addition, their dark back and scapular feathers tend to have broad pale fringes, creating a scalloped look that is quite different from the more uniformly colored Cinnamon. Female Blue-wingeds also typically show some contrast between the darker, more heavily marked breast and the paler, less heavily marked foreneck and throat. Female Cinnamons tend to show little or no contrast in that region.

Likewise, the head and face region of the female Cinnamon has a fairly uniform coloring with very little pattern apparent (Fig. 4.17). Contrarily, the pale face of the female Blue-winged contrasts rather strongly, having a dark crown and dark eye line, thus creating the impression of a bold, pale supercilium (Fig. 4.17). Blue-wingeds also typically have a distinct pale spot at the base of the bill. This area may be lighter in Cinnamons as well, but it is much less apparent (Fig. 4.17). Females of both species usually show a pale, broken eye ring, but this is often whiter and more contrasting in female Blue-wingeds.

Still another character that is useful given comparative experience is the bill, in both size and shape (Fig. 4.17). Cinnamon Teal of both sexes have a bill that is noticeably longer and more spatulate than the bill of Blue-winged Teal, making them look more like a shoveler (although the bill is not nearly as long or as spatulate as that of a shoveler).

Male Cinnamon Teal in eclipse plumage resemble females, but they have dull red eyes, a feature not seen in Blue-winged Teal. The wing patterns of the two species (both sexes) are indistinguishable in the field.

Female Green-winged Teal are easily separated from females of the other two species on the basis of wing pattern. Green-winged Teal have a dull gray panel on the forewing, the green speculum is bordered by a broad buffy or white bar at the base and by a conspicuous white trailing edge. The other two species lack the white trailing edge to the speculum and have a large, contrasting light blue panel

Figure 4.17. Head profiles of female teal: Cinnamon (top center), Blue-winged (lower left), and Green-winged (lower right). Note the different bill sizes and shapes and the amount of contrast in the facial patterns. (Artwork by Shawneen Finnegan.)

in the forewing. Standing or swimming birds can be more difficult, particularly if none of the speculum is visible in the folded wing.

Green-winged Teal are smaller and more compact than the other species, appearing especially short-necked in flight. They have a noticeably smaller bill and a steeper rise to the forehead, giving the head a domed look that is quite different from the more angled, sloping profile of Cinnamon (particularly) and (to a lesser extent) Blue-winged. Female Green-wingeds have a moderately contrasting facial pattern, with a dark eye line and a pale supercilium that is typically less contrasting than that of the Blue-winged but more obvious than any pattern of female Cinnamon (Fig. 4.17). Some individual Green-wingeds may have a distinct whitish loral spot similar to that of the Blue-winged. Green-wingeds have only light markings on the belly, and the contrast between the heavily spotted chest and mottled flanks and the whitish belly and undertail is a good mark.

For further discussion see Wallace and Ogilvie 1977 and Jackson 1991.

## Greater versus Lesser Scaup

Birders who live in inland areas of the West get few chances to see Greater Scaup, thus making the identification of occasional vagrants a difficult task.

Too many birders rely on the difference in the color of head gloss to separate male scaup. Under many light conditions the heads of both species appear plain black. Worse, the purple head of a male Lesser Scaup may appear green under some light conditions. I have never seen the reverse (that is, a Greater Scaup with a purple head), but it may happen. Head color may be considered an accessory field mark but should never be the sole basis for identification.

A much better indication is head and bill shape. The head of Greater Scaup (both sexes) is rounded and has a proportionately large slipperlike bill (Figs. 4.18 and 4.19). The size of the bill combined with the rounded shape of the head tends to deemphasize the size of the head, making it appear somewhat smallish. When viewed in profile, the high point on a Greater's head is the domed forehead. Lesser Scaup, on the other hand, have a distinctly peaked rear-crown and a smaller, less spatulate bill (Figs. 4.20 and 4.21). This combination makes the head more prominent and appear proportionately larger. A Lesser that is actively diving may slick its crown feathers down and may temporarily appear to have a head shape more typical of Greater. The black nail at the tip of the bill tends to be more extensive in Greaters of both sexes, but this mark is often hard to see.

Male Greaters that are sitting on the water can often be picked out from a flock of Lessers by their brighter white sides. The whiteness of the sides in male Lessers is quite variable, but many Greaters are a gleaming immaculate white. Again, this is an accessory mark that should not be used alone.

The often-cited longer white wing stripe that is found in Greaters of both sexes is also a helpful accessory mark, but it does show some overlap. Fortunately, most overlap appears to be between male Lessers and female Greaters.

Figure 4.18. Greater Scaup (female on left, male on right). Note the relatively large bill and low, rounded profile to the head. The white patch on the rear of the female's face is typical of many (but not all) female Greaters. (Photographed in late June at Anchorage, Alaska, by Kevin J. Zimmer.)

Females are best identified by the same structural features of the head and bill already discussed for males. Some female Greaters (particularly worn birds in summer) have light (either white or dirty-buff) patches on the auriculars, a character infrequently found in female Lessers. Female Greaters also average a paler, tawnier brown in overall color, with more white around the base of the bill. Both

Figure 4.19. Female Greater Scaup. Note the relatively large bill and the low, rounded profile of the head. (Photographed in June at Anchorage, Alaska, by Kevin J. Zimmer.)

Figure 4.20. Male Lesser Scaup. Note the smaller bill (in comparison with Greater) and the different head shape (steeper rise to the forehead and more peaked in the rear). (Photo by Barry R. Zimmer.)

Figure 4.21. Female Lesser Scaup. Note the rear-peaked profile to the head, the smaller (compared with Greater Scaup) bill, and the absence of a white patch on the rear of the face. (Photo by Barry R. Zimmer.)

characters are subtle and may show great individual variation. They should therefore be considered only accessory in nature.

## Female Goldeneyes

The separation of female Common Goldeneye from female Barrow's Goldeneye is a frequently encountered problem throughout much of the West. There are few plumage characters that can be used to separate the two species, so birders must rely primarily on structural features. However, these structural differences have been poorly illustrated in some of the standard field guides, some of which have further muddied the waters by misrepresenting the nature of variation in bill color in the two species.

The best characters for identifying female goldeneyes involve head and bill shape and bill color. Head color and upper wing pattern are good secondary characters.

Barrow's Goldeneye has a high, steep forehead that rises almost perpendicularly from the base of the bill (Fig. 4.22). In fact, if one were to trace the angle between the bottom edge of the lower mandible and the forehead, it would approximate a right angle. Barrow's has a somewhat flattish crown, that, when viewed in profile, peaks at the forehead. The feathers at the lower rear of the head are distinctly elongate, creating a puffiness or maned look to the back of the head. The overall effect, again, when viewed in profile, is of a somewhat squarish head. The bill is deep-based, short, and stubby, and, when combined with the steep, high forehead, imparts a distinctive snub-nosed appearance.

The forehead of the Common Goldeneye slopes gradually up from the base of the bill at a much shallower angle, eventually peaking in the center of the crown (behind the eye) before sloping back to the rear of the head just as smoothly. When viewed in profile, the overall effect is of a somewhat triangular head with a smoothly rounded peak (Fig. 4.22). This effect is accentuated by the shape of the bill, which is longer and more gently angled than that of Barrow's and which forms a continuous smooth angle with the slope of the forehead.

Keep in mind that the apparent head shape of an individual bird can vary somewhat from minute to minute if the bird is actively diving, although the major differences in forehead shape between the two species result from underlying skull structure rather than from any transient feather posture. Because head shape is the result of skull structure, it takes an entire year to fully develop, and thus, first-year birds may have a less distinct head and bill shape than do older birds.

Bill color can also be useful, but it is subject to seasonal and geographic variation. From early December through midsummer, female goldeneyes have unique color patterns to the bill. For the remainder of the year the differences are obscured and are more difficult to assess. The use of bill color as a field mark is complicated by geographic variation in Barrow's Goldeneyes, a factor that has been overlooked by many field guides. The bill of adult female Barrow's from western populations is entirely yellowish orange or pinkish orange except for the prominent black nail (which is often protruding). The bill of females from the disjunct

Figure 4.22. Head profiles of female Barrow's Goldeneye (left) versus female Common Goldeneye (right). Compare bill size and color and head shape. (Artwork by Shawneen Finnegan.)

northeastern Canadian population is black from the base to around the nostril, and then deep yellow from there to the tip (except for the black nail). The bill of adult female Commons is mostly black, with a band of yellow orange or orange near the tip that isolates the black nail (which is usually less prominent than the nail of the Barrow's). This band of yellow-orange or orange varies in width from one individual to the next, but it rarely extends back as far as the nostrils (although rare Commons have been reported with all-orange bills).

By summer, the bill color of many adult female Barrow's becomes dull and somewhat mottled with dusky patches. Although individuals with extensive areas of orange or pink in the center of the bill are still likely to be Barrow's, bill color on many individuals will remain inconclusive. Immature birds and eclipse-plumaged males may have an entirely dusky or blackish bill; immature females will gradually develop at least patches of dull orange or pink on the bill during their first fall and winter. Immatures can be separated from adult females by their duller yellow eyes and lack of a white collar.

Head color, when seen in good light, can be a helpful secondary clue. Female Barrow's have a cold chocolate-brown head, whereas the head of the female Common is typically a warmer rufous-brown.

The upper wing pattern differs between females of the two species, but this character can be impossible to assess on flying birds. Females of both species have a dark gray outer wing with a white speculum in the secondaries bordered by mostly white greater coverts. These greater coverts have black tips that form a horizontal black bar that divides the white patch on the wing. In female Commons the median coverts and the lesser coverts are also extensively white, whereas those of female Barrow's are mostly gray.

For more information, see Carney 1983 and Tobish 1986.

## Female Common versus Female Red-breasted Merganser

Female mergansers are superficially similar, but their identification has been complicated by some field guides. Standard guides tend to emphasize the shaggier crest of the female Red-breasted versus the more pronounced throat and neck contrast of the female Common. Although both are usable marks, there are other good characters that in combination can make accurate identification relatively simple.

The head, face, and upper neck of the female Common (Fig. 4.23) are a bright rusty brown. Only the chin is white, and the rust-brown color is uniform throughout. The bright white chin does contrast sharply with the rust of the lower throat and neck, but the posture of a swimming bird often makes this contrast hard to see. In the same vein, however, the white of the chin encroaches into the face on both sides of the head. The margins of this white area are rounded and sharply demarcated, thus forming distinct white ovals extending from the underside of the bill onto the face. These are very easy to see in profile and contrast greatly with the

Figure 4.23. Head profiles of female Common Merganser (top) versus female Red-breasted Merganser (bottom). Note the differences in bill shape, crest shape, and face and throat pattern. (Artwork by Shawneen Finnegan.)

rest of the rusty-brown head. In addition, the upper parts of female Commons tend toward silver-gray, which, when combined with the snow white underparts and very contrasty head, give them an overall clean appearance.

The head, face, and neck of female Red-breasteds have a totally different look (Fig. 4.23). First, the white of the chin is continuous with the white of the breast, and there is no dark coloring on the underside of the neck or throat. Second, although the white of the throat extends onto the side of the face, there is no sharp line of demarcation. Rather, the white fades gradually into the face, as it does on the sides of the neck. Therefore, no distinct white ovals exist, and the boundary between dark and light is blurred and somewhat dingy looking. The overall head and upper neck color is dull rufous-brown, very different from the bright rust of the female Common. In addition, the head and face of the Red-breasted are not uniformly colored; the face is a lighter buff, and the top and back of the head are a darker dull brown. These color patterns, combined with the shaggier crest, give the female Red-breasted an unkempt, dingy appearance that is very different from the bright, clean look of the female Common. The dingy look is accentuated by upper parts that are more dingy gray-brown than the typical silver-gray of Commons.

A few fine points of facial pattern provide further clues that can be useful at close range. Female Red-breasteds usually have a short, pale line running from the bill to just below the eye. No such feature is found in adult female Commons, although juveniles of both species have a similar, but longer, whitish line that extends below and posterior to the eye. Female Red-breasteds also have a pale crescent above and below each eye, forming an eye ring that is broken at the leading and rear edge. Female Commons have essentially an unmarked face on which the only contrast is provided by slightly darker feathering around the eye.

An additional point that may prove useful (particularly when light conditions blot out colors) is the structure of the bill and consequent head profile (Fig. 4.23). The bill of the Common is deeper at the base, giving a more pronounced concave slope to the culmen. This slope is continuous with the flatter, angled forehead, giving the entire head a more streamlined profile. The bill depth of the Red-breasted Merganser is shallower at the base, creating a thinner, straighter-billed look. This also gives the impression of a steeper forehead, because the culmen has less upward slope at its base.

See also Kaufman 1990.

## Immature Eagles

Although adult Bald and Golden eagles are immediately separable, immature birds of the two species are similar enough as to cause confusion. This confusion is enhanced by a less-than-adequate treatment of subadult plumages in many field guides. Most of the problem stems from attempts to pigeonhole immature eagle plumages into a single illustration for each species. Because eagles take 3 to 5 years to attain full adult plumage, such attempts are not only untenable but misleading.

The two species differ in certain structural characters. The inner secondaries of Golden Eagles are noticeably shorter than the other secondaries, lending a constricted or pinched-in look to the trailing edge of the wing where it joins the body. On Bald Eagles, the trailing edge of the wing is straighter and nearly parallel with the leading edge, and it lacks the pinched-in look. The Bald Eagle has a relatively larger head and a noticeably more massive bill than the Golden Eagle. In flight, the head of the Bald Eagle projects much farther beyond the leading edge of the wing, counterbalancing the length of the tail. The smaller head and bill of the Golden Eagle do not project as far beyond the leading edge of the wing; the lesser projection, combined with the pinched-in trailing edge of the wings, makes the tail appear relatively longer. All of these features can be somewhat hard to judge by birders lacking comparative experience. Remember also that juveniles of both species have broader and longer wings than adults (as do juveniles of many large raptors), a feature that can throw off your perceptions of subtle shape differences. Fortunately, several aspects of plumage are more diagnostic and much more objective to judge.

Golden Eagles of all ages have an entirely brown body. Birds molting worn feathers may show asymmetrically scattered white feathers, but these are neither extensive nor prominent. Birds of all ages show a tawny golden nape, legs that are completely feathered, and a bicolored bill that is gray at the base and black at the tip with a yellow cere (a waxy, dense membrane that saddles the base of the maxilla or upper mandible in some birds, especially raptors, and in which the openings of the nostrils are located). Juveniles are darker than older birds and may appear almost black at a distance. Birds in their first year have a sharply contrasting underwing pattern, with bright white patches at the base of the inner primaries and outer secondaries contrasting with the dark-brown coverts and axillars. First-year birds also have a tail that is white at the base with a broad, dark subterminal band and a thin, white terminal fringe. The line of demarcation between the white base and the dark subterminal band is usually sharp, and the white is clean and bright. An important point to note is that the white base of the tail extends completely across, almost always including the outer rectrices. As Golden Eagles age, the tail becomes progressively darker, and the white patches at the base of the inner primaries become progressively smaller. Subadult birds with reduced white in the tail should still have the white extending to include the outer edge of the outer rectrices. Older immatures and adults have tawny greater coverts on the upper wing, forming a tawny bar that contrasts with the darker flight feathers. The wing linings of adult Golden Eagles are entirely dark brown (darker than the remiges), and the tail is dark brown with faintly contrasting gray bars.

The plumage pattern of Bald Eagles is more complex, and birds will not acquire the distinctive adult plumage until they are at least 4 years old. In contrast with those of Golden Eagles, the bill and cere of subadult Bald Eagles are onecolor (slate-gray to horn-yellow), and the legs are not completely feathered. Young Balds also lack the tawny gold nape of the Goldens and have more extensive pale brown upperwing coverts (not reduced to a tawny bar). Juvenile Bald Eagles are not as dark as juvenile Goldens, and they frequently show contrast between the chest (darker brown) and the belly (tawnier, warmer brown). It is also not uncommon for juvenile Bald Eagles to have randomly scattered white feathers throughout the body plumage, which lends a streakier, less uniform appearance.

More diagnostic is the pattern of the underwings and tail. All immature Balds have dingy white patches at the axillars and white diagonal ulnar bars (The ulna, to which the quills of the secondaries attach, is the larger of the two supporting bones of the forearm portion of the wing. Overlying covert feathers along the ulna are contrastingly colored in some birds, creating a conspicuous ulnar bar.), along with a variable number of white remiges. This complex underwing pattern is very different from that of Golden Eagles of any age. The axillars and underwing coverts of Golden Eagles are always dark, and the only white is found at the base of the inner primaries and outer secondaries. The tail of first-year Bald Eagles may be entirely dark, or it may have extensive diffuse white at the base. When present, the white basal area is seldom sharply defined, usually contains extensive dusky internal mottling, and does not extend to include the outer edge of the outer rectrices.

Second- and third-year Bald Eagles show more extensive white to the tail, remiges, belly, and wing coverts than do first-year birds. Most second-year birds have an extensively whitish (dirty-white) belly that contrasts with the dark brown head, throat, and breast, creating a distinctive hooded effect. Many third-year birds are so extensively off-white on the underwing coverts as to present a negative underwing pattern (light linings, dark remiges) reminiscent of Swainson's Hawk (but not nearly as clean or bold). Where extensive white is present in the tail it is less clean, more irregular, and less sharply demarcated than the white found on the tails of young Goldens. Second-and third-year birds also show a variable amount of whitish mottling on the upper back as well as a light eyebrow above dark auriculars.

Flight behavior can be helpful but should not be relied upon for identification. Bald Eagles soar in a flat-winged attitude, whereas Golden Eagles more frequently show a slight dihedral (but Goldens can also fly flat-winged).

For more information see Clark 1983.

## Accipiters

The three species of U.S. accipiters (Sharp-shinned Hawk, Cooper's Hawk, and Northern Goshawk) present one of the most difficult field problems in North America. Only adult Northern Goshawks are easily identified by plumage alone. The rest must be identified by a suite of subtle structural, plumage, and flight characteristics, many of which require some comparative experience to use properly. Even the best birders must be content with recording "*Accipiter* sp.?" occasionally.

These birds present a size continuum, ranging from the small Sharp-shinned Hawk to the large Northern Goshawk, with Cooper's being intermediate. Females of all three species are distinctly larger than males, but there is no overlap in size between species. Female Sharpies may approach male Cooper's in size, whereas female Cooper's approach male Northern Goshawks.

Sharpies are the lightest in weight and relative to body size have proportionately long wings and short tail. The wing loading (weight distribution per surface area of wing) that results from these structural features produces a buoyant flight pattern with much flapping.

Cooper's Hawks are heavier, with proportionately short wings and longish tail (relative to body length). Thus, they have a more powerful flight pattern, with fewer strokes and greater speed.

Northern Goshawks are the heaviest of all, with proportionately long wings and short tail. Their flight is extremely fast and powerful, with fewer required flaps. Because of their size and the few strokes per unit time, Goshawks may appear to be slower fliers than Sharpies. This is an illusion rather than fact; the flight speed of accipiters is proportional to size.

Although the flight characteristics provide a good clue to the identity of an *Accipiter,* they should be used with caution. Individual birds will adjust their flight behavior to existing wind conditions, creating exceptions to every rule.

The real problem identifications in this group are between Sharp-shinned and Cooper's hawks of all ages and between immature Cooper's and immature Northern Goshawk.

### Cooper's versus Sharp-shinned Hawk

Most guides point to the difference in tail shape as the best separator of Sharp-shinned and Cooper's hawks. Cooper's have a distinctly rounded tail (the outer pairs of tail feathers are progressively shorter than the inner pairs) that appears to lack sharp corners even when the bird is perched. The tail appears conspicuously rounded on soaring birds. The Sharpies' tail is typically square-ended (all rectrices are more or less equal in length) and shows distinct corners on perched birds. The tail of many perched individuals may appear notched in the center. Although such distinctions are often useful, they are far from diagnostic. A soaring Sharp-shinned with its tail partially or completely fanned may appear distinctly round-tailed, as will perched birds with incompletely molted tails. Similarly, a Cooper's that is molting the central pair of rectrices may appear to have a notched tail when perched. In summary, a distinctly squared tail will probably allow elimination of Cooper's, but a rounded tail does not safely eliminate Sharp-shinned.

Cooper's Hawks of all ages have a broader, more defined white terminal band to the tail. A white terminal band is also present in Sharp-shinneds, but it is distinctly narrower and less conspicuous. Be aware that feather wear can reduce the width of the band or even eliminate it in both species.

Cooper's Hawks of all ages have a relatively massive head (most apparent on perched birds) that looks squared in profile, but the head of Sharpies is relatively small and rounded. Relative to head size, the eyes of the Cooper's appear small, and they are set far forward, lending a fierce look. Contrastingly, the eyes of the Sharp-shinned are large relative to head size, and they are more centrally positioned, giving a gentler look. In flight, the large head of Cooper's extends noticeably far forward from the leading edge of the wing, which is typically held in a rather straight line. Contrastingly, the smaller head of Sharp-shinneds barely projects beyond the leading edge of the wing, a trait that is accentuated by the tendency of Sharpies to lead with the carpals (wrists) held forward of the rest of the wing.

Another structural character that may prove useful on perched birds is the thickness of the tarsi. Sharp-shinneds have slender, delicate legs, whereas those of Cooper's Hawks are noticeably thicker and more powerful-looking.

Adult Cooper's have a very blackish cap that shows a sharp line of contrast with the slate-gray back. Adult Sharpies are not nearly as dark-capped and show little or no contrast between the cap and the back.

Juvenile Cooper's tend to be very buffy or tawny on the sides of the head and neck. The breast streaking on young Cooper's is finer, sharper, and darker brown. Most juvenile Cooper's Hawks have little streaking on the belly, thus there is a sharp contrast between the heavily streaked chest and the white, mostly unmarked belly. Young Sharpies are more extensively streaked below, and the streaks are larger and blurrier and more of a reddish brown. Juvenile Sharpies tend to be most heavily marked on the belly and thighs, where the streaking is frequently re-placed by barring. Both species typically have unmarked white undertail coverts. Juvenile Cooper's Hawks are usually noticeably mottled with white and buff on the upper parts, whereas juvenile Sharpies are a darker, more uniform brown.

## Cooper's Hawk versus Northern Goshawk

Adult Northern Goshawks, with their gray underparts, blackish head, and flaring white supercilium, are unlikely to be confused with any other *Accipiter*. Juvenile birds, however, can be readily confused with juvenile Cooper's Hawks.

Size alone will probably be sufficient for identification in most cases, but female Cooper's Hawks can approach male Northern Goshawks in size. A careful appraisal of proportions is usually helpful in such cases. Cooper's Hawks are noticeably short-winged and long-tailed, whereas Goshawks are long-winged and short-tailed, presenting a more *Buteo*-like appearance. These shape differences may not be obvious on birds in direct flight but are usually pronounced on soaring individuals.

Immature Goshawks have more pronounced white eyebrows (widest posterior to the eye), much heavier and more extensive belly streaking, and narrower white terminal tail bands than young Cooper's. Immature Goshawks do have dark spotting on their crissums (young Cooper's are typically clean white), but this is often hard to see. A careful examination of the dark bands on the tail could prove useful in identifying perched birds. Both species have three or four dark tail bands alternating with paler brown bands of slightly greater width. On goshawks, the dark marks crossing each feather are irregularly shaped, resulting in wavy, somewhat irregular bands across the tail. The dark marks are also narrowly framed by whitish borders, which serve to highlight the boundaries between the dark and light bands of the tail and accentuate the wavy nature of the bands. Contrastingly, on Cooper's Hawks these bands run straight across the tail, and there is no thin, whitish border to the dark bands, so that contrast between the bands is diminished. The distinctions between the two species in tail pattern are best assessed from above. The outer tail feathers of both species tend to have irregular-shaped bars, which lend a wavy-barred pattern to the undertail of both Cooper's Hawk and Northern Goshawks. Both species also have broad white terminal fringes to the tail.

For contrasting discussions on accipiters refer to Clark 1979, Mueller et al. 1979, and Kaufman 1990.

## Buteos and Other Soaring Hawks

Because there are so many species of *Buteo*, and because there are several possible avenues of misidentification for each species, I have treated each species separately. See also the excellent treatments by Clark and Wheeler (1987).

### Red-tailed Hawk

The Red-tailed Hawk is probably the most common and most variably plumaged species of *Buteo* in the United States. The best path to true competency in identifying buteos is to carefully study every Red-tail seen. More than a few birders have misidentified immature, dark-morph, or rare variant Red-tails for almost every other species of *Buteo*. Typical adults (Fig. 4.24) are identified by the combination of orange or rust-colored tail, distinct brown belly band on otherwise white underparts, large buff or white patches on the scapulars (an excellent mark for perched birds), and a black bar from the shoulder to the wrist (the patagial bar) on the underwings.

Figure 4.24. Red-tailed Hawk (light-morph adult). Note the shape of the bird the and underwing pattern, particularly the black patagial bar. (Photo by Barry R. Zimmer.)

There are countless exceptions to the above generalizations. Many southwestern birds have uniformly brown upper parts without the distinctive light scapulars. Furthermore, many of these same birds lack any trace of a belly band. Many Great Plains birds are extremely pale above and have a tail that is only lightly washed with orange. These individuals are often mistaken for Ferruginous Hawks but can be identified by pale, gray-brown (not rust) shoulders; white (not rust) feathering above the tarsi; a dark patagial bar; lack of prominent white patches on the upper surface of the primaries; and more heavily marked underwings. These pale Great Plains birds are often referred to as "Krider's Red-tailed Hawks"; they do not appear to represent a geographic form, but rather seem to represent a morph within populations.

Dark-morph birds are common in some areas and are frequently misidentified as the rarer "Harlan's" subspecies, or even as other species. These birds typically have an entirely dark brown body (usually with rufous tones; seldom blackish as are Zone-tailed, Black, or dark-morph Rough-leg), with dark wing linings, light remiges with some barring (from underneath), dark undertail coverts, and a reddish tail with a darker subterminal band. "Harlan's Hawks" were formerly considered a separate species that bred in Alaska and northwestern Canada and wintered in the southern Great Plains and Texas. They are now considered to be conspecific with Red-tailed Hawk. "Harlan's Hawks" (compared with dark-morph Red-taileds of other populations) are usually a darker sooty-brown (not rusty) with a dusky gray-white tail (sometimes with a rusty cast) that is often mottled with dark vertical streaking. The tail has a vaguely defined dark terminal band, and the entire underparts of the bird are often mottled with white spotting.

Immature Red-taileds are also highly variable and lack the distinctive reddish tail of most adults (instead having a brownish tail with several narrow, darker bands). The best identifiers of most immatures are the black patagial bar on the underwing and the large white or buff patches on the scapulars, which form a light V on the back when the wings are folded. The color of the head (which may range from dark brown to white) and the amount and distribution of dark streaking below are highly variable.

### Ferruginous Hawk

The Ferruginous Hawk is a large *Buteo* with long broad wings that are somewhat pointed at the tips (Fig. 4.25). The wings of juvenile birds appear narrower than they are because of the proportionately longish tail (noticeably longer than in Red-taileds and adult Ferruginous). Birds of all ages are often first identified by the large white patches on the upper side of the wings (formed by white inner webs of primaries). These create a bold white flash in flight (reminiscent of Crested Caracara) and are larger and more conspicuous than the white windows often seen on the wings of other buteos. Birds of all ages have a large gape that lends an almost owl-like look. This larger gape is best seen on perched birds, with the gape line appearing fleshier and brighter yellow than in other buteos, and extending farther back on the face (on a line with the rear of the eye).

Typical light-morph adults have brown upper parts with distinct rufous highlights formed by rufous edges to the mantle feathers, scapulars, and wing coverts. Below, they are mostly white, with a variable amount of scattered rufous barring on the flanks and belly. The head is whitish, streaked heavily with dark gray (particularly on the nape and crown). Perched birds at a distance usually appear conspicuously pale-headed; the pale-head look is often a good first clue to the bird's identity (most Red-taileds will appear dark-headed at a glance). The tarsal feath-

Figure 4.25. Ferruginous Hawk (light-morph adult). Note the broad, but somewhat pointed, wings and the longish tail. The blackish crescents at the carpals, the contrasting dark (feathered) thighs, and the uniformly pale tail are all good marks. This individual is more heavily barred on the coverts than most. (Photo by Barry R. Zimmer.)

ers are typically rufous (with fine blackish barring), and the largely feathered legs form a dark V in flight that contrasts with the otherwise white underparts. The wings are largely immaculate white below with blackish crescents at the carpals and an individually variable amount of rufous spotting or barring on the underwing coverts. From below, the tail generally appears whitish (frequently washed light-pink or orange) and unbanded, whereas the upper surface usually has a whitish base with a vaguely defined broad rufous band.

Immatures are variable but are typically darker brown above (less rufescent) and often have a buffy head. They lack the rusty leggings of adults but retain the white underwings with black carpal crescents and show some dark spotting on the white leggings. They also tend to show dark spotting (rather than rufous barring) on the underwing coverts. The basal third of the tail is usually whitish, with a broad grayish subterminal band occupying most of the distal two-thirds. The uppertail coverts are white with large dark spots (like the leggings).

Dark-morph birds are usually a darker brown than like-plumaged Red-taileds, although some individuals may be bicolored rufous and chocolate-brown on the underparts. They can also be distinguished from other dark buteos by the entirely pale silvery or gray tail (sometimes with diffuse rusty terminal band). In flight, they can be distinguished by the generally unmarked underside of the primaries and secondaries with a less apparent dark border. The white flash in the upper primaries, the large gape, and structural characters are also useful clues.

Flight characteristics can be helpful. Ferruginous Hawks frequently hover (like Rough-legs), and when soaring they are usually intermediate in wing dihedral between Red-tailed (flatter) and Swainson's (more pronounced).

## Swainson's Hawk

Swainson's Hawk is best told by a combination of wing structure and underwing pattern (Fig. 4.26). Birds of all ages have long, narrow, pointed wings that are unlike those of any other *Buteo*. These appear relatively long on perched birds, extending to or past the end of the tail. The flight attitude is typically a pronounced dihedral, and it is common for the birds to teeter back and forth like a Turkey Vulture.

Light-morph adults have a strong "negative" pattern of contrasting pale wing linings with blackish flight feathers (the reverse of the normal raptor underwing pattern), as shown in Figure 4.26. They are evenly brown above, without the white mottling of the scapulars that is found on Red-tailed. A brown bib encircles the throat and breast, leaving a white chin. The tail is gray with a number of fine, dark bands, and a broader subterminal band.

Dark-morph birds are infrequently seen and seem to be rarer than in other species of *Buteo*. Dark-morphs are told from other dark buteos by shape, lack of sharp contrast to the underwing (the remiges are a dark, dingy gray, whereas the linings are either all one color or a paler or more rufescent brown), grayish tail without bright white bands, pale undertail coverts, and a generally dingy, dark

Figure 4.26. Swainson's Hawk (light-morph adult). Note the characteristic slender, pointed wings; bold negative underwing pattern; and dark bib encircling the white chin. (Photo by Barry R. Zimmer.)

brown body coloring. Rufous-morph birds that are somewhat intermediate in appearance are more common, particularly in certain geographic regions, such as northern Colorado and southern Wyoming. These birds have a dark rufous belly with a contrastingly darker brown bib, although at a distance, or in poor light, the underparts may appear to be uniformly dark. They tend to have a white chin, as do light-morph birds, and paler rufous wing linings. As do dark-morph birds, these individuals also have pale undertail coverts that contrast with the darker belly.

Immatures are variable, with heavy brown streaking below, against a usually bright buffy ground color. Heavy dark malar streaks combine with upper breast streaking to form large, blobby blotches on the sides of the breast. A bold, buffy eye stripe is usually present, although it may be inconspicuous on birds that have a largely pale head. The upper parts are still more evenly colored than those of Red-taileds, and the underwing pattern, although less pronounced than in adults, is still evident. Given the variable nature of plumage in young Swainson's, it is best to concentrate on wing shape and pattern. Most immature Swainson's have a conspicuous white "horseshoe" on the uppertail coverts, which, combined with the dihedral flight attitude, has caused many birders to mistake them for Northern Harriers.

## Rough-legged Hawk

The Rough-legged Hawk is a long-winged, long-tailed *Buteo* (similar in shape to the Ferruginous Hawk, but with slimmer wings) with a confusing array of plumages (Figs. 4.27 and 4.28). Many field guides have greatly oversimplified the morphological variation in this species by illustrating a single light-morph plumage and a single dark-morph plumage. In life, the situation is complicated by

Figure 4.27. Rough-legged Hawk (light-morph). Note the pale head and breast, conspicuous dark eye line, bold black belly band, and broad dusky subterminal band on the tail. The lightly spotted (rather than heavily barred) leggings and lightly marked, pale breast help identify this bird as an immature. (Photographed in mid-November in San Luis Obispo County, California, by Kevin J. Zimmer.)

sexual and age variation superimposed on the typical *Buteo* polymorphisms. There are differing male, female, and immature plumages for both light-morph and dark-morph birds.

Light-morph adults are generally dark brown above, heavily and irregularly mottled with white, gray, and buff. They are more whitish on the head, usually showing a conspicuous pale patch (with a dark center) on the nape, but are generally more heavily streaked with dark than Ferruginous Hawks, and thus tend to appear darker-headed than the latter species (but generally paler-headed than

Figure 4.28. Rough-legged Hawk (light-morph). Note especially the striking black carpal patches, a good feature of all light-morph Rough-leggeds. The solid belly band and the tail pattern mark this bird as a female, and the more heavily marked chest and underwing coverts allow it to be aged as an adult. (Photographed in mid-November in San Luis Obispo County, California, by Kevin J. Zimmer.)

Red-taileds). Many birds have the forehead mostly unstreaked and whitish, lending the appearance of a white "headlight" (perhaps more pronounced in males). Both sexes are heavily mottled with dark feathering on the throat and breast and are heavily barred on the leggings. Males tend to be largely unmarked and whitish on the belly and undertail, contrasting strongly with the barred leggings and almost solidly dark chest (the latter lending a bibbed appearance). In contrast, females have a buffier ground color (rather than whitish) to the underparts and have a broad, blackish belly band (sometimes barred, sometimes solidly colored) that is separated from the dark chest by a buffy, lightly marked "shield" across the lower breast.

The underwings of light-morph adults are distinguished by a large, dark, somewhat square carpal patch that stands out in contrast to the mostly white remiges; this patch is usually larger and more pronounced in females than in males (Fig. 4.28). The flight feathers are tipped dusky, giving a dark trailing edge and tip to the underwing. The wing linings are variably marked with dark brown spots. The upper wings are dark brown and lack the white primary patches that are so prominent in Ferruginous Hawks. Males have a white tail with a variable number of narrow dark bands and a wider dark subterminal band. Females have a wide, white basal tail band, and the remainder of the tail is dark brown. At close range, a narrow, blackish subterminal band can usually be seen against the broader brown band.

Immature light-morph birds are particularly striking (Fig. 4.27). They are pale-headed (varying from creamy-white to buff), with fine dark streaking on the crown and nape and a conspicuous dark eye line. The breast is usually buffy and is only lightly marked with dark streaking or mottling when compared with adults. As do adult females, immatures have a broad, blackish, usually solid, belly band that contrasts strongly with the lightly marked breast and with the leggings, which also tend to be buffy and unmarked (or only lightly spotted, but not heavily barred, as in adults). Immature birds have a tail pattern similar to that of adult females, with a white base and a broad, dark band occupying the distal two thirds. Immature birds lack the narrow blackish subterminal band seen in adult females. Immatures have white patches on the upper primaries similar to those of Ferruginous Hawks. The underwing pattern of immatures is similar to that of adult females except that the wing linings, which are buffy, are only lightly spotted with dark brown.

Dark-morph males are characterized by a blackish overall coloration (darker and colder than dark-morphs of other species) and by underwing and tail pattern. The underwing linings are blackish, and the undersides of the flight feathers are silver-white and heavily barred and are tipped dusky, so that there is a distinct, dark trailing edge to the wing. The tail is blackish, with three or four narrow white bands. Dark-morph females are more of a chocolate-brown, with somewhat more rufescent-brown wing linings. Their tail is broadly white at the base and has a broad blackish terminal band when seen from below, but it looks mostly dark from above. Dark-morph immatures are similar to adult females, but they have white patches on the upper side of the primaries, have much less barring on the underside of the remiges, and may have several narrow, pale bands on the upper tail.

Like the Ferruginous Hawk, Rough-leggeds soar with a moderate dihedral and habitually hover when hunting.

## White-tailed Hawk

White-tailed Hawks of all ages have a unique wing shape; the wings are very long and pointed and very broad (second only to Common Black-Hawk). They project beyond the tail on resting birds. The wings are also somewhat constricted at the base where they join the body. The tail appears relatively short.

Adults are beautiful hawks, with gray upper parts, bright rusty shoulders, immaculate white underparts (sometimes shadow barred with light gray), and a white tail with a single black subterminal band and, usually, some very fine bands that can be seen only at close range. Most obvious in flight is the negative under-wing pattern (dark gray remiges with contrasting white linings) reminiscent of Swainson's. Immature birds are mostly dark brown, often heavily scaled or mottled with white below. They usually have an irregularly shaped whitish patch in the center of the chest and have a white horseshoe on the rump. The undertail coverts are whitish. The underwings are darkest on the linings, paler, but still medium gray on the remiges. The tail is entirely gray with numerous fine dark bands. As is often the case with immature buteos, immature White-taileds have proportionately longer tails than adults, which somewhat alters the overall jizz in flight.

White-tailed Hawks soar with a pronounced dihedral and frequently hover when hunting.

## Common Black-Hawk

Although not a member of the genus *Buteo,* the Common Black-Hawk can be confused with the Zone-tailed Hawk. Structural characters are excellent clues to the identity of Common Black-Hawks of all ages. This species has strikingly wide wings that are proportionately broader than are those of any other U.S. hawk and that are suggestive of a Black Vulture (Fig. 4.29). The tail appears very short, and the bright yellow legs are long. Immature birds have narrower wings and longer tails than adults, but they retain loosely similar proportions.

Adult Common Black-Hawks are further distinguished from dark-morph buteos by their dark slaty (rather than dark-brown) overall color, by their uniformly dark underwings (no striking contrast between wing linings and remiges) with a small white crescent at the base of the outer primaries, and by the tail pattern (black tail with a single wide white band in the center and a very narrow white terminal fringe). The Zone-tailed Hawk, which has much more slender wings and a longer tail, is also slaty gray, but it has a two-toned underwing (blackish linings,

Figure 4.29. Common Black-Hawk. Note the exceptionally broad wings and single wide, white tail band. (Photographed in May at Redrock, New Mexico, by Barry R. Zimmer.)

paler and distinctly barred remiges) and two or three narrower white bands on the tail (which are more gray when viewed from above). Both the cere and facial skin of the common Black-Hawk are yellow, whereas the cere of the Zone-tailed Hawk is yellow and the facial skin is grayish.

Immature Common Black-Hawks are dark brown above, mottled with white and buff. They are tawny-buff below, boldly streaked or mottled with blotchy, dark brown markings. The thighs and undertail coverts are barred dark brown. The head is pale buff with a dark cap, a bold dark postocular stripe, and a bold dark malar stripe. The tail is buff or whitish and narrowly barred with many fine, dark bars and a broader dark subterminal band. The upper wings show large buffy patches in the primaries in flight. The underwings are largely buffy, with barred remiges and a blackish crescent at the carpals.

Common Black-Hawks hunt mostly from perches overlooking the water. They only occasionally soar (unlike Zone-tailed Hawks, which hunt mostly on the wing) and are frequently seen wading in shallow streams in search of crayfish, frogs, and other aquatic prey.

### Zone-tailed Hawk

The Zone-tailed Hawk is slender-winged and is given to soaring with the wings raised in a dihedral like that of the Turkey Vulture (birds flying at high altitudes can be easily passed off as the latter species) (Fig. 4.30). Zone-taileds are told from Common Black-Hawk by the very different shape, distinct bicolored effect on the underwing (as on the Turkey Vulture wing), smaller bill, gray (instead of yellow) facial skin (but the cere is yellow in both species), and long, multibanded tail (only one band may be visible under many conditions, and juveniles may appear plain-tailed under field conditions).

Figure 4.30. Zone-tailed Hawk. Note the narrow wings (as compared with those of the Common Black-Hawk) and the Turkey Vulture–like underwing pattern. (Photo by Barry R. Zimmer.)

## Harris' Hawk

Adult Harris' Hawks are unmistakable. Immatures, with their rusty shoulders, streaky chest, rufous-barred thighs, and rufous underwing linings somewhat resemble immature Red-shouldered Hawks. They can be distinguished by their longer legs, more extensive rufous on the shoulder, lack of barring on the chest and belly, paler undersurface of the remiges, and white at the base and tip of the tail.

## Gray Hawk

Adult Gray Hawks are nearly unmistakable, but in southern Texas they may be confused with male Hook-billed Kites. Hook-billed Kites, however, have more oval shaped wings, a longer tail, an absurdly hooked beak, white eyes (dark in Gray Hawk), and more coarsely barred underparts; the Hook-billed Kite also lacks the neat black border to the underwings. Immature Gray Hawks are similar to immature Broad-wingeds, but they have a conspicuous white "horseshoe" on the rump, a bolder facial pattern (more distinct, pale supercilium; dark eye line; and dark malar stripe), barred (rather than streaked or spotted) thigh feathers, and more tail bands.

## Red-shouldered Hawk

The Red-shouldered Hawk is a medium-sized, long-tailed *Buteo,* with wings that are distinctly rounded at the tips. Adults are readily identified by the black-and-white checkered wings, heavily banded tail, rusty shoulders, orange underparts (very pronounced on California birds), and pale windows (pale patches in the primaries that are usually more conspicuous from below when they arc backlighted, and therefore, partially transparent) at the base of the outer primaries (Figs. 4.31 and 4.32). Individual hawks of many species show pale windows that are typically

Figure 4.31. Red-shouldered Hawk. Note the boldly checkered wings and banded tail. This individual is strikingly orange on the head and underparts, marking it as being of the California race *elegans*. (Photographed in November at Atascadero, California, by Kevin J. Zimmer.)

oval or rectangular, but those of the Red-shouldered are crescent-shaped. Western subspecies (particularly *elegans* of California) are more strikingly bright rufous below and on the head than are eastern populations (especially when compared with the pale Florida subspecies *extimus*), and they have more boldly checkered wings (showing a strong, silvery contrast to the body). The only similar species is the Broad-winged Hawk, which lacks the checkered flight feathers, rusty shoulder, and pale windows and which has a totally different jizz.

Immature Red-shouldereds are similar to young Broad-wingeds, but the wing and tail shapes, crescent-shaped wing windows, rufous underwing linings, more strongly checkered remiges, tail pattern (Red-shouldereds have evenly thick bars throughout; Broad-wingeds have a wider subterminal bar), and the lack of a de-

Figure 4.32. Red-shouldered Hawk. This back-lit bird shows the boldly checkered flight feathers and boldly banded tail as well as the characteristic pale crescents at the base of the outer primaries. (Photographed in September at Atascadero, California, by Kevin J. Zimmer.)

fined black trailing edge to the underwings will prove diagnostic. Broad-wingeds are also whiter below with less marking and have more uniformly colored upper wings with whitish or pale buff underwing linings.

Red-shouldereds of all ages have a somewhat *Accipiter*-like flight, with several quick flaps followed by short glides. They glide with the wings bowed, presenting a distinctive outline. Like accipiters, Red-shouldereds usually hunt from a perch but will occasionally soar. Birds of all ages routinely shiver their tail upon alighting on a new perch—a good behavioral clue.

### Broad-winged Hawk

The Broad-winged Hawk is a small, chunky buteo with broad wings that are pointed at the tips (Fig. 4.33). The tail appears relatively short. The underwings are pearly white (linings occasionally buff) with narrow but distinct, neat black borders and tips. Proportions and flight pattern (along with underwing coloration) will allow separation from the superficially similar accipiters.

Immatures are very similar to young Red-shouldereds but are distinguished by shape; absence of pale, crescent-shaped wing windows; more uniform upper wings; whitish or pale buff (rather than rufous) underwing linings; tail pattern; whiter underparts; and neat black edge to the underwings. Immature Broad-wingeds are even more similar to young Gray Hawks, but their rump lacks the obvious white horseshoe, the face pattern is less striking, the thigh feathers are streaked rather than barred, and the black border to the underwings is more evident.

# Shorebirds

The shorebirds (members of the families Charadriidae, Scolopacidae, Haematopodidae, and Recurvirostridae) present a special challenge to birders everywhere. Although several species are distinctively plumaged and easy to identify in

Figure 4.33. Broad-winged Hawk. Note the broad wings, pointed at the tips, with the underwings pearly white, neatly outlined in black. (Photographed in April in southern Texas by Kevin J. Zimmer.)

all seasons, many others are members of species complexes that involve two or three (or even more) similar species. Members of the genus *Calidris*, the small, brownish gray sandpipers collectively referred to as peeps in the United States and as stints in Europe, are particularly difficult to separate.

Identification of most shorebirds (but especially the peeps, dowitchers, and yellowlegs) is facilitated by (and in some cases is dependent on) at least a basic knowledge of seasonal plumage variation, molt sequences, and patterns of dispersal.

The ability to properly age a shorebird is particularly vital in the identification of many species. Some field guides depict at most only two plumages for each shorebird species: a winter, or basic, plumage and a summer, or alternate, plumage.

In fact, shorebirds have a third plumage, the juvenal plumage, that in most species is distinctly different from either adult plumage. Species that lack a distinctive juvenal plumage are generally those that pose few identification problems to begin with.

Most northbound adult shorebirds in spring are in fresh breeding (alternate) plumage as the result of a partial prealternate molt. Fresh breeding dress is characterized by unworn feathers with clean margins and often with sharp, bright feather edgings of white, gold, or chestnut. Except for occasional individuals that retain their winter plumage into summer (usually because of sexual immaturity), all shorebirds seen from mid-April to early June will be in this plumage, or at least molting into it. This alternate plumage is worn on the breeding grounds and (in most species) on the return migration south in summer or fall. By the time Arctic-nesting species arrive back in the contiguous 48 states, their feathers have been subjected to considerable wear and abrasion. The result is a worn alternate plumage that usually looks tattered and dull. Feather margins are often frayed and in all cases lack the brightly colored edges that were present in spring. Differential feather wear may obliterate any real pattern to upperpart coloration. These individuals lack the sharp, natty appearance seen earlier and thus may totally confuse observers familiar with the other plumage.

Juvenal plumage is acquired by a complete postnatal molt on the breeding grounds and is worn throughout the southward migration. Because the plumage has been only recently attained by the time juvenile birds move south, their feathers have not begun to show the signs of wear that characterize fall-migrating adults.

The feathers of the back, scapulars, tertials, and wing coverts of juveniles of many species are broadly edged with white, buff, gold, or chestnut, lending a bold, clean, appearance that is more reminiscent of spring adults than of those in worn alternate plumage. In some species (for example, Eurasian Dotterel, Curlew Sandpiper, Baird's Sandpiper, Ruff, and Buff-breasted Sandpiper), these feather edgings are especially broad and bold, giving a distinctive spangled or scaly look to the upper parts (Fig. 4.34). To a lesser extent this look is evident in all peeps and to a lesser extent even in some plovers.

Figure 4.34. Baird's Sandpiper in juvenal plumage. Note the characteristic neatly pale-margined scapulars, mantle feathers, and wing coverts, which lend an overall scaly pattern to the upper parts. Note also the projection of the wingtips well past the tip of the tail, a feature exhibited in North American peeps only by Baird's and White-rumped sandpipers. (Photographed in August near Santa Maria, California, by Kevin J. Zimmer.)

Basic plumage is typically somewhat plain (although not ratty until late in winter), with most species having grayer feathers with either dark shafts or centers and with little or no trace of light feather margins. This plumage is attained from a complete prebasic molt by adults and via a partial prebasic molt by juvenile birds. Juveniles of most species retain their scapulars, tertials, and wing coverts from juvenal plumage into first-basic plumage.

Recognition of the three (four including worn alternate) plumage types should go hand in hand with a knowledge of molt timing and general patterns of movement. Adults of almost all shorebirds start migrating south to their wintering grounds earlier than juveniles, sometimes a month or more earlier. Adults of most species that breed in Canada and Alaska will begin appearing in the contiguous 48 states by early to mid-July (some species appear by the end of June), and adults of species that winter in Central or South America, will have passed through for the most part by mid- to late August. Adults typically retain most or all of their alternate plumage until the wintering grounds are reached (the Dunlin and Wilson's Phalarope are among the exceptions). In short, all southward-bound adults of most species will be in worn alternate plumage, and the basic plumage of species that winter far to the south (for example, Baird's and White-rumped sandpipers) will almost never be seen in our area.

Contrastingly, juveniles (in fresh juvenal plumage) migrate later in summer and fall; the earliest individuals arrive in mid- to late July, and the bulk movements occur in August through October. Juveniles also acquire their basic plumage later in fall than do adults, often from October through November rather than in August. Once again, juveniles of most species do not attain basic plumage until they have reached the wintering grounds.

Most areas will have some overlap between migrating adults in worn alternate plumage and migrating juveniles in fresh juvenal plumage. Observers in southern coastal areas need to be particularly alert in late summer through fall because they may encounter three distinct plumages of some species simultaneously. Because these areas serve as wintering grounds for some species (or are at least very close to their wintering grounds), fall-arriving individuals will be molting into basic plumage. Consequently, some species (for example, the Sanderling and the Western Sandpiper) may be present in three plumages: worn alternate, juvenal, and basic, not to mention transitional individuals that are between molts.

There are also sexual differences in the timing of migration by adults of many species. For species with essentially uniparental care, the emancipated sex typically migrates first. These sexual differences do not carry the same importance to birders as do the age differences because the plumage of most shorebirds does not differ between the sexes (phalaropes are an exception).

Careful attention to details of plumage, as well as to dates of arrival will aid tremendously in the identification of many shorebirds. For the difficult species complexes, a knowledge of molt sequence and migration timing may be critical for accurate identification. In all cases, observers should become thoroughly familiar with all plumage variations of the common or expected species in their area before attempting to identify rare species.

## Common Ringed Plover versus Semipalmated Plover

Common Ringed Plover is an essentially palearctic shorebird whose only known North American breeding grounds lie in the northeastern Canadian arctic. In the West, it is known only from Alaska, where it is a rare but regular spring migrant on St. Lawrence Island and a casual vagrant elsewhere in coastal western Alaska (primarily the Seward Peninsula) and the Pribilof and Aleutian islands. In any plumage, the Common Ringed Plover is extremely similar to the Semipalmated Plover, which is common and widespread in Alaska. Each May through June, throngs of birders flush with vagrant fever invade Alaska, many with the mistaken notion that Common Ringed Plover should be expected. When Semipalmated Plovers are encountered in exotic locales such as Nome, St. Paul Island, or Gambell (St. Lawrence Island), many are mistakenly identified as the much rarer Common Ringed. In alternate plumage (the only plumage of the Common Ringed likely to be encountered), the two species can be separated visually given proper views, but vocal confirmation is always desirable. For mainland records of the Common Ringed, vocal confirmation should be considered essential.

Understanding sexual dimorphism in banded plovers is crucial for correctly identifying a vagrant Common Ringed-Plover. Males in alternate plumage have solidly black auriculars and a solidly black breast band, whereas many females in alternate plumage show variable amounts of brown in both areas. There is some indication that female Common Ringeds may frequently closely resemble males in lacking obvious brown in the breast band or auriculars. However, any alternate-plumaged plover of either species that has brown in either of these areas may be confidently identified as a female. Correctly identifying the sex of a given bird is vital to assessing the importance of some characters of facial pattern.

Males are easier to identify. Male Common Ringeds (Fig. 4.35) have a long white stripe that starts above the eye and continues back above the black auricular patch. The auriculars then, are bordered above and below by white, making for a more contrasting facial pattern. Male Semipalmateds (Fig. 4.35) have only a small white spot, a short thin streak, or no white at all above the eye and auriculars. Thus, the auriculars of the Semipalmated are bordered above by dark brown and contrast less. Females of both species have a white eyebrow (often strong in many female Semipalmateds), so this mark is of no use in identifying a female bird.

Many references allude to the wider breast band of Common Ringed as a good mark, and indeed, a wide breast band that is thicker at the corners than in the middle is often the first thing to catch your eye on a Common Ringed Plover. The widest parts of the breast band on Common Ringed are typically at least as wide (or wider) than the white throat and collar that the breast band isolates. However, the apparent width and shape of the breast band of both Common Ringeds and Semipalmateds can change dramatically from one minute to the next as a bird changes posture or behavior. These postural influences work both ways, so that a Common Ringed may appear to have a narrow band and a Semipalmated may appear to have a wider band. A given plover would have to be observed for a lengthy period before any reliable conclusions could be drawn about the width of the breast band.

A good close-range mark is the presence and conspicuousness of a contrasting orbital ring. Male Semipalmateds in alternate plumage have a complete, narrow, yellow (or yellow-orange) orbital ring that is readily seen at close range. This ring is usually less pronounced in alternate-plumaged female Semipalmateds and may be altogether absent in some basic-plumaged and juvenile birds. Common Ringeds typically lack any contrasting orbital ring, but they may show an indistinct partial ring.

A relative character is the coloration of the upper parts, which on the Common Ringed seems to consistently be a shade paler brown than in Semipalmated. The paler brown color to the crown, along with the white supercilium, serves to accentuate the black auriculars of Common Ringed and to make the entire face appear more contrasty (Fig. 4.35).

Figure 4.35. Head profiles of male Semipalmated Plover (upper left) versus male Common Ringed-Plover (lower right). Note the much more prominent white eyebrow and the slightly longer bill of the Common Ringed, as well as differences in orbital rings, neck-band shape and width, and pattern of black and white on the face and forehead. (Artwork by Shawneen Finnegan.)

Common Ringeds do have a longer, somewhat thinner bill than Semipalmateds, a subtle character that is nonetheless apparent (with good views) to those who have critically looked at the bill shape of many Semipalmated Plovers.

Two other distinctions that I have found to be of no use in the field, but which are included here for completeness, involve the length of the white wing stripe and the amount of webbing or palmation between the toes. The white wing stripe of both species is visible only in flight and is slightly longer on the Common Ringed. The webbing between the middle and outer toe of the Common Ringed is reduced and is nearly lacking between the middle and inner toe. In contrast, there is obvious webbing between all toes on Semipalmateds.

Vocalizations remain the most reliable distinction between the two species and appear to be diagnostic. The Semipalmated gives a rich, up-slurred "chur-LEEP" as its usual flight call. The flight call of the Common Ringed is a mellower, softer "POO-wee." The display vocalizations of both species are given in flight as the bird rocks back and forth with its wings held in an exaggerated dihedral. That of the Semipalmated is a somewhat harsh "reep reep reep" repeated many times, and that of the Common Ringed is a softer "puree puree puree" repeated many times.

For further discussions see Chandler 1987, Mullarney 1991, and Dunn 1993.


## Golden-Plovers

The American Golden-Plover and Pacific Golden-Plover were, until recently, considered a single species (the Lesser Golden-Plover). American Golden-Plovers breed across much of arctic and subarctic Alaska and Canada and are common spring migrants throughout the central part of the continent. The bulk of the fall migration is along the Atlantic Coast, as birds head south to the wintering areas in southern South America. Smaller numbers of migrants are seen sparingly throughout the United States. Pacific Golden-Plovers breed in western Alaska and Siberia and winter from southeastern Asia and Australasia to scattered islands in the South Pacific. The bulk of migration occurs across eastern Asia and the Pacific, but small numbers migrate along our Pacific Coast each year, with a very few wintering at select areas in coastal southern and central California. The two species have partially sympatric breeding ranges in Alaska and are sometimes found together in migration along the West Coast. They can be difficult to separate in any plumage, and occasional birds will be encountered that cannot be safely identified to species.

Size and structural differences between the two species are minimal and are largely difficult to judge. Americans are slightly larger overall, but Pacifics have slightly longer bill and legs and may appear proportionately larger-headed and show greater toe projection beyond the tail in flight. One structural feature that is easier to assess (given close views) on resting birds is primary projection. The primaries of Americans project noticeably beyond the tip of the tail, and the tips of four or five primaries are usually visible beyond the tertials. The primaries of Pacifics project to the tip of the tail or just barely beyond, and only one to three (rarely four) primary tips are visible beyond the tertials. This mark must be used with caution and only in conjunction with other marks, because some overlap does exist. Also, this character cannot be judged reliably on birds that are molting their primaries or tertials.

In breeding, or alternate, plumage, males of both species are mostly black below and heavily spangled gold-and-black above. They have a broad white supercilium that continues down the sides of the neck and breast, separating the golden upper parts from the black underparts. In Americans, this white stripe is broader, and it ends abruptly at the shoulder, where it flares in width (Fig. 4.36). This flaring is so pronounced that an American viewed head-on appears to have only a narrow corridor of black in the center of the chest, framed between two large patches of white. On Pacifics, the white stripe is narrower, and it continues past the shoulder, running the length of the sides and flanks and forming a continuous (but somewhat ragged or uneven) boundary between the folded wing and the black belly (Fig. 4.37). The vent of male Americans in full alternate plumage is solidly black, whereas the vent of Pacifics is extensively mottled with white.

Although most males of either species in full alternate plumage can be readily identified by these marks alone, caution is still in order. Most Americans are still in molt during their northbound migration, and they may not complete molt until after they have reached the breeding grounds. Such birds may still show white feathering on the sides and vent that give them more the appearance of the

Figure 4.36. American Golden-Plover in alternate plumage. The white stripe down the side of the neck ends and flares at the sides of the chest. The flanks are black, and there is little contrast between the wing coverts and the mantle. Note also the fairly long primary projection. (Photographed in early June near Nome, Alaska, by Kevin J. Zimmer.)

Figure 4.37. Pacific Golden-Plover in alternate plumage. Note that the white neck stripe continues the length of the sides to the undertail coverts. Note also the shorter primary projection and the contrast between the paler wing coverts and darker mantle. (Photographed in early June near Nome, Alaska, by Kevin J. Zimmer.)

Pacific. Furthermore, females of both species are duller and more mottled with white below and may have indeterminate patterns.

Pacifics are somewhat brighter gold on the back than are Americans because the individual mantle feathers of Pacifics are more heavily marked with gold spots than are the corresponding feathers of Americans. A possible accessory mark that I have found to be relatively reliable for birds on the breeding grounds in June is the presence or absence of contrast between the folded wings and the back. Birds of both species have a variable amount of white spangling mixed with the gold and black of the upper parts. The proportion of white spotting to gold spotting on the wing coverts of Americans seems to match that of the back feathers and scapulars, presenting a uniform appearance to the upper parts. The wing coverts of Pacifics seem to be more heavily spangled with white, setting up a contrast between the darker, more gold-spangled back, and the lighter, more white-spangled wings. This look is accentuated by differences in the ground color of the wing coverts, which, to my eyes, appear grayer and more faded on Pacifics (blacker on Americans). This paler look to the wings could be the result of differences in molt schedule. Pacifics molt into alternate plumage much earlier, usually on the wintering grounds before they migrate. Americans are typically molting as they migrate north and may not complete their molt until after they have reached the breeding areas. Thus, Pacifics seen in Alaska in June should show more signs of feather wear and fading than Americans, and this difference in feather wear may account for observed differences in wing color.

Habitat is one of the best clues to the identity of breeding golden-plovers. In areas where both species nest, Pacifics tend to occupy the lower, wetter, and grassier tundra, often near the coast or in broad, intermontane valleys. Americans are more typically found in higher-elevation tundra that is both drier and rockier. These habitat distinctions do not hold in areas in which only one species of golden-plover is found. For example, at Barrow, where Pacifics do not occur, Americans are common in the low, coastal tundra. Vocalizations are another key to specific identification, although the extent to which certain calls are shared or differ between the two species is not fully understood.

Adult Americans in basic plumage look like smaller, darker versions of Black-bellied Plover, typically lacking any golden color above, and instead, appearing dull, gray-brown above, with a plain grayish breast and dull-whitish belly. Pacifics in the same plumage usually show some golden fringing and spotting on the back, scapulars, and tertials and are often washed with buff on the head or neck, or both, and on the breast.

Juvenal-plumaged birds are typically more distinctive. The upper parts of both species are more heavily marked with gold in this plumage than in adult basic plumage. Some juvenile Pacifics are strikingly golden on the mantle. This coloration is most evident on birds in fresh juvenal plumage, and juveniles of both species may show marked fading of the gold upper parts by midfall. In general, juvenile Pacifics are strongly gold- or buff-tinged on the head, face, neck, and breast, whereas Americans are dull grayish or whitish in the same areas. Americans also typically have a whiter, more distinct supercilium and a less defined dark auricular spot, whereas Pacifics usually have a buffy, less-distinct supercilium, and a darker, more sharply defined auricular spot. Pacifics are also more likely to show fine, dark streaking on the foreneck and breast, whereas Americans often look barred in the same areas. Juveniles of both species will fade as fall progresses, and only Pacifics are likely to be strongly buff or golden anywhere on the head or body after midfall. Virtually all Americans will appear a cold gray-brown and whitish gray by midfall, although they often retain some gold coloration on the rump feathers, which are protected from fading.

For more information see Connors 1983, Connors et al. 1993, and Mlodinow 1993.

## Whimbrel versus Bristle-thighed Curlew

With its wintering grounds consisting of islands scattered across the South Pacific and its nesting area confined to remote areas of western Alaska that can be reached only by bush plane, the Bristle-thighed Curlew remained for decades something of a Holy Grail to birders. Then, in the late 1980s, the U.S. Fish and Wildlife Service discovered a breeding population of curlews north of Nome, near the end of the Taylor Highway (Kougarok Road). Suddenly, it was possible to drive to within hiking distance of this nearly mythical bird. Although the logistics of getting to Bristle-thighed country have gotten easier, the task of finding and correctly identifying this elusive bird remains difficult. Sadly, many birders make the long journey only to leave after having mistaken the very-similar and widespread Whimbrel for their lifer Bristle-thighed. Such mistakes can be attributed partly to the general similarity of the two species, partly to a lack of understanding that Whimbrels greatly outnumber Bristle-thigheds in the Nome region, and partly to the psychological influences that are inevitable when people come expecting to see a Bristle-thighed. Because the separation of these two species is unlikely to be an issue away from Alaska (and more precisely, away from the breeding areas of Bristle-thighed Curlews), the following discussion will center entirely on alternate-plumaged adults and on the resident North American race of Whimbrel.

On the breeding grounds, Bristle-thighed Curlews are often heard before they are seen, and vocalizations provide an easy way of separating the two species. The display song of the Whimbrel (often given on the wing) consists of several spaced, hollow whistles, building in intensity and length and culminating in a long series of bubbly, sputtering notes. The commonly heard flight call is a series of 5 to 10 (or more) identical, flat, whistled notes. Bristle-thigheds sing (often on the wing) a melodic "PURE-PUR-whee-weeit-WEE-WEEIT-WEE-weeit-wee" in which the whistled notes are drawn out and build in intensity and pitch before dropping back down the scale and fading in intensity. The commonly heard flight call is a rich, somewhat ploverlike "PEE-oo-weet," often repeated several times.

Unfortunately, these birds will not always call when you want them to, so visual field marks are still necessary. The two species are essentially similar in size and structure, although Bristle-thigheds are slightly shorter-legged. In general, alternate-plumaged Whimbrels appear uniformly dull-brown above and have fairly indistinct creamy edging, spotting, or notching on the wing coverts, scapulars, tertials, and back feathers. The lower back, uppertail coverts, and tail are a uniform gray-brown with darker brown horizontal bars. The head, neck, and underparts are a paler, dingy white. The head, face, neck, and breast are streaked with brown, whereas the sides, flanks, and vent are strongly barred brown. The head is strikingly patterned with a bold, brown line through the eye and a pair of broad, brown lateral crown stripes separated by a narrow, whitish median stripe. The bill may be entirely blackish or may show extensive fleshy-pink coloring along the basal portion of the lower mandible. The legs are bluish gray.

The best visual character for separating Bristle-thigheds from Whimbrels involves the tail and rump. The rump of Bristle-thigheds is unbarred and cinnamon-buff and contrasts strongly with the darker brown back. The upper tail is orangish to cinnamon (often a shade or two richer in color than the rump) and is banded with several widely spaced, broad dark bars. The rump and upper tail of Whimbrels are both uniformly barred and are the same gray-brown as the back. The contrasting cinnamon-buff tail and rump of Bristle-thigheds is conspicuous on flying birds, but it can be concealed on standing individuals.

In general, alternate-plumaged Bristle-thigheds are warmer and more contrastingly colored above than are Whimbrels. Bristle-thigheds in fresh plumage have broad golden or cinnamon fringes and large cinnamon notches or spots on the dark brown wing coverts, scapulars, tertials, and back feathers. More-worn individuals may appear more uniformly dark brown above. Bristle-thigheds also appear somewhat paler-faced, with the whitish or buffy cheeks and supercilium less streaked with brown than on most Whimbrels, thereby making for a more contrasting facial pattern. The foreneck and breast of Bristle-thigheds are also more densely streaked than are those of most Whimbrels, and the streaking ends more abruptly on the central chest. The lower chest, belly, sides, flanks, and vent are mostly unmarked (the flanks have scattered chevrons rather than the denser barring of Whimbrels) and vary from creamy to strongly buffy. The contrast between the heavily streaked chest and the unmarked belly and sides creates a two-toned or hooded look to the underparts (reminiscent of Pectoral Sandpiper) that is particularly conspicuous on flying birds. By contrast, Whimbrels are boldly barred on the sides, flanks, and vent and thus lack the sharp division between marked and unmarked areas on the underparts.

In flight, Bristle-thigheds show zones of contrast on the upper wing and back. The wing coverts, secondaries, and inner primaries are heavily spotted and notched with buff, gold, or cinnamon. These contrast somewhat with the scapulars and back, which appear darker. The inner part of the wing also contrasts with the outer five primaries (which are not notched or spotted with buff and, thus, appear darker) and especially with the primary coverts, both of which appear distinctly darker. The upper wing of the Whimbrel, like the rest of its upper parts, is more uniform in color, although it too appears darker on the outer primaries and primary coverts.

Some authors have suggested that Bristle-thigheds have more extensive fleshy-pink or dull reddish to the base of the lower mandible. This character appears highly variable (it probably is related to either age or breeding condition), and I have seen several Bristle-thigheds whose bill appears to be entirely black. The Bristle-thighed derives its name from the stiff, bristly feathers at the base of the thighs. These can be seen in the field with very close views, and they are diagnostic when seen.

## Peeps

Many a birder has spent hours on end puzzling over the little brown and gray shorebirds that comprise the genus *Calidris*. Indeed, this group presents many subtle identification problems and offers many opportunities for misidentification by unwary birders. Many of the standard guides are less than adequate aids in identifying these birds, being characteristically oversimplified in their discussion of similar species.

The ability to correctly age peeps is of paramount importance to proper identification. Juvenal-plumaged birds are strikingly different from adults that are present at the same times. Because most records of rare peeps tend to be of juvenile birds in fall, observers would do well to pay particular attention to the juvenal plumages of all peeps. Size, bill structure, wing length, and overall color pattern are also critical marks in assessing peeps of any age group. Absolute familiarity with all plumages of the common species in your area is the best foundation for being able to identify the less common ones. Avoid single-character identifications at all costs. The following discussion will focus on problems in separating the regular species of North American peeps. Be aware that the possibility of vagrant peeps of Eurasian origin can complicate the picture.

**Western versus Semipalmated Sandpiper.** Separating the Western from the Semipalmated Sandpiper is probably the biggest single problem in peep identification in North America (among regularly occurring species). Semipalmated Sandpipers are rare but regular migrants west of the Great Plains (most common in fall), whereas the Western Sandpiper is one of the two most common peeps in this same area (the other is the Least Sandpiper). The Semipalmated does not winter in North America (published Christmas Bird Counts to the contrary), and the Western winters only in southern coastal areas and in a few locales in the Southwest.

Most discussions of separating these species center on bill length. As a rule, Westerns have a noticeably longer bill that droops more at the tip than does that of Semipalmateds. However, bill length in peeps is subject to both sexual and individual variation; females of both species, on average, have a longer bill than males. Female Westerns are unlikely to be mistaken for Semipalmateds, but the shorter-billed males may be easily mistaken if bill length is used as the sole criterion.

More important than absolute bill length is bill shape (Figs. 4.38, through 4.41). The bill of Westerns is broad-based but tapers to a relatively fine point. The bill of many individuals has a noticeable droop to the tip (not unlike the bill of Dunlins), but the bill of others does not. In all cases, the bill of a Western should narrow conspicuously from base to tip. Semipalmateds, on the other hand, have a tube-shaped bill that is thick throughout the length and that does not taper conspicuously. The Semipalmated bill does not terminate in a fine point or in a droop; instead, it has a blunt look and may show a somewhat bulbous tip. These shape differences hold for virtually all Semis encountered in the West and are particularly vital in identifying longer-billed individuals. Semipalmated Sandpipers from the eastern part of the breeding range, which migrate down the Atlantic Coast in

Figure 4.38. Western Sandpiper in alternate plumage. Note the length and shape of the bill. (Photographed in early June near Nome, Alaska, by Kevin J. Zimmer.)

Figure 4.39. Semipalmated Sandpiper in alternate plumage. Note the length and shape of the bill. (Photographed in early June near Nome, Alaska, by Kevin J. Zimmer.)

fall, tend to be longer-billed (and to have a more tapered, pointy bill tip) than the birds that breed in Alaska and show up as rare migrants in the far West. Many of the eastern Semis could be impossible to separate (in the field) from Westerns on the basis of structural characters alone.

There are some consistent plumage differences between the two species. Breeding-plumaged Westerns (Fig. 4.38) are usually light gray with conspicuous chestnut-colored scapulars, auriculars, and crown feathers, giving them a foxy look. Breast spotting extends along the flanks and the spots are shaped like arrowheads or chevrons. Breeding-plumaged Semipalmateds (Fig. 4.39) are typically more brownish with only traces (if any) of rufous on the scapulars, crown, and face. Spotting is confined to the breast and lacks the pronounced arrowhead shape found in Westerns.

Juveniles (Figs. 4.40 and 4.41) of the two species can also be separated on the basis of plumage. Juvenile Westerns are gray and white with contrasting chestnut-colored scapulars and a variable number of mantle feathers (as do many other shorebirds, juvenile Westerns retain wing covert feathers along with some scapulars—but not the chestnut inner ones—and tertials when they molt into first basic plumage). The upperpart feathers are neatly edged with white or reddish. Juvenile Semipalmateds tend toward uniform buffy-brown (not gray) upper parts and lack the distinctive chestnut scapulars of the juvenile Western

Figure 4.40. Juvenal-plumaged Western Sandpipers, with a single juvenal-plumaged Semi-palmated Sandpiper in the center for comparison. Note the shorter bill (with no discernible droop to the tip) of the Semipalmated. (Photographed in August near San Simeon, California, by Kevin J. Zimmer.)

(traces of this coloration may be present). They typically have a bolder pale super-cilium that is set off by a more solidly colored crown (giving more of a capped appearance) and by darker auriculars that extend just above the eye. More striking are the neat, cream-colored edges to all of the upperpart feathers, lending a scalloped or scaly appearance similar to that of juvenile Baird's Sand-

Figure 4.41. Juvenal-plumaged Semipalmated Sandpiper. (Photo by Barry R. Zimmer.)

pipers (but much less pronounced). This effect is more striking in Semi-palmated than in Westerns, perhaps owing to the more uniformly colored upper parts and greater contrast provided by the brown feathers with cream edges (as opposed to gray feathers with white edges). Juvenile Semipalmateds frequently show a buffy wash on the side of the breast (usually somewhat smudged looking and often extending as a large wedge from the shoulder midway onto the breast). This, however, should not be the basis for identification because similar smudges are often seen on juvenile Westerns. Most far West records of Semi-palmateds are of juvenal-plumaged birds from late summer to early fall, and this plumage should be committed to memory.

**Warning:** The plumages described in the preceding paragraph apply to "typical" birds. Occasionally, juvenile Semis are encountered that are much brighter than average. These birds can have broad rufous edges to the tertials, scapulars, wing coverts, mantle feathers, and crown feathers. They can also have a prominent buffy wash to the sides of the chest and may show cream-colored lines down the sides of the back. Such brightly colored birds are still unlikely to be mistaken for Western Sandpipers, but they could readily be mistaken for a (vagrant) juvenile Little Stint. Juvenile Littles should have more-prominent white scapular lines, a thinner (more pointed) bill, and toes that lack any webbing.

Basic-plumaged birds are best identified on the basis of bill shape because many individuals of both species may be virtually identical in plumage. However, as pointed out earlier, adult shorebirds typically delay molt into basic plumage until they reach their wintering grounds. Because Semipalmateds are extremely rare in the United States in winter, basic-plumaged individuals will almost never be encountered. Westerns do winter in southern coastal areas and therefore are commonly seen in basic plumage. This plumage is basically gray and white like the juvenal plumage, but it lacks the rusty scapulars and the crisp, light edges of the upperpart feathers.

The two species can also be separated by call notes. Westerns give a high, thin "jeet," that is readily separated from the low, grating "jrrt" of the Semipalmated (a call similar to that of Baird's Sandpiper). On the breeding grounds, both species give a variety of vocalizations, some of them complex.

**Other Peeps.** As a general rule, the most common peep across most of the interior West is the Least Sandpiper. Therefore, observers should make every effort to familiarize themselves with all of its plumages along with all of the plumages of the nearly as common Western. Such familiarization will greatly facilitate the discovery and correct identification of the more unusual species.

Let's start with the separation of Least from Western. The Least is smaller and has a thinner bill (Fig. 4.42). Westerns are larger and have a longer, broader-based bill. These differences are especially apparent when direct comparison of the two species is possible. The bills of both species taper to a fine point and may droop slightly at the tip. Standard guides emphasize the greenish yellow legs of the Least, as opposed to the black legs of the Western. Although greenish yellow legs will confirm the identification of a Least, the fact that such color is not discernible

Figure 4.42. Juvenal-plumaged Least Sandpiper. Note the bill structure and the neatly pale-edged tertials, scapulars, and wing coverts. (Photo by Barry R. Zimmer.)

does not eliminate this species from consideration. Light conditions and mudcaking may make greenish yellow legs appear dark at any distance.

Least Sandpipers are browner in all plumages than are Westerns (which are gray). Breeding adult Leasts in fresh plumage and juveniles are very brown and have crisp chestnut-and-white edges to the feathers of the upper parts. Breeding adults are further characterized by a bold band of blackish streaks (set against a brownish wash) across the breast, whereas juveniles have a buffy wash (with few streaks) across the breast and are more boldly patterned above. Winter adults are dull brown and lack the bright feather edgings. Their breast is characterized by a band of streaks that is smudged in appearance (not sharp as in spring). Likewise, adults in worn alternate plumage lack the crisp feather edgings and appear dull brown.

Westerns in all plumages are grayer than Leasts. Breeding adults and juveniles have highly contrasting chestnut scapulars; breeding adults also have bright chestnut auriculars and crowns. The breast spotting of adult Westerns in alternate plumage is distinctly different from that of similarly plumaged Leasts, with arrowhead-shaped spots against a white (not a brown) ground color. These extend down the flanks on Westerns but are confined to the breast on Leasts.

Least Sandpipers are separated from Semipalmated Sandpipers by several characters. Leasts have a thinner bill that tapers to a fine point, unlike the thick, tubular bill of the Semipalmated. Like the Western, the Semipalmated has black legs, but again, this mark should be viewed with caution. Winter Semipalmateds are grayer and lack the distinctive breast band of winter Leasts. The buffy, scalloped look of juvenile Semis is also totally different from any plumage of Leasts.

Two other species of *Calidris* that are likely to be confused with Least, Western, and Semipalmated sandpipers are the Baird's and White-rumped sandpipers. The two species are structurally similar; they are noticeably larger than the other species and are differently shaped. Baird's and White-rumped are the largest of the small brown-and-gray peeps; they are much larger than Leasts and are recognizably larger than Westerns.

Both Baird's and white-rumpeds have relatively short legs and long wings, which lend a very horizontal (rather than upright) appearance to the posture of the birds. This horizontal look is almost reminiscent of a small tern on land rather than of a small sandpiper. An excellent mark for separating these two from the other species is the length of the folded wings. In Baird's and White-rumpeds these protrude past the end of the tail, whereas in the other species the wingtips do not even reach the tail tip (Figs. 4.34 and 4.43).

The bill of both Baird's and White-rumped is longer than the bill of the other species but is similar in shape to the finely tapering bill of Leasts. Alternate-plumaged White-rumpeds usually have an orange–flesh-colored base to the lower mandible, a good distinction at close range. The legs of both species are black, leaving the Least as the only small North American *Calidris* with pale legs.

Baird's in all plumages are buffy-colored. Adults in all plumages are somewhat dull (often dull brown owing to feather wear) and lack brightly margined feathers. The bright margins are lacking, especially on birds in worn alternate plumage, whose frayed feathers lend a particularly dull, tattered look. Baird's are buffy-brown above and white below, with a small band of fine darkish streaks overlaid on a buff-washed breast. This buffy breast contrasts with the white chin. Juveniles are very distinctive. Their broad light feather edgings give the upper parts a spangled, scaly appearance that is even more pronounced than on other juvenile peeps (Fig. 4.34) and that is somewhat suggestive of a Buff-breasted Sandpiper (which has a different structure, leg color, and other features). Baird's in all plumages have a broad, whitish (but not clean white) supercilium.

Figure 4.43. White-rumped Sandpiper. The chevrons on the sides and flanks, along with the wingtips projecting beyond the tail, identify this as a White-rumped. This is an adult molting from alternate plumage into basic plumage (note the new generation of scapulars contrasting with the extremely worn wing coverts). (Photo by Barry R. Zimmer.)

White-rumpeds lack the buffy coloring of Baird's, being white below and grayer above with some contrasting rusty feather edgings. They have whiter superciliums, and the breast spots are distinctly arrowhead-shaped and are heavier and more extensive (extending down the flanks) in distribution. They are overlaid on a white (not buffy) background. In all of these respects, White-rumpeds more closely resemble Westerns than Baird's. The clear white rump (not divided by a central bar) of the White-rumped is diagnostic (among peeps) when seen, but reliance on this character alone can lead the observer to confusion with other small to medium-sized shorebirds. The calls of the two species are very different. Baird's has a low, gutteral "grrt," whereas White-rumpeds give a high, thin "seet" that is almost insectlike. Juvenile White-rumpeds lack the distinctive breast spotting of breeding adults, but they can still be distinguished from Baird's by their white rump, calls, lack of scaly back pattern, and extensively chestnut-edged feathers. The white rump, combined with size and shape are the best features for eliminating other peeps from consideration.

Both Baird's and White-rumped sandpipers winter far south of the United States (published Christmas Bird Counts to the contrary), so they are unlikely to ever be seen in basic plumage in our area. Baird's are uncommon to rare spring migrants over much of the West, being more common in late summer and fall than in spring and winter. Most White-rumped records west of the Great Plains (where the species is casual) are from spring. White-rumpeds migrate north much later than other peeps and are more likely to be found in the latter half of May and first days of June than at other times.

For more information see Veit and Jonsson 1984.


## Yellowlegs

Field guides have traditionally instructed birders to identify yellowlegs on the basis of overall size, bill size and shape, and call, with little attention given to plumage differences. In fact, some guides treat yellowlegs (and other shorebirds) as if they have only one plumage. As do most other shorebirds, the two yellowlegs species (Greater and Lesser) have three recognizably different plumages.

1. Basic plumage is attained by adults after breeding or during fall migration (August–September) and is worn until the following April. Juvenile birds molt into first basic plumage later, from October to November.
2. Alternate plumage is worn by breeding adults from April or May through late summer.
3. Juvenal plumage is worn by young birds from fledging until late fall.

Greater and Lesser yellowlegs are highly similar in basic plumage and are best identified at that time by structural and vocal differences. Alternate plumages, however, are very distinctive. The upperpart coloration is of little help in identification (although Greaters are marked a bit more heavily with black), but the underparts are radically different. Lessers have a finely streaked throat and breast and some fine barring on the flanks (which may be concealed). Their belly and lower breast are immaculate white, and the line of demarcation between the streaked upper breast and the plain lower breast is sharp (reminiscent of a Pectoral Sandpiper, but the streaking is less dense). Greaters are boldly streaked with black on the throat and upper breast, and the streaking gives way to dense black spotting and barring on the lower breast, flanks, and belly. They are much more heavily and extensively marked below than are Lessers, and there is no sharp line of demarcation between marked and unmarked areas. Greaters in alternate plumage are actually closer to alternate-plumaged Willets (which have much stouter, straight bills, dark legs, and a bright black-and-white wing pattern).

The two yellowlegs species are also readily distinguished when in juvenal plumage. As a rule, Lessers return south earlier than Greaters (but on the West Coast adult Greaters arrive first), and juveniles follow adults. Juvenile Lessers begin appearing in most western states by late July to early August and will greatly outnumber adults by the end of August. Greaters straggle south more slowly (many winter in the southern United States), and juveniles do not typically outnumber adults until October (remember that these dates are averages and will vary somewhat with latitude).

As it is in the other plumages, the upperpart coloration of the juvenal plumages is of little help in identification. Once again you will have to direct your attention to the underparts. Juvenile Lessers have a grayish wash across the breast and throat. Faint smudgy streaks may or may not be visible against this background. Juvenile Greaters are not similarly washed with gray and instead have a white throat and breast with a distinct bib of heavy black streaks (but the throat is plain and lacks the heavy spotting and barring of the flanks, belly, and lower breast that is seen in alternate-plumaged adults).

In any plumage, Greaters will show whitish spots on the secondaries and inner primaries, whereas the same feathers of Lessers are entirely blackish. Unfortunately, this character is not easy to see in the field.

This discussion of plumage is not meant to discredit or discourage the use of traditional criteria such as size, bill length and shape, and call notes. Indeed, for basic-plumaged birds, these characters are necessary to identification.

Greaters are distinctly larger and have a longer bill that is often slightly upturned. Relative bill length can be judged by comparing the length of the bill with the length of the head. The bill of Greaters is distinctly longer than the head, whereas the bill of Lessers is roughly the same length as the head or very slightly longer. Although bill length is variable for both species, Lessers always have a very straight bill. The overall size of the bird and the and bill length and shape are easily judged when the two species are side by side (or when other, better-known species are present), but they become less helpful when you are dealing with a single bird or with a monospecific group.

Bill color can be helpful because Greaters in basic and juvenal plumage usually show a distinctly bicolored bill; the distal portion is two-thirds to three-quarters blackish, and the basal area is yellow-orange, pinkish, or green-gray. The bill of Lessers is essentially all black, but sometimes there is some lighter gray right at the base in juvenile birds. Leg coloration has been suggested as a useful character, with Greaters often having deep-orange legs. This should be considered an accessory rather than a primary identification aid, because leg color is subject to great individual variation in both species, and perceptions of it may be easily influenced by light conditions.

All calls of Greaters are louder and more resonant than are calls of Lessers. In flight, Greaters typically give three to five rich, "tu-tu-tu" notes, whereas Lessers usually give a sharper, faster call of two or three "tu-tu" notes that is similar to one call of a Short-billed Dowitcher. In addition to the flight calls, both species have more rapidly delivered alarm notes, "tee-tee-tee-tee," that may be uttered repeatedly in a long series.

As mentioned previously, Lessers winter primarily south of the United States. A few individuals winter on our southern coasts and at the Salton Sea, but most wintering yellowlegs in the United States should be Greaters. For more information see Wilds 1982.


## Dowitchers

Dowitchers probably present the most difficult identification problem among the breeding species of North American shorebirds. Field guide illustrations often disagree in their depictions of the two species (Short-billed and Long-billed), and many birders have long given up identifying silent birds. Fortunately, an excellent paper by Wilds and Newlon (1983) summarized the existing knowledge of dowitcher identification, much of which was then known to relatively few birders. Much of the information that follows was first described in their detailed treatment.

As do other shorebirds, dowitchers have three distinct plumages: basic, alternate, and juvenal. Armed with a knowledge of plumage types, geographic variation, and molt sequences, birders can safely identify individuals in alternate and juvenal plumages. However, field identification of basic-plumaged individuals (except by voice) remains tenuous, and the prudent birder will let most individuals go as "dowitcher sp.?."

Dowitcher identification is greatly complicated by the existence of three distinct subspecies (races) of Short-billeds.

1. *Limnodromus griseus griseus* mostly migrates along the East Coast, but some migrate west to the Gulf Coast.
2. *Limnodromus griseus hendersoni* nests in western Canada and migrates from the East Coast west to the Rockies.
3. *Limnodromus griseus caurinus* migrates along the West Coast.

Of these, *caurinus* is the most variable in plumage, and *hendersoni* most closely resembles Long-billeds.

Let's start with basic-plumaged individuals. Adult dowitchers molt into basic plumage after nesting. Molt may begin in transit south and be completed upon arrival on the wintering grounds. Short-billeds generally migrate earlier in fall than do Long-billeds, with adults first appearing in the contiguous 48 states in late June or early July. Adult Long-billeds follow soon after, with the southward movement of juvenile Short-billeds coming about one month later. Most juvenile Long-billeds do not appear until mid-September. Juveniles of both species do not molt into basic plumage until October or November.

All dowitchers in basic plumage are essentially gray and white. There are no consistent known differences between the three subspecies of Short-billeds in basic plumage, and differences from Long-billeds are few and subtle. The black bars on the tail of Long-billeds are usually wider than the light bars, giving the impression of a black tail narrowly barred with white. Short-billeds show a reverse pattern, with the wider white (or cinnamon) bars giving the impression of a white tail barred with black. Unfortunately, the tail barring is difficult to see unless the bird is preening, and intermediate individuals of both species exist (do not be misled by the barred uppertail coverts, which in both species show black and white bars of nearly equal width). The only other consistent plumage distinction concerns the distribution of gray on the throat and breast. Long-billeds are typically washed heavily with gray across the throat and breast (whitish on the chin) and show a fairly defined line of separation between the gray breast and the white belly. Short-billeds usually have less gray on the breast, and it is often distinctly spotted rather than an even wash. The separation of white and gray ventrally on Short-billeds is also less clear. Having said all of this, I would still urge extreme caution in the visual identification of basic-plumaged dowitchers. Separating dowitchers in alternate plumage is easier but still complex. For one thing, it is in this plumage that the three subspecies of Short-billeds appear most different from one another. Also, the alternate plumage of the Long-billed overlaps the corresponding plumage of each subspecies of Short-billed in some respect. All is not lost, however, for careful attention to detail will make identification possible.

The blackish dorsal feathers of Long-billeds in alternate plumage are narrowly edged with rust and tipped with white. Because the rust edgings are narrow, the overall impression given by the upper parts is rather dark (darker than any Short-billed). The underparts of Long-billeds are entirely reddish, except at the beginning of the breeding season, when white tips to fresh feathers form irregular white bars on the breast, belly, and flanks. These bars soon disappear with wear. The throat, breast, and front of the neck are heavily spotted with black, whereas the sides of the breast, the flanks, and the vent region are heavily barred with black (these bars sometimes appear as chevrons or scallops). The central belly is usually unmarked. On many individuals of both species, the black ventral markings may appear as irregular-shaped marks that cannot be labeled as either bars or spots. As is the case on basic-plumaged birds, the black bars on the tail of breeding Long-billeds are wider than the light ones, which are more often orange than white.

The *hendersoni* subspecies of Short-billed is the closest in appearance to the Long-billed. Like the latter species, *hendersoni* is mostly or entirely reddish on the underparts (it may show some white on the vent). Unlike Long-billeds, however, *hendersoni* is very lightly marked below, typically being lightly spotted throughout (spotting is heaviest on the flanks and undertail coverts) with some barring on the flanks. The throat, sides of the neck, and central breast of most individuals are virtually unspotted, lending an overall ventral appearance quite different from that of Long-billeds and from *griseus* and *caurinus*. The black dorsal feathers of *hendersoni* are broadly edged with rust, making the upper parts appear brighter than in Long-billed. The light tail bars are wider than the black ones and are most often white (rather than orange).

The nominate subspecies of Short-billed *(griseus)* is the most different from Long-billed. The throat and breast of *griseus* are a lighter orange than are those of the Long-billed, and the belly and vent are white. This coloring gives a pronounced two-toned effect to the underparts. The breast is densely spotted with black (much more so than on *hendersoni*), and the flanks are moderately to heavily barred. The sides of the neck and breast tend to be spotted rather than barred. The undertail coverts are typically white and spotted, but they may be washed with orange or barred (Wilds and Newlon 1983). Sometimes they have both an orange wash and bars. The black dorsal feathers have narrow rusty edges and are closer in appearance to those of Long-billeds than to those of *hendersoni*. The light bars of the tail, which are most often white, are usually wider than the black ones. The most variable subspecies of Short-billed is *caurinus*. Most individuals are closest in general appearance to *griseus* (with densely spotted breast and white belly and vent), but some birds more closely approximate *hendersoni* (more extensively orange underparts with less marking). The dorsal coloration of *caurinus* is similar to that of *griseus* or Long-billeds, and the light tail bars are usually the widest and are white (sometimes orange). The degree of feather wear can affect the appearance of alternate-plumaged dowitchers.

When in fresh plumage, Long-billeds and the three subspecies of Short-billed may all show white horizontal bars (feather edges) on the otherwise reddish or orange breast. Just as these whitish edges fade with wear, so do the rusty edges of the dorsal feathers. This fading makes the birds progressively darker through the breeding season and effectively blurs any differences between Short-billeds and Long-billeds in upperpart coloration. According to Wilds and Newlon (1983), the black bars of Long-billeds are lost more quickly than are the spots of Short-billeds, so adult Long-billeds may be plain orange-red below by late summer.

The two species are most easily separated when they are in juvenal plumage (Figs. 4.44 and 4.45). The three subspecies of Short-billed are inseparable from one another in this plumage, but all are readily told from juvenile Long-billeds. The most obvious differences involve the scapulars, greater coverts, and tertials. The scapulars of Short-billeds are *broadly* edged with rust or gold (as are all the feathers of the back and wing coverts) and have conspicuous rust or gold internal markings (giving a tiger-bar pattern). Likewise, the tertials (which conspicuously cover the primaries when the wing is folded) of juvenile Short-billeds have prominent internal markings of gold or rust, typically shaped as irregular, wavy lines (Figs. 4.44 and 4.45). The dorsal feathers (including the scapulars) of juvenile Long-billeds are only *narrowly* edged with rust, and the scapulars *lack any internal markings* (Fig. 4.44). Similarly, the tertials of juvenile Long-billeds have narrow, pale margins and also lack internal markings (some individuals show small light spots at the tips of the tertials; Wilds and Newlon 1983). Accordingly, if the scapu-

Figure 4.44. Juvenile Short-billed (left) Dowitcher versus Long-billed Dowitcher (right). Note the bold contrasting (gold) edges to the scapulars, wing coverts, and tertials as well as the bold internal markings on the tertials of the Short-billed. In comparison, the Long-billed has unmarked tertials and narrow, marginally contrasting edges on the scapulars, wing coverts, and mantle feathers. (Photographed in September near Sequim, Washington, by Kevin J. Zimmer.)

Figure 4.45. Juvenile Short-billed Dowitcher. The highly contrasting gold edges of the black-centered scapulars, wing coverts, and mantle feathers are conspicuous, as are the gold internal markings of the tertials. (Photographed in September near Sequim, Washington, by Kevin J. Zimmer.)

lars or the tertials, or both, of a juvenile dowitcher can be seen well, then it should be identifiable as to species. (Note that this distinction applies only to juveniles because alternate-plumaged adults of both species have internal markings on the scapulars and tertials.) Because juvenile dowitchers (like juveniles of other shorebird species) often retain some juvenal tertials and scapulars along with their remiges when molting into basic plumage (October to November), it may be possible to identify birds on this basis well into winter.

Juvenile Long-billeds are basically washed with gray on the head, neck, and breast (possibly with some buff or orange) and have a whitish belly. Any breast spotting is faint when present. Juvenile Short-billeds tend to be much brighter (orange or buff) below, with some fine spotting or streaking on the breast. They also tend to have a darker, rustier crown, which contrasts with a pale supercilium to give a distinctly capped appearance.

Long-billeds and Short-billeds also have some helpful structural and vocal differences. As the names imply, Long-billeds have (on average) a longer bill than do Short-billeds. However, there is enough overlap to make bill length an unreliable field character. Overlap can be attributed to individual variation and to sexual dimorphism; females of both species have a longer bill than do males. Extreme individuals of either type are probably separable by bill length alone. The standard guides adequately describe the typical contact or flight calls of the two species: a Lesser Yellowlegs–like "tu-tu" (sometimes with more syllables) for Short-billeds, and a sharp "keek" for Long-billed. But beware: Long-billeds almost always string several "keeks" together when flushed.

There are some differences between the two species in winter and migratory habitat preferences; Long-billeds more often prefer inland areas, and Short-billeds prefer coastal waters, but overlap is extreme. Clearly, *hendersoni* Short-billeds will be commonly found in freshwater, inland areas, and *caurinus* is a common migrant at the Salton Sea. In Alaska, where the two species breed, the Short-billed is the more southerly breeder, nesting in open bogs within the taiga zone, whereas the more northern-breeding Long-billeds nest in open tundra north of the treeline.

As was previously pointed out, Short-billeds tend to migrate south earlier in summer than do Long-billeds. They also tend to migrate north later in spring. Short-billeds are restricted to coastal locales in winter (primarily at large tidal mudflats) with no verified winter inland records.

## Jaegers

The Jaegers undoubtedly constitute one of the most difficult groups encountered by western birders. The three species (Parasitic, Pomarine, and Long-tailed) are very similar in overall plumage, and all are polymorphic. The identification of adults on the arctic and subarctic breeding grounds is generally straightforward, but jaegers are highly pelagic at other seasons, and at-sea identification of this group can be nightmarish. Not only must you contend with a variety of plumages related to age, seasonal, and genetic variation, but you must do it from a rocking boat and often at great distances in poor light. Nothing will enliven a dull pelagic trip like the sighting of a distant jaeger, because such an event is likely to throw the entire group into spirited debate over the identity of the bird. Indeed, many individuals will have to remain unidentified, especially until you have attained a fair amount of comparative experience. As already mentioned, all jaegers are polymorphic. There are no known consistent sexual dimorphisms, but there are age distinctions. The ability to correctly age jaegers is often vital to proper identification. There is also a range of variation within age groups. Four distinct types of plumage are recognized.

1. Adult alternate plumage. All species have distinct light and dark morphs (although the existence of a dark morph in adults of Long-tailed has yet to be confirmed) and often a continuum of intermediate conditions. All species and morphs are characterized by elongated central tail streamers.

2. Adult basic plumage. This is intermediate between the adult breeding and subadult plumages. It lacks the barred underwings of the latter. Tail streamers are often reduced or absent.

3. Immature (subadult) plumage. This is like a dingy adult plumage, with a less-defined cap and a dusky wash on the face and neck. It is characterized by scalier-looking upper parts, a heavier breast band, shorter tail streamers, and variable amounts of barring on the flanks, underwings, and vent. Jaegers remain in some sort of subadult plumage for 3 or 4 years.

4. Juvenal plumage. This is typically darker and more heavily barred than the other three plumages, and there are short tail points. All species are variably polymorphic in juvenal plumage, often with light, dark, and intermediate morphs. Unlike most gulls, jaegers retain their juvenal plumage through the fall until the wintering grounds are reached.

Subadult stages can be particularly complex, with all species requiring 3 or 4 years to reach adult plumage. The intermediate stages in these cycles are not well understood, and given current knowledge it is impossible to distinguish between first-year and second-year individuals or between second-years and third-years, and so on. Jaegers undergo a complete molt after leaving the breeding grounds. Because the molt is protracted, it is usually not completed until the birds have reached their wintering areas. Hence, we seldom see jaegers in full basic plumage, although many birds in passage will be actively molting.

In all plumages, jaegers are generally separable by structure and flight characteristics, providing the observer has sufficient comparative experience with the group. Long-taileds (Figs. 4.46 and 4.47) are the smallest and most slenderly built of the three species. They have long, very slender wings and are extremely aerobatic, buoyant fliers. In flight they are almost ternlike. Pomarines (Figs. 4.48 through 4.50) are the largest, with bigger, stockier heads (they are more bull-necked) and a thicker more deeply hooked bill that is more angled at the gonys. Pomarines appear to have a thick, heavy undercarriage, and in flight they are more

Figure 4.46. Adult Long-tailed Jaeger in alternate plumage. Note the shape of the black cap, the unmarked breast, and the length of the central tail streamers. (Photographed in early June near Nome, Alaska, by Kevin J. Zimmer.)

direct and powerful (reminiscent of a small South Polar Skua or Western Gull) than the other species. Parasitics (Figs. 4.51 and 4.52) are intermediate, usually larger than Long-taileds, but always bulkier, with shorter, broader-based wings. Their flight is stronger and choppier (more falconlike) with less up-and-down motion to the flight path. They resemble Heermann's Gulls in overall structure and flight characteristics.

The major problems in identification are between Parasitic and Long-tailed on the one hand and between Parasitic and Pomarine on the other. Pomarines and Long-taileds are so different in size, build, jizz, and flight characteristics as to make confusion unlikely. Adults of all species are easiest to identify, whereas juvenal-plumaged and subadult-plumaged birds are most difficult.

Figure 4.47. Adult Long-tailed Jaeger in alternate plumage. Note the slender wings and long central tail feathers. (Photographed in early June near Nome, Alaska, by Kevin J. Zimmer.)

Figure 4.48. Adult Pomarine Jaeger in alternate plumage. Note the strongly hooked, bicolored bill; the extension of the black cap into the malar region (giving a helmeted appearance); the dark back (not contrasting strongly with the cap); the bold, blotchy breast band; the heavily barred flanks; and the spoon-shaped central tail feathers. (Photographed in late June at Barrow, Alaska, by Kevin J. Zimmer.)

Figure 4.49. Adult Pomarine Jaeger in alternate plumage. Note the dark back (barely contrasting with the cap), helmeted look to the cap, bicolored bill, mottled sides, and spoon-shaped central tail feathers. The near absence of any breast band identifies this bird as a male. (Photographed in late June at Barrow, Alaska, by Kevin J. Zimmer.)

Figure 4.50. Adult Pomarine Jaeger in alternate plumage. Note the helmeted look, the bicolored bill, the heavy breast band, the broad wings, the thickset build, and the shape of the central tail feathers. (Photographed in late June at Barrow, Alaska, by Kevin J. Zimmer.)

## Adults

Too many birders rely on the shape and length of the central tail points to identify adult jaegers. Breeding adult Long-taileds have the longest streamers, and these are pointed at the tips (Figs. 4.46 and 4.47). Parasitics also have pointed streamers, but theirs are typically several inches shorter (Figs. 4.51 and 4.52). Pomarines have streamers that are twisted, then flared at the ends (giving a blob-tipped look) (Figs. 4.48 through 4.50). These streamers are nearly as long as those of the Long-tailed, something that is not obvious from most illustrations. Unfortunately, tail streamer length is subject to much variation and is largely dependent on age, wear, and molt condition of the bird. Adults in basic plumage may have very short streamers, and on some individuals the tips of the streamers are broken off. In addition, streamers are difficult to see against a dark background (such as the ocean surface), and they may be invisible on low-flying birds at great distances.

Other plumage distinctions are equally or more helpful. For the moment, let's concentrate on the separation of light-morph birds. Long-taileds are immediately separable from the other species if the upper parts can be seen well. They are light gray-brown on the back, uppertail coverts, and wing coverts, with highly contrasting blackish primaries and a distinct black trailing edge to the secondaries. Pomarines and Parasitics are an essentially uniform dark brown on the upper parts (except for the blackish cap). They also have a dark trailing edge to the secondaries, but it does not contrast markedly with the rest of the wing (which is darker than that of the Long-tailed). In good light, the dark trailing edge can be seen on Parasitics (Fig. 4.52), but it is seldom apparent on Pomarines.

All three species have a blackish cap that contrasts with a yellowish white hindneck, auriculars, chin, and throat. The extent of the cap, its color, and the sharpness of its margins vary among the species and can provide helpful clues on resting birds. The cap of the Long-tailed (Fig. 4.46) is blacker and more neatly defined at its margins than are the caps of the other species, and, because the mantle is paler gray, the cap stands in high contrast. On Long-taileds the bottom edge of the

Figure 4.51. Adult Parasitic Jaeger in alternate plumage (light-morph). Note the shape of the dark cap, intermediate amount of contrast between the cap and back, short central tail feathers, slender bill, and smooth grayish wash to the breast band and flanks. (Photographed in early June near Nome, Alaska, by Kevin J. Zimmer.)

cap cuts straight back on a horizontal line from the gape or from the bottom of the bill before angling up to the back of the crown. The malar area is yellowish white, and the black cap extends all the way to the bill on the forecrown. Pomarines (Figs. 4.48 through 4.50) also have a very black cap, but the edges often appear more ragged and less even than on Long-taileds. On Pomarines, the black also extends to the bill on the forecrown. A major difference is the extent of the cap on the lower part of the face. On Pomarines the cap juts down markedly from the base of the bill into the malar region before angling up to the rearcrown. Thus Poms have more of a helmeted appearance than a capped appearance. Parasitics tend toward a cap that is intermediate in extent (between that of Long-tailed and Pomarine), but their cap is usually dark brown rather than truly black, and the margins are fuzzier and less sharply delineated (Figs. 4.51 and 4.52). The cap of Parasitics pales noticeably on the forecrown, leaving a pale "headlight" on the forehead above the base of the bill.

Underpart coloration is also helpful. Long-taileds are typically immaculate white (with some yellow) on the throat and breast, and they lack a breast band of any type (Figs. 4.46 and 4.47). Both Parasitics and Pomarines are more variable in

Figure 4.52. Adult Parasitic Jaeger in alternate plumage (light-morph). Note the general build, length and shape of the central tail feathers, generally white sides, smooth gray breast band (paler than the upper parts), dark trailing edge to the secondaries, and pale "headlight" on the forehead. (Photographed in early June near Nome, Alaska, by Kevin J. Zimmer.)

their underpart pattern. Most birds of both species have a distinct breast band, immediately setting them apart from all Long-taileds. The nature of the breast band is of particular importance in separating Parasitics from Pomarines. On Parasitic Jaegers that have a breast band, the band invariably appears as a smooth gray or brown wash, without any sign of mottling or blotching (Fig. 4.51). The band is almost always paler than the brown of the upper parts. Conversely, on Pomarines that have a breast band, the band is a dark, chocolate-brown and is often heavily mottled or blotchy in appearance (Figs. 4.48 and 4.50). At its margins the band blends with more mottling or barring that runs from the sides of the chest to the flanks. Female Poms seem to frequently be the most heavily marked in this regard. Less heavily marked Pomarines may have a broken band that appears finely speckled. Contrary to many statements in the literature, some adult Pomarine Jaegers (seemingly only males) lack any semblance of a breast band (Fig. 4.49). Such birds are commonly encountered on Alaska's North Slope in summer, although they always represent a distinct minority of the population.

Long-taileds show some light-gray wash on the flanks. Parasitics have variable amounts of darker brown there, and Pomarines (as already noted) are often heavily marked with smudgy brown bars or are washed extensively with dark brown. The extent of barring or mottling on the sides of the breast and flanks on Pomarines does not always seem to be positively correlated with the extent of the breast band. Some birds that lack a breast band may have extensive mottling or wash on the sides of the breast, although such birds seldom show much barring. Long-taileds have a dusky wash that extends from the vent along the belly all the way to the lower breast. Parasitics also typically have a dusky vent (although a small percentage of birds may be white-vented), but the dusky wash does not extend nearly as far forward on the belly as it does on Long-taileds. Pomarines also a have dusky vent (sometimes much darker), but again, this color does not extend forward nearly as far as on Long-taileds.

The three species of jaegers (in all ages and morphs) have a variable number of outer primaries in which the shaft of the feather is white. When taken together, these white shafts (together with white bases to the inner webs of some primaries in Pomarine and Parasitic) create a white flash that is visible on the upper wing of a flying jaeger. This white flash is largest and most visible on Pomarines, which have from five to eight pale-shafted primaries. It is less striking on Parasitics, which have only three to six pale-shafted primaries. Long-taileds have white shafts on only the outer one or two primaries. The extent of the white flash in the primaries is a relative character that can be supportive evidence in the identification of problem birds. However, because the exact number of pale-shafted primaries is individually variable (and there is overlap between species), and because it is nearly impossible to count the number of pale-shafted primaries on a flying jaeger (except for Long-taileds), this mark remains of little use in the field. Adult Poms and Parasitics, as well as immatures of all three species, have white bases to the undersides of the primaries, creating a white flash to the underwing. This character is of little use, except to rule out adult Long-taileds.

## Dark-Morph Adults

Dark-morph birds present more of a problem, because virtually all plumage distinctions of the light birds are obliterated by dark coloration. The bird's structure, flight characteristics, length and shape of tail streamers, and extent of white flash in the wings are often the primary clues to identity. Dark-morph Parasitic Jaegers are frequently encountered and, in some parts of their breeding range, may even greatly outnumber light-morphs. A typical dark-morph Parasitic tends toward a smoky, gray-brown overall color, against which the black cap and even some semblance of the breast band can often be seen. Such birds often show a bit of yellowish wash to the hind-collar and throat as well. In contrast, dark-morph Pomarine Jaegers (which are generally less common, seldom accounting for more than 5% to 10% of the birds in a given area) tend toward a darker, almost blackish brown color, against which it is difficult to discern any traces of a darker cap or breast band, except at very close range. (But beware: paler individuals that approximate the color tones of a typical dark-morph Parasitic do occur.) Bill color can also be helpful in separating a dark-morph Pom from a Parasitic, because the dark-morph Pom frequently has a bicolored bill (fleshy-pink or dull-reddish base with a dark tip), whereas the Parasitic will typically be entirely dark-billed.

## Juveniles

Juvenile birds are tougher to identify. Juvenile jaegers have polymorphisms that parallel those of their respective adults (and juvenile Long-taileds, unlike adults, do come in light and dark morphs), and many individuals exhibit intermediate characters that cannot be pigeonholed into either the light-morph or the dark-morph category. Juveniles also lack the distinctive tail streamers that often allow immediate identification of adults. It is the juveniles that are most likely to appear as early-fall vagrants on inland lakes and reservoirs and can present major problems in identification.

Juvenile Long-taileds have boldly barred (black-and-white) undertail coverts, underwing coverts, and axillaries. This barring is most pronounced on light birds and is least pronounced on dark ones. Light and intermediate birds have a strongly marbled look to the entire underwing. The upper parts of all juvenile Long-taileds are a cold gray-brown and are narrowly but distinctly scalloped or barred with white or cream fringes on the scapulars, mantle feathers, and wing coverts. This light barring is more distinct than the similar barring of other juvenile jaegers, largely because of the contrast between the dark gray-brown feathers and the creamy-white terminal fringes. The central tail points of young Long-taileds are much shorter than the streamers of adults, and they vary in length. However, they are almost always longer than the tail points of young Parasitics (and they are much longer than those of young Poms) and are either blunt or round-tipped (not sharply pointed). In fact, the entire tail is relatively longer on juvenile Long-taileds than on the other species. Like the adults, young Long-taileds have only the outer one or two primaries with white shafts and show little or no white flash on the upper wing. Like other jaegers (but unlike adult Long-taileds), they do show white crescents at the base of the primaries on the underwing.

The head and nape of paler juvenile Long-taileds are largely or entirely whitish or buff, providing a strong contrast with the mantle. Intermediate birds typically have light grayish areas on the nape and side of the head and an indistinct cap. Darker birds are dark or dusky in these areas, and many birds are uniformly smoky gray on the head, neck, breast, and upper belly but boldly barred black-and-white on the lower belly and vent. Both light and intermediate birds typically have a plain whitish belly, whereas the intermediate individuals often have a dusky breast band or a dusky hood that contrasts with the white belly. Both types have at least some barring on the flanks.

Juvenile Parasitics are equally variable, but again, similarities exist between the different plumage types. As are Long-taileds, Parasitics are barred on the back, scapulars, wing coverts, axillaries, and undertail coverts, with variable amounts of barring on the breast and belly. Likewise, the barring of all surfaces is most pronounced on light birds and is least pronounced on dark ones. In virtually all cases, however, the barring is less distinct than on the corresponding areas of Long-taileds. Juvenile Parasitics do not have a white belly (as do light juveniles of the other species), but beware of subadults, which may. The axillaries, underwings, and undertail coverts are barred less heavily than on either of the other species and the barring is brown-and-white instead of black-and-white. The upper parts are variably barred with buff or chestnut; they do not have the neat whitish bars seen on juvenile Long-taileds. The basic ground color of young Parasitics is also different from that of Long-taileds (and of Poms), being a warm rufous-brown rather than a cold gray-brown. Therefore, the contrast between rufous-brown centers and chestnut or buff terminal fringes on the feathers of the mantle, scapulars, and wing coverts is much less striking than is the contrast seen on these same feather groups on juvenile Long-taileds. Chest barring, when present, is usually somewhat irregular and is typically strongest at the margins and less distinct in the center of the chest. Darker individuals may be uniformly dark rufous-brown (except for the barred vent) on the underparts.

Juvenile Parasitics frequently have a paler, buffy nape that contrasts with the darker brown of the back and crown. They also tend to have fine dark streaking on the head, face and neck. The central tail points are typically short but project noticeably beyond the rest of the tail and come to sharp points.

Juvenile Poms, like juveniles of the other species, are highly variable. Dark birds are mostly blackish brown with barred undertail coverts, uppertail coverts, underwing coverts, and axillaries. Light birds are gray-brown or tawny above with somewhat irregular and indistinct darker barring, except on the rump and uppertail coverts, which are boldly barred light-and-dark. The mantle, scapulars, and wing coverts of these birds frequently appear mottled or checkered rather than neatly barred. Their underwings are broadly barred brown-and-white on the coverts and axillaries. The underparts are more variable and may be uniformly gray-brown, gray-brown lightly barred with whitish, tawny-brown lightly barred with whitish, or either gray-brown or tawny-brown with bolder dark barring. In general, the plumage is somewhat intermediate in color between the colder gray-brown of young Long-taileds and the warmer rufous tones of young Parasitics. The central tail points (which are shorter than in the other species) never protrude noticeably, and these are blunt-tipped rather than pointed.

Kaufman (1990) pointed out a difference in bill shape that is an excellent mark for separating juvenile Long-taileds and Parasitics, provided you get a close view. The nail at the tip of the bill occupies more of the total length of the bill on the Long-tailed than it does on the Parasitic. The ratio of the distance from the tip of the bill to the back of the nail and from the back of the nail to the base of the upper mandible differs markedly between the two species. In Long-taileds the two measurements are more nearly equal, whereas in Parasitics the distance from the back of the nail to the base of the mandible is much greater than the length of the nail. Clearly, this is a mark that has limited application in the field. However, many juvenile jaegers that turn up as vagrants to inland areas seem rightfully bewildered by their predicament and allow birders to approach to very close range. I have not found bill color particularly useful in the identification of juveniles, because all three species frequently have a pale blue-gray bill with contrasting blackish tip.

As stated earlier, subadult plumage progression is complex and poorly understood. Most identifications will have to be based on size and structural characters combined with flight characteristics. The shape of the tail streamers (when these are present) can be extremely useful, as can details of bill structure on birds at exceptionally close range. Many individuals at sea will remain unidentified.

Both Pomarine and Parasitic jaegers are routinely seen on West Coast boat trips in spring and fall. Pomarines are typically more common, particularly far off-shore, and are the only likely jaeger on winter boat trips. The Parasitic is the jaeger most likely to be seen from shore, because it routinely works the nearshore kelp zones. The Long-tailed is rarely recorded compared with the other species, because it moves mostly over deep waters far offshore beyond the continental shelf, and therefore, beyond the range of most one-day boat trips. Long-taileds migrate early in fall; their peak movements are from July through mid-September, coincident with the peak movements of the Arctic Terns and Sabine's Gulls, which they parasitize.

## Identifying Gulls

Gulls as a group present the most challenging identification problem in North America, for several reasons. Some of the more important ones are the following.
1. Delayed acquisition of adult plumage results in lengthy or complex plumage sequences through immaturity.
2. Effects of feather wear on appearances are often extreme.
3. Sexual dimorphism in body size and bill size clouds interspecific differences in these important characters.
4. Some species vary geographically.
5. Hybridization within some species groups is common.

Despite the problems inherent in gull identification, there is cause for optimism. The birder who is willing to work at it can, in fact, safely identify the vast majority of individuals encountered. Fortunately, gulls make excellent subjects for study. They are large, inhabit open habitats, stand still for long periods of time, and typically allow close approach.

The remainder of this discussion will be devoted to understanding the various nuances that make gull identification such a challenge. The most important topics in this regard involve understanding molt sequence and learning how to age gulls. Being able to place a gull in an age class before knowing its specific identity enables you to focus on a smaller set of field marks in making the final identification. It is not only a great shortcut, but it is often a crucial prerequisite. However, knowing whether an individual is an "advanced third-year" or a "delayed fourth-year" is only rarely of importance in identifying it to species. So learn to age gulls as a tool for identifying them, but don't strangle your progress by getting too involved in the minutiae too early on. Learn the typical patterns first and worry about exceptions later. Too many birders give up on gulls altogether because they feel overwhelmed by details. The more you can do to keep it simple in the beginning, the better.

Throughout this section (and in the following detailed accounts of Slaty-backed Gull, Thayer's Gull, and the kittiwakes) you will note the frequent use of qualifiers and modifiers such as "generally," "typically," "most," "often," "many," and so on. The only absolute rule in gull identification is that there are many exceptions to every other rule.

## Molt Sequence

Before you can safely identify gulls, you must be able to age them so that you'll know which set of field marks to look at. Determining the age of a gull requires an understanding of molt sequence in the family. Let's begin by laying out the typical pattern of molt in gulls. Be aware that stated times during which molt is supposed to occur are only averages. There is extreme individual variability in both the initiation and duration of molt, and many individuals will not conform to the timetables presented here. Indeed, most gulls appear to be in a nearly continuous state of molt, without clear breaks.

It should emphasized that the following discussion is based on the currently accepted understanding of molt in gulls. Much remains to be learned, however, about patterns of molt in virtually all seabirds, including gulls, and further study could reveal contradictions to current theory. For instance, there is some evidence that some larger species of gulls may undergo fewer molts in their first year than is currently thought. The most important thing to understand from an identification standpoint, is the general pattern and direction of plumage changes.

The first set of true feathers on a young gull constitute its juvenal plumage. This plumage replaces the natal down and is in turn lost in the first prebasic molt, which occurs during the bird's first fall and is usually completed by the end of October. The first prebasic molt is typically a partial molt, wherein head and body feathers and an individually variable number of wing coverts are replaced. The resulting new plumage is referred to as the first-basic plumage. Subsequently, the bird will undergo an annual spring molt and an annual fall molt throughout its lifetime.

The spring molt, which lasts from February to April, is also a partial molt; the head and body feathers, some wing coverts, and occasionally even the tertials and central tail feathers are replaced, and the remaining wing and tail feathers are retained. The resulting fresh plumage is referred to as alternate plumage.

The fall molt is a complete molt, in which all feathers are replaced, and results in basic plumage. Adults typically begin this molt toward the end of, or immediately after, breeding activities (in late July), but nonbreeding immatures start earlier (June to early July). Most immatures will have completed the process by November, but many adults may not finish their molt until December.

The fall molt begins with the shedding of the innermost primary and progresses outward. The remainder of the plumage is molted within the period of primary renewal (the full growth of the outermost primary comes at or near the end of the molt). The rate is slow, with no more than two or three adjacent primaries growing simultaneously. Be aware that impressions of both wing shape and color pattern can be dramatically altered when a gull is molting its outer primaries.

Secondaries and rectrices are molted in a less regular fashion, and it is not uncommon to see large gaps in the tail or in the trailing edge of the wing, where whole groups of feathers have been lost simultaneously. Wing coverts are also shed in groups, revealing the light bases of underlying remiges. The uncovering of remiges by the loss of groups of feathers accounts for the irregular white bars or patches commonly seen on the upper wings of molting gulls.

As there are for every other aspect of gull identification, there are exceptions to the typical molt sequence. Franklin's Gulls have a typical (partial) prebasic molt into first-basic plumage, but they follow that with a complete spring molt into first-alternate plumage, and another complete molt in fall. Juvenile Sabine's Gulls forgo the fall molt until they have arrived in their wintering areas. Thereafter, they undergo a prebasic molt that is suspended before it is completed, and then they complete the molt of the flight feathers in late winter and early spring concurrent with the partial prealternate molt of head and body feathers.

## Aging

There is generally a positive relationship between the size of a gull and the time it takes to attain maturity. Larger gulls take more time to become adult than do smaller gulls. We commonly refer to gulls as being two-year, three-year, or four-year gulls. What do those designations mean?

Small gulls (e.g., Bonaparte's, kittiwakes) essentially become indistinguishable from adults upon acquiring their second-basic plumage and are hence referred to as two-year gulls. They actually attain their second-basic plumage when they are little more than a year old. The molt sequence is as follows: natal down; postnatal molt into juvenal plumage; prebasic molt (completed during the first fall) into first-basic plumage; prealternate molt (February–April) into first-alternate plumage; prebasic molt (July–October) into second-basic plumage (i.e., adult or definitive basic plumage).

Medium-sized gulls (e.g., Heermann's, Ring-billed, Mew) become adult upon acquiring their third-basic plumage (i.e., when they are slightly more than 2 years old) and are therefore classified as three-year gulls.

The largest species (e.g., Glaucous-winged, Western, Glaucous) become adult upon acquiring their fourth-basic plumage (i.e., when they are slightly more than 3 years old) and are classified as four-year gulls. Molt sequences for three-year and four-year species are the same as outlined above for two-year birds, but they involve one (for three-years) and two (for four-years) additional spring and fall molts. There are occasional exceptions to the "larger takes longer" rule. The Yellow-footed Gull is only a three-year gull despite its large size, and, conversely, the Little Gull is also a three-gull despite its diminutive size.

Do not confuse the preceding terminology with the less frequently used calendar-year terminology. A bird's "first calendar-year" begins at hatching and ends on December 31 of that year. Its second calendar year begins on January 1 after hatching and proceeds to December 31, and so on. This terminology is sometimes useful when a more precise estimate of a bird's age or plumage stage cannot be made. For the most part it is not used in this book.

It is easy to see then why larger gulls tend to cause more problems in identification. A four-year species will wear nine different plumages in its lifetime (juvenal, first-basic, first-alternate, second-basic, second-alternate, third-basic, third-alternate, adult-basic, and adult-alternate) as opposed to seven plumages for a three-year gull and only five for a two-year species.

Not all plumages are equally likely to be encountered in a given region. It has been demonstrated that, in a given population of some species, adults and immatures may have largely separate wintering grounds. Some of the "arctic-breeding" species show pronounced differences in the north-south dispersal of adults and immatures. Thus, whereas adult Thayer's Gulls are not uncommon along the Washington coast in winter, they are rarely seen (relatively speaking) in southern California, where first-year birds predominate. Dispersal patterns may even vary significantly between different age classes of immatures. Immature birds of some species may be more highly pelagic than the adults, and, thus, they may form a disproportionate percentage of the individuals encountered at sea. On the other hand, inland fall records of Sabine's Gulls from the interior of the United States almost always pertain to juveniles, with the adults being seen only offshore.

There is another reason (this one purely statistical) why some age classes are encountered more frequently than others. As an example, let us take Thayer's Gull, a migratory four-year species. Of all the Thayer's Gulls hatched in a given year, a certain significant percentage will not survive long enough to molt into first-basic plumage and migrate south to the wintering grounds. Of those that do, fewer will survive the subsequent spring and fall migrations to return the following year in second-basic plumage. Fewer still will survive an additional year to appear in third-basic plumage. Thus, we should (and do) see more first-year birds than second-years, and in turn, more second-years than third-years. Of course, even fewer individuals from any given cohort make it to full adult-hood, but once there they will go through their full cycle of adult basic and alternate plumages for life (up to 20–25 years). The adult class in a given locale is thus a cumulative category composed of individuals of ages 3 to 25 years. The end result is that the two most frequently encountered age groups of most large gulls are first-year birds and adults.

Unfortunately, for the larger species the situation remains murkier than just dealing with seven or nine discrete plumages. All species of gull exhibit individual variation in the timing of molt, due in part to differences in hatching dates. Given the duration of a molt (3–5 months) and the range of possible hatching dates, it is possible to see all manner of overlap among individuals. Keep in mind that molt is under hormonal control and that sick or injured birds in particular may remain in arrested molt indefinitely. These birds often remain on the wintering grounds through the summer rather than migrating. Thus, it is possible to see basic-plumaged gulls in the middle of summer (a phenomenon also common to loons and shorebirds but less likely to cause identification problems). It has even been demonstrated that many individuals of larger species remain in less than full adult plumage well into their fourth year. Bill coloration seems to be particularly subject to such lag, and there are many instances of gulls of known ages retaining black smudges or bands on their bill well into their fourth or fifth year. For these reasons, bill color may be useless as a character for aging any given individual of the larger gulls.

## Patterns of Plumage Change

Molting is a dynamic process, and the various plumages that we recognize are in many ways simply points along a continuum. No book can hope to illustrate the feather-by-feather changes that occur. Instead, we must learn the discrete plumages acquired through each cycle and then understand the patterns of change that produce them.

If you are new to the challenge of identifying gulls it may be helpful to first think in terms of generic patterns rather than species-specific details. An understanding of the underlying patterns of plumage change common to most species automatically structures an intimidating amount of information into something entirely manageable. Fortunately, the most consistent pattern of plumage change occurs among the subgroup of gulls that also has the most complex molt sequence, the four-year gulls. It is generally easy to assign an individual four-year gull to an age class (first-year, second-year, third-year, adult) without even knowing which species it is. Following are some guidelines to aging four-year gulls that (with minor exceptions) apply to all species in the group. Figures 4.53 through 4.57 illustrate the generalities of changes in plumage and soft parts that take place in large gulls as they age.

**First-Years (Including Juveniles).** In general, if it is a gull and it is entirely or mostly brown, it is a first-year bird. This generalization applies not only to the large four-year gulls but also to the smaller species, (e.g., Heermann's, Mew, Laughing, Sabine's) many of which have juvenal or first-year plumages that are

Figure 4.53. Juvenile Western Gull. Note the all-black bill, dark eyes, and overall dark plumage, all characters that are typical of first-year plumages of large gulls. The brightly spangled upper parts, with broad, sharply contrasting edges of the feathers of the mantle, scapulars, and wing coverts, are typical of juvenal plumage. (Photographed in August at Morro Bay, California, by Kevin J. Zimmer.)

Figure 4.54. Western Gull in first-basic plumage. This all-dark plumage is similar to that of juveniles, but the pattern of the upper parts is less bold and contrasting, and the retained flight feathers show a certain degree of wear. (Photographed in late December near Morro Bay, California, by Kevin J. Zimmer.)

mostly brown. The rule could thus be stated: All entirely or mostly brown gulls are first-year birds, but not all first-year birds are entirely or mostly brown. All of the four-year species have brownish first-year plumage, but these run the gamut from the extremely dark first-year Westerns to the pale, buffy first-year Glaucous and Iceland gulls. Other common features of first-year plumages include dark eyes, mostly or entirely dark bills, and dark tails or tail bands. There are exceptions to these character patterns: first-year California, Glaucous, and some Iceland gulls have a mostly pink bill, and the "white-winged" gulls tend to show little or no tail band (in general, Glaucous and Iceland gulls provide poor fit with generalities pertaining to the other species). For the most part however, dark bill, dark eyes, and dark tail go together with mostly brown plumage as being indicators of first-year status among the four-year gulls.

**Second Years.** Second-year birds of all the larger species share several common features. Prominent among these are graying of the mantle; whitening of the head,

Figure 4.55. Western Gull in second-basic plumage. Typical of most large gulls in second-basic plumage, this bird shows mostly dingy-white underparts, a mostly gray mantle, substantial brown in the wing coverts, a complete dark tail band, and some pinkish color at the base of the bill. (Photographed in late December near Morro Bay, California, by Kevin J. Zimmer.)

Figure 4.56. Western Gull in third-basic plumage. Typical of most large gulls in third-basic plumage, this bird shows a nearly adult pattern of clean white underparts and pure gray upper parts but retains some brown in the wing coverts, a partial dark tail band, and some black in the bill, and it lacks the adult pattern of white mirrors in the black primaries. (Photographed in late December near Morro Bay, California, by Kevin J. Zimmer.)

neck, and underparts; and paling of the bill. As noted above, first-year birds tend to be largely or entirely brown. In the second-year plumages the brown is reduced to varying amounts on the scapulars and wing coverts and often uneven streaking or mottling on the head, neck, and underparts. The mantle should be mostly or entirely gray, and the underparts should show strong signs of becoming white. (The Glaucous-winged Gull is an exception; it remains very dingy gray-brown throughout, and the distinction between the gray mantle and the browner wings may be apparent only in good light.) Likewise, the bills of second-year birds have become pale (usually pinkish), with a variable amount of the tip remaining dark (Again, Glaucous-wingeds are the exception; many individuals retaining the dark bill of first-year plumage.) Species that exhibit distinct tail bands in their first-year

Figure 4.57. Western Gull in definitive basic (adult basic) plumage. As do most large gulls, Western Gulls in definitive basic plumage typically have clean white under parts, clean gray upper parts, an all-white tail, adult bill colors (in this case, bright yellow with a red gonydeal spot), and black outer primaries with the full adult complement of white mirrors or spots. Unlike most large gulls, however, adult Westerns almost always lack head streaking in basic plumage. (Photographed in late December near Morro Bay, California, by Kevin Zimmer.)

plumage will retain their tail bands into the second year. Species that are pale-eyed as adults typically attain pale eyes in their second year.

**Third-Years.** Third-year birds should look essentially adult in terms of being white on the head, neck, and underparts; having the adult mantle, leg, and eye colors; and having the essential elements of adult wing pattern. Signs that they are still not adults include: remnants of a tail band, lack of (or reduced) white mirrors or apical spots in the primaries (assuming such are present in adult plumage), greater amounts of black in the primaries and primary coverts, varying small amounts of black smudging on the bill, and perhaps some brown in the wing coverts. Third-years can be distinguished from second-years by an overall cleaner white appearance to the body, less black in the bill, a much reduced or broken tail band, and little or no brown in the wings.

**Adults.** Fully adult birds will be white-bodied (although several species in adult-winter plumage show variable amounts of brownish streaking or mottling on the head, neck and upper breast), have a yellow bill with red gonydeal spots, have an entirely white tail, and lack brown in the wings.

Many species of three-year gulls have a plumage progression similar to that of the four-year species, but they essentially skip the first-year plumages of their larger relatives. These gulls compress their brown, dark-billed stage into the juvenile period. Their first prebasic molt produces a first-winter plumage that parallels the second-winter stage of the four-year gulls. That is, they are largely white on the head, neck, and underparts (with varying amounts of gray-brown wash, mottling, or spotting) and have a gray mantle, significant amounts of brown in the wing coverts, a white tail with complete dark bands, a less-than-adult primary pattern, and a bicolored bill. Likewise, the second-year plumages of these species parallel the third-year plumages of four-year gulls. That is, they are essentially adult in appearance, with a white body, gray mantle and wing coverts, and mostly white tail. Continuing signs of immaturity include remnants of a tail band, variable black smudging near the bill tip, and imperfect adult primary pattern. Three-year gulls that exhibit this parallel plumage progression include Mew, Ring-billed, and Yellow-footed, and, to a lesser extent, Laughing and Franklin's.

There are few such consistent trends in plumage change among two-year gulls, but there are shared characters among like-aged birds of some species pairs or triplets (e.g., the presence of a carpal bar in first-year plumages).

## Feather Wear

Feather wear is the natural erosion of the feathers due to environmental influences. Sun, salt water, wind, and sand are the primary agents of abrasion. The rate at which a feather abrades is inversely related to the amount of pigment it contains. Thus, white feathers wear most rapidly, with the distinctive white tips of many feather groups destroyed. Brown feathers fade rapidly to tan and then bleach to white. This progression is especially apparent in young Iceland, Glaucous, and Glaucous-winged gulls, which, when very worn, appear almost entirely white. Black feathers are the most resistent to wear but will still fade to brown. The harshness of a gull's environment also determines the rate of wear. Gulls subjected to both intense sun (or prolonged daylight) and strong, sand-blasting winds (in addition to salt water) will exhibit intense wear before individuals from milder climates.

Feather wear can play fiendish tricks on birders. Individuals of the most familiar species can take on bizarre new patterns (Fig. 4.58) or have recognizable ones obliterated.

The effects of wear are most pronounced in early spring (before the spring molt) and again (most drastically) in late summer just before the fall molt. It is at this latter time that the wing and tail feathers (retained from the previous fall) are at their oldest and most worn. Before the onset of fall molt, first-alternate birds (which have retained their remiges and rectrices from juvenal plumage) routinely have many exposed bare shafts in the wings. There may be extreme individual variation in the degree of feather wear among first-year birds, due largely to differences in hatching dates. This asynchrony results in a continuous parade of extremely worn individuals from March through summer's end.

### Sexual Dimorphism

North American gulls appear to be sexually monochromatic, but they do differ sexually in many mensural characters. Males are typically larger than females, and they have a longer, thicker bill, and flatter-crowned head. These differences tend to be most pronounced among the larger four-year gulls, and even then they can vary dramatically in extent from one species to the next. Lone birds are rarely

Figure 4.58. California Gull exhibiting transitional plumage from first-alternate to second-basic. The blotchy pattern results from contrast between old bleached feathers and newer gray ones. Note the extremely worn condition of the primaries and tertials. (Photo by Kevin J. Zimmer.)

safely assignable to one sex or the other. It may be possible to accurately guess the sex of some individuals in a flock. One needs only to look at any flock of Herring or Western gulls to see that some individuals stand out as being larger with flatter crowns and heavier, longer bills, while others appear smaller, rounder-headed, and shorter-billed.

Although it may not be important to be able to sex gulls in the field, it is important to be aware that sexual differences within a species can blur interspecific distinctions in overall size, bill size, and head shape. For example, one of the more noticeable features of Thayer's Gull is its delicate look (relative to the Herring Gull), which is largely due to its round head and short, gently curving bill. Combined with a smaller body size, these characters often allow birders to quickly home in on a Thayer's Gull amidst a flock of Herring Gulls. This small, delicate look is accentuated in female Thayer's, making the identification process easier. Male Thayer's Gulls, however, broadly overlap female Herring Gulls in bill length and thickness, as well as in overall size. This means not only that a male Thayer's could be easily overlooked but also, and more important, that the unwary birder could easily misidentify a female Herring as a Thayer's (especially if it were surrounded by larger male Herrings).

## Geographic Variation

Geographic variation in both mensural and plumage characters is found in several species of gulls and must be taken into account when grappling with an identification. A few examples should suffice.

Western Gulls from Monterey, California, north (subspecies *Larus occidentalis occidentalis*) are distinctly paler-mantled when adult than are birds from farther south (subspecies *L. o. wymani*). They also show moderate amounts of head and nape streaking in winter, whereas southern birds show little to none.

More confusion could result from geographic variation in Glaucous and Herring gulls. Many of the Glaucous Gulls that winter on the West Coast are of the Alaska-breeding subspecies *L. hyperboreus barrovianus* and are noticeably smaller than birds that winter on the East Coast. Female *barrovianus* can be especially small and could easily be misidentified as the much rarer Iceland Gull. Likewise, visitors to western Alaska may encounter Herring Gulls of the Siberian subspecies *L. argentatus vegae*, which have a much darker mantle than North American Herring Gulls. These Siberian Herring Gulls can easily be mistaken for Slaty-backed Gulls.

## Hybridization

Hybridization is the monkey wrench in the already difficult game of gull identification. Many of the larger gulls interbreed, some so frequently that some species groups have become taxonomic nightmares. For proof, one need look no further than the Thayer's Gull. Considered at various times a separate species, a subspecies of Herring Gull, and a subspecies of Iceland Gull, it is but one example of the confusion inherent in gull taxonomy given the amount of gene flow between populations.

Even when taxonomists are not confused, birders can be. Observers on the West Coast have to contend with myriad hybrids, most commonly Western × Glaucous-wingeds (Fig. 4.59). Such individuals are routinely seen as far south as central California, while in parts of the Pacific Northwest hybrids may locally outnumber pure birds of both parental types. The Western × Glaucous-winged phenotype encountered most frequently closely resembles Thayer's Gull and, to observers not familiar with details of body and bill size, could easily be passed off as such. In some parts of Alaska, Glaucous-winged × Herring hybrids are fairly common (these birds routinely winter south along the Pacific Coast to northern California), and Herring × Glaucous hybrids are also occasionally seen. The latest evidence also indicates that Thayer's Gulls and Iceland Gulls interbreed freely throughout the contact zone in northeastern arctic Canada.

Although the taxonomic implications of all of this hybridization are not yet clear, the birding implications are. With such frequent hybridization (involving many species), and with the further problems of second- generation back-crosses, many gulls will be encountered that defy certain identification. Indeed, gulls are

Figure 4.59. Hybrid Glaucous-winged × Western Gull adult (right) and nearly adult Western Gull (left). Note the combination of pale gray mantle and mottled head and neck (typical of Glaucous-wingeds in winter) with jet black wingtips (typical of Western Gull). Herring Gull can be ruled out by the large size and massive bill and by the dark eyes. The plumage features on this standing bird are not dissimilar to those of many adult Thayer's Gulls, but the large overall size and especially the large bill clearly eliminate Thayer's from consideration. (Photo by Kevin J. Zimmer.)

the one group of birds in which even specimens are frequently left unidentified to species.

## Miscellaneous Considerations

Even after age, molt, feather wear, sexual differences, geographic variation, and hybrids have been taken into account, there still remain a few factors to consider. Many adult gulls (and terns) will appear distinctly rosy or pink-tinged below, particularly during the spring and summer. It has been reported that the pink coloration is the result of some substance in the oil of the preen gland and is spread by the birds as they preen. The extent to which dietary, hormonal, and genetic factors influence the degree to which this pink color is differentially expressed between different species and individuals is not known. The color is usually best seen at low-angle light (early mornings or late afternoons) or on high-overcast days. On some species (e.g., Franklin's and Bonaparte's gulls) the pink is more subtle, but in the case of Ross's Gull it is often dramatic.

Partially or wholly albinistic gulls are occasionally encountered, and these can readily be mistaken for Glaucous or Iceland gulls. Even the whitest immature Glaucous or Iceland gulls will show some mottling (often about the vent or underwing) if inspected closely enough. True albinos (with a pink bill) are quite rare, and many albinistic gulls will lack pigment in the feathers but have a black bill or a pink bill tipped with black. In such cases one is forced to rely on bill structure and size and the presence or absence of any barring or mottling on the feathers. Obviously, if you are in an area where "white-winged" gulls are frequently encountered, it is much more likely that a large white gull is a Glaucous or Iceland than an albino of anything else. But, in areas where Glaucous and Iceland gulls are rare, you should rule out the possibility of albinism before closing the book on any white gull.

Oiled birds are a common sight in coastal areas and can cause confusion if seen only at a distance.

Finally, the mantle color of all gulls appears much darker when the birds are standing against a bright background, such as white sand, snow, or ice, than when they are standing against a dark background. This effect is often dramatic enough to make pale-mantled species appear as dark as a Western Gull, especially if the bird is some distance away. Even when gulls are positioned against more neutral backgrounds, it is amazing to see the apparent color differences between two individuals of the same species that are in different positions with respect to the angle of incoming light.

## Tips for Identifying Gulls

All of the foregoing may lead you to believe that identifying gulls is even more difficult than you originally thought. In fact, it probably is more difficult than most birders are aware. Some aspects of gull identification will never be easy, but below are 10 tips that should make the process less difficult.

1. Do your homework before going into the field. Unless you have some idea of what to look for before going afield, you are bound to be overwhelmed once there.

2. Take the time to acquaint yourself with the different feather groups as illustrated by the line drawings in Chapter 2. Then head into the field and see how these feather groups are arranged on the living birds. It may take time to make the transition because living birds can elevate some feather groups (e.g., the scapulars) while concealing others (such as lesser and median wing coverts). The feather groups on living birds are seldom as neat as in the drawings.

3. If possible, try to begin your study of gulls in winter. Gulls of all ages are in fresh plumage after their fall molt, and it is at this time that their patterns are sharpest and the differences between species and age groups will be easiest to discern. In other words, this is the time of year when most of them will look like they do in the books. For many parts of the country, winter is also the time of greatest species diversity, which will make gull study at this time all the more rewarding. Late spring through summer is perhaps the worst time to begin learning to identify gulls. Most individuals are so worn and ratty looking that their characteristic patterns have been eroded or lost. Beginning at this season will likely frustrate and confuse more than help. The challenge of summer identification is best postponed until you are fairly advanced in your study of the group.

4. Be prepared to spend lots of time actively studying gulls in the field. There is no substitute for field experience, and it should be attained at regular intervals. Just as warbler songs in spring can be confusing after you have not heard them all fall and winter, so too can gulls fool you after a long layoff.

5. Learn as much as you can about identifying the common species. This suggestion may seem obvious, but it is often the common birds that we know the least about, simply because we take their presence for granted and never subject them to intense scrutiny. Great familiarity with species expected to occur in your area will cut down on misidentification and will make finding the genuine rarities that much easier.

6. Don't confine your study to stationary birds. Although they may be easier to inspect, they won't reveal all of the important details of wing and tail pattern that are crucial to so many identifications. After you have gleaned what you can from the standing bird, don't be afraid to make it fly.

7. Avoid single-character identifications. This is sound advice for identifying any type of bird, but seldom is it more critical than in the study of gulls. Although some characters may be more or less diagnostic for a given species, always try to confirm your identification with multiple supporting marks. Confirmation by means of supporting marks is especially important if the bird in question is suspected to be a rarity.

8. Take notes. This can be a chore, but it can also be an invaluable tool. Gulls lend themselves well to note taking, being among the few birds that will stand pa-

tiently while you write page after page. Take advantage of this behavior! If this becomes too tedious, try taking a microcassette recorder into the field. You can dictate notes without lowering your binoculars.

9. Spend some time in the field with someone who really knows gulls. This can be a great shortcut to field competency if approached in the proper manner. Do not use the expert as a crutch, but rather as a check of your own identifications. Not only can your companion tell you when and why you are wrong, but he or she can also tell you when your identifications are correct: an important confidence booster that is essential to establishing a firm base.

10. Reconcile yourself to the fact that you will not be able to identify every gull you encounter. Pay special attention to the birds that give you trouble; these are the ones to take the best notes on. As time goes by, you will mark fewer and fewer "gull, species?" in your journal. No matter how expert you become, there will always be gulls that defy pigeonholing. We can still learn much about identification without attaching a label to every individual. Given the frequency of hybridization among gulls, the prudent birder will never completely eliminate "gull, species?" from his or her notes.

## Slaty-backed Gulls

"The Slaty-backed Gull is an exclusively coastal gull of northeastern Asia, breeding around the Kamchatka Peninsula and the Sea of Okhotsk south to northern Japan" (Grant 1986). It is an uncommon to rare migrant and nonbreeding summer visitor to coastal western and northern Alaska and islands in the Bering Sea and the Aleutians, and it is a rare visitor elsewhere in Alaska. In recent years, Slaty-backeds have been turning up in fall and winter with increasing frequency at dumps and harbors in south coastal Alaska. Since about 1985, there have been many documented occurrences of vagrant Slaty-backeds in winter in the lower 48 states. Surprisingly, several of these have come from the interior of the country rather than from the West Coast. The preponderance of reports from the interior is, perhaps, attributable to the fact that any dark-mantled gull will draw attention in much of the interior, rather than to any true pattern of vagrancy. Occasional vagrant Slaty-backeds could easily pass unnoticed amongst the throngs of Western Gulls along the Pacific Coast. Nonetheless, the potential for long-distance vagrancy in this species is now well established, and observers throughout the West would do well to scrutinize dark-mantled gulls closely.

This account is aimed at the identification of the Slaty-backed Gull in Alaska, the only place in North America where it is likely to be seen. Because no other dark-mantled, large gulls are expected to occur in Alaska, I will not dwell on detailed, feather-by-feather comparisons of primary patterns between Slaty-backed and every other dark-mantled gull that occurs in the United States. Rather, I will concentrate on generalities of Slaty-backed identification and will focus on the identification of first-year birds, which remain poorly understood and which provide the greatest challenge to identifying the species in Alaska. At the same time, I will try to clear up some of the misconceptions about Slaty-backed identification that seem rampant among visiting birders.

Current knowledge indicates that the Slaty-backed Gull is a typical four-year gull, becoming an adult with the acquisition of its fourth-basic plumage at slightly more than 3 years of age. Juveniles undergo a partial molt of head and body feathers (and a variable number of wing coverts) in their first fall after hatching. This partial molt results in the first-basic plumage, which is replaced through another partial molt in spring, that produces the first-alternate plumage. It is these first-year plumages that cause birders the most trouble in Alaska, in part because our knowledge of first-year plumages in this species remains primitive and in part because the distinctive dark mantle is absent. The first-alternate plumage will be held through the summer, at which time the bird will undergo a complete molt that finally replaces the faded and worn juvenal flight feathers and some coverts. Thereafter, the immature bird will undergo a complete molt (including all flight feathers and coverts) every fall and a partial molt every spring.

Slaty-backeds are large, heavily built gulls. Typical individuals will be somewhat larger than most Herring Gulls and somewhat smaller than most Glaucous Gulls. Many individuals will appear proportionately hulking, with a long, thick neck, angular forehead, and flat crown. Such birds are also likely to have a relatively massive bill. This is the structural stereotype that has been painted in much of the literature on Slaty-backed Gulls. However, as is the case with virtually all large gulls, Slaty-backeds exhibit extreme individual variation (much of it sex-linked) in many mensural and structural characters. I have seen many indisputable adult Slaty-backeds with a short neck, steep forehead, very rounded crown, and proportionately smallish bill (well within the range of many Herring Gulls).

There are a few structural characters that seem relatively constant for most Slaty-backeds that I have observed. Regardless of overall size, head shape, or bill size, Slaty-backeds in flight appear proportionately full-chested and broad-winged when compared with Herring Gulls (which, as we will see shortly, are the primary identification contenders in Alaska). This appearance applies to the smallest-billed, most delicate-looking Slaty-backeds, as well as to the bruisers. The other relative structural constant is bill shape. The culmen and the bottom edge of the mandible are parallel-sided. There is a moderate angle at the gonys but little evidence (even in the largest-billed individuals) of the kind of marked distal "swelling" that is seen in so many Glaucous-winged and Western gulls. The bill structure is probably closest to that of Glaucous Gull.

Adult Slaty-backeds in alternate plumage are clean white on the head, neck, rump, tail, and underparts. They are a dark, slaty-gray on the back, scapulars, wing coverts, base of the secondaries, and over much of the inner primaries. White marginal coverts form a narrow, white leading edge to the inner wing, and large white tips to the tertials, secondaries, and inner primaries form a broad, white trailing edge to the wing. Slaty-backeds have bright pink legs and feet, pale yellowish eyes surrounded by a reddish orbital ring, and a clear-yellow bill with a red-orange spot at the gonys. Adults in basic plumage have individually variable amounts of brownish streaking, mottling, or wash on the head, neck, and breast and often show some darker feathering surrounding the eye. In addition, many winter adults have a distinctly pinkish cast to the base of the bill. Otherwise, breeding and winter adults are similar.

Mantle color has been a topic of some debate. Examination of both live birds and museum specimens reveals that there is substantial variation in the mantle color of Slaty-backeds. Some individuals may be quite blackish, nearly the color of a Great Black-backed Gull, whereas birds at the pale extreme may be only fractionally darker than a California Gull. Most individuals will be somewhere in the middle, closest perhaps to Lesser Black-backed Gull (subspecies *Larus fuscus graellsii*) or the southern subspecies of Western Gull (*L. occidentalis wymani*). The assertion made by many birders that the black primaries should not contrast markedly with the mantle on Slaty-backeds is without merit. Even the darkest-mantled Slaty-backeds will have contrastingly blacker wingtips, and this contrast will be even greater on typical or pale examples. Adult Slaty-backeds with an average or darker-than-average mantle will generally pose few identification problems in Alaska, given that no other dark-mantled gulls occur there. Paler-mantled birds can be easily confused with Herring Gulls of the Siberian subspecies (*L. argentatus vegae*), which is distinctly darker-mantled than the widespread North American subspecies (*L. a. smithsonianus*) and which is more common in coastal western and northern Alaska than is Slaty-backed. Most of these Siberian Herring Gulls have a mantle that approximates that of a California Gull and, thus, would be at the pale extreme for Slaty-backed. However, all gulls appear darker-mantled against snowy or icy backgrounds, and under such conditions *vegae* Herrings will appear quite dark. These birds are often seen amidst flocks of pale-mantled Glaucous Gulls, which will further the impression that they are darker than they really are.

Careful attention to wing pattern should resolve those occasional instances in which neither mantle color nor structural characters are conclusive. Primary pattern is fairly diagnostic, but it can also be difficult to assess under field conditions. It can, however, be helpful in identifying photos of birds with spread wings. Slaty-backeds have white tips (apical spots) to each of the primaries. The outermost primary (p10) is black, with a long, white mirror across both webs that is only narrowly separated from the white apical spot by a thin, black subterminal bar. P9 is mostly black, often with a small, white mirror on the inner web (usually not visible in the field). Primaries 6–8 are basally black, with elongate "tongues" of slate-gray on the inner webs. These tongues terminate in conspicuous white marks, which are separated from the white apical spots by black subterminal bars. The net effect of these markings is a broken line of white spots that starts at the trailing edge of the wing (in the middle of the primaries) and curls into the center of the blackish wingtip. This line of spots has been likened to a string of pearls and may be easier to see on the underside of the spread wing, particularly on standing birds that raise their wings to stretch. Easier things to judge (but less diagnostic) on flying birds include the exceptionally broad white trailing edge to the secondaries and the lower contrast between the black outer primaries and the mostly dark-gray inner primaries on the upper wing. A study of the underwing pattern is also helpful in separating Slaty-backeds from Herring gulls. The black outer primaries of Herrings contrast vividly on the underwing with the whitish linings and the pale-gray undersides to the secondaries and inner primaries. The gray inner webs of all but the two outermost Slaty-backed primaries conceal the black portions of the outer webs (visible from above), so the wingtip (when viewed from below) appears mostly silvery-gray, with only a small amount of black visible near the outer (leading) edge.

First-year birds present the greatest challenge. They show overlap with first-year *vegae* Herrings in most plumage characters, and only a careful assessment will allow accurate separation of many individuals. When attempting to identify a first-year Slaty-backed, you should pay strict attention to structural characters. Most Slaty-backeds will be larger, heavier-billed, fuller-chested, and broader-winged than most *vegae* Herrings. I find the overall bulk and shape of the bird easier to judge on flying birds than on standing ones. The first plumage feature that most birders notice on a first-summer Slaty-backed is the prominent pale panel on the inner wing. This panel is formed by the wing coverts, some of which are retained from juvenal plumage and all of which are worn and dramatically faded to a pale-buff or off-whitish. Striking as it may be, this covert panel is not a field mark for Slaty-backeds. Similarly bleached coverts are seen in like-aged Herring Gulls.

Contrary to published statements in various references, first-summer Slaty-backeds can, and frequently do, have a contrasting dark-brown secondary bar that is equally as distinct as that of most *vegae* Herrings. They also have strikingly pale inner primaries, as do young *vegae* Herrings (and, again, contrary to some published statements). In fact, the entire upperwing pattern of dark-brown outer primaries contrasting with extremely pale inner primaries and a pale panel of faded wing coverts bordered posteriorly by a dark-brown secondary bar is very similar to that of most first-summer *vegae* Herrings.

A closer look at the wings will reveal some differences. The outer primaries of young Herrings are uniformly blackish brown and show high contrast with the whitish inner primaries from both above and below. The outer webs of the outer primaries of Slaty-backeds are dark brown (not as blackish), but the inner webs are a much paler gray or gray-brown. On the spread upper wing, this pattern has the effect of lightening the wingtip somewhat, because the pale inner webs have a neutralizing effect on the dark outer webs. The effect from below is more dramatic. Because of the way primaries overlap on a spread wing, we can see the entire outermost primary but only the inner webs and tips of the other primaries (the outer webs of each feather are concealed by the inner web of the adjacent feather). Thus, on Slaty-backeds, the pale inner webs of the primaries conceal the dark outer webs, leaving a silvery-gray wingtip except for the dark leading edge (formed by the dark outermost primary, which is wholly visible) and a thin, dark trailing edge formed by the dark tips of the outer six to eight primaries. This underwing pattern is reminiscent of that of first-winter Thayer's Gulls. Another possible difference between first-year Slaty-backeds and *vegae* Herrings involves the presence and distinctness of dark subterminal marks near the tips of the inner three or four primaries. Such marks may more often be present (and when present, may be more discrete) on Slaty-backeds, but more field testing is needed to confirm this difference.

Tail pattern is also helpful in separating first-year Slaty-backeds and *vegae* Herrings. On Slaty-backeds, most of the tail is dark brown, contrasting with the whitish rump and uppertail coverts. The base of the tail is frequently white, or at least mottled white and brown. On *vegae* Herrings, most of the tail is white, setting off a distinct brown subterminal band. Both species will appear to have a banded tail, the distinction being that *vegae* gulls will have a true tail band, whereas many Slaty-backeds will have the entire tail (or nearly the entire tail) dark, appearing as a band only in contrast to the rump and uppertail coverts. There is much potential overlap in this character; many Slaty-backeds show extensive white at the base of the tail and thus have a true tail band. For such birds, the distinction in tail pattern will depend solely on the width of the band. The tail band is almost always noticeably thin on Herrings and broad on Slaty-backeds, but extreme examples of the two species may show overlap.

Slaty-backeds in first-alternate plumage are typically extremely pale except for the contrasting dark tail, outer primaries, and secondary bar. They are somewhat reminiscent of juvenile Great Black-backed Gulls in this regard but show little patterning to the mantle and scapulars. Many first-alternate *vegae* Herrings will also appear uniformly pale and whitish from fading. The tendency is probably greater in Slaty-backeds, because even many juveniles on the natal territories already show a distinctly pale head and neck. Grant (1986) has two excellent photos (numbers 499 and 500) that illustrate pale-plumaged individuals typical of first-alternate Slaty-backeds that are seen in Alaska.

Bill color may also be useful. Young Herring Gulls typically begin to show pink color on the bill by late in their first fall or early in their first winter. By the time they are in first-alternate plumage (and nearly 1 year old) most young Herrings will show significant amounts of fleshy-pink color at the base of the bill. Slaty-backeds, as do Western and Glaucous-winged gulls, seem to retain an all-black bill into their first summer, showing only hints of pinkish at the extreme base or along the cutting edge.

Older immature Slaty-backeds (second- and third-years) should be identifiable by their dark mantle and by structural characters. Second-alternate birds have pale-brown wing coverts that bleach to white, forming a broad panel on the spread wing similar to that seen in first-alternate birds (but whiter). This panel contrasts strikingly with the dark secondary bar, with the dark outer primaries, and especially with the slaty-gray mantle (giving a dark-saddled appearance). The faded-brown or whitish coverts will also be prominent on the folded wing. Many second-alternate birds will still have a mostly dark tail or a broad, solid tail band.

Third-alternate birds will look essentially like adults but will show some brown staining on the wing coverts, blotches of gray-brown on the white underparts, more black in the outer wing, usually some remnants (at least) of the tail band, an incomplete primary pattern (missing mirrors and white tongue tips), and some sign of immaturity in the bill (the bill will vary from pink to yellow to orange, with a black tip, subterminal band, or some irregular dusky marking).

For more information, see Goetz et al. 1986, Grant 1986, and Gustafson and Peterjohn 1994.

## Thayer's Gulls

Thayer's Gull, as a full-fledged species, is a fairly recent addition to the American avifauna, having been officially split from Herring Gull in 1972 (it may yet turn out to be conspecific with Iceland Gull). It breeds from the northern Northwest Territories south and east to Victoria and Baffin islands, western Greenland and the northern edge of the Hudson Bay region. Most Thayer's Gulls winter along the Pacific Coast from southern British Columbia south to northern Baja, with smaller numbers wintering north to southern Alaska and east to the Gulf of St. Lawrence, the Great Lakes, and along the Atlantic Coast south to Florida. Thayer's Gull has been recorded casually from throughout the interior west and from the Gulf Coast. Along the West Coast numbers decrease with latitude, dropping off sharply south of central California.

Thayer's is a four-year gull (as are Herring, Western, Glaucous-winged, California, and Iceland) that attains adult plumage in its fourth winter. First-year birds represent the bulk of wintering California birds and of vagrants found over the rest of the western interior, whereas adults are more common along the Washington and Oregon coasts (Lehman 1980). Second and third-year birds are much less frequently encountered south of Canada (Lehman 1980). Therefore, this treatment will focus on first-year and adult plumages only, with the greater emphasis given to first-year birds (Figs. 4.60 and 4.61).

Structural characters are very helpful in the identification of all age classes of Thayer's Gulls. Most Thayer's are about intermediate in size between California and Herring gulls (but beware of individual variation) and should be noticeably smaller than most Westerns or Glaucous-wingeds. Thayer's tend to have a more rounded, dove like head (Figs. 4.60 and 4.61) that is similar to that of the Mew Gull and that is quite different in appearance from the more angular and flat-crowned look of Herring, Western, and Glaucous-winged gulls (see Figs. 4.62, 4.54, and 4.65, respectively).

Bill differences are even more useful. Compared with other large gulls, Thayer's has a short, almost delicate bill, with a gradually curving culmen and little apparent gonydeal angle. This bill type is very similar to that of the Iceland Gull (see Fig. 4.64) (which is extremely rare in the West) but is quite different from that of typical Herring Gulls, which have a longer thinner bill with a distinctive angling to-

Figure 4.60. Thayer's Gull (center) in first-basic plumage. Note the rounded head and delicate all-black bill (compare with the young Western Gull in the lower right), evenly checkered upper parts, medium-brown folded primaries (rather than black as in the adjacent Western Gull), brown-centered tertials, and pale tips and edges of the folded primaries. (Photographed in late November at Pacific Grove, California, by Kevin J. Zimmer.)

ward the tip. Westerns and Glaucous-wingeds have even more massive bills with sharp gonydeal angles (see Figs.4.54 and 4.65), as do Glaucous-winged × Western hybrids (see Fig. 4.66) (often encountered along the West Coast), which could otherwise be easily mistaken for Thayer's. It must be remembered that females of all large gulls typically have a smaller, more delicate bill and more rounded crown than do males of their own species. Consequently, a female Thayer's should stand out as being especially dovelike in aspect. However, there also is potential for confusing a small, delicate-billed female Herring or Glaucous-winged × Western hybrid for a Thayer's. Therefore, although head and bill structure may be the first

Figure 4.61. Thayer's Gull in first-basic plumage. This individual has darker wingtips than the bird in Figure 4.60. (Photo by Robert Sundstrom.)

Figure 4.62. Herring Gull in first-basic plumage. Compare head and bill structure, bill color (conspicuous fleshy base), constrasting paler head, and darker primaries with the Thayer's Gulls in Figures 4.60 and 4.61. (Photographed in early January at St. Johns, Newfoundland, by Kevin J. Zimmer.)

clue to the presence of a possible Thayer's Gull, they should never be the sole basis for such an identification.

Much of the literature stresses the eye color of adult Thayer's as an important field mark. Thayer's of all ages have brown irises, whereas adult Herring and most adult Icelands have yellow irises. Unfortunately, eye color is hard to distinguish accurately, except at close range and in good light. Also, a few subadult Herrings may exhibit essentially adult plumage while retaining the brown irises of earlier stages (some Icelands also have brownish eyes). It should also be pointed out that adult California and Glaucous-winged gulls as well as northern populations of Western Gulls also have dark eyes. Therefore, eye color should be considered only an accessory mark in the identification of adults and should never be used as the sole basis for identification.

The leg color of all Thayer's Gulls is generally considered to be a deeper, bubblegum-pink than the pink leg color of other similar gulls. This is a subjective mark that should also be considered accessory in nature.

First-year Thayer's are fairly variable in overall plumage. Many birds are mostly or entirely gray-brown, with paler edgings and internal markings on the feathers of the back and wing coverts (giving a marbled look to the upper parts). More commonly, however, first-year birds tend to be quite buffy in overall coloration but with the same marbled look seen in the darker birds. Some individuals show a noticeably white head (as in young Herring Gulls), but most birds are very uniform in color. The best field mark is the color of the primaries. The folded primaries of a first-year Thayer's at rest should be a medium to dark brown above and should be at least slightly to moderately darker than the rest of the wing and mantle (Figs. 4.60 and 4.61). The primaries of First-year Herring, Western, and California gulls are more blackish brown and contrast more strongly with the rest of the wing. The primaries of first-year Glaucous-wingeds are typically the same color as the rest of the wing or (less commonly) are only fractionally darker, and the primaries of young Glaucous Gulls and many young Iceland Gulls are even lighter still. Thayer's also tend to have more conspicuous white or buffy edges to the tips of these primaries than do the other species (Figs. 4.60 and 4.61). These edges are revealed as a series of thin, pale crescents at the tip of each folded primary.

Equally important is the color of the primaries from below. All of the remiges of first-year Thayer's are conspicuously lighter than the wing linings when viewed from below. Thus the underwing of flying birds (Fig. 4.63) has a frosty appearance, a trait that is shared with Glaucous, Iceland, and Glaucous-winged gulls. Contrarily, the outer primaries (at least) of young Herring, Western, and California gulls are darker than the rest of the wing when viewed from below. Young Herrings do show pale windows on the inner primaries. From above, flying Thayer's appear to be nearly concolor on the wings because the more extensive light inner webs of the primaries (concealed when the wing is folded) balance out the thinner, dark outer webs that are so prominent on resting birds. Thayer's does tend to show slight contrast on the upper wing between the duskier outer primaries and the paler inner primaries. It also shows a darker secondary bar. The latter mark is helpful in distinguishing Thayer's from Glaucous-winged and from most Icelands.

The vast majority of first-basic Thayer's should have an entirely black bill from October through February. By February to March some individuals may begin to

Figure 4.63. Thayer's Gull in first-basic plumage. Note the frosty translucence of the underside of the remiges, with only slight dusky tips on the outer primaries. (Photographed in early January near Santa Maria, California, by Kevin J. Zimmer.)

show some paling at the base of the bill (Lehman 1980). By contrast, most first-year Herrings will show noticeable dull pink at the base of the bill by early winter, and first-winter Herrings with an entirely black bill are rare by January. First-basic Icelands frequently appear entirely black-billed at a distance, but at close range these birds can usually be seen to have a contrastingly colored base to the bill (either gray, dull reddish, or olive).

The tail of Thayer's (from above) is a uniform dark brown, with only a small amount of mottling at the base of the outer tail feathers. This coloration contrasts with the lighter, mottled uppertail coverts and in flight gives the appearance of a wide uniformly dark band. First-year Icelands, on the other hand, usually have more mottling to the tail, which is paler and less uniform in color than that of Thayer's. Some first-year Iceland Gulls have a solid (unmottled) tail band, but this is usually a few shades paler than the tail band of Thayer's Gulls.

The color of the primaries is also helpful in identifying adult Thayer's. Resting birds should show clean black wingtips (those of Glaucous-wingeds are pale gray, and those of Iceland vary from white to charcoal-gray) with larger white mirrors (discrete, oval white patches contained entirely within a single primary and surrounded by black) than are found in Herrings. The spread upper wing of flying birds has a striped look to the outer primaries that has been likened to the keys of a piano. The look is created by the alternating black outer webs and largely white inner webs of each feather. From below, the primaries should appear mostly pale, with only a thin black trailing edge to the outer primaries.

Adult Thayer's typically have a mantle that is a shade or two darker than that of Herrings. (Beware the northern population of Western Gulls, which are much lighter-mantled than are southern birds, and which, like Thayer's Gulls, also have dark irises.)

The most likely sources of confusion in your attempts to identify Thayer's Gulls are Herring Gull, Iceland Gull, Glaucous-winged Gull, and Glaucous-winged × Western hybrids. Key points to remember in considering each of these possibilities are summarized below.

For a more detailed treatment of Thayer's Gull identification (including the identification of second- and third-year birds), see Lehman 1980. For a thorough discussion of the complexities of separating Thayer's Gulls of all ages from Iceland Gulls, see Zimmer 1991.

## Thayer's versus Herring Gull

For all ages, size and structural characters (particularly head shape and bill size and shape) are important considerations, but they should always be supported by plumage characters, particularly the primary pattern (as viewed from above and below). In comparison with Herrings (see Fig. 4.62), first-year Thayer's tend to be buffier in overall color, with more sharply checkered upper parts, and they have brown (rather than blackish) folded wingtips, often with a conspicuous pale crescent at the tip of each primary. On first-year Thayer's, the base of the bill should not show conspicuous pink before February. The structure of the head and bill, overall size, and primary pattern should be the primary marks for separating adults. Thayer's should also be darker-mantled than Herrings, and they have brown eyes.

### Thayer's versus Iceland Gull

Field separation of Thayer's and Iceland gulls can vary from straightforward to impossible. The North American–breeding subspecies of Iceland Gull (*Larus glaucoides kumlieni*, "Kumlien's Gull") (Fig. 4.64) is extremely variable morphologically and exhibits individual variation in virtually every character that might be useful in separating it from Thayer's Gull. To make matters worse, "Kumlien's Gulls" and Thayer's Gulls commonly interbreed where their ranges meet, and many hybrids or intergrades will be impossible to separate from extreme variants of the parent types. Fortunately, Iceland Gulls are very rare in the West, and this will remain a largely hypothetical problem for western gull watchers.

First-year Thayer's can usually be separated by the color of the bill and of the plumage. Thayer's have an all-black bill, whereas the bill of Icelands typically has a contrasting-colored base. The Thayer's primaries are noticeably darker than the rest of the wing; most Icelands have paler primaries, but some extreme individuals do not. Thayer's Gulls have a broad, solidly dark tail band; Icelands either lack a tail band or have a paler tail band with significant internal mottling. Thayer's have a strong secondary bar on the spread wing and folded tertials that appear solidly brown, with little or no internal checkering or barring; Icelands usually have significant internal marking on the tertials. Adults must be separated on primary pattern, because eye color (brown in Thayer's, usually golden in Iceland) is an unreliable supporting character.

### Thayer's versus Glaucous-winged Gull

Separation of Thayer's and Glaucous-winged gulls is usually straightforward. Glaucous-wingeds of all ages are significantly larger, with a massive bill and a

Figure 4.64. Iceland Gull in first-basic plumage. The differences between this bird and a typical Thayer's Gull include: even more rounded head and delicate bill (with slightly contrasting base that is not easily seen in this photo), paler overall plumage, paler folded primaries, evenly mottled tertials (without a distinct brown panel in the center), and paler tail. (Photographed in early January at St. Johns, Newfoundland, by Kevin J. Zimmer.)

Figure 4.65. Glaucous-winged Gull in first-basic plumage. Compared with Thayer's Gull, note the heavier build, flatter crown, more massive bill, and paler primaries (the same color as the rest of the wing). (Photographed in late December near Morro Bay, California, by Kevin J. Zimmer.)

blockier head (but beware of small female Glaucous-wingeds). First-year Glaucous-wingeds (Fig. 4.65) have folded primaries that are the same color as or slightly paler than the rest of the wing (rarely a fraction darker than the rest of the wing). Only the palest-primaried Thayer's would have wingtips as light as those of the darkest-primaried Glaucous-winged. Thayer's also has more sharply-patterned upper parts, a conspicuous secondary bar (lacking on Glaucous-winged), and a much darker tail. Adults can be separated by size and structural characters, as well as by wingtip color (black in Thayer's, pale gray in Glaucous-winged).

### Thayer's Gull versus Glaucous-winged × Western Gull Hybrids

Separating Thayer's Gull from Glaucous-winged × Western Gull hybrids can be difficult for all age groups, although size and structure alone will usually allow rapid separation for birders who have comparative experience. Most hybrids will have a massive bill and an angular head (Fig. 4.66) like their parent forms, but occasional smaller females can create confusion. Plumage differences from Thayer's Gulls are often slight and are subject to much variation. First-year hybrids are usually a dingier, gray-brown (rather than the buffy color seen in so many Thayer's) and lack any sharp checkering to the upper parts. They also lack the pale crescents on the tips of the primaries, and in flight the outer primaries often appear duskier. Adults can be separated by a careful analysis of primary pattern, which, although extremely variable in hybrids, is unlikely to ever duplicate the piano keyboard pattern of an adult Thayer's.

## Kittiwakes

The Black-legged Kittiwake has a circumpolar distribution and is one of the most familiar seabirds of northern latitudes. It breeds in large colonies on coastal or is-

Figure 4.66. Hybrid Glaucous-winged × Western Gull in first-basic plumage. The color of the wingtips is similar to that of many Thayer's Gulls (i.e., medium-brown, distinctly darker than the rest of the wing), but note the head shape and massive bill, both typical of Western and Glaucous-winged gulls. (Photographed in December at Pacific Grove, California, by Kevin J. Zimmer.)

land cliffs and is highly pelagic, particularly outside of the breeding season, when birds wander far to the south along both coasts. Vagrants appear periodically on inland lakes and reservoirs. In contrast, the Red-legged Kittiwake is a bird of extremely limited distribution, breeding only on remote islands in the Bering Sea. Away from the breeding colonies, it is highly pelagic and rarely seen, and it is thought to move south to winter in the northern Gulf of Alaska and at the southern ice edge of the Bering Sea. Amazingly, vagrants have been recorded from Oregon, southern California, and even Nevada. Thus, although the field separation of these two species is generally of concern only for birders visiting Alaska, it is not inconceivable that it could become an issue elsewhere in the West.

At first inspection, field separation of the two species of kittiwake may not seem to be much of a problem. As the names imply, the two species differ in leg color. The vast majority of adult Black-leggeds have black legs and feet, as do juveniles and most first- and second-year immatures. However, some Black-leggeds (particularly first-year birds) have dull-yellow, orange-brown, dull flesh-pink, or even dull-reddish legs. Even so, no Black-legged Kittiwake will approach the bright scarlet legs and feet of adult and older immature Red-legged Kittiwakes. Unfortunately, as anyone who has visited the bird cliffs on the Pribilof Islands can attest, it is not always easy to see the legs and feet of a kittiwake that is clinging to a toehold on a vertical cliff face below you. It is even more difficult to see those legs and feet on a flying or swimming bird, which is how most kittiwakes of both species are most likely to be seen away from the breeding grounds. So, with that in mind, let us examine other ways of separating the two species.

As is often the case with gulls, structural characters are useful for separating the two species at any age. Compared with larger species of gulls, both species of kittiwakes appear delicate. When compared with one another, the Black-legged Kittiwake appears fiercer and more rugged, whereas the Red-legged has a gentler, cuter aspect due to differences in head shape and bill size and shape. The Red-legged (Fig. 4.67) has a shorter bill that appears more rounded at the tip. The forehead rises more steeply from the base of the bill, and the crown is more rounded, imparting a more domed look to the head. By comparison, Black-leggeds (Fig. 4.68) have a longer bill, a more angular forehead (less perpendicular), and a flatter crown. These differences in head and bill shape result in a very different look that is somewhat comparable to the differences in head shape between a Herring Gull and a Thayer's or Iceland gull. Once you have developed a feel for these differences, you will find that they are discernible (given reasonably close views) even on flying kittiwakes (Figs. 4.69 and 4.70). Another structural character is that Red-leggeds have shorter legs and thus appear squatter when standing side by side with a Black-legged.

As adults, both species have a yellow bill; dark eyes; an entirely white head, underparts, and tail; a gray mantle and upper wings; a white trailing edge to the sec-

Figure 4.67. Red-legged Kittiwakes (adult on right). Note the high-domed forehead, relatively small bill, and dark, slaty mantle. (Photographed in June at St. Paul Island, Alaska, by Kevin J. Zimmer.)

Figure 4.68. Black-legged Kittiwake (adult). Note the flatter-crowned profile, the longer bill, paler mantle, and black legs. (Photographed in June at St. Paul Island, Alaska, by Kevin J. Zimmer.)

ondaries; and black on the outer primaries that forms a neatly delineated black triangle on each wingtip (the oft-cited "dipped in ink" look). The mantle of the Red-legged is a shade darker gray than the mantle of the Black-legged, and the upper wing is a uniform matching gray except for the black wingtip and the white trailing edge of the secondaries. On Black-leggeds, the wing coverts of the inner wing are the same gray as the mantle (a shade lighter than on Red leggeds), but the secondaries, primaries, and primary coverts are noticeably paler gray, and the primaries and primary coverts that abut the black wingtips are almost white. The result is that the black wingtips of Black-legged Kittiwakes are bordered by the palest feathers of the wing, making for extreme contrast (Fig. 4.70). Conversely, because the secondaries are also such a pale-gray, the white trailing edge contrasts very little and is inconspicuous. The situation is reversed in Red-legged Kittiwakes (Fig. 4.69). Their black wingtips are bordered by medium-gray (rather than

Figure 4.69. Adult Red-legged Kittiwake. The head and bill features are evident even in flight. Note the high contrast between the dark wing coverts and the white trailing edge of the secondaries and, conversely, the low contrast between the dark gray coverts and the black primaries. (Photographed in June at St. Paul Island, Alaska, by Kevin J. Zimmer.)

Figure 4.70. Adult Black-legged Kitti-wake. Structural aspects of the head and bill are apparent even in flight. Note the pale upperwing coverts, which contrast sharply with the black wingtips but which show only weak contrast to the white trailing edge of the secondaries. (Photographed in June at St. Paul Island, Alaska, by Kevin J. Zimmer.)

whitish) inner primaries and, thus, contrast relatively little. On the other hand, because the secondaries are uniformly medium gray for much of their length, the contrast with the white trailing edge is much greater than it is on Black-leggeds.

Similarly, the underwings of Black-legged Kittiwakes are a pale, whitish gray except for the black wingtip. The inner portion of the underwing of Red-leggeds is also pale gray (although slightly darker than on Black-leggeds), but the outer primaries and primary coverts are extensively dark gray, making the entire outer half of the underwing noticeably dark. The marginal coverts of Black-leggeds are whitish, making the leading edge of the wing appear pale when viewed head-on in flight. The marginal coverts of Red-leggeds are darker gray, making the leading edge of the wings appear dark.

Juvenile Black-legged Kittiwakes are striking birds. They are white on the head and underparts and uniformly medium gray on the mantle and scapulars. The white head is suffused with pale gray on the crown and hindneck and is boldly marked by a wide, black hind-collar and a large, blackish smudge on the auriculars. The slightly forked tail is clean white except for a wide black terminal band. In flight, the upperwings exhibit a striking black M pattern formed by the outer primaries and their coverts and by a wide, black carpal bar angling from the wrist to the body. The bill, feet, and legs are black. First-basic birds are similar except that the bill frequently has some greenish yellow coloring, the feet and legs may be some color other than black (dull pinkish, yellow, or brownish orange), and the hind-collar may be reduced in size or replaced by gray in some individuals, whereas other individuals may even have a swath of gray anterior to the black collar, giving a double-collared effect. The black carpal bar may be reduced in extent from juvenal plumage. By the following summer, young kittiwakes (in first-alternate plumage) will show only remnants of the hind-collar, auricular smudge, and tail band; the black carpal bar will be reduced in size and faded to brown; and the bill will be mostly greenish yellow. Most older immatures (second-basic and second-alternate) will resemble adults, but they may show traces of immaturity such as a black tip to the bill or more extensive black on the wingtips (particularly on the primary coverts).

Juvenile and first-year Red-legged Kittiwakes can be separated from Black-leggeds of the same ages by the all-white tail (the Red-legged is the only species of gull in which the tail is all white in first-basic plumage); a less prominent cervical collar; darker gray mantle, scapulars, and wing coverts; and the absence of a prominent black carpal bar on the upper wing. Although most identification literature touts the absence of a carpal bar in first-year Red-leggeds as key in the separation from Black-leggeds, you should not rely solely on this character. At least some first-year Red-leggeds have at least a semblance of a broken, black carpal bar, although, even when present, this bar is not nearly as broad, complete, or conspicuous as the corresponding carpal bar of immature Black-leggeds.

The upperwing pattern of juvenile and first-basic Red-legged is striking in its own way. The outer primaries and their coverts are largely black (gray on the inner webs), contrasting strongly with the inner primaries and secondaries, which are extensively white. Combined with the remainder of the coverts and the bases of the inner remiges, all of which are medium gray, this coloration lends a distinctive tricolored, Sabine's Gull–like appearance to the upper wing.

Juvenile Red-leggeds have a blackish bill, and the legs and feet are dark brown. By first-basic plumage, the bill begins to yellow in color, and the feet and legs go from brown to orange. The plumage is as that of juveniles except that the head is washed with gray and the hind-collar is often reduced in size or absent. By first-alternate plumage, the head is whiter, the unmolted remiges and rectrices are worn and faded, the bill is mostly or entirely yellow, and the legs and feet are red (although typically a duller orange-red that is less intense than the bright scarlet legs and feet of adults). Older immatures can be identified by the same characters used for adults.

## Common versus Arctic versus Forster's Tern

The Common, Arctic, and Forster's complex of *Sterna* terns has long presented a perplexing identification challenge to birders. The complex breaks down into two species-pair problems: (1) Common versus Forster's, and (2) Common versus Arctic. The first problem is of primary interest in the Southwest and on the Gulf Coast. Common Terns are generally rare at any season over much of the Southwest and are constantly overreported by observers who are in fact misidentifying the more common Forster's. Commons are expected on the Gulf Coast, except in winter, when all but a few leave the country. Even so, they have been regularly reported in large numbers by Gulf Coast birders in winter. The Common–Arctic problem is mainly of concern on the West Coast, where Arctics are regular but rare (except offshore, where, for a brief time, they may be common) and observer interest in them is high.

## Structural Differences

Structural differences are useful in identifying birds of all ages. Probably the most consistent and most noticeable structural difference between these terns involves neck length, head size and shape, and bill size and shape (Fig. 4.71). The Arctic Tern has a relatively short neck and small head, with a more rounded crown and a relatively short bill. Forster's and Common terns differ from the Arctic, and more resemble one another, in having a larger head and longer neck, with a flatter crown, and a longer, heavier bill. The bill of Forster's Tern is both longer and deeper-based than that of the Common, but both of these species differ more in these respects from Arctics than they do from one another. These differences in head, neck, and bill structure can be seen on flying birds as well as on resting birds. The larger head and longer neck and bill of Common and Forster's terns combine to make the heads of these species protrude farther beyond the leading edge of the wing, counterbalancing the projection of the main part of the tail (minus the streamers) behind the wing. Conversely, the combination of a smaller head, shorter neck and a shorter bill makes the head of the Arctic Tern project less in front of the wing, making for a more sawed-off or snub-nosed flight profile.

Figure 4.71. *Sterna* terns. Arctic (left), Forster's (right), and wings of the Common (center). Note the differences between Arctic and Forster's in head and bill structure and between all three species in primary pattern. (Artwork by Mimi Hoppe Wolf.)

Adult terns of this species complex have long streamers on the outer tail when they are in alternate plumage. Forster's and Arctics have longer tail streamers than Commons. On standing birds the streamers of a Common barely reach the wingtips, whereas those of Forster's and Arctics extend well beyond the wingtips. Only breeding adults have long streamers; juveniles, subadults, and winter adults either lack the streamers or have streamers that are much shorter than those of breeding adults.

A final structural characteristic that is somewhat difficult to judge (and which should be considered an accessory character only) is tarsal length. Forster's have much longer legs than Arctics, and Commons are intermediate. This difference in leg length is sometimes apparent in mixed flocks that are standing on level terrain. But beware: uneven terrain and temporary differences in posture and the extent to which the feathers of the underparts of a given bird are compressed or fluffed out can greatly influence your perception of leg length.

## Molt Sequence and Sources of Plumage Variation

Before you can make sense of the variation that you see in tern plumages, you must have some understanding of the underlying reasons for the observed variation. For convenience, we can sort the various plumages that an individual tern acquires during its lifetime into four categories: adult alternate, adult basic, juvenal, and subadult. The juvenal plumage is the first true plumage that replaces the natal down of young terns in their first year. This plumage is usually retained through fall migration to the wintering quarters, where the young tern then begins a series of prolonged molts, which will eventually carry it (1 to 3 years later) into adulthood. The series of plumages between the juvenal plumage and the first-adult plumage can be collectively referred to as subadult plumages (immature and predefinitive are other commonly encountered terms). When the tern becomes an adult, it will begin a repeating cycle of alternating plumages. In late winter or early spring it will molt into a definitive alternate plumage before migrating north. This plumage will be held through the breeding season and will then be replaced over the fall and early winter through one or two molts that will result in the definitive basic plumage. Each year, for the rest of its life, the tern will undergo molts that will alternately produce and replace the alternate and basic plumages.

The molt sequence outlined above is not overly different from that of many types of birds. However, terns offer some additional features to the standard equation that make understanding their plumage cycles more difficult. Many terns (unlike most other birds) molt their flight feathers twice each year. This is the case for both Forster's and Common Terns, but not for Arctics. The differences between the three species in the number of molts and in the timing of those molts profoundly influence the observed wing patterns that we rely on for field identification.

The other complication is related to a structural peculiarity of tern feathers and the influence it has on patterns of wear and, consequently, on observed wing patterns. The primary feathers of terns are (when fresh) covered by an ephemeral, powdery "bloom" of tiny white barbules on their upper surface. This extent of the bloom depends on the density of barbules, which varies from one species to the next, but whatever the extent, the bloom conceals the underlying ground color of the primaries, which tend to be some shade of gray or black. As the primaries age, their whitish bloom wears away, resulting in a gradual darkening of the primaries as the true ground color is slowly revealed. With this basic fact in mind, let's return to differences in the number and timing of molts.

The Arctic Tern is the easiest of our three species to understand, because it has the most "normal" molt pattern when compared with most other (nontern) birds. After breeding, Arctic Terns migrate south and undergo their yearly complete molt on the wintering grounds. Because each of the primaries is replaced over a relatively short period, there is little difference between individual feathers in the extent to which the white bloom has worn away by the time the birds migrate north to their breeding grounds. Therefore, in spring and summer, Arctic Terns show a highly uniform upperwing pattern.

Forster's Terns begin molting their flight feathers in July and August, after breeding. The primaries are molted from the inside out, so the innermost primary (p1) is molted first and the outermost primary (p10) is molted last. This molt continues until all of the flight feathers have been replaced, usually by some time in November. The prebasic molt of head, body, and tail feathers takes place concurrently, resulting in the definitive basic plumage. At this time, each of the new primaries is covered with a white bloom, which is particularly dense on Forster's Terns when compared with other species. This white bloom is so dense that it completely conceals the underlying black color of the outer five or six primaries. The basic plumage is worn for about a month before a second molt begins. This molt begins once again with the replacement of the inner primaries, followed by or concurrent with, the molt of head, body, tail, and wing covert feathers into definitive alternate plumage. However, the replacement of primaries is arrested in this molt, so only the inner three to five primaries are replaced. The bird then migrates north to the breeding grounds with two sets of primaries: an inner set, which are freshly molted, and an outer set, which date back to the previous fall. At the beginning of the breeding season, all of the primaries are uniformly pale. But soon after, the whitish bloom on the older, outer primaries begins to wear past a critical threshold, exposing the underlying blackish color. This is first evident on the tips of the outer primaries, which are exposed to light and the elements even when the bird is at rest. The inner primaries and secondaries, which have a paler gray ground color to begin with, are relatively new and thus have a denser bloom. As the summer progresses, increasing contrast is evident between the older, darker outer primaries and the newer, whiter, inner primaries and secondaries. The resulting upperwing pattern is dramatically different from that seen on the same bird at the beginning of the summer.

Common Terns are even more complex in their molt cycle. As do Forster's, Commons begin replacing primaries in July and August after breeding. Unlike

Forster's, however, Commons do not concurrently molt head and body feathers while still on the breeding grounds. After replacing the inner four or five primaries, Commons suspend their molt and migrate south. After arriving on the wintering grounds, they resume molting their flight feathers and begin the molt of head, body, tail, and wing covert feathers into definitive basic plumage. The primary molt is completed in January with the replacement of the outermost primary. Almost simultaneously, the second molt of the inner primaries begins. Soon after, the molt of head, body, tail, and wing covert feathers into definitive alternate plumage begins. The molt of the inner primaries is arrested after the replacement of the inner four or five.

The bird then migrates north to the breeding grounds with two sets of primaries, just as Forster's Terns do. Because the bloom on the primaries is less dense than on Forster's, the primaries do not appear whiter than the wing coverts. However, the newly molted secondaries and inner primaries are just as pale as the wing coverts. The outer set of older primaries, lacking the dense white bloom found in Forster's Terns, appears darker gray, a contrast that will become increasingly apparent through the summer. Eventually, the entire wingtip will appear dark.

Furthermore, because the molt of primaries occurs from the inside out in both the complete molt and the arrested molt, the newest primary (individually variable, but for the sake of example, let's say p5, the fifth primary from the inside) will be adjacent to the oldest primary (in this case, p6). Remember that immediately after the completion of the first molt (with the replacement of p10, the outermost primary), the second molt started and that only the first five primaries were replaced. That means that of the primaries retained from the first molt, the innermost (p6) is the oldest, and it is immediately adjacent to p5, the last of the new primaries to be molted. This sequence greatly influences the wing pattern, because the oldest primary (p6) is the darkest primary and the newest primary (p5) is the palest primary. The contrast created by the juxtaposition of the palest and the darkest primaries appears as an abrupt border that takes the form of a thin, dark wedge leading inward from the trailing edge of the wing.

Now that we have outlined the general sequence of plumages in a tern's development and have discussed the interactions of molt, bloom, and feather wear that combine to bring about the changes in wing patterns that we see through the summer, we can separate these three species of tern on the basis of plumage characters.

## Adults in Alternate Plumage

Arctic, Common, and Forster's terns in definitive alternate plumage are characterized by a complete black cap that stands in high contrast to their gray back; by long streamers on the outer tail; and by an orange-to-red bill (at least at the base), legs, and feet.

The best plumage characters concern differences in color pattern on both surfaces of the wings. The upper wings of Arctic Terns are uniformly pale to medium gray, with a hint of a thin, dark trailing edge to the outer six to eight primaries. As the summer progresses, the primaries remain uniformly pale and do not darken markedly as do the primaries of Forster's and Commons. The lack of a noticeable darkening is due in part to the fact that the underlying ground color of the Arctic primaries is paler and in part to the fact that all of the primaries are roughly the same age.

The secondaries and inner primaries of Common Terns are essentially the same color as the wing coverts, whereas the outer primaries are somewhat darker (making the wingtip the darkest part of the upper wing). A blackish wedge extending forward from the trailing edge of the wing marks the division between old and new primaries. As the summer progresses, the outer five to seven primaries will darken uniformly from wear, leaving late-summer birds with extensively blackish wingtips.

The primaries and secondaries of Forster's Terns are whiter than the coverts, making the wingtip of a flying Forster's the whitest part of the upper wing. The first sign of wear appears at the tips of the outer primaries, which become dark by early summer. As the summer progresses, the edges of each outer primary darken with wear, but the centers remain mostly pale. The net effect is a darkening of the wingtip (which pushes the appearance closer to that of a Common), but the pattern is not uniform because the centers of the primaries remain pale.

The underwing pattern is particularly helpful in the identification process, not only for adults in alternate plumage but also for all other ages and plumages. The important features to note are the pattern of dark-and-light contrast on the trailing edge of the wing and the extent of translucence to the flight feathers. The various species of tern differ in the translucent nature of their flight feathers. Strongly translucent feathers will almost appear to glow on flying terns that are strongly backlit, providing useful clues to identification.

The secondaries and primaries of Arctic Terns are strongly translucent, making the trailing and outer edges of the wing a glowing white when viewed from below. Highlighting this translucent area is a narrow, well-defined, black "pencil-line" on the trailing edge of the wingtips that is formed by discrete blackish tips to the outer six to eight primaries (Figs. 4.72 and 4.73).

Only a small area (if any) of the wing of the Common Tern appears translucent, that being confined to the outer secondaries and inner primaries. The outer primaries are more extensively tipped blackish than are those of Arctics, and the black tips are not as sharply defined. The blackish tips create a broader and a somewhat fuzzy blackish trailing edge to the underwing. Comparing the trailing-edge pattern of a Common Tern with that of an Arctic would be analogous to comparing a drawing outlined by a black, wide-tipped felt marker with that outlined by a black, fine-tipped ballpoint pen.

Forster's Terns show little or no translucence to the underwing, and the pattern of the trailing edge of the primaries nearly duplicates that of the Common Tern, but the trailing edge is somewhat grayer (less blackish) and less defined.

Figure 4.72. Arctic Tern in definitive alternate plumage (adult summer). Note the diagnostic underwing pattern, with translucent remiges and the thin black trailing edge to the primaries. (Photographed in June near Nome, Alaska, by Kevin J. Zimmer.)

The color patterns of the body and tail can also be useful in separating these terns during the breeding season. Forster's Terns in breeding plumage will have white underparts, whereas the breast and belly of Common and Arctic terns are distinctly grayish (contrasting with the white vent and undertail region). These distinctions are often apparent on flying birds, because the gray underparts of Commons and Arctics contrast with the whitish underwing, a contrast that does not exist on Forster's. The gray is typically a shade darker and is more extensive on

Figure 4.73. Arctic Tern in definitive alternate plumage (adult summer). In addition to the primary pattern, note the small, rounded head and delicate bill. (Photographed in June near Nome, Alaska, by Kevin J. Zimmer.)

Arctics, usually extending up to include the throat and thereby isolating the white chin and cheek against the black cap. The gray of Commons is somewhat paler and typically extends only to the breast, leaving the entire throat and lower face white and lessening the contrast of these areas with the black cap. These differences cannot be relied on, because the entire throat of some Arctics is white (approximating the pattern of Commons), and some Commons may be as extensively dark gray below as typical Arctics. (For example, the Siberian subspecies of Common Tern, *Sterna hirundo longipennis,* which is seen regularly in Bering Sea regions of Alaska, is every bit as dark below as the Arctic Tern.)

The amount of contrast between the back, rump, and upper tail should also be noted. The gray back of Arctic and Common terns contrasts strongly with the white rump and upper tail. Forster's Terns are a paler shade of gray on the back, so they show less contrast between the back and the white rump. The upper tail of Forster's is also largely grayish (rather than white). The exact color pattern of the tail itself is diagnostic (except when birds are molting), but it can be difficult to see. The outer edges of the outermost tail feathers of Arctic Terns are narrowly blackish, but these are hard to see except at close range, and the tail of flying birds will usually appear all white. The outer edge of the outermost tail feathers of Common Terns is more extensively blackish than that of Arctics, and these dark edges are often apparent even at fair distances. The tail of Forster's Terns is itself very pale gray, and the outer feathers have the reverse pattern of that seen on Common and Arctic terns. That is, the inner web of the outer feather is dark gray, but the outer web is white. A good memory device is to remember that the tail patterns parallel the upper wing patterns: Arctics are the most uniform, showing no contrast on the upperwing or tail except at close range; Commons have both the outer wing and the outer tail contrastingly darker; and Forster's have both the outer wing and the outer tail contrastingly whiter. Remember also that the tail streamers on a standing Common will typically be concealed by the wingtips, whereas the longer streamers of Forster's and Arctics will extend visibly past the wingtip.

Bill color (and to a lesser extent, leg and foot color) is a helpful clue to the identity of adult terns in summer, but it is not diagnostic, as has been implied by some field guides. The bill, legs, and feet of alternate-plumaged Arctics are a deep, blood-red. The base of the bill, the legs, and the feet of Forster's tend toward a bright orange (or reddish orange), and the tip of the bill is extensively black. Commons are intermediate, with the base of the bill, the legs, and the feet typically being an orange-red to red. The Common's bill is usually, but not always, tipped black. These bill colors hold for the vast majority of individuals encountered, but occasional birds may show overlap with one of the other species.

A mark that can be helpful in identifying standing terns is the shape and extent of the black cap. When an Arctic Tern is viewed in profile, the black cap can be seen to extend down through the eye, nearly to the level of the gape. Only a sliver of white feathering shows between the black cap and the gape at the base of the bill, and the lower border of the black cap cuts straight back across the side of the face.

The cap pattern of the Common Tern is similar, but the black is slightly less extensive, leaving a more noticeable amount of white feathering between the gape and the lower margin of the cap. The lower border of the black cap of Forster's Terns forms an uneven line (as opposed to the straight cutoff of the Arctic and the Common) across the white face. The black is also less extensive, leaving a conspicuous amount of white feathering between the gape and the lower margin of the cap.

## Adult Basic Plumage

Of the three species under consideration, only Forster's undergoes significant molt into definitive basic plumage before late fall. Because the vast majority of Commons and all Arctics winter well south of the United States (and have generally left our area by early October), birders in this country are highly unlikely to encounter these two species in definitive-basic plumage.

Arctics forego molt completely until reaching the wintering grounds, but they may show some darkening to the bill by late summer. Both Forster's and Commons will begin molting the inner primaries in mid- to late summer, but, in Commons, this partial molt of primaries will not be accompanied by any significant change in the color of body plumage or soft parts. Some Commons may show some duskiness to the bill or some white flecking to the forehead, but most will be showing evidence of wear (uniformly dark outer primaries particularly) rather than molt.

Forster's Terns will begin the molt of head and body feathers concurrently with the primary molt. The bill will become blackish (often with some dull orange near the base or along the cutting edge), and the feet and legs will become dusky-orange or brownish. Once the molt of the primaries is complete, the upper wing will be uniformly pale, grayer on the coverts and whiter on the remiges (and will remain this way through spring). The underwing pattern and tail pattern will resemble those of alternate plumage, but the outer tail feathers will be visibly shorter. Of particular importance is the head and face pattern. The black cap of summer will be replaced by a mostly white forecrown, a hindcrown that is variably mottled with gray or dusky feathering, and a well-defined, black "bandit mask" covering the eye and much of the auriculars.

Common Terns in definitive basic plumage will also have a blackish bill (perhaps with some dull reddish along the cutting edge or at the base) and dusky-reddish or orange legs and feet. The gray breast and belly of breeding plumage will be replaced by white, and the rump will be washed with light gray. In all of these respects, it will resemble Forster's at the same season. However, the underwing and tail patterns seen in summer will be retained, although the outer tail feathers will be visibly shorter. The upperwing pattern of winter adults differs from that of breeding birds and of Forster's in having a conspicuous dark carpal bar aong the leading edge of the inner wing. The head and face pattern is also distinctive. The black cap is replaced by a white forehead and forecrown, a black nape, and a black hindcrown that extends forward to encompass the eye. This pattern is normally easily distinguished from the bandit mask of Forster's, but beware of occasional Forster's with more extensive dusky mottling on the hindcrown. Although on close inspection, such birds will always show a distinct black mask that is darker and not connected to the gray mottling, such resolution may not be possible at greater distances.

## Juvenal Plumage

Young terns in juvenal plumage will start appearing at colonies in mid- to late summer. Juveniles of all three species share certain structural distinctions from adults, including a shorter bill, shorter tail (only shallowly forked), and more rounded wingtips. All three species also show varying amounts of brown and buff barring and scalloping to the feathers of the mantle, scapulars, and wing coverts, as well as a buffy or brownish wash to the forehead and irregular brownish streaking and mottling to the nape. Such brown and buff markings create a plumage that is striking but ephemeral, being rapidly faded to gray by September. The distinctive underwing patterns are the same as those seen in adults.

Once the buff or brown wash to the forehead and the streaking to the hindcrown have faded, juveniles will show a head and face pattern like those of their respective adults in winter plumage. Arctics will have a white forehead with a black hindcrown that extends forward through the eye, similar to the pattern of Commons but with more extensive (and more sharply delineated) black through the midcrown and auriculars.

The upperwing patterns of the three species differ noticeably. Juvenile Commons have uniformly gray primaries, a bold blackish carpal bar along the leading edge of the wing between the body and the wrist, a less distinct dusky subterminal bar through the otherwise gray secondaries, and a pale panel on the coverts between the carpal bar and the secondary bar. The carpal bar is distinct even on the folded wing, which also reveals tertials and greater coverts with blackish subterminal crescents or bars. Juvenile Arctics also have a blackish carpal bar, but it is usually narrower and less distinct and may not show on standing birds. Juvenile Arctics typically have whitish (rather than gray) secondaries, without a dark bar. Juvenile Forster's have a fairly uniform gray upper wing, with primaries that darken slightly toward the outer wing and only a hint of a carpal bar (not visible on the folded wing) or a secondary bar.

Juvenile Arctics usually have an all-blackish bill. Forster's bills vary from mostly blackish to orangish with a black tip. Juvenile Commons frequently have a sharply delineated pinkish or orangish base to the bill, set off by a black tip.

## Subadult Plumage

Once juveniles have left their natal territory and migrated south, they molt into their first-basic plumage. From that time until they acquire their definitive alternate plumage (1 or 2 years later), most individuals will remain in the winter quarters rather than migrating north in spring with the adults. Small numbers of subadults will migrate north, at least part way, often remaining south of the breeding grounds to loiter with other nonbreeders on our southern coasts. Still other individuals may accompany adults the entire distance to the breeding areas. Wherever they happen to end up, it is these subadults that often cause problems for birders. The subadult stages rarely offer novel field marks not seen in juvenal or adult plumages. The main problem is that they tend to be out of sync with adults with respect to their molt cycles. Thus, we find subadults near the breeding grounds in early summer with head patterns that adults show in winter and showing amounts of primary wear displayed by adults in August. These subadults are often 2 or 3 months behind in their primary molt and, thus, arrive in summer with worn, blackish primaries at a time when the adults have fresh, gray or whitish primaries. By the end of summer, when adults are showing dark primaries, the subadults have just completed molt into fresh, pale primaries. This is the case only for Forster's and Common terns, because Arctics complete their primary molt well south of the United States. Further trouble is caused by 2-year-old birds, which often look like breeding-plumaged adults but have worn (and thus darker) primaries. Forster's Terns in such plumages are frequently mistaken for Common Terns in places where the latter species is rare.

Because there are numerous possible permutations of plumage and soft-part coloration in subadult birds, all subject to individual variation in expression and timing, I will not cover the subject in detail here. The most important thing is to be aware of the possibility that subadult birds will exhibit either out of season plumages or strange combinations of adult and immature characters. Careful attention to structural characters and details of underwing pattern will usually allow the correct identification to be made.

For further discussions see Grant and Scott 1969, Scott and Grant 1969, Hume and Grant 1974, Russell 1976, Cramp 1985, Kaufman 1987b and 1990, Wilds 1993, and Olsen and Larsson 1995.

## Elegant versus Royal versus Caspian Tern

The Elegant, Royal, and Caspian terns, the largest of North American terns, are often somewhat confusing to beginning birders or to those who have not dealt with one of the species before. With careful attention to a few structural and plumage characters they can often be readily separated.

The three species form a size continuum: Caspian is the largest, Royal is intermediate, and Elegant is the smallest. Size as a distinguishing character is most obvious on Caspian Terns, which are positively massive and, in fact, approach small Herring Gulls in size. Both the Royal and Elegant are much smaller and more slender in build. The Elegant is decidedly smaller and more slender than Royal, but this distinction is used safely only when the two species are side by side. When such comparisons are possible, an additional character that may prove useful on standing birds is relative leg length. The Royal shows little visible leg above the ankle, giving it a squat, close-to-the-ground look. The Elegant shows more leg above the ankle, giving it a longer-legged look. Bill structure and color are more reliable for identifying these terns (Figs. 4.74 through 4.77). Caspians have a very stout bill that is enormous by comparison with the Elegant and is still conspicuously larger than that of the Royal. The bill of Caspian Terns is a deep, blood-red and has a dusky subterminal band and a pale tip that is not always conspicuous. The other two species have a bill that is more orange (less red), and each lacks the dusky band near the tip. Juveniles of both species have a bill that is more yellowish. Elegant Terns have proportionately longer bills than Royals, and their bills are distinctly thinner with more of a droop to the tip and very little angle to the gonys (Figs. 4.75 and 4.76).

The face and head pattern are also important distinguishing points. All three species attain a full black cap during the breeding season, but they show varying degrees of whitening on the forehead and crown later in the year. The black cap is retained for the shortest time by the Royal Tern, which is white-crowned for most of the year. Elegants too will whiten on the forehead and crown after breeding, but they retain more black, making them look less bald than the Royals. At least one of the standard guides has reversed the face patterns of nonbreeding Royals and Elegants. On nonbreeding Elegants the more extensive black of the rear-head and nape extends forward to encircle the eye, making it fairly inconspicuous (Figs. 4.75 and 4.76). On nonbreeding Royals, the black of the rear-head usually stops just short of the eye or meets it posteriorally, making the eye conspicuous against the more extensively white face (Figs. 4.74, 4.76, and 4.77). Note also the shaggier rear crest of the Elegant. Caspian Terns (Fig. 4.77) lighten on the forehead only enough to give a salt-and-pepper impression, but they never attain the pure white

Figure 4.74. Royal Terns in basic plumage. Note the bill structure and the distribution of black on the head and face. (Photo by Kevin J. Zimmer.)

Figure 4.75. Elegant Tern in basic plumage. In comparison with the Royal Tern, note the thinner bill and more extensive black feathering on the face and crest. (Photo by Kevin J. Zimmer.)

forehead and crown of Royals and Elegants. Many Elegants will appear to have a rosy-pink blush to the white underparts. This is typically most apparent on alternate-plumaged birds, but it is frequently seen in late summer and early fall as well.

Wing and tail pattern and structure are also useful aids. Caspians have the widest wings and the least fork to the tail. Their primaries have mostly pale outer webs and mostly dark inner webs, so that the upper surface of the outer part of the wing appears neutral gray, whereas the undersurface of the wingtip appears almost wholly blackish (contrasting with the rest of the underwing, which is

Figure 4.76. Royal Tern (right foreground, with outstretched wing) and Elegant Tern (center) in basic plumage. Compare the bill structure and the distribution of black on the head and face. (Photo by Kevin J. Zimmer.)

Figure 4.77. Caspian Tern (rear center) next to Royal Tern (both in basic plumage). Note the shorter, heavier, red and black-tipped bill of the Caspian. The Caspian also has a more extensively black crown, giving a salt-and-pepper look to the rear crown. Birds in the foreground include four Sandwich Terns and another Royal Tern. (Photo by Barry R. Zimmer.)

whitish). Royals and Elegants by contrast, have more slender wings and a much more deeply forked tail. The tips and outer webs of their outer several primaries are blackish gray, and the inner webs are pale. Thus, their wing pattern is nearly the reverse of the Caspian's. Both Royals and Elegants show a prominent backish wedge on the upper side of the outer primaries, but the underwing is almost completely white except for a dusky trailing edge to the outer primaries. As in other terns, the dark areas of the wing darken with wear in these three species. Juvenile Royals and Elegants show three dark bars (formed by the darker lesser coverts, greater coverts, and secondaries) across the inner portion of the upper wing, and these contrast conspicuously with the pale-gray panel formed by the median coverts. Juvenile Caspians have lightly marked upperwings whose patterns are inconspicuous and only mildy contrasting.

## Common versus Thick-billed Murre

The Common Murre is one of the most common and familiar of alcids, particularly on the Pacific Coast, where breeding colonies extend from northern Alaska south to California. The Thick-billed Murre is an abundant alcid of northern latitudes, overlapping almost completely with the Common Murre in Alaska, but it is rare south of British Columbia on the West Coast, occurring casually south to central California. The two species can be difficult to separate at any season, and distant birds can be impossible.

An important distinction is that Thick-billeds in any plumage are blacker above, whereas Commons are more of an ashy, brownish slate. Although these color differences may not be apparent under some light conditions, they remain one of the better distinctions on flying birds. Particularly helpful on flying birds in alternate plumage is the presence or absence of contrast between the throat and foreneck and the upper parts. Thick-billeds are uniformly blackish on the top of the head, face, throat, and foreneck and show little or no contrast in these areas. Commons are darkest (more blackish) on the chin, throat, and foreneck, and paler, ashier brown on the crown, nape, and hindneck, creating a contrast between upper parts and underparts. Strong sunlight obliterates much of these differences, making birds of both species appear brown-tinted. Low light can have the opposite effect, making both species appear black.

Bill shape is noticeably different between the two species (Figs. 4.78 and 4.79). The Thick-billed has a relatively shorter, stouter bill, with an evenly decurved culmen and the gonydeal angle located at roughly the midpoint on the lower mandible. The bill of Commons is more slender and tapered, with the culmen quite straight along the basal half and decurving distally, and the gonydeal angle is located closer to the base of the bill. Pacific populations of Thick-billeds have a slightly longer and thinner bill than do some Atlantic populations. Most adult Thick-billeds have a whitish or pale-gray stripe along the cutting edge of the upper mandible. This stripe typically becomes less distinct in winter and may be lost entirely on some individuals. Contrary to some published statements, this

Figure 4.78. Thick-billed Murre in alternate (breeding) plumage. In addition to bill structure and the white tomial stripe, note how the white on the foreneck forms an inverted V. (Photographed in June at St. Paul Island, Alaska, by Kevin J. Zimmer.)

Figure 4.79. Common Murres in alternate (breeding) plumage. Note the bill structure and the gentler, more rounded, inverted U formed by the white on the foreneck. Compare also the general tone of the plumage with that of the blacker Thick-billed Murre at the extreme left of the picture. (Photographed in June at St. Paul Island, Alaska, by Kevin J. Zimmer.)

white stripe, which is diagnostic when seen, is noticeable even at some distance (at least on most adults in alternate plumage).

The white of the underparts terminates in a sharp point or inverted V on the black foreneck of alternate-plumaged Thick-billeds, whereas on Commons the white ends in a more gently rounded, shallow, inverted U. This mark is often apparent on both standing (Figs. 4.78 and 4.79) and swimming birds, but it is subject to postural influences and should not be the sole basis for identification. The flanks and sides of Commons are mottled or streaked with gray-brown (not always conspicuously), whereas those of Thick-billeds are unmarked.

Basic-plumaged birds are easier. The chin and lower face of Commons are white, as is the rear part of the cheek, which is divided by a conspicuous blackish post-ocular line. Thick-billeds are more extensively dark-headed and neatly bicolored on the sides of the head. Their black crown extends down the sides of the face through the eye and upper cheek and ends on a straight line projecting rearward from the chin. Commons molt into basic plumage very early, and most birds will have the conspicuous winter face pattern by September. Conversely, Thick-billeds retain their entirely dark head feathering longer, accentuating the differences between the two species in fall.

The greatest difficulty comes with molting birds in transitional plumage. Common Murres begin their prealternate molt in late winter or early spring (at least a few months before Thick-billeds); birds in transition may have the upper half of the head entirely dark and the chin and throat still white (approximating the basic plumage of Thick-billeds). There always seems to be at least a few Common Murres in odd, delayed molt in fall as well.

Juveniles and first-basic birds of both species resemble their respective adults in basic plumage, but they are smaller and shorter-billed. Juvenile and first-basic Commons have the further distinction of having unmarked sides and flanks, unlike adult Commons.

Subadult murres in their first summer after hatching (i.e., when nearly a year old) frequently cause confusion in Alaska. Subadult Thick-billeds essentially retain a first-basic plumage in which the upper parts are more brownish, and most birds show a dark bar or half-collar on the side of the neck (similar to a Craveri's Murrelet). Such "winter-plumaged" birds are commonly seen away from the breeding colonies in June, long before the young of the year have hatched. Common Murres in first-alternate plumage resemble breeding adults, but they can be separated by the paler, browner wings (with worn juvenal feathers) and often by white mottling on the dark chin and throat.

## Kittlitz's Murrelets

The Kittlitz's Murrelet is a poorly known, small alcid that is essentially endemic to Alaska, where it occurs from the coast of the Chukchi Sea south to the Aleutians and eastward along much of the south coast. The center of abundance seems to be roughly from Kodiak Island to Glacier Bay, where it is locally common. They disperse to adjacent seas after breeding, and occasional vagrants are recorded south of the breeding range. Because of its restricted range, it is one of the more highly sought-after birds by summer visitors to Alaska. Unfortunately, overly eager birders often mistake the more widespread and generally more common Marbled Murrelet for Kittlitz's. In any plumage, Kittlitz's is most likely to be confused with Marbled.

Alternate-plumaged adults (the most likely plumage of Kittlitz's to be encountered) of the two species look quite different in the hand or in close photographs, but they can be amazingly difficult to separate under normal field conditions. Of all other alcids only the Long-billed Murrelet of Asia comes close to duplicating the essentially brown and mottled or speckled breeding plumage of the Kittlitz's and Marbled Murrelets.

With good views, the shorter bill of Kittlitz's imparts a distinctly snub-nosed look compared with the Marbled (Fig. 4.80), but this may require some comparative experience to safely assess. The two species also differ in general color tone and pattern. Marbleds appear dark brown above (the feathers of the back are chestnut-brown with black fringes, but these distinctions are seldom apparent in the field) and paler (but distinctly mottled) below. The crown and face are noticeably darker than the chin, throat, and lower cheeks, creating a dark-capped appearance (the dark cap extending through and below the eye). The pale scapulars

Figure 4.80. Marbled Murrelet (top) versus Kittlitz's Murrelet (bottom) (both in alternate plumage). (Artwork by Shawneen Finnegan.)

are often visible and contrast strongly with the dark-brown back and wings. Kittlitz's Murrelets are in fact more streaked, speckled, and mottled than Marbleds (especially on the upper parts), but because this speckling and streaking are fine and uniformly distributed (except on the white belly, which shows only in flight), the effect in the field is one of a more uniform sandy-brown or golden-brown coloration. The scapulars seldom appear as noticeably pale as they do in Marbleds, and the face usually looks pale golden-brown, accentuating the dark eye. Some individuals will give the appearance of having a slightly darker cap, but in such cases the cap is narrow across the crown, not even extending to the eyes, and has a gray tone to it. Although all of these differences are readily seen at very close range, they can be difficult to judge on birds at longer distances, particularly when feathers are wet (a condition that tends to obliterate differences in color tone).

Flying birds, particularly those that are just taking off or landing, are the easiest to identify. Kittlitz's has the entire belly and vent region white (with minimal scattered brown barring on some individuals, but this is rarely visible in the field), contrasting strongly with the dark underwings and the densely speckled chest. Marbleds are variably marked below, with most individuals being heavily scaled or barred with brown all the way to the vent. Some Marbleds, especially molting adults in transition, or subadult birds in a first-alternate plumage, will be more extensively pale on the belly and less densely barred on the chest. Even these birds will rarely lend the impression of having more than half of the underparts clean-white and sharply cut off from the heavily marked throat and chest.

The white outer tail feathers of Kittlitz's are diagnostic and are easily seen when the bird first takes off from the water or spreads its tail when coming in for a landing. They are not normally visible on birds in direct flight. The color of the tail feathers is frequently misinterpreted because Marbleds (which have an entirely dark tail) have white feathering in the uppertail coverts at the sides of the rump, and this can be mistaken for white outer tail feathers, particularly on birds that have just launched into flight.

Basic-plumaged and juvenile Kittlitz's can be separated from like-plumaged Marbleds by their mostly whitish face (white from the throat all of the way up to above the eye); by the broader, more complete white collar and dark breast band; by the thin white trailing edge to the secondaries; and by the white outer tail feathers. Marbleds in the same-aged plumages have a dark cap that extends to below the eye; have only a partial dark breast band and white collar; lack white in the secondaries; and have an entirely dark tail.

Basic-plumaged Least Auklets are also dark above and white below with white in the scapulars, but they are positively tiny on the water (much smaller than Kittlitz's), lack a dark breast band and a white collar, and have an entirely blackish face (the black extends well below the eye).

As do other murrelets, Kittlitz's and Marbleds have the annoying habit of jumping up and flying straight away from an oncoming boat before field marks can be properly noted. You'll definitely want to station yourself on the bow of the boat if you hope to see this bird well.

## Craveri's versus Xantus's Murrelet

Craveri's and Xantus's Murrelets are similar small alcids that present a difficult identification problem to West Coast observers, a problem that is usually compounded by less-than-ideal viewing conditions. Xantus's Murrelet is represented by two subspecies: a southern breeding form *(Endomychura hypoleucus hypoleucus)* that nests on islands off the coast of Baja and western Mexico and a northern breeding form *(E. h. scrippsi)* that nests on islands off the coast of southern California. The former shows up, but rarely, in our waters in fall as the result of post-breeding dispersal; the latter also disperses northward (regularly to Washington) in late summer and fall. Craveri's Murrelet breeds on islands in the Gulf of California and disperses northward in small numbers to southern California (regularly to Monterey) after breeding.

All three forms are very similar in general appearance (Fig. 4.81). They are dark above and light below and lack the white scapulars of the Marbled Murrelet. All three ride low in the water, but, when feeding, they keep their neck held high (not tucked as other murrelets do). Contrary to the way they are pictured in many guides, these murrelets swim so low that they are dark to the waterline, often concealing their white sides.

Xantus's Murrelets of the *hypoleucus* subspecies are readily identified by the distribution of white on the face. These birds have extensively white cheeks, with the white circling up in front of and above the eye, forming a white spectacle that is conspicuous even at great distances (Figure 4.81). The other two forms have incomplete white eye rings (in the form of narrow white crescents above and below the eye) that are much smaller and that can usually be seen only at close range.

Figure 4.81. Murrelets. Craveri's (left), *hypoleucus* subspecies of Xantus's (head only), and *scrippsi* subspecies of Xantus's (right). Compare the distribution of black and white on the face and sides of the chest, as well as the underwing pattern. (Artwork by Shawneen Finnegan.)

The main problem for U.S. birders comes in trying to separate *scrippsi* Xantus's from Craveri's. Most guides emphasize differences between the two in underwing color. Xantus's typically have bright white underwings, whereas those of Craveri's are variable but always much duskier (lightest on the axillaries) (Fig. 4.81). Unfortunately, small alcids typically fly at great speeds with whirring wings, making underwing color a difficult character to judge. The task is made harder by the tendency of murrelets to jump from the path of the boat and fly straight away.

One plumage character that can be helpful in identifying flying or sitting individuals is the dark half-collar of Craveri's that juts down on the side of the neck onto the white breast (Figure 4.81). This mark is reminiscent of the similar half-collar seen in winter-plumaged Spotted Sandpipers and is not found in Xantus's Murrelets. Unfortunately, this half-collar is usually hidden on murrelets that are hugging the water, but it can often be seen just as a bird jumps into flight.

A structural difference that is valuable is the length of the bill. Xantus's has a relatively stubby bill, whereas that of Craveri's is longer and thinner. This difference in bill length is accentuated by a plumage character: the position on the face of the line of demarcation between black and white feathering. On Xantus's the black of the crown extends only as far as the gape line of the bill, and the chin is white. The white feathering immediately adjacent to the base of the black bill serves to isolate the bill and delimit it, accentuating its shorter length. On Craveri's the black of the face extends to the bottom side of the bill, including the feathering at the base of the chin. Because the black feathering completely surrounds the black bill, the effect is one of lengthening the already slightly longer bill because the bill is in essence continuous with the black of the face (Fig. 4.81).

Craveri's also averages slightly darker and browner above than Xantus's. This difference is readily observable in the hand but may be of dubious utility under most field conditions.

## Common versus Lesser Nighthawk

Most birders rely solely on voice or geographic range to identify Common and Lesser nighthawks. Although both methods are often the easiest identifiers, neither is of any help when silent birds are encountered in regions where both species occur. Nighthawks can be identified visually, although the characters used are subtle and may require some practice.

The only visual mark pointed out by most guides is the position of the white bar in the wing. On the Lesser Nighthawk it is closer to the tip, and on the Common Nighthawk it is closer to the body. This distinction is fairly subtle and may require some experience to be used with confidence. Much more distinctive (and unmentioned in most field guides) is the difference in wing shape (Fig. 4.82). The outer primary of Commons is the longest, giving the wings a very tapered, pointed look. The outer primary of Lessers is typically shorter than the adjacent inner one, giving a more rounded appearance. Although the difference is noticeable, it is also relative; that is, the wing of a Lesser will still look pointed compared with that of a Common Poorwill. Beware also that there is much individual variation in wing shape among nighthawks and that, although most individual Common and Lesser nighthawks will conform to the above patterns, there are some ex-

Figure 4.82. Wings of Common Nighthawk (left) versus Lesser Nighthawk (right). Note the structural differences and the position of the white bar. (Artwork by Mimi Hoppe Wolf.)

ceptions. The differences in wing shape are accentuated by the differing wing lengths of the two species: longer in Common, shorter in Lesser. As might be expected, the structural differences of the wings result in different flight characteristics. Commons tend to fly higher and with deeper, more emphatic strokes (reminiscent of Black Tern). Lessers typically cruise lower with a shallower, more fluttery stroke. Again, these distinctions are relative and require some practice to discern.

Other plumage distinctions are complicated by sexual differences in both species and by geographic variation in the Common. Males of both species have a white tail band but females do not. Males also have a white throat, whereas females have a buffy throat. Males of both species have white wing bars, a trait shared by female Commons. Female Lessers have buffy wing bars that are less distinctive. In general, Lessers are more brownish, and Commons are more gray. This coloring is subject to geographic variation in Commons, with eastern birds being darker brown and many western birds being lighter gray. Lessers are more evenly colored above, whereas Commons show contrast between the paler wing coverts and darker back. The two species also differ slightly in underpart coloration. Commons have a whiter base color on the belly and vent with more strongly contrasting barring. Lessers are buffier in those regions, and the barring is less distinctive.

Calls are the most obvious difference. The Common gives a loud, nasal "peent," and the Lesser gives a wavering trill that often varies in pace and intensity. In the Southwest (where the two species overlap), habitat differences are also helpful. Lessers are more common in arid deserts, and Commons are typical of more mesic, usually montane areas. The two often overlap in lowland riparian settings that are bordered by desert. The Common is the more likely species to be seen flying about in the daytime, but Lessers are occasionally seen cruising in the first few hours of daylight.

For more information see Garrett and Dunn 1982.

## Hummingbirds

Fourteen species of hummingbird regularly breed within the area covered by this book, and four others (White-eared, Berylline, Green Violet-ear, and Plain-capped Starthroat) are visitors of varying regularity. Adult males of most species present few problems in identification, but females and immature birds of some species can be problematical. Hummingbirds present some special problems in field identification. Their iridescent colors can appear to change dramatically under different light conditions. A simple turn of the head can make the gorget of a male Rufous Hummingbird go from dull brown to chartreuse to red-orange. Similarly, a male Broad-billed or Magnificent can appear mostly blackish in the shade, only to become a kaleidoscope of color the second it enters the sunlight. To make matters worse, you are likely to see birds whose forehead (and, to a lesser extent, throat and chest) is covered with pollen, which lends strange colors and patterns that do not fit any species. Subtle structural differences in bill length, bill shape, and tail shape are important in the separation of females of some species, but the use of these marks is complicated by the fact that juveniles of most species are shorter-billed than adults and may show slight differences in the shape of some of the tail feathers (particularly the outer ones). Most juveniles initially resemble adult females, but young males of many species go through some transitional stages in which they show blotchy, confusing patterns. Finally, hybridization is more common among hummingbirds than in many other groups, further muddying the picture.

Because there are so many species in this group, and because some of the species can be confused with several other species, I will offer capsule summaries of the potential identification pitfalls one species at a time. The following accounts focus primarily on identifying adult females and immatures.

### Black-chinned Hummingbird

The Black-chinned Hummingbird is one of the most common and widespread of the western hummers, and, as such, it makes a convenient yardstick with which to compare other species. The identification of adult males is straightforward, but females and immature males can be confused with females and immatures of Anna's, Costa's, and Ruby-throated. All four species are essentially green above and some shade of pale grayish below, with dusky auriculars, some white behind the eye, variable amounts of dark speckling on the throat, and most rectrices tipped black-and-white.

Female Black-chinneds and Ruby-throateds are not safely separable in the field on current knowledge. They are extremely similar vocally and in all plumage and structural characters, and neither species should be identified out-of-range except in the hand. Black-chinneds on average are longer-billed (but juvenile Black-chinneds might have a short bill), and are more often grayish green on the forehead (Ruby-throateds are usually greener on the forehead). Compared with Anna's, Black-chinneds are slightly smaller and paler below, lack the green on the sides usually seen in Anna's, have a more patterned look to the face with more extensively dusky auriculars and more noticeable white behind the eye, and have a proportionately longer and thinner bill with more decurvature at the tip. Black-chinneds routinely give a soft "tchew" call note and tend to simultaneously pump and flare their tail when hovering. Anna's usually give a sharper "sik" call note and typically hover with their tail more closed and held down in line with the axis of the body. Costa's are more similar to Black-chinneds but are slightly smaller, with underparts that are usually a paler, cleaner-looking gray. They also have a slightly shorter and straighter bill (but juvenile Black-chinneds can have bill structure identical to that of Costa's) and a more rounded tail. The mark that I find most helpful for separating the two species is back color. Female Costa's usually strike me as appearing distinctly grayish green above, whereas Black-chinneds are more of a true green. As always, light conditions must be taken into account when assessing such features. The call notes of the two species are diagnostic, Costa's gives a hard "tik."

## Costa's Hummingbird

Adult male Costa's Hummingbirds are generally distinctive but could be confused with male Lucifer and Anna's. All three species have elongate gorget feathers that extend down the sides of the face. Lucifer Hummingbirds have a distinctly decurved bill (the Costa's bill is straight) and a deeply forked tail that is normally held folded in a spiky point. It also has a green crown, unlike the other two species. The Lucifer does typically show some white separation on the sides of the neck between the purple gorget and the green nape (as does Costa's, but not Anna's). Anna's is bigger and longer-tailed than Costa's and has a thicker (but similarly straight and proportionately short) bill. Gorget and forehead color are more rose-red in Anna's and purple in Costa's, and the gorget whiskers are distinctly longer in the latter species.

Female Costa's are smaller and paler (less dingy) below than female Anna's, and they lack the green sides. Compared with Black-chinneds they are slightly smaller, with a more rounded tail, and with a shorter, straighter bill. Costa's averages paler gray below and more grayish green above. Note also the vocal distinctions mentioned in the Black-chinned account.

## Anna's Hummingbird

Female Anna's Hummingbirds are similar to Black-chinneds, Ruby-throateds, and Costa's, but they are larger than all three and have dingier, darker gray underparts and mottled greenish sides. Anna's has a proportionately short, straight bill, that is thicker than that of Costa's. Anna's bill looks even shorter relative to its larger body size. By contrast, Black-chinneds look slightly long-billed, with (usually) a slight decurvature at the tip of the bill. Adult female Anna's usually show several red flecks concentrated as a small patch in the center of the throat. This is a distinction from adult females of the other species, but beware that juvenile Anna's lack this red patch, and immature males of the other species may show similar patches. Note also the call note differences mentioned in the preceding accounts.

Male Anna's can be confused with male Costa's (see that account) and with male Lucifers, but they should be readily separable with decent views.

## Ruby-throated Hummingbird

In most of the West, Ruby-throated Hummingbirds are rare vagrants at best. Males are easily identified, although they could conceivably be confused with male Broad-taileds. Ruby-throateds are smaller and have a narrower, shorter tail; their gorget is a scarlet red, and the blackish chin extends back on the sides of the face.

Broad-taileds are heftier and have a broader tail, a rose-red gorget, a bluer-green back, and no black on the chin. In addition, adult male Broad-taileds (except for molting birds) make a piercing metallic trill when they fly. Ruby-throateds fly silently. Females are not separable in the field from female Black-chinneds, although they are slightly shorter-billed (beware of juvenile Black-chinneds, which are also shorter-billed than adults) and greener on the forehead (Black-chinneds more often look grayish green on the forehead). Distinctions from female Costa's and Anna's are as noted for Black-chinned.

## Broad-tailed Hummingbird

Adult male Broad-tailed Hummingbirds are distinctive (see the discussion in the Ruby-throated account) and are usually identified by the piercing metallic trill produced by their wings long before they are seen. Be aware that male Broad-taileds lose the trill for a short period when molting and that both Rufous and Allen's hummingbirds (neither of which is likely to be confused with male Broad-taileds) produce a shrill whine in flight (although this sound is a pale shadow of the trill produced by Broad-taileds).

Females are most easily confused with female Rufous, Allen's, and Calliope, all of which share (along with Broad-tailed) the traits of contrastingly colored rufous or buff sides, flanks, and undertail coverts; some rufous at the base of the rectrices; and the tail typically held cocked horizontally when hovering. Broad-taileds are slightly (but noticeably) larger than Rufous and Allen's, and they are distinctly bigger than Calliope. The size difference is most apparent in overall bulk and in the size of the tail. Broad-taileds are more turquoise green dorsally, without rufous on the back or rump, and they are mostly whitish below with a buffy wash (pale and washed-out in many individuals) on the sides, flanks, and undertail coverts. The throat is lightly speckled dusky. The outer rectrices are rufous at the base, with a black subterminal band and white tips. Rufous and Allen's are more emerald green above and have more contrasting rusty (not buff) sides, flanks, and undertail coverts and extensive rufous in the tail. Adult females and young males tend to show some orange or reddish spotting on the throat, whereas juvenile females may be speckled dusky like Broad-taileds. The darker rufous tones of the sides, combined with the more extensive rufous in the tail and the distinctly smaller and more slender build should allow ready separation of both Rufous and Allen's from Broad-taileds.

## Calliope Hummingbird

Male Calliope Hummingbirds are unique and unlikely to be confused. Females and immatures are like tiny versions of female Broad-taileds, with pale cinnamon-buff sides, flanks, and undertail coverts and with the throat lightly speckled dusky. They have only slight amounts of rufous at the base of the outer rectrices, and this may not be visible in the field. Calliopes look tiny even by hummingbird standards and are particularly short-billed and short-tailed. A good clue is that the folded wingtips project beyond the tail on perched birds. Hovering birds typically hold the tail cocked at or above the horizontal. Broad-taileds, although the most similar to Calliope in plumage, are unlikely to be confused by experienced observers because of the sheer difference in overall size and bulk, tail size, and wingtip projection. Rufous and Allen's are more similar in size, but they have darker rufous (not buff) sides, flanks, and vent and show conspicuous rufous at the base of the tail. Rufous and Allen's also tend to have conspicuous orange or reddish spotting on the throat (but juvenile females have dusky speckled throats).

## Rufous versus Allen's Hummingbirds

Adult male Rufous and Allen's hummingbirds with a full red-orange gorget can generally be distinguished from one another on the basis of back color (rufous in Rufous and green in Allen's). Occasional adult male Rufous Hummingbirds are reported to have a mostly green back, so green-backed males (Rufous or Allen's) outside the normal range of Allen's may require extreme care in identification. Birds with an entirely rufous back are safely identified as Rufous.

Females and immatures of these two species are basically inseparable in the field. In the hand, the two are separated on the basis of the shape of different tail feathers, but rectrix shape varies with sex and age within each species. Other plumage characters are so intraspecifically variable that they are of no help in separating the two species from one another.

## Magnificent Hummingbird

Adult male Magnificent Hummingbirds are unmistakable. Females resemble females of the slightly larger Blue-throated Hummingbird, but they show much less white tipping on the corners of the tail and less white behind the eye. They also have a markedly long, straight bill. Female Blue-throateds have bold white tips on the corners of the tail and a more distinct whitish supercilium; they appear proportionately shorter-billed and longer-tailed. Beware of immature male Magnificents in transitional stages. With purple crown, green gorget, white postocular marks, and pale breast mottled with green, they have been mistaken for the much rarer White-eared Hummingbird. The latter is smaller and proportionately shorter-billed and has a bold whitish postocular stripe, blacker auriculars, and usually at least some reddish color at the base of the bill.

## Blue-throated Hummingbird

Male Blue-throated Hummingbirds, with their large size; large, boldly white-tipped tail; conspicuous white eyebrow; and sky blue throat are unlikely to be confused. Females of this, our largest hummingbird, are unlikely to be mistaken for anything except female Magnificents (see above).

## Broad-billed Hummingbird

The glossy, dark green male Broad-billed Hummingbirds, with their deep blue throat and chest, white vent, forked blue-black tail, and black-tipped, bright red bill are unlikely to be mistaken. Females and immatures are dingy gray below, with a dusky auricular patch, a thin whitish postocular stripe, and a reddish base to the mandible (not always easy to see). They are most likely to be mistaken for female White-eareds, which are shorter-billed and have bolder and broader whitish postocular stripes, more contrastingly dark auriculars, and whiter underparts disked with green. Call notes are helpful: Broad-billeds give a soft chatter that is instantly reminiscent of the chatter of a Ruby-crowned Kinglet, whereas White-eareds have a harder, metallic chatter that is more like the chatter of the Bridled Titmouse.

## White-eared Hummingbird

Adult male White-eared Hummingbirds, with their broad white postocular stripe, purple crown and chin, green gorget, and black-tipped bright red bill, are unmistakable. Many of the birds that show up at feeders in southeastern Arizona are subadult males with duller colors, mottled patterns, and a darker bill. The combination of bold whitish postocular stripe (longer and broader than in other hummers) and short, reddish-based bill should still allow ready identification. Females can be confused with female Broad-billeds (see above).

## Lucifer Hummingbird

Both sexes of the Lucifer Hummingbird have a more distinctly decurved bill than other U.S. hummers, and they have a proportionately long tail. Males have a deeply forked tail, which is usually held closed in a spiky point. Males also have a purplish gorget with long side whiskers like Costa's (but shorter), but they have a green crown. Females have dusky auriculars and a pale postocular stripe, lending a more strongly patterned look than is seen on the face of females of many other species. The underparts are variably buffy: rich and distinct in some individuals, faded and nearly whitish in others. The outer rectrices are basally rufous (often hard to see), with black subterminal bands and white tips. Female Lucifers can be separated from female Black-chinneds by the more decurved bill, usually buffy underparts, stronger face pattern, rufous base to rectrices, and call notes (squeaky chatter).

## Violet-crowned Hummingbird

The Violet-crowned Hummingbird is large, distinctly bronzy above, and nearly immaculate white below and has a thick, bright-red, black-tipped bill. Many birds lack noticeable purple on the crown, but you won't need that mark to identify this bird.

## Buff-bellied Hummingbird

With its bronzy green back, emerald green throat, buffy belly, rufous tail, and black-tipped red bill, the Buff-bellied Hummingbird is unlikely to be mistaken within its limited U.S. range.

# Sapsuckers

Four species of woodpecker of the genus *Sphyrapicus,* commonly known as sap-suckers, occur in western North America. One of these, the Williamson's Sap-sucker, is so distinct in all plumages as to be unlikely to be confused, and thus, is not considered here. The remaining three species, Red-breasted, Red-naped, and Yellow-bellied, interbreed to a limited extent where their ranges come into contact and were formerly treated as a single variable species. The field identification of all three species is complicated by individual variation, sexual variation, and the pos-sibility of various hybrid combinations.

The three species under consideration actually consist of four named forms. Neither the Yellow-bellied Sapsucker nor the Red-naped Sapsucker varies geo-graphically, but the Red-breasted Sapsucker encompasses two subspecies: a north-western form *(S. ruber ruber),* which breeds from southeastern Alaska south along the coastal slope to Oregon, and a more southern from *(S. r. daggetti),* which nests from the Cascades south through northwestern California, the Sierras, and spar-ingly to the mountains of San Diego County. The nominate *ruber* subspecies is largely sedentary, but the more southerly breeding *daggetti* winters throughout the lowlands of California's coastal slope south to Baja. The Red-naped Sapsucker breeds throughout the Rocky Mountains and associated ranges, from southeast-ern British Columbia and southwestern Alberta south to Arizona, west to the east-ern portion of the Cascades and the Sierra Nevada and east to the western edge of the Great Plains. It winters throughout the lowlands of the Southwest and spar-ingly to coastal California. The Yellow-bellied Sapsucker breeds throughout the northeastern United States and through the deciduous forests of Canada west to western Alberta and northeastern British Columbia. It is highly migratory and winters throughout the southeastern and south-central United States and south through Mexico to Central America. It is a regular vagrant west to California.

In the field, these four forms break down into two obvious problem pairs on the basis of plumage similarities. The first identification problem involves the separa-tion of Yellow-bellied from Red-naped sapsuckers. The second problem involves the separation of the two subspecies of the Red-breasted (*ruber* from *daggetti*). A third problem involves the separation of southern Red-breasteds (*daggetti*) from Red-breasted × Red-naped hybrids.

For more information on sapsuckers, see Devillers 1970, Dunn 1978e, DeBene-dictis 1979, Kaufman 1988b and 1990, Landing 1991, and Lehman 1991.

## Yellow-bellied versus Red-naped Sapsucker

The Yellow-bellied and the Red-naped sapsuckers have the same basic head and facial pattern: a red crown bordered by black, black auriculars that continue down onto the sides of the neck, a white postocular stripe that continues back to the nape, a black nape that is interrupted by a white or red horizontal bar, a broad white moustachial stripe, and a black malar stripe that joins with a black breast shield in framing the throat and chin (Fig. 4.83).

Attempts to separate the two species should begin with an effort to sex the individual in question. Throat color and the completeness of the black frame that borders the throat are the keys (Fig. 4.83). Female Yellow-bellieds are the easiest. They have an entirely white throat that is completely framed by the black malar stripes and the black breast shield. No other sapsucker will show this combination. A small minority of female Yellow-bellieds also have a black (rather than a red) crown, another diagnostic mark if present. Female Red-napeds typically have a bicolored throat; the chin and upper throat are whitish, and the lower throat is red. The black frame surrounding the throat is usually complete, although the black malar stripes are frequently thinner than on Yellow-bellieds. Males of both species have an entirely red throat, but they differ in the completeness of the surrounding black frame. The red throat of male Yellow-bellieds is completely contained

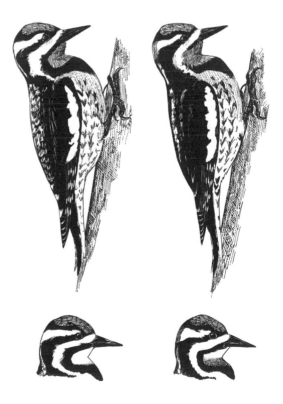

Figure 4.83. Male Yellow-bellied Sapsucker (upper left), male Red-naped Sapsucker (upper right), female Yellow-bellied Sapsucker (lower left), and female Red-naped Sapsucker (lower right). Compare the width of the white facial stripes, broken versus unbroken black "frame" to the throat, throat and nape colors, and distribution of pale coloring on the back. (Artwork by Shawneen Finnegan.)

within the black frame. The red of the throat of male Red-napeds spills over at its margins, interrupting the black malar stripes and often intruding into the black of the breast shield, which then appears less extensive and more ragged around the upper margin than the breast shield of Yellow-bellieds. The fly in the ointment is that female Red-napeds often have very little white on the throat; it sometimes is restricted to just a few feathers at the base of the chin. Such a bird would probably appear in the field to have an entirely red throat, which, when combined with a complete black frame, would approximate the pattern shown by a male Yellow-bellied. Therefore, you should not rely on throat pattern alone but should back up your identification with other marks.

The color of the nape is the first thing that most birders probably look at. Both species have a black nape that is crossed by a horizontal bar. On Yellow-bellieds, this horizontal bar is typically white and is continuous with the white postocular stripe. On Red-napeds (as the name suggests) the horizontal bar that crosses the black nape is usually red and therefore appears separate from the white postocular stripe. Although the great majority of these sapsuckers could probably be safely identified on the basis of nape color alone, there are frequent exceptions. Yellow-bellieds with a red nape are rare but regularly documented (Landing 1991). What's more, some Red-napeds lack red on the nape. The lack of red is probably most common on worn birds in summer, but occasional females in fresh plumage also lack any noticeable red on the nape.

Two other accessory marks can be helpful in the identification of these sapsuckers. The back of Yellow-bellieds is heavily spangled with white, buff, or gold, and this spangling is seemingly randomly distributed, with no apparent pattern. Red-napeds usually have less pale spangling to the back (and thus appear darker-backed), the spangling is usually white rather than buff or gold, and the spangling often (but not always) appears to be concentrated in a couple of mottled "racing stripes" down the sides of the back (leaving the center of the back darker). More subtle is the relative width of the black-and-white striping on the sides of the face. Yellow-bellieds usually have wider white facial stripes than do Red-napeds (Fig. 4.83).

### Red-breasted Sapsucker *(ruber* versus *daggetti)*

The two subspecies of Red-breasted Sapsucker can be readily distinguished from the Yellow-bellied and the Red-naped. Red-breasteds are characterized by a red hood extending over the head, neck, and breast. They lack the black breast shield, nape markings, and strong black-and-white facial striping of Yellow-bellied and Red-naped sapsuckers.

The nominate (northern) Red-breasteds are the most distinctive. They are almost entirely red-headed, with only a slight amount of black in the lores, and the white moustache of other sapsuckers is reduced to a small nasal tuft at the base of the bill (females often show slightly more white than males). The red of the hood is a deep, rich red, which yields abruptly to a strongly yellow-washed belly. The back is mostly black, with pale markings (usually strongly tinged yellow) confined to two narrow stripes down the sides.

Southern *daggetti* are similar but typically have a much longer, more distinct white moustache, some amount of black mottling to the auriculars (usually more pronounced in females), more distinctly black lores, and a white postocular spot. They also tend to have more pale mottling on the back (intermediate between Red-naped and northern Red-breasteds), less yellowish wash on the belly, and a less richly red head. Head color varies from a darker wine-red (almost maroon) to a brighter scarlet-red.

## The Hybrid Problem

There is frequent confusion over possible hybrids. There is little documentation of hybridization between Red-naped and Yellow-bellied sapsuckers. These two species are similar enough in appearance that hybrids would be difficult if not impossible to separate from normal variants of one or the other parent species. The two forms of Red-breasted Sapsucker meet and interbreed extensively in southern Oregon, apparently showing total intergradation in the contact zone. Birds in this region would be expected to span the continuum of morphological variation between the two forms.

The main problems, then, stem from hybridization between Red-breasted and Red-naped and between Red-breasted and Yellow-bellied sapsuckers. The Nominate Red-breasted contacts Yellow-bellied in northern British Columbia, but the extent of hybridization is not clear. Nominate Red-breasted has only very limited contact with Red-naped, and only a small percentage of birds in the contact zone are hybrids. Hybridization is much more extensive between Red-napeds and *daggetti* Red-breasteds.

Hybrid Red-breasted × Red-naped sapsuckers can and do present confusion with both *daggetti* Red-breasteds and with variant Red-napeds with a more extensively red-pigmented head. Most hybrids will appear intermediate between the parental types and, thus, should show stronger black auriculars and more distinct white facial striping (especially behind the eye) than would be typical for *daggetti* and at least a partial black breast shield. The breast shield is probably the key mark, because no *daggetti* should show more than (at most) a small amount of black flecking at the bottom of the red breast. Remember that female *daggetti* will show more black mottling to the cheeks and stronger white facial markings than will males. Occasional Red-naped Sapsuckers with excessive amounts of red on the face and breast may also be problematic. Some hybrids will be indistinguishable in the field from variant Red-napeds and *daggetti* Red-breasteds.

## Immature Sapsuckers

The foregoing discussion has centered on identifying adult sapsuckers. What about immatures? Fortunately, the identification of immature sapsuckers (all of which are largely brown-headed and brown-breasted as juveniles) is rarely a problem. Juvenile Red-breasted and Red-naped sapsuckers molt quickly while on the natal territories into first-basic plumage and will have assumed most of the characteristics of adult plumage long before migrating in fall. Juvenile Yellow-bellieds, by contrast, are slow to molt out of their predominantly brown "immature" plumage, retaining it through the winter and into early spring (often not becoming adultlike until March). The implications are clear: any obviously immature-plumaged sapsucker encountered after September or away from the breeding grounds of one of the western species is probably a Yellow-bellied. (Many young Red-napeds may show some brown scalloping on the breast after migrating, but they will still have an essentially adult head pattern.) Separation of juvenile Red-breasteds (darker, more uniformly brown head and breast) and Red-napeds (lighter-brown head and more scalloped breast) will be of concern only in the limited contact zones.

## *Myiarchus* Flycatchers

The genus *Myiarchus* contains four U.S. representatives of medium to large fly-catchers that differ only subtly from one another in both plumage and structural characters. One species (Great Crested) is essentially eastern in distribution; the others are essentially western. In some areas, as many as three of the species may be sympatric, and vagrant individuals of all four species have been found well outside their normal ranges. For these reasons it is essential that birders be aware of species differences within the genus, even if they live in areas inhabited by only one *Myiarchus* species.

The Great Crested Flycatcher is a common summer resident of deciduous woodlands, orchards, and shelter belts throughout the eastern United States. It breeds regularly west to the west-central Great Plains and central-southern Texas. In the latter region it overlaps the breeding ranges of the Ash-throated and Brown-crested flycatchers. It is an occasional vagrant (mostly in fall) to areas farther west.

The Ash-throated Flycatcher is the most widespread of the three western species. It ranges south from southern Washington along the West Coast to San Diego and east through Nevada, Utah, Arizona, New Mexico, portions of Idaho, Wyoming, and Colorado and the western two-thirds of Texas. It overlaps the range of the Great Crested in central Texas and is an occasional vagrant to both the east and the upper Northwest. It winters in the extreme southwestern corner of Arizona and southeastern California (where it is rare). The habitat preferences of this species are more varied than are those of its congeners. It may be found in sparse shrub-desert, thorn-scrub saguaro deserts, lush lowland riparian forests, and dry oak woodlands of low to middle elevations.

The Brown-crested Flycatcher has a disjunct distribution in the United States. In extreme southeastern California, the Morongo Valley (California), southern Arizona, and southwestern New Mexico, it is a fairly common but local summer resident of saguaro deserts, lowland riparian forests, and streamside deciduous growth in lower montane forests. It is absent from most of southern New Mexico and western and central Texas but is a fairly common summer resident of live oak groves, thorn-scrub, and subtropical forests in southern Texas. In this latter area it is sympatric with both Great Crested and Ash-throated, whereas in the Arizona and New Mexico portions of its range it is sympatric with Ash-throated and Dusky-capped.

The Dusky-capped Flycatcher has the most restricted U.S. range, being limited to southeastern Arizona and extreme southwestern New Mexico. Here, it is a common summer resident of lower montane pine-oak woodlands and lush, lowland riparian forests. It is a casual late fall and winter vagrant to coastal California.

Separating the four species in the field is not easy, but it can be done by using a suite of plumage, structural, and vocal characteristics. It is vital to be aware of a few general trends of molt common to the four species. Alternate plumage is attained by a partial prealternate molt, and basic plumage is attained by a complete molt after breeding. Summering adults are therefore more worn and paler than are fall adults, which are usually brighter yellow on the belly and darker gray on the throat and breast. Juvenal-plumaged birds resemble adults but are generally browner on the back, much rustier on the wings and tail, and paler below. These seasonal differences are important because they affect characters that differ subtly between species. By October to January juveniles have molted mostly into first-basic plumage and will essentially resemble adults.

Bill color and structure are the most useful characters in the field identification of the genus (Fig. 4.84). The bill of Ash-throated, Brown-crested, and Dusky-capped flycatchers typically appears entirely black in the field. The Great Crested usually shows an extensively pale (fleshy or yellow) base to the lower mandible. Although this mark is generally diagnostic, it may be difficult to see on some individuals and is usually lacking on juveniles, which are black-billed. Beware also that occasional Ash-throateds (rarely), Dusky-cappeds (rarely), and Brown cresteds (much more regularly) can have some paling at the base of the lower mandible (although this is typically not as bright or as extensive as in the Great Crested). Southwestern Brown-cresteds (*Myiarchus tyrannulus magister*) have a relatively massive bill that is noticeably longer and thicker than the bill of the other species. The Brown-cresteds found in southern Texas (*M. t. cooperi*) are smaller-billed (closer to Great Crested). The Great Crested has a smaller bill that is still longer and thicker than that of the Ash-throated and Dusky-capped. The bills of the latter two species are closest in size (the Ash-throated bill is slightly larger), but because the body size of the Dusky-capped is distinctly smaller, its bill appears relatively larger in the field. Caution must be used in judging bill size, because all *Myiarchus* species will appear large-billed to birders lacking comparative experience.

The Brown-crested is also the largest and most robust in body size, followed by the Great Crested, Ash-throated, and the distinctly smaller Dusky-capped.

Plumage differences are complex. In general, the Ash-throated is the palest below, being very light gray (often whitish) on the throat and breast, and pale yellow on the belly and vent. (Remember, however, that birds in fresh basic plumage

Figure 4.84. Head profiles of *Myiarchus* flycatchers: Brown-crested, *magister* subspecies (upper left), Ash-throated (upper right), Great Crested (lower left), Dusky-capped (lower right), and Brown-crested, *cooperi* subspecies (center). Note the size of the the bill relative to the size of the head. (Artwork by Shawneen Finnegan.)

are brighter.) Brown-cresteds are generally darker gray on the throat and breast and brighter yellow on the belly and vent than Ash-throateds, but they are lighter and duller in these areas than either Great Cresteds or Dusky-cappeds. The latter two species are darker gray on the throat and breast and brighter yellow on the belly and vent than either Ash-throateds or Brown-cresteds. These color differences make for a highly contrasting line of demarcation between the dark gray of the breast and the bright yellow of the belly of both Great Cresteds and Dusky-cappeds. This contrast is strongest on the Great Crested. On Ash-throateds and Brown-cresteds the lighter colors fade into one another, and the demarcation of gray and yellow is much less pronounced. Once again, it is important to note that fresh fall adults will be darker and brighter below, whereas juveniles will be paler and duller.

Upperpart coloration differs even more subtly. Great Cresteds and Dusky-cappeds are more olive on the back, whereas the other two species are slightly browner. Dusky-cappeds are the darkest above, being especially dark on the crown and nape. Great Cresteds show the most rufous in the primaries and rectrices, whereas adult Dusky-cappeds show almost no rufous coloring in either area (the tail of juvenile Dusky-cappeds is largely rufous). Ash-throateds and Brown-cresteds are comparable in the amount of rufous on the primaries, but the Ash-throated is more extensively rust-colored on the rectrices. Great Cresteds, Ash-throateds and Brown-cresteds all have thin whitish wing bars and conspicuous whitish margins to the wing coverts and tertials. The wing bars of Dusky-cappeds are rustier and inconspicuous, and the tertials and wing coverts are less distinctively margined.

Vocalizations are extremely useful for birds on the breeding grounds but are less useful for fall migrants, which often are silent. All species have a commonly heard one- or two-note call, a longer and more complex dawn song, and a variety of rolling, bickering notes that are most often given during intraspecific encounters.

Brown-cresteds sing a loudly whistled "WILL-for-YOU." Great Cresteds sing a two-phrase song consisting of a low "WHEEyer" followed by a pause and a higher "WHEEyer." Dusky-cappeds sing a varied "whip, WEOO, wee HOO." The song of the Ash-throated is three-syllabled, with a rising then falling inflection. (All song descriptions are from Davis 1962.)

Call notes are more commonly heard and are equally diagnostic. Brown-cresteds deliver a loud "whit" (either singly or in rapid succession); Great Cresteds a loud, upslurred "wheep" ; Ash-throateds a two-syllabled "ka-BRICK" or "ka-WHEER" (vaguely similar to the "chi-queer" of Cassin's Kingbird) and a single-syllabled "pyrrt" ; and Dusky-cappeds a mournful whistled "peeur" (reminiscent of Say's Phoebe).

Foraging differences may be useful secondary clues, but they are often meaningless for migrating or vagrant individuals. In general, the Dusky-capped is the only species prone to hover-gleaning insects from vegetation, although the other species may do so opportunistically. Also, Ash-throateds tend to forage lower in the canopy than do the other species.

Habitat overlap in regions of sympatry is often broad; however, some generalizations are possible. Dusky-cappeds typically range to higher elevations than either Ash-throateds or Brown-cresteds, and, consequently, the Dusky-capped is the most common species in areas where pines grow among live oaks and deciduous species. Brown-cresteds are more restricted to lowlands and ranges upslope only along water courses that provide significant stands of deciduous trees (particularly sycamores). They avoid the sparse, low-shrub deserts that are often occupied by Ash-throateds. When Brown-cresteds are in low-shrub desert they occupy only lush riparian groves of trees or saguaro deserts (which are closer to thorn-forest than other American deserts). In Texas, Great Cresteds typically occupy more-shaded woodlands, Brown-cresteds the drier forest and thorn-scrub, and Ash-throateds the most arid mesquite brushlands. Again, some overlap is found.

For further information see Dunn 1978b,c and Roberson 1980.

## *Empidonax* Flycatchers

Flycatchers of the genus *Empidonax* have traditionally been a source of frustration to birders. The standard advice given to most beginners is, "Don't identify them unless they sing." There is much to be said for this approach, which may work well on the breeding grounds during the peak of territorial activity, but it offers little during the migratory periods when the birds do not sing. When faced with the dilemma of identifying silent empids, cautious birders often throw in the towel and label them simply as "*Empidonax* species?." Less cautious or less knowledgeable birders often make specific identifications based solely on subtle coloration differences pictured in their field guides. Such an approach is essentially useless and may lead to serious errors in presumed knowledge of empid species distribution and abundance at the local level.

Since the early 1980s, active field birders have made great strides in the techniques of identifying species of this genus. Armed with the knowledge of what to look for, they can now accurately identify most silent *Empidonax* to species. Unfortunately, the dissemination of these recent advances in empid identification has left many birders with the impression that all silent empids can and should be identifiable in the field. This is clearly not the case. Caution must remain the watchword, because the new techniques demand that the observer have a fair amount of comparative experience with all members of the group. Even then, if the birds are seen under less than ideal conditions, positive identification may be impossible. This is clearly a case in which a little bit of knowledge is dangerous. Empids should be identified using a suite of morphological, behavioral, and vocal characters, and even then many birds will have to be identified to genus only. Single-character identifications should be strictly avoided. Observers should use extreme caution in identifying out-of-range *Empidonax*. Such identifications should come only after the expected species have been systematically eliminated from consideration.

These flycatchers should not (and arguably cannot) be learned as migrants. They should be studied on the breeding grounds, where you will typically have only a few species of possible empids at any one spot and where visual identifications can be confirmed or rejected on the basis of diagnostic songs. This approach will allow you to form impressions of structural and plumage characters on birds of known identity. These impressions can then be used as yardsticks for comparing other members of the genus. Silent migrants present a real hazard for birders first attempting to learn *Empidonax* flycatchers. In migration, the species possibilities are greater than they are at any one breeding locality, and there is no way to concretely confirm or reject identifications of silent birds of some species on the basis of visual impressions. Because the entire approach to identifying empids is comparative, an initial misidentification with species A creates an inaccurate yardstick for species B, and so on. A domino effect of errors can result from a single initial misidentification. Paradoxically, once you have achieved a certain level of competency in the visual identification of empids, you may find migrants easier to identify than breeders because their plumages are often brighter and less worn.

Vocalizations remain the single best method for identifying adults on the breeding grounds. Because the species-specific songs are well represented on commercially available tapes (and because written transcriptions of such vocalizations are somewhat awkward and unlikely to be perceived the same way by any two people), I will pay little attention to songs in the following discussion. In addition to their primary songs (which are generally heard only on the breeding grounds), empids have simple, one or two note calls that are frequently given at all times of the year. Although generally not as diagnostic (to our ears) as the songs, these vocalizations are strongly suggestive of identity and will allow the easy separation of some species pairs. These calls are, for the most part, inadequately represented on commercial tapes and will be dealt with here.

Structural characters are of particular importance in identifying empids. The length and shape of the bill and its size relative to the size of the head are of primary concern (Fig. 4.85). Note especially whether the bill is broad at the base (imparting a triangular appearance when viewed from above or below) or relatively narrow throughout its length. Note also the color pattern of the bill. An empid may appear to have an entirely dark bill, or the lower mandible may be entirely or partially fleshy-pink or yellowish. On birds with a partially pale lower mandible, note the extent of the pale color, its distribution, and whether it is sharply demarcated from darker parts of the bill.

Head size and shape relative to body size, bill size, and tail length can be important, although difficult to quantify. Some species will appear distinctly big-headed and others evenly proportioned. Impressions of head size are influenced by tail length, which, in turn, is influenced by primary projection (Fig. 4.86). Primary projection is the distance on the folded wing between the tip of the longest primary and the rear of the bunched tertials and secondaries. Some empids have notably long primary projections, which may make the tail appear relatively short (and which, in turn, may make the bird look front-heavy or big-headed). Others have short primary projections, which can accentuate the length of the tail. Although such structural characters can be vital in species identification, beware that individual variation within a species may exceed that of the average variation between species. For instance, virtually all empid males average longer, more pointed primaries than their respective females, and the differences, although slight, may influence our field perceptions of primary projection and other relative proportions.

As mentioned previously, coloration is often of limited use in identifying these flycatchers. The only western species that can regularly be safely identified on the basis of general coloration is the Buff-breasted, which is found in only a few mountain ranges in southern Arizona and New Mexico. Most species exhibit individual variation in color that is strongly influenced by wear, feather condition,

Figure 4.85. Bills (as viewed from below) of *Empidonax* flycatchers. From left to right: Least, Willow, Alder, Acadian, Hammond's, Dusky, Gray, "Western," Yellow-bellied, and Buff-breasted. Note the differences in breadth, length, and extent of dark tip (if any) to the mandible. (Artwork by Shawneen Finnegan.)

Figure 4.86. Least Flycatcher. Note in particular the short bill (with entirely pale mandible), blackish wings with highly contrasting whitish wing bars and edging to the tertials, and short primary projection with relatively rounded tips to the primaries. (Photo by Barry R. Zimmer.)

age, and stage of molt. Also, our perceptions of color may be greatly influenced by ambient light conditions. Strong sunlight in particular, tends to wash out colors, and both strong sun and deep shade can mask areas of contrast in plumage. All empids are variations on some common color schemes: varying tones of olive, brown, or gray above; yellowish to whitish below, with a variably contrasting breast band; darker wings with two pale wing bars; and (usually) a pale eye ring contrasting wih a darker face. As the bird's plumage is subjected to wear, the colors fade. Olives become browner or grayer, grays become paler gray, and yellows turn to white. At the same time, abrasion of the feathers removes the contrasting pale edges and fringes that create much of the pattern of the wing (including the wing bars). Eye rings can change shape or disappear with feather wear. Such wear can even influence our perceptions of structural characters such as head shape and primary projection. The net result is that a group of birds that differ only subtly to begin with, end up converging even more in appearance because of feather wear and fading.

For these reasons, it is important to make a general assessment of plumage condition when attempting to identify an *Empidonax*. Birds in fresh plumage will exhibit greater color saturation, showing greens, browns, and yellows that are darker and more intense than on birds in worn plumage. These in turn, will produce more obvious zones of contrast where differently colored feather tracts converge. Freshly plumaged birds should show broad, sharply defined wing bars and crisp, pale edgings to the tertials and secondaries. The wing bars of some species are distinctly buffy when fresh and later fade to white. If a bird is not in fresh plumage, you should give relatively little weight to the importance of color patterns in making an identification.

A knowledge of molt patterns can be helpful in identifying empids. Juveniles of most species undergo a partial molt of head and body feathers and of a variable number of wing coverts (and in some species even a few flight feathers) in late summer or fall. This may take place on the natal territory (before fall migration) or on the wintering grounds (after fall migration) or it may be partially completed on the natal territory, suspended, and then completed on the wintering grounds. As adults, most empids undergo a complete prebasic molt (that includes all flight feathers as well as head and body feathers) after breeding. Most species delay this molt until after arrival on the wintering grounds (generally south of our borders), but a few species complete the molt while still on the breeding grounds. Molt timing can have major implications for the identification of migrant empids in fall, because adults of most species will be at their most faded and worn, whereas species that molted before migrating (such as Hammond's and Acadian) will be in fresh, clean plumage. Most empids then undergo a partial prealternate molt (not involving flight feathers) on the wintering grounds in early spring, just before migrating north.

For detailed discussions of the identification challenges presented by *Empidonax* Flycatchers see Dunn 1977b–e, Roberson 1980, and, especially, Whitney and Kaufman 1985a,b, 1986a,br, and 1987.

## "Western" Flycatcher Complex

The "Western" Flycatcher complex consists of two species that were formerly considered conspecific (under the name of Western Flycatcher). The Pacific-slope Flycatcher breeds from southeastern Alaska south to Baja, on the Channel Islands off southern California, and east through the Cascades, Coast Ranges, and Sierra Nevada. The Cordilleran Flycatcher breeds from southern Alberta south through the Rocky Mountains and Great Basin region to Mexico, and east to the Black Hills of South Dakota, the Guadalupe Mountains of New Mexico, and the Trans-Pecos region of western Texas. The two species differ vocally and, to a certain extent, in habitat preferences, but they are virtually identical in plumage and structure and cannot be separated visually on current knowledge. Aside from discussing vocal differences, I will treat the two species together, under "Western" Flycatcher in all discussions of plumage and structural characters.

"Westerns" are small to medium-sized empids that appear proportionately large-headed, big-billed, long-tailed, and short-winged. The bill has a wide base and appears triangular when viewed from directly above or below. The lower mandible is entirely and conspicuously fleshy-pink to yellow-orange. The head typically appears distinctly peaked at the rear of the crown.

"Westerns" are distinctly olive above, sometimes with a slight bronzy cast. Juveniles may appear somewhat brownish olive. Birds in relatively fresh plumage are distinctly yellowish on the throat and from the belly up to the center of the chest.

A vague, olive or brownish olive breast band crosses the chest and extends as a wash down the sides. Worn birds (throughout the summer) may show almost no yellow tones below. The most conspicuous plumage feature is the bold yellowish white eye ring, which is typically somewhat flattened and narrow on top and flared at the rear of the eye, giving a distinct teardrop shape. The eye rings of many empids have a top edge that is somewhat thinner than the posterior edge, but nowhere in the genus is the character as pronounced as it is in most "Westerns." The two wing bars vary from dingy-white to slightly yellowish and are somewhat buffier in juveniles. "Western" Flycatchers molt primarily on the wintering grounds.

Pacific-slope and Cordilleran flycatchers differ in their primary songs and calls. The calls are commonly given by migrants as well as breeding birds. Male Pacific-slopes give an emphatic, diphthongal "pseyeep!" that sounds distinctly upslurred. It also gives a sharp, somewhat metallic "szit!" or "szik!" The common call of the male Cordilleran is a more distinctly two-syllabled "tree-IP!" It also gives a short, sharp "seet!"

"Western" Flycatchers are active empids, frequently flicking the wings and tail simultaneously, perhaps more than any other empids except for Hammond's.

Among western-nesting empids they are best identified by the combination of a triangular bill with entirely yellowish lower mandible, distinctly peaked head, teardrop-shaped eye ring, yellowish throat and under parts, and distinctly olive upperparts. They are most similar to Yellow-bellied Flycatcher (see below).

## Yellow-bellied Flycatcher

The Yellow-bellied Flycatcher is the eastern counterpart of the "Western" Flycatcher complex. It is nearly identical structurally to "Westerns," being a small to medium-sized *Empidonax* with a relatively big, wide-based bill, large head, and short primary projection. It is slightly shorter-tailed than "Westerns," and the shorter tail accentuates the front-heavy, big-headed look. The crown usually appears rounded rather than peaked, but the crown of individuals that are alarmed or responding to tape playback may not look rounded because, when alarmed, they routinely erect their crown feathers. Like that of "Westerns," the lower mandible is entirely yellowish orange.

As the name implies, Yellow-bellieds are the most consistently yellow on the underparts (including the throat) of any of the empids (matched only by some fresh "Westerns"), although worn adults can be quite pale (almost whitish) on the belly. Most birds show a distinct olive wash across the breast that continues down the sides. The upper parts are distinctly greenish, and they are brighter than those of most other empids, matched only by some "Westerns" in spring or by freshly molted Acadians in fall. The wings are strongly blackish, showing high contrast with the whitish-edged tertials and secondaries and the yellowish white wing bars. Faded adults will appear browner-winged or dusky-winged, with less contrast. Juveniles often have distinctly buffy wing bars. The eye ring is yellowish white, distinct, and usually of nearly uniform width (slightly thicker posteriorly), although occasional individuals may hint at the teardrop-shaped eye ring seen in "Westerns."

Juvenile Yellow-bellieds undergo a partial prebasic molt on the natal territory and, thus, are in fresh plumage in late summer and fall (appearing distinctly yellower below and greener above than adults at this time). Unlike most empids, adult Yellow-bellieds undergo only a partial (rather than a complete) prebasic molt, and it takes place on the wintering grounds. Consequently, adults in late summer and fall will appear markedly faded and worn. Another unusual feature among Empids is that the Yellow-bellied's prebasic molt is closely followed by a complete prealternate molt in late winter, so adults in spring are in fresh plumage.

Yellow-bellieds give a number of calls in addition to the hoarse (almost froggy) "je-berk" song (which is superficially similar to that of the Least Flycatcher), although none of them are uttered frequently during migration. Most common are a whistled, upward-inflected "preeeep" and a shorter "eep!", both of which are frequently repeated continuously in long series on the wintering grounds in Mexico and Central America. Yellow-bellieds also utter a sneezy "chew!"

Like "Western" Flycatchers, Yellow-bellieds are active empids and are given to much simultaneous wing and tail flicking.

The Yellow-bellied Flycatcher is extremely similar to the "Western" Flycatcher complex, but on average it is more strongly yellow below and green above. The eye ring is more usually circular (rarely teardrop-shaped), and the more-blackish wings give greater highlighting to the contrasting whitish tertial and secondary edgings. The tail is slightly shorter than that of "Westerns," and the shortness of the tail heightens the stubby appearance; the head appears more rounded (not peaked) in profile. Having said all of this, I would still suggest that the identification of an out-of-range Yellow-bellied would need to be supported by vocal characters (or in-hand identification), which are consistently different.

Yellow-bellieds are approached in general plumage characters by Acadian Flycatchers, although even bright examples of the latter should not be as strongly yellowish on the throat. The Acadian (see below) is structurally very different in overall size, bill size and structure, primary projection, and tail structure (the Yellow-bellied's tail is somewhat constricted at the base rather than nearly parallel-sided). The Acadian also differs in some vocal characters. Because Acadians of all ages undergo their prebasic molt on the breeding grounds (before migrating south), they will be in fresh plumage with buffy wing bars at a time when most Yellow-bellieds will appear faded and worn.

## Acadian Flycatcher

The Acadian Flycatcher is a large empid, with a long, wide bill, long primary projection, and a medium-length tail that is broad at the base and nearly parallel-sided. Although the length of the bill may be matched or even exceeded by longer-billed examples of Gray and "Traill's" flycatchers, Acadians consistently average longer in bill length than any other empid and are noticeably broader-billed than is the Gray Flycatcher. The primary projection is also striking on Acadians, and, although short-winged individuals may overlap with longer-winged examples of practically every other empid, the average Acadian will be distinctly long-winged compared with most other species. The tail, although of medium length for the genus, may appear relatively short because of the long primary projection. The lower mandible of the bill is typically entirely yellow-orange, but some individuals may show a dusky tip.

Acadians in fresh plumage average greener olive above than any other empids except Yellow-bellied and "Westerns." The wings are fairly blackish and show high contrast with the two whitish (or yellowish white) wing bars and the whitish-edged tertials and secondaries. The wing bars of adults and juveniles in fall typically are strongly buff. Acadians (except for some worn adults in midsummer) have a well-developed whitish or yellowish white eye ring that is typically of uniform width. The underparts are fairly whitish, particularly on the throat, but many adults in early spring or after the prebasic molt, may be noticeably washed with yellow or yellowish green on the underparts. A hint of an olive-washed breast band is usually evident.

The typical call is a somewhat flat-toned "peet," which is approached only by one of the calls of Yellow-bellieds (which sounds less flat, and is more sharply inflected). The Acadian is not as active as some of the other empids, and it tends to flick its tail and wings less, mostly immediately after changing perches.

## The "Traill's" Flycatcher Complex

The "Traill's Flycatcher complex consists of two species that formerly were considered conspecific (under the English name of "Traill's" Flycatcher): Willow Flycatcher and Alder Flycatcher. The Willow breeds across much of the United States, from coast to coast, and from southern Canada south to the United States–Mexico border. The Alder is generally more northern in distribution (although the two species overlap in the Northeast, Appalachians, Great Lakes region, and parts of southern Canada), occurring throughout most of forested Canada and Alaska. The two species are extremely similar in both structural and plumage characteristics, and, although minor average differences in morphology exist (and extreme examples of each species can be identified), there is overlap in every character. Fortunately, the two species can be separated easily by vocal characters (both songs and calls). Silent migrants are generally best left as "Willow/Alder" or "Traill's sp.," and records of vagrants of either species should be supported by vocal evidence.

Willow and Alder flycatchers are nearly identical in structure. They are large empids and have a large, broad-based bill (most like that of Acadian, but not quite as wide at the base), moderate primary projection, and a medium-length to longish tail that is broad-based and nearly parallel-sided (not constricted at the

Figure 4.87. Willow Flycatcher. Note in particular the relatively long bill, the lack of a prominent eye ring, and the broad-based tail. (Photo by S. J. Lang/VIREO.)

base) (Fig. 4.87). The lower mandible of the bill is frequently entirely fleshy-pink or yellow-orange, but it just as frequently may show a dusky tip.

"Traill's" Flycatchers tend to be drabber than "Westerns," Yellow-bellied, or Acadians. Both Willows and Alders tend toward dull-olive upper parts when in fresh plumage, although some Alders can be a bit more greenish. Both species in fresh plumage tend to show some contrast between the head and nape and the upper back; Willows usually appear darker, and their nape appears paler (often with grayish tones). On average, Willows tend to be a paler olive or a somewhat brownish olive or grayish olive on the upper parts (even in fresh plumage), with a gray- or brown-tinged olive wash across the chest. Alders tend to be a bit darker green on the upper parts and auriculars, with a purer olive wash across the chest. Both species typically have a white throat that contrasts well with the dark sides of the face and the breast band. Both species also tend to have a whitish belly, although juveniles can be strongly washed with yellow. Both species show variation in the expression of the eye ring. Most Alders have a thin, but complete, eye ring that can be anywhere from bold to inconspicuous. Many Willows appear in the field to lack an eye ring altogether, although many others will show at least a partial eye ring. The wing bars and tertial and secondary edges are generally whitish on both species, contrasting strongly with the blackish wings. Birds in fresh plumage may have distinctly buffy wing bars. Both species undergo their molts on the wintering grounds, so adults in late summer and fall may appear dingy and worn.

Vocalizations are definitely the key to separating Willow and Alder Flycatchers. Unfortunately, the song of the Alder has been somewhat misrepresented in most references for many years; it has been made out to be a distinctly three-syllabled "fee-bee-o" (and therefore, more different from the Willow's song than it really is). The Alder actually has a two-syllabled song (as does the Willow) that is distinctly burry and sounds like "frree-BEER!" Many times this is shortened to "brrreer." The Willow, on the other hand, sings an emphatic "FITZ-bew" or a shorter "rrrip." The call notes of the two species are generally more useful in the identification of migrants. The Willow gives a mellow, soft "hwit" that is somwhat like the calls of Dusky, Gray, Least, and Buff-breasted flycatchers. Alder give a sharper "pik" note that is very different from the calls of all other empids except Hammond's and that sounds reminiscent of the pik-note of a Three-toed Woodpecker or the chip of a White-throated Sparrow.

"Traill's" Flycatchers tend to be less active than many smaller empids, and they flick their wings and tail less often (most commonly immediately after changing perches).

Among other empids, "Traill's" Flycatchers are closest structurally to Acadian, but they typically show less primary projection and a slightly thinner bill. They can be further distinguished from Acadian by vocal characters, upperpart coloration (paler, livelier green on the face and upper parts of Acadian; darker, drabber olive, brownish olive, or grayish olive on "Traill's" ), throat contrast (more-contrasting white throat on "Traill's" ), and eye ring (almost always conspicuous and complete on Acadians; frequently incomplete or even absent on Willows and some Alders). In plumage, "Traill's" are approached most closely by the Least Flycatcher, but that species differs appreciably in size, bill length, primary projection, tail length, and vocal characters.

Willow Flycatchers that lack eye rings and that are more brownish or grayish above (most commonly worn birds) can easily be mistaken for wood-pewees because of their size and lack of eye rings. Wood-pewees can be identified by their much greater primary projection, higher-crowned (distinctly peaked) profile, overall size, heavier breast band, vocalizations, and absence of tail flicking.


## Hammond's Flycatcher

Hammond's Flycatcher is often said to be virtually impossible to distinguish from the Dusky Flycatcher, and in plumage the two species may show much overlap. Again, structural differences are more important; the Hammond's is a small, big-headed empid and has a very small bill, long primary projection, and a proportionately short tail. The Dusky is larger, longer-billed, shorter-winged, and longer-tailed. Probably the best mark of the Hammond's is the positively tiny bill compared with those of its congeners. The bill is both short and thin, a distinction that should be apparent to observers who have much comparative experience with the genus. The lower mandible is frequently dull yellow-orange or pinkish flesh-colored along the basal third, but it is just as commonly black or dusky throughout its length. The tail of Hammond's is actually of medium length, but, because the primary projection is so pronounced, the tail appears short, contributing to the compact, stocky look of the bird.

The Hammond's plumage is variable. The upper parts tend to be grayish olive when worn and darker olive in fresh plumage. Both colors contrast with the grayer head and face, giving a saddled look to the back (often found on Dusky Flycatchers as well). The underparts frequently show some yellow on the flanks and belly (but not on the throat), but the presence and extent of yellow are highly variable (yellow is most conspicuous on fresh fall-winter birds). The throat is usually pale gray, and a darker grayish green breast band extends down the sides of the breast, giving the bird a distinctly vested appearance (usually somewhat stronger than on other empids). The creamy-white eye ring is conspicuous, complete, and usually of uniform width, although it is frequently thicker at the posterior end. The wings are dusky, and the wing bars, tertial edges, and secondary edges are a contrasting creamy-white (or strongly buff, on juveniles and on freshly molted adults).

Adult Hammond's undergo a complete prebasic molt on the breeding grounds before migrating south. Juveniles undergo a partial prebasic molt at virtually the same time. Consequently, all Hammond's encountered in fall should be in fresh, bold plumage (neat buffy wing bars, sharply edged tertials, yellowish belly, and maximum head-back contrast) at a time when most other empids appear faded and worn. Hammond's undergo a partial prealternate molt on the wintering grounds before migrating north, but, as in some other Empids, the extent of the prealternate molt is individually variable. Thus, some northbound Hammond's in spring may be appear bright and contrasty, whereas others will look dull and faded.

Of much use is familiarity with the call note, a high, sharp "peek" that is often compared to the similar note of the Pygmy Nuthatch. This note is distinctly different from the calls of all other empids (except Alders, with which it is unlikely to be encountered).

Hammond's is a very active empid; its quick perch changes and habitual tail and wing flicking give it a nervous, hyperactive look. Other empids (including Duskys) flick their wings from time to time, especially upon changing perches, or in response to tape playback. Hammond's, however, does it much more frequently and in more exaggerated fashion (the wings often are raised nearly to the level of the head). This propensity for wing flicking, combined with the stubby, compact shape and the small bill, lends a kingletlike gestalt to this bird. On the breeding grounds, it shows a tendency to forage from perches high in the canopy, a distinction that is not maintained during migration.

Hammond's Flycatcher is most likely to be confused with the Dusky Flycatcher. The call notes of the two species are very different and will allow instant separation if heard. Structural differences are the next best and most consistent clues. Hammond's will typically appear more compact, big-headed, short-billed, short-tailed, and long-winged. The all dusky or mostly dusky lower mandible of Hammond's is a good clue (most Duskies will have an extensively yellow-orange mandible with a dusky tip), although there is some overlap. Plumage differences are trickier and depend on season. In fall, plumage distinctions between the two species are at their greatest, because all Hammond's will be in fresh plumage and Duskies will be worn and faded. At this time, Hammond's will have darker upper parts; contrast between the head and back; bolder, buffier wing bars; a broad edging to the tertials; a yellower belly; and wider and more complete eye rings. Duskies will be paler and grayer above and more uniform between head and back and will have thinner wing bars, little edging to the tertials, a dingy, whitish belly, and narrower and less complete eye rings. A few Hammond's and Duskies winter each year in southern Arizona and New Mexico. At this time, Duskies will be in sharper plumage, because they molt on the wintering grounds, whereas Hammond's will have molted a few months earlier. Plumage differences in spring and summer are minimal, although Hammond's tends to have a darker breast band and sides, imparting a more strikingly vested look.

Hammond's is also similar to the Least Flycatcher, both species being small and big-headed. Least has a slightly longer but noticeably broader-based bill, which is typically more extensively pale on the lower mandible. Least also has noticeably shorter primary extension than the average Hammond's. Differences between the two species in call notes are pronounced, and of a similar nature to the differences between calls of Hammond's and Dusky. Least tends towards a whiter throat (gray in Hammond's) and more uniformly colored upperparts (Hammond's shows greater head-back contrast). Plumage differences between the two species are least pronounced in summer, and most pronounced in fall, when Leasts are still worn and faded, and Hammond's are in fresh basic plumage.

Other Empids can be separated from Hammond's on purely structural grounds (most species being distinctly larger overall and larger-billed), as well as by vocal differences.

## Dusky Flycatcher

The Dusky Flycatcher might appropriately be called the generic *Empidonax*. Structurally, Duskies are intermediate in nearly every character between the extremes found in the genus. They are medium-sized and have a medium-sized, narrow bill (longer than Hammond's and Least, shorter than Gray, Acadian, and "Traill's"), moderate primary projection, and a somewhat longish tail, whose length is accentuated because it is visibly constricted at the base. The lower mandible is mostly yellowish orange to fleshy-pink and has a dusky tip that bleeds into the paler base.

The plumage during spring and summer is typically somewhat drab; the upper parts are grayish olive and show little head-back contrast. The wings are dusky with moderately contrasting whitish wing bars and whitish-edged tertials and secondaries. The underparts are mostly whitish, but the belly is lightly tinged with yellow, and there is an olive-gray wash across the chest. The throat is a pale whitish gray. The eye ring is usually distinct and complete, but it may be broken on some individuals. As the summer progresses, many Duskies fade to the extent that they are gray above and dingy white below and, hence, more resemble the Gray Flycatcher in plumage. Juveniles in fresh plumage are more contrastingly colored, with more-olive upperparts, buffier wing bars, and a more-yellowish belly, but these fade rapidly.

All molts in this species occur on the wintering grounds, so most Duskies seen in the United States will be brighter in spring than in summer or fall. However, the small number of Duskies that winter annually in the Southwest could prove confusing, because they will be much more brightly plumaged than the more-familiar Duskies of other areas.

The call note of Duskies is a soft "whit," quite similar to the calls of Gray, Willow, and Least flycatchers and very different from the sharp "peek!" of Hammond's. Duskies are also intermediate in their degree of activity, being somewhat less lethargic than "Traill's" and Acadian but less active than Hammond's and Least. Duskies frequently flick their tail like other empids, but they only occasionally flick their wings, mostly upon changing perches.

The Dusky is mostly likely to be confused with Hammond's Flycatcher (see the preceding account). In the breeding season, the two species can be distinguished by their primary songs and, to a lesser extent, by habitat and foraging differences. In areas where the breeding ranges of the two species overlap, Duskies tend to occupy drier forests at lower elevations and often forage low among the inner branches of trees. Hammond's prefer wetter, higher-elevation forests and more often use the higher strata of the canopy. Duskies also occupy some of the drier, higher-elevation forests right at timberline and are more likely to be found foraging low in the shrubbery of alpine meadows.

The Dusky can also be easily confused with the Gray Flycatcher, particularly in late summer and fall, when many Duskies appear distinctly gray and white. Gray Flycatchers at the same time should appear even paler gray above and more whitish below. Grays also have a longer bill, with a sharply bicolored mandible (with a pinkish base and a well-delineated black tip) on which the dark tip does not bleed into the pale base, as it does on Duskies. The call notes of the two species are similar, but the Gray has the distinctive habit (unique among empids) of slowly dipping its tail downward (as a phoebe does) rather than quickly flicking it up and then down (as do Duskies and all other empids).

## Least Flycatcher

Like the Hammond's, the Least Flycatcher looks small even for an empid. Unlike the Hammond's, however, the Least has a short bill that is very broad (triangular when viewed from directly above or below) at the base. The lower mandible is extensively yellowish orange to fleshy-pink and has a vaguely defined dusky tip extending over the distal quarter. The Least Flycatcher appears compact and big-headed, with a tail of medium length and a rather short primary projection (Fig. 4.86). The tips of the primaries also appear distinctly rounded and less pointed than the wings of Hammond's and some other empids.

The underpart coloration may vary considerably between individuals. Many birds are quite whitish below (especially on the throat), whereas others may have a white throat contrasting with a dusky or brownish olive upper breast and some hint of yellow on the lower flanks or belly. Most individuals are uniformly brownish olive above (some are fairly gray), although some individuals in fresh plumage can be nearly as greenish as an Acadian. The wings are typically blackish with strongly contrasting white edges to the tertials and secondaries. The wing bars are bold and whitish on fresh adults, dingy-white on worn birds, and distinctly buffy on juveniles. The whitish eye ring is normally bold, complete, and of uniform width.

Adult Leasts undergo a complete prebasic molt on the wintering grounds and, thus, will appear worn and faded in late summer and fall. Juveniles undergo a partial prebasic molt before leaving the natal territory and, thus, will appear fresh-plumaged and brighter in fall.

The call note is an emphatic "pit!" that is somewhat harder sounding than the similar calls of Willow, Gray, and Dusky flycatchers and that has been compared to the chip of a distant "Audubon's" Warbler. The Least is an active empid, with frequent perch changes and more than the average amount of tail and wing flicking.

Of the western empids, the Least is probably closest in appearance to the Hammond's and Dusky. Hammond's Flycatcher is also small and short-billed, but its bill is even shorter than the Least's, is decidedly thinner, and typically is darker (the lower mandible is mostly or entirely dusky). The Hammond's also has a longer primary projection, and the primaries are more pointed at the tips. The Hammond's usually shows more head-back contrast (especially in fresh plumage), a stronger vested appearance, and a grayer throat. The sharp "peek!" call note of the Hammond's is very different from the "pit!" of the Least. The average Dusky is longer-billed and thinner-billed than the Least and usually has a more extensively dark mandible. However, like the Least, it has a relatively short primary projection. The tail of the Dusky is a bit longer and possibly more noticeably constricted at the base. This difference, combined with the longer, thinner bill, gives the Dusky an overall longer, less compact shape. The call notes of the two species are similar, as are plumage characters. On average, the Least will have a whiter throat and blacker wings that contrast more strongly with the whitish-edged tertials and secondaries. Such minor differences may be lost entirely on worn birds of either species.

Among eastern empids, the Least is readily distinguished from Willow, Alder, and Acadian flycatchers on structural grounds (and from the last two by very different call notes). Only the Yellow-bellied is structurally similar, and it differs appreciably in calls and in its overall greenish upper parts and yellowish throat and underparts.


## Gray Flycatcher

The Gray Flycatcher is often one of the easiest empids to distinguish visually. The general impression one gets is that of a largish, but slender and evenly proportioned, *Empidonax*. The bill is long and somewhat narrow (distinctly narrower than that of the Acadian or "Traill's" ). The lower mandible is mostly fleshy-pink or yellowish orange and has a sharply delineated blackish tip that gives it a distinctly bicolored look. The tail is longish, and the primary projection is relatively short.

Many individuals (particularly faded adults in summer) are almost strikingly pale, with silver-gray upper parts and whitish underparts with only a hint of light gray wash on the breast. The general color of such individuals is reminiscent of Lucy's Warbler. Birds in fresh plumage are a bit darker, often with a slight olive tinge to the mantle and breast band and a faint yellowish or creamy-buff wash to the belly. These colors are less pronounced and more ephemeral on spring birds (which undergo a partial prealternate molt on the wintering grounds), and they are more prominent and longer-lasting on the small numbers that winter in the Southwest (and that have undergone a complete prebasic molt after arriving on the wintering grounds). Grays usually show a complete white eye ring that tends to be somewhat inconspicuous owing to a lack of contrast with the pale-gray face. Many individuals show the suggestion of a white spectacle formed by the eye ring and a whitish supraloral stripe between the top of the eye and the forehead. The blackish wings have white edges to the tertials and secondaries and white wing bars (usually somewhat buffier on juveniles). The outer rectrices of Gray Flycatchers have conspicuously white outer webs. These are normally more prominent than the similar pale-gray webs seen on several other empids.

The common call note is a "whit" or "pit" similar to that of the Least, Dusky, and Willow flycatchers. Gray Flycatchers are relatively sluggish empids; they generally perch low and forage near the ground (regularly dropping to the ground for prey). They do not flick their wings often. They do have a distinctive manner of moving their tail. All other empids flick their tail up and down in a motion that is generally too rapid to follow. Grays flick their tail up rapidly, and then slowly wag it downward, more like a phoebe. The breeding grounds habitat (sagebrush desert and foothills, often with pinyon and juniper present) is unusual among empids and is therefore useful in identification.

The Gray Flycatcher is relatively distinct in appearance from most other empids and might be likely to be confused only with the Dusky Flycatcher. The Dusky is smaller, but similarly proportioned, and worn individuals can appear quite gray. The two species also have similar call notes. However, the Gray is usually a distinctly truer and paler gray above (less olive) and whiter below (less yellowish, and with a gray rather than a slightly olive wash to the breast). The Gray's bill is longer, and the lower mandible is more extensively pale and has a more sharply delineated dark tip. The slow tail wagging of the Gray Flycatcher is also an excellent clue.

## Buff-breasted Flycatcher

The Buff-breasted Flycatcher is the most distinctive of North American empids, and it is the only one that has a tiny, localized range; it is limited to a couple of mountain ranges in southeastern Arizona, the Davis Mountains of West Texas, and probably the Animas Mountains of southwestern New Mexico. Hence, it is unlikely to be confused with other species.

The Buff-breasted is a tiny, almost delicate empid and has a short bill of moderate basal width, moderate to long primary projection, and a medium-length tail that is fairly constricted at the base. It may look distinctly round-headed, or it can show a somewhat peaked look to the rear crown. Structurally, it is probably closest to Hammond's Flycatcher, but it has a little less primary projection and a little wider bill. The lower mandible is usually entirely yellowish orange, but it may show a slight amount of dusky coloration to the tip.

In fresh plumage, the species is immediately recognizable by the ochraceous-buff wash across the breast and along the sides. The chin is somewhat paler (off-white or light gray to pale buff), as is the belly. Worn adults in midsummer can be extremely pale on the breast, with little evidence of buff. The upper parts are grayish brown (with a slight olive tinge to the mantle when fresh), and the wings are dusky with mildly contrasting off-white wing bars and tertial and secondary edging (which is strongly buff or cinnamon in juveniles). The eye ring is thin and whitish or pale buff and tends to project slightly on the posterior edge.

Both adults and juveniles undergo their prebasic molt while still on the breeding grounds. This molt is complete in adults and partial in juveniles. Thus, all Buff-breasteds in fall will be in fresh plumage and will have a strikingly buffy breast.

The common call note of the Buff-breasted is a soft, frequently repeated "pwit" that is somewhat more liquid than the similar calls of Dusky, Gray, Least, and Willow flycatchers. Buff-breasteds are active empids that change perches rapidly and flick their tail frequently. They forage at all strata in the open pine forests they inhabit, frequently clinging to grass stems only a foot or so above the ground. There are no serious identification contenders.

## Swallows with a Brown Back

Four species of swallow in the western United States are characterized by brown upper parts in at least one of their plumages. They are the Bank, Northern Rough-winged, Tree, and Violet-green swallows. Each of these species is widespread and common, both as nesting birds and as migrants. Thus, it may seem surprising that they frequently present identification problems for birders. Part of the problem stems from the fact that swallows are most commonly seen in dipping, darting, and whirling flight in their pursuit of flying insects—not the best conditions for appreciating subtle field marks. Sometimes, just keeping them in your binoculars can be a challenge! Problems are also presented by a lack of understanding concerning age and sexual variation in the plumages of Tree and Violet-green Swallows, two species that most birders would not immediately think of as being brown-backed. Adults of both species are iridescent green or bluish above and are not remotely similar to Bank or Northern Rough-winged swallows. However, juvenile Trees and Violet-greens, as well as first-year female Trees, are distinctly brown-backed and capable of being mistaken for the other two species. Fortunately, swallows do occasionally sit still, and better yet, migrating swallows often form mixed-species flocks in which similar species can frequently be found perched side by side.

Let's first consider the identification of perched birds (Fig. 4.88). Size is an immediate clue when more than one species are present. The Bank Swallow is distinctly small compared with the other species; Tree and Northern Rough-winged swallows are the largest and about the same size, and the Violet-green is intermediate (slightly smaller than Northern Rough-winged and Tree swallows).

Upperpart coloration offers another quick clue. Northern Rough-wingeds have uniformly medium-brown upper parts that show virtually no contrast from head to tail. Bank Swallows are a paler gray-brown on the back and rump, and these contrast noticeably with the wings and tail, which are darker brown. Juvenile Tree Swallows are typically a uniform cold gray-brown above, although older immature females may be more of a gun-metal gray with hints of green or blue iridescence (mainly in the crown). Juvenile Violet-greens are also gray-brown above, sometimes with a slightly bronzy cast.

Figure 4.88. Brown-backed swallows. From left to right: immature Tree, Northern Rough-winged, and Bank. On flying birds compare wing and tail shape and color-tone differences between the back, wings, and rump. On perched birds, note the degree of contrast and pattern on the sides of the face, neck, and breast. (Artwork by Shawneen Finnegan.)

Perhaps the most important things to look for are the presence or absence of a breast band, the nature of the breast band if present, and the amount of contrast between the sides of the face and the throat. Northern Rough-wingeds do not have a breast band and are instead washed with gray-brown (adults) or cinnamon-brown (juveniles) from the chin to the upper breast. Viewed in profile, they do not show striking contrast between the medium-brown head and face and the paler gray-brown or cinnamon-brown throat and breast. Juveniles can be further distinguished by the presence of cinnamon wing bars and edging on the tertials. Bank Swallows do have a conspicuous brown breast band that is usually sharply delineated. The band is typically widest in the center, projecting downward from the lower margin as a brown point. Viewed in profile, Bank Swallows show a bold contrast between the brown head and face and a white throat; the white of the throat curves up part way around the auriculars on the sides of the face. Juveniles may have narrow whitish fringes on the tertials. Juvenile Tree Swallows usually have a grayish wash across the breast that may or may not resemble a true breast band. Even when a band appears to be present, it is typically somewhat fuzzy (not sharply defined) and it tends to be darkest at the edges and thins out and becomes paler in the center of the breast. When a juvenile Tree Swallow is viewed in profile, there is a distinct horizontal cutoff between the dark gray-brown head and the white throat. Some juveniles (particularly younger birds) may have the white of the throat curving up around the rear of the auriculars (as do Bank Swallows), but such birds can usually be identified either by the presence of conspicuous white tips on the tertials (also present on adults in fall) or by a fleshy gape (indicating a young bird as opposed to an adult of one of the other species). Some birds have both the white tips and the fleshy gape. Juvenile Violet-greens lack a true breast band, although they are frequently washed gray-brown on the chest. Viewed in profile they present some contrast between the whitish throat and the brown head and typically have the whitish curving up behind the auriculars, with some hint of white above and behind the eye (a shadow of the adult pattern).

What about flying birds (Fig. 4.88)? Bank Swallows look small and have very rapid, shallow wingbeats, which give them a somewhat frenzied look in flight. Although the breast band can frequently be seen against the white breast, it may be difficult to pick it out on flying birds. An easier mark to see is the contrast between the dark wings and tail and the much paler gray-brown rump and back. Northern Rough-wingeds will look larger and bulkier, with longer wings and noticeably slower, floppier wingbeats. They will appear uniformly brown above, without any noticeable contrast. Tree Swallows also appear large and stocky, and their broad-based wings have a distinctly triangular appearance that is different from any of the other swallows. Juveniles are uniformly gray-brown above, without obvious contrast, but first-year females may show random tints of iridescence. More important, Tree Swallows have white feathering from the lower flanks extending upward onto the sides of the rump. These white patches are not nearly as prominent as those of the Violet-green Swallow, but they are easily seen and will allow immediate separation from either a Bank or a Northern Rough-winged Swallow. Similarly, juvenile Violet-green Swallows can be immediately identified in flight by the conspicuous white patches on the sides of the rump. They are long-winged but lack the broad-based, triangular-winged look of the Tree Swallow.

Swallows call frequently in flight, and these calls can be the quickest way to pick a different swallow out of a whirling flock. The calls of Tree Swallows are two-syllabled and richer and more musical than those of the other species, sounding like "chur-lup" or "chu-leep." Violet-green Swallows give a chattering series of distinctly finchlike "chee" notes. Northern Rough-wingeds give a somewhat grating "treet." Bank Swallows have perhaps the most distinctive calls: a low, harsh, buzzy series of notes that sounds more like electrical static than a bird.

For further discussions see Dunn and Garrett 1982b, Wilds 1985, and Lethaby 1996.

## *Aphelocoma* Jays

There are currently four recognized species of jay belonging to the genus *Aphelocoma*. Three of these were formerly considered subspecies of a single wide-ranging species, the Scrub Jay *(A. coerulescens)*. The three newly recognized species are the Florida Scrub-Jay, which is found only in the peninsula of Florida, the Western Scrub-Jay, which ranges over much of the western United States from the Pacific Coast east to the Great Plains and the Edwards Plateau of Texas, and the Island Scrub-Jay, which is restricted to Santa Cruz Island in the Channel Islands off the southern California coast. The fourth species is the Mexican Jay *(A. ultramarina*, formerly called Gray-breasted Jay), which in the United States is found in southern Arizona, in southern New Mexico, and in the Chisos Mountains of western Texas. The Florida Scrub-Jay and Island Scrub-Jay present no problems in identification, because they are sedentary species that are geographically isolated from any other similar jays.

Western Scrub-Jays and Mexican Jays do overlap in range and present an identification problem to many birders. Most of the confusion is the result of geographic variation in both species (primarily in the Scrub-Jay complex) and of the failure of most field guides to adequately address this variation. The Western Scrub-Jay actually consists of two distinctly different subspecies groups. One is a somewhat dull-plumaged group ("Woodhouse's Jay") that inhabits juniper and oak-scrub habitats from southeastern Oregon, southern Idaho, southern Wyoming, western and southern Colorado, and western Oklahoma south through Arizona, New Mexico, and western Texas, and east to the Edwards Plateau. The other is a brighter, more contrastingly plumaged group ("California Scrub-Jay") that is common to abundant in wooded foothills, chaparral, and residential areas from southwestern Washington south through western Oregon, California, and western Nevada to Mexico. The Mexican Jay is also represented in our area by two subspecies, *arizonae* of southern Arizona and New Mexico, and *couchii* of the Chisos Mountains of western Texas. The two subspecies of Mexican Jay differ more in vocalizations and ecology than in morphology, but there are still slight plumage differences. It is the "Woodhouse's" group of the Western Scrub-Jay complex that overlaps Mexican Jay in range, and it is the "Woodhouse's" group that is also most similar to the Mexican Jay morphologically. Unfortunately, field guides have tended to use "California Scrub-Jays" (which differ noticeably from Mexican Jays) as the models for their illustrations of scrub-jays in general, thereby misleading birders into thinking the two species are more different in appearance than they actually are within the zone of overlap.

Most guides picture scrub-jays as having a distinctively brown back but depict the Mexican Jay as being gray-backed. (I am using the term "scrub-jays" generically, because the complex has been split so recently by taxonomists that few field guides as yet treat the various populations as separate.) Although this is generally the case, back color in scrub-jays is subject to much variation, depending mainly on subspecies but also on feather wear and individual variation. "California Scrub-Jays" tend to have a distinctly browner back, whereas "Woodhouse's Jays" are typically quite gray. (Both the Florida Scrub-Jay and the Island Scrub-Jay are also gray-backed.) Mexican Jays vary from uniformly bluish above to blue with a contrasting gray central back.

Better field marks are provided by the contrast or lack of contrast on the face, throat, and breast, although this is again subject to subspecific variation. Mexican Jays are uniformly pale gray below, showing little or no contrast. The throat of all subspecies of Western Scrub-Jay is distinctly white, with a contrasting lower border. The lower breast and belly of "Woodhouse's Jays" are dingy gray (usually somewhat darker and duller than on the Mexican Jay), contrasting with the cleaner white throat and upper breast. The division between white and gray on the breast is streaky in appearance. The belly of "California Scrub-Jays" (and of Florida Scrub-Jays and Island Scrub-Jays) is whitish (much paler than "Woodhouse's" ) and is separated from the white throat by a distinct blue collar, which varies from partial to a complete necklace of blue streaks. (Florida Scrub-Jays are distinctive in having blue, rather than gray, undertail coverts.) In both subspecies groups of Western Scrub-Jay the contrast at the lower margin of the white throat and upper breast is an important character in the field separation of this species from the Mexican Jay.

Another distinguishing character is face pattern, and, again, it varies subspecifically and specifically within the Scrub-Jay complex. Western Scrub-Jays (and Island Scrub-Jays) have a blackish auricular patch that is set off by a thin, white supercilium. The auricular patch is most distinct on Island Scrub-Jays and "California Scrub-Jays," slightly less distinct on "Woodhouse's Jays," and least distinct on Florida Scrub-Jays (which tend to be bluer-faced). The dark auricular patch is further set off by the wider and whiter supercilium of "California Scrub-Jays" and Island Scrub-Jays. "Woodhouse's Jays" have a thinner and shorter supercilium that is often indistinct. The white supercilium of Florida Scrub-Jays is broad and flares to encompass the entire forehead. Mexican Jays show some blackish color on the face, but this is typically limited to the lores, and there is no semblance of a white eyebrow.

Overall, the Mexican Jay is a larger, much more robust jay that is a fairly uniform blue-gray, with no real contrast on the face or underparts. Western Scrub-Jays, although about the same length (because of a longer tail) are distinctly smaller-bodied and thinner and show more contrast on the face, breast, and often the back. Mexican Jays are most closely approached in appearance by the "Woodhouse's Jay" subspecies group, which, compared with "California Scrub-Jays" has a grayer back, a less sharply defined black auricular patch, an indistinct supercilium, a grayer belly, and no blue collar. These can still be separated from Mexican Jays by their white throat's contrasting with the gray belly (and a streaky border between the two), the blackish auriculars, an indistinct white eyebrow (when present), smaller build and proportionately longer tail, and vocalizations (see below). "California Scrub-Jays" and Island Scrub-Jays (neither of which overlap with Mexican Jays) are brighter blue above and paler below and have a more contrasting back patch and a white throat, bold blue collar, black auriculars, and bold white eyebrows. Be aware that all members of the Scrub-Jay complex, when worn, can appear much dingier and less contrasty. Feather wear can obliterate much of the face pattern and breast contrast by midsummer, pushing the superficial resemblance closer to that of a Mexican Jay.

The calls of the two species are very different. Western Scrub-Jays have a variety of harsh, raucous calls, all of which are readily distinguishable from the upslurred, somewhat querulous "weenk, weenk, weenk" of the Mexican Jay. The two species can usually be separated by habitat also, although some overlap does occur. Mexican Jays are typical of open oak and pine-oak woodlands at low to intermediate elevations. In Arizona and New Mexico, they also range into adjacent riparian corridors of sycamores and cottonwoods. In the zone of sympatry, Western Scrub-Jays ("Woodhouse's" ) are usually found in drier pinyon–juniper forests or dense oak-chaparral–covered hills.

Western Scrub-Jays are monogamous breeders, as are Island Scrub-Jays and Mexican Jays of the *couchii* subspecies of western Texas. Mexican Jays in Arizona and New Mexico *(A. u. arizonae),* on the other hand, are cooperative breeders (as are Florida Scrub-Jays); nonbreeding birds share in the care of young that are not their own. These species live in extended family or kinship groups of 3 to 15 birds throughout the year. This sociobiological difference between the subspecies of Mexican Jays is reflected in the morphology of juvenile birds. Nestlings of both subspecies have a pinkish-yellow bill, but the *couchii* birds of western Texas attain an adultlike black bill by the time of fledging. Young birds of the *arizonae* subspecies retain their pinkish-yellow immature bill for up to 3 years. This retention of an immature character in the cooperatively breeding *arizonae* presumably plays a part in maintaining dominance hierarchies by making conspicuous the younger, less experienced birds. Because of the differences in breeding ecology, one would expect to find *arizonae* Mexican Jays in groups all year and Western Scrub-Jays and *couchii* Mexican Jays in pairs throughout the breeding season. Western Scrub-Jays do occasionally indulge in winter flocking that is usually coincident with irruptive movements into low-lying areas during periods of severe food shortage or cold.

The sociobiological behaviors of *arizonae* Mexican Jays would seem to leave them as unlikely vagrants to areas outside of their breeding range, because groups maintain and defend territories year-round. Thus, any fall or winter records from outside the known breeding range should be considered with caution unless extreme care has been exercised in making the identification.

## Female Bluebirds

Although the range of the Eastern Bluebird is different from that of the Western and Mountain bluebirds, there is still enough distributional overlap as to make careful identification of bluebirds a concern in many areas. Males of all three species are so distinctively plumaged as to make identification straightforward. The spotted juvenal plumage of all three species is retained for only a short time and is lost before fall migration. Thus, it is seen only on the breeding grounds where the habitat overlap of any two species of bluebird is minimal. Females present the only real problem in the group, but most standard guides are of little help in separating them.

Easterns and Westerns are structurally and behaviorally more similar to one another than either is to the Mountain Bluebird (Fig. 4.89). Mountains have a longer, thinner bill than either of the other species, proportionately longer tarsi and wings, and a more slender build. These features combine to give Mountains a leaner, more elongated look. Easterns and Westerns have a shorter, thicker bill, proportionately shorter wings and tarsi, and a more rotund or dumpy shape that is accentuated by their hunched posture when perched. The difference in relative wing length is most striking between Mountain and Eastern bluebirds. The wings

Figure 4.89. Female bluebirds. From left to right: Eastern, Western, Mountain. Compare the overall shapes and, particularly, the bills and primary projection. Note also the contrast between the breast and the belly. (Artwork by Shawneen Finnegan.)

of a perched Mountain Bluebird extend to nearly the tip of the tail. The very short wings of the Eastern always fall well short of the tip of the tail. Westerns are intermediate in wing length, but their wings are still typically shorter than are Mountains'. The feeding behaviors of Easterns and Westerns are also similar, and both differ markedly from Mountains. Easterns and Westerns feed extensively in trees (both in the crowns and on inner branches), but they also commonly drop to the ground. Mountain Bluebirds do little foraging in trees, preferring instead to feed mostly on the ground. They differ in their ground feeding from Easterns and Westerns in that they frequently hunt from a low perch (a fencepost or wire) and make repeated short forays, during which they hover over potential prey for several seconds.

Details of plumage provide less subjective clues to species identity. Females of all three species are duller than their respective males. Female Easterns are a dull blue-gray above, sometimes with a brownish wash across the back that contrasts with the rump and the back of the head. Female Westerns are similar (subtly darker) but usually have stronger brownish overtones to the central back. Female Mountains are a lighter blue-gray than the other species and lack the brown back and consequent crown-back contrast.

All three species show extensive blue in the wings and tail, but this blue is darker on Easterns and Westerns and is closer to turquoise in the Mountain. An excellent mark of female Mountains is that most of the wing coverts and secondaries are broadly fringed with white, lending a scalloped look to the folded wing. This is most pronounced in fall after the molt. Females of the other species generally lack the light fringes, but when present they are buff rather than white and not nearly as noticeable.

Of particular importance is the color of the underparts. Easterns are largely reddish brown below (on the breast and flanks) and have a strongly contrasting, clean white vent, belly, and chin. The throat may be either white or reddish brown. Westerns also have a somewhat rusty breast and flanks, but these are more dingy buff as opposed to the brighter reddish colors of the Eastern. In addition, Westerns have a dingy gray or blue-gray throat and chin, and the belly and under-tail coverts are a dirty-white or gray. This coloration results in underparts that lack the sharp contrast between flanks and belly and between breast and chin that are so conspicuous on female Easterns. In general, then, Easterns have a sharper, cleaner look to the underparts than do Westerns (Fig. 4.89).

Female Mountains differ from the other two species in having generally gray or gray-brown underparts. Their chin is paler than surrounding areas, but the throat, breast, and flanks are the same color, and this color generally matches that of the back and head (a pattern that is very different from the contrasting dorsal and ventral surfaces of the other two species). Mountains have a clean white vent and belly that contrast sharply with the flanks and breast (as does the Eastern) (Fig. 4.89), but the contrast is between gray and white as opposed to red-brown and white.

An additional mark that sets female Easterns apart from the other two species is the intrusion of reddish brown from the breast into the neck region. This intrusion of rust coloring has the effect of setting off the bluish auricular region from the back of the head, thus creating an auricular patch that the other species do not have (Fig. 4.89).

Be aware that bluebirds undergo only one molt each year; this is a complete prebasic molt after breeding in late summer. Southbound birds in fall will be in freshest plumage, which may differ somewhat from the more faded plumage worn in spring and summer. Mountain Bluebirds of both sexes (but particularly females) tend to be somewhat buffier (rather than blue-gray) on the underparts when in fresh plumage, and this fact should be kept in mind.

Vocalizations can be helpful. Westerns give a mellow "pew" note, Easterns a two-syllabled "CHUR-lee" (Dunn 1981), and Mountains a note similar to Westerns but flatter in tone.

Mountains and Easterns are more highly migratory than are Westerns, which still show altitudinal migration into the lowlands each winter. The least migratory of all is the highly localized southwestern subspecies of the Eastern Bluebird *(Sialia sialis fulva)*, which is found at high elevations in the Chiricahua, Santa Catalina, and Huachuca mountains and low, along Sonoita Creek (Arizona). This subspecies is not known to migrate. Females of *fulva* resemble those of the nominate Eastern subspecies, but the males are slightly buffier (less red) below than their eastern counterparts.

All three species may be found in open or semiopen habitat during winter and migration, but this tendency is most pronounced in Mountain Bluebirds, which are often seen in large flocks in the middle of treeless prairies, deserts, or cultivated fields.

For more information, see Dunn 1981 and Kaufman 1992a.

## Bendire's versus Curve-billed Thrasher

The separation of Bendire's from the Curve-billed thrasher is another instance in which information presented in many field guides is misleading and results in much confusion. The two marks emphasized by many guides for separating these species are bill shape and length and eye color. Neither mark is infallible, and identifications in the area of sympatry should not be made solely on the basis of these features.

A long, distinctly decurved bill will immediately rule out Bendire's, but a shortish bill that is not distinctly decurved does not automatically eliminate the Curve-billed. Bill length and degree of decurvature are highly variable in Curve-billed Thrashers (less so in Bendire's), and birds located at the opposite extremes of the spectrum can look very different. The culmen is curved in both species. The bottom edge of the lower mandible of Bendire's Thrashers is nearly straight and has the effect of flattening out the curvature of the upper mandible (Fig. 4.90). The bottom edge of the lower mandible of most Curve-billeds is conspicuously curved, increasing the decurved appearance of the entire bill (Fig. 4.91). The de-

Figure 4.90. Bendire's Thrasher. Note the sharply defined chevrons on the breast as well as the relatively short, straight bill. (Photo by Barry R. Zimmer.)

Figure 4.91. Curve-billed Thrasher. Compare the bill structure and underpart pattern with those of Bendire's Thrasher in Figure 4.90. (Photo by John Cancalosi/VIREO.)

gree of decurvature is particularly difficult to judge on singing birds, whose open bills always appear more strongly decurved. Beware also that juvenile Curve-billeds can a have particularly short and straight bill that resembles exactly the bill of an adult Bendire's. More than one birder has joyfully checked off his or her first Bendire's Thrasher, only to watch in dismay as an adult Curve-billed flies up to feed it a grub. Juvenile Curve-billeds can usually be separated from adult Bendire's by several plumage characters (see below).

In summary, many Curve-billeds will be instantly recognizable by their distinctly long and decurved bill. Shorter-billed birds must be examined more closely. Check especially the bottom edge of the lower mandible. If it is straight or nearly so, the bird is almost certainly a Bendire's. If it is distinctly decurved, the bird should be a Curve-billed. Even short-billed Curve-billeds (excluding juveniles) should have a bill that appears heavier than that of Bendire's.

Bill color can also be a useful clue in separating these thrashers. The Curve-billed has an overall darker bill, which tends toward blackish. The bill of Bendire's is grayer overall and typically has a pale, fleshy-pink base to the lower mandible. This is a generally excellent mark when seen; however, it can be difficult to assess accurately in the field. Juveniles of both species may show a conspicuous pinkish gape, which can heighten the resemblance of a short-billed juvenile Curve-billed to an adult Bendire's.

Likewise, eye color can be used as an accessory aid to identification, but it should not be considered diagnostic. Most field guides stress the orange or reddish eye color of Curve-billeds as opposed to the yellow eye of the Bendire's. This "mark" has probably resulted in more misidentified thrashers than any other. Curve-billeds often show a yellowish orange or even a reddish orange iris, but individuals with yellow eyes are also routinely seen. This yellow tends to be more of a golden color than the yellow of the Bendire's, but such impressions are subject to error depending on viewer distance and light conditions. For the most part, eye color is useless and is often misleading.

Plumage characters provide additional clues, although these vary geographically in Curve-billeds and seasonally (through wear) in both species. The two species differ somewhat in general body color. Bendire's is a light, sandy brown above, a color that gives it a warmer appearance (especially on the flanks). Curve-billeds tend toward a grayer shade of brown, giving a colder appearance. Of particular interest is the pattern of the underparts. Both species are (to varying degrees) spotted below. On Bendire's, this spotting takes the form of chevron-shaped marks that are smallest, darkest, and most crisply defined on the lower throat and upper breast and that become larger, paler, and smudgier (while still retaining a chevron shape) on the lower breast and flanks. On Curve-billeds, the spots are typically larger, rounder (not distinctly chevron-shaped) and smudgier (less crisply defined) and are often darkest and most distinct on the lower breast. Birds of central and most of southeastern Arizona (subspecies *palmeri*) are frequently only lightly marked below, whereas Curve-billeds from farther east tend to be more heavily spotted. The pattern of spotting on the underparts of both species is strongly influenced by feather wear. Birds in fresh plumage (from midautumn through early spring) will be the most distinctly marked. As the breeding season winds down, wear will reduce the size of the spots and obscure their shape. By midsummer (when many birders visit southern Arizona), many birds will have lost most traces of their breast pattern.

Fledged juveniles of both species will be in fresher plumage than adults. This is an important consideration when attempting to separate adult Bendire's from short-billed juvenile Curve-billeds. The latter should show crisp streaking on the upper breast, which may approximate the condition found in Bendire's in fresh plumage (fall through early spring). Juvenile Curve-billeds should also have un-worn feather edges, crisp cinnamon edging to the wing coverts and tertials, and some hint of a fleshy gape. Adult Bendire's in the same season should appear no-ticeably worn, with less distinct breast markings and without the cinnamon edges to the wing feathers. The separation of juvenile Curve-billeds from juvenile Bendire's can be a real nightmare, and if these birds are not associating with adults they may not be separable.

Vocalizations are also very useful. Curve-billeds frequently whistle a loud, sharp (almost humanlike) "whit-wheet" (frequently with an extra note) that is instantly recognizable. Bendire's have a low "check" that is infrequently given. The songs of the two species are also different; that of the Curve-billed is separated into dis-tinct trills and warbled phrases, and that of the Bendire's is more of a continuous warble.

For further discussion see Zimmer 1985, Kaufman 1990, and Kaufman and Bowers 1990.

## American versus Sprague's Pipit

Sprague's Pipit is not a particularly difficult bird to identify. However, it has not received adequate treatment in most field guides, and, in some cases, field guide il-lustrations have not even remotely resembled the real bird. In addition, most books also fail to point out the geographic variability of the related American Pipit (formerly, the Water Pipit), thus increasing the likelihood of observer confu-sion where these species are concerned.

Four subspecies of American Pipit (*Anthus spinoletta*) are currently recognized by the AOU (American Ornithologists' Union) as occurring in our area.

1. *A. s. pacificus* (West Coast subspecies that breeds from Alaska south to California)
2. *A. s. alticola* (Rocky Mountain subspecies)
3. *A. s. rubescens* (eastern subspecies that breeds from Newfoundland west to Alaska)
4. *A. s. japonicus* (Siberian subspecies that occurs as a regular visitor to western Alaska and offshore islands)

The Siberian subspecies will not be included in the following discussion be-cause there is virtually no chance that observers would have to worry about separating it from the geographically distant Sprague's Pipit. The other three subspecies of American Pipit differ most conspicuously in alternate plumage. Individuals of *alticola* are the brightest pinkish buff below (with very pinkish buff eye stripes) and are almost entirely lacking in breast or flank streaking. Individuals of *pacificus* represent the other extreme of moderate to heavy breast and flank streaking with yellowish to white (not pinkish) eye stripes and underparts. Typical eastern birds *(rubescens)* are intermediate with respect to amount of streaking and degree of pinkish buff coloring (Parkes 1982). All of the subspecies that breed in North America are somewhat light-gray or gray-brown above with fairly indistinct (often smudgelike) streaking on the back, crown, and nape. In all cases, the supercilium (be it buff or white) contrasts sharply with the darker face and crown. The distinctions between the three North American subspecies are less conspicuous when the birds are in basic plumage (which is attained in fall). The distinctions between *japonicus* and the other three in basic plumage are more pronounced.) All North American individuals are darker (more brown) above and much more heavily streaked below. The streaking takes the form of a broad necklace that extends down the flanks on the sides. Excluding *japonicus*, upperpart coloration is darkest brown in *rubescens* and lightest gray in *pacificus* (Parkes 1982).

In basic plumage, *pacificus* shows reasonably distinct blackish streaking on the crown (Parkes 1982). Underpart coloration is subject to much individual variation, with *alticola* averaging buffier and *pacificus* whiter (Parkes 1982). The most important features to note (regardless of subspecies) are the strongly contrasting supercilium (with darker face), indistinctly streaked back, and heavily streaked underparts (including flanks).

In contrast, Sprague's Pipit is a warm sandy buff (not pinkish buff) color in all seasons (worn birds are darker, particularly on the upper parts). The back and crown are strongly streaked with black and buff, giving it an appearance that is very different from the cold and indistinctly streaked upper parts of any of the subspecies of American Pipit. The distinction between upperpart coloration of the two species is heightened on juvenal-plumaged Sprague's, which have regular buff-gold margins to the black back and scapular feathers, thus giving these birds a scaly look.

Equally distinctive is the nature of the head and face coloration of Sprague's. Although a faint buff supercilium and eye ring are present on this species, the lores and auriculars are almost equally light buff, thus eliminating the impression of any facial markings (except at very close range). This unmarked, buffy face causes the dark eye to look very prominent, a feature that is recognizable at great distances and that is reminiscent of Upland or Buff-breasted sandpipers (Fig. 4.92). This lack of facial pattern is clearly different from the strong-eyebrowed appearance of the American Pipit. Sprague's Pipits are streaked below only on the breast, and even here the streaks are confined to a narrow necklace and are finer in character than the breast streaks of American Pipits. Sprague's (when flying) also displays greater amounts of white on the tail than does American Pipit.

Much has been made of leg color differences between the two species. American

Figure 4.92. Sprague's Pipit. Note the prominent dark eye against the pale, unpatterned face and the scaly back pattern. (Artwork by Dale A. Zimmerman.)

Pipits typically have blackish legs, and Sprague's have pinkish legs. Overreliance on this single character often results in misidentification because the leg color of American Pipits is highly variable and can at least approach the light color of Sprague's (although even pale-legged American Pipits tend toward yellowish rather than pinkish legs). Because the two species are essentially allopatric with respect to breeding ranges, and because breeding habitats are entirely different (Sprague's nests in prairie grasslands, American Pipits in alpine or arctic tundra), confusion on the nesting grounds is unlikely. Hence, the entirely different songs of the two birds are of little help in making the separation. Call notes are useful, however. American Pipits give an oft-repeated "PIP-it" or "PIP-PIP-it" and a "pseet" (both typically uttered in flight), and Sprague's give a loud, squeaky "squeet" (repeated either once or twice).

The habits of the two species are also distinctly different. American Pipits (in winter and in migration) frequent open areas such as plowed fields, mudflats or sandbars, and athletic fields. They are often seen in large flocks and frequently pump their tail up and down. When flushed from cover, American Pipits bound high in the air and return to the ground with a bouncing stair-step descent. Sprague's Pipits frequent grasslands or agricultural fields that offer greater cover (such as alfalfa) and tend to creep furtively about through the vegetation. On the ground, they tend to move quickly away from you with their head and neck held low in front and parallel to the ground (much like longspurs). From time to time they will pause, straighten up, and strain their neck to look around. In this respect, they are reminiscent of Buff-breasted Sandpipers or many plovers. They are more solitary (although frequently migrating in small flocks) and rarely or never pump their tail. When flushed, they fly high and then drop rapidly to the ground in a straight (not bouncing) descent.

For more information see King 1981 and Parkes 1982.

# Wing-Barred Vireos

There are nine regularly occurring species of wing-barred vireo in the United States. Of these, two (Yellow-throated and White-eyed) are not only primarily eastern in distribution but are also reasonably distinct in the field from all other species. Another species, the Black-capped, has a very limited distribution in Texas and Oklahoma and can not be reasonably confused with any other North American bird. Accordingly, those three species will not be treated in this account. Of the remaining six species, one, the Blue-headed Vireo, is strictly an eastern bird, but it does occur as a regular vagrant to the West, and it is similar to other western species (and so, will be included here). The remaining five western vireos are all some combination of gray, white, and olive; all have wing bars and some sort of eye ring; and the plumage of two of the species is geographically variable. These factors combine to make for a group that confuses many birders.

## The "Solitary Vireo" Complex

The "Solitary Vireo" complex is composed of three species—Blue-headed Vireo, Cassin's Vireo, and Plumbeous Vireo, all of which, until recently, were considered subspecies of a single species, the Solitary Vireo. The Blue-headed Vireo is the eastern representative of the complex and is represented by two subspecies, *Vireo solitarius solitarius,* which breeds from northeastern British Columbia east through the boreal forests of southern Canada, the Great Lakes region, and New England; and *V. s. alticola,* which breeds from northeastern West Virginia, western Virginia, and western Maryland south to northern Georgia. The Blue-headed Vireo does not breed within the area covered by this book, but it is fairly common as a wintering bird on the Gulf Coast of Texas, and it is a rare vagrant west of the Great Plains. Cassin's Vireo breeds from southern British Columbia and western Alberta south through northern and western Idaho, northwestern Montana, Washington, and Oregon south through California to Mexico. It is a rare but regular wintering bird in southern California and a regular migrant throughout the area west of the Rockies. Small numbers of migrants occur east to the western Great Plains and the Trans-Pecos region of Texas. The Plumbeous Vireo breeds from southern Idaho, Wyoming, southern Montana, and southwestern South Dakota south to eastern California, eastern New Mexico, the Trans-Pecos region of Texas, and Mexico. It winters primarily in Mexico, with most migration being centered between Arizona to the west and the Pecos River in Texas and New Mexico to the east.

Because the breeding ranges of these vireos are essentially nonoverlapping, confusion as to their identity is most likely to involve migrants away from the breeding grounds. "Solitary Vireos" undergo a complete, prebasic molt in late summer on the breeding grounds (before migration). Juveniles undergo a partial prebasic molt during this same time. All members of the complex are thought to undergo a partial prealternate molt of head, body, and some wing covert feathers while in the winter quarters in March and April (just before migrating north). However, some individuals (like many other species of vireo) may not undergo a prealternate molt. As a general rule, birds will be brightest and most contrasty in fall, somewhat less so in spring, and dullest in summer. Duller, more faded examples in spring may be mostly first-year birds that only underwent a partial molt the previous fall. Because much of the basis for visual separation of these vireos relies on subtle differences in colors and zones of contrast, the possibility of fading and feather wear must be constantly considered when attempting to identify these birds away from the breeding grounds.

The Blue-headed Vireo is the brightest, most colorful member of the group, and adult males in fresh plumage are downright striking. This bird has a gray crown and face (strongly blue-gray on some birds, particularly males) that contrasts strongly with the upper parts, which are typically bright olive-green. Some birds (mostly females or young birds) may show traces of greenish on the nape, crown, and auriculars, but the head of most birds will have a gray-helmeted look in contrast to the greenish back. The dark-gray auriculars also contrast strongly with the throat and bold spectacles, which are snowy-white. The median underparts of most individuals are white, contrasting with the sides, flanks, and vent, which are strongly yellowish. Some individuals of *alticola* may appear slatier gray (rather than greenish olive) on the back and will have less yellow below. Both subspecies have blackish wings with two bold wing bars, which vary from white to yellow to greenish yellow. The tertials and secondaries are also strongly edged with white or greenish yellow, as are the rectrices.

Cassin's Vireo is similar in pattern but is duller overall and less contrasty. It is a duller green above and has a dingier white on the throat and median underparts. The flanks and vent are usually washed with a duller greenish yellow than on the Blue-headed, and the sides of the breast may be grayish olive. The head and back are paler than the Blue-headed's, and they show less contrast. The nape, crown, and auriculars of female and immature Cassin's may be essentially the same color as the olive back. Adult male Cassin's typically have a gray crown and a more olive nape and auriculars, but they still show less contrast to the head and back than do Blue-headeds, because the colors tend to bleed into one another. Similarly, the paler olive cheek of Cassin's does not contrast with the dingy-white throat to the same extent as does the dark-gray cheek and snow-white throat of the Blue-headed. Cassin's has two whitish wing bars, and the tertials, secondaries, and rectrices are usually edged in greenish yellow. Brighter examples of Cassin's can be mistaken for duller Blue-headed (particularly females), but they should be separable on the basis of less contrast between the crown and back, between the cheek and throat, and between the cheek and upper scapulars. Worn Cassin's can appear quite gray above and white below and can be mistaken for Plumbeous Vireos. Such birds will, upon careful inspection, usually show some olive in the upper parts, some greenish wash to the sides, and greenish yellow (rather than white) edges to the tertials and secondaries.

The Plumbeous Vireo is uniformly gray above, with white median underparts and gray sides and flanks. It has two bold white wing bars and bold white spectacles. The tertials and secondaries are edged in white, as are the rectrices. Some birds in good light may show a slight olive cast to the rump or a pale yellowish wash to the vent or lower flanks, or both, but these are not normally visible. Plumbeous Vireos are unlikely to be confused with Blue-headeds. They can, however, be confused with duller examples of Cassin's. On suspect birds, check for olive on the mantle or at the sides of the chest or for greenish edgings to the tertials and secondaries, all of which would indicate Cassin's. Plumbeous Vireos are always gray-backed, are usually gray-washed on the sides of the chest, and have the tertials and secondaries edged in white.

For more information see Dunn and Garrett 1976, Johnson 1995, and especially, Heindel 1996.

## Gray versus Plumbeous versus Bell's Vireo

Of the Gray, Plumbeous, and Bell's vireos, the Gray has the most restricted range and is (generally speaking) harder to find. Birders who are eagerly seeking their first Gray Vireo commonly mistake both Bell's and Plumbeous vireos for their bird. Some of the field guides have not done an adequate job of illustrating or describing the differences in the three species, nor have they dealt adequately with the geographic variation in Bell's Vireos.

The Gray Vireo is entirely gray above and grayish white to white below and has a thin white wing bar across the greater coverts (and sometimes an inconspicuous upper wing bar across the median coverts) and a thin white eye ring. In general proportions, it appears short-winged and long-tailed. The long-tailed appearance is enhanced by the species' habit of flitting about with its tail partially cocked and frequently wagging or jerking the tail like a gnatcatcher or a Bewick's Wren.

The Plumbeous Vireo is similar in tail length, but, because it is substantially longer-winged, it appears relatively short-tailed when compared with a Gray (and it does not share the tail-wagging habit). Plumbeous Vireos are typically a darker gray above, particularly on the crown and auriculars, and they typically show more gray (rather than white) on the flanks. Some Plumbeous Vireos will also show a slight olive cast to the rump or a pale yellowish cast to the lower flanks, two characters not found on Gray Vireos.

The wing bars of Gray Vireos are thinner and less distinct (particularly the upper bar, which may be lacking on some birds), whereas the Plumbeous Vireos usually has two broad, distinct, white bars. Similarly, the secondaries and tertials of Plumbeous Vireos tend to be more conspicuously edged in white, and the wing coverts are blacker, providing much more contrast to the wing than is found in Gray Vireos (which often have a plain, brownish gray look to the wing).

The two species are best separated by their very different facial patterns. Plumbeous Vireos will show bold, highly conspicuous white spectacles that contrast strongly with the dark-gray crown, face, and lower loral region. Gray Vireos have a thin white eye ring (not complete spectacles) that is inconspicuous against the pale gray face and lores.

As summer progresses, both species will become more worn and faded. The wings of Gray Vireos will appear more brownish and may lack any noticeable wing bars, and the eye ring may disappear as well. On Plumbeous Vireos, the previously bold wing bars and spectacles may become less conspicuous, pushing the appearance closer to that of a Gray Vireo.

Habitat preference is a generally useful clue. Grays prefer drier foothills where open pinyon–juniper or live oak woodlands meet more xeric desert brushlands. Plumbeous Vireos tend to inhabit more mesic mixed forests, but the two species may overlap in dry, oak woodlands. In these cases, Grays will usually stick to drier slopes and leave the canyon bottoms to the Plumbeous. Gray Vireos typically forage very low in the interior canopy, seldom venturing into the open or above 6 feet (about 2 meters) in height. Plumbeous Vireos tend to forage higher, but again, some overlap occurs.

Songs are also useful in the discrimination of the two species. The Plumbeous sings a deliberate and slightly burry "chur-REEP, CHUR-yeer" (reminiscent of the Yellow-throated Vireo), in which the syllables of each note are quite clearly enunciated. The Gray's song is also somewhat burry, but it sings a faster "che-ROO CHEE-yoo CHURR chur-WEEP," in which the elements of the song are more closely spaced and the syllables of each element are more run together.

Bell's Vireos may also be mistaken for a Gray Vireo. Bell's Vireo is geographically variable in plumage and is not adequately treated in most guides. There are four recognized subspecies. *Vireo bellii bellii* occupies the northern and eastern portions of the species' range and breeds south to the Gulf Coast and southern Texas (and on into Tamaulipas, Mexico) and west to western Oklahoma and central Texas. *Vireo bellii medius* breeds in the Trans-Pecos region of western Texas (and probably southern New Mexico) and south into Mexico. *Vireo bellii arizonae* breeds from southern Nevada and southwestern Utah to southeastern California (Colorado River Valley), Sonora (Mexico), and east through Arizona to southwestern New Mexico. *Vireo bellii pusillus* breeds in coastal and interior southern California and north regularly to Santa Barbara County. (Many local populations have disappeared in recent decades with the destruction of riparian habitats and the increase in cowbirds.)

Eastern birds (nominate *bellii*) are generally olive above and whitish below, with variable amounts of yellow wash on the flanks and breast. This subspecies most closely approximates the illustrations of Bell's Vireo in most field guides. California birds *(pusillus)* average the grayest of the four subspecies, being entirely gray above (with perhaps some contrasting olive tones to the rump) and whitish to grayish white below (including the flanks). In the Southwest (where confusion with Gray Vireos is most likely), most individuals of both *arizonae* and *medius* are somewhat intermediate in general color, with a pale to medium olive-gray back, lighter gray head (showing some contrast), and whitish or only faintly yellow flanks. Variations from this average are usually toward the grayer end of the spectrum.

Like the Gray Vireo, the Bell's does not have conspicuous spectacles or wing bars. Often, only the lower wing bar is evident at any distance, and even it is not conspicuous. Bell's do have spectacles, but they are faint, and the portion that encircles the underside of the eye is often so light as to be nearly invisible. This feature lends Bell's Vireos more of an eye-striped (albeit faint) appearance than a spectacled one.

Bell's Vireos (like Gray Vireos) have only one annual molt, a complete prebasic molt that takes place on the breeding grounds before fall migration (juveniles undergo only a partial molt into first-basic plumage; subsequent annual molts are complete). Breeding plumage is attained through wear of the winter (basic) plumage. This means that Bell's Vireos will be brightest after late summer and most worn and faded during the spring and summer, when most birders will encounter them. Worn birds will appear grayer (less olive) above and whiter (or at least less yellow) below, and both wing bars and spectacles may be indistinct or lacking. Fledged juveniles will appear brighter, with bolder wing bars and spectacles, than will adults before molting.

One excellent mark is the coloring of the lower mandible. It is probably better than any plumage character for most Bell's, but is usually not mentioned or depicted in field guides. The lower mandible is largely yellowish or fleshy-pink, and this coloring is particularly conspicuous from below. Rare individuals may have an entirely dark bill.

Like Gray Vireos, Bell's are proportionately short-winged and long-tailed. Eastern birds (nominate *bellii*) are proportionately the longest-winged and shortest-tailed subspecies of Bell's, whereas *arizonae* is distinctly shorter-winged and longer-tailed (appearing almost gnatcatcher-like by comparison). The Bell's shares with the Gray the habit of constantly wagging its tail. Bell's Vireos also fan their tails frequently (particularly when disturbed). Bell's are typically found at lower elevations than Grays, being especially characteristic of riparian thickets of mesquite, willow, salt-cedar, and cottonwoods.

Bell's is a persistent singer (even during the hottest hours of the day), and its song is unmistakable. Typically it sings a rapid, speeded-up "cheedle-cheedle-CHEE" (upward inflection as if asking a question) followed by an equally rapid "cheedle-cheedle-CHURR" (downward inflection as if answering its own question). On many occasions, only half the song (usually the second part) is given. Like other vireos, it has a variety of harsh, scolding notes. Bell's is typically very nervous in its actions and will often flit constantly through the underbrush while singing or scolding, without coming into the open.

Bell's Vireos may also be confused with Lucy's Warblers, which share the same habitat in the area of sympatry. The warbler is entirely gray above (except for a brick-red rump patch and crown patch that are usually concealed) and white below and shares the light-faced and faintly eye-striped look of the vireo. However, it lacks spectacles and any real wing bars, has no trace of yellow on the flanks, has a big-eyed look (large dark eyes against a pale face), and a thin, black bill that lacks the vireo hook.

For more information, see Zimmer 1985.

Figure 4.93. Hutton's Vireo. Note the general bulk and bill structure as well as the presence of two distinct wing bars. (Photo by Peter La Tourrette/VIREO.)

## Hutton's Vireo

Hutton's Vireos (Fig. 4.93) are probably more likely to be confused with Ruby-crowned Kinglets (Fig. 4.94) than with other vireos. Southwestern populations of Hutton's average grayer (with olive-gray flanks), whereas West Coast individuals are brighter olive with more yellowish flanks. Birds of both populations will appear grayer when worn (in the latter half of the summer) and will appear more

Figure 4.94. Ruby-crowned Kinglet. Compare the overall structure, bill shape, and wing pattern with those of the Hutton's Vireo in Figure 4.93. (Photo by Shawneen Finnegan.)

olive when in fresh plumage. All members of the species are suggestive of kinglets in being small, plump, and olive-gray above and lighter below and in having an olive or yellow wash on the flanks, a white eye ring, two white wing bars, and dark wings with contrasting white or yellowish edges to the tertials, secondaries, and coverts.

Contrary to the claims of some guides, Hutton's Vireos do not have true spectacles. Rather, they have whitish lores and white eye rings that are broken at the top. The white lores and broken eye ring can be suggestive in separating this species from the Ruby-crowned Kinglet, which typically has darker lores and a bolder, usually more-complete eye ring.

A better mark concerns the color of the wings and the boldness of the wing bars. Kaufman (1979) pointed out that the two wing bars of Hutton's are equally conspicuous, with the area between the bars standing out as the blackest portion of the wing. The kinglet, on the other hand, has a posterior bar (formed by edges to the greater coverts) that is much bolder than the anterior one (formed by edges to the median coverts), and the blackest portion of the wing is a narrow panel posterior to the trailing bar.

Bill structure is an excellent separator. The vireo has a thicker, slightly hooked bill that is somewhat typical of the family. The kinglet has a tiny, straight little bill that looks entirely different. The vireo also has thicker, blue-gray legs and feet, whereas the kinglet has fragile-looking, blackish legs and dull, yellowish or yellow-brown feet (Paulsen 1993).

The vireo is the more sedate of the two species, although it is quite active by vireo standards. Although it does not match the hyper behavior of the kinglet (perpetual motion, with constant wing and tail flicking), the vireo does twitch its wings and tail sometimes, particularly when alarmed. Kinglets chatter frequently, whereas the vireo utters a shorter harsh, scold note (not unlike that of other vireos), a series of three or more low harsh notes, and a repetitious "zu-wheet."

For more information, see Kaufman 1979 and 1993 and Paulsen 1993.


## Baird's versus Savannah Sparrow

In the Southwest, many birders routinely mistake Savannah Sparrows for wintering Baird's. Such errors result less from similarity of the two species than from a combination of three factors:
1.  Field guides emphasize one or two marks.
2.  Savannah Sparrows are extremely variable.
3.  Few Southwestern birders have had field experience with Baird's Sparrow.

Savannah Sparrows breed over most of North America and winter in large numbers across the southern tier of states. By contrast, Baird's Sparrow is an uncommon summer resident of the Dakotas, Montana, and the prairie provinces of Canada. It winters only in western Texas, southern New Mexico and Arizona, and Northern Mexico. It is seldom easy to find on its U.S. wintering grounds. Habitat should provide an immediate clue to the identity of a suspected Baird's. Baird's Sparrows are birds of the grasslands. This is as true in winter as it is on the breeding grounds. Savannah Sparrows also inhabit grasslands but are equally or more common in a variety of agricultural habitats. It is highly unlikely that you will ever find a Baird's Sparrow along a drainage ditch, in a plowed or stubble field, or along a grassy right-of-way, but such habitats may be teeming with Savannahs. Habitat considerations aside, the two species are not as difficult to separate as one might think. Most confusion results from the concentration of standard guides on only one or two marks of the Baird's Sparrow. The feature that is most cited in erroneous reports of Baird's (and one of the two marks most mentioned in field guides) is the necklace of streaks on the breast. Baird's Sparrow does have finer breast streaking than Savannah, and the Baird's streaking is limited to a narrow necklace across the upper breast and some residual streaking that tightly borders the side and flanks. The extent to which the streaking extends posteriorally varies somewhat, but in all cases it fails to extend inward to the central belly or undertail coverts. Savannah Sparrows typically have thicker breast streaks that are blurrier at the margins, and these streaks are usually more widely distributed across the upper breast and down the sides. Many individuals have a convergence of streaks in the center of the breast to form a small but distinct stickpin. Be aware, however, that Savannah Sparrows are among the most variable of all birds and that many individuals not only lack the stickpin but also show a necklace effect similar to that seen on Baird's. The nature of breast streaking should never be the sole criterion for separating these two species.

The field guides also mention the orange median crown stripe of the Baird's (an excellent mark), but they usually fail to illustrate it to full advantage. The Baird's has a broad orange-buff stripe that covers most of the crown and that is bordered by a broad blackish stripe on each side. The orange crown may have some fine dark streaks in the center, but these are not obvious and do little to blunt the conspicuousness of the crown. The nape too is orange, and it is margined posteriorally by a broken border of blackish streaks. The contrast between the color of the nape and the color of the back is obvious. Juveniles tend to be lighter buff on the crown and nape and to have more streaking.

Savannah Sparrows typically have a thinner median stripe that is cream-colored or light-gray and that more often (but not always) has small dark streaks overlaid on the light stripe. On many birds, the light median stripe is laterally bordered by thick, dark brown stripes. If the median stripe is unstreaked, the general appearance is not totally dissimilar to the crown pattern of Baird's. In all cases, however, Savannahs lack the obvious contrast between the nape and the back that is found in Baird's.

Further characters that are highly useful but infrequently mentioned are the color of the upper parts and the facial pattern. Baird's has back feathers that are dark in the center, with thin chestnut inner edgings and broader cream-buff outer edgings. The scapulars and wing coverts have chestnut centers with broad cream-buff fringes. The net effect is a very contrasting back that has a look of dark stripes on a light background. The chestnut adds richness to the overall impression of upperpart coloration. Juveniles have a scalier, more scalloped look, but they still have the light-and-dark contrasting appearance of adults. By contrast, Savannahs have dark back and wing feathers that are thinly edged with gray or gray-brown, lending a darker, duller, more uniform appearance to the upper parts. The tail feathers of Baird's are edged with cream-color on both sides (even the innermost rectrices), giving a much lighter look to the tail that is lacking in Savannahs. Upperpart coloration can be of great importance, because these two species are often only seen flying quickly away just over the tops of the grasses.

The face pattern of the two species is also very different (Fig. 4.95). Baird's has a distinct golden-buff color to the face (not orange like the crown) that is accentuated by the broad, dark lateral crown stripes. The auricular patch is noticeably light and is outlined by a thin, dark border. The posterior border is often reduced to double spots. The anterior border of the auricular patch stands out well and is situated virtually parallel to a thin, dark malar streak. This pattern gives the impression of a double malar-stripe that is very distinctive. Savannahs have a single malar stripe on each side that is wider and less crisply defined than either malar streak of Baird's. The auricular patch is finely but densely streaked with brown, giving the face a darker look. Baird's, then, has a light-buff cheek patch that is outlined by a thin, dark border, whereas Savannah has a dark patch that is more outlined by white or buff. Savannahs typically show some yellow on the lores (Baird's does not), but the extent and intensity of this yellow can vary tremendously.

Figure 4.95. Head profiles of Savannah Sparrow (top) versus Baird's Sparrow (bottom). (Artwork by Shawneen Finnegan.)

# Clay-colored versus Chipping versus Brewer's Sparrow

The separation of Clay-colored, Chipping, and Brewer's sparrows, all members of members of the genus *Spizella*, is a subtle problem that is exacerbated by the illustrations and text in some of the standard field guides. This group presents a problem primarily in the Southwest, where both Brewer's and Chipping sparrows winter in large numbers, and where most birders are unfamiliar with both the plumage and the true pattern of occurrence of the Clay-colored. Identification on the breeding grounds is seldom a problem, because song and, to a lesser extent, habitat, are diagnostic for each species. In addition, Chipping Sparrows in breeding plumage (with their bright rufous crown) are impossible to confuse with the other two species.

Winter birds and fall migrants present more of a problem. As is usual in such cases, most misidentifications involve mistaking the more common species (in this case Chipping or Brewer's) for the rarer one (Clay-colored). Clay-colored Sparrows winter primarily in Mexico, regularly remaining as far north as southern Texas. They are rare in winter elsewhere in the West. Despite their rarity in winter, Clay-coloreds are routinely reported on Christmas Bird Counts, often in large numbers. These reports perpetuate the idea that the species is to be expected in winter, thus compounding the problem. Most legitimate sightings of the species for California and the Southwest are fall (September to October) records, and sightings of suspected Clay coloreds or reports of them outside of this time span should be examined with caution.

## Clay-colored Sparrow

For the most part, field guides have failed to point out the distinctiveness of Clay-colored Sparrows, particularly of birds in first-basic plumage and basic-plumaged adults. Compared with the other two species (Fig. 4.96), the Clay-colored is a bright, sharply patterned, warm-appearing bird. The difference is most apparent on the head and upper breast, but it is also noticeable on the back, wings, and scapulars. The Clay-colored has a sandy-brown auricular patch that is sharply

Figure 4.96. *Spizella* sparrows in basic plumage. Left to right: Chipping, Clay-colored, Brewer's. (Artwork by Dale A. Zimmerman.)

outlined by a thin, dark brown border. The upper margin of this border is formed by the dark postocular line. The anterior border to the auricular patch is formed by a narrow yet distinct dark moustachial streak that widens below the eye. Further isolating and highlighting the auricular patch are a broad, creamy-white (or buff) supercilium above and an equally broad, creamy-white submoustachial stripe below. The latter, in turn, is margined below by a thin dark malar streak that divides the submoustachial stripe from the even whiter throat. The crown is sandy brown with blackish streaks overlaid and a (usually) very noticeable creamy-white median crown stripe dissecting it. The lores are pale, sandy-brown (the dark eye-line does not extend forward from the eye).

The entire head is set off from the body by a broad, well-defined gray nape that is unstreaked and is very conspicuous. This nape creates the same effect as would a large collar (Fig. 4.96). The gray collar of the Clay-colored serves to isolate the head, which gives the general impression of being boldly striped with buff and white. Clay-coloreds typically show a buffy wash of variable intensity (seemingly brighter buff on first-basic birds) to the breast that contrasts sharply with the white throat and adds to the contrasting buff and white pattern of the head and face.

The back and scapulars of the Clay-colored are also quite buffy, with strongly contrasting blackish streaks. This coloration adds to the warm appearance of the bird. The rump is unstreaked but does not contrast with the back (as does the gray nape).

## Chipping Sparrow

In general, fall and winter Chippings are dark grayish birds that lack the bright buff and white overtones of the Clay-colored. On both the back and the crown and face they tend toward a reddish brown color that is very different from the colors of most Clay-coloreds or Brewer's. Juvenile Chippings have very obvious breast streaking, but this remains only until the prebasic molt in midfall. Although Chippings show more contrast in plumage than do Brewer's, the effect still does not approach the bold, striped look of the Clay-colored (Fig. 4.96).

Chipping Sparrows in basic and juvenal plumage share the pale median crown stripe, unstreaked rump, and grayish collar with the Clay-colored. However, the median stripe tends toward light gray or grayish white rather than creamy-white, and the gray collar is not as broad or nearly as obvious as on the latter species. Part of the reason for the less conspicuous collar is that Chipping Sparrows in fall and winter are typically very gray on the breast and face and darker on the back, and therefore the gray of the collar presents little contrast. Also, although both species have an unstreaked rump, the rump of the Clay-colored is essentially the same color as the back, whereas that of the Chipping is medium- gray and contrasts strongly with the rust-brown back.

Chipping Sparrows differ from both Clay-coloreds and Brewer's in a couple of important aspects of facial pattern (Fig. 4.96). The dark eye line of Chipping Sparrows extends from well behind the eye to the bill, giving the species dark lores.

Thus, it has a facial expression different from that of the other two species, which have pale lores and a dark eye line that extends only rearward from the eye. Another important distinction is that the brown auricular patch (which is often streaked with rufous) of the Chipping is not as sharply outlined as are the auricular patches of the other two species. The dark eye line forms a prominent upper margin, but the moustachial streak is indistinct or nonexistent, and thus the anterior lower edge of the auricular patch is not sharply outlined. The malar streak is also less distinct in Chippings than in the other species. Because neither the malar streak nor the moustachial streak is particularly prominent on Chipping Sparrows, the submoustachial stripe is also less prominent owing to the lack of sharply defined margins. The supercilium of Chipping Sparrows is usually more obvious than that of in Brewer's Sparrows, but it is of a grayer ground color and is less obvious than the bright buffy or creamy supercilium of the Clay-colored.

## Brewer's Sparrow

Brewer's is almost more readily identified by a lack of characters than by any outstanding feature. In general, it is a dull bird with a sandy, gray-brown overall coloration that is noticeably different from the warm buff of the Clay-colored or the cold dark gray and rust of the Chipping. However, many fall Brewer's in fresh basic plumage can be surprisingly warm-brown with buff-washed flanks.

Most conspicuous is the general lack of pattern to the face and head (Fig. 4.96). Although Brewer's has a brownish, darkly outlined auricular patch, the stripes on either side of it (supercilium above, submoustachial stripe below) are dull gray rather than creamy-white or bright buff and therefore do not stand out as the stripes of the Clay-colored do. The supercilium, in particular, is inconspicuous. It often contains thin, dark internal streaking that makes it stand out very little. The lores are a pale, sandy brown, as are those of the Clay-colored (but not of the Chipping). The dark moustachial streak (which forms the anterior boundary of the auricular patch) is more prominent than the Chipping's (but slightly less prominent than that of most Clay-coloreds), is evenly thin throughout, and does not flare below the eye (a distinction from most Clay-coloreds). Also, the throat and breast are the same light gray color, leaving virtually no contrast in those areas either. Unlike the other two species, Brewer's usually lacks any obvious pale median crown stripe (there are occasional exceptions), and in the field the impression given is of a sandy-brown crown with many fine, darkish streaks. One feature of the face that does set Brewer's apart is the complete white eye ring (of variable width, but present on virtually all individuals), which is almost reminiscent of the eye ring of the Vesper Sparrow. The other species may show thin crescents below or above the eye, or both, but they never have complete eye rings.

As do the other species, Brewer's has a gray nape, but it differs from them in that the nape is heavily streaked. The fine dark streaks of the nape are extensions of the crown streaking and continue on to the back, largely eliminating any suggestion of a collar. Often the rump (which is the same color as the back) is streaked, too.

One potential wildcard in the identification mix is the "Timberline Sparrow" *(Spizella breweri taverneri)*, a disjunct subspecies of Brewer's Sparrow (treated as specifically distinct by some authors). It breeds in subalpine scrub from east-central Alaska, southwestern Yukon, northwestern British Columbia, and central-western Alberta south to southeastern British Columbia and southwestern Alberta. The winter range and extent of the migratory path of this form are not well understood (migrants have been collected in Arizona, New Mexico, and western Texas). Although the "Timberline Sparrow" remains poorly understood, and concrete identification criteria have yet to be worked out, a few generalizations can be made. "Timberline Sparrows" resemble other Brewer's Sparrows in having a complete white eye ring, streaked nape, and rump concolor with the back. In general, they are darker and more boldly streaked with black on the upper parts and show greater contrast in the facial markings, pushing the resemblance closer to the Clay-colored Sparrow. They are also reported to differ vocally from nominate Brewer's, although the extent of these differences is not clear.

### Tips for Identifying Clay-colored, Chipping, and Brewer's Sparrows

In general, an absence of real contrast anywhere on the body, along with a conspicuous white eye ring suggests Brewer's Sparrow. Dark lores and a gray-and-rust dorsal coloration with a strongly contrasting rump points to Chipping Sparrow. Clay-coloreds are distinctly buffy and clean, with a clearly defined facial pattern and hind-collar. On typical individuals this look is so different from that of the other species that if you find yourself wondering whether a given *Spizella* is a Clay-colored, the chances are that it's not. As is always the case with difficult groups, some individuals of each species will fall outside the normal parameters for one or more field marks; these individuals may defy certain identification.

The calls of the three species are separable with practice. Both Clay-colored and Brewer's have a "tsee" that is thinner than the Chipping's single note. These calls are often heard in migration and winter. Wintering flocks of Brewer's will often engage in sporadic song bouts, which include a variety of prolonged buzzy trills.

For further discussion see Simon 1977, Kaufman 1990, Rosenberg 1990a Pyle and Howell 1996 and Doyle 1997.

# Basic-Plumaged Longspurs

Basic-plumaged longspurs cause birders fits. Although the four species (Lapland, Chestnut-collared, McCown's, and Smith's) fit nearly everyone's definition of "little brown birds," that is not the worst of the problem. Most of the difficulty surrounding the identification of basic-plumaged longspurs stems from the difficulty in seeing them well. Wintering longspurs usually occur in flocks, with other species of longspurs or with Horned Larks. On the ground, they tend to crouch down and blend in so well that they become nearly invisible. Most views consist of a swirling mass of birds bounding high in the air before settling back into the grass, where they become invisible once more.

Aside from these difficulties, it is possible to see wintering longspurs well. Unfortunately, some of the standard guides offer little help in identifying them once seen. Tail patterns are helpful in at least narrowing the choices. McCown's and Chestnut-collared show much more white than the other two, which have their white restricted to the outer two pairs of rectrices (much like a Vesper Sparrow). McCown's typically has an inverted, black T at the end of its tail, and the Chestnut-collared has a centrally located black triangle. The distinctions between the two are frequently obvious, but just as often they are not. It is especially hard to see the exact pattern on an individual that is bouncing around in the middle of a nervous flock. The overall amount of white in the tail is helpful for breaking the four species into groups of two.

Bill size and structure are helpful in identifying sitting birds (Fig 4.97). McCown's has the heaviest, thickest-based bill of the four. It is somewhat different from the more slender bill of the Chestnut-collared (its closest partner on the basis of tail pattern). Likewise, the Lapland has a stouter bill than Smith's, which is its closest partner on the basis of tail pattern alone. Adult McCown's also have a mostly pale-colored (pinkish or yellowish) bill; the bill of other longspurs tends to be darker.

The Lapland is the only one of the four with truly black legs. Smith's has the lightest, and the other two are somewhat intermediate.

Overall structure can also be useful. McCown's has proportionately long wings that nearly reach the end of the short tail. This feature, combined with the big bill, gives McCown's a stocky, somewhat dumpy build. The wings of Lapland and Smith's Longspurs average longer in actual length than those of McCown's, but, relative to tail length, they appear shorter. The Chestnut-collared is shorter-winged, and therefore appears longer-tailed.

Figure 4.97. Head profiles of female longspurs in basic plumage: Smith's (upper left), McCown's (upper right), Chestnut-collared (lower left), Lapland (lower right). Note the subtle differences in bill shape and face pattern. (Artwork by Shawneen Finnegan.)

Plumage distinctions are probably easiest to make among males, which show traces of their breeding colors. McCown's, Chestnut-collareds, and Laplands often have some black smudging on the breast. Laplands will display some trace of their rusty nape, as will Chestnut-collareds (but less conspicuously). McCown's will still have the bright-rusty median wing coverts, a mark that is seldom seen on flying birds. Likewise, Smith's and Chestnut-collareds will show their white shoulder patches, but only at rest.

Laplands of both sexes share some distinctive plumage characters. They are fairly dark above and are whiter below than the other species (being almost entirely white, with perhaps some buff on the breast and flanks). They have a darkish, heavily streaked crown, with the streaks often merging in places to give the impression of a dark cap. Their flanks are usually heavily streaked, whereas females may also show some streaking on the breast. More than any of the other species, Laplands have strong, rust-colored edges to the tertials, greater wing coverts, and (to a lesser extent) the scapulars. Most distinctive is the face pattern (Fig. 4.97), which is similar in both sexes. The face (auriculars) is a unique golden-buff color, not unlike the face of a Baird's Sparrow or of a winter-plumaged Harris's Sparrow. The auricular patch is boldly outlined in black, and highlighted by a bold, buffy eye stripe. There is also a dark malar streak that combines with the outlined, buffy auriculars to yield a facial pattern reminiscent of Baird's Sparrow. No other longspur is similar.

The male McCown's is distinctly grayer below than the other species and also has a grayer rump. The female McCown's is buffier, and often shows little or no rusty wing coverts. It is closest to the Chestnut-collared in appearance, but it can be distinguished by its heavier bill, longer wings and shorter tail, broader buffy eye stripe (Fig. 4.97), and general lack of streaking below. Another difference is the color of buff tones on the two birds. McCown's of both sexes have buffy regions that are best compared to the buff of a female House Sparrow. The Chestnut-collared is a lighter, sandier buff color. Female Chestnut-collared can also be separated from McCown's by their lighter nape (contrasting more with crown and back) and finer dark crown and back streaking (Fig. 4.97). McCown's has blurrier dark streaking on the upper parts, again reminding one of a female House Sparrow.

Smith's of both sexes are somewhat similar to Chestnut-collareds (mainly to females). All are quite buffy, but this color is much stronger on the underparts of Smith's. The whitish chin of Smith's contrasts with the buffy breast, but this pattern is often seen in Chestnut-collareds as well. Smith's generally have broader buffy eye stripes and better defined auricular patches (Fig. 4.97). Their breast streaking also tends to be finer and more gingerly distributed (mostly on the flanks). If there is doubt in your mind in choosing between these two, try flushing the bird, because the tail patterns are very different.

Call notes can be helpful. The Chestnut-collared has the most distinctive call, a finchlike "KIT-tle, KIT-tle," often repeated several times. The other three have a dry rattle (the Chestnut-collared sometimes gives a soft rattle), and the Smith's has a hard, sharp rattle that may be best compared to the winding of a noisy watch. Laplands may also intersperse "tew" notes between rattles.

For further treatment see Dunn 1976b.

## Eastern versus Western Meadowlark

The Eastern and Western meadowlarks are sympatric across much of the eastern edge of the Great Plains, Texas, New Mexico, and Arizona. They are easily distinguished by song. The Eastern's song consists of two penetrating whistles ("SEE-you, SEE-air"), and the Western's is a variable, liquid series of warbles, gurgles, and whistles.

Many people consider the two species to be inseparable by visual characters. Most guides pay token homage to the more extensive white in the tail of Easterns and the more extensive yellow on the cheek of Westerns, but they still suggest using song as the primary criterion. Although this may be all that can be said of differences between Easterns and Westerns at the eastern edge of the sympatric zone, the situation is different in the Southwest.

Eastern Meadowlarks show considerable geographic variation, with eastern populations *(Sturnella magna argutula)* being darker and more richly colored, and southwestern populations *(S. m. lilianae)* being lighter and more similar in general appearance to Westerns. Southwestern birds do show one excellent mark that is consistently different from Westerns: a cream-colored or white, unstreaked cheek patch. Westerns typically show a brown, streaked cheek patch. Although Westerns are somewhat variable in this respect, they are never as clean on the cheek as the Easterns (Fig. 4.98). Another good mark is the color of the dark stripes on the head. On Westerns, these are dark brown with even darker thin streaks overlaid and are not much different from the coloring of the cheek. On Easterns, these stripes are more solidly colored and are much darker black-brown. This darker-striped look really stands out because of the contrast of the very white cheek.

Habitat differences during the breeding season are also important clues to meadowlark identity in the Southwest. In Arizona, New Mexico, and western Texas, Eastern Meadowlarks *(lilianae)* typically dominate grassland areas during

Figure 4.98. Head profiles of *lilianae* Eastern Meadowlark (left) versus Western Meadowlark (right). Compare the relative boldness of the head striping and cheek and malar coloring. (Artwork by Shawneen Finnegan.)

the breeding season, and Westerns tend to settle in agricultural lowlands. Even in winter Easterns are most likely to be found in grasslands (or in grassy swales or playas in the middle of more arid areas); Westerns are common in both more mesic farmlands and more xeric creosote deserts.

For more information see Zimmer 1984.

## *Carpodacus* Finches

The three North American species of *Carpodacus* finch (Purple, Cassin's, and House) can provide western birders with identification problems. Although adult males of the three species are frequently confused, the greater problem comes from adult females and immature birds of both sexes (young male Purple and Cassin's finches retain a female-like plumage until their second fall). This group is of particular concern in parts of the Southwest, where Cassin's Finches are typically uncommon and irregular winter visitors, Purple Finches are rare but regular vagrants, and House Finches are abundant residents.

Some of the best clues to birds of both sexes and all ages are provided by head, bill, and body proportions (Fig. 4.99). House Finches have a smaller head and a smaller bill than the other two species, and their culmen is slightly curved. In profile they appear symmetrical with respect to tail length versus head and bill size. Purple Finches have a noticeably larger (but stubby) bill, and the culmen is also curved. In profile they tend to look big-headed and short-tailed. Cassin's Finches have a longer bill and a straight culmen. The differences in bill shape and length between Cassin's Finches and Purple Finches are most apparent on Purple Finches from the East and Midwest (nominate *purpureus*), which, on average, have a shorter bill and more curved culmen than do Pacific Coast populations (*C. p. californicus*). Cassin's Finches also have longer wings, which extend nearly half the length of the tail. In profile they appear more robust and big-headed than House Finches but longer and less sawed-off than Purples. They also show a marked tendency to erect their crown feathers, thus giving their heads a peaked or crested appearance that is usually absent in the other *Carpodacus* species. Purples and Cassin's also have a distinctly notched tail, a character not seen in House Finches.

Once learned, vocalizations are very helpful. The songs of the three species are fairly distinct, but most of the problems in sorting these birds out do not come during the breeding season but, rather, during winter, when birds are less likely to be singing. More useful clues in the nonbreeding season are the calls. House Finches give a Hooded Oriole–like "wheet" that is markedly different from any call of the other two species. They also give a variety of semimusical, House Sparrow–like chirps. Purple Finches give a rich, vireolike, "CHEE-year" or "CHEE-you," often delivered repeatedly from a perch but also uttered in flight. The more common flight call is a simple, sharp "pik." Cassin's Finches give a drier (less musical), two-syllabled "CHEE-up" or a three-syllabled "ti-di-LIP."

Figure 4.99. Female *Carpodacus* finches. From top to bottom: House, Purple, Cassin's. Note the structural differences and differences in face and head pattern and ventral streaking. (Artwork by Dale A. Zimmerman.)

## Females and Immatures

Both the Purple and Cassin's finches have a more strikingly patterned face than does the House Finch (Fig. 4.99). The latter species has no real face pattern; the entire head is a uniform dull brown with tiny darker streaks overlaid. Cassin's has a brown auricular patch (the margins of which may be slightly blurred, thus making the patch somewhat indistinct on many individuals) that is set off from the brown crown by a whitish or somewhat buffy supercilium of variable width. The auricular patch is bordered below by a paler region that is in turn separated from the lighter throat by a cluster of dark streaks (sometimes vague) in the malar region. This same facial pattern is even more pronounced on the Purple Finch, which has a darker, more defined auricular patch that is bordered above and below by cleaner white stripes that are also broader. The dark malar line of the Purple is also broader and better defined, being more of a solid stripe than a cluster of thin streaks. Eastern and midwestern Purple Finches have whiter stripes bordering the facial patch than do West Coast birds (which are bufffier) and, thus, are all the more striking, being reminiscent of female Rose-breasted Grosbeaks.

The differences in facial pattern between Cassin's and Purple finches are largely ones of degree. The lines of demarcation of the dark crown, auricular patch, and malar region from the light supercilium, lower cheek, and throat are (on average) sharpest on eastern and midwestern Purples *(purpureus)*, intermediate on western Purples *(californicus)*, and fuzziest on Cassin's. The ground color of the light regions of the face tends to be whitest (with the least amount of inlaid fine, dark streaking) on eastern and midwestern Purples and is typically somewhat buffier (often with more fine, inlaid streaking) on both western Purples and Cassin's. The auricular patch of Cassin's often has a slight golden cast to it, whereas that of eastern and midwestern Purple Finches is darkish brown and that of western Purple Finches often has a distinctly olive-brown tone. Many Cassin's Finches have fairly prominent whitish crescents above and below the eye that form a broken (not complete as stated in some literature) eye ring. This feature is seldom found on the other two species.

The underparts provide another important clue to specific identity and are an especially vital consideration in the separation of Purple Finches from Cassin's. All three species are extensively streaked below with brown streaks against a light background. House Finches have an almost dingy look, with blurred streaks that are often somewhat indistinct against a dirty washed-out (brownish white) background. The other two species have streaks that are bolder, crisper (less blurred at the margins), and much more evident against ground colors that are cleaner. Purple Finches have very bold, thick streaks that are usually somewhat blurred at the margins (this blurring seems slightly more pronounced on West Coast birds, whereas the streaking is less bold). These streaks are set against a background color of clean white on eastern and midwestern birds or cream-buff on West Coast individuals. Cassin's Finches tend toward thinner, crisper streaking that is more reminiscent of a Pine Siskin, and this is set against a whitish background (the ground color typically being less cleanly white than on eastern and midwestern Purple Finches) that is often tinged light golden-buff on the flanks.

It is especially critical to note the extent of streaking on the underparts (Fig. 4.99). Cassin's have fine, dark streaking on the undertail coverts, whereas most female Purples lack streaks in this region. Unfortunately, this fairly diagnostic character can be difficult to see. Beware, also, of juvenile Purple Finches, many of which are also streaked on the undertail coverts. Such birds will, if anything, have a slightly smaller, stubbier bill than adults (making them look more like House Finches) and should be readily distinguishable from Cassin's Finches on structural grounds.

Upperpart coloration can also be helpful, because Purple and House finches have a darker ground color than does Cassin's. This makes the back streaking on Cassin's more visible than it is on the other species. Nominate Purple Finches are more contrastingly streaked on the back than are western birds, which are a dingier olive above. The olive cast to *californicus* Purple Finches is often particularly strong on the rump and uppertail regions, something that can frequently be seen when birds are flushed away from you. Cassin's Finches tend toward broader pale (usually yellowish) margins to the greater coverts and flight feathers, making for a more contrasty look to the folded wing. This contrast is especially pronounced on birds in fresh plumage, some of which can show an almost siskinlike (albeit much paler) yellow blaze to the folded remiges.

## Adult Males

Some general differences in both the tone of reddish color and its distribution allow ready separation of most adult males of the three species. Male House Finches are extremely variable in color (some populations more so than others), ranging from a bright, rich red, to a paler vermilion, to a paler-still salmon-orange, to dull yellow. None of these colors is duplicated in the other species, although some intermediate House Finches can approximate the pinkish red hues of some faded male Purple Finches. More important, male House Finches, regardless of their exact pigment, give the impression of being sharply bicolored, with the red (or orange or yellow) head, throat, upper breast, and rump contrasting strongly with the brown auriculars, back, and wings. On some birds the red (or orange or yellow) is restricted to the forehead and supercilium, with the hindcrown and nape matching the brown of the auriculars and back. Other birds are entirely red (or orange or yellow) on the crown. On some birds, the back may be tinged reddish, but this is seldom obvious, and most individuals will appear brown-backed. Likewise, the back usually has blurry darker brown streaks that do not contrast strongly with the ground color. The underparts are dingy white, boldy streaked with blurry brown streaks on the belly and flanks, beginning just below the red (or orange or yellow) of the breast.

Male Purple Finches tend toward a more maroon, wine-red color, which is more evenly distributed over the head, breast, and upper parts. The head, throat, breast, and flanks tend toward a uniform maroon, interrupted only by a brownish auricular patch (more olivaceous-brown in *californicus*), the vague suggestion of a brownish malar region (not present on all birds), and some brownish streaking on the hindcrown and nape. The maroon color extends farther down the breast (on average) than on the other species and is often somewhat flammulated in appearance where it meets the plain white of the lower belly. The upper parts are also uniformly maroon, with overlying broad, dark-brown streaks of medium contrast. The back appears more streaked than does the House Finch's, but the back and rump are more uniformly colored (the House Finch's bright red rump contrasts sharply with the brown back). Similarly, the feathers of the wings are edged maroon, making them blend with the color of the back.

Male Cassin's Finches tend toward rosier shades of red and pink. The distribution of these colors on Cassin's Finch is unique among the three species. The face (except for a brownish auricular patch and a vague brownish malar region), throat, breast, and flanks are a uniform, pale, rosy-pink, which contrasts strongly with the crown and forehead, which are a much brighter rose-red. At a glance, male Cassin's Finches should always look brightest red on the crown (which is often partially erected) and should appear essentially red-capped. This red also contrasts with the brownish nape. The back is a pale pinkish brown, with strongly contrasting darker brown stripes. These stripes are probably no darker than those of Purple Finches, but because the ground color of the Cassin's back is much paler, the dark stripes stand out more. Cassin's often show some fine dark streaking on the flanks but just as frequently may appear to be unstreaked below. As do Purple Finches, male Cassin's have pinkish margins to the wing coverts, making the folded wing blend more uniformly with the color of the back. Both female and male Cassin's have white crescents above and below the eye (usually broader below the eye), forming a broken white eye ring.

For further discussion see Dunn 1976a, Zimmer 1985, and Kaufman 1990.

## Hoary versus Common Redpoll

The taxonomic status of two northern finches, the Hoary Redpoll and the Common Redpoll, has long been debated. Historically, some authors have recognized as many as six species of redpoll in North America. More recently, other taxonomists (e.g., Troy 1985) have advocated lumping all redpolls into a single, morphologically variable species. Currently, the AOU (American Ornithologists' Union) recognizes two species: the Common Redpoll *(Carduelis flammea)* and the Hoary Redpoll *(C. hornemanni)*. Common Redpolls breed across the taiga and tundra zones of Alaska and northern Canada and winter from the southern part of the breeding range south irregularly to the contiguous 48 states. Like many other northern finches, they stage sporadic winter invasions in which large numbers may appear well south of the northern tier of states. The Hoary Redpoll is represented in North America by two recognized subspecies. The nominate form *(C. h.*

*hornemanni*) breeds on Ellesmere and Baffin islands and in the northern half of Greenland. It is a sporadic and rare winter visitor to the northern United States, usually occurring during years of major Common Redpoll invasions. The widespread North American breeding form is *C. h. exilipes*, which breeds in tundra regions across northern Alaska and Canada and which is a sporadic and rare winter visitor to the northern tier of states, again, usually coinciding in its appearances with major movements of Common Redpolls.

Commons and Hoaries have been reported to interbreed wherever their ranges come in contact, and morphological intermediates are reported to be common and even predominate in some regions. Indeed, some morphometric analyses have been unable to find a single morphological character that is diagnostic for either form. However, others have argued that the evidence for extensive hybridization is weak and that many of the purported intermediates are actually based on an incomplete understanding of age and sexual variation in the two forms. Still others have argued that the results of various morphometric analyses have been skewed by improper methodology concerning the definition of character states and how individuals (particularly intermediates) were categorized. A broad range of opinions of how to treat these redpolls exists, ranging from maintaining the status quo, to lumping all forms into one species, to treating nominate *hornemanni* as specifically distinct (and thereby recognizing three species), to lumping Common and *exilipes* Hoaries but splitting nominate *hornemanni*.

Until the taxonomic dust settles, birders must still contend with three realities regarding redpolls: (1) the AOU still recognizes two species; (2) regardless of whether intermediates are common, the morphological extremes also are common and can be identified in the field; and (3) field identification of redpolls at any level will remain difficult at best, and many individuals will be encountered that will be impossible to identify given current knowledge. This account will focus on identifying redpolls that are identifiable: in other words, the morphological extremes. Readers should understand that characters as stated are tendencies, or "average," characters that fit our species limits as currently defined but that for any given character there will be exceptions. Also, this account will focus on generalities of separating Hoaries and Commons, with the emphasis on the Alaskan breeding *exilipes* subspecies of Hoary. I will not devote much attention to differences between *exilipes* and nominate *hornemanni*, in part because the larger, whiter *hornemanni* is easier to distinguish from Common than is *exilipes* and also because field discrimination of redpolls at even the species level (as currently recognized) is tenuous enough without attempting to distinguish between subspecies. Subspecific identifications of redpolls, even by careful observers, should probably be labeled as "probabilities" or as "birds showing characters suggestive of."

With these caveats firmly in mind, let's examine some generalities of redpoll identification and distribution as we currently understand them. The two species exhibit some habitat differentiation within their breeding ranges. Commons breed in both the forested taiga zone and farther north in the tundra regions.

Hoaries are more specialized and seem to be restricted to the tundra zone, often breeding farther north than Commons but just as frequently overlapping with them. Hoaries do not appear to penetrate south into the forested taiga regions.

Both species of redpoll exhibit sexual and age-related variation in plumage characters. Males of both species are apparently more variable in the expression of plumage characters than are females (Troy 1985). Redpolls undergo a single annual molt in late summer. For adults, this is a complete prebasic molt; for juveniles, it is only a partial molt of head and body feathers. Therefore, first-year birds, particularly in winter and spring, may be separable from adults on the basis of their more worn, retained juvenal wing and tail feathers. Freshly molted adults will have crisp white edging to the wing coverts, secondaries, tertials, and rectrices. As summer progresses, redpolls will become darker as these white edges wear away. Male redpolls in fresh plumage appear frostier because of pale fringes to the red or pink feathers of the chest. As the pale fringes wear away, the reds and pinks will intensify in color (usually brightest in spring).

Now for the specifics. Let us look first at size and structural characters, which apply to birds of both sexes and all ages. Common and Hoary Redpolls can not be distinguished in the field on the basis of size. Possible exceptions are provided by Hoaries of the nominate race, which are distinctly large and long-tailed, but birders will be less likely to encounter nominate Hoaries than *exilipes*. There is an average difference in head and bill shape between Common and Hoary redpolls. Hoaries tend to have a steeper rise to the forehead and a flatter crown (Fig. 4.100).

Figure 4.100. Hoary Redpoll (top) versus Common Redpoll (bottom). Note the differences in bill size and shape, general color tone, and distribution of streaking on the rump and sides. (Artwork by Shawneen Finnegan.)

Commons tend to show a more gentle slope to the forehead and a more evenly rounded crown. Bill size and shape are more noticeably different. The Hoary has a shorter bill (often downright stubby) and a straighter culmen, and the Common has a longer bill with a slightly curved culmen (Fig. 4.100). The stubbier bill, combined with the steep forehead and flat crown gives Hoary Redpolls a pushed-in look to the face. Accentuating this look is the color pattern of the bill, which in both species is yellow with a variable amount of dusky coloring to the distal portion of the culmen and the tip (the amount seemingly greater during the summer). The dark tip has the visual effect in the field of cutting off the end of the yellow bill, which on the already stubby-billed Hoary, results in a truly snub-nosed look. Nominate *hornemanni* are longer-billed than *exilipes* and have a deeper base to the bill. The only other structural clue involves the "leggings," or feathers, that cover the tibia; these are often more prominent on Hoaries than on Commons.

Adult males of both species are distinguished by the presence of obvious reddish or pink coloring on the breast. On male Commons the color is typically a deeper reddish pink that not only covers the breast but also extends down the sides and up onto the malar area and cheeks. On male Hoaries the color is a light, frosty-pink (more of a "blush" ) that is more nearly confined to the breast. Remember that males in fresh plumage have pale tips to the reddish feathers, which can make male Commons appear a paler pink.

On average, Hoaries appear paler in general ground color than Commons. This difference is most consistent and most pronounced in adult males, but it holds for many females as well. On male Hoaries, the ground color of the back varies from pale gray (or, at the dark extreme, pale gray brown) to decidedly whitish, with overlying dark streaking. Some females may be quite whitish above as well, but many females and probably all juveniles average darker, more toward a pale gray-brown. On Commons (both sexes and all ages), the ground color of the back varies from gray-brown (at the pale end) to a warmer brown, also with overlying dark streaks. Paler male Hoaries are unlikely to be mistaken, but many females and especially juveniles may show overlap with Commons in general upperpart coloration.

The field mark most often mentioned by field guides is the rump (Fig. 4.100). On Commons of both sexes and all ages, the rump is usually heavily to moderately streaked brown on a paler grayish-white background. Many adult male Commons may have very little or no visible rump streaking but will instead have the rump colored deep reddish pink. On male (and some female) Hoaries, the rump is white or frosty-pink and is typically unstreaked or has only a few fine dark streaks (and thus appears pale and unstreaked under most field conditions). Most female and immature Hoaries have a whitish rump with a light to moderate amount of brown streaking, the darker individuals showing overlap with Commons. Although the rump is often concealed by the folded wings, Hoaries (particularly birds at feeding stations) have a convenient habit of holding their wings slightly drooped so that the rump is exposed.

The amount of streaking on the underparts, particularly on the flanks and undertail coverts, is another important consideration (Fig. 4.100). Most Commons are heavily streaked with brown on the undertail coverts, although some males may have only a single bold streak (usually on the longest covert). Most male Hoaries and many females have unstreaked undertail coverts (or, in many cases, only a single fine streak on the longest covert), whereas many females and probably all immatures have at least a few dark streaks. When streaks are present on Hoaries, they are usually finer and less blurry than the streaks on Commons. Similarly, Commons are usually heavily streaked with bold, gray-brown streaks on the sides of the chest and flanks. Conversely, many male Hoaries show virtually no streaking on the sides of the chest or on the flanks, although many females and most immatures may show light to moderate streaking in these areas (the darker extremes overlapping Commons). When flank and side streaking is present on Hoaries it is usually finer than on Commons.

Head and neck patterns are also suggestive of specific identity. The overall ground color of the head and neck parallels that of the back, and, so, is consistently paler on Hoaries. Furthermore, Commons are usually more heavily streaked with gray-brown on the nape, supercilium, and auriculars, making those areas appear still darker. On many Hoaries (particularly adult males), the nape, supercilium, and auriculars are only lightly streaked, accentuating the paler ground color. On Hoaries these areas are often distinctly washed with buff, and females and immatures may have the buff color extend to the breast as well. The red cap, or "poll," is often smaller on Hoaries than on Commons.

Relatively little attention has been paid to redpoll vocalizations. Both species have several different types of call, some of which are indistinguishable to my ears. Birds on the breeding grounds in Alaska can be distinguished on the basis of some calls, but these do not lend themselves well to written descriptions, and they require some comparative experience to assess. A comprehensive analysis of vocalizations among various populations would make a worthy project that could pay real dividends in field identification as well as shedding light on the gnarled taxonomic controversy.

For more information, see Troy 1985, Knox 1988, Herremans 1990, Lansdown et al. 1991, and Czaplak 1995.

# CHAPTER 5

# FINDING THE WESTERN SPECIALTIES

Chapter 1 concentrates on generalities and concepts of finding birds. It deals with the importance of elevation, habitat, time of year, time of day, knowledge of specific localities, and tapping into birding hotlines. This chapter applies that framework to the specifics of finding the specialty birds of the West.

## What Is a Specialty Bird?

*Specialty bird* (as I have defined the term for this chapter) has a broad, and somewhat arbitrary meaning. My first criterion was that the birds covered must be essentially western birds. Species whose ranges include large areas east of the Mississippi were left out, regardless of how common or rare they are in the West. Thus, birds such as the Red-cockaded Woodpecker, Bachman's Sparrow, and the Brown-headed Nuthatch (all of which are, on a regional basis, considered eastern Texas specialties) were left out, because on the broader scale they are essentially birds of the Southeast. Exceptions were made in the case of some boreal birds (e.g., some owls and northern finches and Black-backed and Three-toed woodpeckers), which in many cases are easier to find (or, are at least more accessible to birders) in the West than in the eastern half of North America. Some of these species regularly invade the eastern states in winter but can be found in Alaska during the nesting season. Exceptions were also made for several seabirds that occur along both the Atlantic and Pacific coasts, but that are more common in the latter area (e.g. South Polar Skua), and or breed in Alaska (e.g. Long-tailed Jaeger), or both. A few exceptions were also made for some Gulf Coast birds that are as easily seen along the Texas coast as any place else in North America (e.g. some herons and terns).

The matter of choosing which of the rare visiting species to include was also somewhat arbitrary. In general, I tried to avoid the following: (1) irruptive northern species whose movements are somewhat irregular, which invade much of the East as well as the West, and which, when present, show up almost anywhere (for example, Evening Grosbeak, crossbills) and (2) Asiatic species whose appearances anywhere on the North American mainland (especially south of Alaska) are extremely rare and unpredictable as to time and place (outside of broad generalities such as "fall on the West Coast," or "May–June in the Aleutians"). Exceptions were made for some Asiatic species of regular occurrence on the North American mainland (i.e., someplace other than the Aleutians and Bering Sea Islands) whose movements over the years fit a somewhat predictable pattern (for example, Sharp-tailed Sandpiper). Similarly, I included many Mexican species that regularly stray into our border states but left out others of less predictable occurrence. Exceptions to the above criteria were made for some irruptive northern species (Bohemian Waxwing, redpolls), which, within their Alaskan breeding ranges, are predictable as to time and place of occurrence. These species are treated in detail only for their breeding ranges, not for the states that they sporadically invade in winter.

Finally, there are some birds that are rightfully considered Western specialties, but that are not included in the following accounts because they are either so widespread in the West (e.g., Western Wood-Pewee) or so common within a smaller region (e.g., Gambel's Quail or Western Gull) that they should be readily found by anyone searching appropriate habitat. I was faced with making somewhat arbitrary decisions as to which species to include. In some cases, an included species was treated solely because of some quirk of microhabitat preference or distribution that I wished to convey, while another species of similar abundance and distribution might have been excluded.

The following species were considered sufficiently widespread or easy enough to find so as to justify not treating them in this chapter: Pacific Loon; Western and Clark's grebes; Sooty Shearwater; Brandt's and Pelagic cormorants; White-faced Ibis; Mottled Duck; Cinnamon Teal; Swainson's and Ferruginous hawks; Prairie Falcon; Scaled, Gambel's, and California quails; Snowy Plover; Black Oystercatcher; Wandering Tattler; Long-billed Curlew; Red Phalarope; Pomarine and Parasitic jaegers; Franklin's, Heermann's, Mew, California, Western, and Glaucous-winged gulls; Royal and Sandwich terns; Band-tailed Pigeon; White-winged and Inca doves; Greater Roadrunner; Western Screech-Owl; Lesser Nighthawk; Common Poorwill; Vaux's and White-throated swifts; Black-chinned, Anna's, Broad-tailed, and Rufous hummingbirds; Acorn and Ladder-backed woodpeckers; Western Wood-Pewee; Black and Say's phoebes; Ash-throated Flycatcher; Cassin's and Western kingbirds; Violet-green Swallow; Steller's and Western scrub-jays; Black-billed Magpie; Mountain and Chestnut-backed chickadees; Oak and Juniper titmouses; Verdin; Bushtit; Pygmy Nuthatch; Rock and Canyon wrens; Western and Mountain bluebirds; Townsend's Solitaire; Sage Thrasher; Plumbeous, Cassin's and Hutton's vireos; Black-throated Gray, Townsend's and MacGillivray's warblers; Western Tanager; Black-headed Grosbeak; Lazuli Bunting; Green-tailed, Spotted, Canyon, and California towhees; Rufous-crowned, Golden-crowned, Brewer's, and Black-throated sparrows; Lark Bunting; Great-tailed Grackle; Bronzed Cowbird; Bullock's Oriole; Cassin's Finch; and Lesser Goldfinch.

## Format

Species accounts vary in length. These accounts are designed to tell you where, when, and in what habitat you can expect to find the birds. I have tried to give as much information on habitat as possible so that readers can discover their own spots for different specialty birds. For common or conspicuous species that are likely to be found just by going to representative habitats at the proper season, no further information is given. For less common or more localized species, a list of recommended locations for finding the birds is provided and broken down by state. These lists include both very general locations (e.g., Yosemite National Park) and highly specific ones (e.g., Willow Lake at Santa Ana National Wildlife Refuge). It is intended that these will provide you with starting points in your searches for various birds. As much as possible I have focused on spots that can be found simply by consulting a standard road map, such as state and national parks, monuments, forests, and grasslands, and national wildlife refuges and state game preserves. Such locations have the added advantage of remaining current longer than privately owned lands, which may be developed. For precise mileages and route descriptions you will still need to consult the proper regional bird-finding guide. Such detail is beyond the scope of this book and has been provided only in a very few instances, for species that are highly localized.

The following abbreviations are used in the species accounts.

Highway (Hwy.)
National Forest (NF)
National Park (NP)
Rare bird alert (RBA)
State Park (SP)
National Wildlife Refuge (NWR)

No one person is familiar enough with every western state to personally write these species accounts. My own experience is heavy in Alaska, North and South Dakota, Texas, New Mexico, Colorado, Arizona, and California. I have much less experience in the other states and so have relied on input from local birding authorities, published bird-finding articles, and the proper regional bird-finding guides as references. In instances where I gleaned information from a published source, I have cited that work in the account. In instances where published information is more than 10 years old, I have tried to verify that the information is still current by checking with local experts.

## Species Accounts

**Arctic Loon.** This is a casual summer resident of Alaska's Seward Peninsula and a rare spring-fall transient along coastal areas in northwestern Alaska and to islands in the Bering Sea. There are only a few confirmed breeding records, from Wales and Kotzebue. The best place in North America to find it is from Northwest Point at Gambell (St. Lawrence Island), during large passages of Pacific Loons in late May and early June. Even then, Arctics will be greatly outnumbered by Pacifics. Smaller numbers pass by the coast at Nome, where Arctics are occasionally seen on the water (most often at Safety Sound or somewhere in the Safety Lagoon complex). This is one of those birds that is reported by overly eager birders far more often than it actually occurs. This species is an accidental fall-spring visitor to coastal areas south of Alaska, but it has been found as far south as central California.

**Yellow-billed Loon.** This is an uncommon and somewhat local summer resident and spring-fall transient of northern and western Alaska, south to the southern Seward Peninsula. It is an uncommon to rare migrant to the rest of coastal Alaska, where non-breeders frequently spend the summer in offshore waters. It winters along the Pacific Coast from Alaska south and is found casually to southern California; occasional vagrants turn up on larger bodies of water almost anywhere in the West. Winters regularly in small numbers in Washington, mostly on quiet bays. Individuals often show site fidelity to a particular spot (check with local birders), but more often they move around a great deal depending on tidal changes. This can be one of the tougher Alaskan specialties to see on a summer trip, because the main center of abundance lies in the mostly inaccessible north and northwest, off the main birding circuit. Then again, you could see individuals in passage at any number of coastal locales. The best bets for seeing migrants in May and June are from Northwest Point at Gambell (St. Lawrence Island, the end of May is usually best), from Wales, or from the base of the Point at Barrow. Yellow-billed Loons nest on tundra lakes near Barrow, but they seldom choose lakes within scoping distance of the few miles of road. One locality that can be driven to where Yellow-billeds have nested in the past is Salmon Lake, located along the Kougarok Road out of Nome. Salmon Lake is usually mostly frozen until mid-June, and the loons are seldom seen there before then. Cordova and the Prince William Sound area are excellent places to see fall migrants (beginning in September) and wintering birds.

**Least Grebe.** This is an uncommon and local resident of small bodies of fresh water in the lower Rio Grande Valley of southern Texas and north along the coast from Brownsville to about Corpus Christi. This grebe seems to undergo irregular population fluctuations, and during some years it can be hard to find. Least Grebes inhabit wood-bordered and open-edged ponds as well as ditches and larger man-made impoundments. Areas with plenty of emergent vegetation are preferred, but not requisite. Try the small lakes at Santa Ana NWR, the freshwater ponds and ditches at Laguna Atascosa NWR, and the ponds and ditches along Highway 281 west from Brownsville. This is casual vagrant elsewhere in the Southwest.

**Black-footed Albatross.** This is a fairly common year-round visitor to the offshore waters of the West Coast. It is most common from May to September, when groups of birds are often seen following fishing trawlers. They commonly settle on the water alongside boats and feed on garbage, fish entrails, or chum tossed overboard. They are almost always seen on spring and summer boat trips (March–July) out of Monterey, California, but numbers in the bay fall off rapidly in late summer, and the species is missed more than it is seen the rest of the year.

Your best chances are from Westport, Washington, where the bird is virtually never missed between April and October and often occurs in substantial numbers.

**Laysan Albatross.** This is a very rare but regular visitor to offshore waters of the West Coast. It summers in waters around the Aleutian Islands of Alaska, from which individuals move south in fall toward their nesting areas on Pacific islands. They appear far offshore (200 or more miles) from Washington by October and off central California by December. Most sightings near shore have come from central California, and most of these have been from December through May (although there are now Monterey Bay records from nearly every month). Trips to the Cordell Banks from Bodega Bay, California have regularly recorded Laysans, but your odds of finding it on any one boat trip are not great. Laysans are fairly regular on winter trips out of Westport, Washington, although many trips at that season are canceled because of bad weather. A summer possibility is the monthly ferry from Homer to Dutch Harbor, Alaska.

**Mottled Petrel.** This is a rare summer visitor to deep waters in the Gulf of Alaska and southern Bering Sea from its breeding areas in New Zealand. In the early and mid-1970s this species was seen in small numbers with some regularity from the Homer-Kodiak-Seward ferry. There have been few confirmed sightings since. The bird's former regularity may have coincided with some cycle of water temperature related to a transient phenomenon of water currents. Mottled Petrels are casually recorded from waters farther south (to southern California) but are probably regular migrants far offshore beyond the range of most one-day pelagic trips. Some November trips out to the Cordell Banks (from Bodega Bay, California) have had luck in finding this species.

**Murphy's Petrel.** The exact status of this species in our waters is uncertain. Since 1989, this bird has been recorded (sometimes more than 50 birds) on several March–June boat trips to deep waters well off central California (generally 30–90 miles offshore). Because few birding boats reach this distance (especially in spring), it is not known whether this is a regular or a recent phenomenon. The bird has now been recorded as far north as Washington in both spring and fall. Murphy's Petrels breed on scattered islands in the South Pacific and enter our waters during the nonbreeding season.

**Cook's Petrel.** The exact status of this species in our waters is uncertain. Most sightings have come between October and December from boats traversing deep waters (2000 or more fathoms; 12,000 ft) far offshore from San Luis Obispo County north to Marin County (particularly from the Davidson Seamount and Cordell Banks), California. However, research boats have also recorded large numbers of Cook's Petrels in the same waters more than 50 miles offshore between March and June. This species breeds on islands off the coast of New Zealand, wintering (our summer) in the North Pacific, at least as far north as the Aleutians.

**Streaked Shearwater.** This is a casual fall vagrant from Asia to the offshore waters of the West Coast. Most records to date have come from pelagic trips out of Monterey, California, usually from mid-September to mid-October. Chase boats have been organized within 24–48 hours after each sighting, but to date, none have been successful.

**Flesh-footed Shearwater.** This is a rare but regular visitor to offshore waters of the West Coast. It breeds on islands off Australia and New Zealand and winters in the Pacific north (at least casually) to the southern Bering Sea and the Gulf of Alaska. In our waters, records are scattered throughout the year, but most birds are seen in fall (August through October). Some autumns seem to yield distinctly more Flesh-footeds than others. In some recent years, at least one or two Flesh-footeds have been recorded on the majority of fall Monterey (California) trips, but over the long term the species has been recorded on only roughly 10% to 15% of all fall trips. In the past, boat trips out of Westport, Washington, have regularly yielded Flesh-footeds in May and from July to October, but, with the decline of active trawling operations, the species has become irregular in the past 3 or 4 years. Flesh-footeds are usually found among concentrations of other shearwaters. They regularly attend fishing boats, and will readily chum-in right next to the boat.

**Short-tailed Shearwater.** This is an uncommon visitor in late fall through winter to offshore waters of most of the West Coast and is an abundant summer visitor to the Gulf of Alaska and adjacent waters. The true status of this bird is greatly clouded by its extreme similarity to the abundant Sooty Shearwater. Specimen evidence suggests that few Short-taileds occur in California before November. At least small numbers probably stay in California waters through much of the winter. Summer ferry crossings in the Gulf of Alaska (try the Homer-Kodiak-Seward crossing) routinely encounter large numbers of Short-taileds. Otherwise, Monterey Bay and Bodega Bay (California) boat trips from mid-November through February, and Westport, Washington, trips in October probably provide as good a chance as any for seeing this bird.

**Pink-footed Shearwater.** This is a common visitor to offshore waters of the West Coast from spring through fall. A sprinkling of birds is generally present from March through July, at which time numbers begin to increase and remain fairly high until late October, when they begin to taper off. Pink-footeds breed on islands off the coast of Chile during our winter months then fan out over the eastern Pacific (north to the southern Bering Sea) during the nonbreeding season. Aside from the Sooty, this is the most common western shearwater, and it is easily seen from boats leaving almost any western port.

**Buller's Shearwater.** This is an uncommon summer-through-fall visitor to offshore waters of the West Coast, from British Columbia (casually north to Alaska) and south to central California. The species is decidedly uncommon south of

Point Conception, California. Buller's Shearwaters breed on islands off the coast of New Zealand, and dispersing postbreeders usually enter our waters in July. Most birds are found from August to November, with a peak in early October. A few may linger in California waters into December. The best chances for seeing it are from pelagic trips taken out of Westport, Washington, and Monterey Bay and Bodega Bay, California, from mid-September through mid-October.

**Black-vented Shearwater.** This species is a fairly common visitor from August through January to offshore California waters (casually north to Oregon) from its nesting islands off of Baja. In some years, numbers may remain well into March. Abundance varies greatly from one year to the next and probably is positively correlated with the strong northward flow of warm currents from west Mexican waters. This shearwater is most common off southern California and is best seen on boats out of San Diego and Monterey. It is typically found somewhat close to shore and can often be spotted from land at appropriate overlooks with the aid of a spotting scope.

**Black Storm-Petrel.** This is a common visitor to the offshore waters of southern and central California (south of Marin County). It breeds from spring through fall on rocky islands off the extreme southern tip of California and northern Baja (notably Los Coronados of Mexico) and in the Gulf of California. A small breeding colony on Sutil Island (near Santa Barbara Island in the Channel Islands) is the only known breeding site in our area. The Black Storm-Petrel is readily seen on San Diego pelagic trips (after late April), and can also be common over the submarine canyons out of Monterey Bay (August through November), where it rafts on the water in large diurnal roosts with hundreds to thousands of Ashy Storm-Petrels (September–October is the peak time). During El Niño events, which bring warm currents farther north along the Pacific Coast, Black Storm-Petrels may remain in the Monterey Bay area into January. This is the storm-petrel most likely to be seen from shore.

**Ashy Storm-Petrel.** This is a fairly common resident from spring through fall (uncommon to rare in winter) of offshore waters of the California coast (more common off the southern and central coast). Most of the world population breeds on the Farallon Islands (California), with lesser numbers breeding on some of the Channel Islands (California) and on Los Coronados Islands (Baja). These birds are most readily seen from August through November, when thousands raft over submarine canyons. The best and most reliable spot is Monterey Bay, but numbers also frequent the Cordell Banks (off Bodega Bay) and the waters near the Farallon Islands. This is probably the most likely storm-petrel to be seen in southern California waters in winter (November–April).

**Least Storm-Petrel.** This is an erratic late-summer and early-fall visitor to offshore waters of California from its nesting rocks off the Pacific Coast of Baja and in the Gulf of California. Numbers vary from one year to the next, and there are occasional years when the species is virtually absent from our waters. In other years, thousands may be present from San Diego (where it is typically most common) north to Monterey Bay. It is rare north of Monterey Bay in any year. The species is present off San Diego in most years, with numbers peaking in August through September. It is more erratic farther north, where its occurrence may be linked to periodic El Niño events that bring warm water currents farther north than usual. When present in Monterey Bay, Least Storm-Petrels are typically found from September through November, associating with the Ashy and Black storm-petrel flocks that gather over the submarine canyons.

**Fork-tailed Storm-Petrel.** This is a common to abundant breeding bird of rocky islands off the southern coast of Alaska and is a fairly common to rare breeder south along the Pacific Coast to northern California (Humboldt and Del Norte counties). Birds are seen year-round in the offshore waters of Alaska, Washington, and Oregon and more rarely off of California, where more records come from late fall and winter pelagic trips. This species is somewhat irruptive in California, with numbers present in some years and almost no birds present in others. It is best seen from summer ferry trips (Homer-Kodiak-Seward, and Homer-Dutch Harbor) in the Gulf of Alaska, where huge numbers occur. It is also seen regularly on pelagic trips out of Washington and Oregon. It is less commonly seen from nearshore waters, such as from tour boats to Kenai Fjords NP, but sometimes is seen from land (particularly from the Homer Spit). Although thousands nest on the Chiswell Islands (Alaska), they are seldom seen there because trips by adults to and from the nests to distant feeding areas are made under cover of darkness.

**Magnificent Frigatebird.** This is a rare, but regular, postbreeding visitor (July through September) to coastal California and Texas and to the Salton Sea (California). Stragglers occasionally find their way into Arizona, particularly along the Colorado River. In Texas, your best bet is to scope wooden pilings and buoys that dot the larger bays. Try the Texas City Dike, Galveston Bay, Lavaca Bay, the Bolivar Ferry, and Corpus Christi Bay. In California, your best chances are to check the Salton Sea and monitor the southern coastal RBAs.

**Red-billed Tropicbird.** This is rare but regular on the offshore waters of the Gulf of Mexico, where it has been recorded annually on Texas pelagic trips the past few years. It is a rare and irregular postbreeding visitor to the offshore waters of southern California. Red-billed Tropicbirds have been found north to the central coast and usually well out to sea. Most records date from August to September. It was formerly regular in the vicinity of San Clemente Island, but in recent years it has been more regular farther north on deep-water trips well offshore. These birds and the less-frequently encountered **Red-tailed Tropicbird** (which is a casual visitor to far offshore waters of southern and central California, mostly from July through September) no doubt occur more regularly on the deeper waters farther offshore (50–100 miles). Your best bets for seeing the Red-billed in California are August–September one-day pelagic trips from San Diego or overnight trips from more northern ports that reach distant waters (e.g., trips from Monterey to the Davidson Seamount). The Red-billed is probably more likely to be seen on summer Texas pelagic trips.

**Brown Booby.** This is a casual postbreeding visitor (July through November, with August and September being most likely) to the Salton Sea, California, and the Colorado River Valley from its breeding rocks in the Gulf of California. This is the rarer of the two boobies expected to occur in California, and in most years none are present. It is certain to be mentioned on local RBAs.

**Blue-footed Booby.** This is a rare and irregular postbreeding visitor (July through November, with August and September being most likely) to the Salton Sea (California), to the Colorado River Valley (California, Arizona), and occasionally along the southern California coast. In the 1960s and 1970s, this species staged periodic invasions into southern California, appearing in numbers in some years. There has been only one such invasion into our area in the past decade, so your chances are not good. It is certain to be mentioned on local RBAs.

**Masked Booby.** This is a rare, but regular, visitor to offshore Texas waters year-round. At times (particularly in summer) it can be fairly common in the Gulf of Mexico. Your best bet is to get booked on a pelagic trip (irregularly scheduled, inquire with coastal Audubon Societies) or hitchhike on a commercial fishing boat. If you can't get on a boat, your only recourse is to stake yourself to the end of a coastal jetty and scope evey buoy and channel marker within sight. Masked Boobies are also occasional vagrants to coastal areas and offshore waters of California, with records scattered through much of the year (although more records are concentrated in the summer months). If present, it is certain to be mentioned on California RBAs.

**Neotropic Cormorant.** This is a fairly common to uncommon resident of mostly freshwater lakes and rivers (but occasionally is found on coastal bays) from the southwestern corner of Louisiana south along the Gulf Coast to Brownsville, Texas, and west along the Rio Grande to about Falcon Dam. It is less common, but still a regular year-round visitor, to reservoirs along the Rio Grande from Laredo, Texas, to Albuquerque, New Mexico. Beginning in the mid-1970s a few pairs began nesting in the vicinity of Elephant Butte Reservoir along the Rio Grande in New Mexico. Since 1982 the population seems to have increased dramatically, and it is not uncommon to see 50 or more birds in a day at such places as Bosque del Apache NWR and Elephant Butte Reservoir and Caballo Reservoir (New Mexico). Neotropic Cormorants are rare year-round visitors to southern Arizona (most commonly found at Patagonia Lake) and are even rarer visitors to southern California (most likely along the lower Colorado River and at the Salton Sea).

**Red-faced Cormorant.** This is a fairly common coastal resident from the Pribilofs south to the Aleutians and east along south coastal Alaska to Prince William Sound. It nests on seacliffs, often close to other seabirds and winters throughout the breeding range and beyond to southeastern Alaska. It is easily seen on the Pribilofs (St. Paul and St. George), on the Aleutians, at Dutch Harbor, around Resurrection Bay, at the Chiswell Islands and Kenai Fjords NP, on Kachemak Bay, on the Barren Islands, and (less easily) near Cordova.

**Reddish Egret.** This is an uncommon resident of salt marshes and beaches along the Gulf Coast from Brownsville (Texas) to southern Florida. In Texas, it nests on offshore islands that are covered with dense, low shrubs and trees. The Reddish Egret is more restricted to salt water than any other U.S. heron or egret. Because it prefers open habitats, it is easily seen. Look for it in appropriate habitats anywhere along the Texas coast, but especially at Bolivar Flats, Galveston Island SP, Rockport, Corpus Christi, Laguna Atascosa NWR, and along the Queen Isabella Causeway (connecting Port Isabel to South Padre Island). It is also a rare, but regular, vagrant to southern California (primarily the San Diego and Salton Sea areas).

**Roseate Spoonbill.** This is a fairly common to uncommon resident of marshes, ponds, and coastal mudflats along the Gulf Coast from Brownsville, Texas, to southern Florida. It is more common on the upper and central Texas coast than on the lower coast. It nests on dry coastal islands alongside other species of waders. Most individuals leave for the winter, making the bird somewhat hard to find at that season. Apparently the wintering birds are best found in the river deltas at the end of the larger bays, such as Trinity Bay near Baytown and Corpus Christi Bay (Holt 1993). At other times of the year it should be easy to find at Galveston Island SP; Sabine Marsh; Bolivar Flats; Corpus Christi; and Anahuac, Aransas, and Laguna Atascosa NWRs.

**Wood Stork.** This is an uncommon postbreeding visitor (July through September) to freshwater marshes, lagoons, and rice fields along the Texas Gulf Coast and to the Salton Sea in California. It is often seen circling high overhead like a vulture or perching on the upper branches of large trees (often dead ones in standing water). In Texas, try Anahuac, Welder, Aransas, and Laguna Atascosa NWRs; Welder Wildlife Refuge; the Sabine Marsh; and the rice fields west of Houston. Salton Sea birds are most easily found around Redhill and at Finney and Ramer lakes.

**Fulvous Whistling-Duck.** This is an uncommon and decreasing summer resident (some winter) of rice fields and freshwater lakes and marshes along the Texas coast. It is seen in the lower Rio Grande Valley as a migrant. It is also an uncommon to rare summer visitor to the Salton Sea in California (where it has nested), with small numbers sometimes occurring throughout the winter. In Texas, try Anahuac (in summer), Laguna Atascosa (during migration), and Santa Ana (during migration) NWRs; Welder wildlife Refuge; the Corpus Christi area; and (possibly the best spot) the rice fields east and west of Houston.

**Black-bellied Whistling-Duck.** This is a fairly common summer resident of tree-lined ponds along the lower Rio Grande Valley from Rio Grande City to Brownsville and along the Gulf Coast north to Corpus Christi, Texas. This duck winters in smaller numbers in the extreme southern portions of that range along the Rio Grande delta. When wintering birds are located they are often in large flocks. This species has also become a regular but localized summer resident in the Santa Cruz and lower San Pedro river valleys of southern Arizona. In Texas look for it at Lake Corpus Christi, at Welder Wildlife Refuge, and at Laguna Atascosa and Santa Ana NWRs. The best places in Arizona are all near the town of Nogales; try the ponds at Kino Springs, the Drive-In Theater ponds, and (especially) the Nogales sewage ponds. Black-bellied Whistling-Ducks are also very rare post-breeding (summer through fall) vagrants to the Salton Sea in California.

**Trumpeter Swan.** This is an uncommon breeder on lakes and ponds in the taiga zone of interior Alaska and a rare resident of scattered lakes and marshes in the Northwest, northern Rockies, and northern Great Plains. The isolated Alaska population is somewhat migratory and tends to winter from southeastern Alaska to the coasts of Washington and Oregon (individuals occasionally show up as far south as California). Once nearly extirpated, this bird is making a comeback, in part because of reintroduction programs. Look for it at the following locations:

1. Alaska. Lakes along the Parks Hwy. between Wasilla and Denali NP (particularly just south of Cantwell); lakes along the Denali Hwy. between Cantwell and Paxson; Midway Lake (between Tetlin Junction and Northway Junction) and Yarger Lake (7.5 miles southeast of Northway Junction) along the Alaska Hwy. (Springer 1993); Kenai NWR (Armstrong 1983); barley fields and lakes around Delta Junction from late April through early May (Springer 1993); the Copper River Delta near Cordova (spring through fall); and lakes and marshes throughout the Kenai Peninsula during spring and fall migration.

2. Washington (Wahl and Paulson 1977). Turnbull NWR (nests) and Beaver Lake, Clear Lake, and DeBay Slough (0.2 mile north and 1 mile west of Clear Lake) in Skagit Cove (winter). Flocks of a few to hundreds are widespread on the "flats" on Washington rivers that empty into north Puget Sound, from Marysville north to the British Columbia border. Sightings in Washington are increasing. Trumpeter Swans often mix with Tundra Swans.

3. Oregon (Evanich 1990). Malheur NWR (introduced population); and in winter, look for scattered birds among flocks of Tundra Swans at the Trojan Nuclear Power Plant Grounds (about 45 miles north of Portland on the east side of U.S. Hwy. 30), Suavie Island (about 10 miles north of Portland off U.S. Hwy. 30, at

the confluence of the Columbia and Willamette rivers), and in farm fields south of Forest Grove.

4. Montana. Red Rock Lakes NWR (the source of birds introduced to other areas) and Yellowstone NP.

5. Wyoming (year-round). National Elk Refuge (along Flat Creek on U.S. Hwy. 191) near Jackson and at several locations in Grand Teton NP and Yellowstone NP.

6. South Dakota. Lacreek NWR.

7. Idaho (Svingen and Dumroese 1997). Teton Valley southwest of Driggs (winter), Camas NWR near Hamer (nesting), Harriman SP north of Ashton (year-round).

**Ross's Goose.** This is an uncommon and local winter resident of freshwater marshes and agricultural lands in the interior of California. It breeds in arctic Canada. The bulk of the world population winters in the Sacramento (try Sacramento NWR) and San Joaquin (try San Luis NWR) valleys. Ross' Goose is less common among the vast Snow Goose flocks at the Salton Sea. It is also easily found in winter (November through April) at Bosque del Apache NWR (New Mexico) and, in smaller numbers, at Bitter Lakes NWR (New Mexico). Small numbers winter on the Texas coast, where they must be picked from among the Snow Goose flocks. In Texas, try Anahuac NWR, the Attwater Prairie-Chicken NWR, San Bernard NWR, and the Katy rice fields west of Houston. Stray individuals and small groups often winter along the California coast, where they will usually be noted on local RBAs. As birders begin to scan Snow Goose flocks more closely, Ross's Geese are being found regularly in small numbers throughout much of the interior West, wherever flocks of migrant geese stop to rest and feed.

**Emperor Goose.** This is an uncommon breeder in wet lowland tundra, often near the coast, from the northern Seward Peninsula south along the western Alaskan coastline to the Yukon-Kuskokwim River Delta. The bulk of the world population breeds in the Yukon-Kuskokwim Delta region (including the Yukon Delta NWR), which, unfortunately, is difficult to access. Only small numbers breed on the Seward Peninsula and on remote parts of St. Lawrence Island, but migrants can often be seen from mid-May through mid-June off Northwest Point at Gambell (St. Lawrence Island), and (less reliably) at coastal lagoons near Wales and Nome (Safety and Woolley lagoons). The return migration takes place in August and September. Emperor Geese winter primarily from the Aleutians east along the Alaska Peninsula to Bristol Bay and Kodiak, sparingly farther east along south coastal Alaska and south along the Pacific Coast to (rarely) northern California. They are rare but regular in winter along Puget Sound and coastal Washington. Wintering birds spend much of their time on rocky beaches. Large concentrations of fall migrants can be seen from August to October at Izembek NWR near Cold Bay (serviced by daily flights from Anchorage). Good numbers of Emperors also winter at Cold Bay (best seen along the beaches near the mouths of Russell and

Trout creeks; Lethaby 1994) and at Kodiak (best seen at the mouth of the Buskin River, at Womens Bay, and at Kalsin Bay-Cape Chiniak; Lethaby 1994).

**Brant.** All birds in our area are referable to the western *nigricans* group, formerly considered a separate species, "Black Brant." The Brant is a common to uncommon summer resident of coastal tundra in western and northern Alaska. It is a common migrant along coastal portions of the Seward Peninsula, where numbers can usually be found at coastal lagoons at Wales and Nome (especially at Safety Lagoon) in both spring and fall (with some nonbreeders spending the summer). A large population breeds in the Yukon-Kuskokwim Delta region. Huge numbers stage in the eelgrass marshes at Izembek Bay near Cold Bay from August through October before heading south. It is a fairly common winter resident (usually at major bays) and migrant along the length of the West Coast. It is rarely found inland but often appears in late summer at the Salton Sea (California). This "sea goose" favors large coastal bays, preferring to feed in shallow water and on mudflats, often around river mouths.

**Muscovy Duck.** This is a rare, but increasing, year-round visitor along the lower Rio Grande in southern Texas. The numbers of these widespread neotropical ducks increased in adjacent northeastern Mexico in 1990s, seemingly in response to conservation efforts and nest-box programs by Ducks Unlimited of Mexico. Unlike the familiar domesticated Muscovies (which wouldn't fly even if you set off dynamite under them), these wild birds are generally exceedingly wary and often bolt into flight as soon as people come into view. Domesticated birds often have significant amounts of white scattered irregularly through their plumage, a character not found on wild birds. The best areas to look are all along the river below Falcon Dam, including below the spillway, at Salineño, at Santa Margarita Ranch, and from Santa Margarita Bluffs.

**Eurasian Wigeon.** This is a rare but regular winter visitor along the length of the West Coast, usually with large flocks of American Wigeon. The Eurasian Wigeon is a dependable bird in large American Wigeon flocks in western Washington from mid-October until March. Samish Bay and the flats of the Samish River near Edison are particularly good sites. The San Diego River flood control channel (opposite Sea World) and Morro Bay (California) host a few Eurasian Wigeons every winter. Scattered individuals turn up amidst American Wigeon flocks throughout the West, but they are not predictable. This is the most regular of vagrant waterfowl to reach Alaska from Siberia. In most summers a pair can be found somewhere near Safety Lagoon at Nome, and small migrant groups regularly turn up on lakes and marshes on St. Paul Island in May and June.

**Tufted Duck.** This is a very rare but annual winter visitor (October through April) to bays and lakes along the West Coast. It is most common in fall around Vancouver, British Columbia (try Lost Lagoon in Stanley Park), but also regularly is found south to the bay area in California. Many individuals return to the same lakes for several consecutive years and remain for long periods of time. Tufted Ducks are often found among scaup or Ring-necked Duck flocks. Your best bet is to check local RBAs. This species is also a frequent spring and early-summer vagrant to western Alaska from Siberia. They frequently turn up in May and June on various lakes on St. Paul Island, the Pribilofs.

**Spectacled Eider.** This is a rare and declining summer resident of coastal tundra in northern and western Alaska. It winters in the western Bering Sea. The North American population of this spectacular duck has declined precipitously since the 1980s, for reasons that are largely unknown. It nests sporadically on the Seward Peninsula (Shishmaref and Wales), but the bulk of the Alaskan population breeds on the North Slope and in the Yukon-Kuskokwim Delta region. It was formerly common at Barrow, but nesting birds have become scarce in recent years. Barrow is still the most accessible spot where breeding birds might be found, and many more birds pass over the base of Point Barrow en route to more distant breeding areas. The Yukon Delta NWR, Hooper Bay and Prudhoe Bay are other possibilities for nesting birds. Your chances are probably just as good from Northwest Point at Gambell (St. Lawrence Island) in late May through mid-June, when small numbers of Spectacleds pass by. This species is also seen (although less predictably) as a migrant along the coast at Nome, mostly between Safety Lagoon and Solomon (and more often after mid-June, possibly representing a return of failed breeders or nonbreeders).

**Steller's Eider.** This is an uncommon and apparently declining summer resident of lowland tundra ponds and lakes along Alaska's north coast, south locally to the Yukon-Kuskokwim Delta region. It does not appear to nest regularly on the Seward Peninsula, although migrants and summer visitors are frequently seen at Nome and Wales (at coastal lagoons and along the immediate coast). It winters in the Pribilofs and Aleutians, east to Kodiak and (sparingly) to Prince William Sound. It is casual farther south, with vagrants recorded to northern California. Nonbreeders sometimes summer at coastal locales south of the breeding range (e.g., coastal coves and the Salt Lagoon at St. Paul Island). It is best seen at Barrow (where nesting pairs are scattered about the tundra) and at Gambell (migrants pass by Northwest Point in May–June).

**King Eider.** This is a fairly common summer resident of lowland tundra ponds and lakes in arctic Alaska, only rarely breeding as far south as the Seward Peninsula. It is a common migrant and uncommon summer visitor to coastal western Alaska, and a rare migrant along Alaska's south coast. It winters in the southern Bering Sea south to the Aleutians and the Alaska Peninsula and, rarely, farther east along south coastal Alaska. It is casual south to California in winter. Barrow is the easiest place to see breeding King Eiders. A few pairs are scattered about the tundra, and small flocks are routinely seen passing by along the coast and across the base of the Point. Large numbers also pass by Northwest Point at Gambell (St. Lawrence Island) in May and June. Small numbers breed at Prudhoe Bay, and migrants and nonbreeding summer visitors are frequently seen along the coast at Nome, Wales, and St. Paul Island (Pribilofs). Cold Bay and Kodiak are likely spots in winter.

**Harlequin Duck.** This is a fairly common to common breeder along fast-flowing rivers and streams in western, central, and southern Alaska. Adults and grown offspring move to the coast after breeding. There, they join nonbreeders, sometimes forming flocks of 50 or more. Nonbreeders spend the entire year in coastal areas. Harlequins winter north to the Pribilofs and Aleutians.

It is an uncommon breeder along fast-moving rivers and streams in the high country of Washington, Oregon, Idaho, Montana, and Wyoming. It moves to areas of rocky coast (where the winter is spent) after nesting. There, it is seen feeding in the roughest part of the surf. It winters south to central California (regularly to the Monterey area, but is more common farther north).

**Barrow's Goldeneye.** This is an uncommon to fairly common summer resident of forest lakes and ponds from central Alaska south to Oregon, northern Montana, and northwestern Wyoming. It winters on large inland lakes, bays, and rivers and along the West Coast, often considerably south of the breeding range (regularly to the San Francisco Bay area in California, as vagrants farther south).

**Masked Duck.** This is a very rare and irregular year-round visitor (which occasionally nests) to freshwater ponds and ditches with emergent vegetation (and usually grassy borders) in the lower Rio Grande Valley of Texas and along the Gulf Coast. Santa Ana NWR, Welder Wildlife Refuge, Brazos Bend SP, Aransas NWR, Attwater Prairie-Chicken NWR, and Anahuac NWR have had their share of past records, but this bird is impossible to predict. It is certain to be mentioned on local RBAs if present.

**Hook-billed Kite.** This is a rare resident of subtropical forests along the lower Rio Grande Valley of southern Texas. The most consistent areas are Santa Ana NWR (watch from trails around Pintail Lake or from the levee), Bentsen SP (along either the Rio Grande or Singing Chaparral Nature Trails or from the levee west of the entrance road), and the woodlands from Falcon Dam downstream to the Santa Margarita Ranch. Check the local RBAs for current hot spots. These kites feed on tree snails, which tend to be distributed in patches. Once a kite discovers a productive feeding area, it often establishes definite foraging patterns (to the point of flying over precise stretches of park or refuge roads at roughly the same time every day). You would do well to note the exact times and places of kite sightings that are passed along by other birders.

**White-tailed Kite.** This is a fairly common to uncommon resident of brushy grasslands and agricultural areas in southern Texas, central and coastal California, and coastal Oregon. It is rare and local in small satellite populations in surrounding states such as Arizona, New Mexico, Washington, and Oklahoma. This bird seems to undergo periodic population fluctuations. From the late 1960s through the early 1980s the U.S. population increased measurably, and White-tailed Kites colonized many areas formerly unoccupied. During this time they were a common sight along California freeways and not at all difficult to find. During the 1990s, kite populations in some areas declined substantially, and the species is now hard to find in areas where it was formerly common.

**Common Black-Hawk.** This is an uncommon to rare summer resident (from mid-March to early October) of cottonwood-willow-sycamore woodlands along permanently flowing streams in southeastern and central Arizona, southwestern New Mexico, and the Davis Mountains of Texas (it is casual north to southern Utah). It is occasionally seen in southern Texas and at Big Bend NP in migration. The current Arizona hot spots are Aravaipa Canyon (north of Tucson) and along the San Pedro River north of Dudleyville, although the species is actually more common farther north in areas that are not accessible to the public, or are off the popular southeastern Arizona birding circuit. In New Mexico, try along the Gila (at Redrock and Cliff and along the road to Bill Evans Lake), San Francisco, and Mimbres rivers. The Texas population consists of one or two pairs that breed along Limpia Creek near Fort Davis. This bird does most of its hunting from branches overlooking the water. It is also not uncommon to find one either standing on a sandbar or actually wading through water as it searches for crayfish, frogs, and other aquatic prey. These hawks tend to be very skittish around the nest, and extreme caution should be exercised to avoid disturbing nesting birds.

**Harris' Hawk.** This is a locally common but decreasing resident of mesquite brushlands in southern Texas, extreme southern New Mexico (uncommon), and south-central Arizona (uncommon). This hawk is generally easier to find in Texas than in New Mexico or Arizona.

1. Texas. Easy to find at Santa Ana NWR, the King Ranch, around Falcon Dam, along Hwy. 83 west of Mission to Laredo, and between San Antonio and Laredo on State Hwy. 16 and U.S. Hwy. 59. Small numbers persist in patches along the river west to El Paso.

2. New Mexico. Rattlesnake Springs (Carlsbad Caverns NP), Harroun Lake (Eddy County), and U.S. Highway 80 between Road Forks and Rodeo (including the San Simon Cienega).

3. Arizona. Best seen north and west of Tucson in desert dominated by saguaro and palo verde. Often seen perched on telephone poles along Hwys. 77 and 79 north of Tucson to Aravaipa Canyon and Florence, respectively. Also commonly seen on Tohomo O'odham Nation lands and on poles along Thornydale Road and adjacent sideroads (northwest Tucson) and at scattered spots in the Sulphur Springs Valley.

**Gray Hawk.** This is an uncommon and local summer resident (March through September) of riparian forest (consisting of cottonwoods, sycamores, and willows) at low elevations in southeastern Arizona. Most of the U.S. population is located along the San Pedro and Santa Cruz rivers and their tributaries, but most people see their first one along Sonoita Creek near Patagonia. At least a couple of pairs of hawks are present in this general area every year, and they are fairly easy to find from April through September. Try also at Kino Springs (north of Nogales off State Hwy. 82), River Road east of Nogales, and along the San Pedro River east of Sierra Vista off State Hwy. 90. Because of the rarity of this bird in the United States, please do not go near a nest or tarry long in the vicinity of an obviously agitated pair. This species is also a rare but regular winter visitor to the lower Rio Grande Valley of Texas. Look for it at Bentsen SP, Santa Ana NWR, and below Falcon Dam.

**Roadside Hawk.** This is a casual visitor to the lower Rio Grande Valley of southern Texas. It is one of those species that is reported far more than it should be. There is a good reason why this species is named Roadside Hawk. Throughout its extensive range (Mexico south to Argentina) it is a common and conspicuous raptor, generally inhabiting open country and perching along roads, busy highways, and river edges. Roadside Hawks are neither difficult to see nor particularly difficult to identify. Contrarily, many of the reports of Roadside Hawk from Texas are of extremely wary birds in some obscure immature plumage. It seems more than coincidental that most of these reports are made by birders who have never seen a Roadside Hawk in Latin America. If present, this species is certain to be mentioned on local RBAs.

**White-tailed Hawk.** This is an uncommon resident of coastal prairies and grassy mesquite–live oak savannas in southern Texas. Some of the better places to look are along U.S. Hwy. 77 from Kingsville to Raymondville (King Ranch), along State Hwy. 16 from Zapata to Hebbronville, the area on and around Aransas NWR, Attwater Prairie-Chicken NWR near Eagle Lake, and along State Hwy. 35 in Aransas and Refugio counties.

**Zone-tailed Hawk.** This is an uncommon to rare summer resident (late March to early October at the extremes) of steep-walled desert canyons, pine-oak-juniper montane woodlands, and lush cottonwood and sycamore forests along streams over much of Arizona, New Mexico, western Texas, and the western Edwards Plateau of Texas. This bird is often found in the same habitats as the Common Black-Hawk but is perhaps more typical of drier, more mountainous areas.

1. Texas. Lost Maples SP, Campwood Road (Ranch Road 337) out of Leaky (Edwards Plateau), McKittrick Canyon in Guadalupe Mountains NP, almost anywhere in the Davis Mountains, and along the Boot Springs Trail (near Pinnacle Pass) in Big Bend NP (perhaps the best Texas spot). Throughout winter (October–April) individuals are often seen in the lower Rio Grande Valley, particularly below Falcon Dam downstream to Santa Margarita Ranch.

2. New Mexico. Try the area around Los Alamos; the Gila River at Redrock and Cliff; Bandalier National Monument; and the Guadalupe, Burro, and Peloncillo Mountains.

3. Arizona. Guadalupe Canyon, Aravaipa Canyon, Cave Creek Canyon to the Southwest Research Station (Chiricahua Mountains.), Sonoita Creek near Patagonia, the Pinaleno Mountains, Harshaw Canyon east of Patagonia, and Madera Canyon (Santa Ritas).

4. California. A few individuals often winter in coastal southern California and will be listed on local RBAs if present.

**Crested Caracara.** This is an uncommon resident of mesquite brush country, coastal prairies, and grassy mesquite–live oak savannas in southern Texas and along the Texas coast to about Rockport (rare farther east). It is also a rare resident of saguaro desert and mesquite country in extreme south-central Arizona (Tohono O'odham Nation Lands to about Gila Bend. The dump at Sells is the standard spot.). In Texas it is perhaps easiest to see near Freer, along State Highways 16 (especially from Zapata to Hebbronville) and 44, and along U.S. Hwy. 59. Try also along Hwy. 83 from San Ygnacio to Mission, around Falcon Dam, along Hwy. 77 through the King Ranch, and at Laguna Atascosa, Attwater Prairie-Chicken, and Aransas NWRs.

**Aplomado Falcon.** This was formerly a resident of desert-grasslands and brushlands from southern Texas west to Arizona, but its last known natural nesting in this country was in 1952. Although Aplomado Falcons have been reported frequently by birders, there have been only a few confirmed sightings since about 1960. These have come from western Texas and New Mexico. There have been no substantiated sightings from Arizona since 1940. A captive breeding and reintroduction program has been under way at Laguna Atascosa NWR in southern Texas for several years, and released birds from that program are seen with some regularity in surrounding areas. Local RBAs will be certain to have details of any vagrant Aplomados if present.

**Gyrfalcon.** This is an uncommon to rare and often nomadic resident of open country in northern, western (including the Alaska Peninsula and Aleutians west to Umnak), and central Alaska. It is usually confined to lowland and alpine tundra with domes, seacliffs, or river escarpments for nesting. It feeds primarily on ptarmigan and (to a lesser extent) on seabirds and shorebirds. Unlike many other raptors, Gyrfalcons do not show a great deal of site tenacity, and they frequently change nest sites from year to year. They are morphologically variable, with dark birds, white birds (rare), and a variety of intermediate types all being found in our area. Gray birds with buffy underparts seem to predominate in much of Alaska. Gyrfalcons winter throughout the breeding range, but there is much individual movement, and the birds that occupy a site in winter may not be the ones that nested there. Gyrfalcons also winter far south of the breeding range, regularly (at least in small numbers) reaching the northern tier of western states. When present, wintering birds are certain to be mentioned on local RBAs, even in Alaska. Try the following locations:

1. Alaska. vicinity of Polychrome Pass, Eilson Visitor Center and all points in between at Denali NP; high cliff faces and bluffs overlooking river valleys along any of the roads out of Nome; eastern end of the Denali Hwy.; atop Eagle Summit northeast of Fairbanks along the Steese Hwy. (Springer 1993); and the Cold Bay-Izembek NWR area.

2. Washington. The most dependable area is in Skagit County on the flats of the Samish River near Bow, Edison, and Padilla Bay (a few birds are usually present from December to early March).

3. Oregon (Evanich 1990). The south jetty of the Columbia River (northwestern Clatsop County; winter).

**Plain Chachalaca.** This is a common, but local, permanent resident of subtropical woodlands in extreme southern Texas. It is easiest to find at Santa Ana and Laguna Atascosa NWRs, Bentsen SP, and the Sabal Palm Sanctuary, where they are protected. It is also common along the Rio Grande below Falcon Dam, but these birds are more wary (as are all species of chachalacas throughout Latin America), perhaps because of poaching. Their raucous dawn choruses are an unforgettable facet of any trip to "the Valley."

**Spruce Grouse.** This is a fairly common to uncommon resident of coniferous and mixed forests and spruce bogs in Alaska and an uncommon to rare resident of montane spruce-fir forests in the Northwest (Washington, Oregon, Idaho, Montana, and northwestern Wyoming). Even where this bird is fairly common it can be hard to find because of its protective coloring and quiet nature. Once you have found one, you can often view these usually tame birds at leisure. They are most often seen along gravel roads at dawn or dusk, but they may be glimpsed crossing trails or perched in trees. They are easiest to find in Alaska, where they occur in black spruce bogs, more-upland white spruce and birch or cottonwood associations, and the lush Sitka spruce forests of the south coastal and southeastern regions. They are generally easier to find in late summer and fall, when hens and their grown broods are about. Fall is also the time when grouse are making the transition to a winter diet of spruce needles, which requires more grit to digest. Hence, the grouse are even more likely to frequent roadsides in fall. Some suggested spots include the following:

1. Alaska. It is almost impossible to pick a specific spot, since much of the southern half of the state is good Spruce Grouse habitat. I've had the best luck searching campgrounds and trails on the Kenai Peninsula, between Anchorage and Seward. Here, they seem to prefer areas with abundant downed timber and a lush understory of devils club, horsetails, and various kinds of berry-producing plants.

2. Idaho (Svingen and Dumroese 1997). Sawtooth National Recreation Area (Stanley Lake and Iron Creek Trailhead near Stanley and Pettit Lake area), along Forest Road 129 near the Trinity Recreation Area (Elmore County), Goose Lake

area (Adams County northwest of McCall), Red River Wildlife Management Area (Idaho County), Chamberlain Basin, southwest of Cascade Reservoir along Forest Road 451.

3. Montana (Pettingill 1981, McEneaney 1993). Forest service campgrounds around Georgetown Lake west of Butte, along higher portions of Thief Creek (west of I-15 on Birch Creek Road, north of Dillon), the east side of Glacier NP (Forest Service Campground near Summit Siding, and along the Pike Creek logging road south of U.S. Hwy. 2), the west side of Glacier NP (trail to Avalanche Lake west of Logan Pass and the forest around MacDonald Pass along U.S. Hwy. 12 west of Helena).

4. Oregon (Evanich 1990). Wallowa Mountains (June–October) from Cove to the Moss Springs Guard Station via Mill Creek Road–National Forest Road 6220; Wallowa SP; and the Bonny Lakes trail in the Eagle Cap Wilderness Area (east from Joseph).

5. Washington (Wahl and Paulson 1977). Methow Wildlife Recreation Area east of Winthrop, Sherman Pass on State Hwy. 20 in Ferry County, the Little Pend Oreille Wildlife Recreation Area (Stevens County), Sullivan Lake and Calispell Peak (Pend Oreille County), and Tiffany Mountain (northwest of Okanogon). Tiffany Mountain is the current hot spot for finding Spruce Grouse. It is accessible after snowmelt in mid- to late June.

**Blue Grouse.** This is a fairly common resident of coniferous forests throughout much of the West, from southeastern Alaska south (locally) to northern Arizona, north-central New Mexico, and south-central California. There are several subspecies, comprising two subspecies groups. A primarily coastal form (*fuliginosus* group, also known as "Sooty Grouse" ) occurs from coastal southeastern Alaska south in coastal ranges and the Cascades to northern California and in the Sierra Nevada of California and adjacent western Nevada. A montane form (*obscurus* group, also known as "Dusky Grouse" ) occurs from montane areas of southeastern Alaska south through the Canadian Rockies, eastern Washington, and the Rocky Mountain chains to Arizona and New Mexico. Males of the *fuliginosus* group are darker in overall coloration and have dull, yellowish neck sacs. Males of the *obscurus* group are paler gray, with maroon-colored neck sacs. Birds of this group occurring from the Canadian Rockies through eastern Washington, northeastern Oregon, Idaho, Montana, and northwestern Wyoming can be further distinguished by the absence of the terminal gray tail band found in the other forms.

Blue Grouse inhabit a wide range of habitats, from lush coastal rain forests in the Pacific Northwest to stunted subalpine fir at 11,000 ft (3353 m) in the Rockies. In general, their distribution is closely associated with that of true firs (*Abies*) and of Douglas fir (*Pseudotsuga*), but in some parts of their range (e.g., northern Colorado and southern Wyoming) they will occupy (in the breeding season) dense oak thickets in sagebrush-covered foothills. During the nesting season they seem to prefer somewhat open conifer woodlands that are mixed with deciduous trees (such as aspen) and grassy or shrubby meadows. In many areas Blue Grouse undergo a reverse elevational migration, moving upslope (sometimes several thousand feet) to denser coniferous woodlands in fall and winter.

Like the Spruce Grouse, this bird is best spotted along gravel roads (early or late in the day) or by slowly walking forest trails and bordering meadows. The trick is in finding them; once spotted they are often ridiculously tame. They are widespread in appropriate habitats. Glacier Bay NP, Alaska (grouse are often in the parking lot at the Glacier Bay Lodge at Bartlett Cove); Grand Canyon NP and the Kaibab NF (Arizona); Yosemite NP (California); Rocky Mountain NP and Mesa Verde NP (Colorado); Black Canyon of the Gunnison National Monument (Colorado); Glacier NP (Montana); Yellowstone NP (Montana and Wyoming); Dinosaur National Monument (Utah and Colorado); Zion NP and Bryce NP (Utah); Hurricane Ridge in Olympic NP (Washington); Mt. Rainier NP (Washington); and Grand Tetons NP (Wyoming) are just a few of the many well-known spots where Blue Grouse can be found.

**Willow Ptarmigan.** This is a fairly common resident of well-vegetated tundra (mostly at low to mid elevations), muskeg, and low willow thickets in openings in taiga forest virtually throughout Alaska (west to the central Aleutians). It overlaps broadly with Rock Ptarmigan in some areas, but generally is separated by microhabitat. Willow Ptarmigan prefer more mesic areas with taller and denser shrubs. Their preferred food is leaves and buds of the various species of dwarf willow (supplemented by berries and insects when available).

These birds are easiest to see early in the breeding season (April through the beginning of June), when males are vocally advertising their territory from conspicuous perches (either atop willows or in the center of roads). At this time males, are readily identified by their bicolored appearance: reddish head, neck, and breast contrasting strikingly with a white body. Willow Ptarmigan are monogamous, and once mating has taken place and females are on eggs, both sexes abruptly become much more difficult to find (roads where 20–30 ptarmigan were seen in the last week of May might yield only one or two in the first week of June). The cryptically plumaged females spend much of their time incubating, and the males (who no longer have to worry about attracting a mate or excluding other males) retreat back off the roads and commence molting into the more cryptic plumage that they will retain for the rest of the summer. Once the young have hatched, these ptarmigan again become more conspicuous, and family groups (including the males, which, unique among grouse, assist in caring for the young) are frequently seen. In winter, Willow Ptarmigan retreat from the harsher parts of their breeding range, forming huge flocks in protected sites with an abundance of exposed willows.

The best places to find this species during the late spring and summer months are along any of the roads out of Nome (Kougarok is best); anywhere above treeline where shrubs abound along the road through Denali NP, including the latter half of the section that is open to public vehicular traffic; and along the east end of the Denali Hwy. near Paxson. As do most other gallinaceous birds, ptarmigan seem to undergo periodic population fluctuations, and, in down years, can be much harder to find. Sometimes, what appears to be a down year is simply one in which the breeding season started earlier, and birds are present in numbers but are just inconspicuous.

**Rock Ptarmigan.** This is a fairly common to uncommon resident of alpine and open tundra throughout most of Alaska, including west along the Aleutian chain to Attu. It overlaps broadly with Willow Ptarmigan in some regions, but in others it occurs only at higher elevations. In areas of overlap the two species can be separated by microhabitat. Rock Ptarmigan prefer more xeric, sparsely vegetated tundra (the "dwarf shrub mat" of Kessel 1989), often with a significant rock component. Rock Ptarmigan occur not only above Willow Ptarmigans on higher, more exposed ridges and domes, but they also separate out in valleys, where the Rocks are found along boulder-strewn gravel-bar complexes of rivers and streams, and the Willows are in adjacent dense willow-alder thickets. The preferred food of Rock Ptarmigan consists of leaves and buds of dwarf birch (supplemented by insects and berries when available).

As are Willow Ptarmigan, Rocks are much easier to find early in the breeding season, when males are advertising from prominent perches (roadsides, gravel berms along streams, and open ridgetops). Unlike the Willows, male Rock Ptarmigan court and breed in a mostly white plumage (very unlike the red-headed appearance of male Willows) that turns to an increasingly dirty-looking buff as the breeding season progresses. The best places to find Rock Ptarmigan in spring and summer are along the Teller and Kougarok roads out of Nome (check particularly in river valleys with broad, open gravel bars and in upland tundra with an abundance of lichen-covered rocks); in Denali NP around and above Highway Pass, Thorofare Pass, and the Eilson Visitor Center; along higher portions of the east end of the Denali Hwy. near Paxson; and atop Twelvemile Summit and Eagle Summit along the Steese Hwy. northeast of Fairbanks (Springer 1993).

**White-tailed Ptarmigan.** This is a fairly common, but local, resident of alpine tundra on high peaks throughout southern Alaska (west to the Kenai Peninsula) and much of the Rockies, Cascades, and adjacent ranges. Even in areas where this bird is common, it can be hard to find because of its protective coloring. Once found, they can be approached to within a few feet. Most birders see their first one in Colorado, along Trail Ridge Road in Rocky Mountain NP (one of the few places where you can drive to White-tailed habitat). Other places include Mt. Evans (west of Denver) above Summit Lake, Loveland Pass at the Summit of Hwy. 6 (near Dillon Reservoir), and Guanella Pass (out of Georgetown) around the summit parking lot. The latter location is the place to try in winter when other areas are closed. Outside of Colorado, try the following locations:

1. Alaska. Along the Richardson Hwy. at Thompson Pass (near Valdez), ridges over Palmer Creek near Hope (West 1994), around the edges of glaciers and ice fields in Denali NP, and generally anywhere in true alpine habitat high in the Chugach Mountains.

2. Montana (McEneaney 1993). Logan Pass in Glacier NP (trail to Hidden Lake Overlook).

3. New Mexico (Zimmerman et al. 1992). Above timberline in the Sangre de Cristo Mountains, particularly from the Valle Vidal tract of the Carson NF out of Costilla (inquire at the Questa Ranger District headquarters in Questa); and along the trail to Santa Fe Baldy (on the road to the Santa Fe Ski Basin, reintroduced population).

4. Washington (Wahl and Paulson 1977). Mt. Rainier NP at Second Burroughs Mountain (reached from Sunrise), Slate Peak Lookout off Hart's Pass (State Hwy. 20), on Mount Baker (west of Bellingham), and along the Freezeout Ridge Trail on Tiffany Mountain (west of Okanogan).

5. Wyoming (Pettingill 1981). The Snowy Range of the Medicine Bow Mountains. (west from Laramie on State Hwy. 130, then north to Brooklyn Lake and take the trail to Brooklyn Ridge; also Medicine Bow Peak).

**Notes on Observing Lekking Grouse.** Certain behaviors are required of birders when visiting grouse and prairie-chicken leks. A scouting trip to the lek the afternoon before is a good idea, so that you can visualize where you will be parking your car, where the sun will be relative to the birds, and so on. On the morning of your visit you will need to arrive at the lek well before first light so as not to spook the birds. If your car is to be positioned close to the lek, it would be best to dim your lights when covering the last 50–100 yards (46–91 m). Once you are in position, quiet and lack of movement are called for. The birds will accept your vehicle as a blind, but excessive movement or noise will frighten them. It is imperative that you remain in your vehicle until the birds are finished displaying, or at least until they are showing obvious signs of disinterest in displaying. Their lack of interest will be obvious, because instead of dancing the males will be crouched quietly or showing more interest in eating than in courtship. It is common for these birds to stop momentarily at sunrise to face the sun, but they will soon resume displaying. If you start your car engine before the birds are finished, they will likely fly. Such disturbances, when repeated by many birders, can result in the birds' abandoning the lek. In some areas the forest service or refuge personnel may provide blinds for viewing grouse displays. Reservations are often required to use such blinds. Your behavior in using the blinds should mirror that outlined above for viewing from vehicles.

**Sage Grouse.** This is a fairly common but declining resident of sagebrush-covered hills and flats over much of the western interior. Unlike other prairie grouse, this species can be relatively easy to find away from the leks. The following spots are just a few of the reliable areas:

1. Wyoming (Scott 1993). The Farson area (go north 3 miles from Farson on U.S. Hwy. 191 and take any road or track east toward Big Sandy Reservoir); from just east of Casper (exit 182 off I-25), go south on State Hwy. 253 8.2 miles to Natrona County Road 605 and turn left to the lek, which is 0.1 mile down the road on the right; sagebrush flats around Jackson Hole and the National Elk Refuge.

2. Colorado. Arapaho NWR; public display ground at Coalmont off State Hwy. 14; several leks scattered around the town of Walden (particularly around Lake John); north of Hayden along County Road 80 and north toward California Park. Your best bet is to check with the Division Wildlife agents in Walden and the Steamboat Springs area.

3. California. Clear Lake NWR, Honey Lake Wildlife Area, Ash Creek Wildlife Area in the Big Valley District of Modoc NF, and Bodie State Historical Park (north of Lee Vining), where grouse can be found in late summer walking around the deserted streets of the old ghost town.

4. Idaho (Pettingill 1981, Svingen and Dumroese 1997). Area surrounding Macon Lake (north of Shoshone), Sand Creek Wildlife Management Area (Fremont County, 9 miles north of St. Anthony), Midvale area (Washington County).

5. Oregon (Pettingill 1981, Evanich 1990). Malheur NWR (check at refuge headquarters for current sites); the road from Fort Rock to Fort Rock SP; Hart Mountain National Antelope Refuge (northeast of Plush, where you should inquire about road conditions); and Virtue Flats (from I-84, east from Baker on State Hwy. 86 for 6.5 miles, then 2.5 miles south on Ruckles Creek Road, and another 0.5 mile south on a spur road to the lek, which is on private property and must be viewed from the road).

6. North Dakota. U.S. Hwy. 12 west from Bowman (especially north and south of Marmarth: try West River Road south of Hwy. 12 from just west of Marmarth).

7. Nevada. North of Tonopah off State Hwy. 376 (from U.S. Hwy. 6 go 13 miles north and turn right to Belmont. From Belmont go 12.3 miles north on a dirt road, turn left, and go 2.3 miles to the lek; Cressman 1995) and Ruby Lake NWR.

8. Montana (Pettingill 1981, McEneaney 1993). South of Miles City on U.S. Hwy. 312; Bowdoin and Red Rock Lakes NWRs; the Dillon area (from Dillon, leks located off State Hwy. 278 about 22 miles west to Ermont and 1 mile east; and 31 miles west of Dillon near Dyce Creek).

9. Utah (Sorensen 1991b). Parker Mountain (Wayne County) and Park Valley (western Box Elder County).

**"Gunnison" Sage Grouse.** The AOU currently treats this as-yet-unnamed form as an isolated population of Sage Grouse. Several recent studies (including some in press at the time of this writing), however, provide convincing evidence that the "Sage" Grouse found in the Gunnison Basin of Colorado and (marginally) in southeastern Utah are, in fact, specifically distinct from other Sage Grouse populations. The Gunnison Sage Grouse are markedly smaller than other Sage Grouse, and the males differ in having smaller and whiter neck ruffs; whiter and more distinctly cross-banded rectrices; and different vocalizations. Displaying male Gunnison Sage Grouse also erect the filoplumes of the nape above the head in a sort of crest, whereas these feather lie lax on the back of the nape in displaying males from other populations. Genetic differences have also been reported. Information on other differences between Gunnison Sage Grouse and other Sage Grouse is still being documented, and accessible sites for viewing Gunnison Sage Grouse are being located. Your best bet is to contact the Gunnison office of the Colorado Division of Wildlife for more information: Gunnison Service Center, 300 West New York, Gunnison, Colorado 81230, (970) 641-7061. For more background information on Gunnison Sage Grouse see Hupp and Braun 1991.

**Greater Prairie-Chicken.** This is a rare and local resident of tall-grass prairies in a narrow corridor of the Great Plains states from North Dakota to Texas. It is best found on the display grounds in spring (March through June in the North, February through April in the South), when courtship activity is at its peak. Afterward the birds disperse and are difficult to find. Booming activity typically begins shortly before dawn and continues for only 1 or 2 hours after first light. Some of the better known areas are the following:

1. North Dakota. Sheyenne National Grasslands around Lisbon.

2. Colorado. Found primarily in the sandhill country of Yuma County, where foraging birds are frequently seen along roadsides at dawn and again late in the day. Many leks are located on private land around the town of Wray. Inquire locally for directions and permission to visit.

3. Nebraska (Pettingill 1981). Valentine NWR and near Burwell (go north on State Hwy. 11 for 18.5 miles, then 0.5 mile west), the Bessey Division of the Nebraska NF (Rosche 1994a,b), and mileposts 138 and 146 along U.S. Hwy. 183 south of Bassett (Rosche 1994a,b).

4. Kansas (Pettingill 1981, Zimmerman and Patti 1988). Flint Hills NWR (contact the Kansas Department of Wildlife and Parks in Emporia, P.O. Box 1525, Emporia, KS 66801, for locations of leks and permission to visit); the Konza Prairie Research Natural Area near Manhattan (make prior arrangements through: Director, Konza Prairie Research Natural Area, Division of Biology, Kansas State University, Manhattan, KS 66506); near Cassoday (northeast of Wichita: the Kansas Department of Wildlife and Parks maintains a blind, which can be reserved by contacting their office at 316-755-2711; Janzen 1995a,b); and along State Hwy. 150 between Elmdale and Marion.

5. Oklahoma (Tulsa Audubon Society 1986). Lake Okmulgee Recreation Area; bluestem grasslands northeast of Tulsa off U.S. Hwy. 75; grasslands around Sooner Lake, 20 miles north of Stillwater on U.S. Hwy. 177 (contact the Payne County Audubon Society in Stillwater for specific sites); grain fields and tall-grass prairie near the tiny towns of Grainola and Hardy (northeast of Ponca City).

6. Texas. The coastal subspecies *Typmpanuchus cupido attwateri*, or "Attwater Prairie-Chicken," is highly localized and steadily declining. During the 1990s, the best place to see it was the Attwater Prairie-Chicken NWR near Eagle Lake, but the public has recently been denied access to parts of the refuge inhabited by the prairie-chickens, with the hopes of minimizing disturbance. Access could change. Your best bet is to contact the Refuge Manager, Attwater Prairie-Chicken National Wildlife Refuge, PO Box 518, Eagle Lake, TX 77434, or, phone 409-234-3021.

7. South Dakota (Rosche 1990). From Valentine, Nebraska, take U.S. Hwy. 83 north into South Dakota. Three miles north of the state line turn east on a paved

road and watch on the north side of the road in the next mile for a lek. Birds may also be seen along the gravel road on the west side of Hwy. 83.

**Lesser Prairie-Chicken.** This is a local, uncommon to rare resident of shortgrass prairie and sand-sage prairie with shinnery oak in the panhandle country of Texas and Oklahoma, eastern New Mexico, extreme southeastern Colorado, and southwestern Kansas. It is best found on the display grounds from March through May (April is usually best), when courtship activity is at its peak. The birds disperse for the rest of the year and are often hard to find. Even at display grounds the birds are found for only an hour or two after dawn. Some reliable areas are the following.

1. Oklahoma. Arnett (drive east at dawn on U.S. Hwy. 60 for 1.0 mile, then south on U.S. Hwy. 283 for several miles, taking any side roads and listening for chickens along the way).

2. Kansas. Cimmaron National Grasslands (pick up map and directions to observation blinds at the U.S. Forest Service headquarters in Elkhart).

3. New Mexico. Caprock (40 miles east of Roswell on Hwy. 380 to a roadside rest stop on the right, then anywhere from 1 to 5 miles north on the gravel road directly across from the rest stop), Milnesand area and around Elida (check with State Game and Fish office in Roswell for directions at the latter two locales.)

4. Colorado. Comanche National Grassland (8 miles east of Campo, then 2 miles south, and 4 miles east to public display grounds. Visitors are requested to first obtain reservations by contacting Comanche National Grassland, U.S. Forest Service, P.O. Box 127, Springfield, CO 81073, or phone 719-523-6591.)

**Sharp-tailed Grouse.** This is a fairly common resident of grasslands, sagebrush prairies, and brushy forest edges from central Alaska south to much of the northern Great Basin and northern Great Plains regions east into northern Minnesota. Like other prairie grouse, Sharp-taileds are best observed on leks from April to mid-June. Sharp-taileds are less site-faithful than other prairie grouse, often moving the location of their leks every few years. If you wish to see the spectacular dances of these birds, your best bet is to contact local birders or state wildlife agencies for the location of currently occupied leks. Sharp-taileds are still readily seen in proper habitats away from leks, particularly by driving gravel roads early or late in the day. Try the following locations:

1. Alaska. Muskeg and brushy forest edges in the interior taiga zone of central Alaska. Most often seen along roads and railroad tracks early in the morning and again late in the day. Perhaps most commonly seen along the Richardson Hwy. from Fairbanks to Delta Junction.

2. Colorado. Two subspecies occur in Colorado. The "Plains Sharp-tailed" (*Tympanuchus phasianellus jamesii*) formerly occurred in shrub-prairies over much of eastern Colorado (west to the Front Range). A higher-elevation form, the "Columbian," or "Mountain," Sharp-tailed Grouse (*T. p. columbianus*), inhabits sagebrush foothills with extensive oak thickets in the high-basin parklands of the northwest. Both subspecies have declined in the state because of habitat loss, but

the decline of the "Plains Sharp-tailed" has been more severe. They are currently rare residents of Douglas County, although reintroduction programs are under way. The "Columbian Sharp-tailed" are locally fairly common in Routt and Moffat counties, although many of the leks are located on private lands. Your best bet is to check with Colorado Division of Wildlife personnel in the Hayden-Craig-Steamboat Springs area for information on currently accessible sites. Another alternative is to drive Twenty Mile Road (between Steamboat Springs and Hayden, next to the Hayden power plant) south from U.S. Hwy. 40 at dawn, stopping frequently to listen for the cackling sounds of displaying Sharp-tailed.

3. Montana (Pettingill 1981, McEneaney 1993). Medicine Lake, Benton Lake, Charles M. Russell, and Bowdoin NWRs; Medicine Rocks SP (south of Baker); Fox Lake Wildlife Management Area (near Lambert); and Beaver Creek County Park (south of Havre)

4. Nebraska (Pettingill 1981). Fort Robinson SP, the Bessey Division of the Nebraska National Forest, Crescent Lake (phone 308-762-4893) and Valentine (phone 308-376-3789) NWRs (both of which maintain viewing blinds for leks), north of Cody off U.S. Hwy. 20 (Rosche 1990), and west of Eli along U.S. Hwy. 20 (Rosche 1990).

5. North Dakota. The Badlands in and around both units of Theodore Roosevelt NP and on Chase Lake/Arrowwood, Long Lake, J. Clark Salyer, Lostwood, and Des Lacs NWRs.

6. Utah (Pettingill 1981). The Cache Valley east of Wellsville.

7. Wyoming (Scott 1993). Wagon Box Road south of Story, Bird Farm Road south of Big Horn, and State Hwy. 335 west of Big Horn.

**Montezuma Quail.** This is an uncommon resident of grassy hill country forested with pines, oaks, and junipers. It is found in western Texas, southern Arizona, and southern New Mexico. This bird is not easy to find. In fact, your first one will probably find you. The best technique is to drive very slowly along roads through appropriate habitat, keeping watch for quail on the shoulders. These birds do not flush unless nearly stepped on, and even then they tend to run swiftly into cover at the first opportunity. They do seem to cluster around pools of water, particularly during the dry season. They are perhaps easier to find in mid- to late summer, when breeding pairs and fledged coveys are more conspicuous. Some reliable areas follow.

1. Texas. The campgrounds at Davis Mountains SP, the scenic loop through the Davis Mountains (Hwy. 17 to 18 to 166), and the road to the McDonald Observatory.

2. New Mexico. Along Forest Road 63 (the Geronimo Trail) through the Peloncillo Mountains; North Fork Canyon along Forest Road 39 in the Magdalena Mountains; the Fort Bayard Military Reservation off U.S. Hwy. 180 8 miles east of Silver City; around Pinos Altos; near the Gila Cliff Dwellings National Monument; and around Fort Stanton (northwest of Lincoln off U.S. Hwy. 380).

3. Arizona. Hwy. 82 between Patagonia and Nogales, Ruby Road to California Gulch (particularly near Peña Blanca Lake), the vicinity of the Appleton-Whidell

Research Ranch at Elgin (call the manager at 605-455-5522 for permission to visit), the area around the Southwest Research Station and the road to Paradise (Chiricahua Mountains.), lower Miller and Garden Canyons (Huachuca Mountains).

**Mountain Quail.** This is a fairly common but secretive resident of montane chaparral, dense brushy edges of montane coniferous forest, and mountain meadows bordered by conifer forest. It is found in coastal ranges from British Columbia to southern California, and in interior ranges (for example, Sierra Nevada) of California and western Nevada. It was introduced into eastern Washington and Oregon and into western Idaho. Although resident, birds tend to migrate locally to lower elevations. This bird is much shyer than other U.S. quail, so seeing them can be a problem. Males call from open perches (usually rocks), but the call is somewhat ventriloquial and, therefore, hard to pin down. The best time to see them is in mid- to late summer after the young have hatched. At these times whole coveys can often be seen along mountain roads. The following are some of the better spots:

1. California. The road to Mount Pinos; Palomar Mountain: Hurkey Creek Campground and the forest around Big Bear Lake in the San Bernardino Mountains; Placerita Canyon SP, Switzer Picnic Area, Charleton Flats, and Chilao Recreation Areas in the San Gabriel Mountains; brushy slopes above Yosemite Valley in Yosemite NP; Cuyamaca Rancho SP (near San Diego); La Cumbre Peak off San Marcos Pass (north of Santa Barbara); and the high country of Kings Canyon and Sequoia NPs.

2. Nevada (Pettingill 1981). Incline Village at the north end of Lake Tahoe.

3. Oregon (Evanich 1990). West of the Cascades (including the western slope). Try William L. Finley NWR, Saddle Mountain SP, Scoggins Valley Park, Lake Selmac County Park (20 miles southwest of Grants Pass off U.S. Hwy. 199), Roxy Ann Butte near Medford, Foster Reservoir (east of Sweet Home), and Larch Mountain (east of Portland).

4. Washington (Wahl and Paulson 1977). Between Lyle and Centerville (Klickitat County), and the W. T. Wooten Wildlife Recreation Area in the Blue Mountains of Columbia County. Very local on the Olympic Peninsula near McCleary and Indianola.

**Yellow Rail.** This is an uncommon and local summer resident of fens (spring-fed swales with quaking mats of vegetation over saturated soil), grassy marshes, and wet meadows in the extreme northern Great Plains, the upper Midwest, and Canada. The Yellow Rail avoids the deep marshes with lots of standing water that are preferred by other rails. It winters in hayfields, rice fields, and freshwater and saltwater marshes along the Gulf Coast from the central Texas coast to Florida and north along the lower Atlantic Coast. Occasionally this bird is seen during migration, usually by farmers mowing their hayfields or at controlled burns of tall-grass fields. Louisiana birders have had some success in recent years by finding rice fields that are being mowed and taking up lookout positions ahead of the combines. This technique could work well on the upper Texas coast, although the prime time for rice harvesting (August) precedes the arrival of migrant Yellow Rails. Recommended breeding sites include: the area between Agency Lake and Fort Klamath, Oregon (specific spots include the meadow behind the Ft. Klamath National Historical Site interpretive sign just east of town and the roadsides of Dixon, Nicholson, Weed, and Seven-mile roads; Evanich 1990), and J. Clark Salyer NWR and appropriate habitat in Benson County, North Dakota. One specific site in the latter county is a sedge meadow 2 miles north of Minnewaukon along U.S. Hwy. 281 (Faanes 1984). Use of a tape recorder to lure in breeding birds is the surest and least obtrusive way to see Yellow Rails. In migration and on their wintering grounds (such as the rice fields east and west of Houston; Anahuac, San Bernard, and Aransas NWRs; Galveston Island SP; Sabine Marsh; and the Freeport area), you are almost entirely dependent on seeing one flushed by a combine or by walking one up yourself. The latter strategy should acquaint you with fire ants and possibly rattlesnakes, but it is not likely to do much else.

**Black Rail.** This is an uncommon to rare and local inhabitant of freshwater, brackish, and saltwater marshes (California, Arizona, and Texas) and wet sedge meadows (Kansas). It is probably much overlooked because of its extremely secretive nature. California and Arizona populations are resident; upper Texas coast birds are basically winter residents; and Kansas birds are summer residents (the best spot in Kansas is probably Quivera NWR, located 8 miles north of Zenith off U.S. Hwy. 50; Zimmerman and Patti 1988). California birds are essentially of two populations. One inhabits pickleweed marshes at the margins of large bays on the central and southern coast (for example, Upper Newport Bay, Morro Bay, Suisun Marsh, and the Palo Alto Baylands Preserve in San Francisco Bay). The other is found in marshes along the Colorado River near the Imperial Dam (California-Arizona border). The latter birds should be looked for at Mittry Lake (on the Arizona side) and around West Pond just southwest of the California end of the dam. Hearing Black Rails at these locations is one thing (nighttime is best); seeing them is another. Coastal birds are best observed during extremely high tides when they (like other rails) are forced out of cover by rising water. The most popular place for seeing this species in California has been the Palo Alto Baylands Reserve (reached from U.S. Hwy. 101 in Palo Alto by taking the Embarcadero exit east). This reserve has a boardwalk that goes into the marsh habitat, but you will still need an exceptionally high tide to have much luck (the endangered "California" race of the Clapper Rail can also be found here). In other areas, your best bet is to use a tape recording, to which this species is fairly responsive (again, night is best).

**Whooping Crane.** Whooping Cranes are rare and endangered. The historical population breeds in the bogs of Wood Buffalo NP (Alberta) and winters on Aransas NWR on the Gulf Coast of Texas. Individuals and small groups en route to either place during migration are occasionally chanced upon (usually at wildlife refuges in the Great Plains). The wintering birds at Aransas can often be distantly seen from the observation tower, but your best bet is to book passage on the M. V. *Skimmer,* which departs twice daily (November–April) from the Sand Dollar Pavilion on the south side of Copano Bay in Fulton. The cranes are generally easy to see from the boat between November and early April. An attempt was made in the 1970s and 1980s to establish a second, more western population of Whoopers. This management program used Sandhill Cranes at Gray's Lake NWR in Idaho to incubate Whooper eggs taken from Wood Buffalo Park. The Sandhills became foster parents to the young Whoopers, which then followed the Sandhills south in fall to the wintering grounds in New Mexico. Most of these birds spent the winter at Bosque del Apache NWR. The program has been discontinued owing to a lack of success in getting the Whoopers to breed (at least in part because the Whoopers tended to imprint on Sandhills). At last word, the "western" population of Whooping Cranes was down to about five birds.

**Pacific Golden-Plover.** This is a fairly common summer resident of low-lying tundra (either coastal or in interior valleys) in western Alaska, from Wales south to the Kuskokwim River delta. It is a fairly common spring and fall migrant throughout western Alaska and on offshore islands, locally in fall south along the immediate Pacific Coast to southern California (where it is uncommon). This species is a rare spring migrant along the Pacific Coast south of Alaska. Most Pacific Golden-Plovers winter on islands in the south Pacific, but small numbers winter annually in southern and central coastal California. The species is a rare to accidental vagrant (mostly in fall) eastward as far as the Atlantic Coast. It was formerly considered conspecific with the American Golden-Plover, the enlarged complex being called "Lesser Golden-Plover." The two species overlap as breeding birds in much of western Alaska. Where they are sympatric (as on the Seward Peninsula), Pacifics occupy wetter, grassier tundra at lower elevations, whereas Americans occupy higher, drier tundra with sparser vegetation and more rocks. In migration and winter, Pacifics frequent shortgrass pastures, sod farms, pickleweed marshes, and (to a lesser extent) sandy beaches and mudflats. Breeding birds are probably best seen along the Teller and Council Roads out of Nome, Alaska. Migrants can be seen almost anywhere that the species is found in Alaska. South of Alaska, in migration try the following locations.

1. Washington. Ocean Shores (Grays Harbor County), especially at the Oyhut Game Range and Damon Point at the south end of the Ocean Shores Peninsula; and at Leadbetter Point, Pacific County, (from late July through October and in April and May, with fall migrants greatly outnumbering spring migrants in both locations).

2. Oregon (Mlodinow 1993). Bandon (Coos County) and Clatsop Spit (Clatsop County) (from late July through October and in April and May).

3. California. Birds can be seen during migration and winter at all of the following except on pastures near Humboldt Bay, Humboldt County, (where they occur during migration only). Lawson's Landing at Dillon Beach and fields (particularly the Spaletta Plateau) on Point Reyes (Marin County), pastures along Bet-

teravia Road and near the Guadalupe Sewage Ponds in the Santa Maria Valley (Santa Barbara County), sod farms near Port Hueneme (Ventura County) and in the Tijuana River valley (San Diego County), and Anaheim Bay (Orange County).

**Wilson's Plover.** This is a fairly common summer resident of salt flats, intertidal dunes, and mudflats along the Gulf and lower Atlantic coasts. In our area, it winters only along the lower and central Texas coast, where it is rare. In general, this is a late-March through mid-October bird. Some prime Texas spots include Bolivar Flats, West Galveston Island, Rockport Beach, South Padre Island at the end of the Queen Isabella Causeway, and Laguna Atascosa NWR. Wilson's Plover is a casual vagrant to southern California.

**Common Ringed Plover.** This is a rare but regular spring migrant to St. Lawrence Island (Alaska) and a casual spring and fall migrant to the Seward Peninsula, the Pribilofs, and the Aleutians (Alaska). Small numbers breed in the northeastern Canadian arctic. In our area, it is most regular in late May and early June at Gambell (St. Lawrence Island), where one or more birds are seen in most years. Birders should use great caution in identifying this species in North America. It is very similar in plumage to the widespread Semipalmated Plover, and even some of the vocalizations are somewhat similar. Overly enthusiastic birders routinely misidentify Semipalmated Plovers for Common Ringeds on the Alaskan mainland, where the former species is a common breeding bird and the latter species is highly unlikely to occur.

**Mountain Plover.** This is an uncommon and local summer resident of high plains and xeric shortgrass prairie in a narrow corridor of states from Montana to western Texas. These birds like prairie where the grass is almost carpet-short. They are incredibly cryptic when not moving, so you should stop frequently in appropriate habitat to scan. The Mountain Plover winters (sometimes in large flocks) in plowed fields, shortgrass pastures, and oil fields in southern Texas and central and southern California. In summer try the following locations:

1. Colorado. Almost anywhere in appropriate habitat in Weld County, but especially on the Pawnee National Grassland; along U.S. Hwy. 287/385 between Lamar and Springfield; off Burnt Mill Road south of Pueblo, north of State Hwy. 96 in Crowley County, and between Sugar City and Cheraw in Crowley and Otero Counties.

2. Wyoming (Scott 1993). The Laramie Plains, including around West Carroll Lake northwest of Laramie, Hutton Lake NWR south of Laramie, and the Old Laramie River Road (take U.S. Hwy. 30 north 20 miles to Bosler, turn west across the tracks at the south end of town and go south on the Old Laramie River Road). Try also the Oregon Basin between Cody and Greybull, the Shirley Basin (especially between State Hwys. 77 and 487 south of Casper), the Powder River Basin, the Green River Basin, and the Big Horn Basin.

3. Montana (Pettingill 1981). The Charles M. Russell NWR and west of Harlowton.

4. New Mexico (Zimmerman et al. 1992). The Grasslands Turf Ranch near Los Lunas (off State Hwy. 6, just west of its junction with I-25, about 20 miles south of Albuquerque: spring migration in March–April and fall migration in August–October), the Green Chaparral Turf Ranch 6 miles east of Moriarty along I-40 (migration: ask permission at ranch headquarters before birding), and Capulin Mountain National Monument (north of Capulin).

5. Nebraska. Vicinity of Bushnell.

6. Texas. The Rita Blanca National Grasslands in the northwestern panhandle and in the grasslands near Fort Davis.

In winter try the following locations:

1. California. Plowed fields around the south end of the Salton Sea, near Blackwell's Corner in Kern County, the Carrizo Plains in the interior of San Luis Obispo County, the Cholame Valley (off State Hwy. 46 in southeastern Monterey County) and in the oil fields along Betteravia and Black roads in Santa Maria (Santa Barbara County).

2. Arizona. Agricultural fields in the Sulphur Springs Valley, particularly around Elfrida.

3. Texas. Appropriate habitat near San Antonio (check with local birders).

**Eurasian Dotterel.** This is a rare but regular spring and summer visitor to the mainland of western Alaska and to St. Lawrence Island and a casual spring and summer visitor to northern Alaska. It is likely that at least small numbers of these palearctic plovers breed (although possibly only irregularly) in these remote and undercovered regions, as evidenced by numerous June records of paired birds from appropriate habitat. Pairs were found on the same ridgetop (east of Milepost 25, Kougarok Road) near Nome in successive Junes from 1972 to 1974. The preferred nesting habitat for these birds is alpine tundra, with only dwarf-stature vegetation and lichen-covered rocks. The best bet for finding this species in North America is to visit Gambell (St. Lawrence Island) from late May to mid-June. Check especially atop the mountain east of the village and on the grassy flats near the airstrip and at the south end of Troutman Lake. Eurasian Dotterels are casual to accidental fall migrants along the Pacific Coast south to central California and are certain to be listed on local RBAs if present.

**Northern Jacana.** This is a casual visitor to ponds in the lower Rio Grande Valley of southern Texas and along the lower and central Texas coast. Until 1977 there was a resident colony on Manor Lake (west of Freeport). This colony was apparently wiped out by a severe freeze, and no jacanas have been seen there in recent years. However, it does afford ideal potential breeding habitat: a reedy border with a thick growth of water hyacinths. Recent records have been of individual birds at scattered locales. There is even one Arizona record from a pond on Guevavi Ranch near Nogales in 1985–86. If present, this species is certain to be listed on local RBAs.

**Bristle-thighed Curlew.** This is a rare and local summer resident of dwarf shrub tundra meadows in western Alaska. Bristle-thighed Curlews winter on islands in the South Pacific, their migration route being almost entirely over the Pacific Ocean. Thus, they are seldom seen on our shores away from nesting areas, except in a few locations in coastal Alaska where the species stages for a short time before the southward migration in late summer. The first nest of this species was not discovered until 1948, and it is still known to breed in only two areas, the interior of the Seward Peninsula and the Nulato Hills on the north Yukon River delta. Birds arrive on the nesting grounds in mid- to late May and have usually completed nesting by late June. By July they are already starting to gather in groups, and most individuals will have migrated by mid-August.

The most accessible place to see Bristle-thighed Curlews is toward the far end of the Kougarok Road (Taylor Highway) out of Nome. In most years there is one pair of curlews nesting on the mountain opposite Coffee Dome at Milepost 73 (on the west side of the road). Additional pairs of curlews nest at the end of the Kougarok Road (about 84 miles out of Nome), atop domes on both sides of the Kougarok River. Try the near side of the bridge and west of the road, or across the river and up a conspicuous tractor cut that leads up a dome to the east. Be aware that the hiking conditions at any of these locations range from strenuous to very difficult. The tundra appears deceptively easy from the road, but the tussock formations can be treacherous, and you are a long way from help if you encounter a problem. Grizzly bears are frequently seen in the area. The curlews have huge territories, and finding them at any of the above locations can involve several miles and many hours of difficult hiking. Once a bird has been flushed, it may fly well over a mile before putting down again. The curlews are best located by listening for their distinctive calls, most often given in flight. The most frequently heard call is a loud whistled "TOO-wheet" or "TEE-oo-wheet," frequently given as part of a longer, much more complex vocalization. Curlews vocalize much more frequently before egg laying than after, and if you time your visit for late May or very early June you are more likely to catch the male doing display flights. At these times your best strategy may be simply to walk back and forth along the road on either side of the Kougarok River, listening and watching for displaying males. Later in June the birds become much more cryptic, and about the only time they vocalize is when a raven, hawk, or jaeger passes overhead. Be aware that Whimbrels, which look virtually identical to Bristle-thighed Curlews at a distance (but which sound very different), outnumber Bristle-thigheds at each of the localities mentioned above.

Other options for seeing Bristle-thighed Curlews are more difficult (nesting areas), or less certain (staging areas). Try the following locations:

1. Safety Lagoon complex along the Council Road near Nome. Small numbers of postbreeders stage for a short time in July and August.

2. Middleton Island (northern Gulf of Alaska). Small numbers of curlews often settle here for a few days in early to mid-May en route to the breeding areas. The island is reachable by charter flights from Anchorage or Kenai.

3. Curlew Lake. This breeding area is reachable by a one-hour floatplane charter from Bethel (which is serviced by daily flights from Anchorage). Try also along the road from St. Marys (southeast of Curlew Lake) to Mt. Village.

4. Coastal Yukon-Kuskokwim rivers delta. This area is reachable by boat from the villages of Hooper Bay, Chevak, and Scammon Bay or by floatplane charter from Bethel. Small flocks can be seen staging here in July and August before their southbound migration.

5. Random vagrants may be encountered at St. Paul Island (Pribilofs) in mid- to late May or along the Homer Spit in July and August, but these options can't be planned and are entirely based on luck.

**Bar-tailed Godwit.** This palearctic species is a fairly common summer resident of tundra meadows in western Alaska, from the Yukon-Kuskokwim delta north to the Seward Peninsula, and (less commonly) east toward the North Slope. Like the Bristle-thighed Curlew, this species is a transoceanic migrant, arriving in Alaska by mid-May. Migrants are commonly seen in the Aleutians and the Pribilofs, rarely eastward along south coastal Alaska (spring migrants are particularly rare, late-summer migrants are more regular). The species is a casual fall migrant (accidental in spring) to beaches and estuaries along the length of the Pacific Coast, with more records coming from Washington (nearly annual over the past decade) and Oregon than from California.

The most accessible breeding locality for this species is Nome. Here, breeding pairs of godwits are widely, but sparsely, distributed across mesic upland tundra, typically with abundant tussock-hummock formations and shrubs of dwarf stature. They tend to breed in the same areas favored by Whimbrels and, to a lesser extent, by Bristle-thighed Curlews. They are seldom found in the low, wetter tundra near the coast. At Nome, godwits are more readily found at the mouth of the Nome River and on the mudflats surrounding the Safety Lagoon complex than on the tundra breeding grounds. It is not clear whether the birds that mass on these coastal mudflats are all nonbreeders; some of them might be breeding birds feeding far from their nesting territories. Regardless, the godwits are easy to find at these coastal locales, and when tides are favorable you may find hundreds.

**Black Turnstone.** This is a locally common summer resident of saltgrass meadows and wet meadows (particularly around the edges of lagoons or river estuaries) in coastal lowlands along the west coast of Alaska, from southern Kotzebue Sound south to the Yukon-Kuskokwim delta. The main breeding areas seem to be on the north side of the Seward Peninsula and in the Yukon-Kuskokwim delta region, neither of which is overly accessible. Late migrants and nonbreeders are often seen in late May through June at Safety Lagoon near Nome. The bulk of the population migrates along the southern Alaska coast in May and again in July and August.

It is much easier to find outside of the breeding season, when it is a common to abundant winter resident and spring and fall transient the length of the West Coast (wintering north to south-coastal and southeastern Alaska). Birds are typically found on rocky coastlines, along rock jetties, and on breakwaters, and they are sometimes seen on sandy beaches (particularly where they can feed amongst beached mats of kelp). The Black Turnstone is present in spring until early May (as far south as southern California), with the first fall birds returning by mid-July. It is almost impossible to miss thereafter.

**Surfbird.** This is an uncommon summer resident of alpine tundra in the mountains of much of central and interior Alaska, west to the Seward Peninsula. These birds nest on rocky, wind-swept tundra with dwarf mats of vegetation, and to see them on their breeding grounds usually requires a substantial off-road hike. Two of the more accessible spots are along the Steese Hwy. northeast of Fairbanks at Twelvemile Summit (at about milepost 84; park and hike the Pinnell Mountain Trail up to the west) and farther along at Eagle Summit (even better because more good habitat is closer to the road) (Springer 1993). Other places (usually requiring more walking) to try include along the top of Primrose Ridge and ridges above the Eilson Visitor Center at Denali NP and atop appropriate domes and ridgetops along the Kougarok (mileposts 23 and 40), Council (mileposts 50 and 60), and Teller (beyond milepost 20) roads out of Nome. Surfbirds are much easier to see during migration along the coast of southern Alaska, from late April through May in spring and again from July through September in fall. Try rocky coastline and gravel shores around Prince William Sound, Resurrection Bay, and Kachemak Bay, particularly along the Homer Spit. Small numbers (possibly failed breeders or nonbreeders) can often be found in May and June along the shores of Cook Inlet at Anchorage (scope the mudflats at Earthquake Park, opposite Westchester Lagoon, and at various lookouts along the Seward Highway, but do not attempt to venture onto the flats).

Surfbirds are fairly common winter residents of rocky coastlines along the length of the West Coast (north to southern Alaska and Kodiak Island). Typically less common than Black Turnstones, they also arrive slightly later in fall and are found at the same places as the latter species. They are not hard to find.

**Red-necked Stint.** This is a rare summer resident of coastal (mostly) tundra on the Seward Peninsula of Alaska and a casual breeder along the north coast to Barrow. Small numbers seen regularly in May and June at coastal lagoons, estuaries, and river mouths along the Seward Peninsula (and anywhere on St. Lawrence Island) may be visitors or breeders. Elsewhere in Alaska the species is a rare but regular migrant along the western coast, in the Aleutians, and on the Pribilofs. It is a casual to accidental fall vagrant along the length of the West Coast, where it is most often found from late July through September. The most accessible place where this bird is likely to be found is in the vicinity of Nome (Alaska) from late May through June. Check especially at the mouth of the Nome River and at Safety Lagoon. Pairs may be by themselves, but just as often you will encounter one or more birds in large mixed-species groups of shorebirds (particularly flocks with lots of Western Sandpipers). Red-necked Stints have also been confirmed to breed at Wales. The species is also a regular spring migrant at Gambell (St. Lawrence Island), at St. Paul Island (the Pribilofs), and in the Aleutians. South of Alaska, check local RBAs. The species was formerly called "Rufous-necked Stint."

**Sharp-tailed Sandpiper.** This is a locally uncommon to rare fall migrant (August–October) along the coasts of the Chukchi and Bering seas and the north Pacific Ocean of Alaska south (including offshore islands in the Bering Sea) to the Aleutian chain and east to Kodiak Island. During peak periods (mid-August to mid-September) flocks numbering more than 100 individuals have been recorded from Safety Lagoon near Nome, and scores have been seen on St. Paul Island. The preferred habitats of these migrants are wet coastal meadows and tidal flats. The Sharp-tailed Sandpiper is a very rare to casual fall migrant elsewhere in coastal Alaska and is a very rare to casual spring migrant anywhere in the state (mostly in western Alaska). It is a very rare but regular fall migrant (September to November) along the length of the West Coast, where virtually all sightings are of juveniles, usually moving with flocks of Pectoral Sandpipers. South of Alaska it is found most regularly around Vancouver, British Columbia and Ocean Shores, Washington, but a few typically reach California every year. South of Alaska, Sharp-taileds are found in saltmarsh habitat, flooded pastures, and wherever groups of Pectoral Sandpipers might gather. In coastal Washington they are typically found in *Salicornia* marshes from Ocean Shores to the mouth of the Columbia River and less often, but regularly, near Puget Sound. Check local RBAs.

**Rock Sandpiper.** This Bering Sea specialty is a locally fairly common summer resident of alpine and coastal tundra in central western Alaska (from the north side of the Seward Peninsula south to Hooper Bay), the islands of the Bering Sea, and the Aleutian chain. There are three described subspecies from North America: *Calidris ptilocnemis tschuktschorum* (St. Lawrence and Nunivak islands and the Alaskan mainland from the Seward Peninsula to the Yukon delta), *C. p. ptilocnemis* (the Pribilofs, St. Mathew, and Hall Islands), and *C. p. couesi* (Aleutians east to the Alaska Peninsula). The more widespread *tschuktschorum* is locally common in alpine tundra (mostly on more xeric, rocky ridges) on the north side of the Seward Peninsula (particularly on Cape Mountain near Wales) but is uncommon in the southern part of the peninsula. They breed on the higher slopes inland from Nome but are seen there mostly as spring migrants in the latter half of May and again in July and August, when postbreeders move down from the slopes to the coast. Birds of this subspecies are usually easy to find at Gambell (St. Lawrence Island), particularly around the base of the mountain. Mainland Rock Sandpipers migrate primarily along the west coast of Alaska, and large numbers can be found staging around the Yukon-Kuskokwim delta in late summer. They are fairly common along the Homer Spit in spring and fall migration and are common winter residents there. They winter from south coastal Alaska south locally to Bodega Bay, California. Wintering birds become less common from north to south and are to be looked for in the same places as Black Turnstones and Surfbirds. Wintering populations from at least Washington south have been in apparent decline over the last decade.

Probably the best place to see breeding Rock Sandpipers is on St. Paul Island in the Pribilofs. There, the large, pale, nominate subspecies *(ptilocnemis)* is a common and conspicuous part of the avifauna, and, in the absence of many other breeding shorebirds, it occupies a wide range of habitats. Both island subspecies of Rock Sandpiper *(ptilocnemis* and *couesi)* are more sedentary than mainland *tschuktschorum,* but at least some birds of both subspecies winter away from their breeding grounds along the Alaska coast (nominate birds breed at least south to Juneau).

**Long-tailed Jaeger.** This is a locally common summer resident of open tundra regions of northern and western Alaska (including some of the Bering Sea islands) and south through the Brooks Range to central Alaska. It will nest in lowland coastal tundra but generally is more common in upland and alpine tundra. It migrates in flocks in spring, when it is not uncommon to encounter 20–50 birds resting on the tundra or even along the road outside of Nome. Nowhere is this bird easier to see than Nome, where it is impossible to miss from late May to early August. Other good spots include Kotzebue, Wales, Denali NP (beyond Polychrome Pass), the east end of the Denali Hwy., the Dalton Hwy., and Prudhoe Bay.

It is a rare fall (August through September) migrant through offshore waters along the length of the West Coast. This is the most pelagic of the jaegers, and it is very hard to find south of the breeding grounds. The optimum times for seeing it are in late August and early September (California) or late July to early September (Washington), which coincide with the peak southbound movement of Arctic Terns. It is a very rare vagrant to inland bodies of water throughout the West.

**South Polar Skua.** This is an uncommon to rare visitor to offshore waters along the length of the Pacific Coast from spring through fall. Even taking several pelagic trips won't guarantee a sighting of this bird. Your best chances are on trips out of Westport, Washington, where skuas are seen on more than half of the July–October trips taken and on the annual September boat trip out of Morro Bay (skuas are seen on about 80% of these trips). The best time to search out of Monterey, California, is from September through October, when birds are regularly seen but are still missed more often than not. They are occasionally seen as late as December and as early as June. There are few spring records from Monterey, although spring seems to be the better time for finding skuas in southern California (e.g., out of San Diego). You are more likely to see skuas from Monterey than from points farther south, and you won't have to go as far offshore to do it.

**Thayer's Gull.** This species breeds in the Canadian high arctic. It is a fairly common to rare winter resident (October through March) along the length of the West Coast (rarely as far north as south coastal Alaska). It becomes less common with decreasing latitude (most coastal California Christmas Bird Counts record from one to several birds; some Washington CBCs record a few hundred). In Washington, Thayer's Gulls winter in greatest densities along the eastern Strait of Juan de Fuca and Puget Sound (where they are particularly fond of river mouths and harbors) and less commonly along the outer coast. Unlike many other western gulls, this one is not restricted to the coast. It routinely shows up several miles inland, and one or two can often be found at the Salton Sea (California). It is also a rare but regular vagrant to inland areas throughout the West and is becoming increasingly common on the western Great Lakes. The taxonomic status of this gull is still being debated. It hybridizes extensively with Iceland Gull where the ranges of the two forms meet, and it seems likely that the two will be treated as a single species (Iceland Gull) in the future.

**Slaty-backed Gull.** This is a rare, but regular, migrant and May–September visitor to coastal western and northern Alaska, including offshore islands (Aleutians, Pribilofs, St. Lawrence). It is a casual fall–winter visitor to south coastal Alaska (Kodiak, Homer, Ketchikan), with a few recent records from British Columbia and Washington. A few of these birds can usually be found around Nome every summer. The most likely spots are the city landfill, the harbor area, the mouth of the Nome River, Safety Sound (scope the sandy barrier strip in the late evenings when large flocks of gulls often gather), and along the coastline between the Safety Sound bridge and Solomon. Small numbers are also seen with regularity at Gambell (St. Lawrence Island) and (less frequently) at St. Paul Island. When identifying this species be careful to distinguish it from the more common Siberian subspecies of Herring Gull *(Larus argentatus vegae)*, which is distinctly darker-mantled than North American Herring Gulls (subspecies *smithsonianus*) and which can look darker still against a backdrop of snow or ice.

**Yellow-footed Gull.** This is an uncommon but increasing postbreeding visitor to the Salton Sea (California) from its breeding ground in the Gulf of California. Peak numbers arrive in July and leave by October, but a few remain through the winter. In winter, check Obsidian Butte and Red Hill at the south end of the sea and around the vicinity of Salton City on the western shore. From July through September it is relatively easy to find.

**Red-legged Kittiwake.** This is a highly localized Bering Sea endemic, breeding from the Pribilofs (St. Paul and St. George) to parts of the Aleutian chain (Buldir, Bogoslof, and Fire islands). It winters at sea in the North Pacific and is a casual to accidental vagrant farther south. It is easy to see in the summer at St. Paul and St. George islands (the Pribilofs).

**Ross's Gull.** This Siberian breeder is a rare but regular migrant and spring–fall visitor to nearshore waters of the Seward Peninsula and St. Lawrence Island (it is a casual visitor to the Pribilofs). It is most often seen from Northwest Point at Gambell in late May through mid-June, particularly when the sea ice is close to shore. It is less frequent at Nome, where individuals occasionally put down along the coast near Safety Sound. The best way to see this bird is to visit Barrow in fall for the annual passage of thousands of Ross's Gulls from the Chuckchi Sea into the Beaufort Sea. The precise timing of this passage is weather-dependent and, therefore, somewhat variable. However, between mid-September and early October your chances of seeing at least a few of these beautiful gulls between town and the Point are good. For more details, see Maynard 1989.

**Sabine's Gull.** This is a locally fairly common breeder in coastal wet meadows and saltgrass meadows of northern and western Alaska, from Kotzebue (small numbers may breed farther north) south to Bristol Bay. It is most common on the northern Seward Peninsula and in the Yukon-Kuskokwim delta regions (Yukon Delta NWR), neither of which is particularly accessible. Sabine's Gulls are fairly common migrants along coastal western and northern Alaska, from May through mid-June and again from August through October. During these times they are frequently seen at Nome (Safety Sound and adjacent coastline), Wales, Gambell (St. Lawrence Island), and Barrow.

It is a fairly common to uncommon spring (April through May) and fall (July through October) migrant over offshore waters along the length of the West Coast. It is highly pelagic and only rarely recorded from shore. It is a rare but regular fall vagrant to inland lakes throughout the West (most of these birds are juveniles). This striking gull can be seen on boat trips out of any western port, but the ones from Westport, Washington (where it is rarely missed on May or mid-August through mid-October trips), and Monterey, California (September–October is best) are probably your best bet.

**Ivory Gull.** This species breeds in the Canadian high arctic. It is an uncommon migrant to Bering Sea and Chuckchi Sea waters, mainly from October through June. The movements of these gulls are closely attuned to the movements of sea ice. When the ice is near shore at Gambell (St. Lawrence Island), Ivory Gulls are regularly seen in small numbers. The best time seems to be from mid-May to early-June, but the position of the ice in spring and early summer changes dramatically not only from year to year, but also from day to day, making the presence of the gulls unpredictable. Fall (September–November) is probably also good. Ivory Gulls are occasionally seen on the mainland from Wales to Nome and at Barrow (late September through October, when the Ross's Gulls are also migrating, is probably best). Ivory Gulls are notorious scavengers on remains of killed animals and may visit beached carcasses or blubber faithfully over a period of several days.

**Gull-billed Tern.** This is a fairly common to uncommon and local resident (very scarce in winter) along the Gulf Coast from Brownsville (Texas) to Florida and along the Atlantic Coast (in summer). It is an uncommon to rare summer resident at the Salton Sea, California (where 100–150 pairs breed). On the Gulf, it nests on spoil banks left over from canal dredging operations. It is most often seen over salt marshes, bays, and wet coastal grasslands. It is fairly easy to find at such places as the Bolivar Peninsula, Galveston Island SP, and Freeport, Rockport, Aransas, and Laguna Atascosa NWRs.

**Elegant Tern.** This is a fairly common postbreeding visitor from Mexico to beaches, estuaries, bays, and open ocean along the West Coast north to northern California. It is easy to find from July to October, when most dispersal occurs. Numbers drop rapidly in November, but in some years small numbers may remain well into December. Some birds nest on San Diego Bay and at Bolsa Chica in Orange County, where they can be seen locally from March on (try the South Bay Marine Biological Study Area on the Silver Strand and Imperial Marsh in San Diego, and Bolsa Chica State Ecological Reserve off Hwy. 1 north of Huntington Beach in Orange County). During years when El Niño events bring warm-water currents far to the north, Elegant Terns may be found (exceptionally) all the way to British Columbia.

**Arctic Tern.** This is a common summer resident over much of Alaska (less common in the northern part of the state) and south to British Columbia (a few pairs have nested at Everett, Washington, for the past decade or more). It breeds (often colonially) on gravel bars of rivers and streams, on coastal barrier strips and lagoon edges, and in saltgrass and wet meadows. It is impossible to miss (in summer) on the Kenai Peninsula (from Anchorage to Seward and Homer) and at Nome and is easily seen elsewhere along coasts or at inland rivers and lakes. It is an uncommon spring (April–May) and fall (mid-August to mid-October) migrant along the entire West Coast, almost always well offshore. Your best chance by far is from a boat (early fall is best).

**Aleutian Tern.** This is a fairly common but local breeder of northern and western Alaska, from Kotzebue south to the Aleutians and east along south coastal Alaska to Kodiak, Homer, and Yakutat Bay. It winters at sea, the precise area still uncertain. It breeds in small colonies, usually on sandy barrier strips, islands in lagoons, or in saltgrass or wet meadows, sometimes in mixed colonies with Arctic Terns. Colony sites often shift from one year to the next, frequently because of human disturbance. Try Nome (Safety Lagoon and Safety Sound areas), Kotzebue (near the airport; Lethaby 1994), Homer (from the Homer Spit, and also nesting at marshes off Kachemak Drive and near Anchor Point, West 1994), Kodiak (heads of Womens, Middle, and Kalsin bays; Lethaby 1994), Cold Bay and Izembek NWR (Lethaby 1994), and the east and west sides of the Copper River delta (Haney et al. 1991). The peculiar, House Sparrow–like chirping calls of these terns will often allow identification long before you can note the plumage characters necessary to separate them from the abundant Arctic Terns.

**Black Skimmer.** This is a common but somewhat local resident (fewer in winter) along our portion of the Gulf Coast. It is an uncommon to rare postbreeding visitor along the southern California coast (regularly north to Santa Barbara

County), with a few hundred pairs nesting at the Salton Sea (arriving in April and usually departing by November), San Diego (resident), and, in recent years, at Bolsa Chica State Ecological Reserve in Orange County. Skimmers inhabit sand and shell beaches, bays, and estuaries. They are easily seen along the Texas coast at such places as Bolivar Flats, Galveston Island, Rockport, Corpus Christi, Laguna Atascosa NWR, and from the Bolivar Ferry and the Whooping Crane boat. In California try the Salton Sea; the Bolsa Chica State Ecological Reserve; in San Diego County, the Silver Strand, Imperial Marsh, San Elijo Lagoon, and San Diego River Channel at West Mission Bay; and in Santa Barbara, the outfall pond on the beach at the base of Santa Barbara Street.

**Pigeon Guillemot.** This is a fairly common to common summer resident of coastal waters from northern Alaska south along the Bering Sea coast to the Aleutians, east along south coastal Alaska, and south along the Pacific Coast south to central California (Santa Barbara Island and to San Luis Obispo County on the mainland). It forages in bays, harbors, open surf, off rocky headlands and around offshore rocks. After nesting, the birds disperse over the open sea and are uncommonly encountered through the winter. This species is more localized at the southern end of its range but is widespread and easily found from May through August from northern California north. Reliable spots in summer include the following:

1. California. Morro Rock (Morro Bay) and Montana de Oro SP (San Luis Obsipo County); Point Lobos Reserve SP, from the observation deck at the Monterey Bay Aquarium, and from pullouts along Ocean View Boulevard in Pacific Grove (Monterey County); Point Reyes; and Humboldt Bay.

2. Oregon and Washington. Easily seen from almost any rocky headland, in the vicinity of offshore islands, and (in Washington) from many of the state's ferries. It is common year-round on upper Puget Sound.

3. Alaska. Glacier Bay NP, Kenai Fjords NP, Resurrection Bay, Kachemak Bay, and Gambell (St. Lawrence Island). At the latter spot, Pigeon Guillemots can be compared with the more northern and eastern Black Guillemot.

**Marbled Murrelet.** This is a fairly common to uncommon resident along the West Coast from the Aleutian Islands, the Alaska Peninsula, and south coastal Alaska south to central California (Santa Cruz County). It is most often seen in coastal waters but very near shore, as from coastal overlooks or ferries along inside passages. This small alcid is unusual in that it nests on the mainland, either on the ground on a talus slope (only in northern parts of its range, where forest is lacking) or on a branch of a tall conifer in a coastal redwood or fir forest. Some reliable spots are the following:

1. Alaska. Common to abundant from shore and tour boats at Seward, Homer, and other south coastal and southeastern ports, particularly around Glacier Bay, Resurrection Bay, Kachemak Bay, and Kenai Fjords NP.

2. California. Pigeon Point (40 miles north of San Francisco on Hwy. 1), the harbor in Crescent City, North Jetty from North Bay of Humboldt Bay (Pettingill

1981), and the coast immediately south of the mouth of the Russian River in Sonoma County (60 miles north of San Francisco) off Hwy. 1 (Parmeter 1974).

3. Oregon (Pettingill 1981, Evanich 1990). Cape Meares SP, northern Tillamook Bay, Boiler Bay State Wayside (along U.S. Hwy. 101, 2 miles north of Depoe Bay), Yaquina Head 3 miles north of Newport on U.S. Hwy. 101, Umpqua Lighthouse SP, Coquille Point in Bandon, and Cape Arago SP.

4. Washington. Along Hood Canal in winter, on bays near Port Townsend or Sequim, the Keystone Ferry from Port Townsend to Whidbey Island, or the San Juan ferry. It is more easily found in winter than at other times.

"Marbled Murrelets" have also occurred as winter vagrants to a number of inland reservoirs and lakes throughout the country. To date, all of these records have pertained to the Asiatic form *(Brachyramphus marmoratus perdix)*, which is now recognized as a distinct species, the Long-billed Murrelet (*B. perdix*) Long-billed Murrelets are easily overlooked in areas where Marbled Murrelets are expected, and it is only recently that observers have documented their occurrence along the West Coast. Most records of Long-billed Murrelets in North America have come between late June and January, a period that would coincide with post-breeding dispersal. The occurrence of this bird in our area is unpredictable, but observers should carefully scrutinize all "Marbled Murrelets" for possible Long-billeds. For more information see Mlodinow 1997.

**Kittlitz's Murrelet.** This is a fairly common but local breeder in coastal mountains of western and southern Alaska. Unlike most alcids, which nest in large, noisy colonies along the immediate coast or on offshore islands, these murrelets routinely commute many miles inland to nest as solitary pairs on alpine scree slopes. They feed in nearshore waters, and tend to concentrate in ice-filled waters particularly near the entrances to tidewater glaciers. The easiest place by far to see this species is from one of the tour boats that visit Glacier Bay in southeastern Alaska. It is less common, but still regular, on Resurrection Bay and adjacent parts of Kenai Fjords NP near Seward (where you will still probably need to take a tour boat) and on Kachemak Bay, including from the Homer Spit, where it can sometimes be found feeding close to shore in tidal rips. It is much harder to find in winter, when most birds are found well offshore from the southern Bering Sea through the Aleutians and east to Glacier Bay.

**Xantus's Murrelet.** This is fairly common in offshore waters of southern California and Baja. The northern-nesting subspecies, *Endomychura hypoleucus scrippsi,* nests on the Channel Islands (California) and is commonly seen in southern California waters during the nesting season (March through July). After nesting, Xantus's disperses northward, commonly as far as Monterey Bay, where individuals are regularly seen on pelagic trips from August through October. Some birds make it as far north as Washington, where they are infrequently seen from fall boat trips. After October they are only occasionally encountered, but there are Monterey Bay records from nearly every month of the year. Xantus's Murrelets are best seen from spring boat trips out of San Diego north to Santa Barbara. After that, your best bet is Monterey Bay from August through October. The southern subspecies *(hypoleucus)* nests on islands off Baja and is occasionally seen in California waters, most frequently off San Diego but occasionally north to Monterey.

**Craveri's Murrelet.** This is an uncommon to rare postbreeding (August through October) visitor to the offshore waters of southern and central California (north regularly to Monterey Bay, rarely much farther north than San Francisco). It nests on rocky islands off the coast of Baja. Its movements are somewhat irregular and may be dependent on the movement of warm ocean currents north from Mexican waters. In some years, it is encountered in numbers (with a sprinkling of birds lingering in Monterey Bay into January), whereas in others it is truly hard to find. Like other murrelets, this one tends to fly straight away from an oncoming boat, making identification particularly difficult. Craveri's Murrelets are extremely tough to spot on the water if there is even a moderate amount of surface chop. Your best chances for seeing this bird are from boats out of San Diego north to Monterey, from August through October.

**Ancient Murrelet.** This is a locally common breeder from the Aleutian Islands and Kodiak in southern Alaska, south to at least the Queen Charlotte Islands of British Columbia. It is a variably fairly common to uncommon winter resident of offshore waters along the West Coast from the Pribilof Islands (Alaska) and the breeding areas south to central California (it is uncommon to rare along the southern California coast) and is more common farther north. In summer, this bird is best seen from tour boats out of Seward and Homer or from the ferries that operate between Homer and Dutch Harbor or between Homer, Kodiak, and Seward. Boat trips to Kenai Fjords NP (out of Seward) often turn up a few Ancients in the waters near the Chiswell Islands. Winter birds are best seen from pelagic trips operating from Washington south to Monterey Bay, California. This bird arrives in Monterey Bay in early October and may stay until April. Peak numbers, which vary greatly between years, occur from November on through the winter. Ancient Murrelets are occasionally seen from shore (via a spotting scope) at coastal overlooks such as Point Pinos (Pacific Grove), Montana de Oro SP (San Luis Obispo County), and Pigeon Point (on Hwy. 1 north of Santa Cruz) in California; from Boiler Bay State Wayside (along U.S. Hwy. 101, 2 miles north of Depoe Bay) and Barview Jetty County Park (Tillamook County) in Oregon (Evanich 1990); and from Point Roberts, Point Hudson (Port Townsend), or Keystone Ferry in Washington (best from mid-November through December). Ancient Murrelets have shown a tendency for vagrancy to inland lakes and reservoirs in winter.

**Cassin's Auklet.** This is a locally common breeder and offshore resident from the western Aleutian Islands east and south along the entire West Coast (it is more common from Santa Barbara, California north). It nests on rocky islands and forages on the open ocean. It winters from southern Alaska south to Baja. In the southern part of its range it is less common in summer (away from the immediate vicinity of breeding islands) and is distinctly more common from August to April, when breeders are augmented by migrants from more northerly populations. It is not hard to see from pelagic trips from Washington to California. Your best bet in Alaska is probably from ferries between the mainland and Dutch Harbor.

**Parakeet Auklet.** This is a common summer resident of large, mixed-species alcid colonies on offshore islands and (to a lesser extent) coastal seacliffs off western Alaska in the Bering Sea, in the Aleutians, and east to the Chiswell Islands and Barren Islands. It is more common in the western part of its range, where it is easily seen in numbers at St. Paul Island (the Pribilofs), Gambell (St. Lawrence Island), and Dutch Harbor. Small numbers can be seen from tour boats around the Chiswell Islands and Resurrection Bay. In the Bering Sea, birds return to the nesting colonies in mid- to late May and leave by mid-September. It winters in offshore waters from the Pribilofs and Aleutians south to (casually) southern California. Your chances of seeing this bird outside of the breeding season are not good.

**Least Auklet.** This is an abundant summer resident of Bering Sea islands, the Aleutians, the Shumagins, and the Semidi Islands. It nests in dense colonies on talus slopes and in beach boulder rubble. From mid- to late May (when birds arrive at colonies) until September (when they depart), swarms of these tiny alcids can be easily seen at St. Paul and St. George (Pribilof Islands) and Gambell (St. Lawrence Island). After breeding, birds disperse to offshore waters, where they winter from the Pribilofs south through the Aleutians.

**Whiskered Auklet.** This is a locally common to uncommon summer resident of islands in the Aleutian chain (west to Buldir), where it nests on rocky cliffs, talus slopes, and in beach boulder rubble. It nests both in pure colonies and in mixed-species colonies with other alcids. Birds typically arrive at breeding colonies by mid-May. After breeding, birds disperse to offshore areas in the southern Bering Sea, around the Aleutians, and east to Kodiak. Because of the inaccessibility of the breeding islands, the Whiskered Auklet is one of the most difficult North American birds to see. Your best bet is to take the ferry from Seward or Homer to Dutch Harbor. (The ferry runs once a month from June through August, with stops at Kodiak and Cold Bay; contact the Alaska Marine Highway System, PO Box 25535, Juneau, AK 99802, 800-642-0066 or 907-465-3946.) Another good bet is to plan a stay of several days at Dutch Harbor and to take day trips by boat to nearby nesting areas in the Baby Islands. (Contact the Grand Aleutian Hotel, Pouch 503, Dutch Harbor, AK 99692, 800-891-1194. They routinely organize boat trips to see the auklets.) The ferry option may produce hundreds (perhaps thousands) of Whiskered Auklets, but if the passage between Cold Bay and Dutch Harbor is not navigated in daylight, you could strike out completely. Make sure to consult the ferry schedules before booking (although even this precaution is no guarantee, since weather delays could severely alter planned schedules). The day trips from Dutch Harbor are probably the surest thing, but even there you will want to allow a few days in case weather makes getting to the proper areas impossible for a day or two.

**Crested Auklet.** This is an abundant summer resident of Bering Sea islands (from the Diomedes south) and the Aleutians east to the Shumagins and the Semidi Islands. It nests in dense, mixed-species colonies with other alcids, amongst talus slopes, beach boulder rubble, and in crevices on cliff faces. From mid- to late May (when they arrive at colonies) until September (when they depart), they are easy to see at St. Paul Island (the Pribilofs), Gambell (St. Lawrence Island), and Dutch Harbor and from ferries operating between Dutch Harbor and Kodiak or the mainland. Staggering concentrations can be seen daily off Northwest Point at Gambell (St. Lawrence Island). After breeding, birds disperse to offshore waters, where they winter from the southern Bering Sea to the Aleutians and east to Kodiak.

**Rhinoceros Auklet.** This is a locally common breeder on offshore islands from south coastal Alaska south to central California. In summer it is usually uncommon away from the immediate vicinity of breeding rocks, at least during daylight hours. During the breeding season it is easily seen from one of the boats that go to Kenai Fjords NP, Alaska (particularly around the Chiswell Islands and Aialik Bay); on Protection Island, Washington; and on the Farallon Islands, California. Away from the vicinity of breeding islands, Rhinos are most often encountered as winter residents (October through April), often forming huge loose flocks, at such places as Monterey Bay (California). During these times they are easily seen on pelagic trips originating from most California ports (south to San Diego). They are uncommon north of California in winter, but they are easy to see from Washington-based and Oregon-based pelagic trips taken between April and October. They are also frequently seen in these states from shore. Look for them along the coast wherever alcids congregate. They are also easily seen from the ferries that navigate the various inside passages of the Washington coast. They are scarce in upper Puget Sound in winter, becoming more common near Everett, Seattle, and other locations along the lower sound.

**Tufted Puffin.** This is a locally abundant to uncommon summer resident of offshore seastacks and rocky islands from the Diomedes south through the Bering Sea to the Aleutians, east along south coastal Alaska, and south (locally) to northern California (it is an uncommon to rare breeder on California islands south to Anacapa Island, Ventura County). During the breeding season, it forages in the vicinity of the nesting rocks (seldom far away from these sites). After nesting, individuals disperse far out to sea and are seen only irregularly (and in small numbers) in fall and winter. Check with coastal birders from Crescent City, California, north for the location of current nest rocks. Many fall pelagic trips turn up one or more puffins, but they can't be counted on.

1. Alaska. They are easily seen in large numbers from tour boats to Kenai Fjords NP (Seward) and Glacier Bay NP, from the Homer-Kodiak-Seward ferry, and from the Homer-Dutch Harbor Ferry. They can also be seen in good numbers from Northwest Point at Gambell (St. Lawrence Island) and sitting at close range on the nesting cliffs at St. Paul Island and St. George Island (the Pribilofs).

2. Washington (Wahl and Paulson 1977). In Admiralty Inlet (reached by ferry from Keystone, Whidbey Isand to Port Townsend); Tatoosh Island offshore from Cape Flattery, and James Island offshore from Rialto Beach (Clallum County); and Protection Island NWR (can be approached to within 200 yards by boat from May through August).

3. Oregon (Evanich 1990). Haystack Rock at the south end of Cannon Beach, Cape Meares SP, Yaquina Head Natural Area and Lighthouse (2.5 miles north of Newport), Coquille Point near Bandon, Cape Blanco SP, and Goat Island (offshore from Harris Beach SP near Brookings).

**Horned Puffin.** This is a locally common summer resident of mainland cliffs, offshore seastacks, and rocky islands from the Diomedes south through the Bering Sea to the Aleutians, east across south coastal Alaska, and south along the Pacific Coast to the Queen Charlotte Islands (British Columbia). It disperses to offshore waters after breeding, wintering from the Bering Sea and Aleutians south to southern California, where it is considered very rare. Nonbreeders are rarely but regularly seen well offshore as far south as California in spring and summer. It is easy to see in Alaska near breeding colonies, particularly at St. Paul Island (the Pribilofs), Gambell (St. Lawrence Island), Kenai Fjords NP and Resurrection Bay (from Seward), and from the ferries to Kodiak and Dutch Harbor. Your chances of finding this bird in the nonbreeding season are not great.

**Red-billed Pigeon.** This is an uncommon summer resident, rare and local in winter in the lower Rio Grande valley of southern Texas. It is easiest to find along the Rio Grande from San Ygnacio southeast to below Falcon Dam. It is also seen occasionally at Santa Ana NWR and, with increasing regularity, at the youth camp at Bentsen SP. This bird will be seen either perched high in a treetop or in direct, fast flight above the river or forest. For this reason it is preferable to search along the riverbanks, where visibility is high. When birding through dense patches of forest growth, your only likely views will be of a large dark bird flashing by overhead. From time to time south Texas birders locate large roosts (usually along Hwy. 83 north of Zapata) where the birds can be seen at dawn and dusk. These are usually reported on the valley RBAs.

**Common Ground-Dove.** This is a locally fairly common to rare resident of brushy thickets, woodlands, and agricultural areas of southern California, Arizona, New Mexico (rare), and Texas. It is usually seen on the ground in thickets or at edges of clearings. The stubby tail gives it a sawed-off look in flight. Look for it along the Rio Grande valley (it is most common from Big Bend NP to Brownsville) and at Laguna Atascosa NWR in Texas; along Sonoita Creek near Patagonia, around Kino Springs (north of Nogales along Hwy. 82), and in the Nogales area in Arizona; at Redrock (rare) in New Mexico; and in the Imperial and Colorado river valleys of southern California.

**Ruddy Ground-Dove.** This is a rare but regular fall and winter visitor from Mexico to border areas from southern Texas to southern California. The number of records of this little dove have increased dramatically in recent years, possibly as a result of our having a better understanding of where and how to look for it. Most records have been of individuals, pairs, or small groups of birds at oases in deserts or agricultural valleys in desert regions, and most of these birds have been associated with flocks of Inca Doves. Check RBAs from Brownsville to El Paso (Texas) and in Arizona and southern California.

**White-tipped Dove.** This is a locally common resident of the subtropical woodlands of the lower Rio Grande valley of southern Texas. It is typically found in dense growth, where its ghostly call (much like the sound produced by blowing across the mouth of a bottle) is often heard but where the bird can be hard to see. When alarmed, it usually drops to the ground from its low perch and walks rapidly away. It is easiest to see at Santa Ana NWR, Bentsen-Rio Grande Valley SP, below Falcon Dam, and at the Sabal Palm Grove Sanctuary (Brownsville), but it is present throughout the valley.

**Groove-billed Ani.** This is a locally common summer resident of subtropical forest and brushland in the lower Rio Grande valley of southern Texas. Some individuals winter as far up the Gulf Coast as Louisiana, but the species is typically difficult to find anywhere before late April. It is a frequent vagrant outside of the breeding range. Look for it at Santa Ana and Laguna Atascosa NWRs, Bentsen SP, and downriver from Falcon Dam. These birds are cooperative breeders and, as such, are usually encountered in small groups.

**Flammulated Owl.** This is an uncommon to common summer resident of coniferous and mixed forests of middle to high elevations in the Northwest, Southwest, southern Rockies, and Pacific Coast. Throughout most of its range, the Flammulated Owl is a transition zone bird. In the southern part of its range, it is found in ponderosa pine woodlands and in pine-oak woodlands, including mountain riparian areas with sycamore, juniper, and cypress. In much of the West, it is found where ponderosa, sugar, Jeffery, or coulter pines are intermixed with Douglas-fir, white fir, and aspen. Despite its abundance in some areas, it is still difficult to find because of its small size, nocturnal habits, and retiring nature. This bird will often sit in one spot and vocalize for hours. That's the good news. The bad news is that vocalizing Flammulateds usually perch high in conifers and hug the trunk, meaning that your spotlight beam will have to penetrate dozens of branches to illuminate this tiny owl. The call, a single low hoot repeated incessantly, is quiet, yet deceptively far-carrying. It is also somewhat ventriloquial and hard to pin down. At very close range, you can hear a harmonic that makes the call sound two-syllabled. When you hear this, the bird is probably right overhead. Flammulated Owls are insectivorous, specializing on large moths. They are migratory throughout their U.S. range, arriving in western Texas and southern Arizona as early as late March, but in many northern areas not until late May. By July, few Flammulateds are still vocalizing, and they become almost impossible to find. Birds seem to depart all breeding areas by October. Day-roosting Flammulateds are found with some regularity at migrant traps in the lowlands (spring and fall), particularly at desert oases.

**Whiskered Screech-Owl.** This is a locally common resident of oak and pine-oak woodlands from 3500 to 7000 feet (1067–2134 m) in the mountains of southeastern Arizona. It is rare in the Peloncillo Mountains (and possibly also in the Animas Mountains) of adjacent New Mexico. It is typically found at higher elevations than sympatric populations of Western Screech-Owls. The Whiskered Screech-Owl is strictly nocturnal. It is best located by listening for its calls, which may consist of a monotone series of hoots (similar to the hoots of the Western Screech, but without the acceleration at the end) or a duet call similar in cadence to Morse code. It is easy to find in upper Cave Creek Canyon and along the road to the Southwest Research Station (Chiricahuas), in Madera Canyon (Santa Ritas), and in Miller and Carr Canyons (Huachucas).

**Snowy Owl.** This species breeds in the tundra regions of western and northern Alaska, south to Hooper Bay and the Yukon-Kuskokwim river delta. Breeding populations are closely tied to levels of vole and lemming populations, and in years of rodent scarcity the owls may be absent from many areas within the nesting range, particularly south of the North Slope. This species does not regularly breed at any of the localities on the standard Alaskan birding circuit, except for Barrow. In most years, it is easy to see on any of the short roads out of Barrow (during peak years of lemming abundance you might see 50 or more owls each day), but during crash years they can be difficult even here. Migrants are seen with some frequency on St. Paul Island (the Pribilofs) in May and early June. Snowy Owls enter the "lower 48" mostly during irregular winters when they stage invasions that may bring individuals deep into the interior of the West. Some individuals reach the northern Great Plains every winter. When present, they are highly visible in open country as they perch on telephone poles, on road signs, and in plowed fields during the day.

**Northern Hawk-Owl.** This is an uncommon resident of boreal forests to treeline in Alaska (and east across Canada), most commonly in the central part of the state. This diurnal owl routinely selects conspicuous perches high atop spruce trees (or even telephone poles in winter), but chances are that you will grow tired of looking at spruce trees long before spotting your first Hawk-Owl. Although diurnal, they are more apt to perch in the open on cool, overcast days or during the twilight hours. Finding this bird, even in the heart of its breeding range, is largely a matter of persistence or luck. Some of the more consistent spots have been in Denali NP (try the first several miles of the park road, which visitors are allowed to drive), along the Denali Hwy. (from Cantwell to Paxson), and along the Glenn Hwy. (between Anchorage and Glenallen) and Parks Hwy. (between Anchorage and Fairbanks). This bird is more common around Fairbanks than it is around Anchorage, but you would do well to check with local birders in both cities as to current locations.

**Northern Pygmy-Owl.** This is an uncommon but widespread resident of mixed-conifer, pine–oak, and oak–juniper woodlands west of the Great Plains. There are two subspecies groups. One group includes the subspecies *Glaucidium gnoma californicum, grinnelli,* and *swarthi.* This group occurs from southeastern Alaska south along the coast to southern California and through the interior Great Basin, Sierra, and Rocky Mountain ranges south to central Arizona. The other group, nominate subspecies, *G. g. gnoma,* is found throughout the border ranges in southern Arizona and on into Mexico. The two groups differ in morphology and vocalizations and have been treated by some taxonomists as separate species (Northern Pygmy-Owl for the *californicum*-group, and Mountain Pygmy-Owl for the nominate *gnoma*). The widespread "Northern Pygmy-Owl" is best distinguished by its voice, a slow (compared with *gnoma*) "toot" repeated over and over. The "Mountain Pygmy-Owl" has a faster-paced, double-noted "toot-toot, toot-toot . . . ," also repeated incessantly. All members of this complex are chiefly diurnal but are most active (and vocal) at dawn and dusk. They respond well to imitations of their calls, often teeing up high in a conifer, where they tend to draw the attention of smaller birds, which, in turn, mob the owl. The range-restricted "Mountain Pygmy-Owl" can be found in the Chiricahua, Santa Rita, and Huachuca mountains of southeastern Arizona. Try particularly at Cave Creek Canyon, at Rustler Park, and along the road from Onion Saddle to Rustler Park (Chiricahuas); at Madera Canyon (Santa Ritas); and in Garden, Sawmill, and Carr canyons (Huachucas).

**Ferruginous Pygmy-Owl.** This is a rare resident of (and visitor to) saguaro deserts in southern Arizona and subtropical scrub woodlands and live oak mottes in the lower Rio Grande valley of southern Texas. Most of the small U.S. population probably occurs on large ranches (such as the King Ranch) in southern Texas, most of which are inaccessible to birders. Some of these ranches are in the process of allowing access to ecotourists, although you may have to visit as part of an organized tour. Joining such a birding tour may be your best bet for this species (and for the Tropical Parula). The only other areas that have been consistent are along the Rio Grande below Falcon Dam to Santa Margarita Ranch, where a few pairs have been present in most years; and on the grounds of El Canelo Inn, just north of Raymondville on the west side of U.S. Hwy. 77. Occasional pairs have been found in southern Arizona, mostly around northwest Tucson and Organ Pipe Cactus National Monument, but the birds are not known to be present in most years. This bird is chiefly diurnal (but most active at dawn and dusk) and responds well to tape recordings or whistled imitations of its call (a rapid "toot-toot-toot . . . " repeated incessantly). Watch and listen for scolding titmice, gnatcatchers, and the like, all of which will energetically mob one of these owls and which can lead you to the spot.

**Elf Owl.** This is a locally common summer resident of saguaro deserts, subtropical forest-brushlands (southern Texas), riparian cottonwood or sycamore woodlands, and low- to middle-elevation oak forests in southern Arizona, New Mexico, and Texas. It barely reaches the deserts of southeastern California, where a few pairs persist in cottonwood-willow–tall mesquite associations along the Colorado River valley (particularly in the Needles area). Birds arrive in Arizona and New Mexico in late March and in southern Texas a week or more earlier. The Elf Owl nests in old woodpecker holes in saguaro cacti, trees, and telephone poles. It is strictly crepuscular or nocturnal and is best found by waiting at nest holes at dusk. Locations of these birds are often passed through local birding grapevines in southern Arizona and Texas. Elf Owls are also easily located by their calls, which are reminiscent of the chattering laugh of a robin or the muffled yelping of a small puppy. By mid- to late July, most Elf Owls are no longer vocalizing, and at this time they can be very difficult to find. By September most birds will have left the breeding areas. Good locations are the following:

1. Arizona. Saguaro National Monument, lower Madera (Santa Ritas) and Cave Creek (Chiricahuas) canyons, the village of Portal, Harshaw Canyon near Patagonia, and Guadalupe Canyon.

2. New Mexico. Along Forest Road 63 (the Geronimo Trail) in the Peloncillo Mountains; at Guadalupe Canyon; along the Gila River near Cliff, Gila, Redrock, and Bill Evans Lake; and along the San Francisco River near Glenwood.

3. Texas. Rio Grande Village at Big Bend NP and Bentsen SP.

**Burrowing Owl.** This is a fairly common to uncommon but local summer resident of prairies, grasslands, shrub deserts, coastal plains, and agricultural lands throughout the West (south of Canada). It is resident in the southern portion of the West and migratory elsewhere. Throughout much of its range, this species is closely associated with the presence of large numbers of burrowing rodents, particularly prairie dogs, in whose old burrows the owls frequently nest. Where large colonies of prairie dogs persist, Burrowing Owls too, are loosely colonial. They will also use culverts, the burrows of ground squirrels and badgers, or holes that they themselves excavate in loose soil. Burrowing Owls are largely nocturnal in their foraging, but they keep sentinel outside their burrow during the day, standing either atop the nest mound or on a fencepost. They are not uncommon around human habitation, frequently being found on golf courses, at airports, and around ongoing construction sites. Possibly the highest densities of these owls occur in the agricultural lands surrounding the south end of the Salton Sea. Conversely, numbers have crashed in some parts of the northern range.

**Spotted Owl.** This is an uncommon to rare resident of montane (mostly) forests in the West, primarily in Arizona, New Mexico, California, Oregon, and Washington. In Oregon, Washington, and northern California, it mostly occupies humid, old-growth conifer forests of fir, cedar, hemlock, and redwood. In southern California and the Southwest, it is more often found in steep, shaded canyons bordered by drier live-oak and pine forests. Some of the better spots include the following:

1. Arizona. Cave Creek Canyon (Chiricahuas), upper Madera Canyon (Santa Ritas), Harshaw Canyon near Patagonia, and Miller and Scheelite canyons (Huachucas). Most birders have probably seen their first Spotted Owl along the trail up Scheelite Canyon, where a pair can usually be found roosting somewhere between the one-quarter and three-quarter mile markers. Please remember that this pair of birds has been enjoyed by thousands of birders and that your behavior toward the birds can ensure that birders will enjoy them for years to come. Do not approach them too closely; do not use flash photography; and do not play tapes to the birds.

2. New Mexico. The Pinos Altos Mountains (particularly around Cherry Creek and McMillan Campgrounds and Lake Roberts), the Guadalupe Mountains, and along State Hwy. 152 in the Black Range.

3. Texas. Guadalupe Mountains NP.

4. California (in part, from Holt 1990 and Westrich and Westrich 1991). The Switzer Picnic Area (San Gabriel Mountains), Palomar Mountain SP (near San Diego), Lake Fulmor (off State Hwy. 243 in the San Jacinto Mountains south of Banning), Green Valley Lake (off State Hwy. 18 in the San Bernardino Mountains), north and east of Fawnskin (along State Hwy. 38 in the San Bernardino Mountains), Santa Anita Canyon (Los Angeles County, out of Pasadena), Redwood NP, Nojoqui Falls County Park near Solvang, Bothe-Napa Valley SP (in Ritchey Canyon), Samuel P. Taylor SP (Marin County), Tomales Bay SP, along the trail to Alice Eastwood Camp in Muir Woods National Monument (near San Francisco), Yosemite Valley in Yosemite NP, Sinkyone Wilderness SP (Mendocino County), Humboldt Redwoods SP, Prairie Creek Redwoods SP (U.S. Hwy. 101, Humboldt County).

5. Oregon (Evanich 1990). In suitable habitat in the coast ranges (especially southwest of Eugene near Alma) and on the west slopes of the Cascades. Your best bet is to contact local birders or Oregon Department of Fish and Wildlife personnel for current spots.

6. Washington (Wahl and Paulson 1977). In Mt. Rainier NP, along State Hwy. 20 near Rainy Pass, along trails from the Hoh Ranger Station (29 miles north of Kalaloch in Jefferson County), and along the the Kulshan Cabin Trail (Mount Baker area in Whatcom County; inquire at the Glacier Creek Ranger Station).

**Great Gray Owl.** This is an uncommon to rare and local resident of boreal forest and spruce bogs of central and southern Alaska. Isolated small populations are also known from the montane fir forests of select western mountain ranges in

Oregon, California, Idaho, Montana, and Wyoming. It is more common in the forests of northern Canada and Alaska, but even there it can be hard to find. In Alaska, your best bet is to check with birders in Fairbanks for directions to staked-out territories. In the southern part of their range, Great Gray Owls are most often seen at the edges of large, montane meadows ringed by mixed fir–pine forests. They are best seen at dusk (dawn can also be good), when they emerge from the shaded forest interior to hunt rodents in the grassy meadows. At these times they can frequently be seen sitting atop dead snags (low to medium height) at the meadow edge. The Great Gray Owl is sometimes seen during irregular winter invasions into the northernmost tier of states. At these times, individuals are sometimes conspicuous and easy to find (check local RBAs). South of Alaska, try the following locations:

1. Oregon (Evanich 1990). The Fort Klamath area (particularly the dump and adjacent cemetery south of town off State Hwy. 62); Spring Creek Road (from La Grande go northwest on I-84 to the Spring Creek Road exit, turn south, and go about 3 miles to a parking area near the first conspicuous fork in the road); and the Anthony Lakes area (west of I-84 at North Powder; look especially at Floodwater Flats Meadows and at the picnic area at Grande Ronde Lake).

2. California. Most often found in fir forests bordering grassy meadows in Yosemite NP (check particularly around Tuolumne, Peregoy, and Crane Flat Meadows and around Bridalveil Creek Campground).

3. Montana (McEneaney 1993). Yellowstone NP, Glacier NP (east side, near the campground at Summit Siding on U.S. Hwy. 2), Georgetown Lake (northwest of Butte and Anaconda on State Hwy. 1), Red Rock Lakes NWR, Kings Hill (located along U.S. Hwy. 89 south of Great Falls), and the Bozeman area.

4. Wyoming (Scott 1993). The Jackson Hole and Grand Tetons NP area, and Yellowstone NP (the road from Canyon Village west toward Norris Junction is best).

5. Idaho (Svingen and Dumroese 1997). Along Bear Basin Road west of McCall (Valley County), between Ashton and lower Mesa Falls along ID 47 (Fremont County).

**Boreal Owl.** This is an uncommon to rare and seldom-seen resident of boreal forests, chiefly in Canada and Alaska. This species tends to vocalize early in spring (January to May, depending on latitude), when snow still covers the ground at most breeding locales (and when many roads into appropriate habitat are still closed). By the time warm weather arrives and birders become active, the owls are largely silent and well into nesting. Females brood the young continuously until they are feathered enough to regulate their own body temperature. Before that time, females can easily be seen at staked-out nest holes. Once the female stops brooding, adult attendance at the nest is usually limited to a few feeding trips each night, most often during the darkest hours. In Alaska, your best bet is to check with local birders in Anchorage and Fairbanks regarding the location of staked-out nests. In the past two decades, isolated small populations have been found nesting at high elevations (from 5000 to 11,000 ft, 1524–3353 m) in Washington, Oregon, Idaho, Montana, Wyoming, Colorado, and New Mexico. These birds inhabit subalpine and transition-zone conifer forests dominated by Douglas-fir, subalpine fir, lodgepole pine, and Engelmann spruce. Small numbers sometimes reach the northern tier of western states during irregular winter invasions. In spring and summer try the following locations:

1. Alaska. Virtually anywhere in the central and southern parts of the state where spruce forests are intermixed with birch, poplar, and cottonwood.

2. Colorado. Cameron Pass along State Hwy. 14 (between Fort Collins and Walden) has been the traditional spot, although there are doubtless many other areas.

3. Idaho (McClung 1992). From the Kaniksu NF of the northern panhandle south through the Bitteroot Mountains and Salmon NF to Salmon and McCall.

4. Montana (McEneaney 1993). Lolo Pass (33 miles west of Lolo on U.S. Hwy. 12), Lost Trail Pass (south of Missoula on U.S. Hwy. 93), Cooke City (winter), Yellowstone NP, Glacier NP, and the Flathead NF.

5. New Mexico. The San Juan and Sangre de Cristo mountains. One specific spot is Canjilon Mountain (inquire about road conditions at the ranger station in the small town of Canjilon, just east of U.S. Hwy. 84; Zimmerman et al. 1992).

6. Oregon (Evanich 1990). In the Blue Mountains (northeastern part of the state) about 12 miles northeast of the small resort town of Tollgate. Similar habitat exists in the Moss Springs Eagle Cap Wilderness Area east of Cove, near Bonny Lakes in the Wallowa Mountains east and south of Joseph, and near Anthony Lakes (west of I-84 from North Powder), all of which are in the same general region and could harbor as yet undiscovered populations of Boreal Owls.

7. Washington. The Blue Mountains and northern Cascades.

8. Wyoming (Scott 1993). Grand Teton NP and east along Hwy. 26 (near Togwotee Pass), on either side of Teton Pass along State Hwy. 22 west of Wilson, and north of the Colorado border in the Medicine Bow NF (try along State Hwy. 130 west of Centennial).

**Pauraque.** This is a locally common resident in subtropical scrub forest and brushy thickets of agricultural areas in the lower Rio Grande Valley of southern Texas and along the lower Texas coast. It is strictly nocturnal or crepuscular but can often be flushed from the ground during the day by walking through dense cover. It is easily located by its call, an unmistakable "go-wheer" or "go-go-go wheer." Pauraques are best seen by driving back roads at night and looking for the ghostly reflection of their eyes as they sit on or alongside the road. They are easiest to find at Bentsen SP, but look also at Falcon Dam SP, below Falcon Dam, and at Santa Ana and Laguna Atascosa NWRs.

**Buff-collared Nightjar.** This is a rare and local summer resident of middle-elevation desert canyons in southern Arizona. For years, this species was known in the United States only from Guadalupe Canyon (Arizona–New Mexico). Since the late

1970s it has been found in several other localities, including near Catalina SP, in Aravaipa Canyon, in California Gulch off Ruby Road (Pajarito Mountains north and west of Nogales), and in McCleary Wash below Madera Canyon (Santa Ritas). Most birders have seen their Buff-collared at the McCleary Wash site, which has hosted a pair almost every year since 1983. Unfortunately, the presence of a staked-out accessible pair has caused people to quit looking for Buff-collareds elsewhere, and they undoubtedly occur in a number of other locations. As are other caprimulgids, this species is best located by listening for its distinctive call. However, this bird tends not to call much until the moon has risen above the canyon walls, at which time it may call continuously. It also calls more frequently when the moon is full or nearly full. This bird often responds well to tape recordings, but the pair below Madera Canyon has been subjected to so many recordings tape over the years that they rarely respond (birders are requested not to play nightjar tapes in McCleary Wash). Buff-collared Nightjars hunt from perches, most commonly from dead branches that project above surrounding vegetation. From there, they sally out after insects, often returning several times to the same favored perch. The birds are best spotted by using a powerful spotlight to look for orange eyeshine atop likely dead snags.

**Black Swift.** This is an uncommon and local summer resident of mountain areas at scattered localities across the West. The easiest way to find one is to stake out a nesting colony site (on cliff faces, usually behind waterfalls or overlooking the ocean) at dawn or dusk to catch the birds as they leave or return to their nests. In between, these birds scatter to often-distant foraging areas, where seeing them is much less certain. During the bouts of cool rainy weather that seem to persist in summer across much of the Northwest, Black Swifts can often be seen low over the ground in valley areas. Some of the better places include the following:

1. Colorado. Black Canyon in Gunnison National Monument (nests), Loch Vale in Rocky Mountains NP (nests), and the town of Ouray (they are commonly seen over the town in the early evening).

2. Montana (McEneaney 1993). McDonald Valley in Glacier NP (Avalanche Creek Picnic Area) and near the town of Libby.

3. California. Santa Anita Canyon in the San Gabriels, Big Falls in Mill Creek Canyon in the San Bernardinos, McArthur-Burney Falls Memorial SP northeast of Redding (Westrich and Westrich 1991), Bridalveil Falls in Yosemite NP, falls in King's Canyon and Sequoia NPs, and (in smaller numbers) at scattered sites along the Big Sur coastline off Hwy. 1 between Monterey and Morro Bay.

4. Washington (Wahl and Paulson 1977). Hurricane Ridge in Olympic NP, Cape Flattery, the Skagit Valley, the area around Newhalem (commonly seen over town in early evening), Lake Wenatchee (Chelan County), and over Puget Sound (in migration or during low cloud cover).

5. Oregon (Evanich 1990). Salt Creek Falls (about 21 miles east of Oakridge off State Hwy. 58).

6. Utah (Sorensen 1991b). Squaw Peak Trail in Provo Canyon (north of Provo off I-15 and U.S. Hwy. 189) and near the Mt. Timpanogos Trail, Bridalveil Falls and Stewart Falls (on the Alpine Loop in the Wasatch Mountains).

**Green Violet-Ear.** This is a casual summer visitor to feeders in (most frequently) the Austin, Texas, area. However, this widespread neotropical hummingbird can basically show up anywhere in the country (there are records from Wisconsin to Arkansas). It is certain to be mentioned on RBAs if present.

**Broad-billed Hummingbird.** This is a fairly common summer resident of oak woodlands, desert canyons, and low-elevation riparian forests in southeastern Arizona, primarily west of the Huachuca Mountains. It is rare in winter at feeders from Tucson to Nogales. It is easy to find in Guadalupe Canyon, along Sonoita Creek near Patagonia, in lower Madera Canyon (Santa Ritas), and at the feeders in Ramsey Canyon (Huachucas). It is not often seen in the Chiricahua Mountains and is an occasional vagrant to Big Bend NP (Texas) and the California coast. It responds well to imitations of screech-owls and pygmy-owls.

**White-eared Hummingbird.** This is a rare summer visitor to the mountains of southeastern Arizona (and casually to western Texas and southern New Mexico). It is most often seen at feeders in Ramsey (Huachucas) and (to a lesser extent) Cave Creek (Chiricahuas) canyons, but it may occur more frequently in higher-elevation pine and pine-oak forest, where both feeders and observers are less common. Check local RBAs.

**Berylline Hummingbird.** This is a very rare but semiannual visitor from Mexico to southeastern Arizona. Most records are from feeders in Ramsey (Huachucas), Madera (Santa Ritas), and Cave Creek (Chiricahuas) canyons (from April through August), but the species has bred near the Southwestern Research Station and at the Chiricahua National Monument in the Chiricahua Mountains and in Ramsey Canyon. It is certain to be listed on RBAs if present.

**Buff-bellied Hummingbird.** This is a fairly common to uncommon resident (decidedly less common in winter) of southern Texas. It is easiest to find at feeders in Brownsville, McAllen, and Harlingen; at the Sabal Palm Grove Sanctuary (Brownsville); and at flower gardens surrounding the old refuge headquarters at Santa Ana NWR, but look also at patches of tubular flowers (particularly tree tobacco) anywhere in the valley and at live-oak mottes on the King Ranch.

**Violet-crowned Hummingbird.** This is a rare summer resident of desert-riparian forest and oak woodlands in southeastern Arizona and southwestern New Mexico and is a rare postbreeding visitor to feeders in southeastern Arizona. Breeders do not typically arrive until after mid-May. This bird is particularly keyed into sycamores. It is seen most regularly as a breeder in Guadalupe Canyon, where it is most common in the Arizona portion of the canyon. It probably also nests annually along Sonoita Creek near Patagonia. It is a regular postbreeding visitor to feeders throughout southeastern Arizona (most regularly at Patagonia, at Portal, and in Ramsey and Madera canyons), primarily in mid- to late summer, but there are increasing numbers of records from other months, including throughout the winter. In recent years, it has been easiest to see at feeders in Patagonia.

**Blue-throated Hummingbird.** This is a fairly common summer resident of forested canyons (usually along streams) in the mountain ranges of southeastern Arizona and is uncommon to rare in the Chisos and Guadalupe mountains of western Texas. It is rare in southern New Mexico. Blue-throateds are easy to find in summer at feeders and along streams in Cave Creek Canyon (Chiricahuas), Madera Canyon (Santa Ritas), and Ramsey Canyon (Huachucas) in Arizona. At least a few individuals often overwinter at these locales. In Texas, try the Boot Springs trail in Big Bend NP (particularly along the streambed at Boot Springs itself) and McKittrick Canyon in Guadalupe Mountains NP. Males call loudly and repeatedly (a penetrating "seep" ) from perches within tree canopies.

**Magnificent Hummingbird.** This is a fairly common summer resident of pine–oak woodlands, mixed-conifer forests, and sycamore-dominated riparian corridors in oak woodlands in the mountain canyons in southeastern Arizona. It is rare, but regular in similar habitats in southern New Mexico and in the Guadalupe and Davis mountains of western Texas. It is easiest to see at feeders in Cave Creek (Chiricahuas), Ramsey (Huachucas), and Madera (Santa Ritas) canyons in Arizona, where at least a few individuals usually overwinter. Try also in the high country of the Guadalupe Mountains (Texas–New Mexico) and at feeders around Mogollon, New Mexico, and Fort Davis, Texas.

**Plain-capped Starthroat.** This is a casual summer–fall visitor from Mexico to southeastern Arizona, usually at feeders or flowering agaves (century plants) in lower canyons and arid foothills. There have been several records from the Chiricahua Mountains. It is certain to be reported on the Arizona RBA if present.

**Lucifer Hummingbird.** This hummer of the central plateau of Mexico is an uncommon to rare summer resident and spring–fall visitor to our southernmost borderlands. In our area, it is most common in the Chisos Mountains of Big Bend NP (Texas), where it is an uncommon summer (March through September) resident. There, it is usually found in the desert foothills (above 4000 ft, 1219 m) along arroyos, canyons, and on drier slopes. Early in spring, birds are often seen feeding on red-flowering *Penstemon* at lower elevations, but they move up to higher elevations as the agaves (century plants) begin to bloom. The orange-flowering shrub *Anisacanthus,* which is common along many foothill washes, is a preferred plant later in summer. Small numbers of Lucifers move into the oak-juniper woodlands at higher elevations after breeding. The best locations in Big Bend NP for seeing this bird are along the Window Trail below the Chisos Basin, along the trail to Blue Creek Canyon, and in larger arroyos and canyons near Panther Junction. In some years, birds have visited feeders around the Panther Junction employee residence area. Watch also in suitable habitat in the new Big Bend Ranch State Natural Area (west of the National Park), in the Black Gap Wildlife Management Area (east of the National Park), and at feeders at the privately owned Cibolo Creek Ranch, 32 miles south of Marfa (you must be a guest to bird here).

Lucifer Hummingbirds are also rare to casual visitors (from April to October) to hummingbird feeders in southeastern Arizona, primarily at Portal (Chiricahuas), Madera Canyon (Santa Ritas), Ramsey Canyon (Huachucas), and Patagonia. Since 1980 a small population has been known to nest on private land in the Peloncillo Mountains of New Mexico. These birds are found in similar habitat to that occupied in Big Bend: dry foothill slopes with ocotillo, agave, juniper, and oaks. Similar habitat is to be found on the slopes above lower Cave Creek Canyon (Chiricahuas), and it seems likely that the species may breed there. Feeders at Portal are certainly the best bet for seeing this bird in Arizona.

**Costa's Hummingbird.** This is a fairly common breeding bird of desert arroyos and coastal and low-mountain chaparral in southern California and Arizona (north sparingly to southern Nevada and Utah). Nesting may commence as early as January and end by April in some areas (notably the eastern interior populations). Listen for the high-pitched whine made by males as they perform their circular display flights. Males often become hard to find later in spring and summer after postbreeding dispersal. Then, you will be left to grapple with sorting out the females and immatures from the nearly look-alike Black-chinned Hummingbirds. Attention to call notes will be most helpful. Costa's give a hard "tlk," and Black-chinneds, a very different "chew." Also an annual but uncommon winter resident of the extreme southern California coast and Colorado Desert region, east through southern Arizona to (casually) El Paso, Texas.

**Calliope Hummingbird.** This is an uncommon to fairly common summer resident of montane conifer forests and adjacent meadows and valley riparian areas (often with willows, alders, and cottonwoods) from British Columbia through much of the Northwest, south to southern California. Migrants can turn up almost anywhere, from montane areas to deserts (although seldom along the coast). It is rare but regular at feeders in the Southwest, from Arizona to western Texas in late summer and early fall. It winters primarily in Mexico, although small numbers have been turning up at feeders along the Gulf Coast in recent winters.

**Allen's Hummingbird.** This is a locally common spring–summer resident of oak woodlands, coastal riparian vegetation, coastal chaparral, and residental areas of coastal California and extreme southern Oregon (north to Cape Arago). Males arrive in the breeding areas very early (from late December to early January in southern California, by March in Oregon) in the year and typically depart by June. Most breeders remain close to the coast, but in some areas Allen's Hummingbirds are found 30 miles (or more) inland. The exact status of the species in inland areas after the adult males depart is clouded by the arrival in July of migrant Rufous Hummingbirds, the females and immatures of which cannot be distinguished in the field from like-aged Allen's. Occasional adult males are found at feeders in the mountains of southeastern Arizona in summer, indicating that there is some inland movement of migrants. A small population on the Palos Verdes Peninsula and nearby offshore islands (San Clemente, Catalina, Santa Rosa, and Santa Cruz) is nonmigratory.

**Elegant Trogon.** This is a rare summer resident (some individuals occasionally winter) of low- to middle-elevation forests in the mountains of southeastern Arizona. This bird probably also nests in the Animas Mountains of southwestern New Mexico, which, at the time of this writing, are closed to public entry. It is a rare vagrant elsewhere in southern New Mexico and Texas. It prefers riparian corridors in more-mesic canyons with madrones, sycamores, and pines, but it will forage in adjoining drier oak forest. Despite its bright colors, this bird can be difficult to find if it is not calling. The call is far-reaching, but often deceptively ventriloquial, and sounds like a cross between an oinking pig and a hen turkey. It is most easily found in Cave Creek Canyon (Chiricahua Mountains); Ramsey, Garden, and Sawmill canyons (Huachuca Mountains); upper Madera Canyon (Santa Rita Mountains); and Sycamore Canyon (Pajarito Mountains). It may winter regularly (in small numbers) in the Pajaritos.

**Eared Trogon.** This is an extremely rare summer–fall visitor (and apparently occasional breeder) to mountains of southeastern Arizona. In its native Mexico this species is a resident of pine-oak forests. It was first recorded in the United States in 1977, with scattered records since then from the Huachuca, Chiricahua, and Santa Rita mountains. Pairs have at least attempted to nest in upper Ramsey Canyon (Huachucas), although no successful nestings have been documented. Most records have involved possible postbreeding birds in mountain canyons (particularly Cave Creek Canyon, Chiricahuas) from late summer through fall. These individuals seem particularly attracted to the fruits of madrone trees. It is certain to be mentioned on local RBAs if present.

**Ringed Kingfisher.** This is an uncommon but increasing resident along the Texas Rio Grande and around associated resacas (isolated oxbows of the river) and ponds, from just north of San Ygnacio to Brownsville. It is easiest to find along the river immediately below Falcon Dam, and at Salineño, Santa Margarita Ranch, and the Santa Margarita Bluffs. In recent years it has become regular at Santa Ana NWR, and individuals have wandered as far north as Austin and as far east as Aransas NWR. These kingfishers are quite vocal, typically giving a loud, "machine-gun" rattle when they fly.

**Green Kingfisher.** This is an uncommon and local resident along the Rio Grande from Del Rio, Texas, south to Brownsville and is a rare resident along streams and rivers from the Edwards Plateau country (Texas) west to the Pecos River. In recent years it has been a rare and localized resident along the San Pedro River and Sonoita, Arivaca, and Cienega creeks in southeastern Arizona. It is easiest to find in southern Texas along the stretch of river immediately below Falcon Dam. There, it is best to look in the morning when low water levels expose numerous potential perches. This bird can be very secretive as it sits concealed along some shady bank. Its presence is often first revealed by its call, an inconspicuous ticking "thk."

1. Texas. Below Falcon Dam, from the spillway to Santa Margarita Ranch; Santa Ana NWR; along the Rio Frio (particularly near Neals Lodge at Concan and at Garner SP); along the Nueces River between Uvalde and Camp Wood (State Hwy. 55); at Pedernales Falls SP; and along the Guadalupe River west of Kerrville (along State Hwy. 39 and Farm Road 1340 near Hunt).

2. Arizona. Along the San Pedro River east of Sierra Vista (San Pedro House) off Hwy. 90, the Kino Springs ponds north of Nogales off Hwy. 82 (make sure to first ask permission at the pro shop), and in the Patagonia-Sonoita Creek Preserve. These sites are unoccupied in some years.

**Lewis's Woodpecker.** This is a locally fairly common to uncommon breeder in open woodlands of oak, ponderosa pine, and (especially) cottonwoods along riparian corridors, over much of the West, from British Columbia, Montana, and western South Dakota south to southern California (San Luis Obispo County), central Arizona and New Mexico, and extreme southeastern Colorado. It withdraws from much of the northern breeding range in winter and irregularly invades lowland areas south of the breeding range in southern California, Arizona, and New Mexico. In some areas (particularly in oak woodlands), Lewis's Woodpeckers may breed in loose colonies for a few years and then disappear for one to several years. This fluctuation could be related to cycles of acorn production by the oaks (these birds eat a lot of acorn mast, particularly in winter), or it could be part of a much broader expansion and contraction of range related to population fluxes of the birds themselves. Lewis's Woodpeckers spend much of their time making aerial sallies after flying insects, and they are most often seen atop conspicuous perches, such as dead snags in treetops or on telephone poles. In pine forests, Lewis's often gravitate to recently burned areas for nesting. In fall and winter they often descend on orchards and pecan groves. These birds are unusually silent for woodpeckers, neither vocalizing nor drumming with much frequency.

**Gila Woodpecker.** This is a common resident of saguaro deserts and lowland riparian woodlands in the arid country of southeastern California, southern Arizona, and southwestern New Mexico. It is easy to find in the Tucson vicinity (particularly around the Saguaro National Monument and the Arizona-Sonora Desert Museum); along Sonoita Creek near Patagonia; in Aravaipa, Sabino, and Guadalupe canyons; and along the San Pedro River east of Sierra Vista. In New

Mexico, it is best seen along the Gila River near the settlement of Redrock. It is harder to find in California, where it is restricted to the Colorado River valley and a few spots around the Salton Sea.

**Golden-fronted Woodpecker.** This is a common resident of agricultural areas, mesquite brushlands, riparian forest, and subtropical scrub forest from southern Oklahoma through central Texas to the lower Rio Grande Valley, and west sparingly to Big Bend NP. It is frequently seen from the highways perched on telephone poles or palm trees. It is nearly impossible to miss on a trip to southern Texas, especially at such places as Laguna Atascosa NWR, along U.S. Hwy. 77 south of Corpus Christi, anywhere in the Brownsville area, the Sabal Palm Grove Sanctuary, Bentsen-Rio Grande Valley SP, Santa Ana NWR, below Falcon Dam, and at Pedernales Falls SP. In the past 15 years this species has become increasingly common in riparian woodlands west of the Pecos River and is now fairly common near Marathon, at Rio Grande Village in Big Bend NP, and along cottonwood-lined streams that cross State Hwy. 118 between Big Bend and Alpine.

**Red-naped Sapsucker.** This is a fairly common and widespread summer resident of deciduous and mixed woodlands from British Columbia south through Idaho, Montana, Washington and Oregon east of the Cascades, northeastern California, most of Nevada, Wyoming, and Colorado to central Arizona and New Mexico (and at least rarely to the Guadalupe Mountains of western Texas). It winters from southern California (rarely farther north), Arizona, New Mexico, and western Texas south. In the breeding season, this species is most common in aspen forest, but it also occurs in cottonwood-willow-alder associations in valleys and basins and in coniferous forests with stands of aspens along streams or marking former fire or landslide events. It is seldom found in pure coniferous forest. In migration and winter it is often found in riparian thickets, pine forests, orchards, and pecan and walnut groves. It was formerly considered conspecific with both Yellow-bellied and Red-breasted sapsuckers (with which they occasionally hybridize). It is not hard to find.

**Red-breasted Sapsucker.** This is a locally fairly common to uncommon resident of conifer and mixed woodlands of coastal and interior California, Oregon (mostly west of the Cascades), and Washington. It is also found locally in southeastern Alaska and western Nevada. In winter, it is often found south of the normal breeding areas and at lower elevations (frequently in deciduous woodlands or orchards). Formerly it was considered conspecific with Yellow-bellied and Red-naped Sapsuckers. It is not hard to find.

**Williamson's Sapsucker.** This is an uncommon breeder in montane coniferous forests over much of the West, from British Columbia south to (locally) southern California and central Arizona and New Mexico. As do other sapsuckers, Williamson's withdraws from the northern parts of its range in winter. It is a resident in the southern part of its breeding range, but even there it may exhibit a downslope altitudinal migration. It is an uncommon to rare winter resident and migrant south of the breeding range from southern California, Nevada, Arizona, and New Mexico south. In parts of its breeding range (e.g., in Colorado) and in much of its winter range, this is very much a bird of the ponderosa pine forest, but over most of its range (e.g., the Sierras, the Pacific Northwest, and the northern Rockies) it is more a bird of higher-elevation lodgepole pine and fir forests, often with aspen intermixed. Wintering birds in the Southwest are frequently found in the pinyon–juniper belt in the foothills, as well as in lowland deciduous forest. It is not very vocal.

**Nuttall's Woodpecker.** This is a common resident of low to middle-elevation forests and chaparral-covered slopes in western California. It is most common in rolling, oak-covered hills but is also found in riparian areas dominated by willows or cottonwoods, or both, and in pine–oak associations. It often announces its presence with a loud, mechanical whinny that starts out as if the bird is cranking up an old engine. This sound is very different from anything uttered by the morphologically similar Ladder-backed Woodpecker. The two species occupy mostly separate ranges, but in the narrow area of overlap Nuttall's are found in riparian corridors, whereas Ladder-backeds are in desert (such as Joshua Tree forest). Try Old Mission Dam Historical Site near San Diego; Torrey Pines State Reserve (La Jolla); San Elijo Lagoon (from Lomas Santa Fe in Solano Beach to the end of Rios Avenue); Mount Laguna in the Laguna Mountains; Griffith Park in Los Angeles; Big Sycamore Canyon in Point Mugu SP; Placerita Canyon SP; Switzer Picnic Area and Charlton Flats in the San Gabriels; Dorothy May Tucker Wildlife Sanctuary (off Modjeska Canyon Road) and Irvine Regional Park (both near Orange in the Santa Ana Mountains); Big Morongo Canyon Preserve (State Hwy. 62 north of I-10); Santa Barbara Botanic Gardens; Lake Cachuma; Nojoqui Falls County Park; Montaña de Oro SP (Los Osos); Oceano Campground at Pismo State Beach; Morro Bay SP; Pfeiffer Big Sur SP; Andrew Molera SP; Robinson Canyon (off Carmel Valley Road near Carmel); the Diablo Mountains south of Livermore along Mines Road; and Mount Diablo SP near Berkeley.

**Strickland's Woodpecker.** This is a fairly common resident of oak and pine–oak forests at low to middle elevations in southeastern Arizona and the Peloncillo Mountains of New Mexico. Its calls include a sharp "peek" and a chattering rattle, both of which are similar to (but recognizably different from, for experienced birders) the similar calls of the more widespread Hairy and Ladder-backed woodpeckers. This is one of those irritating birds that seems to be everywhere when you're not looking for it and nowhere when you are. Some of the more consistent spots are in Cave Creek Canyon (especially around the South Fork trailhead and near Sunny Flats Campground) in the Chiricahuas; Madera Canyon (especially around Bog Springs Campground and the lower picnic grounds) in the Santa Ritas; and in Garden, Sawmill, and Scheelite Canyons on Fort Huachuca and Ramsey Canyon in the Huachucas. A less specific, but possibly just as productive, course would be to canvas some of the drier oak-covered hillsides above the canyons. Strickland's Woodpeckers are reasonably common in this zone, although not many other birds are. Good examples of this habitat are to be found in the Chiricahua Mountains along the road from the Southwestern Research Station to Onion Saddle and along stretches of the Paradise Road between Onion Saddle and Portal. If nothing else, you should see lots of Black-throated Gray Warblers for your efforts. People looking for Strickland's Woodpecker in New Mexico should try along Forest Road 63 (the Geronimo Trail) in the Peloncillo Mountains.

**White-headed Woodpecker.** This is a fairly common to uncommon resident of pine and pine-fir forests (above 4000ft, 1219 m) of California, western Nevada, Oregon, and Washington. Try the following locations:

1. California (in part from Schram 1998). Cuyamaca Rancho SP (Paso Picacho Campground); Palomar Mountain near San Diego; Hemet Lake near Palm Springs; Mount Laguna in the Laguna Mountains; Hurkey Creek Campground (along Hwy. 74), and Humber County Park in the San Jacinto Mountains; Green Valley and Grout Bay Campgrounds near Big Bear Lake in the San Bernardinos; McGill Campground and along the road to Mount Pinos (off Mil Portrero Road between Gorman and State Hwy. 166); Piute Mountain Road north of Mojave off State Hwy. 14; Charlton Flats and Chilao Campground in the San Gabriels; Calaveras Big Trees SP; Sugar Pine Point SP and D. L. Bliss/Emerald Bay SP (Lake Tahoe area; Westrich and Westrich 1991); Yuba Pass on State Hwy. 49; and Lassen Volcanic, Sequoia, Kings Canyon, and Yosemite NPs.

2. Nevada. Incline Village at the north end of Lake Tahoe.

3. Oregon (Pettingill 1981, Evanich 1990). Cold Spring Campground off State Hwy. 242 and Indian Ford Campground off U.S. Highway 20 (both northwest of Bend and west of Sisters), Ochoco Ranger Station (east of Prineville); Fort Klamath area and Klamath Forest NWR; the Sumpter area; Starr Campground (on State Hwy. 397, 14 miles south of John Day); and Crater Lake.

4. Washington (Wahl and Paulson 1977). Lake Wenatchee, Entiat Valley 16 miles north of Wenatchee off U.S. Hwy. 2197, Chelan Butte Lookout near Chelan (off U.S. Hwy. 97), Brender Canyon (west from Cashmere in Chelan County), the Methow River Valley near Twisp along State Hwy. 20 (Pettingill 1981), and Wenas Creek Campground, between Ellensberg and Naches off the Umtanum Road.

**Three-toed Woodpecker.** This is an uncommon to rare resident of pine–fir forest in the Northwest, Rocky Mountains, and various ranges over most of the central and northern mountain states. Three-toed and Black-backed Woodpeckers tend to colonize major burn areas or conifer forests stricken with blights that leave many trees dead or dying. For several years after such an event, these woodpeckers may be locally fairly common, capitalizing on the wood-boring beetles (mostly cerambycids) that, in turn, take advantage of the newly dead trees. Eventually, these tree-kills are no longer as attractive to the beetles, and the woodpeckers leave. Three-toeds are not particularly vocal, but they do frequently utter a Robinlike "kep" or "kup" note (less frequently an angry, buzzy chatter). Three-toeds spend a lot of time flaking bark from the trees on which they feed. This activity leaves tell-tale signs of their presence, in the form of reddish patches where the grayer surface bark has been removed. A stream of bark fluttering down from a tree is often the only sound made by a foraging Three-toed. This species is also given to foraging on or near the ground and is frequently seen creeping about on downed timber.

Three-toed Woodpeckers are geographically variable in appearance. Birds from Alaska south to Oregon, Idaho, and northwestern Montana (*Picoides tridactylus fasciatus*) are moderately barred on the flanks and across the white central back. Southern Rocky Mountain birds (*P. t. dorsalis*) have little to no barring in the back and more closely resemble Hairy Woodpeckers. Eastern birds (*P. t. bacatus*) are so heavily barred on the back as to appear black-backed. These latter birds are also blacker on the face and flanks and could be mistaken at a glance for Black-backed Woodpeckers, with which they overlap.

1. Alaska. Widespread. Check virtually any conifer-forested campground, trail, or side road off any of the highways out of Anchorage, Fairbanks, Seward, and Homer. Seemingly most common in stands of diseased or beetle-infested spruce on the Kenai Peninsula. Also frequently found within or near the Anchorage city limits at such places as Chugach Mountains SP (Upper Huffman Trailhead) and Kincaid Park.

2. Arizona (Babbitt 1995). De Motte Park Campground and Fire Point and Marble Viewpoint (east of State Hwy. 67, take Forest Road 610 to Forest Road 219) in the Kaibab NF.

3. Colorado (in part from Holt and Lane 1988). Brainard Lake, Echo Lake Park, Grand Mesa, Rocky Mountain NP, along Greenhorn Road in the Wet Mountains; along Michigan Creek near Jefferson, and Deadman Lookout west of Fort Collins.

4. Idaho. Widespread in appropriate habitat statewide. Svingen and Dumroese (1997) list numerous spots.

5. Montana (Pettingill 1981, McEneaney 1993). MacDonald Pass (west of Helena on U.S. Hwy.12); Battle Ridge Campground off Bridger Canyon Road near Bozeman; Yellowstone NP; from Lewistown to Crystal Lake; and Glacier NP.

6. New Mexico. Sandia Crest (above Albuquerque), Silver Creek Divide (Mogollon Mountains), from Sandy Point to Hummingbird Saddle (Mogollon Mountains), Pajarito Mountain Ski area in Bandelier National Monument, and the upper reaches of the road to the Santa Fe Ski Basin (particularly along the trail to Santa Fe Baldy).

7. Oregon (Pettingill 1981, Evanich 1990). Lodgepole pine forests in the Blue and Wallowa mountains and on the east slope of the Cascades. Try Lost Lake Campground (Santiam Pass) off U.S. Hwy 20; Spring Creek Road (east of Meacham off I-84); Anthony Lakes Ski Area in the Elkhorn Mountains; Starr Campground (on State Hwy. 397, 14 miles south of John Day); and the Wallowa Mountains west and south of Enterprise.

8. South Dakota. Harney Peak and burn areas anywhere in the Black Hills.

9. Utah (Sorensen 1996). In the Uinta Mountains at Trial Lake and Mirror Lake (east of Kamas along State Hwy. 150) and at the top of Big Cottonwood Canyon in the Wasatch Mountains.

10. Washington (Wahl and Paulson 1977). The Paysayten Wilderness (on the east side of the Cascades), the forest above Mill Creek Canyon in the Blue Mountains, and Chinook Pass Summit (on the east side of Mt. Rainier NP).

11. Wyoming (Pettingill 1981, Scott 1993). The Big Horn Mountains (Tic Flume and Dead Swede Campgrounds along U.S. Hwy. 14), Canyon Creek Road off U.S. Hwy. 16 (Big Horns), the Medicine Bow Mountains, the Pinnacles Campground at Brooks Lake in the Shoshone NF, Lower Green River Lake campground on State Hwy. 352 north and west of Pinedale, and any burn areas in Grand Tetons and Yellowstone NPs.

**Black-backed Woodpecker.** This is an uncommon to rare resident of conifer forests in the northwest and Pacific Coast states and locally in the Rocky Mountains and associated ranges. It overlaps in many areas with the Three-toed Woodpecker. In most areas of overlap, one species or the other is decidedly more common. In Alaska, Black-backeds are most common in the central part of the state (particularly around Fairbanks and outlying areas), but even there (as elsewhere in Alaska), they are generally greatly outnumbered by Three-toeds. The latter species also predominates in much of the Rocky Mountains and associated ranges. Conversely, Black-backeds outnumber Three-toeds in the Black Hills of South Dakota and Wyoming, and in parts of the Pacific Northwest (e.g., in the Cascades). As do Three-toeds, Black-backeds rapidly colonize burn areas and other tree-kills, but they move on when the beetle populations diminish. They are similar to Three-toeds in behavior but are less inclined to forage on the ground or on fallen timber. Try the following locations:

1. Alaska. Any significant burn area in conifer forest, particularly in the central part of the state. Your best bet is to contact the local State Division of Forestry office in Fairbanks and ask them for locations of recent burns (Springer 1993).

2. California. Yuba Pass (on State Hwy. 49, 9 miles east of Sierra City); D. L. Bliss/Emerald Bay SP (Lake Tahoe); Bridalveil Creek Campground, Lake Tenaya, Peregoy Meadow and Siesta Lake in Yosemite NP; the Marble Mountain Wilderness in Klamath NF (Westrich and Westrich 1991); and Devils Garden Ranger District in Modoc NF (Westrich and Westrich 1991).

3. Idaho. Widespread in appropriate habitat. Svingen and Dumroese (1997) list numerous spots.

4. Montana (Pettingill 1981). Trail to Avalanche Lake in Glacier NP, MacDonald Pass (U.S. Hwy. 12 west from Helena), the University of Montana Biological Station at Yellow Bay on the east shore of Flathead Lake (east and north of Polson on State Hwy. 35), and Yellowstone NP.

5. Nevada. Lehman Caves National Monument and Incline Village (at the north end of Lake Tahoe).

6. Oregon (Pettingill 1981). Vicinity of Lost Lake Campground on U.S. Hwy. 20 (near Santiam Pass), the Wallowa Mountains (west and south of Enterprise),

the trail to Mount Scott (off Rim Drive) in Crater Lake NP, and Lodgepole Pine forests around Davis Lake (Ramsey 1978), Spring Creek Road (east of Meacham off I-84; Evanich 1990), the northern lakes on the Cascades Lakes Highway (Deschutes NF Road 46, west of Bend; Evanich 1990).

7. South Dakota. Spearfish Canyon, Jewel Cave National Monument, and burn areas anywhere in the Black Hills.

8. Washington (Wahl and Paulson 1977). Widespread and uncommon breeder, particularly in subalpine habitats. Try Trout Lake (Klickitat County), Mt. Rainier NP, Mt. Adams, or recent burns in the Wenatchee Mountains or Moses Meadow in Okanogan NF.

9. Wyoming (Scott 1993). Along the trail around Devils Tower (Black Hills) and in major burn areas in the northwest, particularly in Grand Tetons and Yellowstone NPs.

**Gilded Flicker.** Formerly treated by taxonomists as conspecific with "Yellow-shafted" and "Red-shafted" flickers (the enlarged species being called "Northern Flicker" ), this form has recently been reelevated to separate species status. Although somewhat intermediate in appearance between Yellow-shafted and Red-shafted types, Gildeds are distinctly smaller, with a bright cinnamon crown, and they differ in some vocalizations and are ecologically distinct, being restricted to saguaro desert and adjacent riparian woodlands. This bird is a common resident of the saguaro deserts of Arizona west of the San Pedro River to the Colorado River valley, where it is much less common in the cottonwood–willow riparian belt along the river. The species is considered endangered on the California side of the river. It is easy to find around the desert-landscaped residential areas of Tucson (try along Thornydale Road off Ina Road in northwestern Tucson), at the Saguaro National Monument, Arizona-Sonora Desert Museum, Aravaipa Canyon, around the San Xavier Mission south of Tucson, Kino Springs near Nogales, and along the San Pedro River east of Sierra Vista.

**Northern Beardless-Tyrannulet.** This is an uncommon and somewhat local summer resident of mesquite-, willow-, and cottonwood-lined watercourses in southeastern Arizona and a year round resident of subtropical mesquite woodlands along the Rio Grande and mesquite-oak savannas of extreme southern Texas. Some Arizona birds remain all winter (perhaps more than is known owing to the inconspicuous appearance and nature of the bird). This nondescript bird is often overlooked and is best found by listening for its loud, descending "ee-ee-ee . . . " song. It is easier to find in Arizona, where it should be looked for along Sonoita Creek (and near the roadside rest stop 4 miles south of Patagonia) near Patagonia, in California Gulch, Guadalupe Canyon, Sycamore Canyon, Florida Wash below Madera Canyon, Catalina SP (north of Tucson), Aravaipa Canyon, Muleshoc Ranch Preserve (north of Willcox), and in appropriate habitat along the Santa Cruz and San Pedro rivers. In Texas, it is most regular at Anzalduas, Bentsen-Rio Grande Valley SP, Santa Ana NWR and in the mesquite–oak savannas of the King Ranch and surrounding areas.

**Greater Pewee.** This is an uncommon summer resident of pine and pine–oak forests at higher elevations in central and southeastern Arizona and (less commonly) in southwestern New Mexico. It is best located by listening for its unique whistled "ho-SAY-ma-RIA" song. The pewees seldom sing much after early morning, but they can still be located by their repeated (and excited-sounding) "pippip-pip" notes. The easiest places to find them are in Sawmill, Carr, and upper Miller Canyons (Huachuca Mountains); Rustler Park and the Barfoot Trail (Chiricahua Mountains); Rose Canyon Campground (Santa Catalina Mountains); and the Bog Springs, Mount Wrightson, and Josephine Saddle trails in Madera Canyon (Santa Rita Mountains). This bird is a rare but regular winter visitor or resident in pecan groves and other lower-elevation woodlands below the mountains where it breeds. It is harder to find in New Mexico, but at least a few pairs can often be found in the Gila NF around McMillan Campground (west of Pinos Altos on State Hwy. 15), along the road to Signal Peak (Forest Road 154 off State Hwy. 15), and in the Mogollon Mountains near Mogollon.

**Hammond's Flycatcher.** This is a fairly common summer resident of montane coniferous forests over much of the West, from central Alaska south through Washington, Oregon, Idaho, western Montana, northwestern Wyoming, east-central California, central Nevada and Utah, western Colorado, and northern Arizona and New Mexico. This species is most common in closed-canopy, shaded forests of fir and spruce. In some regions it is also found in lodgepole pine and Douglas-fir associations and in denser stands of ponderosa pine. Groves of aspen within coniferous forest are also utilized, particularly in the spruce forests of Alaska. In all areas, this species seems to prefer forests with sparse understory growth. Hammond's Flycatchers are much more birds of shaded, closed forest than are the look-alike Dusky Flycatchers, which, in turn, are birds of open, sunny forest with numerous clearings and a significant shrubby understory. Hammond's is a fairly common to uncommon migrant throughout much of the West, including to lowland areas. It is a regular migrant through southwestern desert oases but is generally rare along the coast north of southern California. Small numbers winter every year in southern Arizona and New Mexico, usually in low- to middle-elevation riparian corridors dominated by cottonwoods and sycamores.

**Dusky Flycatcher.** This is a common summer resident of coniferous and mixed montane and foothill forests over most of the West, from the Yukon south to southern California, central Arizona, and central New Mexico, and east to the eastern edge of the Rockies and to the Black Hills. Duskies seem to require open, sunny forest with a significant shrubby understory. At lower elevations they occupy open groves of ponderosa or Jeffrey pine, pinyon–juniper woodland, and foothill shrublands (dominated by thickets of Gambel oak, sagebrush, serviceberry, and mountain mahogany). At higher elevations (particularly on the east slope of the Sierras) they are common in open stands of lodgepole pine and whitebark pine, especially around edges of clearings. From mid-elevations to timberline, they are common in dense riparian stands of willow and aspen. The

Dusky Flycatcher is a fairly common to common migrant virtually throughout the West (west of the Great Plains and the Pecos River in Texas), except west of the coastal ranges and Cascades, where it is generally rare. Small numbers winter most years in southern Arizona and southern California, often in riparian vegetation. It is not hard to find.

**Gray Flycatcher.** This is an uncommon to fairly common summer resident of pinyon-juniper woodlands, big sagebrush and mountain mahogany shrublands, and open ponderosa pine forests (often with shrubby clearings and well-spaced trees) throughout the Great Basin and adjacent areas. It occurs from south-central Washington, eastern Oregon, southern Idaho, and southwestern Wyoming south through Nevada, Utah, western Colorado, the eastern ranges of California, northern Arizona, central New Mexico (at least locally to Silver City in the southwest) and the Davis Mountains of west Texas. It is an uncommon migrant to lowland and foothill habitats throughout the breeding range and to the deserts of southern California, Arizona, New Mexico, and western Texas. It winters in oak-juniper foothills, riparian corridors, and mesquite thickets from southern Arizona south into Mexico. It is the most common wintering *Empidonax* in Arizona. It is not difficult to find in proper habitat.

**Cordilleran Flycatcher.** This formerly was considered conspecific with the Pacific-slope Flycatcher, the enlarged complex having been called "Western Flycatcher." This form is a locally fairly common summer resident of montane coniferous and mixed forests throughout much of the West. Cordillerans breed from southern Canada south through the Rocky Mountains (east to the Black Hills of South Dakota) to southern Arizona, southern New Mexico, and western Texas, and west through the Great Basin ranges to eastern Oregon and eastern California. Cordilleran Flycatchers prefer shaded coniferous or mixed forests, particularly in canyons with streams. The presence of rock ledges and overhangs, steep dirt banks, or outbuildings (old cabins or sheds) for nest placement is also important. It is a fairly common to uncommon migrant throughout the breeding range and through adjacent lowlands. It apparently is less common in spring as a migrant through lowland areas of southern Arizona than is the Pacific-slope Flycatcher. (Cordillerans migrate mainly through the foothills and mountains.) It is not hard to find in summer.

**Pacific-slope Flycatcher.** This formerly was considered conspecific with the Cordilleran Flycatcher, the enlarged complex having been called "Western Flycatcher." This form is a fairly common summer resident of shaded woodlands (coniferous, deciduous, and mixed) from southeastern Alaska south along the Pacific Coast to Baja, and east to the Cascades (Washington and Oregon), coast ranges, and Sierra Nevada. An isolated race breeds on the Channel Islands off southern California. The Pacific-slope Flycatcher is particularly common along riparian corridors in live oak and mixed woodlands. As with Cordilleran Flycatchers, the presence of water and cut banks, rock ledges, and man-made structures (outbuildings, carports, and so on) for nest placement is important. Pacific-slopes are fairly common to common migrants throughout the breeding range and adjacent lowlands and east regularly at least to the deserts and lowland riparian corridors of southeastern Arizona (where they apparently outnumber Cordillerans in spring). The true status and distribution of migrants have yet to be determined because it is impossible to separate silent Pacific-slopes from Cordillerans. The Pacific-slope winters casually in southern California, usually in riparian vegetation. There is at least one verified winter record from New Mexico, from floodplain habitat. It is easy to find in the breeding season.

**Buff-breasted Flycatcher.** This is a fairly common but local summer resident of pine-oak forests in the Huachuca and Chiricahua (irregularly) mountains of Arizona and the Animas Mountains of New Mexico. These birds seem to be loosely colonial, with several pairs nesting close to each other, while other seemingly good habitat goes unoccupied. The small cup nest is usually placed on a horizontal limb of a Chihuahua pine 15–30 ft (4.6–9.1 m) above the ground and is often quite easy to find. Buff-breasteds often forage low to the ground (below 5 ft, 1.5 m) and can be located by their slightly liquid "pwit" notes. The easiest place to find them is in Sawmill Canyon (at the top of Garden Canyon) on Fort Huachuca, but they can also be found readily in upper Carr and Scotia canyons (Huachucas) and, in some years, near the Southwestern Research Station and Rustler Park in the Chiricahua Mountains. They are occasionally recorded from the upper Santa Ritas in spring and summer, but these may just be wandering individuals. In 1999 this species was found nesting in the upper elevations of the Davis Mountains Mount Livermore Preserve (a Nature Conservancy property), Texas. Details of public access have yet to be worked out.

**Vermilion Flycatcher.** This is a fairly common but local summer resident along watercourses in desert and other arid lands of southwestern Utah, southeastern California, Arizona, New Mexico, and western and central Texas south to the lower Gulf Coast. It winters in the southern portion of its U.S. range, and there is even a certain amount of northward dispersal in winter. The Vermilion Flycatcher prefers willow- or mesquite-lined ponds and cottonwood–willow–sycamore riparian woodlands. It is easy to find in Arizona along Sonoita Creek at Patagonia, along the San Pedro and Santa Cruz rivers, at Kino Springs, Aravaipa Canyon, and Guadalupe Canyon, among other spots. It is less common in winter, but it can still be found at Kino Springs, Arivaca Creek, and Sonoita Creek. In New Mexico, try along the Gila River at Redrock, in Guadalupe Canyon, and at Rattlesnake Springs near Carlsbad Caverns. In Texas, it is easiest to find along the Rio Grande at Big Bend NP (particularly at Rio Grande Village and Cottonwood Campground), but try also along the Guadalupe River and the Rio Frio in the hill country.

**Dusky-capped Flycatcher.** This is a common summer resident of live oak mountain woodlands (as well as pine–oak woodlands and streamside oak–sycamore associations) in southeastern Arizona and extreme southwestern New Mexico. It generally occurs in higher-elevation, drier forests than the Brown-crested and Ash-throated, but the three species overlap in many areas, including in lowland riparian woodland. Listen for its mournful, whistled "peeur" at such Arizona spots as Cave Creek Canyon (Chiricahuas); Madera Canyon (Santa Ritas); Guadalupe Canyon; Garden, Miller, and Ramsey canyons (Huachucas); and along Sonoita Creek near Patagonia. In New Mexico, it is found only in Guadalupe Canyon, the Peloncillo Mountains, and the Animas Mountains.

**Brown-crested Flycatcher.** This is a fairly common summer resident of riparian cottonwood-sycamore (and oak-sycamore) woodlands (to 6500 ft, 1981 m) and saguaro deserts in southern Arizona and southwestern New Mexico and of subtropical mesquite woodlands in southern Texas. It is less common along the Colorado River and in Morongo Valley (California). This *Myiarchus* is more restricted to areas with large trees (or at least tall cacti) than is the Ash-throated, which also thrives in desert scrub habitats. The Brown-crested is easy to find at the following locations:

1. Arizona. The Saguaro National Monument; Arizona-Sonora Desert Museum; Aravaipa Canyon; along Sonoita Creek (Patagonia) and the San Pedro River (east of Sierra Vista off Hwy. 90); and Guadalupe, Cave Creek, and lower Garden and Madera canyons.

2. California. Big Morongo Canyon Preserve (off State Hwy. 62 north of I-10).

3. New Mexico. Look along the Gila (particularly at Redrock) and San Francisco rivers, but this species is less common there than in Arizona or Texas.

4. Texas. At Santa Ana NWR, Bentsen-Rio Grande Valley SP, and below Falcon Dam.

**Great Kiskadee.** This is a common resident of subtropical woodlands and brush near water in the Rio Grande Valley of southern Texas (Laredo to Brownsville). This bird generally forages from branches overlooking the river or small ponds. It is easy to find around the various small lakes at Santa Ana NWR, along the river at Bentsen-Rio Grande Valley SP, at almost any resaca (isolated oxbow of a river) in Brownsville, and along the river itself from Falcon Dam to Santa Margarita Ranch and upstream to the town of San Ygnacio.

**Sulphur-bellied Flycatcher.** This is an uncommon summer resident of sycamore and oak woodlands in the mountain canyons of southeastern Arizona. It is closely tied to streamsides with sycamores. This species is one of the last of the nesting birds to arrive in spring and may not be present before mid-May. Its arresting, squeaky calls (at least one of which sounds like a rubber duck being squeezed) are frequently heard when the bird itself is concealed and motionless in the upper reaches of the canopy. Sulphur-bellieds are easy to find in Cave Creek (Chiricahuas), Madera (Santa Ritas), and Garden and Ramsey (Huachucas) canyons.

**Tropical Kingbird.** This is a rare and local summer resident of lowland riparian areas in southeastern Arizona. It is most often found in the vicinity of Nogales and around small cottonwood- or willow-lined ponds between Nogales and Tucson. In recent years the tree-lined ponds at the Kino Springs Golf Course (about 5 miles north of Nogales on the south side of Hwy. 82; make sure to ask permission at the pro shop) have been the most reliable spots, but try also around the small pond by the San Pedro House (entrance on the south side of Hwy. 90, east of Sierra Vista and just before the bridge over the San Pedro River) and Arivaca Cienaga (a unit of Buenos Aires NWR west of I-19 and south of Tucson). In the past few years a few pairs have nested in southern Texas in the vicinity of Brownsville, where care must be taken to distinguish them from the nearly identical (and common) Couch's Kingbirds. For the past few years a pair has also nested at Cottonwood Campground in Big Bend NP, Texas. Reports of Tropical Kingbirds from Texas should be substantiated by tape recordings or detailed descriptions of vocalizations. Tropical Kingbirds are also regular fall vagrants (occasionally overwintering) along the West Coast (check local RBAs).

**Couch's Kingbird.** This is a common summer resident (rare in winter) of subtropical woodlands and brushlands in the lower Rio Grande Valley of southern Texas. This bird is easy to find below Falcon Dam, at Santa Ana NWR, at Bentsen-Rio Grande Valley SP, and in agricultural areas in between.

**Thick-billed Kingbird.** This is an uncommon and local summer resident of riparian sycamore–cottonwood woodlands in southeastern Arizona. Noisy and prone to perching in the tops of trees, it is not hard to find. The best spots are Guadalupe Canyon (Arizona New Mexico border), the roadside rest stop on Hwy. 82 4 miles south of Patagonia, the Patagonia-Sonoita Creek Preserve, Arivaca Creek, and along the San Pedro River near Dudleyville. On occasion, one or two birds have taken up residence for a few months in Cottonwood Campground, Big Bend NP, Texas.

**Scissor-tailed Flycatcher.** This is a common summer resident (from March to October in coastal Texas; dates are more restricted farther north and west) of open and semiopen country in Texas (the eastern two-thirds of the state only), Oklahoma, Kansas, and southern Nebraska. It is uncommon and local in southeastern New Mexico. Scissor-taileds are nearly impossible to miss when you are driving cross-country for any distance through these areas. Southward-migrating birds stage in impressive concentrations on the coastal prairies of southern Texas in September.

**Rose-throated Becard.** This is a rare and local summer resident of riparian woodlands in southeastern Arizona. These birds seem to prefer areas with large cottonwoods or sycamores, or both, from which they suspend their football-sized nest. The most consistent spot has been along Sonoita Creek from the Circle Z Guest Ranch to the Patagonia-Sonoita Creek Preserve. (The nest is usually visible across the creek from the roadside rest stop 4 miles south of Patagonia on Hwy. 82.

NOTE: Do not cross any fences here. The land across the fence is Circle Z property and only registered guests are allowed access.) Other places that have hosted nesting becards include lower Sycamore Canyon (be prepared for a long, hot hike) and Arivaca Creek. The becards often do not arrive until after May 1 (sometimes much later) and seem to be entirely absent in some years. Check local RBAs for updated status. This species also occasionally nests in the lower Rio Grande Valley of southern Texas (Santa Ana NWR, below Falcon Dam). If it is present there, it is sure to be mentioned on local RBAs.

**Sky Lark.** This is a rare to casual migrant to the Aleutians, the Pribilofs, and St. Lawrence Island. In 1995 at least two pairs attempted to breed on St. Paul Island (the Pribilofs). All Alaskan records are referable to the Asiatic subspecies *Alauda arvensis pekinensis*. The European subspecies, *A. a. arvensis*, is an introduced resident of Vancouver Island, British Columbia, and San Juan Island, where it is very localized. The airport on Vancouver Island has been a traditional location, but you would do best to check with local birders for current spots. This species has decreased in numbers in recent years because of habitat loss.

**Cave Swallow.** This is a common but local summer resident of southern, central, and western Texas and of Carlsbad Caverns, New Mexico. Once restricted to caves and sinkholes in the Edwards Plateau region of Texas, this bird has in recent years made major range expansions in nearly every direction by nesting in highway culverts and under overpasses. It is now common as far west as El Paso, Texas, and is spreading into the Rio Grande Valley of southern New Mexico. Cave Swallows return to these areas by late February, much earlier than the Cliff Swallows with which they would otherwise have to compete for nesting sites. As a result, the latter species has been displaced from several sites that it formerly occupied.

**Green Jay.** This is a common resident of subtropical woodlands in the lower Rio Grande Valley of southern Texas. Like most neotropical jays, it can be elusive, but it is generally easy to see at Santa Ana NWR, Bentsen-Rio Grande Valley SP (particularly coming into feeding stations in the trailer campground), the area below Falcon Dam, and along the river west to San Ygnacio.

**Brown Jay.** This is an uncommon and local resident of subtropical mesquite woodlands in the lower Rio Grande Valley of southern Texas. At present Brown Jays are basically restricted to a several-mile stretch of river below Falcon Dam, and there is some indication that this small population is on the decline. Like most other neotropical jays, Brown Jays are cooperative breeders that live in group-defended territories. They are best located by their noisy calls ("PIA PIA"), which are almost hawklike. Juvenile birds can be identified by their yellow (as opposed to black) bill. Try the old hobo camp below Falcon Dam, overlooks of the river at Salineño and Chapeña (particularly from the El Rio RV park), Santa Margarita Ranch, and the Santa Margarita Bluffs.

**Island Scrub-Jay.** This was recently split from other members of the scrub-jay complex. This form is restricted to (and is common on) Santa Cruz Island (part of Channel Islands NP) off the southern California coast. In comparison with other scrub-jays, it is recognizably larger, a darker (more intense) blue above, and more contrastingly white below, with a more distinct necklace of streaks around the sides of the chest. Much of the best jay habitat is included in a large preserve owned by the Nature Conservancy, and access is limited. Check with the park concessionaire (Island Packers, 1867 Spinnaker Drive, Ventura, CA 93001; phone 805-642-1393) regarding the scheduling of boat trips to the Nature Conservancy's Santa Cruz Island Preserve. Island Packers runs trips several times each week to the east end of the island, where the jays are regular but less common. Local Audubon chapters in Santa Barabara and Ventura also sponsor boat trips to Santa Cruz Island from time to time. More information on access can be obtained from: Superintendent, Channel Islands National Park, 1901 Spinnaker Drive, Ventura, CA 93001; phone 805-658-5730. Signs along I-101 in Ventura will direct you to the appropriate exit for Channel Islands NP excursions.

**Mexican Jay.** This is a common and conspicuous resident of oak and pine-oak woodlands (and often adjacent riparian growth) in select mountain ranges of the Southwest. There are two subspecies found in our area. Arizona and New Mexico populations are of the subspecies *Aphelocoma ultramarina arizonae,* a cooperative breeder that lives in extended family or kinship groups year-round. Young *arizonae* retain their yellowish bill for up to 3 years. Birds nesting in the Chisos Mountains of western Texas are of the subspecies *A. u. couchii,* which, apparently is not a cooperative breeder. Juvenile *couchii* attain their (adultlike) black bill by the time they have fledged. The western birds are paler than the eastern ones, and the two forms differ in some vocalizations. Whether these differences warrant recognition of the two forms as separate biological species is a matter of ongoing taxonomic debate. The common English name has recently reverted back to Mexican Jay from Gray-breasted Jay. The western subspecies *(arizonae)* is easy to find in the lower and middle elevations of the Chiricahua, Santa Rita, Santa Catalina, and Huachuca mountains of Arizona and in the Pinos Altos, Peloncillo, and Burro mountains of New Mexico. It is also readily found in sycamore-cottonwood riparian woodlands along Sonoita Creek near Patagonia, in Guadalupe Canyon (Arizona-New Mexico), and along the Gila River in New Mexico. The eastern subspecies *(couchii)* is easily found in the wooded sections of the Chisos Mountains in Big Bend NP, Texas. Unlike Western Scrub-Jays and Steller's Jays, Mexican Jays only rarely wander outside of their breeding areas in fall and winter.

**Pinyon Jay.** This is a common, but somewhat nomadic, resident of foothill and lower montane open conifer woodlands over much of the West, particularly in the Great Basin and central and southern Rockies (east to the Black Hills of South Dakota). This jay is strongly associated with pinyon pine and juniper woodlands and associated sagebrush communities, but in some areas (e.g., Mono Lake, California) it is also found in open Jeffrey pine or ponderosa pine forests. Pinyon Jays nest in loose colonies; they form discrete pair bonds but also routinely forage in groups. After the breeding season, groups consolidate into huge roving flocks (often numbering hundreds of birds) that move restlessly over a large home range in search of food. Their primary food over much of their range is the nut of the pinyon pine. In years when the pinyon nut crop (piñones) is poor, large numbers of these jays may move erratically outside of their normal range, invading adjacent regions (including lowland deserts and plains). They are most easily found in fall and winter when flocking (listen for their peculiar, nasal "queah" and mewing calls, both of which carry for long distances). They are much less conspicuous during the breeding season.

**Clark's Nutcracker.** This is a locally common resident of montane spruce-fir and pine-fir forests at high elevations throughout much of the West, from Canada south to southern California and central Arizona and New Mexico, and east to the eastern edge of the Rockies. These birds are extremely nomadic, nesting early in the year and then following the ripening cone crop of various conifers throughout the summer, fall, and winter. Some birds move upslope after breeding and can be found in stunted, subalpine fir forest and even onto alpine tundra. Many others move downslope into open ponderosa and Jeffrey pine woodlands and even into pinyon-juniper. By winter, most birds will have moved into these lower zones. Nutcrackers also undergo sporadic irruptions into lowland areas, but irruptions may happen only once every several years or more. Noisy and conspicuous, they are not hard to find. At campgrounds and scenic overlooks in many National Parks, nutcrackers will commonly eat from human hands.

**Yellow-billed Magpie.** This is a locally common resident of open oak savannas and associated riparian corridors and ranchland in the Sacramento and San Joaquin valleys of central California (from Shasta County south to Kern County) and in coastal valleys from the San Francisco region south to Santa Barbara County. These magpies nest in loose colonies and forage in noisy groups of anywhere from a few birds to 20 or more. They are virtually always present at the I-101 roadside rest stop (best on the southbound side) about 16 miles north of Paso Robles (near the San Luis Obispo-Monterey County line). Other spots include Nojoqui Falls County Park and the Solvang area; Lopez Lake near Arroyo Grande; anywhere in the vicinity of Santa Margarita and Santa Margarita Lake (San Luis Obispo County); Carmel Valley east of Carmel; and (from Westrich and Westrich 1991) Joseph D. Grant Park (Santa Clara County); Del Valle Park near Livermore; the vicinity of the San Juan Bautista Mission and Fremont Peak SP (near Hollister); Black Butte Lake (west of Orland off I-5); Lake Oroville State Recreation Area (near Oroville); Colusa-Sacramento River State Recreation Area (near Colusa); throughout the Davis and Sacramento areas; Oak Grove Regional Park (north of Stockton); Turlock Lake State Recreation Area (21 miles east of Modesto); and Merced and Los Banos NWRs (near the towns of the same names).

**Northwestern Crow.** The taxonomic status of this bird has been questioned. Many people consider it to be a subspecies or clinal variant of the American Crow. At present "pure" birds seem to be common coastal residents from about the north end of Puget Sound (Washington) north to south coastal Alaska and west to Kodiak Island. Apparent intergrades are more common to the south, and, in Washington, only birds from near the Straight of Juan de Fuca and northern Puget Sound and north are likely to be Northwesterns. Even in the Alaskan portion of its range (where there are no other crows), these birds seldom stray far from the immediate coast or offshore islands. They are most frequently seen foraging along beaches, picking through the strand. They are easy to find at Seward, Homer, Cordova, Glacier Bay, and Kodiak (Alaska). In Washington, listen carefully to birds on the San Juan Islands or (for example) along the Port Angeles waterfront.

**Tamaulipas Crow.** This is a common, but highly localized, winter resident around Brownsville, Texas. It is easiest to find at the Brownsville Dump, where large numbers are present from November through March. In recent years small numbers have nested, with some birds present throughout the year. It was formerly treated as conspecific with the vocally different west-Mexican populations (Sinaloa Crow), the enlarged complex being called "Mexican Crow."

**Chihuahuan Raven.** This is a common resident of southwestern deserts and grasslands (it is migratory in the northern portion of its range). In many areas (e.g., southern New Mexico) it replaces the more montane Common Raven in most low-elevation habitats (often sharing agricultural lands in the river valleys with American Crows). In other areas (e.g., southeastern Arizona and the Trans-Pecos region of Texas), both ravens are found at low elevations, but the Chihuahuan is more typical of desert-grasslands, while the Common occupies purer shrub deserts and saguaro deserts. Your first Chihuahuan will probably be sitting on a fenceline or telephone pole.

**Mexican Chickadee.** This is an uncommon to fairly common but local resident of pine-oak and pine-fir forests at high elevations in the Chiricahua Mountains of Arizona and the (at present) inaccessible Animas Mountains of New Mexico. The best areas in the Chiricahuas are just above and below Onion Saddle, at Pinery Canyon Campground, and in Rustler Park, particularly along the Barfoot Trail. As is the case with other species of chickadees, these birds become relatively quiet and inconspicuous when breeding. They are generally more conspicuous later in summer when noisy family groups are wandering throughout the high country. After breeding, many individuals wander to lower elevations (e.g., South Fork of Cave Creek Canyon) to spend the fall and winter. They are occasionally found in the Peloncillo Mountains (Arizona-New Mexico) in winter. They respond well to imitations or tapes of the Northern Pygmy-Owl.

**Gray-headed Chickadee.** This is a rare and localized resident of spruce–willow associations from northern Alaska east across northern Yukon to Mackenzie and south to western and central Alaska. The range of this nearly mythological bird is poorly understood, and many older nonspecimen records are probably based on misidentified Boreal Chickadees. The one reliable spot that has emerged in recent years is the Kelly Bar at the confluence of the Noatak and Kelly rivers. Reaching it requires a bush charter flight from Kotzebue. This is a popular area with sport fishermen, and the air charter services in Kotzebue are familiar with the location. These birds are not always easy to find, so you should be prepared to camp for at least a few days (there are no services or facilities of any kind at the Kelly Bar). The weather is routinely cold and wet even in summer, and bears are common. The Gray-headed Chickadees can be found in the dense willows that line the rivers, in the spruce zone beyond, or in the interface between the two habitats. Most birders visit in late summer (after the young chickadees have fledged), a time when noisy family groups of tits are likely to be more conspicuous. Like most chickadees, these birds are likely to be relatively quiet and secretive while nesting is under way earlier in the summer. Be aware that Boreal Chickadees are present as well.

**Bridled Titmouse.** This is a common resident of middle-elevation oak–juniper woodlands, and sycamore-cottonwood riparian forests in southeastern Arizona and southwestern New Mexico. There is some movement in winter from higher-elevation sites to adjacent lowlands.

1. New Mexico. Guadalupe Canyon; along Forest Road 63 in the Peloncillo Mountains, in Gallinas Canyon off State Hwy. 152 in the Black Range; in appropriate habitat around Silver City and Pinos Altos; in the Burro Mountains along Forest Road 851; and along the Gila River near Cliff, Gila, Redrock, and Bill Evans Lake. Two areas that are good in winter (but that lack breeding birds) are Percha Dam SP and nearby Las Animas Creek.

2. Arizona. Easy to find at lower and middle elevations in the canyons of the Chiricahuas, Santa Ritas, Santa Catalinas, and Huachucas and in the riparian forest along Sonoita Creek (near Patagonia) and in Guadalupe Canyon.

**Verdin.** This is a common and easily found resident of Southwestern shrub deserts and ambient riparian stands of mesquite and tamarisk. In the Chihuahuan Desert of New Mexico and Texas it is best searched for in arroyos, where the larger shrubs and trees provide more potential nesting sites. It is easily located by its calls, a whistled "tee-tee-tee" and well-spaced or run-together sharp chips.

**Cactus Wren.** This is a common resident of desert scrub, from south-central California, southern Nevada, and southwestern Utah south and east through southern Arizona and New Mexico and western Texas south to the lower Texas coast. It is particularly common in deserts where tall cacti and desert trees (saguaro and cholla cactus; Joshua trees; tall mesquite, ironwood, and palo verde) add much vertical layering to the plant community. In deserts dominated by low shrubs (e.g., much of the Chihuahuan Desert), Cactus Wrens are mostly confined to large arroyos (washes) that contain tall mesquite, desert willow, and sumac for nesting and foraging sites. A population in coastal southern California inhabits coastal sagescrub with patches of prickly pear. These wrens are big and noisy, and their football-sized nests are conspicuous. They are easy to find.

**American Dipper.** This is a fairly common resident of swift-flowing montane streams from northwestern Alaska (Seward Peninsula) south to the Alaska Peninsula, Aleutian Islands, south coastal Alaska and east and south throughout the West, east to the Black Hills of South Dakota, and south to southern California and central Arizona and New Mexico. Although resident, these birds regularly move to lower elevations in winter, and vagrants are occasionally found in lowlands far removed from breeding habitat. Although they are restricted to streams, rivers, and the immediate edges, Dippers can prove hard to find simply because their territories are often large. In spring they are best found by locating the nest, a large ball of moss and mud plastered conspicuously under a bridge, on the side of a flood control gate, or on a rocky ledge above the water. Once an active nest is located, just wait. If there are young in the nest, the parents will likely be making frequent feeding trips. Otherwise, your recourse is to simply walk lots of stream edge or scan from overlooks. Lots of good-looking habitat is Dipper-less. One clue to the presence of Dippers is whitewash (dubbed "Dipper doo") on favorite perch rocks in the middle of the streams. Because Dippers frequently forage under water, you will need to scan back and forth over the same stretch of stream a few times to be sure of covering it well. With a little persistence they are easy to find.

**Arctic Warbler.** This is a locally common summer resident of tall and medium-shrub thickets in western and central Alaska, north to the Brooks Range. Arctic Warblers seem to prefer dense thickets of alder, dwarf birch, and various dwarf willows in which the shrub height varies from 3 to 8 ft (1–2.4 m). They also spill over into taller, streamside thickets of willow and alder. This bird is one of the latest-breeding birds to arrive in Alaska, and, because it migrates east across the Bering Sea, migrants arrive in the northern and western parts of the U.S. range first. On the Seward Peninsula, migrants typically arrive sometime during the first week of June, but, in some years, they may not arrive until mid-June. There are often a few early-arriving individuals, followed a few days later by a mass movement. Birds arrive in the Denali region about one week later. These warblers are easily located when present, by their persistent, reverberating trills. By mid- to late August they will have migrated back to Asia. Arctic Warblers are easily found in appropriate habitat along the Kougarok and Teller roads (and locally along the Council Road) at Nome, at several places in Denali NP (perhaps best at Igloo Creek), along the Denali Hwy. east of Cantwell, and along the Glenn Hwy. 100 miles or more east of Anchorage.

**Black-tailed Gnatcatcher.** This is an uncommon resident of desert scrub and ambient riparian groves of saltbush, mesquite, and tamarisk in the extreme Southwest. It is particularly fond of arroyos and desert washes, especially in sparser desert, where washes support the only tall or dense stands of shrubs. It occurs in more arid, lower-elevation sites than the Blue-gray Gnatcatcher.

1. Arizona. Saguaro National Monument, Arizona-Sonora Desert Museum, residential areas of northwest Tucson, Aravaipa Canyon. Sabino Canyon, and Florida Wash below Madera Canyon (Santa Ritas).

2. California. Dense saltbush-tamarisk stands bordering the Salton Sea and along the Colorado River (Imperial Dam and Laguna Dam) and Anza-Borrego Desert SP (check Yaqui Well).

3. Nevada. Along a dry wash north of Hwy. 160, 17.5 miles west of its junction with I-15 (south of Las Vegas; Cressman 1989) and in Sunset Park, Las Vegas (Mowbray and Cressman 1991).

4. New Mexico. Dripping Springs Natural Area and La Cueva on the west mesa of the Organ Mountains (east of Las Cruces); arroyos on the Jornada Experimental Range (east of Las Cruces).

5. Texas. Desert washes and Rio Grande Village at Big Bend NP.

6. Utah (Sorensen 1991b). Beaver Dam Wash and the Lytle Ranch preserve off State Hwy. 91 just north of the Arizona border (west of St. George).

**California Gnatcatcher.** This is an uncommon and local resident of coastal sage scrub communities from southern California (Los Angeles, Orange, San Bernardino, Riverside, and San Diego Counties) south through Baja. This species (formerly considered conspecific with the Black-tailed Gnatcatcher) is threatened in the U.S. portion of its range by habitat destruction brought about by coastal development. California Gnatcatchers are best located by listening for their nasal "mewing" calls, which are quite different from the thin "spizz" or "spee" notes of Blue-gray Gnatcatchers (which winter in coastal sage scrub). Try the following locations:

1. San Diego County. San Elijo Lagoon (take the Lomas Santa Fe exit off I-5 in Solana Beach, proceed to Rios Avenue, turn right, park at the end of Rios and take trails leading downhill to the south side of the lagoon. The gnatcatchers can be anywhere along the brushy hillsides or on the brushy flats bordering the lagoon.); Otay Lakes (take I-805 to Telegraph Canyon Road, then go east 8 miles. The best areas are around the west and north edges of lower Otay Lake; Willick and Patten 1992); Lake Hodges (Willick and Patten 1992); Lake Jennings County Park (Willick and Patten 1992).

2. Orange County (Willick and Patten 1992). Crystal Cove State Park (along Hwy. 1 between Corona del Mar and Laguna Beach. From MacArthur Boulevard in Newport Beach go south on Hwy. 1 for 2 miles and turn right into the Pelecan Point parking area. Trails lead from there.); Upper Newport Bay Ecological Reserve; Oak Canyon Nature Center in Anaheim Hills.

3. Riverside County (Willick and Patten 1992). Lake Skinner (about 7 miles northeast from Temecula; take Rancho California Road east from I-15).

4. Los Angeles County (Holt 1990). Palos Verdes Peninsula. (Take Palos Verdes Drive south to Forrestal Drive. Turn on Forrestal Drive and park at the end of the road. Walk through the gate and then up the dirt road to the right. This area could be developed out of existence in the not too distant future.)

**Black-capped Gnatcatcher.** This is a casual visitor and summer resident of south-eastern Arizona. It has nested along Sonoita Creek near Patagonia, in Chino Canyon in the Santa Ritas, and in Sycamore Canyon. There have been relatively few confirmed records since 1986. Nesting habitat (at least in Arizona) is desert riparian growth with mesquite, desert hackberry, and (sometimes) sycamores. Because of the extreme similarity of this species to both Black-tailed and Blue-gray (depending on season and sex of the bird) gnatcatchers, birders should exercise great caution in attempting to identify Black-capped Gnatcatchers anywhere within the United States.

**Bluethroat.** This is a locally uncommon to fairly common summer resident of shrubby thickets in northern and western Alaska, from the central Brooks Range through the Seward Peninsula. Bluethroats are partial to low shrub thickets of dwarf willow and dwarf birch that grow in protected draws and along minor drainages in upland tundra areas. They also use medium shrub thickets along valley watercourses and on protected slopes. They arrive on the breeding grounds in late May and begin nesting immediately. For a short period early in the nesting cycle, males are conspicuous as they perform fabulous skylarking displays above the thickets. The loud, cricket like calls that are a part of every male's vocal repertoire are usually your first clue to the bird's presence. Bluethroats are mimic-thrushes, and no two males sing exactly the same song, although they may incorporate shared elements. If you listen closely to a male in full song you will hear elements of neighboring birds' voices (particularly Arctic Warblers, American Tree Sparrows, and redpolls). Once males are past the time of peak vocalization (and females are incubating eggs), Bluethroats can become very difficult to find. Furtive by nature, they skulk through the dense shrubbery, foraging on the ground beneath the cover of vegetation. Short of chartering a bush flight to the Brooks Range, your best bet by far for seeing this bird is along the Kougarok Road out of Nome. Bluethroats occur as close as 17 miles to town, but they become decidedly more common from about Salmon Lake to the end of the road. They can also be found in appropriate habitat near the end of the Teller Road. Migrants are frequently seen at Gambell (St. Lawrence Island).

**Northern Wheatear.** This is an uncommon and local summer resident of dry, rocky upland and alpine tundra throughout much of Alaska. Much of the habitat favored by these birds is generally inaccessible or difficult to access because of the distance from roads. Wheatears arrive on the Seward Peninsula in late May and probably a week or more later in the interior of Alaska. Try along ridge tops above the Eilson Visitor Center and Highway Pass in Denali NP, at Twelvemile Summit and Eagle Summit along the Steese Hwy. northeast of Fairbanks (Springer 1993), and at high points along all three roads out of Nome. There is usually a pair or two on Anvil Mountain, just a few minutes drive from Nome, and at the turnoff to Woolley Lagoon at MP 41 on the Teller Road. By mid-August, Wheatears are already staging for their return migration to Asia, and small groups may be encountered at coastal locales on the Seward Peninsula. Migrants are frequently seen in late May and early June at Gambell (St. Lawrence Island).

**Clay-colored Robin.** This is a very rare year-round visitor to the lower Rio Grande Valley of southern Texas, where individuals have occurred at all of the major birding locations. Most records are from winter, but pairs have nested at Brownsville and (presumably) at Bentsen-Rio Grande Valley SP. Like other robins, it is most likely to be found around fruit-bearing shrubs or trees. Over the years some visiting Clay-coloreds at Bentsen-Rio Grande Valley SP have become habituated to feeders in the trailer campground, where popcorn has been the handout of choice. Check local RBAs.

**Rufous-backed Robin.** This is a very rare fall–winter visitor (there are only a few spring–summer records) from Mexico to southeastern Arizona, where it is most often found in dense riparian vegetation, hackberry groves, and ornamental fruit-bearing trees and shrubs. It may associate with winter flocks of American Robins, but it is almost always shier and is unlikely to remain in the open. Records have come from widely scattered localities, but the Patagonia-Nogales area has produced several recent records (particularly along Sonoita Creek and at Kino Springs). It is certain to be mentioned on local RBAs if present.

**Varied Thrush.** This is a common (but often hard to see) summer resident of coastal and interior conifer forests from northern and western Alaska south to Washington, Oregon, northern Idaho, northwestern Montana, and northern California. It is most common in old-growth, coastal rain forest (particularly in coastal redwoods in the southern part of its range, and in Sitka spruce forests of the Kenai Peninsula in Alaska), but in some areas (e.g., Washington) it is equally or more common as a breeder in subalpine conifer forest. It also breeds in stunted balsam poplar and tall alder thickets beyond the spruce zone in northern Alaska (as on the Seward Peninsula near Nome). Singing birds sometimes tee-up at the tops of conifers, but more often they are partially concealed and difficult to spot. The unusual song (composed of well-spaced, ethereal notes on different pitches) can be maddeningly ventriloquial. Varied Thrushes winter from southern Alaska south, in irregular numbers to well south of the breeding range in California. South of the breeding range, wintering Varied Thrushes concentrate in shaded, well-wooded canyons, where they can often be found foraging in leaf litter. They also concentrate in areas with abundant berry crops (particularly those of madrones). Individuals are frequent winter vagrants east to the Great Lakes.

**Aztec Thrush.** This is an extremely rare, but almost annual, postbreeding visitor from western Mexico to southeastern Arizona and western Texas. There are now more than 20 U.S. records of this bird since the first one was recorded in 1977. The vast majority of these records are from July and August, with most records coming from mountain canyons (roughly 5000–7000 ft, 1524–2134 m, in elevation) in Arizona (Huachucas, Santa Ritas, and Chiricahuas). Aztec Thrushes in Arizona seem to frequent canyons in pine–oak woodlands, often sticking to sycamore-shaded streams. Madera Canyon has had more records than any other spot. Most of the Texas records have come from Big Bend NP and vicinity (particularly from trails in the Chisos Mountains). Aztec Thrushes seen in the United States have generally been solitary, but they may also associate with American Robins. This species frequently feeds on the ground, where it takes insects from leaf litter, but it also frequents fruiting trees and shrubs (madrones, manzanitas, and others) and will hover-glean tent caterpillars. There is one winter record from Cave Creek Canyon (Arizona) of a bird that fed extensively on *Pyracantha* and hackberry fruits. It is certain to be mentioned on local RBAs if present.

**Wrentit.** This is a common resident of coastal sage communities and chaparral-covered slopes from southern California into Oregon (almost up to the mouth of the Columbia River). It is locally fairly common in dense willows lining creeks and rivers, particularly near coastal areas. It is less common in streamside thickets and brushy openings in conifer forests. Its rattly, accelerating song is often heard in appropriate habitat, but the bird itself can be hard to see well. It often responds well to pishing.

**Long-billed Thrasher.** This is a common resident of subtropical forest and mesquite brushlands in the lower Rio Grande Valley of southern Texas (found west to Del Rio). This bird is easy to find from San Ygnacio to Brownsville (including at Falcon Dam, Bentsen-Rio Grande Valley SP, and Santa Ana NWR) and locally up the coast (for example, Laguna Atascosa NWR) to the Rockport area.

**Bendire's Thrasher.** This is a fairly common to uncommon and local summer resident of open deserts and agricultural brushlands in the Southwest. Its center of abundance is Arizona, but it is most common west of Tucson, and, therefore, off the normal southeastern Arizona birding circuit. Here, it tends to inhabit somewhat sparser shrub desert than does the Curve-billed Thrasher, although the two species can be found almost side by side in some of the saguaro-dominated residential areas of northwestern Tucson. In the Mojave Desert of California it is often found in Joshua Tree forest. This species is highly migratory (a small population in south-central Arizona is resident), with birds arriving in Arizona by February.

They are easiest to find from February through April, when song activity is at its peak. Most breeding areas are deserted from September through January.

1. Arizona. Northwest Tucson (try side streets off of Thornydale Road, but remember that virtually all of this area is private property), the Avra Valley north and west of Tucson (this is one of the few wintering areas; check along mesquite hedgerows), adjacent to the San Xavier Mission near Tucson, and along Stateline Road and other roads along the base of the east side of the Chiricahua Mountains.

2. New Mexico. High desert-grasslands along the road from Redrock to the Burro Mountains; U.S. Hwy. 80 from Road Forks to Rodeo; side roads off Stateline Road near Rodeo; south of Gallup along State Hwy. 602 (Zimmerman et al 1992); along the first few miles of State Hwy. 6 west of its junction with I-25 (about 20 miles south of Albuquerque; Zimmerman et al. 1992); and along State Hwy. 338 in the Animas Valley.

3. California (Schram 1998). Butterbredt Canyon (Kern County), Joshua Tree National Monument (try Ryan Campground), and on the road to Cima and Kelso (25 miles east of Baker off I-15).

4. Colorado (Andrews and Righter 1992). Rare and local summer resident in the foothills of the San Luis Valley, near La Garita and San Luis. Apparently a recent colonist.

**Curve-billed Thrasher.** This is a common, but irregularly distributed, resident of deserts, grasslands, foothills, and agricultural brushlands in the Southwest. It is common in the mesquite-grasslands of southern Texas, but farther west it is intimately tied to the distribution of cholla cactus, in which it often nests. Where such cacti are abundant (as in the Sonoran Desert of Arizona, the mesa grasslands of central New Mexico, and the desert grasslands surrounding the Guadalupe Mountains of western Texas and southern New Mexico) this thrasher is a conspicuous resident. Adjacent arid lands that lack cholla (for example, much of the Chihuahuan Desert of western Texas and southern New Mexico) typically host Curve-billeds in winter, but they lack breeding birds. Curve-billeds are easiest to see around Tucson, Arizona, where they are abundant, even in residential areas. Unlike other species of desert thrashers, Curve-billeds are conspicuous birds, frequently perching atop shrubs, cacti, telephone wires, fences, and rooftops. They call attention to themselves with their loud, whistled "whit-WHEET" calls. Even their nests are conspicuous.

**California Thrasher.** This is a common resident of chaparral-covered hills and streamside thickets along the southern three-quarters of coastal California. It is often hard to see well because of its shy nature, but it is not hard to find in appropriate habitat near such population centers as San Diego, Los Angeles, Santa Barbara, and Monterey.

**Crissal Thrasher.** This is a fairly common resident of desert washes; riparian stands of saltbush, mesquite, sumac, and tamarisk; and low mountain chaparral up into the pinyon–juniper belt in Arizona, New Mexico, western Texas, south-eastern California, and extreme southern Nevada and Utah. It is widespread but secretive and often hard to find. It is probably most easily found along the Rio Grande (and in adjacent shrub deserts and desert-grasslands) from El Paso (Texas) to Socorro (New Mexico). This species begins nesting very early (in January or February) and may exhibit somewhat of a bimodal reproductive pattern, with a first nesting completed by late March, followed by a break until the mid-summer rainy season, and then another nesting. Between nestings, they are typically unresponsive to taped calls. Singing birds perch in the tops of trees or shrubs but are quick to drop to the ground and run away.

1. Texas. Big Bend NP, Hueco Tanks SP.

2. New Mexico. Anywhere along the Rio Grande from the Texas border north to Socorro, the Jornada Experimental Range (east of Las Cruces), the lower portions of Aguirre Springs Recreation Area (east side of the Organ Mountains) and its entrance road, the Dripping Springs Natural Area and La Cueva (west slope of the Organ Mountains), Bitter Lakes and Bosque del Apache NWRs, Rattlesnake Springs (south of Carlsbad), along the Pecos River north of Brantley Lake (Zimmerman et al. 1992), and along Forest Road 851 in the Burro Mountains.

3. Arizona. Vicinity of Portal, particularly in washes along the lower portion of the road from Portal to Paradise (Chiricahuas); Florida Wash below Madera Canyon (Santa Ritas); tamarisk-mesquite groves adjacent to the San Xavier Mission (near Tucson); Molino Basin on the Mt. Lemmon road (Santa Catalinas); and higher desert above the San Pedro River.

4. California. In salt cedar (tamarisk) along the Colorado River Valley, especially at Cibola NWR (south of Blythe) and near Laguna and Imperial Dams; in saltbush and tamarisk around the Salton Sea, including near Finney and Ramer lakes and along Hwy. 195 west and south of Mecca; and at Anza-Borrego SP.

5. Utah (Sorenscon 1991b). The Beaver Dam Mountains (along State Hwy. 91 west of St. George) and Beaver Dam Wash and the Lytle Ranch Preserve (just north of the Arizona state line, off Hwy. 91).

6. Nevada. Floyd Lamb SP (off U.S. Hwy. 95, 12 miles north of Las Vegas; Mowbray and Cressman 1989); and Sunset Park, Las Vegas (Mowbray and Cressman 1991).

**Le Conte's Thrasher.** This is an uncommon and local resident of the sparse shrub deserts of southeastern California, southwestern Arizona, southern Nevada, and the San Joaquin Valley of central California. In the latter locale it inhabits open saltbush desert. Elsewhere it can be found in open stands of either saltbush or creosotebush. As do other desert thrashers, this one begins singing very early in spring, and is easiest to find before April. It is extremely shy, and when pursued, it tends to fly some distance low to the ground, and then hits the ground running (often with tail cocked like a miniature roadrunner). Many people find their first one among the disjunct San Joaquin Valley population around the tiny town of Maricopa (Kern County). Try the following locations:

1. Arizona. Unfortunately, many of the best areas are on Tohono O'odham Nation lands, where access is tenuous at best. (Reservation police can and will run birders off for no apparent reason.) The best spot is the intersection of Baseline Road and Salome Road (reached by taking I-10 west from Phoenix, turning south onto State Hwy. 85 to Gila Bend, then west on Baseline Road to where it intersects Salome Road). Some people have also had luck in the Avra Valley west of Tucson.

2. California. Along the road to Cima (25 miles west of Baker and south of I-15; Holt 1990), near Palmdale in the Antelope Valley, Anza-Borrego Desert SP, Butterbredt Canyon and Red Rock Canyon SP in Kern County (Holt 1990), and near Maricopa (particularly along Petroleum Club Road from Hwy. 33 to Cadet Road).

3. Nevada (Mowbray and Cressman 1989). About 2 miles north of U.S. Hwy. 95 along the road to the Desert NWR and Corn Creek about 25 miles north of Las Vegas (thrashers are in sagebrush north of the road; the south side is private property).

**Yellow Wagtail.** This is a locally common summer resident of tundra with dwarf-stature shrubs and tussock-forming sedges and of ambient riparian thickets of taller shrubs in much of northern and western Alaska. It is readily found at Nome, Kotzebue, Wales, and Gambell (St. Lawrence Island); along parts of the Dalton Hwy.; and in the Yukon Delta NWR. Of these, the most accessible place is Nome. Yellow Wagtails arrive in the Nome area in late May, often in large waves, and can be found foraging in the coastal sand dunes along the Council Road. From there, they spread out across the tundra and are easily seen along any of the roads out of Nome. Listen for their loud "squeet" calls, frequently doubled or tripled in flight, and for their wiry, penetrating songs. Migrants are seen regularly in coastal western Alaska, and in the Pribilofs and Aleutians.

**White Wagtail.** This is a rare and local summer resident of northwestern Alaska, primarily at scattered sites on the Seward Peninsula and nearby offshore islands, including St. Lawrence Island. White Wagtails are mostly found around coastal villages, where they nest in abandoned buildings, gold dredges, and oil drums, and in boulder rubble that lines jetties, breakwaters, and gravel pits. They frequently forage in beach strand and garbage dumps and are most often seen hurtling overhead in undulating flight, calling as they go. These birds have large territories and can be difficult to pin down. They are probably best looked for at Nome, Teller (anywhere in the village), Gambell (anywhere in the village, and especially around the boatyards and town dump), and Wales. Of these, Nome is the most accessible. There is usually a pair nesting along the breakwater in the harbor area, but try also at old gold dredges on the outskirts of town, near the native village at the mouth of the Nome River, and at the gravel pit operation at Cape Nome (Council Road). Vagrants have been seen in fall and winter south to California.

**Red-throated Pipit.** This is an uncommon to rare and local summer resident of block-fields and dwarf-shrub mat tundra (mostly on the slopes of mountains) in northwestern Alaska, from Cape Lisburne south to Wales (and occasionally to Nome), and on St. Lawrence, Sledge, and Little Diomede Islands. It is fairly common on Cape Mountain at Wales. Otherwise, the only dependable spot that is readily accessible is Gambell (St. Lawrence Island). At Gambell, anywhere from two to five pairs can be found scattered along the base of the mountain east of the village. Migrants typically arrive during the last few days of May. They are usually on the rock-strewn lower slopes but routinely venture into the adjacent boneyards to forage. Listen for the complex song, which is usually given in flight, and for the thin "speee" note given by flushed birds as they bound away. There are only a few confirmed nesting records from Nome, although the species undoubtedly breeds regularly. There is an abundance of good-looking habitat, although in most years no birds are turned up by birders. Try drier, rocky tundra along the Teller and Kougarok roads beyond the 30-mile marks. The Red-throated Pipit is a very rare fall vagrant (usually in agricultural fields with flocks of American Pipits) along the West Coast. Most records are from California and are concentrated in late October and early November. However, it is not recorded every year. If present, it is certain to be mentioned on local RBAs.

**Sprague's Pipit.** This is a fairly common but somewhat local summer resident of mixed-grass prairies in North Dakota, Montana, northwestern South Dakota, and the prairie provinces of Canada. It is found both in typical mixed-species, medium-height grasslands and in the grassy meadows bordering alkaline lakes. The latter areas often harbor very high densities of pipits. Breeding birds perform display flights at dizzying altitudes, often appearing as little more than a speck circling overhead. Birds flushed from the ground (the normal way of seeing them in winter) typically give a loud "squeet" on takeoff, ascend rapidly to a fair height, then drop vertically, as if shot, to the ground. In summer try the following locations.

1. North Dakota. Des Lacs, J. Clark Salyer, and Arrowwood/Chase Lake NWRs; and anywhere in appropriate habitat in Burke, Mountrail, Ward, McHenry, Pierce, Kidder, and Stutsman Counties.

2. Montana (McEneaney 1993). Bowdoin and Medicine Lake NWRs; prairie around the town of Molt (west of Billings); Terry Badlands (between Glendive and Miles City: take the Terry exit off I-94, go 2 miles north on Hwy. 253 and turn west); Fox Lake Wildlife Management Area (21 miles west of Sidney on Hwy. 200); along Cutover Road in Pine Butte Swamp Preserve (a south turn off Teton River Road, 17.5 miles west of U.S. Hwy. 89, north of Choteau); Mission Lake (20 miles east of Browning on U.S. Hwy. 2); and the Blackfeet Potholes along U.S. Hwy 2 between Browning and East Glacier.

The species winters locally in the grasslands of extreme southern Arizona (for example, San Rafael Valley and the Sonoita region) and New Mexico (Animas Valley); in grassy pastures, meadows, fallow fields, and alfalfa fields from central Texas (Attwater Prairie-Chicken NWR is excellent) to Louisiana; and in coastal grassland from Louisiana south to Laguna Atascosa NWR (Texas).

**Bohemian Waxwing.** This is an uncommon and nomadic resident of mixed and coniferous woodlands from western and northern Alaska (to treeline) south to central Washington, northern Idaho, and northwestern Montana. It winters almost throughout the breeding range (withdrawing from the northern and western parts of its Alaska range) and erratically much farther south, at least occasionally, almost throughout the West. It is easiest to see during these winter invasions, when flocks or small groups (sometimes intermixed with Cedar Waxwings) descend on mountain and prairie towns (particularly in the northern tier of states from Washington to North Dakota) to feast on the fruits of mountain ash, juniper, chokecherry, highbush cranberry, crab apple, and elderberry. In summer it is easiest to find in Alaska, but even here pairs may seem few and far between. It is best seen in the taiga zone of central Alaska, where large swampy expanses of black spruce and or white spruce are intermixed with birch, cottonwood, and poplar. Here, they perch high atop spruce trees or other prominent lookouts, from whence they sally out after flying insects. Good general areas for seeing them include the Parks Hwy. from Wasilla to Fairbanks, Denali NP, the Denali Hwy. from Cantwell to Paxson, the Richardson Hwy. from Anchorage to Fairbanks, and the Glenn Hwy. from Anchorage to Glenallen.

**Phainopepla.** This is a fairly common to locally abundant resident of riparian forests, mesquite groves, and oak–juniper foothill forests in the desert Southwest and coastal southern California. It withdraws from the northern portion of its range in winter. This species is very unusual in that birds from some desert populations have been shown to nest early in spring and then migrate west toward the coast for a second nesting. Likewise, many individuals move altitudinally (upslope) after their first nesting. Because of this propensity for seasonal movement in many populations, the local abundance of this species can change dramatically through the year and may vary radically from place to place. This species is strongly associated with various species of mistletoe, each of which tends to be host-specific. In Texas and New Mexico, mistletoes are most commonly found as parasites of oaks and cottonwoods, whereas in Arizona, other species also commonly parasitize palo verde and mesquite.

**Black-capped Vireo.** This is an uncommon and local summer resident of scrub-oak and juniper communities (particularly those in successional stages) in the plateau country of central Texas and Oklahoma. This bird is elusive, and although it is often quite vocal (sings persistently through the heat of the day, much like other vireos), it can be extremely difficult to see well in the dense oak thickets. Popular areas for finding it in Texas include Lake City Park in Austin, Neal's Lodge near Concan, County Road 674 from Rocksprings to Brackettville (Holt 1992), Kickapoo Cavern State Natural Area (about 22 miles north of Brackettville), the Kerr Wildlife Management Area (along Ranch Road 1340 near Hunt; Holt 1992), Dewberry Hollow (south of Kerrville off State Hwy. 16, take East Spicer Drive to West Spicer Drive; Holt 1992), Johnson Canyon (12 miles south of Kerville on

Hwy. 16), Pedernales Falls SP, the Lost Maples State Natural Area, in Friedrich Wilderness Park (west from San Antonio off I-10 and Camp Bullis Road; Holt 1992), and along the Window Trail in Big Bend NP. You might also check with local birders in Austin and San Angelo for current hot spots. In Oklahoma it is best found in the Wichita Mountains of Comanche, Caddo, Canadian, and Blaine counties (Grzybowski 1991). This bird arrives in late March to early April, three to four weeks later than its fellow "hill country" specialty, the Golden-cheeked Warbler.

**Gray Vireo.** This is an uncommon and local summer resident of arid hillsides and canyons with scattered trees, from Colorado and Utah south. This bird is found in a variety of dry, open, or semiopen wooded habitats, ranging from live-oak forests to xeric mesquite and juniper-spotted hills and mesas. However, it is probably most closely associated with pinyon-juniper forest. There may be some quirk of microhabitat, such as spacing between trees or percent cover by shrubs, that dictates the localized distribution of this bird. Many areas seem to support a few pairs of vireos for a few years and are then abandoned. This species is almost never encountered as a migrant. Try the following locations:

1. Arizona. As a general rule, this species is absent from the standard southeastern Arizona birding circuit. The only reliable spot in southeastern Arizona is Redington Pass, about 20 miles northeast of Tucson off Redington Road. Farther north try Slate Creek Divide (between Phoenix and Payson on State Hwy. 87 just south of the intersection with Hwy. 188), in the vicinity of Sacred Mountain on U.S. Hwy. 89 north of Flagstaff (as you drop down into pinyon–juniper habitat), along the road between Carefree and Seven Springs (north and east of Phoenix), just south of Sedona in pinyon-juniper, and generally, anywhere between 3000 and 5000 ft (914–1524 m) in pinyon–juniper habitat on the Mogollon Rim.

2. California. Occurs in the Grapevine, Kingston, Clark, New York, Laguna (southern slopes), San Jacinto, and San Bernardino (drier northeastern slopes) mountains (Garrett and Dunn 1981). Try (Holt 1990, Schram 1998): Cedar Canyon Road in the foothills of the Providence Mountains east of Kelso; off Bob's Gap Road (from Wrightwood, along State Hwy. 2 in the San Gabriel Mountains, take Route N4 north toward Valyermo and turn right onto Bob's Gap Road, then right again just before the Limekiln Ruins); Rose Mine Road (east side of Baldwin Lake off State Hwy. 18 in the San Bernardino Mountains); Pinyon Flats Campground in the San Jacinto Mountains; and Kitchen Creek Road (east of San Diego off I-8, 6.5 miles east of the Sunrise Hwy. exit).

3. Colorado (Holt and Lane 1988). Devils Kitchen and Monument Canyon in Colorado National Monument (west of Grand Junction); near the Utah state line and I-70; and Escalante Canyon (west of Delta).

4. Nevada. Along the road to the Mount Potosi Boy Scout Camp, south of Hwy. 160, 18 miles west of its junction with I-15 (south of Las Vegas; Cressman 1989).

5. New Mexico (in part from Zimmerman et al. 1992). Slaughter Canyon (Carlsbad Caverns NP, south of Rattlesnake Springs); near Sitting Bull Falls in the Guadalupe Mountains; lower portions of the Aguirre Springs Recreation Area

(east slope of the Organ Mountains); Forest Road 851 in the Burro Mountains; Rattlesnake and Reese Canyons (about 15 miles north of Navajo Dam on State Hwy. 511); Oso Canyon in the Jicarilla Apache Reservation portion of Carson NF (near the eastern forest boundary, 5.5 miles north of U.S. Hwy. 64, on Forest Road 310).

6. Texas. The Window Trail, Blue Creek Canyon Trail, and Campground Canyon in Big Bend NP (Chisos Mountains), near the entrance to McKittrick Canyon NP (Guadalupe Mountains), Cibolo Creek Ranch 32 miles south of Marfa (you must be a guest to bird the Ranch), and in Kickapoo Cavern State Natural Area (north of Brackettville).

7. Utah. Zion, Canyonlands, and Arches NPs; and the Beaver Dam Mountains along State Hwy. 91 west of St. George (Sorenson 1991a).

**Yellow-green Vireo.** This is a casual summer visitor or resident of woodlands in southern Texas and a casual fall migrant to southern California. This Mexican species is not recorded every year from the United States. Recent records of territorial birds in Texas have come from Laguna Atascosa NWR, the Brownsville area (where it formerly was regular), and the Austin area. It is certain to be mentioned on RBAs if present. It formerly was considered conspecific with the Red-eyed Vireo.

**Virginia's Warbler.** This is a common summer resident of brushy slopes (primarily in the transition zone to 9000 ft, 2743 m) from the Great Basin southward. This bird is most common in areas where deciduous oak thickets (such as Gambel's oak) grow among live oak and pinyon–juniper woodlands. In Arizona, New Mexico, and Colorado (and perhaps elsewhere) it should be looked for in the same places where Spotted Towhees nest. It is not particularly difficult to find once you locate the proper breeding habitat. It is an uncommon to rare migrant in lowlands throughout its range.

**Colima Warbler.** This is a locally common summer resident of oak woodlands in a small portion of the Chisos Mountains of Big Bend NP (Texas). This bird occurs nowhere else in the United States. The bulk of the population is found in Boot Canyon and along its drainages, where Arizona cypress and maples are mixed among the junipers and live oaks. To be assured of finding this bird, you must hike the 5.5-mile (one-way) trail to Boot Springs, which takes off from the parking lot in the Chisos Basin. The birds are easiest to find in April and May when singing is at its peak, but with patience they can still be found through August. After nesting they are nonvocal but can still be located by their sharp chip notes (similar to those of a Virginia's or Nashville warbler).

**Lucy's Warbler.** This is a common summer resident of southwestern riparian forests and ambient mesquite or tamarisk thickets. It is also found in densely vegetated parts of the Sonoran Desert of southeastern Arizona, particularly along arroyos with taller and denser stands of mesquite and desert hackberry. This cavity-nesting warbler is somewhat inconspicuous. Its songs are reminiscent of those of the Yellow Warbler (with which it shares the wetter riparian areas), but it is best located by its sharp "chik" notes, similar to those of Nashville and Virginia's warblers. It responds well to pishing or owl imitations, often being the first bird to appear. It is easy to find at the following locations:

1. Arizona. Along Sonoita Creek near Patagonia, at Kino Springs north of Nogales off Hwy. 82, along the San Pedro River (San Pedro House) east of Sierra Vista off Hwy. 90, behind the San Xavier Mission and in Sabino Canyon near Tucson, along Florida Wash below Madera Canyon (Santa Ritas), and in the arroyos around and below Portal (Chiricahuas).

2. New Mexico. Mangas Springs (northwest of Silver City off U.S. Hwy. 180); along the Gila River at Cliff, Gila, Redrock, and along the road into Bill Evans Lake; Guadalupe Canyon; and in mesquite borders of Percha Dam SP.

3. Texas. In riparian thickets along the road from Ruidosa to Candelaria (northwest from Presidio) and sometimes around the edges of Cottonwood Campground in Big Bend NP.

4. California. Locally common along the Colorado River Valley (try between Imperial and Laguna dams and at Mittry Lake Wildlife Area); Big Morongo Canyon Preserve (off State Hwy. 62 north of I-10).

5. Nevada. Sunset Park, Las Vegas (Mowbray and Cressman 1991).

**Tropical Parula.** This is a rare resident of subtropical forest and live oak mottes in the lower Rio Grande Valley of southern Texas. Many pairs nest on the King Ranch, but at present the only way to gain access is to go with an organized tour group. There is often a pair nesting at the roadside rest stop along Hwy. 77 south of Sarita (the rest stop is in the divider of the highway; look for the warbler on the west side of the highway). There are also recent nesting records from Anzalduas County Park near McAllen. In some winters the bird is seen at scattered locales in the valley, particularly at Santa Ana NWR, Bentsen-Rio Grande Valley SP, and the Sabal Palm Grove Sanctuary where it is most often found associating in mixed flocks with titmice, kinglets, and warblers.

**Hermit Warbler.** This is a fairly common summer resident of moist, old-growth conifer forests along the coasts of Oregon, Washington, and northern California. The Hermit Warbler also breeds in some drier interior mountain ranges such as the Sierras in California. It is a fairly common migrant through the southwestern mountains in spring (April–May), where it is most often seen with mixed-species groups of birds, particularly in association with migrant Townsend's Warblers. It migrates south very early (beginning in mid-July) in fall and can actually be common in the Arizona mountains (uncommon in New Mexico) in early August, with numbers tapering off into October. Migrants also appear in the lowlands, and individuals winter along the southern two-thirds of California coastline.

**Golden-cheeked Warbler.** This is a fairly common but local summer resident of juniper woodlands and the hilly Edwards Plateau region of central Texas (which harbors the entire world's breeding population). These warblers require old-growth stands of juniper (locally called "cedars" ) mixed with a number of deciduous oaks (Sexton 1992). They return (from wintering areas in the highlands of northern Central America early in spring (the first week of March) and are fairly easy to find until mid-June, by which time song activity drops off tremendously. Even singing birds can be difficult to see well, given the low, fairly closed canopy of the juniper-covered hillsides. The buzzy song is reminiscent of that of the Black-throated Green Warbler. Favored locales include Lake City Park (Austin); Friedrich Wilderness Park (San Antonio); County Road 674 from Rocksprings to Brackettville (Holt 1992); Kerr Wildlife Management Area (along Ranch Road 1340 near Hunt; Holt 1992); Pedernales Falls, Garner, Kerrville, and Lost Maples SPs; and Johnson Canyon south of Kerrville. Check with Austin or San Antonio birders for directions to current Golden-cheeked hot spots.

**Grace's Warbler.** This is a fairly common summer resident of conifer forests from southern Colorado and Utah south through Arizona and New Mexico. It also breeds in the Guadalupe Mountains and Davis Mountains of western Texas. This bird is closely tied to ponderosa pines. In the lower mountain ranges where live oaks predominate, Grace's Warblers are found only where pockets of ponderosa pines exist. In pure stands of pine forest in Arizona and New Mexico, Grace's is often the most common breeding bird (along with Pygmy Nuthatch). They are also found at high elevations where firs interdigitate with the pines. These birds often stick to the higher portions of the trees and are particularly prone to singing from the uppermost tufts of pine needles. Once you have learned the song (variable, but usually some sort of accelerating, "chippy" trill), they will seem to be everywhere in appropriate habitat.

**Gray-crowned Yellowthroat.** This is a casual visitor to the lower Rio Grande Valley of southern Texas. It could show up anywhere in brushy habitats. This is another of those birds that is reported far more than it should be. Overly enthusiastic birders report this species every year from southern Texas, but most of these reports turn out to involve Common Yellowthroats with some minor plumage variation. It is certain to be mentioned on RBAs if present.

**Red-faced Warbler.** This is a fairly common summer resident of conifer and mixed forests in the mountain ranges of central and southern Arizona and southwestern New Mexico. It is a casual spring and fall migrant in lowlands surrounding the breeding range. Seldom found in pure stands of pine, it is more common at higher elevations where fir or spruce or both are also present. However, it is often found lower, in areas dominated by live oaks. When searching the high country, pay special attention to the draws, where fingers of Gambel's oak (a deciduous species) run through otherwise pure conifer forest. These are often the best places for Red-faced Warblers. Reliable spots include the following:

1. New Mexico. Along State Hwy. 15 in Cherry Creek Canyon (Pinos Altos Mountains), Iron Creek Campground off State Hwy. 152 (Black Range), Water

Canyon off State Hwy. 60 west of Socorro (Magdalena Mountains), and the Mogollon Mountains.

2. Arizona. Rustler Park (particularly along the Barfoot Trail), along the road above Onion Saddle, and in Pinery Canyon (Chiricahua Mountains); along the Mount Wrightson Trail in Madera Canyon; and in upper Miller, Scheelite, upper Carr and Sawmill canyons (Huachuca Mountains).

**Painted Redstart.** This is a common summer resident of pine–oak forests and riparian sycamore–cypress associations in the mountain canyons and adjacent slopes of southern Arizona and New Mexico. In some years a few pairs nest along Boot Springs in the Chisos Mountains in Big Bend NP (Texas). In mild winters (particularly), small numbers may overwinter in some of the larger canyons of the southeastern Arizona mountain ranges. It is only occasionally seen in lowlands as a spring and fall migrant. This vocal, flashy, and conspicuous bird seems to be particularly partial to canyons with streams. It nests on the ground, typically on a slope with overhanging mats of grass and pine needles. It is easy to find in Cave Creek, Madera, Ramsey, Miller, and Garden canyons in Arizona; along State Hwy. 15 in Cherry Creek Canyon (Pinos Altos Mountains), off State Hwy. 152 in Gallinas Canyon (Black Range), at the Gila Cliff Dwellings National Monument, and in Whitewater Canyon off U.S. Hwy. 180 near Glenwood, in New Mexico; and in some years, at Boot Springs in Big Bend NP (Texas).

**Golden-crowned Warbler.** This is a casual winter visitor to the lower Rio Grande Valley of southern Texas. Records have come from Brownsville, the Sabal Palm Grove Sanctuary, Santa Ana NWR, and a few other scattered sites. It is certain to be mentioned on RBAs if present.

**Rufous-capped Warbler.** This is a casual spring–ummer visitor to middle-elevation canyons in the mountains of southeastern Arizona and western Texas. The first U.S. record (in 1973)was from below Falcon Dam in southern Texas. Since then, Texas records have come mostly from Big Bend NP (Pulliam Ridge in the Chisos Basin, and Santa Elena Canyon) and other parts of the Trans-Pecos region. Arizona records to date have come from the Chiricahua, Huachuca, Pajarito, and Whetstone mountains. It is certain to be listed on RBAs if present.

**Olive Warbler.** This is a fairly common but somewhat local summer resident of high mountain (more than 7000 ft, 2134 m), mixed-conifer forests in southeastern Arizona and southwestern New Mexico. It is an uncommon to rare winter resident throughout much of its U.S. breeding range, usually at lower elevations in adjacent foothills. This bird seems to prefer forests where Douglas-fir, white fir, and even blue spruce occur with ponderosa pines, although it can occur in fairly pure stands of the ponderosa pine. It typically forages somewhat high in the trees. Males sing a loud, ringing song; individuals of both sexes and all ages utter mellow, short whistled "pew" notes that are reminiscent of bluebird contact notes. Olive Warblers respond well to tapes or imitations of the Northern Pygmy-Owl.

1. Arizona. Look for it along the Barfoot Trail in Rustler Park and anywhere along the road above Onion Saddle (Chiricahua Mountains); at Rose Canyon Campground on Mount Lemmon (Santa Catalina Mountains), in Sawmill and upper Carr Canyons (Huachuca Mountains); and along the Mount Wrightson Trail in Madera Canyon (Santa Rita Mountains).

2. New Mexico. Try Emory Pass along State Hwy. 152 (Black Range), along State Hwy. 15 at McMillan Campground, and along the side road (Forest Road 154) to Signal Peak (Pinos Altos Mountains).

**Hepatic Tanager.** This is a fairly common to uncommon summer resident of pine–oak, mixed-conifer, and oak–juniper woodlands in the mountains of western Texas, New Mexico, and Arizona. It is a casual winter resident in extreme southern Arizona lowlands and middle elevations. It is seldom seen as a transient anywhere in lowlands. At times this bird's song can sound amazingly like that of the more common Black-headed Grosbeak. Apparently the birds can be fooled too, for the grosbeaks will often respond to tapes of the tanager! Listen for its single-note "chuck" call, which is very different from the multisyllabic calls of Western and Summer tanagers. The Hepatic is easy to find in summer at the following locations:

1. Texas. McKittrick Canyon and the Bowl (Guadalupe Mountains NP), the Chisos Basin and trails above it (Big Bend NP), and the Madera Canyon Picnic Ground (Hwy. 118 in the Davis Mountains).

2. New Mexico. Little Walnut Picnic Area (Silver City), the Guadlupe Mountains, the Burro Mountains, and Aguirre Springs Recreation Area (Organ Mountains, east of Las Cruces).

3. Arizona. Madera Canyon (Santa Ritas), Garden, Sawmill, and upper Carr canyons (Huachucas); Cave Creek Canyon to Onion Saddle (Chiricahuas).

**Flame-colored Tanager.** This is a casual summer visitor and occasional breeder in the Chiricahua, Santa Rita, and Huachuca mountains of southeastern Arizona from the mountains of western Mexico. It was first recorded from Cave Creek Canyon (Chiricahuas) in 1985, when an adult male established a territory and mated with a female Western Tanager (eventually fledging two young). It was not recorded again until 1992, when birds were found in Madera (Santa Ritas) and Ramsey (Huachucas) canyons. Since then, there have been multiple sightings from both Madera and Ramsey canyons. In Mexico and Central America this species inhabits montane live-oak, pine-oak, and broad-leafed evergeen woodlands to elevations of 9000 ft (2743 m) and higher. Both sexes can be distinguished from other tanagers by the combination of bold white wing bars and tertial tips, dusky auricular patch, large blackish bill, and boldly dark-streaked upper parts. Males of the west Mexican race are flaming orange about the head and breast (fading on the lower abdomen); females are yellow or yellowish olive. The three-syllabled call note closely resembles that of the Western Tanager. Flame-coloreds are certain to be mentioned on RBAs if present.

**Pyrrhuloxia.** This is a fairly common resident of thorn-scrub deserts and adjacent riparian and agricultural lands in southeastern Arizona, southern New Mexico, and southern and western Texas. Within this range the species has a somewhat spotty breeding distribution. There are areas in southwestern New Mexico, extreme western Texas, and extreme southeastern Arizona where this bird is common in winter but only a rare breeder. In winter it occurs in groups (sometimes numbering 10–20 birds), often moving up out of lowland (river valley) breeding areas into higher-elevation desert-grasslands, particularly along the base of mountain ranges and foothills. Within its range it is easy to find almost anywhere with dense stands of either mesquite or acacia.

1. Texas. Big Bend NP (especially around the edges of Rio Grande Village and desert oases such as Dugout Wells and the Old Sam Nail Ranch); FM Road 2221 north of La Joya (west of Mission on U.S. Hwy. 83); Falcon SP and side roads off U.S. Hwy. 83 near Falcon Dam; Amistad National Recreation Area; Kickapoo Cavern State Natural Area; Seminole Canyon State Historical Park (try the Rio Grande Trail; Holt 1992); Davis Mountains SP; Balmorhea State Recreation Area; brushy areas along the Rio Grande, at Hueco Tanks SP, and in the canyons of the Franklin Mountains (along the lower portions of Trans-Mountain Road) near El Paso (more common in winter); and in the lower portions of the Guadalupe Mountains NP.

2. Arizona. Anywhere around Tucson (particularly the Saguaro National Monument, Arizona-Sonora Desert Museum, Catalina SP, residential areas of northwest Tucson (try off of Thornydale Road and its many side roads).

3. New Mexico. Oliver Lee SP (south of Alamagordo; Zimmerman et al. 1992), Bitter Lakes NWR (fall and winter), Rattlesnake Springs (south of Carlsbad); near Las Cruces along the Rio Grande, on the Jornada Experimental Range, along the west mesa of the Organ Mountains, and along the east slope of the Organ Mountains along the road into Aguirre Springs Recreation Area (more common at all of these sites in fall and winter); on the mesa above Redrock and the Gila River; and in the saltbush flats bordering Bosque del Apache NWR (more common in winter).

**Blue Bunting.** This is a rare to casual winter visitor to the lower Rio Grande Valley of southern Texas. A very few records come from farther north along the Gulf Coast. Most records are from Bentsen-Rio Grande Valley SP (usually of birds visiting feeding stations in the trailer campgrounds), Santa Ana NWR, and Anzalduas County Park (near McAllen). It is certain to be listed on Valley RBAs if present.

**Varied Bunting.** This is an uncommon to fairly common but local summer resident of dense thorn-scrub desert in southern Arizona and New Mexico, along the

Rio Grande Valley of Texas from Big Bend south and east to the lower Gulf Coast, and from the Trans-Pecos region of western Texas east onto the southwestern portion of the Edwards Plateau. In some years, small numbers may overwinter in parts of the Big Bend region. This bird is often found near water (along stream courses or in dense thickets bordering stock tanks or ponds) and is more frequently found on slopes, or in canyons or arroyos, than on flats. Family groups often congregate in weedy patches or in fruit-bearing desert hackberry trees. Varied Buntings are easiest to locate when the males are singing early in the morning. Reliable locations include the following:

1. Arizona (where it may not arrive until after mid-May). Chino Canyon, Proctor Road and Florida Wash (below Madera Canyon) in the Santa Rita Mountains, Guadalupe Canyon, brushy hillsides above Sonoita Creek near Patagonia (particularly at the roadside rest stop on Hwy. 83 just south of town), Kino Springs (north of Nogales off Hwy. 83), and California Gulch and Sycamore Canyon off of Ruby Road (north and west of Nogales off I-19).

2. Texas. The Window Trail (Chisos Basin), the lower several miles of the road to the Chisos Basin, the Blue Creek Canyon Trail, and the Old Sam Nail Ranch at Big Bend NP (Texas); the Big Bend Ranch State Natural Area (Presidio County); the road from Ruidosa to Candelaria (northwest from Presidio); Cibolo Creek Ranch 32 miles south of Marfa (you must be a guest to bird the ranch) Kickapoo Cavern State Natural Area; Seminole Canyon State Historical Park (Holt 1992); and Laguna Atascosa NWR.

3. New Mexico. Guadalupe Canyon and Carlsbad Caverns NP (especially in Walnut Canyon and below the visitor center).

**Olive Sparrow.** This is a common resident of subtropical forest and thornscrub in the lower Rio Grande Valley of southern Texas (Del Rio to Brownsville) and northeast along the lower Texas coast. Its loud song (a series of sharp chips, starting slowly then accelerating as if a marble had been dropped on a hard floor) is easily heard, but the bird is difficult to see as it scoots along the ground through the dense brush. Look for it at San Ygnacio, below Falcon Dam, the Santa Margarita Ranch, at Bentsen-Rio Grande Valley SP, at Santa Ana NWR, and at Laguna Atascosa NWR (along the wooded nature trails).

**Abert's Towhee.** This is a locally common resident of desert riparian habitat with dense cover in Arizona, southwestern New Mexico, southeastern California, southwestern Utah, and extreme southern Nevada. This species is perhaps most commonly found in cottonwood-willow-mesquite associations along the major river systems of the Southwest. It is also found in riparian habitat dominated by tamarisk and saltbush, and, in such places as Phoenix, it is even found in agricultural and residential areas. This bird is often shy and given to hiding in streamside thickets, but it is still easily found in appropriate habitat along the Gila, San Pedro, Santa Cruz, and Colorado Rivers in Arizona; along the Gila River near Redrock in New Mexico; and around the Salton Sea in California. At the latter locale it is found in scrubby mesquite, tornillo, and saltbush edges and borders of fields, not necessarily associated with riparian habitats. Some of the easier places to find it along the standard southeastern Arizona birding circuit are near the San Pedro House along the San Pedro River just east of Sierra Vista (off State Hwy. 90), at Kino Springs (north of Nogales off Hwy. 82), and along Sonoita Creek in the Patagonia area (Patagonia-Sonoita Creek Preserve and across from the roadside rest stop on Hwy. 82 south of town).

**White-collared Seedeater.** This is a very rare winter (December–March) visitor to the lower Rio Grande Valley of southern Texas. Virtually all recent records have been from west of Falcon Dam, either from the first roadside rest stop north of San Ygnacio along U.S. Hwy. 83 (the rest stop overlooks the river), from the city park in Zapata, or near the tiny town of San Ygnacio itself. The most consistent spots in San Ygnacio have been in the patches of cane and brush along the river at the end of Washington Street and Grant Street. However, the birds are often seen right in town and could appear anywhere in weedy or brushy habitats.

**Five-striped Sparrow.** This is a rare and highly localized summer resident (some may winter) of southeastern Arizona. This species has rather strict habitat requirements, being found on dry, rocky slopes (and in draws) that are densely vegetated with catclaw-acacia and ocotillo. The very small U.S. population is subject to some fluctuation, and not all sites are occupied each year. Like other members of the genus, this one appears to be at least partially rain-stimulated in its breeding cycle. Birds typically become much more vocal after the onset of July rains, and, in dry years, there may be no song or nesting activity before that time. Five-striped Sparrows can be almost impossible to detect when they are not singing, in large part because of the nearly inpenetrable nature of their preferred habitat. The most consistent spots in recent years have been California Gulch and lower Sycamore Canyon (both off Ruby Road in the Pajarito Mountains, north and west of Nogales off I-19). In past years, Chino Canyon (Santa Rita Mountains) has also proved productive.

**Botteri's Sparrow.** This is an uncommon and local summer resident of grasslands in southeastern Arizona and the lower Texas coast. In the former area, Botteri's inhabits open grassland with scattered mesquite and ocotillo. It sings from an elevated perch, often buried in the middle of a shrub. The Texas population is found in mesquite- or huisache-peppered savannas, as well as in bunch-grass and prickly pear–covered flats along the coast. Texas birds are present from April to August. Arizona birds are more of a mystery, and seem to be rain-stimulated in their breeding efforts as are their close relatives, the Cassin's Sparrows. At any rate, Arizona birds are probably present from early May on but are most easily found during their peak singing period, which coincides with the midsummer rainy season. In Arizona try the grasslands below Madera Canyon (Santa Ritas), the research ranch at Elgin, the grasslands along lower Garden Canyon Road (Fort Huachuca), the grasslands along Hereford Road (east of Hwy. 92 and south of Sierra Vista) west of the San Pedro River, the Nature Conservancy Canelo Hills Cienega Preserve (south of Sonoita off Hwy. 83), and the first several miles along the road to Gardner Canyon (Santa Ritas). In Texas try the Gunnery Range Tour at Laguna Atascosa NWR and appropriate habitat along State Hwy. 186 between Raymondville and Port Mansfield.

**Cassin's Sparrow.** This is a common summer resident of arid grasslands and mesquite-grass savannas from eastern Colorado and western Kansas south through Oklahoma, New Mexico, Texas, and Arizona. In Texas, where the species is common from the lush grasslands of the panhandle to the bunch grass-dotted coastline of the Gulf (and is found across an elevational gradient of 5000 ft, 1524 m), birds are present and nesting as early as March. Populations in Oklahoma, Kansas, and Colorado also follow a traditional pattern of spring through summer nesting. Populations in western Texas, western New Mexico (west of the Pecos River), and Arizona are present (at least in reduced numbers) through the winter but are often not in evidence until the onset of summer rains, which usually begin in July. Just one good rainstorm in spring (March–May) can be enough to stimulate an outburst of song activity for several days. Breeding males are conspicuous because of their aerial flight displays (they also sing from perches). This species winters throughout much of its southern range, but because of its drabness and retiring habits during the nonbreeding season, it is seldom encountered.

**Rufous-winged Sparrow.** This is an uncommon and local resident of southeastern Arizona, principally around Tucson, the Tohono O'odham Nation lands, and the base of the Santa Rita Mountains. It seems to favor washes or flat deserts with a lush growth of tall shrubs or trees (e.g., mesquite and palo verde) and good amounts of grass for cover. Like other *Aimophila*, it may be at least partly rain-stimulated in its breeding efforts. Not all sites are occupied every year, and your best bet may be to check with Tucson birders for current locations. Some fairly reliable spots include the eastern unit of Saguaro NP (north of I-10 and east of Tucson; sparrows are fairly common along the loop road), near the junction of Thornydale and Tangerine in northwest Tucson, almost anywhere in appropriate habitat between Tucson and Green Valley (try the first rest area on the west side of I-19 south of Green Valley), Florida Wash (below Madera Canyon), the lower part of the road from Continental to Madera Canyon, Gardner Canyon (Santa Rita Mountains), behind the Circle K store in Mammoth, and along Speedway Blvd. 5 or more miles east of its junction with Wilmot Road in Tucson.

**Black-chinned Sparrow.** This is an uncommon bird of chaparral-covered slopes in California, extreme southern Nevada and Utah, southern Arizona and New Mexico, and extreme western Texas. Birds in Texas, New Mexico, and the eastern part of Arizona are resident; those in California, Nevada, and Utah are summer residents only; and those in southwestern Arizona are a wintering population only. In California this bird occupies true chaparral; elsewhere it occupies slopes with similar physiognomic plant associations (including scrub-oak thickets, manzanita, pinyon pine and juniper, mountain mahogany, and Apache plume). Even in areas where the species is resident, there is a pronounced downward altitudinal migration in winter. The best time to find these birds is from April to June, when their loud, Field Sparrow–like songs are delivered from prominent perches.

1. California (in part from Schram 1998). Mount Palomar and the Old Mission Dam Historical Site near San Diego; Crystal Cove SP along Hwy. 1 between Corona del Mar and Laguna Beach (Holt 1990); in the Laguna Mountains near Cibbet's Flat Campground off Kitchen Creek Road (about 47 miles east of San Diego; Holt 1990); the Switzer Picnic Area, Chilao Recreation Area and Mill Creek Canyon in the San Gabriel Mountains; in the San Jacinto Mountains along Hwy. 243 south of Banning (Holt 1990); Big Sycamore Canyon in Point Mugu SP; upper end of Quatal Canyon Road (1 mile south of Ventucopa off Hwy. 33; Holt 1990); various points along Cerro Noroeste Road (between Hwy. 166 and I-5), especially near Valle Vista Campground; La Cumbre Peak off San Marcos Pass (Hwy. 154) north of Santa Barbara; and Mount Diablo SP near Berkeley.

2. Arizona. The Paradise Road above Portal (Chiricahua Mountains, summer), Molino Basin in the Santa Catalinas, the Mule Mountains north of Bisbee (summer), Florida Wash below Madera Canyon (winter), and lower Cave Creek Canyon (winter).

3. Nevada. Along the road to the Mount Potosi Boy Scout Camp, south of Hwy. 160 about 18 miles west of its intersection with I-15 (south of Las Vegas; Cressman 1989).

4. New Mexico. Aguirre Springs Recreation Area in the Organ Mountains (east of Las Cruces), the Burro Mountains, Carlsbad Caverns NP, and the Guadalupe Mountains.

5. Texas. The Chisos Basin in Big Bend NP, McKittrick Canyon in the Guadalupe Mountains, Hueco Tanks SP (winter), and in canyons along Trans-Mountain Road in the Franklin Mountains near El Paso (winter).

6. Utah (Sorensen 1991b). The Beaver Dam Mountains along State Hwy. 91 west of St. George.

**Sage Sparrow.** This is an uncommon to fairly common and somewhat local breeder in a variety of arid and semiarid habitats over much of the Great Basin and California. The Sage Sparrow complex consists of four recognized subspecies within the western United States. One of these, *Amphispiza belli clementeae*, is found only on San Clemente Island off the southern California coast. It is resident. The other three forms are much more widespread and, because they differ vocally, morphologically, and ecologically, are good candidates for being elevated to full species status. The darker *A. b. belli* ("Bell's Sparrow") is an uncommon resident of coastal sagebrush and inland foothill chaparral communities from the coastal ranges inland to the western slopes of the Sierra Nevada and associated interior foothills. It occurs from at least Marin County south to San Diego County.

The two interior forms are paler and more heavily streaked above and have a heavier malar stripe. The smaller *A. b. canescens* ("Saltbush Sparrow") breeds in saltbush *(Atriplex)* flats in the central interior valleys of California, from the San Joaquin Valley and the Carrizo Plain east to western Nevada and south to the western and southern borders of the Mojave Desert. It is partially migratory, with birds withdrawing in winter from the northern parts of the range and wintering farther south in California and east into western Arizona. The most widespread form is *A. b. nevadensis* ("Sagebrush Sparrow"), which breeds in sagebrush communities over much of the Great Basin, east of the Cascades and Sierra Nevada, and west of the Rockies, from central Washington, southern Idaho, southwestern Wyoming, and northwestern Colorado south to northeastern California, southern Nevada and Utah, and northern Arizona and New Mexico. It winters from the southern part of the breeding range south into Mexico. These wintering birds are found in creosotebush deserts along with Black-throated Sparrows, but they are more common in saltbush flats, particularly where grasses are intermixed. Sage Sparrows of all types run with their tail cocked like a little thrasher or roadrunner. They respond well to pishing, often teeing up in the top of a shrub to investigate. They are not difficult to find.

**Baird's Sparrow.** This is an uncommon and somewhat local summer resident of mixed-grass prairies and weedy fields in the Dakotas, Montana, and the prairie provinces of Canada. It is an uncommon to rare winter resident of grasslands in southeastern Arizona (particularly in the Sonoita, San Rafael, and Sulphur Springs valleys) and western Texas (grasslands around Valentine and Marfa and in Big Bend NP). In winter, this species behaves much like other grassland sparrows, flushing from underfoot, dropping into the grass, and then running (mouselike) rapidly away. This bird arrives rather late on the breeding grounds (in late May; migrants are still coming through Arizona in mid-April) and is best seen during June and early July, when song activity is still high. Look for it at the following locations:

1. Montana (McEneany 1993). Bowdoin, Benton Lake and Medicine Lake NWRs; the Chief Joseph Battlefield area (south of Chinook along Secondary Road 240); and along the road to Lonesome Lake (8 miles northwest of Big Sandy).

2. North Dakota. Des Lacs, Lostwood, Long Lake, and J. Clark Salyer NWRs; Little Missouri National Grassland (near Medora).

3. South Dakota. The S. H. Ordway Prairie (Nature Conservancy land near Leola).

**Le Conte's Sparrow.** This is a fairly common but local summer resident of wet meadows, fens, grassy bogs, and lake and pond edges in the extreme upper Midwest (Minnesota, Michigan, Wisconsin), northern Great Plains (North Dakota, Montana), and Canada. It winters in similar habitats, as well as in coastal marshes and grasslands and a variety of weedy fields throughout much of the south-central United States. This bird is very secretive and is given to skulking or running through mats of reeds or grass. When flushed, it typically flies only a short distance before dropping to the ground, at which time it quickly vacates the area on foot. Population levels on the breeding grounds are somewhat cyclic, with more birds present in wet years. In North Dakota, look for it anywhere in appropriate habitat in the eastern and (more locally) northwestern parts of the state, particularly in Kidder and Stutsman counties and from McHenry County east through Grand Forks County. For specific spots, try Des Lacs, Arrowwood, and J. Clark Salyer NWRs. It is fairly easy to find in eastern Texas and along the Gulf Coast from mid-October through mid-April. Check especially at Galveston Island SP, the Attwater Prairie-Chicken NWR (near Eagle Lake), and the Yellow Rail Prairie at Anahuac NWR. At least in Texas, wintering Le Conte's Sparrows seem partial to fields with an abundance of little bluestem, a reddish knee-high grass.

**Nelson's Sharp-tailed Sparrow.** This is an uncommon and local summer resident of wet meadows and lake and pond edges in North Dakota and barely into northeastern South Dakota. It is rarely seen in migration. It winters in saltwater and brackish marshes, primarily along the Gulf Coast (with very small numbers wintering in a few bays along the California coast). Like the Le Conte's Sparrow (with which it shares many breeding areas), this species undergoes population fluctuations in tune with weather cycles. Unlike Le Conte's, Nelson's Sharp-tailed are typically more common in drought years when low water levels expose more emergent vegetation for nesting. Sharp-taileds tend to breed in wetter habitats than Le Conte's, frequently exploiting the marsh zones with standing water. Away from the actual water's edge, they are more often found in areas with coarser grass such as cattails and bulrushes. Also, like the Le Conte's, this species is typically shy and elusive, although it more frequently perches in plain view. Look for it anywhere in appropriate habitat in northern and eastern North Dakota (particularly in Benson, Ramsey, Nelson, Kidder, and Stutsman counties). For specific spots, try Des Lacs, Arrowwood, and J. Clark Salyer NWRs in North Dakota. In winter in Texas try Anahuac and Aransas NWRs, the marshes at Sabine and Bolivar Flats, and Galveston Island SP; in California try the edges of the pickleweed marsh at Morro Bay SP (where it is rare, but regular). The presence of wintering birds in California is usually mentioned on local RBAs. Wintering birds on the Gulf Coast are often quite territorial, especially in April just before migrating. At this time it is not uncommon to hear them singing repeatedly, and the birds are usually quite responsive to tapes and pishing. This species was formerly considered conspecific with forms nesting in coastal salt marshes on the Atlantic Coast (now differentiated as "Saltmarsh Sharp-tailed Sparrows"), the entire complex then being referred to as Sharp-tailed Sparrow."

**Seaside Sparrow.** This is a fairly common resident of salt and brackish marshes along the Gulf and Atlantic coasts. In our area it breeds commonly along the Texas coast from about Corpus Christi north (it winters south to Brownsville). In spring, males sing from the tops of vegetation. At other times these birds stick to cover, where they run about on the mud bars and banks at the edge of channels in the marsh. They are best seen by sitting quietly at the edge of a channel and waiting for a bird to run into the open. They also respond well to pishing. Try the marshes at Sabine, Sea Rim and Galveston Island SPs, Bolivar Flats, and Anahuac and Aransas NWRs.

**Yellow-eyed Junco.** This is common resident of spruce–fir, mixed conifer, and pine–oak forests in the mountains of southeastern Arizona and the Animas Mountains of southwestern New Mexico. It often moves to lower elevations in winter but does not form large flocks as do other juncos. It is easy to find at Rustler Park and above Onion Saddle in the Chiricahuas; at Mount Lemmon in the Santa Catalinas; along the Mount Wrightson Trail, at the Santa Rita Lodge and (in some years) at the lower picnic sites in Madera Canyon (Santa Ritas); and along Sawmill and Carr canyons in the Huachucas. This species displays a bewildering repertoire of vocalizations, and you may well find yourself tracking down numerous song variants.

**McCown's Longspur.** This is an uncommon to common but local summer resident of short-grass prairies and stubble and fallow fields from the southern prairie provinces of Canada south through Montana, western North Dakota, Wyoming, and northern Colorado. This species occupies grazed areas and more xeric, short-grass prairie (often with prickly pear cactus) than does the Chestnut-collared. Various types of retired croplands are commonly used in some areas. Look for it from April through September at the following locations:

1. Colorado. Pawnee National Grassland (particularly on the west side, north and east of Nunn).

2. Montana (Pettingill 1981, McEneaney 1993). At Benton Lake NWR (near Great Falls), Bowdoin NWR (east of Malta), Fox Lake Wildlife Management Area (21 miles west of Sydney), along U.S. Hwy. 191 north from Harlowton, Mission Lake (20 miles east of Browning on U.S. Hwy. 2), near the Chief Joseph Battlefield east of Havre and south of Chinook, and the Lake Elwell Recreation Area near Tiber Dam (60 miles west of Havre and southwest of Chester).

3. North Dakota. Near Marmarth (take Hwy. 12 west of town and turn south on West River Road; longspurs are particularly common near the state line), Bowman-Haley Dam NWR, and the south unit of Theodore Roosevelt NP.

4. Wyoming (Scott 1993). On the plains west of Laramie along Hwy. 130, along the plains northeast of Cheyenne on U.S. Hwy. 85 (common), and south of Van Tassel off U.S. Hwy. 20 (turn south off the highway onto a gravel road just beyond the railroad track crossing).

5. Nebraska (Rosche 1990). Along a north-south gravel road just south of U.S. Hwy. 20 and immediately east of the Wyoming line.

In winter (October–April) this bird is commonly found in plowed fields with Horned Larks. The center of winter abundance is in Oklahoma and Texas; the species is uncommon to rare in New Mexico and Arizona. McCown's is the common wintering longspur in the Texas panhandle, where huge flocks can be found in the plowed fields surrounding Amarillo. In Arizona, it is best found by scanning irrigated fields in the Sulphur Springs Valley, particularly along Hwy. 191 north of El-frida. In New Mexico (Zimmerman et al 1992), it is best found at the Green Chap-arral Turf Ranch (6 miles east of Moriarty, exit 203 of I-40; ask permission first) and the Grasslands Turf Ranch (20 miles south of Albuquerque off I-25; take exit 203 for Los Lunas and go west on State Hwy. 6 to the first dirt road going north).

**Lapland Longspur.** This is a common to abundant summer resident of tundra re-gions over much of mainland Alaska (particularly in the northern and western parts of the state) and its offshore islands, including the Aleutians, the Pribilofs, and other Bering Sea islands. It is impossible to miss at Barrow, Prudhoe Bay, Nome, Kotzebue, Wales, Gambell (St. Lawrence Island), St. Paul and St. George (the Pribilofs) and other outposts. It is less common, but still easy to spot, in tun-dra along the Denali Hwy. between Cantwell and Paxson, in the alpine areas of Denali NP (Highway Pass, Primrose Ridge, and ridges above the Eilson Visitor Center), and at Twelvemile Summit and Eagle Summit on the Steese Hwy. east of Fairbanks.

It is a variably common to rare migrant and winter visitor throughout much of the West, usually in agricultural fields, sod farms, and prairies, and often among flocks of Horned Larks or other species of longspur.

**Smith's Longspur.** This is an uncommon and local summer resident at scattered locales in northern Alaska (primarily the Brooks Range) and, disjunctly, in south-eastern central Alaska (Wrangell Mountains, Susitna River highlands, southern edge of the Alaska Range). Birds in the Brooks Range occupy valley meadows with tussock-forming sedges. Populations in central Alaska seem to prefer drier ridgetop tundra but may also utilize wetter muskeg. The most accessible places to find this bird in Alaska are scattered along the Denali Hwy. between Cantwell and Paxson. One traditional site is on the north side of the Denali Hwy. just a couple of miles beyond Brushkana Creek Campground, but birds are more numerous near the east end of the highway. The owners of the Tangle Lakes Lodge (mile 22, from Paxson) cater to birders, and their lodge makes an excellent base for visiting nearby longspur sites (phone or fax 907-688-9173).

Smith's Longspur is an uncommon to rare and local winter resident (mid-October to April) of grasslands, pastures, and airport fields over much of the southern Great Plains (southern Nebraska south into Texas). Try mowed hayfields around Lyon County State Fishing Lake northeast of Emporia, Kansas (Zimmer-man and Patti 1988); and in Oklahoma (Tulsa Audubon Society 1986), prairies north and east of Tulsa and Skiatook, around the Hulah Dam site in Osage County, and in fields east of Pryor off State Hwy. 20. It is occasionally seen in mi-gration at points farther north, sometimes in small flocks. Your best bet is to check with birders in Oklahoma City for current hot spots.

**Chestnut-collared Longspur.** This is a fairly common to common summer resi-dent of mixed-grass prairies, meadow zones around lake edges, hayfields, and pastures throughout most of the northern Great Plains. This species tends to breed in more lush tall-grass areas than does the McCown's. It winters across much of the southern Great Plains (southern Colorado and Kansas through central Texas) and west through the desert grasslands of New Mexico and Arizona to California. In winter it is more often found coming to stock tanks in true grassland areas and is less likely to be found in plowed fields than is McCown's or Lapland. In summer try the following locations:

1. Colorado. Pawnee National Grassland (particularly around lake edges, and along Road 114 in the first mile east of U.S. Hwy. 85 north of Ault). They are frequently seen on fence lines along State Hwy. 14 west of Briggsdale.

2. Montana (Pettingill 1981, McEneaney 1993). Medicine Lake, Bowdoin, and Benton Lake (near Great Falls) NWRs, Mission Lake (about 20 miles east of Browning on U.S. Hwy. 2), near the Chief Joseph Battlefield south of Havre, Fox Lake Wildlife Management Area (21 miles west of Sidney on State Hwy. 200).

3. North Dakota. Bowman-Haley Dam, Des Lacs, Lostwood, Long Lake, Arrowwood, Chase Lake, and J. Clark Salyer NWRs.

4. South Dakota. U.S. Hwy. 85 north of Belle Fourche, side roads off U.S. Hwys. 83 and 18 in the south-central part of the state, and side roads off U.S. Hwys. 83 and 14 and State Hwy. 47 north and east of Pierre.

5. Wyoming (Scott 1993). Along U.S. Hwy. 85 northeast of Cheyenne and in grasslands south of Van Tassel off U.S. Hwy. 20 (just west of the railroad track crossing in Van Tassel turn south on a gravel road).

6. Nebraska (Rosche 1990). Along an east-west gravel road just south of Walgren Lake State Recreation Area (south of U.S. Hwy. 20 about 3 miles east of Hay Springs) and along a north-south gravel road south of U.S. Hwy. 20 immediately east of the Wyoming border (Chestnut-collareds replace McCown's along this road the farther south you go).

In winter (October–April), try the Cimarron National Grassland (Morton County) in Kansas; Wichita Mountains NWR in Oklahoma; the areas surrounding Amarillo and Valentine (western Texas) in Texas; the Green Chaparral and Grasslands turf ranches (see directions under McCown's Longspur), the Animas Valley, Jornada Experimental Range (near Las Cruces), and State Hwy. 26 from Deming to Hatch (especially near Nutt) in New Mexico; and the Sonoita Plains (around the town of Sonoita), San Rafael Valley (near Patagonia), and the Sulphur Springs Valley (near Willcox) in Arizona.

**Snow Bunting.** This is an uncommon to common but local summer resident of coastal tundra along much of the northern and western shores of Alaska and on offshore islands (although generally absent from the coastline over most of the Seward Peninsula). In these areas Snow Buntings are frequently seen in native villages and small towns, nesting in abandoned buildings, equipment, and old oil drums, and sometimes in bird boxes. It is an uncommon to common but local summer resident of alpine tundra, particularly in block fields, scree slopes, and lava formations over the Seward Peninsula and much of the interior of the state, although many of these sites are generally inaccessible. It is easy to see at Barrow, Prudhoe Bay, Gambell (St. Lawrence Island), and St. Paul (the Pribilofs). Small numbers can usually be found in the highest, rockiest tundra along the roads out of Nome.

It winters in varying numbers from central and southern Alaska (rarely north to Nome) south through the northern tier of western states at least to southern Oregon (irregularly to northern California), northern Utah, Colorado, and central Kansas, and only casually farther south. In winter months they are most often found in weedy or stubble fields and along beaches of large lakes and the Pacific Ocean.

**McKay's Bunting.** This is an uncommon to rare and highly local summer resident of islands in the Bering Sea. The centers of abundance are Hall Island and St. Matthew Island, which are occasionally accessible by booking passage on nature-oriented cruise-ship tours of the Bering Sea (some itineraries call for Zodiac landings on these otherwise inaccessible islands). The species is a rare and sporadic breeder at Gambell (St. Lawrence Island), with relatively few records from recent years. Occasionally a pair turns up on St. Paul Island (the Pribilofs). These birds occupy the same habitats used by breeding Snow Buntings and frequently hybridize with the latter. McKay's Bunting is an uncommon to rare migrant and winter visitor along the western coast of Alaska, from Nome to Cold Bay and Hooper Bay. It is a very rare to casual winter visitor elsewhere in Alaska and south sporadically to Washington, where it is certain to be reported on RBAs if present.

**Tricolored Blackbird.** This is a locally common summer resident of freshwater tule and cattail marshes along the coast and central valley of California and marginally into southern Oregon. It often breeds in dense colonies. After nesting, Tricoloreds can be hard to find because of their tendency to wander, especially to agricultural areas.

1. California. The Tijuana River Valley from San Diego (winter); Upper Newport Bay; Lake Sherwood (near Thousand Oaks); marshes on Point Mugu; Goleta Slough in Santa Barbara; Mojave Narrows Regional Park (San Bernardino County); the Moonglow Dairy off Dolan Road at Moss Landing (fall and winter); Neary's Lagoon Native Area in Santa Cruz; fields on Point Reyes (huge flocks gather in winter); and San Luis, Lower Klamath, Clear Lake, and Tule Lake NWRs.

2. Oregon (Ramsey 1978, Evanich 1990). Klamath Wildlife Management Area, the Lower Klamath NWR, and Agency Lake and Lynn Newbry Park (near Medford).

**Hooded Oriole.** This is a fairly common summer resident along the Rio Grande Valley of Texas, in southwestern New Mexico, southern Arizona, and north along coastal California. In Texas this bird seems to be declining in numbers, while in California it is expanding its range northward. This oriole is found in a variety of habitats. In Texas it is found primarily in subtropical woodlands along the Rio

Grande to Big Bend NP, where it occupies the large riparian stands of cotton-woods. In Arizona it is often found in riparian woodlands as well as in saguaro deserts. Throughout its range it is commonly found in city parks and residential areas, concentrating in areas with various species of fan palms, which it uses for nesting. Hooded Orioles readily habituate to taking sugar water from humming-bird feeders, and lodges or homes with an array of such feeders are often the most productive places to watch for this species. It is casual in winter in southern Arizona, usually at hummingbird feeders near Tucson or Nogales.

**Streak-backed Oriole.** This is an extremely rare fall and winter visitor to southeastern Arizona and southern California. Arizona records have come from numerous locations near Tucson, Green Valley, Arivaca, Patagonia, and Dudleyville. From 1993 to 1995 a pair nested in the lower San Pedro River Valley at Dudleyville, and another pair attempted to nest in the Pinal Air Park pecan groves northwest of Tucson. Basic-plumaged Hooded Orioles are frequently mistaken for this species. It is certain to be reported on local RBAs if present.

**Altamira Oriole.** This is a fairly common but local resident of subtropical forest and brush in extreme southern Texas, from San Ygnacio to Brownsville. It can be readily seen below Falcon Dam, at the Santa Margarita Ranch, Bentsen-Rio Grande Valley SP, and Santa Ana NWR. At Bentsen it frequently nests around the campgrounds and feeds at hummingbird feeders put up by the campers.

**Audubon's Oriole.** This is a rare and local resident of subtropical forest-brushland along the Rio Grande in southern Texas. Look for it along the river at San Ygnacio, below Falcon Dam, at the Santa Margarita Ranch, and at Santa Ana NWR (this is the poorest of the spots listed). Of these areas, below Falcon Dam is the best. (Try the boat landing at the settlement of Salineño and the stretch of river immediately below the dam.) This oriole is best located by following its song—an almost humanlike variable whistle—to the bird, which is often perched high in a tree near the river's edge.

**Scott's Oriole.** This is a fairly common summer resident of desert grasslands (especially those with abundant soaptree yuccas); pinyon–juniper foothills; and live oak, oak–juniper, and pine–oak woodlands throughout much of the Southwest (from central Texas west to California and north through Nevada and Utah to extreme southwestern Wyoming). It is a rare winter visitor (often to hummingbird feeders) to southern California and Arizona. It is not difficult to find.

1. Texas. Kickapoo Cavern State Natural Area, the Chisos Basin in Big Bend NP, Davis Mountains SP, Hueco Tanks SP, the canyons of the Franklin Mountains off Trans-Mountain Road in El Paso, and McKittrick Canyon and Guadalupe Mountains NP.

2. New Mexico. At the Dripping Springs Natural Area and La Cueva Picnic Area on the west slope of the Organ Mountains (east of Las Cruces); Aguirre

Springs Recreation Area, including the entrance road (east slope of the Organ Mountains); the Jornada Experimental Range near Las Cruces; the western end of State Hwy. 152 near Bayard; the Fort Bayard Military Reservation (8 miles east of Silver City off U.S. Hwy. 180; Zimmerman et al. 1992); around the town of Pinos Altos; along the Gila River Valley near Cliff, Gila, Bill Evans Lake, Mangas Springs, and Redrock; along Forest Road 851 through the Burro Mountains, along the road from Lordsburg to Redrock; Whitewater Canyon near Glenwood; the Peloncillo Mountains; and Guadalupe Canyon.

3. Arizona. Vicinity of Portal and along the Paradise Road above Portal (Chiricahua Mountains), Madera Canyon (Santa Ritas), Ramsey Canyon and in yucca grasslands along Hwy. 92 south of Sierra Vista (Huachucas), and Molino Basin (Santa Catalinas).

4. California (in part from Holt 1990). Anza-Borrego Desert SP, Butterbredt Springs, Big Morongo Canyon Preserve (off State Hwy. 62 north of I-10) and Joshua Tree National Monument, Pinyon Flats in the San Jacinto Mountains, Ballinger Canyon Road and Quatal Canyon Road east of State Hwy. 33 (south of State Hwy. 166), the Antelope Valley, and along the road from I-15 south to Cima and Kelso (east of Baker).

5. Nevada. Along a dry wash on the north side of Hwy. 160, 17.5 miles west of its junction with I-15 (south of Las Vegas; Cressman 1989); along State Hwy. 156 to Lee Canyon (south of U.S. Hwy. 95 north of Las Vegas; Mowbray and Cressman 1989).

6. Utah (Sorenson 1991b). The Beaver Dam Mountains along State Hwy. 91 west of St. George.

7. Wyoming (Scott 1993). Powder Rim (west of Baggs).

**Gray-crowned Rosy-Finch.** This is a fairly common but local resident of rocky alpine tundra on scattered high mountains of the West and Northwest. This is the most widespread of the Rosy-Finches (breeding from the Brooks Range and the Seward Peninsula of Alaska south to central California) and perhaps the one most likely to be seen in huge flocks roaming the lowlands in winter. In the Pribilofs and Aleutians, Gray-crowned Rosy-Finches are the ecological equivalent of House Sparrows, nesting in towns and villages in crevices and cavities of abandoned buildings, machinery, oil drums, and bird boxes, as well as along coastal cliffs and rock jetties.

1. Alaska. St. Paul Island (the most accessible spot), islands in the Aleutian chain, cliff faces and block fields along the higher portions of the Kougarok and Council roads at Nome, edges of Sunrise and Sunset glaciers in Denali NP, and (in winter and migration) along the Homer Spit.

2. California. Tioga Pass in Yosemite NP (especially along the margins of Saddlebag Lake); the Mammoth Pass area (reached from Casa Diablo Hot Springs on U.S. Hwy. 395, 42 miles northwest of Bishop); the trail up Mount Whitney (from the road up Lone Pine Canyon: off U.S. Hwy. 395, 59 miles south of Bishop); and at Lower Klamath, Tule Lake, and Clear Lake NWRs in winter.

3. Colorado. Squaw Mountain (October–November) and Red Rocks Park (winter).

4. Montana (Pettingill 1981). Logan Pass and the Hidden Lake Trail off of the pass in Glacier NP (summer) and at feeders in Butte in winter (McEneaney 1993).

5. Oregon (Pettingill 1981, and Evanich 1990). The Crater Lake area (Rim Village, Llao Rock, Dutton Ridge, Vidae Ridge, the trail to Garfield Peak from the Crater Lake Lodge, Mount Scott, and the east face of Applegate Peak in summer; and look for large flocks roaming the lowland, especially the Pumice Desert north of the lake, in winter); on the high peaks of the Cascades, including Jefferson, Three Sisters, Hood (near Timberline Lodge), Washington, and McLoughlin; and between Enterprise and Zumwalt (roadside flocks in winter).

6. Washington. Mount Baker and trails leading up from Paradise and Sunrise in Mount Rainier NP. Winter flocks often roost in rimrock formations in canyons in eastern Washington. Good spots have been Frenchman Coulee just east of the Columbia River and along the east shore road of Grand Coulee.

7. Idaho (Svingen and Dumroese 1997). Boise area (Barber Park, Lucy Peak Park: winter roosts) and the Ketchum/Sun Valley area in Blaine County (check feeders and rocky ridges in the town of Triumph, November–April).

**Black Rosy-Finch.** This is an uncommon resident of alpine tundra on scattered high peaks in the northern Rockies, Northwest, and Great Basin. It generally breeds farther north and west than the Brown-capped Rosy-Finch. This is generally the hardest rosy-finch to find. Like the other species, this one feeds at the edges of snowfields (on windblown insects that are immobilized by the cold of the snow) and is often found in the vicinity of talus slopes and rock outcroppings. Also like the others, these birds descend to lower elevations in winter. Good areas include the following:

1. Colorado. Squaw Mountain (October–November), Red Rocks Park (uncommon to rare in winter), feeders in Georgetown (winter), Walden (winter), and the Gunnison area (winter).

2. Wyoming (Pettingill 1981). The summit of Mount Washburn in Yellowstone NP, the Jackson Hole Aerial Tram out of Teton Village to the summit of Rendezvous Mountain, Bear Tooth Pass on U.S. Hwy. 212 45 miles east of Tower Jct. (Scott 1993), and high country in the Grand Tetons and Big Horn Mountains in general.

3. Utah (Pettingill 1981, Sorensen 1991b). Above Mirror Lake (Bald Mountain trail head) 33 miles east of Kamas on State Hwy. 150.

4. Idaho (Pettingill 1981, Svingen and Dumroese 1997). U.S. Hwy. 93 from Haily to Samon, Boise area (Barber Park: Lucky Peak Park, winter roosts), the Ketchum/Sun Valley area in Blaine County (at feeders or on rocky ridges in the town of Triumph from November through April).

5. Oregon (Pettingill 1981, Evanich 1990). Steens Mountain (reached via Steens Mountain Loop Road east from Frenchglen) and the area between Enterprise and Zumwalt (winter roadside flocks).

6. Nevada. The Ruby Mountains. Take the Island Lake trail from the head of Lamoille Canyon to Island Lake. Climb the talus slopes toward Thomas Peak and search the talus and unmelted snowfields. The finches are common here after fledglings have left the nest in midsummer.

**Brown-capped Rosy-Finch.** This is a fairly common resident of alpine tundra of scattered mountain ranges in Colorado, Wyoming, and New Mexico. Brown-cappeds sometimes move to lower elevations in winter, where they can be seen along roadsides in foothills. The center of abundance is Colorado, where the following locations should be searched: Summit Lake on Mount Evans, Trail Ridge Road in Rocky Mountain NP, Pass Lake on Loveland Pass, Squaw Mountain (they come to feeders in winter; try October and November while the road is still drivable), and Red Rocks Park (uncommon to rare in winter). In winter they are best seen around Gunnison. In New Mexico, in summer try the trail to Santa Fe Baldy (off the road to the Santa Fe Ski Basin) and the high peaks of the Sangre de Cristo Mountains, and in winter try the area at the top of the ski lift in the Sandia Mountains (Albuquerque). In Wyoming look for them on Medicine Bow Peak and Brooklyn Ridge off of State Hwy. 130 (Snowy Range Pass) in the Snowy Range of the Medicine Bow Mountains (Pettingill 1981).

**Common Redpoll and Hoary Redpoll.** These two redpolls are currently considered separate species, although some taxonomists have urged treating them as a single variable species. Common Redpolls are common to uncommon breeders in shrub habitats throughout much of Alaska, but they are distinctly less common beyond the taiga zone in the northern part of the state. Hoary Redpolls are more restricted to the tundra regions of northern and western Alaska, breeding from Barrow and the North Slope south through the Seward Peninsula and south in western Alaska to Hooper Bay and the Yukon-Kuskokwim Delta region. Within this area they are common in low and medium shrub habitats. Common Redpolls are easy to find in Anchorage and Fairbanks (even in residential areas) and in all areas in between (including Denali NP) and on the Kenai Peninsula. Hoaries are easily found at Barrow and throughout the Seward Peninsula (common at Nome). Both forms can be found at Nome, with Hoaries being decidedly more common. Redpolls winter throughout their breeding range, although they generally retreat from more northern areas. Their occurrence in any one area in winter is unpredictable from year to year, and even sometimes from week to week. They occur irregularly (sometimes in large numbers) in winter south to the northern tier of western states, being found in weedy fields, ditches, birch trees, and shrubs, and at bird feeding stations. Common Redpolls always greatly outnumber Hoaries during these winter invasions.

**Lawrence's Goldfinch.** This is an uncommon and local (somewhat erratic) resident of dry pine-oak forest and montane chaparral over most of southern and central California. It is particularly common in the foothills of inland valleys where blue oaks and digger pines are the dominant trees and where various chaparral species contribute to a shrubby understory. Willow-lined creeks and small drainages within these drier regions are also used. These goldfinches are conspicuous for a short time in early spring (March–April), when their bell-like calls and complex songs fill the air. After breeding, the birds become very nomadic and can be difficult to find. This species seems especially attracted to water, and the key to finding them (particularly in summer) is often to find a semipermanent water source in an otherwise dry region. Look for deep spots along mostly dry creek beds that may retain water later into the long dry season (May–October). Stock tanks and water troughs in the oak savanna ranch country are also choice spots. Such spots may attract dozens to scores of Lawrence's Goldfinches in July and August. Later in fall these birds disperse so much (presumably mostly southward) that finding them is largely a matter of luck. They are seldom found in coastal areas, more regularly sticking to weedy fields and brushy areas inland. They regularly winter in southern Arizona (mostly along the Santa Cruz River and its tributaries), but abundance varies considerably between years. Try the road to Palomar Mountain; lower portions of the Laguna and San Jacinto mountains; Placerita Canyon SP, Charlton Flat Picnic Area, Chilao Recreation Area, and Switzer Picnic Area in the San Gabriels; Ballinger Canyon off State Hwy. 33 (north of Ventucopa); the area around Lopez Lake, Santa Margarita Lake and along State Hwy. 229 south of Creston in San Luis Obispo County; eastern portions of Carmel Valley Road (east from Carmel) and above Robinson Canyon in Monterey County; Caswell Memorial SP and Del Puerto Canyon near Patterson (south of Stockton; Westrich and Westrich 1991); the Diablo Mountains south of Livermore along Mines Road (Remsen 1973); and Folsom Lake State Recreation Area.

# Bird Species Mentioned in the Text

Red-throated Loon (*Gavia stellata*)

Arctic Loon (*Gavia arctica*)

Pacific Loon (*Gavia pacifica*)

Common Loon (*Gavia immer*)

Yellow-billed Loon (*Gavia adamsii*)

Least Grebe (*Tachybaptus dominicus*)

Horned Grebe (*Podiceps auritus*)

Eared Grebe (*Podiceps nigricollis*)

Western Grebe (*Aechmophorus occidentalis*)

Clark's Grebe (*Aechmophorus clarkii*)

Light-mantled Albatross (*Phoebetria palpebrata*)

Laysan Albatross (*Phoebastria immutabilis*)

Black-footed Albatross (*Phoebastria nigripes*)

Northern Fulmar (*Fulmarus glacialis*)

Murphy's Petrel (*Pterodroma ultima*)

Mottled Petrel (*Pterodroma inexpectata*)

Cook's Petrel (*Pterodroma cookii*)

Streaked Shearwater (*Calonectris leucomelas*)

Cory's Shearwater (*Calonectris diomedea*)

Pink-footed Shearwater (*Puffinus creatopus*)

Flesh-footed Shearwater (*Puffinus carneipes*)

Buller's Shearwater (*Puffinus bulleri*)

Sooty Shearwater (*Puffinus griseus*)

Short-tailed Shearwater (*Puffinus tenuirostris*)

Black-vented Shearwater (*Puffinus opisthomelas*)

Audubon's Shearwater (*Puffinus lherminieri*)

Fork-tailed Storm-Petrel (*Oceanodroma furcata*)

Leach's Storm-Petrel (*Oceanodroma leucorhoa*)

Ashy Storm-Petrel (*Oceanodroma homochroa*)

Band-rumped Storm-Petrel (*Oceanodroma castro*)

Black Storm-Petrel (*Oceanodroma melania*)

Least Storm-Petrel (*Oceanodroma microsoma*)

Red-billed Tropicbird (*Phaethon aethereus*)

Red-tailed Tropicbird (*Phaethon rubricauda*)

Masked Booby (*Sula dactylatra*)

Blue-footed Booby (*Sula nebouxii*)

Brown Booby (*Sula leucogaster*)

Brown Pelican (*Pelecanus occidentalis*)

Brandt's Cormorant (*Phalacrocorax penicillatus*)

Neotropic Cormorant (*Phalacrocorax brasilianus*)

Double-crested Cormorant (*Phalacrocorax auritus*)

Red-faced Cormorant (*Phalacrocorax urile*)

Pelagic Cormorant (*Phalacrocorax pelagicus*)

Anhinga (*Anhinga anhinga*)

Magnificent Frigatebird (*Fregata magnificens*)

Tricolored Heron (*Egretta tricolor*)

Reddish Egret (*Egretta rufescens*)

Black-crowned Night-Heron (*Nycticorax nycticorax*)

Yellow-crowned Night-Heron (*Nyctanassa violacea*)
White-faced Ibis (*Plegadis chihi*)
Roseate Spoonbill (*Ajaia ajaja*)
Wood Stork (*Mycteria americana*)
Turkey Vulture (*Cathartes aura*)
Black-bellied Whistling-Duck (*Dendrocygna autumnalis*)
Fulvous Whistling-Duck (*Dendrocygna bicolor*)
Emperor Goose (*Chen canagica*)
Snow Goose (*Chen caerulescens*)
Ross's Goose (*Chen rossii*)
Brant (*Branta bernicla*)
Trumpeter Swan (*Cygnus buccinator*)
Tundra Swan (*Cygnus columbianus*)
Muscovy Duck (*Cairina moschata*)
Eurasian Wigeon (*Anas penelope*)
American Wigeon (*Anas americana*)
Mottled Duck (*Anas fulvigula*)
Blue-winged Teal (*Anas discors*)
Cinnamon Teal (*Anas cyanoptera*)
Green-winged Teal (*Anas crecca*)
Canvasback (*Aythya valisineria*)
Ring-necked Duck (*Aythya collaris*)
Tufted Duck (*Aythya fuligula*)
Greater Scaup (*Aythya marila*)
Lesser Scaup (*Aythya affinis*)
Steller's Eider (*Polysticta stelleri*)
Spectacled Eider (*Somateria fischeri*)
King Eider (*Somateria spectabilis*)
Common Eider (*Somateria mollissima*)
Harlequin Duck (*Histrionicus histrionicus*)
Surf Scoter (*Melanitta perspicillata*)
Oldsquaw (*Clangula hyemalis*)
Common Goldeneye (*Bucephala clangula*)
Barrow's Goldeneye (*Bucephala islandica*)
Smew (*Mergellus albellus*)
Common Merganser (*Mergus merganser*)
Red-breasted Merganser (*Mergus serrator*)
Masked Duck (*Nomonyx dominicus*)
Osprey (*Pandion haliaetus*)
Hook-billed Kite (*Chondrohierax uncinatus*)
White-tailed Kite (*Elanus leucurus*)

Bald Eagle (*Haliaeetus leucocephalus*)
Northern Harrier (*Circus cyaneus*)
Sharp-shinned Hawk (*Accipiter striatus*)
Cooper's Hawk (*Accipiter cooperii*)
Northern Goshawk (*Accipiter gentilis*)
Gray Hawk (*Asturina nitida*)
Common Black-Hawk (*Buteogallus anthracinus*)
Harris's Hawk (*Parabuteo unicinctus*)
Roadside Hawk (*Buteo magnirostris*)
Red-shouldered Hawk (*Buteo lineatus*)
Broad-winged Hawk (*Buteo platypterus*)
Swainson's Hawk (*Buteo swainsoni*)
White-tailed Hawk (*Buteo albicaudatus*)
Zone-tailed Hawk (*Buteo albonotatus*)
Red-tailed Hawk (*Buteo jamaicensis*)
Ferruginous Hawk (*Buteo regalis*)
Rough-legged Hawk (*Buteo lagopus*)
Golden Eagle (*Aquila chrysaetos*)
Crested Caracara (*Caracara plancus*)
American Kestrel (*Falco sparverius*)
Merlin (*Falco columbarius*)
Aplomado Falcon (*Falco femoralis*)
Gyrfalcon (*Falco rusticolus*)
Peregrine Falcon (*Falco peregrinus*)
Prairie Falcon (*Falco mexicanus*)
Plain Chachalaca (*Ortalis vetula*)
Sage Grouse (*Centrocercus urophasianus*)
"Gunnison" Sage Grouse (*Centrocercus* sp.)
Spruce Grouse (*Falcipennis canadensis*)
Willow Ptarmigan (*Lagopus lagopus*)
Rock Ptarmigan (*Lagopus mutus*)
White-tailed Ptarmigan (*Lagopus leucurus*)
Blue Grouse (*Dendragapus obscurus*)
Sharp-tailed Grouse (*Tympanuchus phasianellus*)
Greater Prairie-Chicken (*Tympanuchus cupido*)
Lesser Prairie-Chicken (*Tympanuchus pallidicinctus*)
Mountain Quail (*Oreortyx pictus*)
Scaled Quail (*Callipepla squamata*)
California Quail (*Callipepla californica*)
Gambel's Quail (*Callipepla gambelii*)

Montezuma Quail (*Cyrtonyx montezumae*)
Yellow Rail (*Coturnicops noveboracensis*)
Black Rail (*Laterallus jamaicensis*)
Clapper Rail (*Rallus longirostris*)
King Rail (*Rallus elegans*)
Sandhill Crane (*Grus canadensis*)
Whooping Crane (*Grus americana*)
Black-bellied Plover (*Pluvialis squatarola*)
American Golden-Plover (*Pluvialis dominica*)
Pacific Golden-Plover (*Pluvialis fulva*)
Snowy Plover (*Charadrius alexandrinus*)
Wilson's Plover (*Charadrius wilsonia*)
Common Ringed Plover (*Charadrius hiaticula*)
Semipalmated Plover (*Charadrius semipalmatus*)
Kilideer (*Charadrius vociferus*)
Mountain Plover (*Charadrius montanus*)
Eurasian Dotterel (*Charadrius morinellus*)
Black Oystercatcher (*Haematopus bachmani*)
Northern Jacana (*Jacana spinosa*)
Greater Yellowlegs (*Tringa melanoleuca*)
Lesser Yellowlegs (*Tringa flavipes*)
Willet (*Catoptrophorus semipalmatus*)
Wandering Tattler (*Heteroscelus incanus*)
Whimbrel (*Numenius phaeopus*)
Bristle-thighed Curlew (*Numenius tahitiensis*)
Long-billed Curlew (*Numenius americanus*)
Bar-tailed Godwit (*Limosa lapponica*)
Marbled Godwit (*Limosa fedoa*)
Black Turnstone (*Arenaria melanocephala*)
Surfbird (*Aphriza virgata*)
Sanderling (*Calidris alba*)
Semipalmated Sandpiper (*Calidris pusilla*)
Western Sandpiper (*Calidris mauri*)
Red-necked Stint (*Calidris ruficollis*)
Little Stint (*Calidris minuta*)
Least Sandpiper (*Calidris minutilla*)
White-rumped Sandpiper (*Calidris fuscicollis*)

Baird's Sandpiper (*Calidris bairdii*)
Pectoral Sandpiper (*Calidris melanotos*)
Sharp-tailed Sandpiper (*Calidris acuminata*)
Rock Sandpiper (*Calidris ptilocnemis*)
Dunlin (*Calidris alpina*)
Curlew Sandpiper (*Calidris ferruginea*)
Buff-breasted Sandpiper (*Tryngites subruficollis*)
Ruff (*Philomachus pugnax*)
Short-billed Dowitcher (*Limnodromus griseus*)
Long-billed Dowitcher (*Limnodromus scolopaceus*)
Wilson's Phalarope (*Phalaropus tricolor*)
Red Phalarope (*Phalaropus fulicaria*)
South Polar Skua (*Catharacta maccormicki*)
Pomarine Jaeger (*Stercorarius pomarinus*)
Parasitic Jaeger (*Stercorarius parasiticus*)
Long-tailed Jaeger (*Stercorarius longicaudus*)
Laughing Gull (*Larus atricilla*)
Franklin's Gull (*Larus pipixcan*)
Little Gull (*Larus minutus*)
Black-headed Gull (*Larus ridibundus*)
Bonaparte's Gull (*Larus philadelphia*)
Heermann's Gull (*Larus heermanni*)
Mew Gull (*Larus canus*)
Ring-billed Gull (*Larus delawarensis*)
California Gull (*Larus californicus*)
Herring Gull (*Larus argentatus*)
Thayer's Gull (*Larus thayeri*)
Iceland Gull (*Larus glaucoides*)
Lesser Black-backed Gull (*Larus fuscus*)
Slaty-backed Gull (*Larus schistisagus*)
Yellow-footed Gull (*Larus livens*)
Western Gull (*Larus occidentalis*)
Glaucous-winged Gull (*Larus glaucescens*)
Glaucous Gull (*Larus hyperboreus*)
Sabine's Gull (*Xema sabini*)
Black-legged Kittiwake (*Rissa tridactyla*)
Red-legged Kittiwake (*Rissa brevirostris*)
Ross's Gull (*Rhodostethia rosea*)
Ivory Gull (*Pagophila eburnea*)

Gull-billed Tern (*Sterna nilotica*)
Caspian Tern (*Sterna caspia*)
Royal Tern (*Sterna maxima*)
Elegant Tern (*Sterna elegans*)
Sandwich Tern (*Sterna sandvicensis*)
Common Tern (*Sterna hirundo*)
Arctic Tern (*Sterna paradisaea*)
Forster's Tern (*Sterna forsteri*)
Aleutian Tern (*Sterna aleutica*)
Black Skimmer (*Rynchops niger*)
Common Murre (*Uria aalge*)
Thick-billed Murre (*Uria lomvia*)
Black Guillemot (*Cepphus grylle*)
Pigeon Guillemot (*Cepphus columba*)
Long-billed Murrelet (*Brachyramphus perdix*)
Marbled Murrelet (*Brachyramphus marmoratus*)
Kittlitz's Murrelet (*Brachyramphus brevirostris*)
Xantus's Murrelet (*Synthliboramphus hypoleucus*)
Craveri's Murrelet (*Synthliboramphus craveri*)
Ancient Murrelet (*Synthliboramphus antiquus*)
Cassin's Auklet (*Ptychoramphus aleuticus*)
Parakeet Auklet (*Aethia psittacula*)
Least Auklet (*Aethia pusilla*)
Whiskered Auklet (*Aethia pygmaea*)
Crested Auklet (*Aethea cristatella*)
Rhinoceros Auklet (*Cerorhinca monocerata*)
Horned Puffin (*Fratercula corniculata*)
Tufted Puffin (*Fratercula cirrhata*)
Red-billed Pigeon (*Columba flavirostris*)
Band-tailed Pigeon (*Columba fasciata*)
White-winged Dove (*Zenaida asiatica*)
Inca Dove (*Columbina inca*)
Common Ground-Dove (*Columbina passerina*)
Ruddy Ground-Dove (*Columbina talpacoti*)
White-tipped Dove (*Leptotila verreauxi*)

Greater Roadrunner (*Geococcyx californianus*)
Groove-billed Ani (*Crotophaga sulcirostris*)
Barn Owl (*Tyto alba*)
Flammulated Owl (*Otus flammeolus*)
Western Screech-Owl (*Otus kennicottii*)
Eastern Screech-Owl (*Otus asio*)
Whiskered Screech-Owl (*Otus trichopsis*)
Great Horned Owl (*Bubo virginianus*)
Snowy Owl (*Nyctea scandiaca*)
Northern Hawk Owl (*Surnia ulula*)
Northern Pygmy-Owl (*Glaucidium gnoma*)
Ferruginous Pygmy-Owl (*Glaucidium brasilianum*)
Elf Owl (*Micrathene whitneyi*)
Burrowing Owl (*Athene cunicularia*)
Spotted Owl (*Strix occidentalis*)
Great Gray Owl (*Strix nebulosa*)
Boreal Owl (*Aegolius funereus*)
Lesser Nighthawk (*Chordeiles acutipennis*)
Common Nighthawk (*Chordeiles minor*)
Common Pauraque (*Nyctidromus albicollis*)
Common Poorwill (*Phalaenoptilus nuttallii*)
Chuck-will's-widow (*Caprimulgus carolinensis*)
Buff-collared Nightjar (*Caprimulgus ridgwayi*)
Whip-poor-will (*Caprimulgus vociferus*)
Black Swift (*Cypseloides niger*)
Chimney Swift (*Chaetura pelagica*)
Vaux's Swift (*Chaetura vauxi*)
White-throated Swift (*Aeronautes saxatalis*)
Green Violet-ear (*Colibri thalassinus*)
Broad-billed Hummingbird (*Cyanthus latirostris*)
White-eared Hummingbird (*Hylocharis leucotis*)
Berylline Hummingbird (*Amazilia beryllina*)
Buff-bellied Hummingbird (*Amazilia yucatanensis*)
Violet-crowned Hummingbird (*Amazilia violiceps*)

Blue-throated Hummingbird (*Lampornis clemenciae*)

Magnificent Hummingbird (*Eugenes fulgens*)

Plain-capped Starthroat (*Heliomaster constantii*)

Lucifer Hummingbird (*Calothorax lucifer*)

Ruby-throated Hummingbird (*Archilochus colubris*)

Black-chinned Hummingbird (*Archilochus alexandri*)

Anna's Hummingbird (*Calypte anna*)

Costa's Hummingbird (*Calypte costae*)

Calliope Hummingbird (*Stellula calliope*)

Broad-tailed Hummingbird (*Selasphorus platycercus*)

Rufous Hummingbird (*Selasphorus rufus*)

Allen's Hummingbird (*Selasphorus sasin*)

Elegant Trogon (*Trogon elegans*)

Eared Trogon (*Euptilotis neoxenus*)

Ringed Kingfisher (*Ceryle torquata*)

Green Kingfisher (*Chloroceryle americana*)

Lewis's Woodpecker (*Melanerpes lewis*)

Acorn Woodpecker (*Melanerpes formicivorus*)

Gila Woodpecker (*Melanerpes uropygialis*)

Golden-fronted Woodpecker (*Melanerpes aurifrons*)

Williamson's Sapsucker (*Sphyrapicus thyroideus*)

Yellow-bellied Sapsucker (*Sphyrapicus varius*)

Red-naped Sapsucker (*Sphyrapicus nuchalis*)

Red-breasted Sapsucker (*Sphyrapicus ruber*)

Ladder-backed Woodpecker (*Picoides scalaris*)

Nuttall's Woodpecker (*Picoides nuttallii*)

Hairy Woodpecker (*Picoides villosus*)

Strickland's Woodpecker (*Picoides stricklandi*)

Red-cockaded Woodpecker (*Picoides borealis*)

White-headed Woodpecker (*Picoides albolarvatus*)

Three-toed Woodpecker (*Picoides tridactylus*)

Black-backed Woodpecker (*Picoides arcticus*)

Northern Flicker (*Colaptes auratus*)

Gilded Flicker (*Colaptes chrysoides*)

Northern Beardless-Tyrannulet (*Camptostoma imberbe*)

Greater Pewee (*Contopus pertinax*)

Western Wood-Pewee (*Contopus sordidulus*)

Eastern Wood-Pewee (*Contopus virens*)

Yellow-bellied Flycatcher (*Empidonax flaviventris*)

Acadian Flycatcher (*Empidonax virescens*)

Alder Flycatcher (*Empidonax alnorum*)

Willow Flycatcher (*Empidonax traillii*)

"Traill's" Flycatcher (*Empidonax traillii / alnorum*)

Least Flycatcher (*Empidonax minimus*)

Hammond's Flycatcher (*Empidonax hammondii*)

Gray Flycatcher (*Empidonax wrightli*)

Dusky Flycatcher (*Empidonax oberholseri*)

Pacific-Slope Flycatcher (*Empidonax difficilis*)

Cordilleran Flycatcher (*Empidonax occidentalis*)

"Western" Flycatcher (*Empidonax difficilis / occidentalis*)

Buff-breasted Flycatcher (*Empidonax fulvifrons*)

Black Phoebe (*Sayornis nigricans*)

Eastern Phoebe (*Sayornis phoebe*)

Say's Phoebe (*Sayornis saya*)

Vermilion Flycatcher (*Pyrocephalus rubinus*)

Dusky-capped Flycatcher (*Myiarchus tuberculifer*)

Ash-throated Flycatcher (*Myiarchus cinerascens*)

Great Crested Flycatcher (*Myiarchus crinitis*)

Brown-crested Flycatcher (*Myiarchus tyrannulus*)

Great Kiskadee (*Pitangus sulphuratus*)

Sulphur-bellied Flycatcher (*Myiodynastes luteiventris*)

Tropical Kingbird (*Tyrannus melancholicus*)

Couch's Kingbird (*Tyrannus couchii*)

Cassin's Kingbird (*Tyrannus vociferans*)

Thick-billed Kingbird (*Tyrannus crassirostris*)

Western Kingbird (*Tyrannus verticalis*)

Scissor-tailed Flycatcher (*Tyrannus forficatus*)

Rose-throated Becard (*Pachyramphus aglaiae*)

White-eyed Vireo (*Vireo griseus*)

Bell's Vireo (*Vireo bellii*)

Black-capped Vireo (*Vireo atricapillus*)

Gray Vireo (*Vireo vicinior*)

Yellow-throated Vireo (*Vireo flavifrons*)

"Solitary" Vireo (*Vireo solitarius / plumbeus / cassinii*)

Plumbeous Vireo (*Vireo plumbeus*)

Cassin's Vireo (*Vireo cassinii*)

Blue-headed Vireo (*Vireo solitarius*)

Hutton's Vireo (*Vireo huttoni*)

Red-eyed Vireo (*Vireo olivaceus*)

Yellow-green Vireo (*Vireo flavoviridis*)

Gray Jay (*Perisoreus canadensis*)

Steller's Jay (*Cyanocitta stelleri*)

Green Jay (*Cyanocorax yncas*)

Brown Jay (*Cyanocorax morio*)

Florida Scrub-Jay (*Aphelocoma coerulescens*)

Island Scrub-Jay (*Aphelocoma insularis*)

Western Scrub-Jay (*Aphelocoma californica*)

Mexican Jay (*Aphelocoma ultramarina*)

Pinyon Jay (*Gymnorhinus cyanocephalus*)

Clark's Nutcracker (*Nucifraga columbiana*)

Black-billed Magpie (*Pica pica*)

Yellow-billed Magpie (*Pica nuttalli*)

American Crow (*Corvus brachyrhynchos*)

Northwestern Crow (*Corvus caurinus*)

Tamaulipas Crow (*Corvus imparatus*)

Sinaloa Crow (*Corvus sinaloae*)

Chihuahuan Raven (*Corvus cryptoleucus*)

Common Raven (*Corvus corax*)

Sky Lark (*Alauda arvensis*)

Purple Martin (*Progne subis*)

Tree Swallow (*Tachycineta bicolor*)

Violet-green Swallow (*Tachycineta thalassina*)

Northern Rough-winged Swallow (*Stelgidopteryx serripennis*)

Bank Swallow (*Riparia riparia*)

Cliff Swallow (*Petrochelidon pyrrhonota*)

Cave Swallow (*Petrochelidon fulva*)

Carolina Chickadee (*Poecile carolinensis*)

Black-capped Chickadee (*Poecile atricapillus*)

Mountain Chickadee (*Poecile gambeli*)

Mexican Chickadee (*Poecile sclateri*)

Chestnut-backed Chickadee (*Poecile rufescens*)

Boreal Chickadee (*Poecile hudsonicus*)

Gray-headed Chickadee (*Poecile cinctus*)

Bridled Titmouse (*Baeolophus wollweberi*)

Oak Titmouse (*Baeolophus inornatus*)

Juniper Titmouse (*Baeolophus griseus*)

Tufted Titmouse (*Baeolophus bicolor*)

Verdin (*Auriparus flaviceps*)

Bushtit (*Psaltriparus minimus*)

Red-breasted Nuthatch (*Sitta canadensis*)

White-breasted Nuthatch (*Sitta carolinensis*)

Pygmy Nuthatch (*Sitta pygmaea*)

Brown-headed Nuthatch (*Sitta pusilla*)

Cactus Wren (*Campylorhynchus brunneicapillus*)

Rock Wren (*Salpinctes obsoletus*)

Canyon Wren (*Catherpes mexicanus*)

Bewick's Wren (*Thryomanes bewickii*)

House Wren (*Troglodytes aedon*)

Marsh Wren (*Cistothorus palustris*)

American Dipper (*Cinclus mexicanus*)

Ruby-crowned Kinglet (*Regulus calendula*)

Arctic Warbler (*Phylloscopus borealis*)

Blue-gray Gnatcatcher (*Polioptila caerulea*)
California Gnatcatcher (*Polioptila californica*)
Black-tailed Gnatcatcher (*Polioptila melanura*)
Black-capped Gnatcatcher (*Polioptila nigriceps*)
Bluethroat (*Luscinia svecica*)
Northern Wheatear (*Oenanthe oenanthe*)
Eastern Bluebird (*Sialia sialis*)
Western Bluebird (*Sialia mexicana*)
Mountain Bluebird (*Sialia currucoides*)
Townsend's Solitaire (*Myadestes townsendi*)
Clay-colored Robin (*Turdus grayi*)
Rufous-backed Robin (*Turdus rufopalliatus*)
American Robin (*Turdus migratorius*)
Varied Thrush (*Ixoreus naevius*)
Aztec Thrush (*Ridgwayia pinicola*)
Wrentit (*Chamaea fasciata*)
Gray Catbird (*Dumetella carolinensis*)
Sage Thrasher (*Oreoscoptes montanus*)
Brown Thrasher (*Toxostoma rufum*)
Long-billed Thrasher (*Toxostoma longirostre*)
Bendire's Thrasher (*Toxostoma bendirei*)
Curve-billed Thrasher (*Toxostoma curvirostre*)
California Thrasher (*Toxostoma redivivum*)
Crissal Thrasher (*Toxostoma crissale*)
Le Conte's Thrasher (*Toxostoma lecontei*)
European Starling (*Sturnus vulgaris*)
Yellow Wagtail (*Motacilla flava*)
White Wagtail (*Motacilla alba*)
Black-backed Wagtail (*Motacilla lugens*)
Red-throated Pipit (*Anthus cervinus*)
American Pipit (*Anthus rubescens*)
Sprague's Pipit (*Anthus spragueii*)
Bohemian Waxwing (*Bombycilla garrulus*)
Cedar Waxwing (*Bombycilla cedrorum*)
Phainopepla (*Phainopepla nitens*)
Olive Warbler (*Peucedramus taeniatus*)
Nashville Warbler (*Vermivora ruficapilla*)
Virginia's Warbler (*Vermivora virginiae*)

Colima Warbler (*Vermivora crissalis*)
Lucy's Warbler (*Vermivora luciae*)
Tropical Parula (*Parula pitiayumi*)
Yellow-rumped Warbler (*Dendroica coronata*)
Black-throated Gray Warbler (*Dendroica nigrescens*)
Golden-cheeked Warbler (*Dendroica chrysoparia*)
Townsend's Warbler (*Dendroica townsendi*)
Hermit Warbler (*Dendroica occidentalis*)
Grace's Warbler (*Dendroica graciae*)
Kirtland's Warbler (*Dendroica kirtlandii*)
MacGillivray's Warbler (*Oporornis tolmiei*)
Common Yellowthroat (*Geothlypis trichas*)
Gray-crowned Yellowthroat (*Geothlypis poliocephala*)
Red-faced Warbler (*Cardellina rubifrons*)
Painted Redstart (*Myioborus pictus*)
Golden-crowned Warbler (*Basileuterus culicivorus*)
Rufous-capped Warbler (*Basileuterus rufifrons*)
Hepatic Tanager (*Piranga flava*)
Summer Tanager (*Piranga rubra*)
Scarlet Tanager (*Piranga olivacea*)
Western Tanager (*Piranga ludoviciana*)
Flame-colored Tanager (*Piranga bidentata*)
White-collared Seedeater (*Sporophila torqueola*)
Olive Sparrow (*Arremenops rufivirgatus*)
Green-tailed Towhee (*Pipilo chlorurus*)
Spotted Towhee (*Pipilo maculatus*)
Eastern Towhee (*Pipilo erythrophthalmus*)
Canyon Towhee (*Pipilo fuscus*)
California Towhee (*Pipilo crissalis*)
Abert's Towhee (*Pipilo aberti*)
Rufous-winged Sparrow (*Aimophila carpalis*)
Cassin's Sparrow (*Aimophila cassinii*)
Bachman's Sparrow (*Aimophila aestivalis*)
Botteri's Sparrow (*Aimophila botterii*)
Rufous-crowned Sparrow (*Aimophila ruficeps*)

Five-striped Sparrow (*Aimophila quinquestriata*)
American Tree Sparrow (*Spizella arborea*)
Chipping Sparrow (*Spizella passerina*)
Clay-colored Sparrow (*Spizella pallida*)
Brewer's Sparrow (*Spizella brewer*)
"Timberline" Sparrow (*Spizella brewer taverni*)
Field Sparrow (*Spizella pusilla*)
Black-chinned Sparrow (*Spizella atrogularis*)
Vesper Sparrow (*Pooecetes gramineus*)
Lark Sparrow (*Chondestes grammacus*)
Black-throated Sparrow (*Amphispiza bilineata*)
Sage Sparrow (*Amphispiza belli*)
Lark Bunting (*Calamospiza melanocorys*)
Savannah Sparrow (*Passerculus sandwichensis*)
Grasshopper Sparrow (*Ammodramus savannarum*)
Baird's Sparrow (*Ammodramus bairdii*)
Le Conte's Sparrow (*Ammodramus leconteii*)
Nelson's Sharp-tailed Sparrow (*Ammodramus nelsoni*)
Saltmarsh Sharp-tailed Sparrow (*Ammodramus caudacutus*)
Seaside Sparrow (*Ammodramus maritimus*)
Fox Sparrow (*Passerella iliaca*)
Song Sparrow (*Melospiza melodia*)
Harris's Sparrow (*Zonotrichia querula*)
Golden-crowned Sparrow (*Zonotrichia atricapilla*)
Dark-eyed Junco (*Junco hyemalis*)
Yellow-eyed Junco (*Junco phaeonotus*)
McCown's Longspur (*Calcarius mccownii*)
Lapland Longspur (*Calcarius lapponicus*)
Smith's Longspur (*Calcarius pictus*)
Chestnut-collared Longspur (*Calcarius ornatus*)
Snow Bunting (*Plectrophenax nivalis*)
McKay's Bunting (*Plectrophenex hyperboreus*)

Northern Cardinal (*Cardinalis cardinalis*)
Pyrrhuloxia (*Cardinalis sinuatus*)
Rose-breasted Grosbeak (*Pheucticus ludovicianus*)
Black-headed Grosbeak (*Pheucticus melanocephalus*)
Blue Bunting (*Cyanocompsa parellina*)
Lazuli Bunting (*Passerina amoena*)
Indigo Bunting (*Passerina cyanea*)
Varied Bunting (*Passerina versicolor*)
Dickcissel (*Spiza americana*)
Bobolink (*Dolichonyx oryzivorus*)
Tricolored Blackbird (*Agelaius tricolor*)
Eastern Meadowlark (*Sturnella magna*)
Western Meadowlark (*Sturnella neglecta*)
Great-tailed Grackle (*Quiscalus mexicanus*)
Bronzed Cowbird (*Molothrus aeneus*)
Hooded Oriole (*Icterus cucullatus*)
Streak-backed Oriole (*Icterus pustulatus*)
Altamira Oriole (*Icterus gularis*)
Audubon's Oriole (*Icterus graduacauda*)
Baltimore Oriole (*Icterus galbula*)
Bullock's Oriole (*Icterus bullockii*)
Scott's Oriole (*Icterus parisorum*)
Gray-crowned Rosy-Finch (*Leucosticte tephrocotis*)
Black Rosy-Finch (*Leucosticte atrata*)
Brown-capped Rosy-Finch (*Leucosticte australis*)
Pine Grosbeak (*Pinicola enucleator*)
Purple Finch (*Carpodacus purpureus*)
Cassin's Finch (*Carpodacus cassinii*)
House Finch (*Carpodacus mexicanus*)
Red Crossbill (*Loxia curvirostra*)
White-winged Crossbill (*Loxia leucoptera*)
Common Redpoll (*Carduelis flammea*)
Hoary Redpoll (*Carduelis hornemanni*)
Pine Siskin (*Carduelis pinus*)
Lesser Goldfinch (*Carduelis psaltria*)
Lawrence's Goldfinch (*Carduelis lawrencei*)
Evening Grosbeak (*Coccothraustes vespertinus*)
House Sparrow (*Passer domesticus*)

# BIBLIOGRAPHY

Andrews, R., and R. Righter. 1992. *Colorado birds: A reference to their distribution and habitat.* Denver: Denver Museum of Natural History.

Armstrong, R. H. 1983. *A new expanded guide to the birds of Alaska.* Anchorage: Alaska Northwest.

Babbitt, C. J. 1995. Birding the Kaibab Plateau, Arizona. *Winging It* (7)6: 1–5.

Bailey, S. F. 1991. Bill characters separating Trumpeter and Tundra swans: A cautionary note. *Birding* 23:89–91.

Bartol, D. A. 1974. Inserts: Mountain Plover. *Birding* 6:17.

Binford, L. C. 1971. Identification of Northern and Louisiana waterthrushes. *California Birds* 2:1–9.

Binford, L. C., and J. V. Remsen Jr. 1974. Identification of the Yellow-billed Loon *(Gavia adamsii). Western Birds* 5:111–126.

Cade, T. J. 1955. Variation of the Common Rough-legged Hawk in North America. *Condor* 57:313–346.

Carney, S. M. 1983. Species, age, and sex identification of nearctic goldeneyes from wings. *Journal of Wildlife Management* 47:754–761.

Chandler, R. J. 1987. Yellow orbital eye ring of Semipalmated and Ringed plover. *British Birds* 80:241–242.

Clark, W. S. 1979. Communications. *American Birds* 33:909.

Clark, W. S. 1981. Flight identification of common North American buteos. *Continental Birdlife* 2:129–143.

Clark, W. S. 1983. The field Identification of North American eagles. *American Birds* 37:822–826.

Clark, W. S., and B. K. Wheeler. 1987. *A field guide to the hawks.* Boston: Houghton Mifflin.

Connors, P. G. 1983. Taxonomy, distribution, and evolution of golden plovers. *Auk* 100:607–620.

Connors, P. G., B. J. McCaffery, and J. L. Maron. 1993. Speciation in golden-plovers, *Pluvialis dominica* and *P. fulva:* Evidence from the breeding grounds. *Auk* 110:9–20.

Cramp, S., ed. 1985. *Birds of the western Palearctic.* Vol. 4. Oxford: Oxford University Press.

Cressman, J. L. 1989. Birdfinding insert: Gray Vireo and Scott's Oriole. *Winging It* (1)8:9.

Cressman, J. L. 1995. Birdfinding insert: Sage Grouse, Belmont, Nevada. *Winging It* 7(5):7–8.

Curson, J. 1994. Identification forum: Separation of Bicknell's and Gray-cheeked thrushes. *Birding World* 7:359–365.

Czaplak, D. 1995. Identifying Common and Hoary Redpolls in Winter. *Birding* 27:447–457.

Davis, L. Irby. 1962. Songs of North American *Myiarchus. Texas Journal of Science* 13: 327–344.

DeBenedictis, P. 1979. Gleanings from the technical literature. *Birding* 11:178–181.

Devillers, P. 1970. Identification and distribution in California of the *Sphyrapicus varius* group of sapsuckers. *California Birds* 1:47–76.

Doyle, T. J. 1997. The Timberline Sparrow. *Spizella (breweri) taverni*, in Alaska, with notes on breeding habitat and vocalizations. *Western Birds* 28:1–12.

Dunn, J. 1975. Field notes: The identification of immature orioles. *Western Tanager* 41(4):7.

Dunn, J. 1976a. Field notes: The *Carpodacus* finches. *Western Tanager* 42(9):4.

Dunn, J. 1976b. Field notes: The identification of longspurs. *Western Tanager* 42(5):4–5.

Dunn, J. 1976c. Field notes: The identification of pipits. *Western Tanager* 42(3):5.

Dunn, J. 1977a. Field notes: Female grosbeaks. *Western Tanager* 43(6):5.

Dunn, J. 1977b. Field notes: The genus *Empidonax*. *Western Tanager* 43(7):5.

Dunn, J. 1977c. Field notes: The genus *Empidonax*. *Western Tanager* 43(8): 5, 7.

Dunn, J. 1977d. Field notes: The genus *Empidonax*. *Western Tanager* 43(9):4.

Dunn, J. 1977e. Field notes: The genus *Empidonax*. *Western Tanager* 43(10):5, 7.

Dunn, J. 1978a. Field notes: The *Endomychura* murrelets. *Western Tanager* 44(8):8–9.

Dunn, J. 1978b. Field notes: The *Myiarchus* flycatchers. *Western Tanager* 44(3):4–5.

Dunn, J. 1978c. Field notes: The *Myiarchus* flycatchers. *Western Tanager* 44(4):5.

Dunn, J. 1978d. Field notes: Plain-winged vireos. *Western Tanager* 44(10):9.

Dunn, J. 1978e. The races of the Yellow-bellied Sapsucker. *Birding* 10:142–149.

Dunn, J. 1979a. Field notes: Immature Red-shouldered and Broad-winged hawks. *Western Tanager* 45(8):13.

Dunn, J. 1979b. Field notes: Northern and Louisiana waterthrushes. *Western Tanager* 45(10):7.

Dunn, J. 1981. The identification of female bluebirds. *Birding* 13:4–11.

Dunn, J. L. 1993. The identification of Semipalmated and Common Ringed plovers in alternate plumage. *Birding* 25:238–243.

Dunn, J. L., and K. L. Garrett. 1976. The races of the Solitary Vireo. *Western Tanager* 43(1):5.

Dunn, J. L., and K. L. Garrett. 1982a. Field notes: Horned and Eared grebes. *Western Tanager* 48(5):8.

Dunn, J. L., and K. L. Garrett. 1982b. Field notes: Tree, Bank, and Rough-winged swallows. *Western Tanager* 48(9):8–9.

Dunn, J. L., and K. L. Garrett. 1983a. The identification of thrushes of the genus *Catharus*, Part one: Introduction. *Western Tanager* 49(6):1–2.

Dunn, J. L., and K. L. Garrett. 1983b. The identification of thrushes of the genus *Catharus*, Part two: Hermit Thrush. *Western Tanager* 49(7):4, 9.

Dunn, J. L., and K. L. Garrett. 1983c. The identification of thrushes of the genus *Catharus*, Part three: Swainson's Thrush. *Western Tanager* 49(8):7–9.

Dunn, J. L., and K. L. Garrett. 1983d. The identification of thrushes of the genus *Catharus*, Part four: Veery and Gray-cheeked Thrush. *Western Tanager* 49(9): 1–33.

Dunn, J. L., and K. L. Garrett. 1983e. The identification of wood-pewees. *Western Tanager* 49(4):1–3.

Dunn, J. L., and K. L. Garrett. 1997. *A field guide to the warblers of North America*. Boston: Houghton Mifflin.

Dunn, J. L., and B. J. Rose. 1992. A further note on Arctic Loon identification. *Birding* 24:106–107.

Eckert, K. 1993. Identification of Western and Clark's grebes: The Minnesota experience. *Birding* 25:304–310.

Evanich, J. E., Jr. 1990. *The birder's guide to Oregon*. Portland: Portland Audubon Society.

Faanes, C. 1984. Inserts: Yellow Rail. *Birding* 16:118I–J.

Farrand, J., Jr., ed. 1983. *The Audubon Society master guide to birding*. 3 vols. New York: Knopf.

Garrett, K. L., and J. Dunn. 1981. *Birds of southern California: Status and distribution*. Los Angeles: Los Angeles Audubon Society.

Garrett, K. L., and J. L. Dunn. 1982. The identification of Common and Lesser nighthawks. *Western Tanager* 48(1):1, 3.

Goetz, R. E., W. M. Rudden, and P. B. Snetsinger. 1986. Slaty-backed Gull winters on the Mississippi River. *American Birds* 40:207–216.

Grant, P. J. 1981. Identification of Semipalmated Sandpiper. *British Birds* 74:505–509.

Grant, P. J. 1986. *Gulls: A guide to identification*. 2d ed. Calton, England: T. and A. D. Poyser.

Grant, P. J., and R. E. Scott. 1969. Field identification of juvenile Common, Arctic, and Roseate terns. *British Birds* 62:297–299.

Grzybowski, J. A. 1991. A closer look: The Black-capped Vireo. *Birding* 23:216–219.

Gustafson, M., and B. Peterjohn. 1994. Adult Slaty-backed Gulls: Variability in mantle color and comments on identification. *Birding* 26:243–249.

Haney, J. C., J. M. Andrew and D. S. Lee. 1991. A closer look: rare, local, little-known and declining North American breeders, Aleutian Tern. *Birding.* 23:347–351.

Harrison, P. 1985. *Seabirds: An identification guide.* Rev. ed. Boston: Houghton Mifflin.

Harrison, P. 1987. *A field guide to seabirds of the world.* Lexington, Mass.: Stephen Greene Press.

Hayman, P., J. Marchant, and T. Prater. 1986. *Shorebirds: An identification guide.* Boston: Houghton Mifflin.

Heindel, M.T. 1996. Field identification of the Solitary Vireo complex. *Birding* 28:458–471.

Herremans, M. 1990. Taxonomy and evolution in redpolls *Carduelis flammea-hornemanni:* A multivariate study of their biometry. *Ardea* 78:441–458.

Holt, H. R. 1990. *A birder's guide to southern California.* Colorado Springs, Colo.: American Birding Association.

Holt, H. R. 1992. *A birder's guide to the Rio Grande Valley of Texas.* Colorado Springs, Colo.: American Birding Association.

Holt, H. R. 1993. *A birder's guide to the Texas coast.* Colorado Springs, Colo.: American Birding Association.

Holt, H. R. 1997. *A birder's guide to Colorado.* Colorado Springs, Colo.: American Birding Association.

Holt, H. R., and J. A. Lane. 1988. *A birder's guide to Colorado.* Colorado Springs, Colo.: American Birding Association.

Hume, R. A., and P. J. Grant. 1974. The upperwing pattern of adult Common and Arctic terns. *British Birds* 67:133–136.

Humphrey, P. S., and K. C. Parkes. 1959. An approach to the study of molts and plumages. *Auk.* 76:1–31.

Hupp, J. W., and C. E. Braun. 1991. Geographical variation among Sage Grouse populations in Colorado, Wilson Bulletin 103:255–261.

Jackson, G. D. 1991. Field identification of teal in North America: Female-like plumages—Part 1. *Birding* 23:124–133.

Jackson, G. D. 1992. Field identification of teal in North America: Female-like plumages—Part 2. *Birding* 24:214–223.

Janzen, P. 1995a. Where to find birds in Sedgwick County, Kansas. *Winging It* 7(7):1, 4–7.

Janzen, P. 1995b. Where to find birds in Sedgwick County, Kansas Part 2. *Winging It* 7(8):8–11.

Johnson, N. K. 1995. Speciation in vireos. I. Macrogeographic patterns of allozymic variation in the *Vireo solitarius* complex in the contiguous U.S. *Condor* 97:903–919.

Jordan, M. 1988. Distinguishing Tundra and Trumpeter swans. *Oregon Birds* 14:37–40. [Reprinted with minor changes in *Birding* 20:223– 226.]

Kaufman, K. 1979. Field identification of Hutton's Vireo. *Continental Birdlife* 1:62–66.

Kaufman, K. 1983. Identifying Streak-backed Orioles: A note of caution. *American Birds* 37:140–141.

Kaufman, K. 1987a. The practiced eye: Notes on female orioles. *American Birds* 41:1–4.

Kaufman, K. 1987b. The practiced eye: Terns overhead. *American Birds* 41:184–187.

Kaufman, K. 1988a. The practiced eye: Immature night-herons. *American Birds* 42:169–171.

Kaufman, K. 1988b. The practiced eye: Red-naped Sapsucker and Yellow-bellied Sapsucker. *American Birds* 42:348–350.

Kaufman, K. 1990. *A field guide to advanced birding.* Boston: Houghton Mifflin.

Kaufman, K. 1992a. The practiced eye: Bluebirds. *American Birds* 46:159–162.

Kaufman, K. 1992b. The practiced eye: Western Kingbird identification. *American Birds* 46:323–326.

Kaufman, K. 1992c. The practiced eye: Identifying monochrome grebes in winter. *American Birds.* 46:1187–1190.

Kaufman, K. 1993. The practiced eye: Identifying Hutton's Vireo. *American Birds* 47:460–462.

Kaufman, K., and R. Bowers. 1990. The practiced eye: Curve-billed Thrasher and Bendire's Thrasher. *American Birds* 44:359–362.

Kessel, B. 1989. *Birds of the Seward Peninsula, Alaska.* Fairbanks: University of Alaska Press.

King, B. 1981. The field identification of North American pipits. *American Birds* 35: 778–788.

Knox, A. G. 1988. The taxonomy of redpolls. *Ardea* 76:1–26.

Landing, J. E. 1991. On Yellow-bellied Sapsuckers with red napes. *Birding* 23:20–22.

Lane, J. A. 1976. *A birder's guide to southern California.* 3d ed. Denver: L & P Press.

Lane, J. A. 1983. *A birder's guide to the Rio Grande Valley of Texas.* 4th ed. Denver: L & P Press.

Lane, J. A. 1983. *A birder's guide to southeastern Arizona.* 4th ed. Denver: L & P Press.

Lane, J. A., and H. L. Holt. 1979. *A birder's guide to eastern Colorado.* 3d ed. Denver: L & P Press.

Lane, J. A., and J. L. Tveton. 1980. *A birder's guide to the Texas coast.* 3d ed. Denver: L & P Press.

Lansdown, P., N. Riddiford, and A. Knox. 1991. Identification of Arctic Redpoll *Carduelis hornemanni exilipes.* *British Birds* 84:41–56.

Lehman, P. 1980. The identification of Thayer's Gull in the field. *Birding* 12:198–210.

Lehman, P. 1991. Notes on plumage variation in adult Red-naped and Red-breasted sapsuckers. *Birding* 23:23–26.

Lethaby, N. 1994. *A bird finding guide to Alaska.* Nick Lethaby. Photocopy.

Lethaby, N. 1996. Identification of Tree, Northern Rough-winged and Bank swallows. *Birding* 28:111–116.

Lockewood, M. W., W. B. McKinney, J. N. Paton and B. R. Zimmer. 1999. *A birder's guide to the Rio Grande Valley.* Colorado Springs, Col.: American Birding Association.

Madge, S., and H. Burn. 1988. *Waterfowl: An identification guide.* Boston: Houghton Mifflin.

Maynard, W. R. 1989. Jewels of the north. *Birding* 21:200–204.

McCaskie, G., J. L. Dunn, C. Roberts, and D. A. Sibley. 1990. Notes on identifying Arctic and Pacific loons in alternate plumage. *Birding* 22:70–73.

McClung, J. M. 1992. Boreal Owls in Idaho: Birds on the edge. *Birding* 24: 78–84.

McEneaney, T. 1993. *The birder's guide to Montana.* Helena, Mont.: Falcon Press.

McLaren, I. A. 1995. Field identification and taxonomy of Bicknell's Thrush. *Birding* 27:358–366.

Mlodinow, S. 1993. Finding the Pacific Golden-Plover *(Pluvialis fulva)* in North America. *Birding* 25:322–329.

Mlodinow, S. G. 1997. The Long-billed Murrelet *(Brachyramphus perdix)* in North America. *Birding* 29:461–475.

Morlan, J. 1991. Identification of female Rose-breasted and Black-headed grosbeaks. *Birding* 23:220–223.

Mowbray, M. V., and J. L. Cressman. 1989. Birdfinding insert: Las Vegas, Nevada. *Winging It* (1)5:9–10.

Mowbray, M. V., and J. L. Cressman. 1991. Birdfinding insert: Las Vegas, Nevada. *Winging It* (3)7:9–10.

Mueller, H. D., D. D. Berger, and G. Allenz. 1979. The identification of North American accipiters. *American Birds* 33:236–240.

Mullarney, K. 1991. Identification of Semipalmated Plover, a new feature. *Birding World* 7:254–258.

National Geographic Society. 1999. *National Geographic Society field guide to the birds of North America.* 3rd ed. Washington, D.C.: National Geographic Society.

Olsen, K. M., and H. Larsson. 1995. *Terns of Europe and North America.* Princeton, N.J.: Princeton University Press.

Ouellet, H. 1993. Bicknell's Thrush: Taxonomic status and distribution. *Wilson Bulletin* 105:545–571.

Parkes, K. C. 1982. Further comments on the field identification of North American pipits. *American Birds* 36:20–22.

Parmeter, B. D. 1974. Inserts: Marbled Murrelet. *Birding* 6:125–126.

Paton, J. N., and B. R. Zimmer. 1996. *Birds and birdfinding in the El Paso area.* El Paso: J. N. Paton. Photocopy.

Patten, M. A. 1993. Notes on immature Double-crested and Neotropic cormorants. *Birding* 25:343–345.

Patten, M. A., and M. T. Heindel. 1994. Identifying Trumpeter and Tundra swans in the field. *Birding* 26:306–318.

Paulsen, I. 1993. Point/Counterpoint: "New" kinglet field mark. *Birding* 25:223.

Paulson, D. 1993. *Shorebirds of the Pacific Northwest.* Seattle: University of Washington Press and Seattle Audubon Society.

Peterson, J., and B. R. Zimmer. 1998.*Birds of the Trans Pecos.* Austin, Texas: University of Texas Press.

Peterson, R. T. 1980. *A field guide to the birds.* Boston: Houghton Mifflin.

Peterson, R. T. 1990. *A field guide to Western birds.* 3rd ed. Boston: Houghton Mifflin.

Pettingill, O. S. 1951. *A guide to bird finding east of the Mississippi.* New York: Oxford University Press.

Pettingill, O. S. 1981. *A guide to bird finding west of the Mississippi.* 2d ed. New York: Oxford University Press.

Pough, R. H. 1957. *Audubon Western bird guide.* New York: Doubleday.

Pyle, P., and S. N. G. Howell. 1996. *Spizella* sparrows: Intraspecific variation and identification. *Birding* 28:374–387.

Pyle, P., S. N. G. Howell, R. P. Yunick, and D. F. DeSante. 1987. *Identification guide to North American passerines.* Bolinas, Calif.: Slate Creek Press.

Ramsey, F. L. 1978. *Birding Oregon.* Corvallis: O.S.U. Book Stores.

Ratti, J. 1981. Identification and distribution of Clark's Grebe. *Western Birds* 12:41–46.

Reinking, D. L., and S. N. G. Howell. 1993. An Arctic Loon in California. *Western Birds* 24:189–196.

Remsen, J. V., Jr. 1973. Inserts: Lawrence's Goldfinch. *Birding* 5:17–18.

Ritchison, G. 1983. The function of singing in female Black-headed Grosbeaks *(Pheucticus melanocephalus):* Family-group maintenance. *Auk* 100:105–116.

Robbins, C. S., B. Brunn, and H. S. Zim. 1983. *Birds of North America: A guide to field identification.* New York: Golden Press.

Roberson, D. 1980. *Rare birds of the West Coast.* Pacific Grove, Calif.: Woodcock Publications.

Roberson, D. 1982. The changing seasons. *American Birds* 36: 948–953.

Roberson, D. 1989. Point/counterpoint: More on Pacific versus Arctic loons. *Birding* 21:154–157.

Roberson, D. 1993. A note on hybrid white Geese. *Birding* 25:50–53.

Rosche, R. C. 1990. Birding pristine Nebraska. *Winging It* 2(6):1–2, 4–6.

Rosche, R. C. 1994a. Birding in western Nebraska, Part 1. *Birding* 26:178– 189.

Rosche, R. C. 1994b. Birding in western Nebraska, Part 2. *Birding* 26:416– 423.

Rosenberg, G. H. 1990a. Arizona birding pitfalls. Part 1. Species we take for granted. *Birding* 22:120–129.

Rosenberg, G. H. 1990b. Arizona birding pitfalls. Part 2. The Mexican Connection. *Birding* 22:176–184.

Russell, W. 1976. Field identification notes *(Sterna* terns). *Birding* 8: 347–348.

Schram, B. 1998. *A birder's guide to southern California.* Colorado Springs, Colo.: American Birding Association.

Schulenberg, T. 1989. Point/counterpoint: More on Pacific versus Arctic loons. *Birding* 21:157–158.

Scott, O. K. 1993. *A birder's guide to Wyoming.* Colorado Springs, Colo.: American Birding Association.

Scott, R. E., and P. J. Grant. 1969. Uncompleted moult in *Sterna* terns and the problem of identification. *British Birds* 62:93–97.

Sexton, C. 1992. A closer look: Golden-cheeked Warbler. *Birding* 24:373– 376.

Simon, D. 1977. Identification of Clay-colored, Brewer's and Chipping sparrows in fall plumage. *Birding* 9:189–191.

Simon, D. 1978. Identification of Snow and Ross' geese. *Birding* 10: 289–291.

Sorensen, E. 1991a. Birding in Utah: Part 1. *Birding* 23:10–19.

Sorensen, E. 1991b. Birding in Utah: Part 2. *Birding* 23:134–144.

Sorensen, E. 1996a. Birding Utah: Part 1. *Winging It* 8(3):1, 4–7.

Sorensen, E. 1996b. Birding Utah: Part 2. *Winging It* 8(4):1, 4–8.

Sorensen, E. 1996c. Birding Utah: Part 3. *Winging It* 8(5):1, 4–7.

Springer, M. I. 1993. *Birdwatching in eastcentral Alaska*. Fairbanks, Alaska: FALCO.

Starks, D. S. 1981. Inserts: Black Rosy Finch. *Birding* 13: 54U–V.

Storer, R., and G. Nuechterlein. 1985. An analysis of plumage and morphological characters of the two color forms of the Western Grebe *Aechmophorus*. *Auk* 102:102–119.

Svingen, D., and K. Dumroese. 1997. *A birder's guide to Idaho*. Colorado Springs, Colo.: American Birding Association.

Taylor, R. C. 1995. *A birder's guide to southeastern Arizona*. Colorado Springs, Colo.: American Birding Association.

Terrill, S. B., and L. S. Terrill. 1981. On the field identification of Yellow-green, Red-eyed, Philadelphia, and Warbling vireos. *Continental Birdlife* 2:144–149.

Tobish, T. 1986. Separation of Barrow's and Common goldeneyes in all plumages. *Birding* 18:17–27.

Troy, D. M. 1985. A phenetic analysis of the redpolls *Carduelis flammea flammea* and *C. hornemanni exilipes*. *Auk* 102:82–96.

Tucson Audubon Society. 1995. *Davis and Russell's finding birds in southeast Arizona*. Tucson, Ariz.: Tucson Audubon Society.

Tulsa Audubon Society. 1986. *A guide to birding in Oklahoma*. Tulsa, Okla.: Tulsa Audubon Society.

Veit, R. R., and L. Jonsson. 1984. Field identification of smaller sandpipers within the genus *Calidris*. *American Birds* 38:853–876.

Wahl, T. R., and D. R. Paulson. 1977. *A guide to bird finding in Washington*. Bellingham, Wash.: T. R. Wahl. Photocopy.

Wahl, T. R., and D. R. Paulson. 1987. *A guide to bird finding in Washington*. Bellingham, Wash.: T. R. Wahl. Photocopy.

Wallace, D. I. M. 1974. Field identification of small species of the genus *Calidris*. *British Birds* 67:1.

Wallace, D. I. M. 1976. A review of waterthrush identification. *British Birds* 69:27.

Wallace, D. I. M., and M. A. Ogilvie. 1977. Distinguishing Blue-winged and Cinnamon teals. *British Birds* 70: 290–294.

Walsh, T. 1988. Identifying Pacific Loons. *Birding* 20:12–28.

West, G. C. 1994. *A birder's guide to the Kenai Peninsula, Alaska*. Homer, Alaska: Pratt Museum and Birchside Studios.

Westrich, L., and J. Westrich. 1991. *Birder's guide to northern California*. Houston, Tex: Gulf Publishing Company.

Whitney, B., and K. Kaufman. 1985a. The *Empidonax* challenge, Part 1: Introduction. *Birding* 17:151–158.

Whitney, B., and K. Kaufman. 1985b. The *Empidonax* challenge, Part 2: Least, Hammond's and Dusky flycatchers. *Birding* 17:277–287.

Whitney, B., and K. Kaufman. 1986a. The *Empidonax* challenge, Part 3: "Traill's" Flycatcher: The Alder/Willow problem. *Birding* 18:153–159.

Whitney, B., and K. Kaufman. 1986b. The *Empidonax* challenge, Part 4: Acadian, Yellow-bellied, and Western flycatchers. *Birding* 18:315– 327.

Whitney, B., and K. Kaufman. 1987. The *Empidonax* challenge, Part 5: Gray and Buff-breasted flycatchers. *Birding* 19:7–15.

Wilds, C. 1982. Separating the yellowlegs. *Birding* 14:172–178.

Wilds, C. 1985. Unravelling the mysteries of brown swallows. *Birding* 17:209–211.

Wilds, C. 1993. The identification and aging of Forster's and Common terns. *Birding* 25:94–108.

Wilds, C., and M. Newlon. 1983. The identification of dowitchers. *Birding* 15:151–166.

Willick, D. R., and M. A. Patten. 1992. Finding the California gnatcatcher. *Birding* 24:234–339.

Zimmer, K. J. 1979. *A birder's guide to North Dakota.* Denver, Colo.: L & P Press.

Zimmer, K. J. 1984. Point/counterpoint: Eastern vs. Western meadowlarks. *Birding* 16:155–156.

Zimmer, K. J. 1985. *The Western birdwatcher.* Englewood Cliffs, N.J.: Prentice Hall.

Zimmer, K. J. 1990. The Thayer's Gull complex. Pages 114–130 *in* K. Kaufman, *A field guide to advanced birding.* Boston: Houghton Mifflin.

Zimmer, K. J. 1991. Plumage variation in "Kumlien's" Iceland Gull. *Birding* 23:254–269.

Zimmerman, D. L., M. A. Zimmerman, and J. N. Durrie eds. 1992. *New Mexico bird finding guide.* Rev. ed. Albuquerque: New Mexico Ornithological Society.

Zimmerman, J. L., and S. T. Patti. 1988. *A guide to bird finding in Kansas and western Missouri.* Lawrence: University Press of Kansas.

# Index

Accipiters (*Accipiter*), 30–31, 104–106, 117
Age dimorphism, 39
Aging
  of gulls, 150–157
  of jaegers, 141
  of shorebirds, 117–120
  of terns, 181–183
Alaska Marine Highway System, 17
*Alauda arvensis*
  *A. a. arvensis*, 337
  *A. a. pekinensis*, 337
Albatross(es), 19, 29, 33, 40
  Black-footed, 20, 270–271
  key characters in identification, 49
  Laysan, 20, 271
  Light-mantled (Sooty), 20
Alcids, 5, 9, 19, 20, 29, 192, 195, 311
  key characters in identification, 51
Alpine Zone, 2
American Avocet, 64
American Birding Association (ABA), 14, 18
American Dipper, 5, 342
*Amphispiza belli*
  *A. b. belli*, 362
  *A. b. canescens*, 363
  *A. b. clementeae*, 362
  *A. b. nevadensis*, 363
Anatomy of feather groups, 35–39
Anhinga, 44
*Anthus spinoletta*
  *A. s. alticola*, 239–240
  *A. s. japonicus*, 239–240
  *A. s. pacificus*, 239–240
  *A. s. rubescens*, 239–240
*Aphelocoma*
  *coerulescens*, 231
  *ultramarina*
    *A. u. arizonae*, 231–234, 338
    *A. u. couchii*, 231–234, 338
Audubon Society
  of Los Angeles, 17, 69
  of Portland, 17

Auklet
  Cassin's, 309–310
  Crested, 311
  Least, 197, 310
  Parakeet, 310
  Rhinoceros, 311
  Whiskered, 310–311
Avocets, 44
  American, 64
Axillaries, defined, 35

Behavior, as aid to identification, 44–45
  escape, 45
  foraging, 44–45
  mating displays, 45
  nest-building, 45
*Birding* (magazine), 13–14
*Birding by Ear* (Walton and Lawson), 21
Birding grapevines, 14–17
Bird topography, 36–39
Bitterns, 45
Blackbirds, 10, 29, 41
  Tricolored, 368
Black Brant, 279
Black Oystercatcher, 6, 30, 268
Black Skimmer, 306–307
Bluebirds, 5, 9, 234, 236
  Eastern, 234–236
  key characters in identification, 54
  Mountain, 234–236, 268
  Western, 234–236, 268
Bluethroat, 344
Bobolink, 4, 45
Boobies, 12, 275
  Blue-footed, 9, 275
  Brown, 9, 275
  Masked, 20, 275
Boreal species, invasions of, 10
*Brachyramphus perdix*, 195, 308
Brant, 279
Buff-collared Nightjar, 13, 24,
  319–320

Bunting
  Blue, 10, 358
  Indigo, 11
  key characters in identification, 55
  Lark, 268
  Lazuli, 268
  McKay's, 368
  Snow, 367–368
  Varied, 358–359
Bushtit, 53, 268
*Buteo lineatus*
  *B. l. elegans*, 116
  *B. l. extimus*, 116
Buteos (*Buteo*), 31–32, 39–40, 61,
    106–115

Calendar-year terminology, defined, 152
*Calidris ptilocnemis*
  *C. p. cousei*, 302–303
  *C. p. ptilocnemis*, 302–303
  *C. p. tschuktschorum*, 302–303
Calling birds, 20–22
Canadian Zone, 2
Canopy feeding, 44
Canvasback, 35, 90
Caprimulgids, 7, 42
  key characters in identification, 52
*Carduelis*
  *flammea*, 262
  *hornemanni exilipes*, 263–265
  *hornemanni hornemanni*, 262–265
*Carpodacus* finches, 258–262
  key characters in identification, 56
*Carpodacus purpureus*
  *C. p. californicus*, 258–262
  *C. p. purpureus*, 258–262
Cere, defined, 102
Charadriidae, 117
Chickadees, 5, 9, 20, 43–44, 340
  Black-capped, 53
  Boreal, 341
  Carolina, 53
  Chestnut-backed, 268
  Gray-headed, 341
  Mexican, 340
  Mountain, 268
Chuck-will's-widow, 43
Chumming, 18
Clark's Nutcracker, 339
Clinal variation, 36
Color and plumage patterns, 35–42
  molt and plumage sequence, 40–42
  variations, 36–40
    dimorphisms, 39
    geographic, 35–36
    polymorphisms, 39–40

Common Black-Hawk, 32, 107, 113–114, 282
Common Pauraque, 319
Common Poorwill, 7, 43, 199, 268
Coots, key characters in identification, 50
Cormorants, 18, 29, 35, 44, 49, 82, 83, 85
  Brandt's, 85–87, 268
  Double-crested, 82–87
  key characters in identification, 49
  Neotropic, 82–84, 275–276
  Pelagic, 85–87, 268
  Red-faced, 85–87, 276
Corvids, 28–29, 34
Cowbirds, 45
  Bronzed, 268
Cranes, 10, 44–45
  key characters in identification, 50
  Sandhill, 296
  Whooping, 295–296
Creepers, 9, 44
Crested Caracara, 108, 284
Crissum, defined, 35
Crossbills, 267
  Red, 10
  White-winged, 10
Crows, 29
  American, 28, 43
  key characters in identification, 53
  "Mexican," 340
  Northwestern, 43, 340
  Sinaloa, 340
  Tamaulipas, 340
Cuckoos, 42
  key characters in identification, 51
Curlews, 44
  Bristle-thighed, 125–127, 299–300
  Long-billed, 30, 268
  Whimbrel, 125–127, 299
Cursorial foraging, 44

Dabbling ducks, 44–45
  key characters in identification, 50
*Dendragapus obscurus*
  *fuliginosus* group, 286
  *obscurus* group, 286
Dickcissel, 4
Dimorphisms
  age, 39
  sexual, 39
Documenting rare birds, 63
Doves, 42
  Common Ground-Dove, 312–313
  Inca, 268, 313
  key characters in identification, 51
  Ruddy Ground-Dove, 313
  White-tipped, 313
  White-winged, 268

Dowitchers, 36, 42, 44, 47, 118, 136–140
    Long-billed, 47, 64, 136–140
    Short-billed, 37, 47, 136–140
Ducks, 6, 29, 39, 41, 45
    Canvasback, 35, 90
    dabbling (puddle), 44–45, 50
    diving, 35, 44–45, 50
    Eiders (see Eiders)
    Goldeneyes (see Goldeneyes)
    Harlequin, 281
    key characters in identification, 50
    Mallard, 60
    Masked, 281
    Mergansers (see Mergansers)
    Mottled, 268
    Muscovy, 279
    Oldsquaw, 10
    Ring-necked, 35, 280
    Scaup (see Scaup)
    Scoters (see Scoters)
    Shoveler (Northern Shoveler), 95
    Smew, 13
    Teal (see Teal)
    Tufted, 35, 279–280
    Wigeon (see Wigeon)
    See also Whistling-Ducks
Dunlin, 119, 218
Dunn, Jon, 69

Eagles, 30, 102
    Bald, 102–104
    Golden, 102–104
Eclipse plumage, 41
Egrets, 44
    Cattle, 60
    key characters in identification, 49
    Reddish, 39, 44, 276
Eiders, 35, 50
    Common, 90
    King, 280–281
    Spectacled, 280
    Steller's, 280
Elevation, 2–3
Empidonax flycatchers, 35, 42–43, 46–47, 52–53,
        213–228, 333
    identification, general considerations,
        213–217
    key characters in identification, 52
Escape behaviors, 45
Ethics, 22–26
    and observing lekking grouse, 289
Eurasian Dotterel, 118, 298
European Starling, 5

Falcons (Falco), 4, 30, 31, 32
    American Kestrel, 33

Aplomado, 284
    Gyrfalcon, 37, 284–285
    Merlin, 37
    Peregrine, 37
    Prairie, 60, 268
Fallouts, 11
Feather anatomy, 35–39
Feather topography, 35–39
Feather wear, in gulls, 157–158
Field Guide to Advanced Birding, A (Kaufman),
        69
Field Guide to Western Birds (Peterson), 21
Field Guide to Western Bird Songs, A, 21
Field journals, 58–66
    how to keep, 59–66
    notes section in, 63
    reasons for, 58
    species list in, 60–63
Field notes. See Field journals
Field Notes (magazine), 13, 63
Finches, 9–10, 12, 29, 39, 41, 262, 267
    Carpodacus, 56, 258–262
    Cassin's, 3, 258–262, 268
    House, 3, 258–262
    key characters in identification, 56
    Purple, 3, 258–262
Flickers
    Gilded, 331
    Northern, 37, 331
    "Red-shafted," 331
    "Yellow-shafted," 331
Flight characteristics
    importance in identification, 29–34
    of pelagic birds, 33–34
    of raptors, 29–33
Flycatchers, 10, 36, 41–42, 44, 46, 210, 213, 214
    Acadian, 215–227
    Alder, 43, 215–223, 226
    Ash-throated, 5–6, 210–213, 268, 335
    Brown-crested, 5, 210–213, 335
    Buff-breasted, 13, 215, 222, 227–228, 334
    Cordilleran, 217–218, 333–334
    Dusky, 215, 222–228, 332–333
    Dusky-capped, 211–213, 334–335
    Empidonax (empids), 35, 42–43, 46–47,
        52–53, 213–228, 333
    Gray, 215, 219–220, 222, 224–228, 333
    Great Crested, 210–213
    Great Kiskadee, 43, 335
    Hammond's, 215, 217–218, 222–226, 228, 332
    key characters in identification, 53
    Least, 215 216, 219, 222, 224–228
    Myiarchus, 5, 42, 52, 210–212, 335
    Northern Beardless-Tyrannulet, 331
    Pacific-Slope, 217–218, 333–334
    Scissor-tailed, 34, 336

—S
—N
—L

Flycatchers (*continued*)
Sulphur-bellied, 335
"Traill's," 219–227
Vermilion, 45, 334
"Western," 215, 217–221, 333
Willow, 43, 215, 220–222, 225–228
Yellow-bellied, 215, 218–221, 226
Foliage gleaning, 44
Foraging strategies, 44–45
active searcher, 44
sit-and-wait, 44
Form and structure, 28–35
body proportions, 35
trophic, 29
wing/tail shape and flight characteristics,
29–34
of pelagic birds, 33–34
of raptors, 30–33
Frigatebirds, 12, 34
Magnificent, 9, 274

Gallinaceous fowl, 39
key characters in identification, 51
Gallinules, key characters in identification, 50
Garrett, Kimball, 69
*Gavia arctica*
*G. a. arctica*, 74
*G. a. viridigularis*, 74
Geese
Brant, 279
Emperor, 278–279
key characters in identification, 50
Ross's, 39, 92–94, 278
Ross's × Snow hybrids, 94
Snow, 39, 92–94, 278
Geographic variation in plumage, 36–37
Gestalt birding, 45–47
definition of, 45–46
problems in use of, 47
*Glaucidium gnoma*
*G. g. californicum*, 315
*G. g. gnoma*, 315
*G. g. grinnelli*, 315
*G. g. swarthi*, 315
Gnatcatchers, 20, 34, 45, 244, 246
Black-capped, 54, 344
Black-tailed, 6, 54, 343
Blue-gray, 343
California, 343–344
key characters in identification, 54
Godwits, 44
Bar-tailed, 37, 300
Marbled, 30
Goldeneyes, 10, 35, 50, 98–100
Barrow's, 98–100, 281
Common, 98–100

Goldfinches, 373
key characters in identification, 55
Lawrence's, 372–373
Lesser, 268
Gorget, definition of, 52
Grackles, 41, 45
Great-tailed, 268
Gray Catbird, 11
Greater Roadrunner, 5, 268
Great Kiskadee, 43, 335
Grebes, 9, 35, 44–45, 73, 78
Clark's, 49, 77–79, 268
Eared, 35, 49, 60, 79–80
Horned, 35, 49, 79–80
key characters in identification, 49
Least, 270
Western, 49, 77–80, 268
Groove-billed Ani, 313
Grosbeaks
Black-headed, 56, 268, 357
Evening, 3, 10, 267
key characters in identification, 56
Pine, 3, 10
Rose-breasted, 11, 56, 260
Ground-Doves
Common, 312–313
Ruddy, 312
Grouse, 6, 45, 289
Blue, 286–287
"Columbian Sharp-tailed," 292–293
"Dusky," 286
"Gunnison" Sage, 290–291
lekking, 289
"Plain's Sharp-tailed," 292–293
Sage, 289–290
Sharp-tailed, 292–293
"Sooty," 286
Spruce, 285–287
Gular pouch, defined, 83
*Guide to Birdfinding East of the Mississippi, A*
(Pettingill), 14
*Guide to Birdfinding West of the Mississippi, A*
(Pettingill), 14
Guillemots
Black, 307
Pigeon, 307
Gulls, 5–6, 9–12, 18, 29, 34, 38–42, 46, 68, 141,
150–179
age terminology, 152–157
aging of, 152–157
Black-headed, 13
Bonaparte's, 152, 161
California, 155, 158, 165, 168, 170–171, 268
feather wear, 157–158
Franklin's, 152, 157, 161, 268
geographic variation, 159

Glaucous, 10, 152, 155, 158–159, 161, 164–165, 170–171
Glaucous-winged, 152, 156, 158, 164, 167–175, 268
Glaucous-winged × Herring hybrids, 160
Great Black-backed, 165, 167
Heermann's, 152, 154, 268
Herring, 82, 159–160, 164–173, 176, 189, 304
Herring × Glaucous hybrids, 160
hybridization, 159–161
Iceland, 81, 155, 158–161, 168–173, 176, 304
identification, general considerations, 150–163
Ivory, 305
key characters in identification, 51
"Kumlien's," 173
Laughing, 9, 154, 157
Lesser Black-backed, 165
Little, 13, 152
Mew, 46, 152, 154, 157, 268
miscellaneous considerations, 161
molt sequence, 151–152
Ring-billed, 152, 157, 168
Ross's, 161, 304–305
Sabine's, 12–13, 20, 150, 152–154, 179, 305
sexual dimorphism, 158–159
Slaty-backed, 68, 150, 159, 163–168, 304
Thayer's, 10, 81, 150, 153, 159–160, 167–176, 303–304
tips for identification, 161–163
Western, 37, 58, 142, 152–156, 159–172, 175, 268
Western × Glaucous-winged hybrids, 160, 169, 172, 174–175
Yellow-footed, 9, 58, 152, 157, 304

Habitat recognition
elevation and, 2–3
key plant species and, 3–4
nest site availability and, 4–6
Haematopodidae, 117
Hawks, 9, 20, 29, 31, 32, 39, 41, 46, 68
Broad-winged, 115–117
Common Black-Hawk, 32, 107, 113–114, 282
Cooper's, 104–106
Ferruginous, 5, 32–33, 107–113, 268
Gray, 115, 117, 283
"Harlan's," 107
Harris's, 115, 282
"Krider's" Red-tailed, 107
Northern Goshawk, 104–106
Northern Harrier, 32–33, 110
Red-shouldered, 115–117
Red-tailed, 5, 32, 37, 106–112
Roadside, 283
Rough-legged, 32–33, 107–113

Sharp-shinned, 104–105
soaring, 30–31, 33, 61, 106
Swainson's, 32, 60, 103, 109–110, 113, 268
White-tailed, 32, 113, 283
Zone-tailed, 5, 33, 107, 113–115, 283–284
Herons, 6, 9, 25, 44, 45, 267
Great Blue, 89
key characters in identification, 50
Little Blue, 60
Tricolored, 44
Hotlines, 15–17. See also Birding grapevines
Hudsonian Zone, 2
Hummingbirds, 4, 8, 12, 20, 28–29, 34, 39, 42, 45, 62, 200–201
Allen's, 8, 203–204, 323–324
Anna's, 201–203, 268
Berylline, 9, 200, 321
Black-chinned, 5–6, 42, 201–205, 268, 323
Blue-throated, 61, 204, 322
breeding of, 8
Broad-billed, 200, 205, 321
Broad-tailed, 12, 28, 61, 202–204, 268, 324
Buff-bellied, 206, 321
Calliope, 12, 203–204, 323
Costa's, 8, 42, 201–205, 323
Green Violet-ear, 200, 321
key characters in identification, 52
Lucifer, 4, 202, 205, 322–323
Magnificent, 200, 204, 322
Plain-capped Starthroat, 200, 322
post-breeding dispersal of, 9
Ruby-throated, 201–203
Rufous, 8, 12, 200, 203–204, 268, 324
Violet-crowned, 9, 205, 321–322
White-eared, 9, 200, 204–205, 321
Humphrey and Parkes molt terminology, 41

Ibis, 44
key characters in identification, 50
White-faced, 60, 268
Icterids, 34, 39
key characters in identification, 56
Identification
accessory information in, 47
behavior in, 43–45
color and plumage patterns in, 35–42
molt and plumage sequence, 40–42
problems with, 28–29
variation in, 36–40
difficult, 67–266
form and structure in, 28–35
body proportions, 35
trophic, 29
wing/tail shape and flight characteristics, 29–34
Gestalt (or jizz), 45–47

Identification (*continued*)
    key characters in, by group, 48–57
    preparation and, 47–48
    psychological influences on, 57
    techniques of, 27–57
    vocalizations in, 42–43
Immature, definition of, 42

Jaegers, 12, 29, 34, 39–40, 46, 140–150
    key characters in identification, 50
    Long-tailed, 20, 34, 140–150, 267, 303
    Parasitic, 34, 140–150, 268
    Pomarine, 34, 140–150, 268
Jays, 9, 37
    *Aphelocoma*, 53, 231–234
        *coerulescens*, 231
        *ultramarina*, 231
        *ultramarina arizonae*, 231–234, 338
        *ultramarina couchii*, 231–234, 338
    Brown, 22, 337
    Gray, 3, 53
    Green, 22, 337
    key characters in identification, 53
    Mexican, 231–234, 338
    Pinyon, 338–339
    "Scrub," 231
    Steller's, 2, 268, 338
    "Woodhouse's," 231–233
    *See also* Scrub-Jays
Jizz, 45–47
    definition of, 46
    problems in use of, 47
Journals. *See* Field Journals
Juncos, 12
    Dark-eyed, 37
    key characters in identification, 56
    Yellow-eyed, 365
Juvenile, definition of, 42

Kenai Fjords Tours, Inc., 18
Kestrels, 31
    American, 33
Killdeer, 60, 62
Kingbirds
    Cassin's, 268
    Couch's, 42, 336
    key characters in identification, 52
    Thick-billed, 336
    Tropical, 42, 335–336
    Western, 6, 268
Kingfishers, 5, 44
    Green, 325
    key characters in identification, 52
    Ringed, 324
Kinglets, 9, 44–45, 48, 53, 354
    key characters in identification, 54
    Ruby-crowned, 46, 205, 247–248

Kites, 30–34
    Hook-billed, 10, 115, 281
    White-tailed, 33, 282
Kittiwakes, 150, 152, 174–179
    Black-legged, 10, 20, 174–179
    Red-legged, 175–179, 304

Lane, James A., 14
Lane birdfinding guides, 14
*Large Gulls of North America, The* (video), 69
Larks, 45
    Horned, 254, 365–366
    Sky, 13, 15, 337
*Larus*
    *argentatus smithsonianus*, 165, 304
    *argentatus vegae*, 159, 165–167, 304
    *fuscus graellsii*, 165
    *hyperboreus barrovianus*, 159
    *occidentalis occidentalis*, 159
    *occidentalis wymani*, 159, 165
Lekking grouse, 289
Life zone concept, 2–3
*Limnodromus griseus*
    *L. g. caurinus*, 136–140
    *L. g. griseus*, 136–140
    *L. g. hendersoni*, 136–140
Longspurs, 10, 45, 254–256, 365–366
    Chestnut-collared, 4, 254–257, 365–367
    key characters in identification, 56
    Lapland, 10, 254–257, 366–367
    McCown's, 4, 254–256, 365–366
    Smith's, 254–257, 366–367
Loons, 9, 29, 35, 44–45, 69–71, 73, 153
    Arctic, 69, 73–76, 269–270
    Common, 69–74
    key characters in identification, 48–49
    Pacific, 69–76, 268–269
    Red-throated, 69–73, 76
    Yellow-billed, 69–74, 270

Magpies
    Black-billed, 268
    key characters in identification, 53
    Yellow-billed, 339
Mating displays, 45
Meadowlarks, 64, 257
    Eastern, 43, 257–258
    key characters in identification, 56
    Western, 43, 257–258
Mergansers, 100–101
    Common, 100–101
    Red-breasted, 100–101
Merlin, 37
Merriam, Clinton H., 2
Migration
    Bering Sea, 11–12

birding in, 10–13
Trans-Gulf, 10–11
Mimids, 20, 29, 34, 41
key characters in identification, 54
*See also* Thrashers
Molt·
definition of, 40
partial, 40–41
plumage sequence and, 40–42
in *Empidonax* flycatchers, 217
in gulls, 151–157
in shorebirds, 118–120
in terns, 181–183
typical, 40–41
synchronous, 40
terminology, 41
Morphs, 39–40
Murre
Common, 192–195
Thick-billed, 192–195
Murrelets, 197
Ancient, 309
Craveri's, 20, 195, 197–199, 309
Kittlitz's, 195–197, 308
Long-billed, 195, 308
Marbled, 195–197, 307–308
Xantus's, 197–199, 308–309
*Myiarchus* flycatchers, 5, 42, 210–212, 335
key characters in identification, 52
*Myiarchus tyrannulus*
*M. t. cooperi*, 211–212
*M. t. magister*, 211–212

*National Geographic Society Field Guide to the Birds of North America*, 68

Nests
building behaviors and, 45
desertion of, 25
failure of, 8–9, 25
site availability for, 4–6
Nighthawks, 44, 199–200
Common, 42, 199–200
Lesser, 5, 42, 199–200, 268
Night-Herons, 87
Black-crowned, 87–89
Yellow-crowned, 87–89
Nocturnal birding, and time of day, 7
*North American Birds* (magazine), 13–14, 63
Northern Beardless-Tyrannulet, 331
Northern Cardinal, 43
Northern Fulmar, 20, 40
Northern Harrier, 32–33, 110
Northern Jacana, 298
Northern Wheatear, 344–345
Nutcrackers, 53
Clark's, 339

Nuthatches, 9, 20, 44
Brown-headed, 53, 267
key characters in identification, 53
Pygmy, 3, 53, 223, 268, 355
Red-breasted, 3
White-breasted, 3

Oldsquaw, 10
Orioles, 10, 41, 45
Altamira, 45, 369
Audubon's, 369
Baltimore, 11
Bullock's, 268
Hooded, 258, 368–369
key characters in identification, 56
Scott's, 369–370
Streak-backed, 369
Osprey, 32
Owls, 7, 9–10, 20, 22, 30, 42, 267
Barn, 5
Boreal, 10, 318–319
Burrowing, 5, 7, 316
calls of, 22
Eastern Screech-Owl, 22, 39
Elf, 5, 8, 316
Ferruginous Pygmy-Owl, 5, 7, 22, 24, 315–316
Flammulated, 8, 313–314
Great Gray, 3, 7, 10, 13, 317–318
Great Horned, 2, 5, 22
key characters in identification, 52
"Mountain Pygmy-Owl," 315
Northern Hawk-Owl, 10, 314
Northern Pygmy-Owl, 3, 7, 22, 315, 340, 357
pygmy, 321
screech, 5, 321
Snowy, 7, 10, 314
Spotted, 317
Western Screech-Owl, 22, 42, 268, 314
Whiskered Screech-Owl, 42, 314

Parids, 41
key characters in identification, 53
Passerines, 20, 39, 41, 42, 45
breeding of, 7–8
migration of, 10–12
Peeps, 118, 127, 131, 133, 134
Pelagic birds, 17–19
migration of, 11–12
wing/tail shape and flight characteristics, 33–34
Pelagic birding, 17–20
Pelicans, 44
Brown, 9
key characters in identification, 49
Petrels
Cook's, 271

Petrels (*continued*)
  Mottled, 271
  Murphy's, 271
  *Pterodroma*, 34, 49, 68
Pewees
  key characters in identification, 53
  Greater, 43, 331
  *See also* Wood-Pewees
Phalaropes, 13, 120
  Red, 12–13, 268
  Wilson's, 12, 30, 64, 119
Phainopepla, 351
Phases, 39–40
Phoebes, 5, 225, 227
  Black, 268
  Eastern, 53
  key characters in identification, 53
  Say's, 268
*Picoides tridactylus*
  *P. t. bacatus*, 329
  *P. t. dorsalis*, 329
  *P. t. fasciatus*, 329
Pine Siskin, 10, 260
Pigeons
  Band-tailed, 2, 9, 268
  key characters in identification, 51
  Red-billed, 312
Pipits, 45
  American, 239–241
  key characters in identification, 54
  Red-throated, 349–350
  Sprague's, 4, 239–241, 350
  "Water," 239
"Pishing," 20
Plain Chachalaca, 43, 285
Plant-bird associations, 3–4
Plovers, 44, 118, 120–121, 241
  American Golden-Plover, 122–125, 296
  Black-bellied, 125
  Common Ringed, 68, 120–122, 297
  Eurasian Dotterel, 118, 298
  golden-plovers, 122–125
  Killdeer, 60, 62
  Lesser Golden-Plover, 122, 296
  Mountain, 4, 297–298
  Pacific Golden-Plover, 122–125, 296–297
  Semipalmated, 60, 210–122, 297
  Snowy, 60, 268
  Wilson's, 30, 297
Plumage, 41
Polygamous breeders, defined, 8
Polymorphisms, 39–40
Post-breeding dispersal, 8–9
Prairie-Chickens, 289–292
  "Attwater," 291
  Greater, 291–292

lekking, 289
  Lesser, 292
Primary projection, defined, 215
Procellarids, 5
Ptarmigan
  Rock, 287–288
  White-tailed, 288–289
  Willow Ptarmigan, 287–288
*Pterodroma* Petrels, 34, 68
  key characters in identification, 49
Puddle ducks, key characters in identification, 50
Puffins
  Horned, 312
  Tufted, 311–312
Purple Martin, 5
Pygmy-Owls, 321
  Ferruginous, 5, 7, 22, 24, 315–316
  "Mountain," 315
  Northern, 3, 7, 22, 315, 340, 357
Pyrrhuloxia, 358

Quail
  California, 268
  Gambel's, 268
  Montezuma, 293–294
  Mountain, 294
  Scaled, 5, 268

Race, 36
  plumage, variation in, 36–37
Rails, 7, 42
  Black, 7, 295
  Clapper, 37, 50
  key characters in identification, 50
  King, 50
  Yellow, 294–295
Rain stimulated breeding, 9
Raptors, 10, 25, 40, 45, 102
  key characters in identification, 51
  wing/tail shapes and flight characteristics of, 29–33
Rare Bird Alerts (RBAs), 15–17
Ravens
  Chihuahuan, 340
  Common, 340
  key characters in identification, 53
RBAs (Rare Bird Alerts), 15–17
Recurvirostridae, 117
Redpolls, 262–268, 344, 372
  Common, 10, 262–266, 372
  Hoary, 10, 262–266, 372
  key characters in identification, 55
  *See also Carduelis*
Reeve, 40
Remiges, defined, 40

Robins
  American, 345
  Clay-colored, 10, 345
  Rufous-backed, 345
Rose-throated Becard, 45, 336–337
Rosy-finches, 370–371
  Black, 371–372
  Brown-capped, 372
  Gray-crowned, 370–371
Ruff, 40, 118

Sanderling, 120
Sandpipers, 44, 118
  Baird's, 60, 118–119, 131, 133–134
  Buff-breasted, 118, 133, 240–241
  *Calidris*, 38, 118, 127, 133
  Curlew, 118
  Dunlin, 119, 128
  Least, 30, 60, 128, 131–133
  Pectoral, 60, 127, 302
  Rock, 302–303
  Sanderling, 120
  Semipalmated, 60, 64–65, 127–133
  Sharp-tailed, 302
  Spotted, 198
  Stilt, 64
  Upland, 240
  Western, 60, 62, 64, 120, 217–134, 301
  White-rumped, 119, 133–134
  *See also* Peeps; Shorebirds; Stints
Sapsuckers, 206–210, 326
  hybrid problem, 209
  immatures, 209–210
  Red-breasted, 206–210, 326
  Red-breasted × Red-naped hybrids, 206,
    209
  Red-naped, 206–210, 326
  *Sphyrapicus*, 206
  Williamson's, 206, 326–327
  Yellow-bellied, 206–210, 326
Scaup, 35, 50, 96, 280
  Greater, 96–98
  Lesser, 96–98
Scolopacidae, 117
Scoters, 10, 35, 50
  Surf, 62
Screech-Owls, 5, 321
  Eastern, 22, 39
  Western, 22, 42, 268, 314
  Whiskered, 42, 314
Scrub-Jays
  "California," 231–233
  complex, 232–233
  Florida, 231–233
  Island, 231–233, 338
  Western, 231–234, 268, 338

"Woodhouse's," 231–233
  *See also Aphelocoma*; Jays
Seabirds, 68. *See also* Pelagic birds
Seasickness, 19
Sexual dimorphism, 39
Shearwater, Debra Love, 17
Shearwater Journeys, 17
Shearwaters, 29, 33, 34, 81
  Audubon's, 20
  Black-vented, 273
  Buller's, 272–273
  Cory's, 20
  Flesh-footed, 272
  key characters in identification, 49
  Pink-footed, 272
  Short-tailed, 20, 80–82, 272
  Sooty, 80–82, 268, 272
  Streaked, 272
Shorebirds, 9–12, 25, 29, 30, 41–50, 62, 68, 117,
    127, 131, 134, 153
  key characters in identification, 50
  molt sequence and plumage variation in,
    118–120
  patterns of dispersal and, 118–120
  tidal fluctuations and, 6–7
shoveler, 95
Shrikes, key characters in identification, 54
*Sialia sialis fulva*, 236
Skuas, 19
  South Polar, 20, 142, 267, 303
Smew, 13
Solitaire
  key characters in identification, 54
  Townsend's, 268
Songbirds, 6, 11. *See also* Passerines
Sonoran Zone, 2
Sparrows, 9–10, 12, 20, 34, 41, 43–45, 363
  *Aimophila*, 361
  American Tree, 344
  Bachman's, 24–25, 267
  Baird's, 4, 248–250, 256, 363
  "Bell's," 362
  Black-chinned, 361–362
  Black-throated, 5, 268, 363
  Botteri's, 9, 43, 360–361
  Brewer's, 4, 251–254, 268
  Cassin's, 9, 43, 45, 361
  Chipping, 251–254
  Clay-colored, 251–254
  Field, 362
  Five-striped, 13, 360
  Fox, 37
  Golden-crowned, 268
  Grasshopper, 37
  Harris's, 256
  House, 256, 258, 306, 370

Sparrows (*continued*)
  key characters in identification, 56
  Lark, 36
  Le Conte's, 363–364
  Nelson's Sharp-tailed, 364
  Olive, 359
  Rufous-crowned, 268
  Rufous-winged, 361
  Sage, 362–363
  "Sagebrush," 363
  "Saltbush," 363
  Saltmarsh Sharp-tailed, 364
  Savannah, 37, 248–250
  Seaside, 364–365
  "Sharp-tailed," 364
  Song, 37
  *Spizella*, 251, 254
  "Timberline," 254
  Vesper, 255
  White-throated, 222
Specialty birds, 267–373
  criteria for inclusion among, 267–268
Species accounts, in field journals, 65
*Sphyrapicus ruber*
  *S. r. daggetti*, 206–210
  *S. r. ruber*, 206–208
*Spizella breweri taverni*, 254
Spoonbills
  key characters in identification, 50
  Roseate, 44, 276
"Squeaking," 20
*Sterna hirundo longipennis*, 186
Stilts, 44
Stints
  Little, 131
  Red-necked, 301–302
  Rufous-necked, 302
  *See also* Peeps, Sandpipers
Storks, 44
  key characters in identification, 50
  Wood, 9, 12, 276
Storm-petrels, 19–20, 29, 34, 46
  Ashy, 273–274
  Band-rumped, 20
  Black, 9, 273–274
  Fork-tailed, 20, 274
  key characters in identification, 49
  Leach's, 37
  Least, 9, 19–20, 273–274
*Sturnella magna*
  *S. m. argutula*, 257
  *S. m. lilianae*, 257
Subadult, definition of, 42
Subspecies (race)
  definition of, 36
  plumage variations in, 36–37

Sulids, 39, 40, 42, 44
  key characters in identification, 49
Summer, birding in, 7–9
Surfbird, 6, 301
Swallows, 29, 34, 44–45, 228–231
  Bank, 5, 228–231
  Cave, 5, 45, 337
  Cliff, 5, 37, 45
  key characters in identification, 53
  Northern Rough-winged, 228–231
  Purple Martin, 5
  Tree, 5, 228–231
  Violet-green, 5, 228–231, 268
Swans, 35, 89–92
  key characters in identification, 50
  Trumpeter, 89–92, 277–278
  Tundra, 89–92, 277
Swifts, 4, 29, 44
  Black, 5, 7, 320–321
  Chimney, 52
  key characters in identification, 52
  Vaux's, 52, 268
  White-throated, 268
*Synthliboramphus hypoleucus*
  *S. h. hypoleucus*, 197–198, 309
  *S. h. scrippsi*, 197–198, 308

Tanagers, 10, 39
  Flame-colored, 357–358
  Hepatic, 41, 57, 357
  key characters in identification, 57
  Scarlet, 11
  Summer, 41, 57
  Western, 268, 357
Tape recorders
  bird calls and, 21–22
  ethics and, 23–25
Taxonomic hierarchy, 28
Teal, 94
  Blue-winged, 60, 94–96
  Cinnamon, 94–96, 268
  Green-winged, 95–96
Terns, 6, 25, 29, 34, 44, 46, 68, 161, 179–189, 192, 267
  Aleutian, 306
  Arctic, 20, 150, 179–189, 303, 306
  Black, 200
  Caspian, 189–192
  Common, 179–189
  Elegant, 189–192, 306
  Forster's, 179–189
  Gull-billed, 305–306
  key characters in identification, 51
  molt sequence and plumage variation in, 181–183
  Royal, 189–192, 268

Sandwich, 192, 268
*Sterna*, 35, 179
*Sterna hirundo longipennis*, 186
Thrashers, 6, 238, 348
  Bendire's, 54, 236–239, 346–347
  Brown, 54
  California, 347
  Crissal, 6, 24, 347–348
  Curve-billed, 54, 236–239, 346–347
  Le Conte's, 348–349
  Long-billed, 54, 346
  Sage, 268
  *See also* Mimids
Thrushes, 10–11, 37, 41
  American Robin, 345
  Aztec, 346
  Bluethroat, 344
  *Catharus*, 37
  Clay-colored Robin, 345
  key characters in identification, 54
  Northern Wheatear, 344–345
  Rufous-backed Robin, 345
  Townsend's Solitaire, 268
  Varied, 345–346
Time of day, 6–7
Time of year, 7–13
Titmouse (titmice), 20, 44, 354
  Bridled, 5, 205, 341
  key characters in identification, 53
  Juniper, 5, 53, 268
  Oak, 53, 268
  Tufted, 37, 53
Towhees, 44
  Abert's, 359–360
  California, 268
  Canyon, 6, 268
  Eastern, 43
  Green-tailed, 268
  key characters in identification, 55
  Spotted, 268, 353
*Toxostoma curvirostre palmeri*, 238
Transition Zone, 2
Trogons
  Eared, 324
  Elegant, 24, 324
  key characters in identification, 51
Trophic structures, 29
Tropicbirds, 34, 44
  key characters in identification,
    49
  Red-billed, 9, 19–20, 274–275
  Red-tailed, 274–275
Turnstones, 44
  Black, 6, 300–301
*Tympanuchus*
  *cupido attwateri*, 291

*phasianellus columbianus*, 292–293
*phasianellus jamesii*, 292–293
Tyrannulet, 53

Ulnar bar, definition of, 103

Vagrants, 25
  Asiatic (Siberian, Palearctic), 11–12, 68,
    267–268
  eastern, 11
Verdin, 6, 53, 341
Vireos, 10, 20, 41, 44, 46, 48, 53, 242, 243
  Bell's, 244–246
  Black-capped, 242, 351–352
  Blue-headed, 242–244
  Cassin's, 242–244, 268
  Gray, 244–246, 352–353
  Hutton's, 247–248, 268
  key characters in identification, 55
  Plumbeous, 242–245, 268
  Red-eyed, 353
  "Solitary," 242
  *Vireo bellii*
    *V. b. arizonae*, 245–246
    *V. b. bellii*, 245–246
    *V. b. medius*, 245
    *V. b. pusillus*, 245
  *Vireo solitarius alticola*, 242–243
  *Vireo solitarius solitarius*, 242–243
  White-eyed, 242
  Yellow-green, 353
  Yellow-throated, 242, 245
Vocalizations, importance in identification,
    42–43
Vultures, 30
  Black, 113
  Turkey, 33, 109, 114–115

Waders, 35, 39
Wagtails
  Black-backed, 55
  key characters in identification, 55
  White, 55, 349
  Yellow, 349
Wahl, Terry, 17
Wandering Tattler, 6, 268
Warblers, 10–11, 20, 25, 39, 41, 43–45, 48, 68,
    354
  Arctic, 24, 342, 344
  Black-throated Gray, 268, 328
  Black-throated Green, 355
  Colima, 8, 353
  Common Yellowthroat, 43, 355
  Golden-cheeked, 3, 8, 352, 354–355
  Golden-crowned, 356
  Grace's, 3, 355

Warblers (*continued*)
    Gray-crowned Yellowthroat, 355
    Hermit, 354
    key characters in identification, 55
    Kirtland's, 4
    Lucy's, 5, 227, 246, 353–354
    MacGillivray's, 268
    Nashville, 353
    Olive, 3, 356–357
    *Oporornis*, 55
    Painted Redstart, 356
    Red-faced, 4, 355–356
    Rufous-capped, 356
    Townsend's, 268, 354
    Tropical Parula, 354
    Virginia's, 353
    Yellow-rumped, 37
Waterfowl, 9, 10, 11, 12
Waterthrushes, 55
Waxwings
    Bohemian, 10, 268, 351
    Cedar, 351
    key characters in identification, 55
*Western Birdwatcher, The* (Zimmer), 69
Western Field Ornithologists (WFO), 17
*Western Tanager* (newsletter), 69
Whimbrel, 125–127, 299
Whip-poor-will, 7, 43
Whistling-Ducks
    Black-bellied, 277
    Fulvous, 276–277
White-collared Seedeater, 10, 360
Wigeon
    American, 279
    Eurasian, 279
Willet, 60, 135

*Winging It* (newsletter), 14
Wing loading, definition of, 104
Wing/tail shape and flight characteristics, 29–34
Winter, birding in, 9–10
Woodpeckers, 4, 9, 20, 42, 44, 45, 206
    Acorn, 4, 268
    Black-backed, 3–4, 267, 328–331
    Gila, 5, 325–326
    Golden-fronted, 326
    Hairy, 327
    holes, 5
    key characters in identification, 52
    Ladder-backed, 6, 268, 327
    Lewis's, 325
    Nuttall's, 327
    Red-cockaded, 4, 267
    Strickland's, 327–328
    Three-toed, 3–4, 222, 267, 328–330
    White-headed, 328
Wood-Pewees, 222
    Eastern, 42–43, 53
    Western, 43, 53, 268
Wrens, 20, 34, 45
    Bewick's, 5, 244
    Cactus, 6, 341–342
    Canyon, 268
    House, 5
    key characters in identification, 54
    Marsh, 41
    Rock, 268
Wrentit, 24, 346

Yellowlegs, 89, 118, 134–136, 140
    Greater, 134–136
    Lesser, 134–136